DISCOVER
NATIVE AMERICA

DISCOVER NATIVE AMERICA

ARIZONA, COLORADO, NEW MEXICO, AND UTAH

Expanded Edition

Tish Minear
and
Janet Limon

Hippocrene Books, Inc.
New York

For information, address:
HIPPOCRENE BOOKS, INC.
171 Madison Avenue
New York, NY 10016
www.hippocrenebooks.com

ISBN of 1995 edition: 0-7818-0327-6

Library of Congress Cataloging-in-Publication Data

Minear, Tish.
  Discover Native America : Arizona, Colorado, New Mexico, and Utah /
Tish Minear and Janet Limon. -- Expanded ed.
      p. cm.
  Includes index.
  ISBN-13: 978-0-7818-1198-9
  ISBN-10: 0-7818-1198-8
  1. Indians of North America--Southwest, New--History--Guidebooks. 2.
Indians of North America--Southwest, New--Antiquities--Guidebooks. 3.
Southwest, New--Guidebooks. I. Limon, Janet. II. Title.
  E78.S7M57 2008
  917.904'33--dc22

                                                          2007050871

Printed in the United States of America.

Acknowledgments

Many people helped us to write this book. In particular, we owe our gratitude to Dianne Perkins for her illustrations, Bruce Minear for his maps, and Jim McCall, Jeannie Sandoval, and Sara White for their photographs. In addition, Pat Fossen, Matthew Shake, Merilyn Truxal-Hamburg, Jenny Ward, and Dave Ward reviewed parts of the text for accuracy, although any remaining errors are strictly our own. Throughout the development of the book, time and again we were also aided and encouraged by people willing to go above and beyond their job descriptions to answer our questions and point us in the right direction, whether for information or photographs. We thank each of you for your contributions in making this a better book.

Without the dedication and skill of the professionals at Hippocrene Books, Inc. this book would never have become a reality. Without the unwavering support of our families and friends through the long hours of writing and research, this book would not have been possible. And without the synchronicities that fill all creative projects with surprises, this book would be far less complete. Thank you.

Contents

PREFACE

WHEN CHRISTOPHER COLUMBUS landed at the West Indies in 1492, he named the people he met "Indians" in the mistaken belief that he had reached India. In a gesture of hospitality, Chief Guacanagari and the other Arawaks helped Columbus unload his ship, which had run aground. Since that time, most reports have emphasized the clash between the two cultures rather than their friendly encounters. The truth is, without the aid of Native Americans, it would have been close to impossible for Europeans to have survived in this new world.

Over time, the understanding of what actually happened between the indigenous peoples of North America and the European newcomers has shifted. Two hundred years ago, most written accounts called the Indians "savages." Today, many point toward European acts of savagery. Both sides were at times motivated by revenge, fear, and prejudice, and both committed atrocities. Each side also rose above these emotions to act in the spirit of cooperation and compassion, but it was not enough to prevent the massive destruction of the tribal communities. In appalling numbers, the native people were killed, by starvation, bullets, disease, or despair.

Despite considerable challenges created by decades of cultural devastation, native roots still survive. Individuals and tribal organizations are now applying the strength and wisdom of their traditions to the realities of the modern world and in the process are creating vibrant new lifestyles. It is this new Native America that is yours to discover.

We are not Native Americans, but regardless of cultural heritage, we are all connected through our human family. If something good can come from the centuries of injustices, maybe it is that we can now learn to live in peace and shared prosperity, working together to create a better future for our children. This is the hope to which we dedicate this book.

SECTION I

SOUTHWEST NATIVE AMERICAN HISTORY

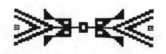

OVERVIEW

ANTHROPOLOGISTS ONCE CLAIMED that Paleo-Indians migrated on foot in waves of small family groups to North America around 11,500 years ago. It was believed that by following animal herds and gathering indigenous plants, the first Americans crossed the Bering land bridge from Asia, then funneled between the ice sheets and spread south and east. This date has been pushed back by thousands of years and the "land bridge" theory challenged by the possibility of oceanic migrations.

Many indigenous peoples dispute that they migrated from a distant continent, believing instead that they emerged into this world at places made by the Creator especially for them. From the beginning, they say they lived with reverence for the creation and respect for self and community. Many of the groups had names for themselves that meant simply "The People." Emphasis was placed on establishing and maintaining an intimate bond with the land. One's identity was interconnected to the natural world and everyone and everything in it. In addition to a supreme being, there were spirits of animals, plants, locales, the weather, and other natural phenomena. Aided by offerings, ritual, and ceremonies, individuals could communicate with and be guided by these powers. This concept of interconnection was often symbolized by the circle, which was found naturally in the cycle of the seasons and a human life and was echoed in the medicine wheel, the tipi, the hogan, the sweat lodge, the ceremonial dance, and the drum.

According to archaeologists, the small families of earliest indigenous Americans followed the "seasonal round," wearing trails behind animal herds and harvesting ripe roots, seeds, and berries along the way. Theirs was a portable lifestyle, utilizing shelters that were easy to erect from materials available on site or leaving more permanent pithouses at favorite campsites. Over time, The People learned to weave baskets for carrying their few possessions precious enough to move but left behind items like heavy grinding stones that would assuredly be there for the next season.

Around 6500 B.C., the Desert Archaic culture developed in the Four Corners region. It was marked by an increase in foraging for food as the changing climate eliminated many of the large mammals on which the people had depended.

By around 1100 B.C., the knowledge of how to cultivate maize began its rapid spread

Circles like the one on this petroglyph at Three Rivers Ruins have been used as symbols since ancient times.

from Mesoamerica into what is now the United States. Along with squash and beans, this vital crop supported the subsequent development of the Ancestral Pueblo (Anasazi), Hohokam, and Mogollon civilizations. Smaller groups such as the Sinagua, Mimbres, Fremont, Salado, and Patayan also evolved, each with similarities and unique characteristics. Pithouses and caves were their initial dwellings, to be followed by apartment-style pueblos. Bows and arrows were used to hunt small game, and distinctive pottery was crafted for cooking and storage vessels. Later, cotton garments and weaving became an integral part of their lives.

Distinct nomadic groups developed simultaneously. On the Great Plains they used ancient hunting methods to cull the vast buffalo (bison) herds, while in the mountains, they relied on the smaller game herds, like deer and elk, which grazed in the grassy parks.

The cultures of the Southwest and the Great Plains changed irreversibly with the arrival of Europeans, who brought with them devastating diseases and more sophisticated weaponry. While importing the means for active destruction of traditional lifeways, Europeans also introduced horses, sheep, cattle, new crops, and metal tools to indigenous culture. The Spanish were the first Europeans to arrive, following the lead of Coronado and his expedition of 1540. Over the next three hundred years, Spain laid claim to all the land in the Southwest, as well as that which would become Oregon and California. Meanwhile, the French claimed the land from the Mississippi River to the Rocky Mountains. All of this became part of the United States over the course of fifty years, first with the vast Louisiana Purchase of 1803, followed by the 1848 Treaty of Guadalupe Hidalgo ending the U.S.-Mexican War, and finally with the 1853 Gadsden Purchase.

For the indigenous peoples trying to preserve their traditional way of life, the change of governments initially meant little, but as wagon trains carried American immigrants across Indian land, game and resources became contested. When Indians demanded payment, the U.S. government promised compensation in exchange for assurances of peaceful passage and acceptance of boundaries around the immigrant trails and army posts.

Before long the promise of gold, land, and a better life became too good for the settlers to resist, and tensions between native and newcomer escalated. After the end of the Civil War, soldiers seasoned on Union battlefields were available to come to the West to suppress the native people. In 1868, with the completion of the transcontinental railroad, what was once a trickle of European settlement was now a tidal wave. Manifest Destiny was a reality.

In general, U.S. government policy was to ignore Indians in settled farming villages unless their locations interfered with prospectors or settlers. Because of this, the subsequent changes in Pueblo lifestyle were not as drastic as those for the nomads, who were actively subdued and eventually forced to settle on reservations designated by the government.

These reservations were often marginal lands that lacked water and the other resources necessary to sustain a traditional life. No longer able to provide for themselves, Native Americans were promised food and supplies from government agencies and soon became dependent on them. Tragically, many of these supplies were either never sent or were stolen by dishonest agents, so little help for Indians materialized. The blow to The People's self-respect and physical health was devastating, as hunger, resentment, stagnation, and hopelessness grew.

In 1887, the Dawes Act was passed to "civilize" Indians by making them into farmers, even though many of the hunting groups considered it a demeaning occupation. Reservations were carved into small individual parcels, and the rest of the land was opened to settlers. Even the small parcels were often lost when unscrupulous whites leased or bought them for low sums from desperate and trusting Indians. By 1933, tribal holdings had shrunk from 150 million acres to 60 million acres.

Meanwhile, many of the children were sent to government boarding schools to learn how to assimilate into the dominant culture. There, native culture was openly derided, and speaking in a native tongue could bring a beating. It was called the "termination" era, and it lived up to its name by shattering what was left of communal tribal bonds and severely curtailing the natural resources necessary for self-sufficiency.

By the beginning of the twentieth century, alcoholism, poverty, disease, malnutrition, and despair were common among Indians. By 1910 there were only 210,000 Indians left, and they were being referred to as the "Vanishing Americans."

After World War I, a climate of reform began to grow in Washington, D.C. Full citizenship that still recognized tribal affiliation was granted in 1924 to all Indians born in the United States, and partial self-government was extended with the Indian Reorganization Act of 1934. Twenty years later a wrenching policy halted this progress when the government granted one-time payments and terminated support and social programs for over one hundred indigenous groups. Even though The People had little preparation to make the transition into mainstream American society, many were forced to relocate from reservations to cities.

During the civil rights movement of the 1960s and 1970s, a new spirit of activism arose. Organizations like the Native American Rights Fund began successful legal and lobbying battles to win the return of ancestral lands and payment of cash settlements. Since

An honor guard of Native American veterans begins each powwow.

then, several pieces of legislation have granted more control to tribal governments and reaffirmed the sovereignty of the individual Indian nations.

Much of Native America is now experiencing a cultural and economic renaissance. New sources of revenue have been found in tourism, gaming, business, and development of natural resources. In addition, native peoples are gaining political clout in the western states.

As The People travel into the future, instead of relegating their sacred traditions to the backseat, they often rely on them as a trusted front-seat navigator. Today, a Native American might live on a reservation or in a city. He might leave his reservation home for school, then return to use his skills to better the community. During the week he may work with computers in a nearby city and then on weekends don tribal dress and dance at powwows.

The journey continues to be fraught with grave challenges, but crossing the bridge between two worlds is a new generation. As this younger generation asks what it means to be a Native American in the twenty-first century, they will create the answers, nourished by roots that are deep enough to sustain the changes of the future.

CHAPTER 1

HISTORY OF THE INDIANS
IN ARIZONA

ARIZONA HAS A RICH and varied history of indigenous peoples. From the grand canyons in the north to the arid deserts in the south, a wealth of different environments brought forth from the inhabitants a mosaic of creative responses to the quest for survival.

THE APACHE

They called themselves *Tinneh* or *Inde,* meaning "The People"; their neighbors called them Apache, a Zuni term for "the Enemy" and a Yuma word for "fighting men." As rugged as the Arizona landscape, this vital and tenacious people earned a reputation as the fiercest tribe in the Southwest. The Spanish, Mexican, and American governments all tried to exterminate them, but each one failed.

The Apache, like their close relatives the Navajo, are southern Athabaskans. It is believed they originally came from western Canada, following the buffalo herds into the Southwest sometime between A.D. 1000 and 1500. Once they arrived, they adapted their nomadic lifestyle to conditions in the high, timbered peaks, often visiting the nearby deserts and plains for food and encampment during severe winters. From the inaccessible mountain strongholds, the Indians ventured forth to trade with their friends and raid their enemies.

Over time, the Apache clustered into six divisions based on geography: Jicarilla, Lipan, Kiowa-Apache, Mescalero, Western (Coyotero), and Chiricahua. These were further divided into small independent groups that developed local linguistic and cultural characteristics.

Depending on location, each group adopted characteristics of both the Plains Indians and the Rio Grande Pueblos, combining limited farming with hunting in varying degrees. Usually at peace with each other, they visited for social dances, puberty rites, and marriages.

The smallest unit was the extended family, which consisted of a handful of related households led by a headman. Internal cooperation was essential for survival, and fortune, or lack of it, was shared equally by all. Because leaders held power at the discretion of their followers, none had coercive powers, even in battle. A chief had little influence outside of his own local group, and few ever spoke for more than a small number of people.

Life in an Apache camp was generally warm and friendly. Early observers described them as cheerful, honest, talkative, and the type of people who place a premium on laughter and jokes. Generosity was also prized, especially among the leaders.

Labor for men and women was strictly divided. The men made the weapons and medicine objects and were responsible for hunting, raiding, and attending group councils. It was their intense love of family and homelands that turned these protectors into fierce warriors, and their courage, cunning, endurance, guerilla warfare tactics, and intimate knowledge of the land that made them almost invincible.

The women did not normally take part in raids. Instead, they tended camp, cared for the children, and wove baskets with great precision, beauty, and skill. Twined burden baskets and water jars were fashioned from mulberry, willow, cottonwood, and sumac.

Beadwork was used on a variety of items, including moccasins, dolls, necklaces, and war shirts. Items such as war shields, boot-length moccasins, and medicine pouches were also painted, the designs incorporating religious symbols depicting the supernatural and natural forces in nature. Both muted and bright colors were derived from the earth and from plants: walnut juice for brown; mahogany roots for red; charcoal for black; and clay for blue, white, and yellow.

From an early age, a boy engaged in strenuous activities such as wrestling, foot racing, and tug-of-war to prepare him for life as a warrior. By fourteen he had begun his serious training. Discipline and obedience were stressed, as was increased preparation for physical hardships. This included swimming in ice-filled lakes and running long distances to build endurance for the seventy miles a day that he would travel as a seasoned warrior.

Puberty rites consisted of solitary fasting and praying or of group ceremonies, both with the purpose of contacting a guardian spirit and cultivating strength and courage. At puberty, a boy also joined his first raiding party, at which time he would be watched for signs of disobedience, dishonesty, cowardice, or gluttony. After successfully completing four raids, a novice was officially considered a warrior, which meant he could marry and enjoy the privileges attendant to that rank.

Girls were also trained to be physically hardy, and they engaged in such activities as running and swimming year-round. When a girl reached puberty, she became the center of an elaborate coming-of-age ritual that is still one of the Apache's most important ceremonies.

Another popular ritual is the nighttime curing ceremony, held to restore a patient's harmony with the natural order that is considered the foundation of health. During the shaman-led ceremony, people who are important to the patient gather to offer songs, speeches, food, and pollen blessings. Because the healing powers work best in a positive atmosphere, all is accompanied by laughter and jokes.

The Spanish were the first Europeans to meet Apaches. Through policies ranging from extermination to colonization, the Spanish tried to wrest control of the land north of the Rio Grande from the Apache. After years of bloody conflict, the two cultures eventually learned to coexist. By 1786, the Spanish presidio system of forts and missions stretched across the Southwest, and the government's rationing system had effectively forced many Apaches into dependency.

Apache wickiups are dome-shaped dwellings made of brush.

In 1821, the success of the Mexican Revolution changed the nationality of the troops in Apacheria. The presidio system broke down, and Indians who had settled near forts out of necessity now left to hunt for food. Raiding of settlements resumed.

In 1848, with the end of the Mexican-American War, the face of the enemy changed again. Almost overnight, all of Apache territory north of the Gila River became part of the United States. The U.S. border was pushed even farther south with the Gadsden Purchase in 1853. American settlers soon followed.

Relations between the United States and the Apache fluctuated. Some Apaches, like Geronimo and his Chiricahua followers, fought the white man for years and were involved in the final Indian wars in the United States. Other Apaches enlisted as army scouts for General Crook and were pivotal in the army's eventual success over the Apache. Acting as guides, fighting renegade Indians, and maintaining order on the reservations, these scouts received army pay plus forty cents a day to ride their own horses and carry their own food on expeditions. For uniforms they wore the Apache war gear of calico shirts, loose-fitting cotton trousers, and breechcloths. Sometimes they substituted army boots and socks for moccasins.

The first encounters with the United States were generally peaceful, but as settlement increased, so did the stories of betrayal and hostility on both sides. While some Apaches tried to maintain peaceful relations with the newcomers, others, in particular the Chiricahua, returned to their traditional lifestyle of raiding settlements. The new border worked to the advantage of Apache raiders, allowing them to alternately raid Mexican settlements and return to Arizona Territory for safety or to flee south to the mountains of Sonora to evade the United States army.

Led by Cochise, the Chiricahua were prosperous in the mid-1850s. He and his people controlled most of southeastern Arizona and frequented the Chiricahua and Dragoon Mountains, as well as the area just south of the border. A man of intelligence and honesty, it was his betrayal by the army in 1861 that began the Apache Wars. Inflamed by the incident, Cochise spent the next ten years leading numerous bloody raids until he finally surrendered in 1872.

Apache resistance was aided by the outbreak of the Civil War, which led to the abandonment of the Butterfield Overland mail route and two forts in the area. By late summer of 1861, the only whites left in southern Arizona were at a few isolated mines.

When the army returned in 1862, it did so with a vengeance. Under the command of Colonel James Henry Carleton, the United States established Fort Bowie at Apache Pass and began pursuing Apaches. Carleton's philosophy was one of unconditional surrender or extermination. In less than a year, he successfully subdued many of the Mescalero and forced them onto the Fort Sumner Reservation in the Bosque Redondo, where the alkaline water was unfit to drink, the marginal land failed to produce crops, and the poor supply of wood provided scant fuel to keep away the bitter cold.

In 1865, the situation worsened when Navajos completing the infamous Long Walk joined the Mescaleros. The land could not support these increased numbers, and cultural animosity between the two enemies heightened the tensions. After three years, the Apache had had enough of drought, failed crops, and Comanche raids. They eluded the guards and fled back to the mountains.

Up until 1875, the Apache remained clustered on several reservations, including the Chiricahua, who had surrendered under a peace treaty negotiated by Cochise in 1871. In 1875, all of the Apaches, along with a number of Yavapais, were herded to a hot, desolate, and sandblasted area in the Gila River valley known as San Carlos. Between suspicion and distrust among the inhabitants, the Spartan living conditions, and the corruption of the white merchants and agents, the situation eventually exploded.

Many Indians escaped to the Sierra Madre in Mexico and resumed their raiding way of life. Geronimo, a Chiricahua whose own hatred had been kindled when Mexicans murdered his wife and children, was among them. His final surrender to General Miles in September of 1886 ended the last large-scale Indian resistance in the United States.

Four days later, all of the Chiricahuas, including those living peacefully on the reservations and the scouts who had aided in the capture of Geronimo, were packed off to prison in Florida. Later, they were sent to Alabama and then to Fort Sill in Oklahoma. It would be twenty-eight painful years of physical and cultural destruction before they would be allowed to return to the Southwest. In 1873 there had been 1,675 Chiricahuas; by 1913, there were only 258.

Today, most Apaches live in Oklahoma and on reservations in Arizona and New Mexico. The Apache language is still commonly spoken, and renewed cultural pride is evident in the resurgence of traditional customs and ceremonies.

THE HOPI

The Hopituh, "Peaceful Ones," are related to the Pueblo people of New Mexico. Believed to be descendants of the Ancestral Puebloans, they arrived at the three treeless mesas that comprise the Hopi Reservation around A.D. 100 and have lived there ever since, surrounded by their sacred landmarks.

According to Hopi legend, three worlds existed before this one, but they were all destroyed because of man's evil. When the Fourth World was formed (the one we inhabit today), the Hopi entered it from the Sipapuni, a spot near the confluence of the Colorado and Little Colorado rivers.

Hopi women's shawl design

Ma'saw, the guardian of the Fourth World, met the Hopi. In return, they agreed to be stewards of the world. Led by omens and spiritual signs given to their priests, they migrated throughout the Southwest, leaving their footprints in the form of petroglyphs, sacred trails, and shrines.

Eventually, the Hopituh arrived at their homeland on the Hopi Mesas. It is a place where dramatic monsoon rains sweep across the plateaus, disappearing as quickly as they come.

As dry land farmers, the Hopi used the annual ten inches of rainfall to raise a hardy variety of corn, beans, squash, melons, and other crops. In small fields, they dug holes four feet apart with sticks and dropped in a few corn seeds. When the corn germinated, it grew in isolated clusters, its unexpected green contrasting with the drab, sandy hillsides.

After the corn was harvested and dried, women pounded it between stone manos and rough metates. One of the delicacies made from this cornmeal was piki, a mixture of cornmeal, water, and wood ash that was baked on a hot, greased *duma* (a slab of sandstone). It took a skillful cook to dip her hand in the batter and quickly spread it over the *duma* without getting burned. Almost immediately, the piki was done, lifted off the polished stone, and rolled into a crackling, cylindrical treat. It took a proper *duma* to make good piki, and these special stones were passed down from mother to daughter with great pride.

For the traditional Hopi, every action is considered sacred. In underground ceremonial chambers (kivas), the people maintain a complex system of numerous rituals, with each clan responsible for one or more of them. Ceremonies to ask for rain, to promote health, and to produce well-being are held, some with katsinas (also spelled kachinas), supernatural beings representing the spirits in all things.

For part of the year, the katsinas stay with the people. The rest of the time, they return to their homeland, the sacred San Francisco Peaks. From there, they ascend to the stars, carrying the prayers of the people with them. Hopi men spend hours carving and painting representations of the katsinas out of cottonwood roots. Even the very young are given these katsina dolls, not so much to play with as to help them learn the intricacies of their forms.

The Hopi perform their elaborate ceremonies not only for themselves but also for the entire world. They believe their collective purpose in the universe is as keeper of the sacred way and that their traditions must be honored to maintain the vital balance that supports all life on earth.

They also believe that, just as the three previous worlds were destroyed by man's errant ways, this world, too, will end. Only the faithful, living and dead, will survive to enter the Fifth World, a purified land where love will prevail. The destruction will come in a time when people have once again abandoned truth and allowed evil to rule. On that day, the great dances will have been forgotten and the rituals no longer understood.

But today, there is still time to experience one of these majestic ceremonies—the katsinas resplendent in their colorful costumes and masks as they emerge from the kivas to enact the movements of their spirit selves, the hypnotic chanting of the dancers moving in unison, and the rhythm of the drums pulsing with the heartbeat at the center of the universe.

And although some Hopis have adopted Western jobs, clothing, and language, many still come home to their beloved mesas and ancestral villages, where their belief system and the Hopi place in it has changed very little.

THE MOGOLLON

The Mogollon (*moggy-YON*) populated southeastern Arizona, southwestern New Mexico, and northern Chihuahua, Mexico, from possibly as early as 200 B.C. to about A.D. 1450. Several Mogollon groups, all culturally related, developed through three distinct phases, although each at slightly different times.

Traditionally hunters, the Mogollon, "Mountain People," first lived in caves or rock alcoves. Around A.D. 250, they began to move into pithouses, which were holes dug three or four feet deep into the ground, framed with logs, and then covered with mud and sticks. Between five and twenty dugouts were often clustered together into new settlements built on mesa tops or long defensible ridges. A ceremonial kiva, either circular or D-shaped, was dug in the center of the cluster.

Mogollon pottery was crafted from brown-coiled clay that was smoothed, covered with a slip, and then fired in hot coals. Bowls, jars, and pots were all popular household items. Baskets and cradles were woven from yucca and sotol, and sleeping mats were fashioned from reed or straw.

Petroglyphs left by people of the prehistoric Mogollon culture

Using a digging stick as their main tool, the Mogollon did a limited amount of cultivation of beans, squash, corn, tobacco, and cotton on hillside terraces and in river floodplains where nature did the work of irrigation for them. To supplement their crops, they gathered wild roots, nuts, and berries such as pinyon nuts, mariposa lily bulbs, walnuts, sunflower seeds, and chokecherries. Initially, spears and *atl-atls* (spear-throwing sticks) were used to hunt small game, but they were eventually replaced with bows and arrows.

Beginning around A.D. 550 with the Late Pithouse period, larger and rectangular pithouses began to appear at Mogollon settlements. Pottery became more decorative, with red designs painted on brown backgrounds. Later backgrounds were white and the designs black or red. The use of the spear was phased out, and the bow and arrow became the primary hunting apparatus. Trade expanded, especially with groups westward near the Pacific Ocean, and contact with Ancestral Puebloans in the north probably increased. For unknown reasons, some Mogollon groups also gave up on farming at this time and reverted to hunting and gathering for food.

Around A.D. 1000, the Mogollon culture entered the vibrant Mimbres Mogollon period, where several large pueblos with five hundred or more rooms that face an open plaza were built. Grasshopper Ruin in Arizona is one example. Many small kivas were dug in these pueblos, either nearby or within individual room clusters. In the larger communities, great communal rooms also appeared. Society became more complex and stratified and individual skills more specialized.

In farming, extensive irrigation systems were developed, and the size of cultivated fields expanded. Stunning black-on-white painted pottery was developed and widely traded with neighboring cultures. Fine lines, naturalistic figures, and geometric designs are the earmarks of this Mimbres pottery, along with a "spirit" hole punched in the bottom of pots that were placed over the faces of the dead.

By around A.D. 1450, the Mogollon, like other prehistoric Southwest groups, had abandoned their homelands. Drought, overuse of natural resources, disruption of trade networks with the Ancestral Puebloan culture, disease, and warfare may have all contributed to the culture's demise. Were the people absorbed by existing Ancestral Pueblo groups? Are their descendants the modern Zuni and Hopi? At present, no one knows for sure.

THE NAVAJO

They call themselves *Diné* or *Dineh,* meaning "The People," and their land is *Diné Bikeyah* (*dih-NEH beh-KAY-ah*). When these Athabaskans arrived in the Southwest somewhere between A.D. 1300 and 1600, they had few possessions and followed the simple life of the nomadic hunter. At one time they lived with the Paiute, but they left over religious differences and moved south. They also spent time with their relatives, the Apache, but eventually came to settle here within the boundaries of their sacred mountains: Sisnaajini (Blanca Peak), Tsoodzil (Mount Taylor), Dook'o'osliid (San Francisco Peaks), and Dibé Nitsaa (Mt. Hesperus).

Their new neighbors, the Pueblo Indians, taught them pottery making and weaving techniques, new ceremonies, and a lifestyle incorporating agriculture. With the arrival of the Spanish and later the Mexican government, the Navajo continued to borrow what was

Navajo men near Shiprock, probably between 1930 and 1945

useful to them, learning silversmithing and acquiring sheep and horses. As the Navajo's herds grew, so did their prosperity.

In summer, most Navajos lived at higher elevations in ramadas—wall-less shelters made of branches and sticks. In winter, the house was a hogan constructed of logs, mud, and earth; more modern hogans are often built of boards, but still with the door facing east to the rising sun. By the early 1700s, many Navajos had clustered in small extended families at Canyon de Chelly.

Although early Spanish and Mexican military presence in the area had been sporadic, when the United States gained possession of the territory in 1846, the situation changed, and hostilities between Navajos and settlers escalated. In 1860 Chief Manuelito and his followers attacked Ft. Defiance in Arizona. A few years later, the United States government launched a full-scale campaign against the Navajo.

Troops led by Colonel Kit Carson systematically destroyed Navajo homes, fields, and livestock. Carson's orders were to starve the people into submission, and by 1864, he had succeeded. Around eight thousand men, women, and children were herded together and forced to walk over three hundred miles to Fort Sumner in eastern New Mexico. Food was scarce, clothing and shelter even scarcer.

Many died on the tortuous "Long Walk," but for those who survived, life was no easier. In captivity, thousands fell to disease and to a continued shortage of food, fuel for warmth, and water. Finally, after four long years of banishment, the survivors signed a treaty allowing them to return to the safety of their cherished homeland. Their numbers had been reduced by one-fourth.

The adaptability and durability of the Navajo people have enabled them to recover from their exile and adjust to the modern world so well that they are now the largest federally recognized tribe in the United States, containing over 225,000 members. Part of their strength has come from a strong sense of tradition, much of which has been passed from generation to generation in the form of stories.

According to Navajo legend, in the beginning was the First World, a small floating island in a sea of mist. The creatures of this world were Mist Beings, containing only the essence of what they were to become. Coyote, called Child of the Dawn, was one of the Holy People, as were First Man and First Woman. Quarreling among the different beings forced them to move into the Second World, emerging upward through an opening in the east. Unfortunately, the evils of the First World went with them.

After entering the Second World, these beings discovered other beings were already living there and also fighting amongst themselves. The refugees continued their journey into the Third World, where a flood eventually forced them to flee to the Fourth World by climbing up a reed planted by First Man.

In the Fourth World, Changing Woman created the first four Dineh clans from various parts of her body. A ceremony called *Kinaalda*, "Walked into Beauty," was held for her when she reached puberty so she would be able to have children. Her twin sons, Monster Slayer and Child Born of Water, later killed monsters that were terrorizing the Dineh.

After they emerged, the Holy People formed four sacred mountains from the soil they brought with them from the Third World. They also made fire from a Third World piece of flint, gave the Navajo the gift of corn, built the first hogan of five logs (which some say still exists near the Place of Emergence) and taught Navajos how to weave.

From that time on, as Navajos journey through life, they are surrounded by the Holy People, who teach them how to live and the ceremonies and rituals necessary to maintain a harmonious relationship with these powerful beings.

Of all the Navajo, the medicine man most excels in the knowledge of complex ceremonies. Part of his knowledge includes the technique of sandpainting, which utilizes sand colored by charcoal, gypsum, ocher, seeds, pollens, and meal to create intricate designs that are used to help restore harmony and health to the patient. Some of these paintings are so elaborate, it takes fifteen men a full day to make just one. At the conclusion of a curing ceremony, the painting is taken apart in the reverse order of the way it was created.

Singing is also used to maintain a harmonious life, as well as to mark the important milestones of life. Hundreds of chants exist, and some form the basis of precise and elaborate ceremonies, or "sings," that last for several days. A part of the Nightway Chant is one of the more well known of these songs:

> In beauty I walk;
> I walk with beauty before me;
> I walk with beauty behind me;
> I walk with beauty above me;
> I walk with beauty below me;
> I walk with beauty around me ...

In these simple words is the expression of harmony and connection with the earth that a Navajo strives to maintain while following his or her pathway through life. Living once again between the sacred peaks that define the Navajo Nation, many are still able to walk surrounded by that beauty.

THE PEOPLE OF THE DESERT

Southwestern Arizona is blanketed by the Sonora Desert, 120,000 square miles of forbidding inferno that also engulfs large portions of the Baja peninsula, Southern California, and the state of Sonora, Mexico. Water is scarce here; in places, precipitation is less than three inches a year. To live, people must adapt.

For thousands of years, from about 9000 B.C. to 500 B.C., the inhabitants of the Sonora Desert were hunters and plant gatherers who belonged to the Cochise culture. By

2000 B.C., they had learned to farm. Maize was their first crop, and it very likely came to them from Mesoamerica.

Early corn was as small as a finger, but its cultivation was a turning point for the Cochise, and it soon became the basis of their economy. In addition to its high nutritional content, corn has a high yield. As the excess grain was traded to other cultures, increased interaction with neighbors encouraged technological development. When agriculture settled into a central role in society, the people were coaxed to establish permanent villages, and new rituals emerged to insure the harvest.

Possibly by 300 B.C., a distinct group, the Hohokam ("Those Who Have Vanished"), appeared in the desert plains between the Salt and Gila rivers, either having migrated from Mesoamerica or having evolved from the Desert Archaic hunter-gatherers who lived there before them.

To water their corn, squash, amaranth, cotton, tobacco, chilies, and beans Hohokam farmers built the most extensive system of canals ever found in North America—over six hundred miles of them. Some of these canals were as large as fifty feet wide and ten feet deep. With elaborate care, using nothing more than wood and stone tools for digging and baskets for hauling the tons of rock and sand, they dug out the earth, following the slope of the land and the course of the river. They then lined the canals with clay to keep them watertight. Hundreds of years later, the Swilling Irrigation Canal Company would use this ancient system to form the basis of the Phoenix water system.

In addition to building canals, the Hohokam were also artists. Fine cotton textiles were woven into tapestries and gauze, and ornaments were made from stone beads inlaid with turquoise from Northern New Mexico and seashells from the Gulf of California. Around A.D. 100, the Hohokam discovered an innovative technique to etch these shells with the fermented juice of the saguaro cactus, four hundred years before Europeans learned to use a similar technique for decorating metal armor.

Hohokam pottery was a red-on-buff color that sparkled with the addition of mica and, later, polychromatic colors. Designs were highly stylized pictures of animals such as fish, lizards, snakes, and rabbits, and of peaceful activities such as dancing and lovemaking. So far, no images of war have been found in their pottery or rock art.

The Hohokam stayed for 1,400 years or so, populating a third of what is now Arizona, from the San Pedro River in the southeast to the central Verde Valley. During that time, they showed strong cultural ties to Mexico, and in many ways, they funneled influences from these highly developed civilizations to other cultures in the Southwest.

Population reached its height somewhere between A.D. 1100 and 1450, when the small villages grew into large towns such as Casa Grande and Pueblo Grande. Then, after more than a millennium of peace and prosperity, the Hohokam culture vanished like dust on the desert wind. By the time Fray Marcos de Niza arrived from Spain in 1539, they had been gone for almost a hundred years.

Theories about their disappearance abound, ranging from droughts to raids by hostile nomads. The cultures that were left were simpler, with more self-sufficient lifestyles.

One culture that may have developed from the Hohokam was the Salado of the Tonto Basin. The Salado built walled, multistoried pueblos of cobbles and mud and crafted polychrome pottery in a mixture of earthy colors. The Salado prospered in the fifteenth century but disappeared soon after, leaving behind an intriguing array of perishable items, such as reed cigarettes, hairbrushes, pot rests, agave quids (a chewed wad of the plant), and cloth kilts and ponchos. Climate change, salt buildup in fields, violence, shifting trade centers, and competition for resources from newcomers may have contributed to the decline of the Salado.

When the Spanish arrived in the early sixteenth century, among the groups of native people who greeted them were the Akimel O'odham (formerly called the Pima), who many believe are descendants of the Hohokam. These "People of the River" lived along the river systems in south central Arizona in *rancherias*—small villages of desert brush and mud huts. The *ki* (their name for this type of dwelling) was usually about fifteen feet in diameter and had a flat roof. There was no opening in the top for smoke to escape, but since the fire was kept small, much of it was either absorbed by the earthen walls or escaped through the door. Villages also contained numerous ramadas.

Earth ridges subdivided Akimel O'odham fields into rectangles (about 200 by 100 feet) that were then irrigated using the canals left by the Hohokam. Their dress, dwellings, and ceremonies also reflected Hohokam influence.

Generally tall, dark skinned, and broad faced, the Akimel O'odham wore cotton breechcloths and kilts and tattooed their cheeks and chins using cactus thorns and charcoal. History was recorded on calendar sticks that kept track of years with notches and important events with carved symbols. Several people at a time kept the sticks, which were considered sacred and were rarely shown in public, and the sticks were often buried with their owners.

Contrary to many native groups, the Akimel O'odham used alcohol ceremonially. The beverage was called *navait* and was prepared by fermenting juice from the saguaro cactus fruit. During the New Year festival in springtime, great quantities of *navait* were drunk to ensure the coming of rain.

The saguaro fruit was also used as food, and mesquite pods were ground into flour that formed a large part of the Akimel O'odham diet. Maize was another staple, as was wheat after its introduction by the Spanish. Fish and small game such as quail, rabbit, and javelina supplemented the plant food.

The kitchen belonged to the woman of the house, and it was well stocked with a variety of baskets she had woven. Wrapping a foundation of cattails with willows and decorating it with black fiber from cultivated devil's claw plants, an Akimel O'odham woman could skillfully weave watertight baskets of great artistic and utilitarian value. Even today, Akimel O'odham baskets are prized.

Tohono O'odham house
near San Xavier, 1900

To honor this important activity, the Basket Dance was held. It not only celebrated the coming of spring, but it allowed the women to display the baskets they had crafted during the winter.

Another ceremony, the Quail Dance, was performed by children. It tells the story of a baby quail that wanders away from its mother and is nearly eaten by a coyote. As the offspring of the quail mother learned to follow closely behind her, Akimel O'odham children learned the value of obeying their parents.

In the sixteenth century, Spanish soldiers and missionaries claimed much of what was then Indian land. The Akimel O'odham and their allies, the Tohono O'odham (*Toe-HO-no AH-tomb*) and Maricopa, greeted these Europeans with friendship, providing them food, water, and shelter. To convert the Indians and exploit their labor, the Spanish established Pimeria Alta, an administrative district consisting of missions and presidios.

After the arrival of the Spanish, the Akimel O'odham joined with the Maricopa in a powerful confederation to protect themselves against attack by enemy tribes. This alliance later aided the United States Army, both in the Civil War and in fights against the Apache, Yavapai, Quechan, and Mojave (Mohave). Although the power of the confederation ebbed in 1908 with the death of its last general, Antonio Azul, the military tradition continued through World War I and World War II, when Ira Hayes, a nineteen-year-old Akimel O'odham, helped to raise the American flag on Iwo Jima.

After the region became part of the United States in the nineteenth century, more travelers came to explore the new territory, and it was the generosity of Akimel O'odhams that enabled them to survive their journey through the Sonora Desert. Of all native peoples met

Mohave girl with beadwork necklace, circa 1906

on the westward migration, they were often remembered as the most honest, cheerful, and hospitable to immigrants.

Travelers such as General Kearny and his Army of the West, Forty-niners bound for California, settlers looking for land, and passengers on the Butterfield Overland Stage all relied on the water, pumpkins, squashes, and melons of the Akimel O'odham, as well as their protection from hostile tribes. In one year alone, the Indians provided 400,000 pounds of wheat to the Overland Stage Company.

As settlement in Arizona increased, so did the encroachment on Akimel O'odham lands. In 1859, the tribe secured the Gila River Reservations. In 1879, this area was expanded and the Salt River Reservation added. These reservations contained some of their traditional homelands, but they did little to protect the water upstream. As Anglo settlements diverted increasing amounts of river water, little was left for downstream farmers to grow food. Eventually, the Akimel O'odham experienced massive crop failures, starvation, and terrible poverty.

Today the Akimel O'odham share their land with their traditional allies, the Maricopa. For over one hundred years they have been involved in an ongoing legal battle to secure water rights to their land. Although they engage in limited farming, raising of livestock, production of crafts, and small industry, most look for jobs off the reservation.

Along with water, the Akimel O'odham have lost much of their culture, including some of the rituals and stories of their oral tradition. And these people who were always there to aid the frightened, desperate settlers, and who loyally fought for the United States government in every war since the Civil War, are today searching for ways to gain back their economic independence.

Close cultural and linguistic relatives of the Akimel O'odham are the Tohono O'odham, "People of the Desert." Traditionally, this group lived in southern Arizona and northwestern Sonora. Each of their widely scattered villages was politically autonomous and included two locations, a winter home near a mountain spring that enabled the people to hunt for deer and a summer home on a floodplain that allowed for marginal farming. Highly dependent on desert plants for food, the Tohono O'odham marked the beginning of the year with the June saguaro harvest.

In general, the Tohono O'odham lived peacefully with the settlers, but they still lost much of their land to the newcomers. Their main reservation was established in 1917 but did not include the most productive of the Indian's traditional lands. Since then, encroachment on their surface and underground water supplies from burgeoning metropolitan Tucson, Arizona, has added an additional burden.

Today, the Tohono O'odham Reservation, the second largest reservation in the United States, is the year-round home to less than one-third of its members. Unemployment on the reservation is high. As the tribe explores new avenues of revenue, including the gaming industry, many of the people preserve their craft of skilled basketry.

THE PEOPLE OF NORTHWEST ARIZONA

Paleo-Indian hunters arrived in the canyon country of Northwest Arizona as early as 12,000 B.C. They were followed around 8000 B.C. by the Desert Archaic people, who explored the deep, winding recesses of the Grand Canyon, took refuge in its caves, and left behind stone spear points and "split-twig" figurines fashioned into images of deer and bighorn sheep.

Centuries later, probably by 300 B.C., the Ancestral Puebloans had arrived on the scene, living in the Arizona Strip, hunting bighorn sheep and deer, harvesting wild pinyon nuts and agaves, and eventually maintaining a complex religious and social life. The population peaked somewhere between A.D. 1050 and 1150, at which time drought and other factors forced them to move elsewhere, possibly to the Hopi Mesas. Left behind were over two thousand archaeological sites.

As Ancestral Puebloan influence waned, the nomadic Southern Paiute entered the Arizona Strip. They made seasonal visits to the North Rim of the Grand Canyon, spending their summers in the high country of the Kaibab Plateau and seeking warmer, lower elevations in the winter. Their culture was similar to that of the early Archaic, a hunt-

Hualapai couple taken about 1906, with home in background

ing/gathering tradition with some limited farming. Evidence of their passing is seen in the form of yucca roasting pits, brownware pottery sherds, and the shallow, circular depressions of their campsites.

On the South Rim of the Grand Canyon, between A.D. 600 and 1150, people of the Cohonina culture lived a simple lifestyle in plain stone and wooden houses. Two hundred years later, the Cerbat, a group with possible cultural ties to the Cohonina, migrated from the west onto the South Rim. These hunters and gatherers lived in caves or brush shelters, ranging as far upstream as the Little Colorado River. They also planted crops in the fertile soil beside permanent springs. Some speculate that these groups were the ancestors of the Havasupai and Hualapai (also called Walapai), who, along with the Yavapai, constitute the Yuman-speaking Pai people. The Havasupai and Hualapai consider themselves members of the same tribe, while the Yavapai have traditionally been their enemy.

The Pai people exemplify the Desert Culture, blending an agricultural and a hunting/gathering society. In spring, the Pai would gather in the canyon bottoms to plant and tend their crops of corn, beans, squash, peaches, cotton, sunflowers, and tobacco; in winter, after the harvest celebration, they would disperse to the countryside for the men to hunt rabbit and deer and the women to gather seeds and pinyon nuts.

The tribes were loosely organized into bands that followed a headman—a person who led by persuasion more than by coercion. Religious life shared similarities with the Pueblo, including the use of prayer sticks and masked dancing. Trade was also a vital part of life, in particular with the nearby Hopis, who prized the salt and ocher found in the Grand Canyon.

The Havasupai, "People of the Blue-Green Water," settled in the remote Havasu Canyon—part of the Grand Canyon just below the confluence of the Colorado and Little Colorado rivers. West of the Havasupai were the Hualapai, "Pine Springs People." Their bands were more dispersed and extended from the western Grand Canyon to the banks of the Colorado River below its emergence from the canyon.

Spanish missionaries were the first known Europeans to make contact with the Pai people. When the Franciscan Father Garces visited the Havasupai in 1776, he described them as happy, industrious, and peaceful.

However, extensive contact between the two cultures did not occur until after 1865, when gold was discovered in the Hualapai and Cerbat mountains. Prospectors and cattlemen soon descended on the area, sparking the Hualapai Wars. In a few short years, the Hualapai were defeated and marched to prison at La Paz on the lower Colorado River. In 1883, the Hualapai Reservation was established near Peach Springs on the South Rim of the lower Grand Canyon. Today, the tribal economy is based on arts and crafts, tourism, timber sales, limited farming, and cattle ranching.

The Havasupai, who had avoided confrontation by withdrawing into the Grand Canyon, were confined to a reservation there in 1882. Like that of the Hualapai, this land-holding was small and did not include their traditional gathering lands on the plateau, which had been claimed by ranchers. In 1975, their winter homelands were returned to them, and today the reservation totals about 188,077 acres.

THE PEOPLE OF THE VERDE VALLEY

The Verde Valley snuggles in the heart of Arizona, between the Mogollon Rim of the Colorado Plateau in the northeast and the Black Hills in the southwest. An abundance of water makes it a verdant paradise compared to the deserts to the south, and numerous cultures have chosen to call it home.

At least eight thousand years ago, hunters and gatherers left projectile points, scrapers, manos (hand-held grinding rocks), and metates (grinding stones) in the valley. Around 1,300 years ago, permanent settlements and agriculture appeared, with people living in pithouses and farming the surrounding mesa tops and alluvial bottomlands. Undecorated, utilitarian pottery was crafted, and Hohokam-style ball courts were built. A trade network developed to funnel the salt, argillite, and copper of the valley to the Hohokam people in the south and possibly the Ancestral Puebloans in the north.

Around the twelfth century, a culture called the Sinagua (Spanish for "without water") emerged. The Sinagua (*seen-AH-wah*) people were dry-land farmers, as well as hunters and gatherers. The agave plant, which grows abundantly in the Verde uplands, was an important food source for the Sinagua. In spring, when the plants were at their sweetest, women and children harvested the juicy stalks with flake knives and removed the tough outer leaves. The trimmed agave was then eaten raw or first roasted in a pit that was lined with heated rocks and covered with grass and dirt.

The Sinagua were fine craftsmen, fashioning bone needles and awls, cotton clothing, shell and turquoise ornaments, and stone axes, knives, and hammers. Their pottery was plain and porous, but their homes were skillfully built in a style similar to the Kayenta Anasazi. Their widely scattered villages were commonly erected on hilltops, like the one at Tuzigoot National Monument, or in cliff overhangs, like the one at Montezuma Castle.

By the fifteenth century, their population became increasingly clustered into fewer but larger centers with buildings several stories high and consisting of an average of thirty-five rooms. So far, dozens of these major pueblos have been found in the valley.

The Sinagua flourished for several hundred years, and then they simply disappeared. By A.D. 1425, all of their settlements had been abandoned. Theories range from drought, to soil erosion, to disease, to enemy raids, but the mystery of the Sinagua remains unsolved. Some may have migrated to live with the people who became ancestors to the Hopi. Some may have stayed to become the Yavapai (*YAH-vah-pie*), who, along with small bands of nomadic Tonto Apaches, were the tribes the Spanish found when they first entered Verde Valley.

The Yavapai and the Tonto Apache have many similarities. Traditionally, both cultures were hunters of small game and gatherers of wild plants who also engaged in limited farming. Each tribe was split into small family units that searched for food and water over vast areas, often traveling twenty miles a day. Occasionally, the groups would congregate for socializing, weddings, and rituals.

The cycle of wild plants dictated the people's seasonal movements. The staple of their diet was the agave, and they used it much as the Sinagua had done before them. Yucca was also used extensively, for food, soap, needles, game balls, baskets, and houses. Weaving baskets was a prized skill, and the artisans created numerous versatile shapes to provide durable and lightweight storage containers.

Contact with the Spanish was limited, but when gold was discovered on the Hassayampa River in 1863, American prospectors converged on the area. Settlers soon followed, along with military forts to protect them.

As the land became increasingly settled, the ability of the Yavapai and Tonto Apache to forage was curtailed, and the once self-sufficient people quickly became destitute. In 1871, a reservation was established for them along the river near Camp Verde. Malnourishment and epidemics soon reduced their numbers by a third. In 1875, they were marched 150 miles away to the San Carlos Reservation, where they joined other Apache groups.

A few Yavapais and Tonto Apaches were allowed to return to their homelands in the Verde Valley in 1900. Today, they live on the Camp Verde, Prescott, and Fort McDowell reservations. In the surrounding valley, hundreds of village sites built by those who preceded them stand as mute reminders of an earlier time, when the people laughed and shared their stories around the agave roasting pits.

CHAPTER 2

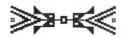

HISTORY OF THE INDIANS
IN COLORADO

THE PLAINS INDIANS

In eastern Colorado, much of the scenic drama comes from the sky, which is vast, bright blue, and prone to thunderous clouds sweeping in from the west. Living with such a sky makes one view life differently. Freedom becomes more than a concept. As one gets used to roaming freely in all directions, it seems to become part of the bones.

The Plains Indians lived with no fences and endless sky by moving with the cycles of the land: the spring thaw and winter freeze; the flowering of prairie plants; the ebb and flow of the bison (buffalo) herds, some so huge they covered fifty square miles. After they acquired the horse from the Spanish, following these cycles became easier. Buffalo meat now became the staple, and the Indians learned to use the entire animal to support their nomadic lifestyle. Skins were sewn into tipis and robes, sinews made thread and bowstrings, stomachs converted to cooking pots, and hooves were boiled for glue. In all, there were at least eighty-eight uses for the buffalo.

Traditionally, every aspect of a Plains Indian's life was permeated with religious reverence and respect. Part of manhood involved seeking mystical visions. Safety in war and success in hunting required a special vision quest for a guardian spirit. The rituals of vision-seeking often involved fasting and self-torture as a form of sacrifice in exchange for physical and spiritual well-being. These trials also tested a warrior's bravery and ability to withstand pain.

Plains Indian men spent much of their time hunting for food, fighting enemies, and being involved with one of the several military societies in each tribe. From the time they were boys, they played games to build athletic skills. In addition to his first buffalo hunt, a boy's life was highlighted by his first war party, where he hoped to be able to "count coup"—that is, to touch the enemy with his hand or a coup stick. This act was far more dangerous than killing an enemy and was considered a braver deed.

Although men gained prestige by their ability to feed and protect the tribe, this influence did not necessarily translate into wealth and power. To be a chief meant a willing-

Cheyenne camp with cooking tripod and drying rack, probably between 1880 and 1910

ness to sacrifice for the good of the community, and part of that responsibility included sharing possessions with the less fortunate. In addition, because harmony in the community was highly valued, decisions were often arrived at by consensus rather than decree.

Women were in charge of domestic tasks, including gathering and preparing food and dressing buffalo hides. They also made the tipi and most of its contents and subsequently owned them. Typically, if an object was not used in war, the hunt, to smoke, or possibly to make music, it was made by a woman. When the camp moved, the woman disassembled her portable home and loaded it onto a travois (two poles with a platform in between used for dragging loads), along with the kitchen equipment, clothing, and other household items.

Women also provided decorative touches in the home that held special meaning. Each color and design used in her elaborate beadwork and quill embroidery had deep religious significance, while her tipi paintings provided the pictorial representations of important events to document the family's history.

The Native Americans that dominated the Colorado Plains until the mid-1700s were Apaches. At that time, Indians farther north and east began moving into the area, having been previously displaced by the European settlement of the eastern coastal areas. The first newcomers to the plains were the Comanche and Kiowa, and they pushed the Apaches southward. By the early 1800s, they had in turn been displaced by the Arapaho and Cheyenne.

Both the Arapaho and Cheyenne were Algonquian-speaking tribes and longtime allies. Before moving to the plains, they had crafted pottery and lived as farmers. But in the 1700s they "lost the corn," as it is described in the Cheyenne oral tradition, and were forced south and west by hostile tribes. As they moved onto the plains, the men became skilled buffalo hunters and fierce warriors. With this change of lifestyle, the nations prospered.

In the early 1830s, bands of Arapaho and Cheyenne developed friendly trade relations with Bent's Fort, a large trading post on the Arkansas River in southeast Colorado. To support this commerce, these southern groups settled near the post. In contrast, the Northern Cheyenne remained centered near the headwaters of the North Platte and Yellowstone rivers; the Northern Arapaho stayed primarily in northern Colorado and southern Wyoming.

Indian-Anglo relations deteriorated rapidly after the 1859 discovery of gold near Cherry Creek. Perhaps inevitably, as the number of settlers grew, so did the frequency of hostile encounters between the two cultures. To the immigrants in search of new opportunity, the current residents were a nuisance at best and life-threatening at worst.

From before Sand Creek until Summit Springs, the next ten years told a story of increasing hatred and bloody war that ended in the demise of the Cheyenne's way of life. By 1869, with many of their leaders dead, the buffalo herds depleted, and starvation imminent, most of them had surrendered to the U.S. Army. By 1877, all had been removed to a reservation in Oklahoma.

Reservation life was fraught with hunger and disease. In 1878, the Northern Cheyenne, led by Dull Knife, Little Wolf, and several others, fled north to their homelands. Many died or were killed along the way, but eventually the survivors were able to secure land in Montana. This is where the Northern Cheyenne headquarters is today.

While Cheyenne groups were fighting settlers, most of the Arapaho were trying to avoid confrontation. The northern bands withdrew above the Platte River into Wyoming and Montana, and in 1878, they settled with the Shoshoni on the Wind River Reservation. Once bitter enemies, these two tribes were able to make livable adjustments to each other. Today the Northern Arapaho actively maintain many of their tribal traditions.

In contrast, by 1869, the Southern Arapaho had joined the Southern Cheyenne in Oklahoma. The government abolished their reservation in 1890, leaving the people to fend for themselves in the mainstream culture. Since that time, these groups have faced a difficult struggle for survival, both physically and culturally.

In the 1800s, both the Cheyenne and the Arapaho knew the threat to their existence posed by the newcomers. In response, some chose the path of war, while others opted for the way of peace. In the end, both choices led to suffering and grief.

The sky on the High Plains is still grand, monumental, and prone to sweeping thunderheads. In some places you can even hear the coyotes howl. But the buffalo no longer roam freely. And the tribes who once lived with the endless sky now live with the reality of fences.

THE UTE OF COLORADO

Indians lived in the mountains of Colorado as far back as prehistoric times, long before Europeans invaded their daunting heights. By the late 1200s and early 1300s, the semi-nomadic Ute had arrived there. Living a life that left little mark on the land, they made their camps in the warmer, lower elevations and visited the higher mountains to hunt and fish. Named "Deer Hunting Men," "The Mountain People," and "Yutah" by others, they called themselves simply "The People." Their soft, melodious Uto-Aztecan language relates them to the Aztec, Comanche, Hopi, Akimel O'odham, Tohono O'odham, and Paiute.

Early Ute history is still unclear, and unlike many other groups in the Four Corners states, the tribe has no migration stories telling of their travels before they reached these traditional lands. It is certain, though, that they are the oldest continuous residents of Colorado.

In historic times, the Ute numbered as many as ten thousand people and were divided into seven bands: the Mouache, Capote, Tabeguache (Uncompahgre), Uintah, Weeminuche, Parianuche (Grand River), and Yamparicas (White River). They ranged west into central Utah, along the eastern Front Range of the Rocky Mountains, north along the Green River in Wyoming, and south into New Mexico.

Eagles are powerful symbols in many Native American cultures.

Eagle

Traditionally, Utes followed the seasonal pattern of hunter-gatherers, with small groups following the game herds on which they depended and then visiting favorite campsites to collect the ripened roots, seeds, and berries they knew were nearby. Sometimes they planted their own seeds to harvest when they passed through the next year. Game was lured into box canyons, stampeded over low cliffs, and channeled into ambush by using low stone walls or long nets. Rabbits were smoked from their holes, and big game was slowed in deep snow.

Their homes were light and easy to erect, made of brush and branches, or sometimes built over a pit. These domed or triangular wickiups could be eight feet tall and were heated by an inside firepot. Group harmony was essential, and the people learned to cooperate for the good of all. Property was freely shared, but it was impolite to admire someone else's possessions, because it often caused the other person to feel obligated to give it away.

From spring to autumn each small group followed the elk, deer, and small buffalo herds to high mountain meadows, their few possessions hung from shoulder ropes or tumplines around their foreheads, or strapped to a travois pulled by dogs. As winter winds approached, the families followed the animals to sheltered lower valleys. Once there, they joined other bands to face winter's harsh tests together, passing the time with storytelling and gambling games. After festivals that celebrated the arrival of spring and reaffirmed tribal unity, the people again dispersed to follow the herds.

One of the oldest of these ceremonies is the Bear Dance, called *Mama-kwa-nkhap*. It is said that once, long ago, a Ute saved a bear from starving by waking him from deep hibernation. To reward the man, the bear taught him this dance to mark winter's end and the renewal of spring. For the sake of their long-standing friendship, and in exchange for the people performing the Bear Dance, the bear agreed to use its magic to help find food.

The Bear Dance consists of several days and nights of singing, dancing, and a celebration of new life and old friends. The dancers form two lines, the men facing south and the women facing north. Then, to the accompaniment of the growling rumble of the *moraches* (sticks of notched bone or wood rubbed together), the lines move backward and forward in a slow, rhythmical wave. The shuffle and sway is reminiscent of a bear sharpening its claws for the coming hunt, and the music is to awaken the bear from hibernation so it can find food and a mate. Each day the duration of dancing and the number of dancers increases, until everyone except the smallest children is involved. The ceremony culminates in a community-wide feast and numerous weddings.

Ute life was revolutionized in the 1600s by the Spanish horse. Instead of hunting the small clusters of game in the mountain valleys, with horses they could harvest the huge bison herds on the Great Plains. Food and supplies became abundant and defense against Spanish slavers and Indian neighbors easier. Now able to remain together in large groups year-round, tribal cohesion and social structure were enhanced, and Ute leaders were able to consolidate their power. Ute warriors and raiders soon became respected for their bravery, stealth, and cunning.

By 1641, the Spanish had launched a campaign to stop Ute raids. Although not soundly defeated, the Indians were convinced it was wiser to leave the settlers alone. They turned to trading instead, and their expertly tanned animal hides adorned with porcupine quills and beadwork, their patterned woven baskets, and slaves captured from other tribes were exchanged for iron and steel tools and utensils, flint to make fire, wool blankets, pottery, and beads.

As the Ute adapted their lifestyle to the horse, they borrowed much of the culture of the Plains Indians. Clothing, tipis, and eagle-feather war bonnets all became popular, and soon horses were the measure of wealth. Both women and men owned them, and some families had hundreds. They were pampered, honored, and often painted for special occasions. Races were held between bands, with heavy betting on favorites. The horses were even treated with water from the hot springs, which were of great importance to the Utes.

Around the turn of the century, the Ute adopted the Sun Dance from the Great Plains tribes. With its emphasis on personal purification, it acts as a vehicle for spiritual renewal for participants, who channel this healing power to the community through their prayers. Today, the Sun Dance and the Bear Dance are the most important tribal ceremonials.

Chief Ouray and his wife Chipeta pose for a formal portrait in Washington, DC, January 1880.
Walker Art Studio

When the United States took control of the mountains in Colorado, the government negotiated a treaty with the Ute. Settlers, however, coveted their rich lands and competed with the Ute for water and food, further displacing the game on which the Indians relied.

As the number of Anglos in the region grew, so did the frequency of conflict. After gold was discovered in 1858 at the mouth of Cherry Creek, miners poured into the mountains, following the streams farther back into Ute strongholds to find the mother lode. Not content to take the gold and leave, the prospectors built camps and towns with little regard for treaties.

Distrust between the two groups increased, and although one treaty after another was negotiated, each was eventually broken by the newcomers. Through the years, Chief Ouray, an Uncompahgre Ute leader who believed that resisting white settlement was futile, managed to gain many concessions from the United States government. As he did so, he acquired numerous admirers and friends, as well as detractors who believed he was "selling out."

In 1879, a Ute uprising (called the Meeker Massacre by settlers) against the repressive policies of a newly appointed government agent resulted in the deaths of Nathan Meeker and ten employees at the White River Agency. Meeker's wife and daughter, as well as another woman and her children, were kidnapped.

Although the captives were eventually released, public outcry against the Ute increased, and they were banished to a reservation in Utah. A final treaty in the 1880s relegated the Colorado and northern New Mexico Utes to a strip of land 15 miles wide and 140 miles long, roughly paralleling the Colorado–New Mexico border. This land was further reduced when the allotment system opened the reservation to homesteading.

Today, the Weeminuche band lives on the Ute Mountain Ute Reservation, which is headquartered at Towaoc, Colorado. The Mouache and Capote bands reside on the Southern Ute Reservation, headquartered at Ignacio, Colorado. A small group of Weeminuche also lives on the White Mesa Reservation in southeast Utah.

Since the latter part of the nineteenth century, the northern Ute bands in both Utah and Colorado have lived on the Uintah-Ouray Reservation, headquartered at Ft. Duchesne, Utah. A separate section in the area of Desolation Canyon has since been added.

CHAPTER 3

HISTORY OF THE INDIANS
IN NEW MEXICO

THE ANCIENT ONES

The Four Corners is the high plateau country where the states of Colorado, Utah, New Mexico, and Arizona meet. Nomads lived here in centuries past, gathering wild rhubarb, lambs-quarters, and pinyon nuts and hunting rabbits and other small game with long spears and spear-throwing sticks called atl-atls. Somewhere around 100 B.C., the dramatic shift from a nomadic to an agrarian lifestyle began, and a new culture was born. Hundreds of years later, the Navajo named it "Anasazi," which means "Enemy Ancestor" or "Foreigner." Today, the Pueblo people prefer the term "Ancestral Pueblo."

The precious gift of maize, probably brought north from Mesoamerica, was a main impetus for the Ancestral Puebloans to forge a new way of life. To stay near their fields, they learned to build energy-efficient pithouses of mud and sticks, clustering them into small and widely dispersed villages.

Weaving developed into a skilled craft of extraordinary proficiency. Burden baskets, trinket baskets, flat baskets, cooking baskets, and those so tightly woven they could be lined with pitch to store water were crafted by the people we now call Basketmakers. These expert weavers also fashioned sacks without seams, carrying straps, and nets for trapping small animals. Despite the increasing importance of agriculture, the people continued to eat the mice, rabbits, wild sheep, and deer in the area and gather wild plants.

Wild turkeys were domesticated and their feathers fashioned into warm blankets and clothing. The juniper tree's soft bark became diapers, and the yucca plant provided fruit to eat, roots for soap, and fibers strong enough to make sandals and aprons.

Today it is believed that by about A.D. 700, the Basketmaker culture had evolved into that of the Pueblo Anasazi. As farming slowly became central to the people's lives, the people learned to build ditches and check dams for irrigating the fields. With stores of surplus corn, squash, beans, and cotton, the harvest needed protection from rodents and insects. Coiled pottery was crafted with plain and corrugated surfaces and then decorated with geometric, symbolic, or animal motifs. Extensive trade networks developed, bringing macaw feathers, shell, turquoise, copper bells, and other exotic goods to enrich their lives.

Farming also brought new gods to worship. With the rain, sun, and soil now holding their fate, the Indians became sky watchers, peering at the heavens for clues to guide the rhythm of their agricultural lives. Complex ceremonies, religious rituals, and a way of life that focused on the seasonal cycle were the result.

Aboveground houses of adobe and stone replaced the pithouses, which may have evolved into the ceremonial and social gathering place of the underground kiva. Pueblos were built, with adobe houses clustered around an open-air plaza. The buildings were used mainly for storage and sleeping, with daily activities taking place in the plaza or on the rooftops.

By around A.D. 1100, farming was its most productive and efficient, craftsmanship its most masterful. Pottery, jewelry, and ceremonial objects of beauty and durability added artistic touches to daily life and new items to trade.

While the Alhambra and Westminster Abbey were rising in Europe, some groups moved from the mesa tops to sheltered and hidden alcoves. This time fine masonry skills were employed to build magnificent apartment complexes three and four stories high. Nestled under natural ledges for protection from the wind and set on the west side of the canyons to catch sun in the winter and shade in the summer, these cliff dwellings were energy-efficient homes. One of the largest of these solar communities was Cliff Palace in Mesa Verde.

Other Ancestral Puebloans built pueblos curved gracefully around a central plaza. In the wash of an erratic river in New Mexico, a group of settlements now known as Chaco rose from the canyon floor. Skilled architects directed the design of the buildings, their rubble-filled double walls rising four or five stories with hundreds of thousands of dressed stones chinked with smaller ones to form patterns. Great kivas were built to accommodate communal events, and Chaco became the apex of the sophisticated Ancestral Puebloan society.

In the thirteenth century the Ancestral Puebloans gradually disappeared from the area, leaving behind tens of thousands of relics. By A.D. 1300, only fragments and ruins were left to tell the story of their once-great civilization. It is generally believed they migrated south and west to more hospitable land, becoming the ancestors of the modern-day Hopi and other Pueblo Indians in Arizona and New Mexico.

Two grinding bins, each with a mano (stone grinder) and metate (grinding surface), at Gran Quivera Ruin in Salinas National Monument

But why did the people leave? Some speculate it was warlike nomads who entered the area and drove off the Ancestral Puebloans. Others blame the arrival of a new religion, epidemics, trade disruption, the breakdown of leadership, or internal pressures for causing social changes. One theory points to a burgeoning population that led to overcrowding and the depletion of natural resources. When climate change brought shortened growing seasons and a twenty-year drought, there was no margin for error. The houses remained, but the people could not. Or maybe, as the Pueblo people say, they were instructed by their gods to play out the pattern of migration, which eventually led them to the places they now call home.

The red sandstone of the Colorado Plateau that once provided the building material for this cultural flowering fades back into the earth a little more each year. But much of the Ancestral Puebloan's handiwork still remains, preserved by the dry desert air and nestled under rock ledges, crumbling on mesa tops, and lying concealed in arroyos. Exquisite artwork, magnificent cities of stone, and thousand-year-old furs and feathers have been found in the ruins of what was once abundance. In time, these ruins may reveal answers and more secrets hidden in the land of the Ancient Ones.

THE PEOPLE OF EASTERN NEW MEXICO

Before George McJunkin, a cowboy and former slave, took a trail ride one day in 1925 across eastern New Mexico, the common theory was that people had lived in North America for only two thousand years. Then McJunkin discovered human-crafted spear and lance points lying beside the bones of an extinct bison. Almost overnight, anthropological theories were revolutionized to include the newfound Folsom culture. Years later, timelines had to be revised further when evidence of the even earlier Clovis culture was found.

People of the Folsom culture roamed the rich grasslands of northeastern Colorado and southeastern New Mexico around ten thousand years ago. The Ice Age was waning, and the Folsom hunters used superbly crafted, grooved stone lance heads to kill the giant bison, mammoths, mastodons, elephants, four-toed horses, and giant ground sloths of the time.

By 5000 B.C., the climate had changed and become hot and dry. The Folsom culture disappeared and was replaced by the Archaic, a group of wild-plant foragers and small-game hunters. Archaic people cooked their food by stone boiling, which involved dropping hot stones into clay-lined baskets to heat the water. Eventually, they learned to cultivate corn and began settling in villages.

The succession of dominant cultures continued as south-central New Mexico became a busy trade and travel corridor between the northern Pueblos and the Plains tribes. Beginning in the twelfth century, the area became a refuge for people escaping prolonged drought in the fertile Rio Grande Valley. Even after the decline of the Ancestral Puebloan culture in places like Chaco Canyon, building here continued on a monumental scale. In the Galisteo Basin southeast of Santa Fe stand Pueblo Largo, with an estimated 480 rooms, and San Cristobal Pueblo, with as many as 600 ground floor rooms in walls up to four or five stories high. Both are enormous in comparison to the 332 rooms and kivas at Pueblo Bonito, the largest settlement in Chaco Canyon. And both were visited by the nomadic raiders of the Apache, and later the Kiowa and Comanche.

Military life of the 19th century is re-enacted at Fort Union.

By 1700, the Comanche had begun their migration southward to eventually settle in the southern plains. After the Spanish introduced Comanches to horses, the tribe gained a reputation as the best horse thieves around. Comanche men developed unmatched riding skills, and each strove to own two sets of horses: one trained for war, the other for buffalo hunting.

By the 1750s, Comanches were the lords of the southern plains. Comanche herds often numbered over 250 horses—larger than those of any other tribe—and they were used to build a powerful buffalo hunting and trading culture that ranged over one thousand miles in a wealthy inland empire the Spanish called "Comancheria."

Warriors raided as far south as Durango in Old Mexico and traded horses and captives as far north as Canada. In the east they ranged from Cross Timbers, where the plains give way to the timbered east in Kansas, to the Rocky Mountains. As a buffer group, they halted the northern and eastern advance of the Spanish and the southern and western advance of the French, thus preventing these European powers from meeting and claiming the territory for their own.

Life for a Comanche was similar in many ways to that of other nomadic Plains Indians. Since the men were often absent for hunting or raiding, the women were responsible for maintaining the camp. They skinned and butchered game, dried meat, prepared and tanned hides, made clothing and tools, and raised the children.

For years, the U.S. government tried to confine the Comanche to reservations. Like the other nomadic tribes of the plains, defeat would eventually come more from hunger than bullets. As more troops and settlers marched into the Comancheria, the great southern buffalo herd almost disappeared, and the land became unable to sustain the people's traditional lifestyle.

Today, many of the Comanche live in southwestern Oklahoma. Tribal headquarters is in Lawton near Fort Sill. Aspects of the traditional culture still survive, including the language, which was used by sixteen code talkers during World War II to cloak military messages. And every summer, members from around the country return to Oklahoma for Comanche Homecoming as they strive to renew their ancestral ties and affirm that they are still Comanche.

THE PUEBLOANS

The nineteen Pueblos in New Mexico all share similarities in religion, lifestyle, and economy, although each retains a unique identity in terms of language and customs. Their three main languages are Keres, Tano, and Zuni, with the Tanoan language consisting of three dialects: Tewa, Tiwa, and Towa.

The Pueblo people trace their ancestry to earlier groups in the area, including the Ancestral Puebloans, who by A.D. 1150 had begun to migrate southward from the Four Corners. For years, they lived in scattered, self-sufficient adobe villages, worshipping the gods of their ancestors, tilling their fields in peace, and cooperating with each other.

Society was matrilineal, and when a man married, he moved in with his wife's family. The woman owned all household property, including the seeds for planting and often the resulting crops. She was also responsible for transforming the numerous varieties of corn into hominy, cornbread, tortillas, tamales, *atole*, succotash, and cornmeal mush. Men were weavers, and they tended the fields and conducted religious ceremonies to maintain harmony between the individual, the community, and the natural world.

For both men and women, life centered on religion. Each person belonged to a moiety, a social and ceremonial society that held a specific responsibility for the common good. In many of the eastern Pueblos, there were two main moieties, one of Summer People and one of Winter People.

Everything in the world was believed to have a spiritual essence, and all was believed to be interrelated. To mediate between the spirit world and the physical world, elaborate and exacting rituals were performed, and prayer sticks (*pahos*) were often used to carry messages to the spirit world.

One of the overriding forces that shaped Pueblo religious views was the cultivation of corn. Its seasonal cycle was of vital importance, with prayers and ceremonials evolving around the need for rain and for thanksgiving, and for the astronomical observations necessary to determine the proper time for planting and harvesting.

The people believed they entered this world from the world below. This point of emergence is symbolically represented by a hole called the *sipapu* found in every kiva. The Great

Native Americans and white tourists at Zuni Pueblo between 1880 and 1900

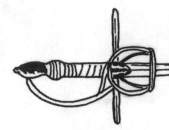

Conquistador Sword

Spirit accompanied them in their emergence, told them when and where to migrate once they entered this world, and taught them rules by which to live. The Great Spirit also warned them of coming danger and instructed them to build protected villages. In accordance with the Great Spirit's instructions, a cacique was placed in charge of the community's spiritual life. Even today, this theocratic leader remains as the head of the community in all but a few instances.

By 1525, Apache and Navajo nomads from the north had entered New Mexico and begun raiding and trading with their Pueblo neighbors. They were followed by conquerors carrying the banner of Spain and seeking to proclaim religious and cultural dominion over the native inhabitants. The 1540 expedition of Coronado was the first incursion, and one of Coronado's initial acts was to massacre much of the population of Arenal, one of the pueblos in the Tiguex province on the Rio Grande.

Spanish colonizers followed, led by Don Juan de Oñate in 1598. Catholic priests were among them, intent on converting the pagan natives. Sacred kivas were destroyed and religious leaders executed in the process.

To feed the colonists, the Spanish government confiscated crops, sometimes leaving the Indians to starve. Poverty and hunger were exacerbated by taxes the native people, now Spanish subjects, were obligated to pay to the Crown, sometimes in the form of manual labor. Thousands were enslaved and forced to work in the mines, fields, and missions, where brutality was common. Just as deadly was the unintentional transmission of European diseases to which the native population had no immunity.

On August 10, 1680, the Puebloans fought back, uniting in a rebellion under the leadership of representatives from each village and a man named Popé (Po'Pay) from San Juan Pueblo. Within days, the land was purged of Spaniards, who were either killed or driven south towards Mexico. The churches were sacked and burned, and about 400 Spanish settlers and 21 priests were killed. Indian casualties were about 350.

In less than fifteen years, the Spanish returned to formulate an uneasy peace, with some Pueblos cooperating with the Spanish and many others actively resisting reconquest. Hundreds of Indians were executed or sold into slavery; others fled to live with the neighboring Navajo or with their Pueblo relatives, the Hopi.

Despite several minor revolts, relations between the Spanish and Pueblos gradually improved, partly because of an increased Spanish tolerance for the Indian way of life. When Apache and Navajo raids increased, the Spanish and Puebloans formed an alliance against their common enemy.

Soon Spanish customs became a part of Pueblo life. Wheat became an important addition to the diet, and every home included an *horno*, an outdoor beehive-shaped oven

Horno ovens are used by the Indians of the Southwest to bake bread.

used for baking bread. Spanish became a common language, and even clothing styles changed as some Pueblo women adopted the shawls and lace of Spain.

While it ruled, the Spanish government established land grants that assured the continued Pueblo ownership of villages and land. In 1620, each Pueblo was given a silver-headed cane of authority, blessed by the church and intended to be passed on to newly selected officials. The office of governor was introduced, and since then, this individual has acted as the administrative leader of the community. Other governing officials include a lieutenant governor and tribal council members.

The Spanish reigned until 1821, when Mexico declared its independence and took control of the Pueblo territory. In 1848, Americans displaced the Mexicans, when the Treaty of Guadalupe Hidalgo ended the war between Mexico and the United States. In spite of the change of government, the Pueblos were able to retain their historic villages for the most part, although their surrounding land was often lost.

For the next few years, the settled Pueblo population suffered from extensive raids by the Navajo, Ute, Apache, and Comanche. It wasn't until after the American Civil War that the U.S. Army was able to focus its attention on the region and quell the raids. The end of Apache hostilities came in 1886, with the capture of Geronimo.

After the Pueblo people lost their land, economic self-sufficiency through traditional farming became difficult at best. In more recent times, controversy over water rights has added to this problem. In addition, Pueblo Indians were not recognized as U.S. citizens until the twentieth century—deprived of jobs, credit, education, they were discriminated against socially and economically.

In response, the Pueblos have looked to other business enterprises, including tourism. Some are now independent business owners, and many sell superbly made arts and crafts through stores and private homes at the pueblos and in neighboring towns. Since the 1980s, the gaming industry has created a source of reliable revenue for the Pueblos that is being used to fund improvements in infrastructure, education, housing, business, and other areas. Agriculture is still important for some, but many adults also commute to work in the surrounding cities of Santa Fe, Albuquerque, and Los Alamos.

Today, each Pueblo remains autonomous and is governed by a combination of the ancient tribal and European systems. In most cases, the cacique and his assistants select the governor and his staff annually, with past governors then becoming part of the tribal council. Each Pueblo also sends a representative to the All-Indian Pueblo Council, which was established centuries ago for mutual defense.

The governor now holds four canes: the original one presented in colonial times by the Spanish Crown; the Abraham Lincoln cane, which was granted by the United States in 1863; a cane given in 1980 by Governor Bruce King of New Mexico; and a Spanish cane presented in 1987 by King Juan Carlos of Spain. The lieutenant governor holds an additional cane received from Mexico after its independence. All of these symbolize the leadership, justice, and legitimate authority of the Pueblo governments.

Many Pueblo people have adapted aspects of the Catholic faith. In particular, on feast days for patron saints, Christmas and Easter, and for the sacraments such as weddings and baptism, the rites of Christianity are honored. However, the complex Pueblo religion also thrives, and numerous sacred ceremonials are held throughout the year. Ancient beliefs form the basis of religious life for many, and in the sacred kivas the people still drum to the ancient rhythms of the land.

San Geronimo Catholic church at Taos Pueblo

CHAPTER 4

HISTORY OF THE INDIANS
IN UTAH

THE FREMONT

The Fremont was a mysterious prehistoric culture that for eight hundred years dominated a region spanning the Colorado, Virgin, and Escalante rivers and north across Utah. The culture became known as the Fremont in 1928, when Noel Morss discovered a settlement along the Fremont River that he considered distinct from other early Native American cultures.

Since the initial discovery, Fremont cultural remnants have been found in Utah, Nevada, Colorado, and Idaho. The earliest finds date back as far as A.D. 1150. The northern groups shared many traits with tribes of the plains; in the south, the predominant influence seems to have been the Ancestral Puebloans.

The Fremont people were both farmers and hunter-gatherers. Game animals included prairie dogs, rabbits, bighorn sheep, and gophers. Some plants were harvested directly from nature, such as edible seeds, roots, tubers, juniper berries, and pinyon nuts. Others were cultivated, including dent corn, a unique variety highly resistant to drought and climate extremes. The Fremont people also employed extensive irrigation systems.

Archaeologists use several markers to distinguish the Fremont as a separate culture. First, they wore unusual leather moccasins made from the hide of a deer leg, with the dew claw left to protrude from the heel, possibly for padding or to act as a hob nail for traction. Juniper bark may have been stuffed inside these moccasins to provide winter insulation.

Another distinctive characteristic is their coiled, unpainted, black or gray pottery, with bits of clay added in the designs. The Fremont people also crafted unfired clay Pilling figurines—small but elaborate statues reminiscent of bread dough ornaments. Many of these were shaped like humans and painted with minerals for details.

In addition, the Fremont used caves for food storage, not for habitation. Remnants of their granaries can still be seen tucked high in canyon walls, but the grand cliff dwellings so common to the Ancestral Puebloans are nowhere to be found.

Petroglyphs at Dinosaur National Monument

Perhaps the most dramatic, and unique, reminder of these ancient people is their rock art, which includes thousands of figures pecked and painted on the rocks near their dwelling, storage, and chipping sites. Bighorn sheep were a popular subject, but some of the most unusual images are trapezoidal humanlike beings adorned with elaborate head-dresses, jewelry, and belts. Many carry wild plants or huge shields and have bodies and faces tattooed or painted with geometric designs. Some of the most intriguing examples of these somber figures can be seen at Horseshoe Canyon (also called Barrier Canyon) in Canyonlands National Park.

Several theories speculate about the origin of the Fremont. They may have evolved from the earlier Desert Archaic peoples; they may have originally come from groups living in the plains of the western United States; they may have branched off from the Ancestral Puebloans and created unique adaptations to the Utah environments.

By A.D. 1300, the Fremont culture had largely disappeared. Did they join the local Paiutes? Did they return to their Ancestral Puebloan relatives? Did they become the modern Ute and Shoshone peoples? The fate of the Fremont remains a mystery.

THE GOSHUTE

Isolated in their home in the Great Basin, the Goshute learned to hunt and gather a living from seemingly barren alkaline desert dotted only with sagebrush. Family groups were usually self-sufficient, but cooperation between families was not uncommon, and large game was shared by the village. Like some of their Shoshonean relatives, the Goshute survived by utilizing everything edible they could find, including small rodents and insects they dug from the ground. Early explorers called them "Digger People," and few appreciated the economy, knowledge, and skill it took to eke out a living in such meager surroundings.

At first, contact with European civilization was sporadic, probably starting with Mexican slavers looking for captives. It wasn't until Mormon settlers arrived in 1847, followed by the Pony Express and Overland Stage, that their lives were affected on a more profound scale. As farmers and ranchers began taking more of the desirable land with water and forage, the Goshute's fragile existence started to unravel. Local militia and the military forcibly quelled the Indian's attempts to resist, and by 1863, the people had no choice but to allow free access to their land by the military, railroads, mines, mills, stage lines, telegraph lines, ranches, and timber interests. In exchange for these concessions, they were to receive $1,000 a year for the next twenty years.

Loss of resources meant the loss of the Goshute way of life, and many tried supplementing hunting and gathering with farming and ranching. When attempts to relocate them to other reservations failed, all annuities from the 1863 agreement were cut off.

Today the Goshutes (numbering about 420 people) have two reservations, one that straddles the Utah-Nevada border at the base of Deep Creek Mountain about sixty miles southeast of Wendover, Utah, and one at Skull Valley. The barren land here has been designated a waste zone by the State of Utah and has been used as a dumping ground for low-level nuclear waste, nerve gas storage, and weapons testing by the U.S. government. Recently some of the elders agreed to allow temporary storage of nuclear waste on their land, hoping to use the promised cash to improve the lives of their people. This controversial decision has resulted in lengthy litigation that is still unresolved.

THE PAIUTE

The Paiute, who call themselves *Nuwuvi,* "The People," may have migrated to Utah from Death Valley around A.D. 100; or, they may be related to the earlier resident Fremont, who decorated parts of the Four Corners states with their unique petroglyphs. Regardless of their origin, they eventually came to occupy southeastern Utah, northeastern Arizona, southern California, and the Nevada deserts.

The basin and range geography in which the Paiute lived produced a harsh and varied land. In the deeply carved canyons, springs and small streams provided water for agave and cactus. In higher country, forests of pinyon, fir, spruce, and aspen flourished. In the broad dry valleys, mesquite and the creosote bush predominated.

As Paiutes wandered through these various landscapes, they learned to make do with what nature offered. If they lived near a lake, fish was often part of the evening meal. When bighorn sheep, deer, and antelope grazed nearby, the men hunted them. And if the only animals available were lizards, mice, and insects, these too were gratefully used. Rabbits, which were numerous and easy to kill, became a staple food. The meat and ground bones were eaten, and the skins were woven into soft, warm blankets.

The Paiute also gathered plants for medicine, raw materials, and food. Some of these, like amaranth, corn, sunflowers, and beans, were adapted from the wild and planted in the oases along waterways and by springs. Sometimes the old and very young stayed to tend the crops; sometimes the fields were only visited to weed and harvest.

The Paiute lived in small groups, which ranged widely. These mobile, extended families lived in easy-to-erect conical wickiups and open areas roofed with brush, branches, rushes, and bark. Later, canvas or animal skins were stretched over the framework.

Women became adept at gathering willow, sumac, and yucca and pulled the fibers through their teeth to soften and separate them for crafting into baskets. By weaving in the dark fibers of devil's claw plants, they created designs.

Paiute girls carry basket water vessels using a tumpline around their heads. 1874 Hillers, John K.

These light, easily carried containers were fashioned into an astonishing variety of shapes. The harvest was transported in burden baskets strapped to the back, while pinyon nuts were winnowed in flat baskets and roasted with hot coals in fan-shaped ones. Water was stored in pitch-covered vessels, and babies were carried in those woven like cradleboards. Some baskets were shaped like tennis rackets, while others resembled conical hats.

When Father Silvestre Velez de Escalante and Father Francisco Atanasio Dominguez traveled through the Southwest in 1776, they described the Paiutes as intelligent, shy people who were willing to guide, feed, and help them. Later Spaniards exploited their peaceful nature and carried away their children to be sold as slaves. The Ute, cousins of the Paiute, also conducted regular raids against them for captives to sell in Santa Fe.

Early American travelers often regarded the Paiutes as cowardly and beggars. In 1844, John C. Fremont called them "diggers," an insult that stuck. When Mormons arrived in the mid-nineteenth century, they called the Paiute the "Lamanites" and considered them members of the lost tribes of Israel who should be treated in a "civilized" manner so they could be guided to end their so-called savage ways. Towns and missions were built and Paiute children were bought as indentured servants to be worked, taught, and converted to the Mormon religion.

Although contact with Anglos brought trade, cloth, iron-tipped arrows, and a few new plants to the Paiute, it also brought settlers who gradually overwhelmed traditional Paiute fields, springs, and meeting sites. As their range and resources narrowed, many took low-paying jobs in the fields and homes of the settlers. Others sought to hold to their traditional ways and joined with tribes across the Colorado River. Eventually, the government gave them reservation land, most of it with little available water and only marginal hunting and gathering resources.

In the late 1880s, a Paiute holy man named Wovoka had a vision. If the people performed the Ghost Dance, the land would be cleansed of the white culture and restored to its natural bountiful state. The indigenous people could again practice the old ways. The message spread quickly to other tribes, but it was brutally crushed in 1890 when at Wounded Knee, South Dakota, hundreds of Sioux dancing the Ghost Dance were massacred by U.S. troops.

Today, the Paiutes are concentrated in four main places: the San Juan Paiute on the Navajo Reservation, the Kaibab band in Arizona, the Las Vegas and Moapa bands in Nevada, and the five Southern Paiute groups in Utah living in scattered settlements around towns like Richfield, Cedar City, and Kanosh.

With help from their Mormon neighbors, the Kaibab group was able to stay in traditional territory. They now have government housing, a tribal office, a community center, and social services. A cash settlement, shared with other Paiutes in 1965, helped them improve their educational and economic opportunities.

The traditional homelands of the San Juan Paiutes in northern Arizona and southern Utah were annexed to the Navajo Reservation in 1884 and 1933. Today, they are part of a complicated lawsuit involving the Hopi and Navajo over who will live on and use the land claimed by each of them.

Because of their isolation, the lifestyle of the San Juan Paiutes remains the most traditional of all Paiutes. Many still greet the morning sun and feed the spring bonfires dedicated to the Thunder People who bring the rain. They continue to weave devil's claw into the patterns of their wedding baskets, selling them to their Navajo neighbors, who believe the baskets have special powers. When other Paiutes want their children to learn the language and ways of their ancestors, they send them to study with the San Juan Paiutes.

THE SHOSHONE

The Shoshone were once hunter-gatherers well adapted to survival in their homelands. After they obtained the horse from the Plains Indians, they were able to hunt buffalo and raise their standard of living.

Living by the Great Salt Lake and in the valleys of northern Utah, the Northwestern Shoshone were drastically affected by the arrival of Mormon farmers and the resulting loss of resources taken by settlers. California-bound emigrants and gold seekers traveled through their homelands on the way to Montana and brought additional disruption to their lives. In response, young Shoshone warriors led by a man named Bear Hunter began leading raids against the intruders.

On the morning of January 29, 1863, a military force from Fort Douglas brutally assaulted the 450 men, women, and children encamped with Bear Hunter at Bear River. Between 250 and 400 Shoshone, including Bear Hunter and at least 90 women and children, were killed in what is now considered one of the worst slaughters in American Indian history.

Eventually, many of the survivors were baptized into the Church of Jesus Christ of Latter-day Saints and helped to establish the town of Washakie, fifty miles north of Brigham City. The remaining Shoshone moved to Fort Hall Reservation in Idaho.

It was not until 1980 that the Northwestern Shoshone gained federal recognition. It now holds a 187-acre land base, 40 percent of which is in a cemetery, along with some land held in trust by the Bureau of Indian Affairs. Tribal offices for the 383 members are in Brigham City, Utah, and in Pocatello, Idaho.

With little land and few people, the Shoshone have looked to creative enterprises for economic development. Foreign language translations for the U.S. government, construction companies, and energy development have all provided important sources of revenue. The Shoshone have also secured monetary pledges from the U.S. government to build a visitor center, memorial park, and monument on the thirty-three acres they own at the

Beadwork was traditionally an important activity for Ute women.

Bear River Massacre site. Other land is being developed for an industrial park, interpretive center, travel plaza, and casino resort.

THE UTE OF UTAH

The Ute were called "Yutah" by Europeans. It comes from an Apache word that means "one that is higher up," and this is where the state of Utah got its name. The Ute moved seasonally to take advantage of the hunting and gathering in Provo Valley and beyond, often fishing the freshwater lakes and drying the abundance of their catch to sustain them over the winter or for trade. They wove plant fibers into skirts and sandals, and fashioned rabbit skins and leather into leggings, skirts, and shirts. Their homes were easily erected brush wickiups and ramadas. After the arrival of the horse around 1680, Ute hunters bagged larger mammals, warriors excelled in raiding, and traders became important middlemen for the horse and slave trades.

When Mormons settled Salt Lake Valley and began competing for the limited resources, the displaced Ute began raiding the isolated communities. More suffering and disruption came with the Walker War of 1853–54 (which was ignited by the death of Chief Walkara's cousin at the hands of a settler), as well as with the failed attempts to settle the Ute as farmers and the Black Hawk War, begun in 1865 by a Ute named Black Hawk in retaliation for a Mormon insult.

By 1869, the starving Ute moved to the Uintah and Ouray Ute Reservation and lost their nomadic hunter-gatherer lifestyle. Searching for a way to preserve their native identity, many embraced the Sun Dance and Peyotism. More recently, oil, gas, land leases, and the sale of watershed runoff have benefited their economy, and restoration of legal jurisdiction over land owned in the pre-allotment reservation has increased their political power.

Today, tribal headquarters is in Fort Duchesne. See Chapter 2, "The History of the Indians in Colorado," for more about the Ute.

SECTION II

DISCOVERING NATIVE AMERICA

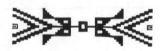

HOW TO USE THE TRAVEL GUIDE

Some tips on how to use this guidebook:

Although we do mention other sites, this book focuses on places that have a direct Native American connection. Some of these were chosen to acknowledge the strong ties indigenous peoples had and continue to have with the land that nurtured and supported them. Areas that preserve natural features provide a glimpse into the kind of places they fought so hard to retain.

We have clustered the sites around core cities that make convenient places to stay while in a specific area. These towns are listed in the text in alphabetical order. In addition, immediately under the name of the core city, we have listed the Native American sites in and near that town.

We have listed alphabetically the contact information for each travel chapter at the end of that chapter.

We have made every effort to include accurate information; however, availability of services, hours, telephone numbers, dates of events, and other information can and does change. Even historical and archaeological "facts" are sometimes revised. We recommend you check ahead before making special plans.

Since most tourist attractions are not open on major holidays, we do not make note of that. Christmas, New Year's Day, and Thanksgiving are common times to close, and state facilities are usually closed on state holidays.

Maps are included at the beginning of each travel chapter to point to the general location of the sites. The map numbers in each chapter are keyed to the core cities. Since these maps are not detailed enough to depend on in more remote areas, we recommend you purchase a general road map or one with more details about the various Indian lands. The Southern California American Automobile Association (AAA) prints one of the entire Four Corners regions called "Indian Country," which covers the Navajo, Hopi, Havasupai, Hualapai, Zuni, Jicarilla Apache, and many smaller reservations. North Star Mapping publishes a road map of the Navajo and Hopi Nations, plus some of the adjacent reservations.

Since Native American languages were typically not written, there is often not one agreed-upon spelling for a word. We have chosen a spelling that seems to be most acceptable to native peoples.

Occasionally, we refer to a native group by the name the people use to describe themselves rather than the one that might be more familiar to you because the familiar name is considered derogatory by the people it references. Instances of this include Tohono O'odham rather than Papago and Akimel O'odham rather than Pima. Others are referenced in the text. In addition, there is no consensus on what to call the indigenous people in general. Since many individuals refer to themselves as "Native American" and "Indian," we use these terms interchangeably. Likewise, the Navajo word "Anasazi" is the term preferred by the Navajo, while the Hopi and Pueblo descendants of that culture prefer "Ancestral Puebloan." Both terms are in general usage, and we use both in this guide.

Travel to the Southwest has some unique aspects. For your safety, please be aware of the following:

Because towns may be separated by large distances, and because some small towns may not have services available, plan ahead for when you will need to fill your gas tank and your stomach. Also realize that cell phone coverage is spotty in many rural areas.

Be alert for flash flooding, which can turn the dry wash across the road into a torrent of mud, rocks, and sticks in an instant, even when the thunderstorm is far upstream.

Because of the extreme summer heat in the desert and canyon country, it is advisable to avoid prolonged exposure to the sun during the middle of the day. *Always* carry drinking water. Sunscreen and a hat are also important.

In remote places, make lodging reservations early to avoid being stranded.

Secure your valuables and lock your car. Theft on reservations continues to be a problem, especially in isolated parking areas.

Windows at Guisewa Ruins provide a glimpse to the past.

VISITING THE PUEBLOS AND RESERVATIONS

As was the case in the past, a variety of native cultures exist today, each with its own individual language, customs, and religion. "Indian Country" is now anyplace individuals gather to share their common ancestry and connect with their roots. It can be on a reservation or at a community center in the middle of a large city, where many Native Americans now make their homes. As in all cultures, individual attitudes vary, ranging from traditionalists who strive to maintain the lifeways of their ancestors to modernists whose goal is to assimilate into mainstream America.

Some non-Indians have sought to become part of Native American culture by pursuing its customs and rituals. They have been encouraged by certain individual Indians who share their spiritual practices in the hope of transmitting values they believe are vital to the future of humanity. Other Native Americans strongly criticize what they call "Indian wannabes," making the claim that these "new-agers" are engaged in a modern form of genocide by stealing one of the few things left to Native Americans—their religion. The National Congress of American Indians is one group that has denounced non-Indians who profit commercially as so-called shamans or experts on Indians, pointing out that they have failed to grasp the impossibility of divorcing native spirituality from the history, culture, and well-being of each tribe.

Because of its emphasis on communal life, native religion has strengthened the community and enabled groups not only to adapt to the harsh environment but also to survive the appalling destruction of both people and lifeways that began with the arrival of the Spanish in 1540. Although the effects of centuries of cultural disintegration and forced government dependency have been impossible to escape completely, Native America is in a cultural renaissance. With this resurgence has come new pride in traditions, languages, and native contributions to contemporary society, as well as a renewed dedication to economic self-reliance.

Tourism is one of the most lucrative vehicles for this economic self-reliance but is fraught with dilemma. Tribes thrive from the added revenues tourists bring, and Indian tradition emphasizes extending the hand of friendship to visitors, but the reservations are first and foremost the homes of people who, like most, value their privacy and the sanctity of their sacred places. The destruction of these sanctuaries, the real or perceived rudeness by visitors, and the violation of rituals, both intentional and unwitting, have all increased with the tourist traffic.

Priscilla Torivio-Jim uses designs from her Acoma heritage to create her pottery.

One way to support the native communities you visit is to take your business directly to tribal enterprises and individual artisans. When touring, hire an Indian guide to lead you through his or her homeland. The personal perspective imparted can never be learned from a non-Indian or by reading a book. Learn about the variety of cultures by visiting different communities and meeting the residents. You may be surprised by their friendliness and willingness to share their cultural heritage.

The question remains as to whether tourism will bring the native and non-native cultures closer to mutual understanding and support or be yet another wedge driven between the two. As a tourist, you will be a part of the answer.

Although each community may have specific rules for visitors, in general, most ask that you adhere to the following:

> Remember that you are a guest, so travel with respect for the land and the inhabitants. The pueblos and reservations are not theme parks.

> The center of the reservation is often tribal headquarters. Inquire here about local customs and regulations and to obtain the necessary licenses and permits for such things as entrance and recreation. The tribal offices can also tell you which events are open to the public.

> Honor the sanctity of holy places, whether they are kivas, cemeteries, or sacred mountains, and do not enter them. These places carry the same significance to a Native American as the Vatican does to a Catholic or Mecca to a Muslim.

> Do not enter a private residence unless you are invited.

> Do not enter any area marked "off limits."

> In national parks located on reservations, personal-use photography is allowed. However, many communities require a permit for photography, sketching, and recording. In some instances, all photography is prohibited, which means you should leave your camera in the car and out of sight to avoid it being confiscated. Even when photography is permissible, always ask before taking a picture of an individual or his or her land or private residence. And don't be surprised if you are asked for a fee in return.

> Wear modest clothing (no bare midriffs, shorts, revealing clothes).

> Most reservations have strict rules against alcohol, drugs, littering, firearms, and sometimes pets. Off-road and off-trail travel is also often prohibited.

> Do not disturb or remove plants, artifacts, or feathers.

> Obey the traffic laws, especially in places where children are playing or when an open-range policy means you could be confronted by a herd of sheep around the next turn.

> Remember that you are visiting a different culture, and English may not be the main language spoken. About 250 Indian languages are still in use throughout the United States. Consider learning a simple greeting in your host's language as a show of goodwill.

> Communication may have different ground rules, and a cultural exchange that you take for granted, such as eye contact or a firm rather than a light handshake, may be considered rude. It is also often considered impolite to point with a

finger, so use a nod of your head instead. In general, polite listening is often considered a virtue, especially when an elder is talking.

And last, but certainly not least, keep an open mind, a relaxed attitude, and a sense of adventure.

One of the best ways to gain a deeper understanding of each culture is to attend a public ceremony. Please remember that these are often religious observances and the participants are fulfilling a spiritual role. Behave as if you were in church by maintaining silence and saving your questions for later. In addition, keep the following in mind:

If photography is allowed, do not use a flash, as it distracts the dancers.

Do not interrupt the dancers or touch their regalia.

The ceremonies do not adhere to a strict time schedule, and it is considered impolite to ask what time the ceremony will begin.

Applause is not always appropriate, so follow the lead of Indians in the audience.

Leave the chairs in front for older members of the host community.

Turn off all cell phones and leave your pets at home.

ARCHAEOLOGICAL SITES AND MUSEUMS

Thousands of prehistoric sites exist in the Four Corners states, many in unexpected places. Because most of the stabilized ones are in national monuments, national parks, or historic parks, and because vandalism is an increasing problem, we have not included specific directions to some of the more remote sites. Visitors can obtain information from the local sources we have listed.

In addition to the ruins of pueblos and other structures, the prehistoric peoples of the Southwest left numerous scattered panels of rock art. These are petroglyphs chipped into rock often coated with a black or brown surface called "desert varnish" and pictographs that are painted with minerals on the smooth red sandstone of eastern Utah.

Despite repeated attempts to interpret these ancient records, for the most part their meanings remain a mystery. Interpretations vary wildly. Some believe the rock art was spiritual in nature, etched on sacred spots and portraying shamans and the spirits that aided them in their journeys to gain wisdom and health for the community. Others believe the art records special events such as coming-of-age ceremonies, astronomical and seasonal guides, clan territorial boundaries, and trail markings. Some even claim that the art is simply an ancient form of doodling.

The science of archaeology provides a window to the prehistoric human past. Because the context in which an artifact is found is vital to understanding it, once a site has been disturbed, much of its value is lost forever. And because these fragile sites are nonrenewable resources, destroying, vandalizing, or altering them in any way is a federal crime. Even buying an item illegally obtained is a crime. The federal Archaeological Resources Protection Act provides a penalty for such actions of $20,000 and ten years in prison for first-time offenders.

According to experts, it is the thousands of seemingly innocent acts that are often re-

Archaeologists work to uncover the story of the past.

sponsible for destroying these resources, so keep these rules in mind when visiting a prehistoric site:

Do not visit sites that are closed to the public.

Do not touch or in any way disturb artifacts, no matter how small.

Stay off the wall, roofs, and middens (low mounds nearby that indicate the trash pile) of ruins unless they are specifically marked as accessible; do not touch the plaster or lean against windows and doorways. Stay on the trails; foot traffic near the walls causes erosion. In addition, eating and camping should be at least three hundred feet from the site.

All of the following cause irreparable damage to rock art: touching (oil and moisture on hands deteriorate it), making rubbings, building a fire nearby, adding your own rock art, and chalking, repecking, or repainting to make the image more visible.

Don't leave trash or "offerings" at the site.

Remember that when these resources disappear, they will be gone forever. If you witness anyone vandalizing a site or removing artifacts, report them. A reward is often available for information that leads to a conviction.

ARTS AND CRAFTS

Traditionally, Native Americans have expressed their spirituality, cultural traditions, and connection to nature through their art. In contrast to Western societies, art has not been viewed as separate from utility, and in many Indian languages, a word for art did not even exist.

The pot used to cook breakfast required the correct spirit to survive the handling and heat and to infuse the food with nourishment and inspiration. That spirit was incorporated into the pot by the skill of the artisan and his or her personal connection with spirit. Symbols and colors were often used to express the power of the artist's vision, as well as to act as a conduit for the spirit to enter the life of the owner.

Art has also been an integral part of Native American economies, as each tribe gained skills in making a particular item that could be traded to other groups. Individual artists gained status and respect by using their skill to enhance the reputation of the group.

Even though the Indian Arts and Crafts Act of 2000 states that an item advertised as an Indian product must be made by either a member or a certified artisan of a federally recognized tribe, buying Native American arts and crafts can be fraught with pitfalls. One of the problems is labeling. Perhaps the most authentic work would be created from raw material gathered in traditional ways from nature and then fashioned completely by hand by a full-blooded tribal member. But what about the urban potter who is a quarter Pueblo and uses materials bought from a national distributor? Or the Navajo who uses acrylics to decorate the figures of Hopi katsinas that were machine-crafted? Or the 50 percent Indian mixed-blood and non–tribal member who handcrafts pieces of silver jewelry and sets them with imitation stones?

Another problem in the trade of Native American arts and crafts is the dishonesty of sellers and ignorance of buyers. Worldwide business interests have rushed to cash in on the popularity of Native American art and have even been successful at renaming towns in the Phillipines "Hopi" and "Zuni" so they can stamp items made there with those names and then sell them as authentic at a huge profit.

Many stores carry both authentic and non-authentic items, and staff members do not always know which is which. Store personnel might also be unaware of the origin of an item or may have themselves been hoodwinked by a dishonest or unscrupulous trader.

Perhaps the best advice is to buy what you like but know what it is you are buying. There is nothing wrong with purchasing an inexpensive piece as long as you are not expecting museum quality. In keeping with the nature of true Indian art, find a piece that speaks to you, either through the symbols, colors, designs, or feel of the piece, and one that opens a door to your own deeper connection with spirit.

The more information you know about a piece, the more likely you will end up with what you want. Although price often reflects quality, it is no guarantee. When purchasing an expensive item, ask for background information about the artist, his or her culture, and how the piece was made. For historical pieces, find out what the item was used for originally and how it was acquired. The value of the artwork is increased it if is signed by the artist and accompanied with a certificate of authenticity. Also look for the artist's "hallmark" on the piece.

Some of the best places to purchase Indian arts and crafts are from trading posts, stores, and individual artists on the various reservations, where prices are often cheaper than in the cities. Another advantage of shopping on the reservation is that you can hear from the source the meanings of the incorporated symbols and designs, as well as other related stories about the work. The tribal headquarters usually has information on people who sell from their homes and by mail.

Established art fairs like the Santa Fe Indian Market produced by the Southwestern Association for Indian Arts require their exhibitors to adhere to strict quality standards.

Many different types of Native crafts are displayed at this powwow booth.

Larger museums, such as the Heard Museum in Phoenix and the Museum of Northern Arizona in Flagstaff, also have quality controls. In addition, look for tribal cooperatives such as the Navajo Arts and Crafts Enterprise. Other reputable dealers who offer authentic items are in regional art centers such as Santa Fe, Sedona, and Phoenix. Local chambers of commerce can be reliable sources of information, as can other businesses in the area, which are usually well aware of their neighbors' reputations.

Other places to find information are the U.S. Department of the Interior's Indian Arts and Crafts Board, which has a listing of galleries in each state that sell authentic Native American pieces. The Indian Arts and Crafts Association is an association of distributors, museums, collectors, and creators of Native American arts and crafts whose members pledge that what they represent is authentic. The association also sells an inexpensive packet of brochures detailing how to buy Indian arts and crafts.

Following is information about some of the crafts and the groups that produce them. More specific information is included in the travel chapters. Realize that Native American art is a living tradition that continues to evolve, and contemporary Native American artists excel in all art media, from photography to sculpture.

BASKETRY (Akimel O'odham, Apache, Hopi, Jemez Pueblo, Paiute, Santo Domingo Pueblo, Tohono O'odham, Ute) Since 8000 B.C., baskets have been used in North America for cradling children, gathering, trapping, cooking, serving, storing, and transporting. They have also played a part in religious ceremonies, and in many cultures, having the skill to make a basket took on an unprecedented importance.

Even today, fine baskets are in high demand. The Hopi create wicker and plaited yucca items, and the Jicarilla and Western Apache, Ute, Jemez and Santo Domingo Pueblos, and Paiute still maintain their weaving traditions, although on a limited scale. The Akimel O'odham and Tohono O'odham expertly weave baskets from the devil's claw plant, willow, and bear grass. In addition, in response to a growing scarcity of these traditional materials, some of them have begun weaving miniature baskets out of horsehair. The Havasupai, Hualapai, and Yavapai also weave a small number of baskets.

When considering price, look for consistency of shape and color in the basket, as well as the placement and proportion of the design. The finer the weave (i.e., the greater number of stitches and coils per inch) and the more complex the design, the more valuable the basket.

BEADWORK (Apache, Ute) Beadwork evolved from quillwork after traders introduced glass beads, and the two crafts use many of the same designs. A quality beaded piece should have no knots showing, a uniformity of size and color of beads, and no loose beads. In addition, the backing should be in good condition and not show through, and the beading should lay flat. Apache and Ute artisans still create fine pieces of beadwork today.

FETISHES (Zuni) Fetishes are objects carved from stone, antler, or shell as representations of plants, animals, or forces of nature and are considered to have the power of those objects. Fetishes have been used since prehistoric times for luck, curing illness, protection, and fertility.

Although many tribes carve these items, the Zuni are considered the most skillful. Fetishes are an honored and integral part of their lives and are even sometimes symbolically given food and water. The bundle tied to the back of a Zuni fetish (usually a piece of coral, turquoise, or an arrowhead) is such an offering.

Newer styles of carving are generally more realistic and detailed than the older ones. Look for the skill of the representation, the material from which it is carved, and the name of the artist to gauge the value.

HEISHI (Santo Domingo Pueblo) *Heishi* (pronounced *he-she*) is a type of bead comprising seashells, coral, jet, pipestone, or other stone broken into small pieces. After a hole is drilled in the center, the beads are ground and polished into a uniform size and then strung together into a necklace or earrings. Some of the oldest jewelry found in the Four Corners region was made from *heishi*, using shells traded from the Gulf of California.

The finest *heishi* today is from Santo Domingo Pueblo. A good quality piece will be well strung and made with uniform beads. The smaller the bead, the more expensive the strand usually is.

KATSINAS (Hopi) Katsinas are considered the spirit essence of all things, both animate beings like plants and animals and inanimate objects such as the moon. The Hopi believe hundreds of these spirits exist, and for part of the year, they visit the people and intercede on their behalf. During this time, they are embodied in ceremonies by masked and costumed dancers. Although primarily a Hopi belief, katsinas also appear in the dances of other Pueblos, in particular the Zuni.

Katsina also refers to the carved and painted wooden figurines that represent these spirits and that are given to children for educational purposes or to girls and women as a blessing. Hopi artisans carve them from dried cottonwood roots using a saw, hammer, chisel, knife, and rasp. The katsina doll is then smoothed with sandpaper, coated with fine clay, and painted, today usually with acrylics. The paraphernalia is added last.

Earlier figures are not as intricately carved as later ones and are often seen in static positions. Although some carvers are skilled enough to create a finely tuned katsina out of a single piece of wood, most use several pieces and glue them together. Katsinas both old and new carry expensive price tags. Recently, less expensive machine-cut katsinas made by other tribes have been offered for sale.

Maria Martinez and her son Popovi Da created beautiful San Ildefonso pottery (1961).

POTTERY (Hopi, Navajo, Rio Grande Pueblos, Tohono O'odham) Around two thousand years ago, farmers in the Four Corners area began to make storage vessels, cooking pots, and ceremonial jars out of clay. The earliest pieces were generally a plain gray, but before long, an astounding variety of forms and designs had developed.

In general, traditional potters do not use a wheel. Instead they employ a coil-and-scrape method, whereby long ropes of clay are coiled into the shape of the pot and then are scraped and smoothed. Designs are either carved or painted on the vessel. One of the newest techniques to emerge is called "sgraffitto," which involves carving a design after firing. Another new pottery technique is that of making "storyteller" figures.

The majority of the pottery made today is for decorative, not functional, purposes. Pueblo and Maricopa artisans excel at the craft, although few Maricopa potters are active today. Look for a balanced and pleasing shape (a coiled pot will not be perfectly symmetrical), a smooth finish, and a skillfully rendered design that enhances the shape.

SANDPAINTING (Navajo) Sandpaintings are made by sprinkling colored sand composed of ground stones into an intricate design on the earth. They were originally part of Navajo healing ceremonies, created by a medicine man and then destroyed immediately following the ceremony. Permanent sandpaintings were not fashioned until this century, partly as a means of preserving a vanishing tradition.

Since the mid-1970s, Navajo artisans have been exploring nonreligious subjects and different techniques to create "sand art." Today, even those who depict traditional designs often incorporate small changes that alter them from the sacred original.

Look for the uniformity and fineness of the sand and the lines, as well as the complexity of the design.

SILVERWORK (Hopi, Navajo, Rio Grande Pueblos, Zuni) The Navajo were the first Southwestern Native Americans to use metal work, a skill they learned from Spaniards and Mexicans. Interest in the craft expanded during their exile at Fort Sumner, when many learned blacksmithing and made their first jewelry from copper and brass. Silversmithing gained popularity among the Navajo after their return to Arizona in 1868, and the craft later spread to the Hopi, Zuni, and other Pueblos.

Silver jewelry is often set with turquoise, a semiprecious stone that varies in hardness, color, and markings. Usually found soft and porous, the small percentage naturally hard enough to cut and polish is of increased value. Today, some of the turquoise is "stabilized"—that is, immersed in a plastic resin. It is commonly used to make *heishi* necklaces and earrings (see Beadwork), but jewelry made with it is generally of less value than that of unstabilized stones.

Markings range from a pale blue to a deep green with the most valuable being a deep blue webbed with black. Before the Spanish came to North America, Indians dug turquoise with stone hammers and antler picks at places like Cerrillos, a mine that extended two hundred feet underground. Today non-Indians mine the vast majority of it. Knowing the mine of origin can enhance the value of a stone.

Styles of jewelry have evolved from adaptations of Spanish and Plains Indian styles. Navajo artists emphasize heavy pieces with fluid silver designs around the stones; the squash blossom necklace that many associate with Southwestern jewelry is of their design. The Zuni are known for their delicate lapidary work. The Hopi often use a technique called overlay and frequently incorporate animal designs into their pieces.

When buying silver jewelry, be sure the silver is sterling and the turquoise authentic.

TEXTILES (Hopi, Navajo) The earliest textiles were made by Basketmaker people, who used finger-weaving techniques to crate nets, bags, and other necessities. By around A.D. 1000, the use of loom weaving and domesticated cotton had been learned from cultures in Mesoamerica.

Navajo women card, spin, and weave wool for a rug between 1921 and 1931.

The Pueblo Indians considered cotton a sacred crop. Thus, weaving became a spiritual activity restricted to men in the kiva. Because most of the complex techniques they devised were lost during the Spanish domination, Pueblo weaving has almost died out. Hopi weavers, however, still craft fine pieces today.

Around 1500 A.D., the Navajo learned to use Pueblo-style looms and Spanish wool for skillfully crafting blankets that soon became highly prized trade items. In the late 1800s, traders suggested design improvements to increase the value of the textiles. In addition to patterns that developed then, such as Two Grey Hills, Ganado Red, and Teec Nos Pos, modern weavers often use distinctive individual patterns and pictorials that depict ceremonies, events in daily life, or words to live by.

To gauge the value of a textile, look for balance and symmetry of design, color resonance, and evenness and tightness of the weave.

THE POWWOW

The powwow is an important social occasion, when family and friends come together to honor their heritage. The term comes from the eastern Algonquian word *pau-wau,* which refers to a curing ceremony. This passed into English as *powwow* and came to refer to a social gathering of dancing and singing. Most of the powwow activities evolved from Plains Indian ceremonial dances held to celebrate successful hunts and battles.

Powwows are attended by locals, as well as visitors from around the country. Many communities sponsor at least one large event a year, usually in summer. Smaller celebrations are also often held throughout the year. The large commercial events are held on a specific date each year, in auditoriums and parks in the cities and outside on the reservations.

Powwow pageantry begins with the Grand Entry, a colorful spectacle that involves all the dancers, from the oldest to the youngest, entering the arena in their regalia. They are led by the Honor Guard, comprising veterans carrying the United States' and state flags, and the Feathered Staff representing the Indian peoples. Next are honored guests, tribal leaders, politicians, and the royalty—young women chosen to represent their communities.

They are followed by the dancers, who sweep into the arena accompanied by the rhythm of the drumbeat and the powerful chanting of the singers. The male traditional dancers often lead the procession, their hawk and black-tipped golden eagle feathers bobbing with movements that portray a hunter tracking his prey or a warrior stalking an enemy. Next are the male grass dancers, with brilliantly colored strings of yarn swaying to smooth movements. The flashy "fancy dancers" follow, with feather bustles blending into a twirl of color.

The traditional dancers also lead the female participants, as the fringe on their beaded, ankle-length buckskin dresses sways gently to the rhythm of their graceful, precise steps. Other traditional women dancers wear dresses of red or dark blue wool embroidered with elk teeth.

The female jingle dancers are clad in form-fitted dresses of bright cloth and decorated with hundreds of "jingles"—tin cones that are often made from lids of snuff or chewing tobacco containers. With each step, the cones jingle, just as the cowry shells, elk teeth, or deer toes (halves of hoofs) did on dresses in times past, when this style was first given to an Ojibwa girl in a vision.

The colors of the female fancy dancers are as brilliant as those of the men. Their out-fits are decorated with beads and sequins; beautifully embroidered shawls drape over their shoulders to be held like outstretched wings. Children are also part of the procession, wear-ing everything from traditional to fancy dress.

When all the dancers have entered the arena, they pause for a prayer and a song. Then they dance together, an intertribal communion of friendship and joy. Several Grand En-tries are held during a multi-day powwow, with the largest one usually on Saturday night.

Special exhibition dancing includes difficult styles such as the Hoop Dance, which uses ten to twenty unconnected hoops to create intricate shapes. During social dances, the au-dience is sometimes invited to participate. In contest dancing, participants are judged on style and outfit. Missing a drumbeat, dropping part of one's regalia, or failing to stop on the last beat are all causes for disqualification. Drumming contests between singing groups are also held.

Other events that take place at powwows include Honor Songs and giveaways, which are sponsored to mark a special occasion, an individual accomplishment, or a deceased family member. In addition, many powwows have arts-and-crafts booths, food vendors, a rodeo, gambling games, athletic tournaments, parades, and other special events. Be aware that vendors prefer that you pay in cash, although many also accept credit cards.

If you visit a powwow, realize that they often do not adhere to a strict schedule. The audience is requested to stand in silence during the Grand Entry and during Honor Songs. Alcohol and drugs are forbidden, and conservative dress is expected. Photography for per-sonal use is usually permitted, except during ceremonial dances, prayers, and certain Honor Dances. Listen to the master of ceremonies for announcements about those times. Also, it is courteous to ask before photographing or videotaping an individual dancer. And if you need to get to the other side of the arena, walk around the perimeter, not through the center.

A powwow dancer
in his regalia

CONTACT INFORMATION

Indian Arts and Crafts Association
4010 Carlisle Blvd NE, Suite C, Albuquerque,
    NM 87107
505-265-9149 • www.iaca.com

Indian Arts and Crafts Board
U.S. Department of the Interior
www.doi.gov/iacb

Southwestern Association for Indian Arts
www.swaia.org

National Museum of the American Indian
    (Smithsonian)
Fourth Street & Independence Ave., S.W.,
    Washington, DC 20560
202-633-1000 • www.nmai.si.edu

Native Energy
Help offset the carbon dioxide impact of your
    travel by donating to build Native Ameri-
    can wind farms.
PO Box 539, Charlotte, VT 05445
800-924-6826 • www.nativeenergy.com

Native Music and Links
www.nativeradio.com

List of Powwows throughout the U.S.
www.powwows.com

500 Nations
Information on U.S. and Canadian tribes and
    events
http://500nations.com

SECTION III

TRAVEL GUIDE

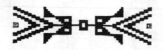

ARIZONA

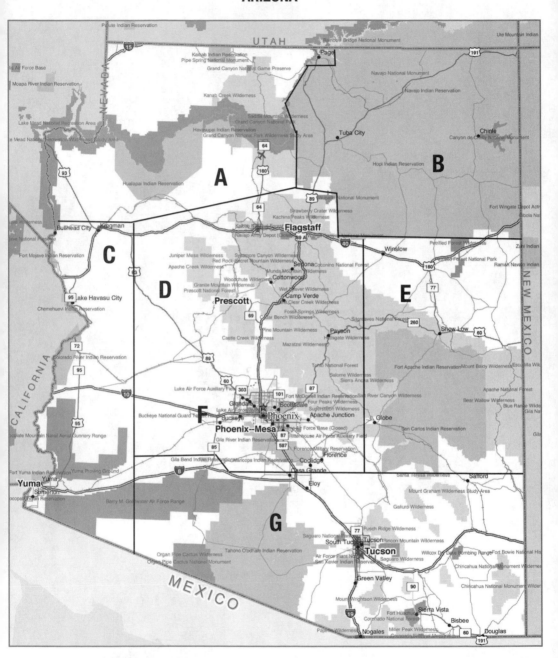

A. **Grand Canyon Country**

B. **Hopi/Navajo**

C. **Arizona's West River Coast**

D. **Central Arizona**

E. **East Central Arizona**

F. **Metropolitan Phoenix**

G. **Southern Arizona**

COLORADO

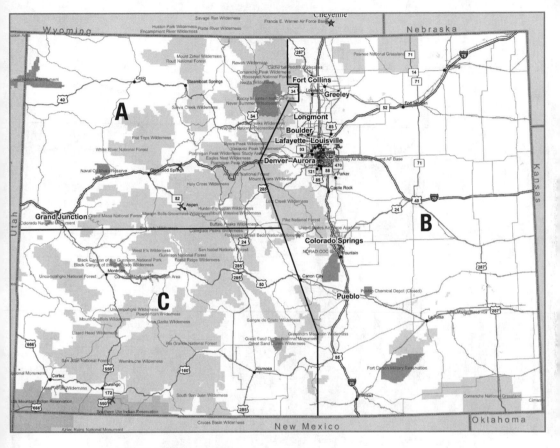

A. Northwest Colorado
B. Colorado's Front Range/High Plains
C. Southwest Colorado

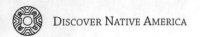
NEW MEXICO

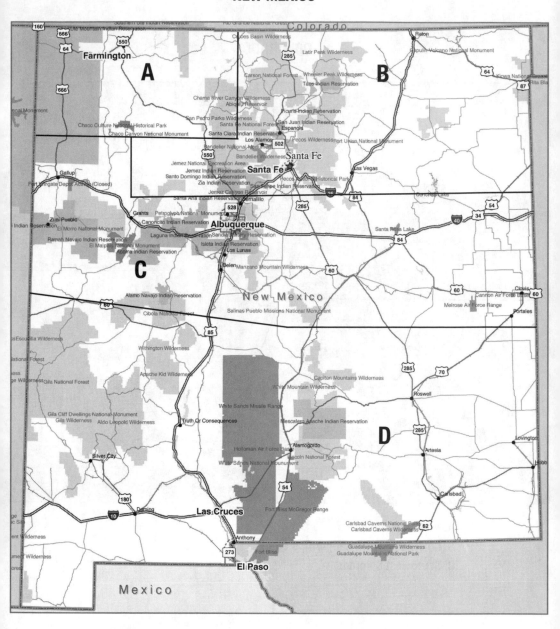

A. Northwest New Mexico

B. Northeast and North Central New Mexico

C. New Mexico's I-40 Corridor

D. Southern New Mexico

UTAH

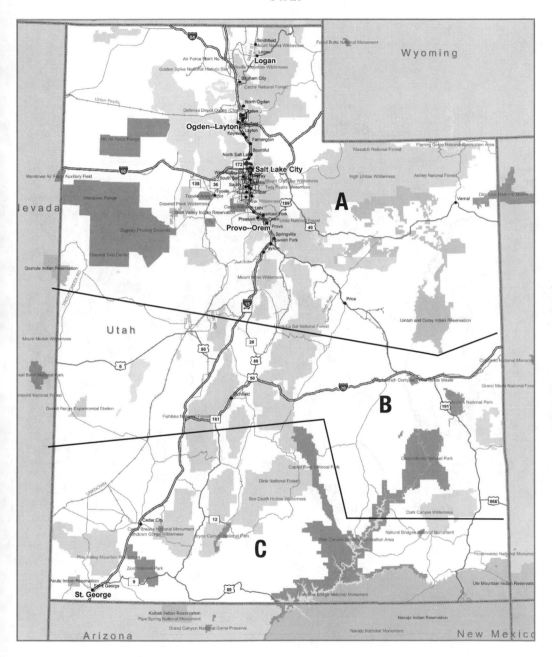

A. **Northern Utah**
B. **Central Utah**
C. **Southern Utah**

GRAND CANYON COUNTRY

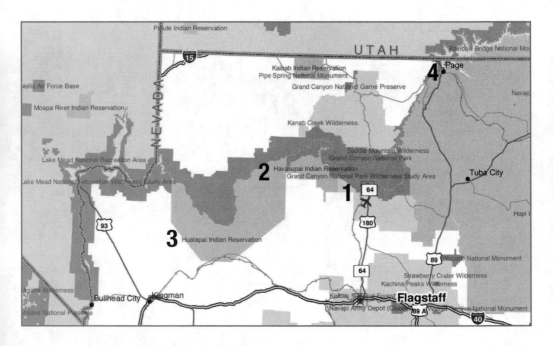

1. Grand Canyon National Park
2. Havasupai Reservation
3. Hualapai Nation
4. Page

CHAPTER 5

∿∿∿∿∿∿

GRAND CANYON COUNTRY

FOR MILLIONS OF YEARS, the mighty Colorado River has been carving out the land in northwestern Arizona, progressively revealing older and older pages of its past. The Grand Canyon is the most dramatic evidence of the river's handiwork, and it is indeed grand. Considered one of the Seven Natural Wonders of the World, it is breathtaking by anybody's standards.

From the Grand Canyon, the land stretches north into the canyons, cliffs, and plateaus of the arid Arizona Strip, which encompasses 5 million acres of northwestern Arizona. Pinyon-juniper woodlands and shrublands abound here, although in lower elevations you'll find plenty of cactus and creosote bushes, and in the higher elevations, ponderosa pine, aspen, and fir trees. The only year-round stream in the Arizona Strip is the Virgin River, which flows from southern Utah into Lake Mead. The permanent population is as sparse as the water and clusters in widely scattered towns like Page and Colorado City.

For possibly twelve thousand years, people have roamed the Grand Canyon. So far, over 4,800 archaeological sites have been discovered. Early visitors left behind handholds in the steep rock walls and prehistoric trails that still lead from rim to riverbed. Some of the earliest artifacts found in the canyon were made by Archaic hunters and gatherers. They are enigmatic deer and bighorn sheep figures fashioned from split willow or skunkbush twigs and dating from 2,000 to 4,000 years ago. Later groups built semipermanent villages on canyon terraces, and by A.D. 1000, at least three separate peoples were flourishing here. Today, only the Havasupai and Hualapai actually live within the canyon, while millions of annual day-trippers return home to more prosaic surroundings.

GRAND CANYON NATIONAL PARK
Map #1

South Rim: Bright Angel Trail/Bright Angel Pueblo, Desert View, East Rim Drive, Grand Canyon Village, IMAX Theater, Tusayan Ruin & Museum, West Rim Drive, Yavapai Point & Museum
North Rim: Cliff Spring Trail, North Rim Parkway
Nearby: Colorado City, Kaibab Paiute Reservation, Parashant National Monument (Nampaweap), Pipe Spring National Monument, Vermilion Cliffs National Monument

The views at the Grand Canyon are unforgettable.

In 1540, when Coronado's men explored the Southwest, Hopi guides led them to the South Rim of the Grand Canyon. Although they knew the place intimately from annual religious pilgrimages to the canyon to collect salt, the Indians refused to show the Spanish how to reach the bottom or cross to the other side.

You can still follow ancient Indian routes into the canyon's interior, but finding the solitude the Hopi experienced on their spiritual quests here might be more difficult. The crush of visitors in the park can be daunting, especially on the South Rim. In summer, two-mile waits at the entrance station are possible.

The North Rim receives only a fraction of the tourists and can provide a completely different experience, as well as another perspective of the canyon itself. Because annual moisture on the North Rim is almost ten inches more than on the South Rim, it looks luxuriant in comparison, with its forest of fir, spruce, ponderosa pine, and aspen. The North Rim is also over one thousand feet higher, with a resulting cooler climate.

Park officials on both rims offer extensive daily programs on the anthropology, geology, and natural history of the canyon. Look for up-to-date information in *Grand Canyon: the Guide,* a seasonal newspaper available at the park that lists shuttle bus routes, interpretive programs, hikes, and other park information. Separate editions are printed for the North and South rims. An online trip planner is also available at the national park's Web site, along with downloadable maps.

SOUTH RIM OF THE GRAND CANYON

Highway access to the South Rim of the Grand Canyon is on AZ64. From Flagstaff, take either US180 north to AZ64 and the east entrance, or I-40 west to AZ64. Once on AZ64, follow it north to the town of Tusayan and the south entrance of the park. From Utah, follow US89 south to the junction with AZ64, and turn west (right) onto AZ64, which becomes East Rim Drive in the Park. Riding the Grand Canyon Railway with its steam locomotive pulling vintage train cars is another way to arrive. It leaves from Williams, Arizona.

The town of **Tusayan** (*TOO-say-an*) lies just outside the south entrance to the national park. If you want to spend the night nearby but not in the park itself, this is a good place to stay. While here, visit the *National Geographic Visitor Center* to watch the excellent *Grand Canyon: The Hidden Secrets*, a half-hour IMAX movie covering the history, wildlife, recreation, and scenery of the canyon. The interactive Base Camp 1 exhibit recreates the experience of being deep in the canyon, and the center sponsors naturalist-led hikes.

Grand Canyon Village, about 3 miles north of the south entrance, is the hub of the South Rim. It has complete visitor services, including lodging, food, a pet kennel, medical clinic, taxi, service station, bank, dry cleaners, and post office.

Canyon View Information Plaza at Mather Point on the east side of the village has information, restrooms, pay phones, bookstore, and a shuttle bus stop. Exhibits provide a good overview of the park, and the canyon's rim is a short walk from here.

Yavapai Point and Observation Station, three-quarters of a mile northeast of Canyon View Information Plaza, has spectacular panoramic views of the canyon and a series of mounted binoculars. The small museum focuses on the local geology and flora and fauna.

For a closer look at the canyon's interior, look for the powerful telescope at Lookout Studio near Bright Angel Lodge. For more in-depth knowledge of the canyon, visit the national park library, located in the headquarters building.

In summer, a free shuttle service transports tourists around the park. Three routes are covered: Hermits Rest, Village, and Kaibab Trail. Look for a colored square near each door or the display on the front of the bus for the route. Stops are marked throughout the park.

Two scenic drives leave from the Village: **West Rim Drive,** accessible only by shuttle, travels 7 miles to Hermit's Rest and has several excellent viewpoints along the way, and East Rim Drive, which leads 26 miles to the east entrance of the park. (West Rim Drive is closed for repairs until November 2008.)

East Rim Drive includes Grandview Point and other well-known viewpoints. Each affords a unique and superlative view across the 18-mile-wide canyon. Watching a sunrise or sunset from one of them is an unforgettable experience.

Tusayan Ruin and Museum, about 23 miles east of Grand Canyon Village, depicts the Ancestral Puebloan culture with artifacts. Exhibits also cover modern Indian cultures in the area, and guided tours are offered throughout the day.

Outside the museum, a short self-guided trail (paved and wheelchair accessible) leads to the ruins of a plaza, living quarters, storage rooms, and two kivas built around A.D. 1185 by Kayenta ancestors of the modern Pueblo Indians. About thirty people once tried to make their home here, but perhaps the poor soil, low rainfall, and scarce drinking water discouraged them. Only thirty years after the Kayenta had moved in, they had moved on.

A mule train winds back up Bright Angel Trail from the bottom of the Grand Canyon.

The last stop before leaving the park is **Desert View**. Over 7,500 feet, the top of the tower here is the highest point on the South Rim. Desert View Watchtower, a re-creation of the prehistoric watchtowers once prevalent in the Southwest, affords a tremendous view of the canyon and western portions of the Painted Desert. The tower also houses a collection of Indian art from various sources. In the Hopi room are reproductions of a Snake Altar and objects used in the ceremonial Snake Dance. A large circular painting portrays the Snake Legend, which tells the origin of the dance. Other of the murals by Hopi artist Fred Kabotie reproduce petroglyphs and pictographs from various Southwest ruins. Desert View also has a curio shop, food concession, general store, service station, and campground.

The Grand Canyon is over 277 miles long, and Grand Canyon National Park encompasses 1,904 square miles. In addition to touring by car, you can explore it by horse, helicopter, airplane, mule, river raft, or kayak. For an up-to-date list of concessionaires, call or write Grand Canyon National Park Lodges (part of Xanterra Parks and Resorts). Reservations need to be made well in advance.

The park also has numerous hiking trails. South Kaibab and Bright Angel Trails lead to the bottom. Just remember that hiking up out of the canyon will probably take you twice as long as it did to hike down into it, especially on a hot day. Also be aware that you may experience a variety of weather depending on your elevation, which can range from an average of 7,000 feet on the rim to 2,400 feet at the bottom of the canyon.

Bright Angel Trail leads to the bottom of the canyon along the same route the Havasupai followed to their fields and to the spring at Indian Gardens. The trailhead is just west of Bright Angel Lodge next to the mule corral. Bright Angel is a popular trail, but steep. Don't attempt the hike to the bottom unless you are in excellent physical condition. The initial high altitude, the extreme change in elevation, and the summer heat make physical exertion here more difficult than you might think.

For an easier alternative, hike the first portion of the trail to Mile-and-a-Half Rest-house, which is only 3 miles round-trip. Continuing from here, the path becomes strenuous as it leads 8 miles farther down to the Colorado River. Narrow and with a precipitous drop, parts of the trail are most easily traversed on the back of a mule. Guided trips are available through the park concessionaire, Xanterra Parks and Resorts. Minimum height to join a trip is four feet seven inches; maximum weight is two hundred pounds. Reservations are needed well in advance.

Traveling from rim to river, the trail descends through several life zones and strata of the earth. Like a cake of eons, one stacked atop another, the walls of the Grand Canyon create a picture of the past. Layers of exposed limestone are littered with the fossil imprints of billions of ancient marine creatures, and the yellow sandstone is etched with the wavy lines of hardened sand dunes and the footprints of small animals. The red shale is abundant with plant fossils and the imprints of dragonflies. Hidden in the depths of the canyon are brittle rocks starred with mica and seams of rose quartz that count among the oldest exposed rock on earth—2 billion years old.

At the bottom is the grand architect of it all, the Colorado River. A suspension bridge here spans the river to Phantom Ranch, which provides limited dormitory lodging. Camping at Bright Angel Campground and ranger-led programs are also available at the bottom of the canyon.

The bridge is the only crossing of the river for the 200 miles between Navajo Bridge and Lake Mead. The ruins of **Bright Angel Pueblo** are about 40 yards west of the bridge, at the top of a talus slope east of the confluence of Bright Angel Creek and the Colorado River. The small pueblo was constructed around A.D. 1050 from blocks of schist. Three or four families lived here for several decades, hunting and farming beside the river. A kiva and five additional rooms were added between A.D. 1100 and 1140.

Although the feeling of isolation at the bottom of the canyon may make it a haven from the crowds, the climate is similar to that in central Mexico. Summer days can be intolerably hot, with an average high temperature that exceeds 100 degrees. Early October is one of the best times to make the trek.

Another way to see the bottom of the canyon is by river raft. Trips of two to twenty-two days leaving from Lees Ferry are available, with a few shorter ones embarking from Phantom Ranch. The peak rafting season is from April to October. Although there are numerous companies operating tours, it is wise to make reservations at least a year in advance. The Grand Canyon Chamber of Commerce and hotels in the village list companies that offer river trips, as well as guided air, bus, and hiking tours.

Camping on the South Rim is available at Desert View, with fifty campsites open May to October, and at Mather Campground in Grand Canyon Village with 320 campsites, open year-round. Reservations for Mather Campground or the adjacent Trailer Village can be obtained up to six months in advance from National Park Service Campground and Tour Reservations. Desert View Campground is on a first-come, first-served basis only. For camping in the inner canyon, contact the Backcountry Information Center. For advance reservations (available four months in advance), call for a registration form, visit the park Web site, or fax a request. No reservations are taken over the telephone and availability is limited. If you arrive at the park without a reservation, there is a small chance you can still obtain one by visiting the Backcountry Reservations Office south of the visitor center. Guided overnight trips are also offered by Grand Canyon Field Institute.

Bright Angel Lodge displays a geologic fireplace with stones stacked as they are layered in the canyon. Reservations can be booked up to twenty-three months in advance. Other lodging is at the historic El Tovar Hotel (also bookable twenty-three months in advance), at Phantom Canyon Ranch at the bottom of the canyon (bookable thirteen months in advance), and at four other lodges. Make reservations through Grand Canyon National Park Lodges (Xanterra).

Roads and most facilities on the South Rim are open year-round. Perhaps the best time to visit, however, is in autumn, when the heat and crowds have dissipated and the snows have not yet arrived.

NORTH RIM OF THE GRAND CANYON

The one-thousand-foot higher elevation on the North Rim brings a different perspective of the canyon. **North Rim Parkway** (AZ67) travels south from Jacob Lake for 30 miles to the national park entrance, then 13 miles to the canyon rim through the dense forest and flower-drenched meadows of the Kaibab Plateau. The road is usually closed by snow from mid-October through mid-May.

The parkway continues to Bright Angel Point, Grand Canyon Lodge, and the visitor center. Two roads lead from here past several trailheads and sensational viewpoints along the way. The pueblo ruins near the *Walhalla Overlook* were left by the Kayenta ancestors of the Pueblo people before A.D. 1150. *Cliff Spring Trail*, a 1-mile round-trip down a ravine to Cliff Spring, passes a small Ancestral Puebloan granary. The trail begins from Angel's Window Overlook, a small pullout on the curve of Cape Royal parking lot and Walhalla Overlook. Ask park rangers for conditions on other trails to little visited places.

North Rim Parkway ends at Grand Canyon Lodge (bookable twenty-three months in advance) and a campground, which offer the only accommodations on the North Rim. For reservations at the lodge, contact Grand Canyon National Park Lodges (Xanterra). North Rim campground reservations can be made through National Park Service Campground and Tour Reservations up to six months in advance. Both the lodge and campground are open mid-May to mid-October.

North Rim Visitor Center, adjacent to the lodge, has displays, books for sale, and information on ranger programs and backcountry permits. Advance reservations for permits can be made through the same Backcountry Reservations office that handles requests for the South Rim.

Gasoline, dining, a general store, laundry facilities, a post office, and showers are also here, as well as concessionaires offering mule rides, bus tours, guided hikes, and river tours. One hour, half-day and full-day mule trips into the canyon are offered between June and mid-October. All trips have a minimum age and a maximum weight limit. Contact Grand Canyon Trail Rides in the lodge.

Other developed campgrounds, two motels, and Kaibab Lodge are located north of the park toward Jacob Lake. Camping is allowed in the surrounding Kaibab National Forest and in DeMotte National Campground, ten miles north of the canyon rim.

Kaibab Visitor Center in Jacob Lake has information about the National Forest. Here you will also find a 3-D model of the Grand Canyon, as well as maps and exhibits.

Ravens pose on the edge of the Grand Canyon. This bird is found in many Native American stories.

NORTH OF GRAND CANYON NATIONAL PARK

At the turn of the millennium, two new national monuments were created in northern Arizona out of 1.3 million acres of wilderness. Over a million of those acres are now protected in **Parashant National Monument**, west of and adjacent to the Grand Canyon. The monument is administered jointly by the Bureau of Land Management (BLM) and the National Park Service (NPS). In addition to showcasing a rich biological diversity and millions of years of geological history, it preserves a varied prehistory and history of human habitation and use.

Despite the remoteness and forbidding terrain of canyons, lava flows, mountains, and buttes, people have been here for at least eleven thousand years. Paleo-Indian big-game hunters came first. Eventually, they gave way to hunter-gatherers. After corn was introduced from Mexico around three thousand years ago, these nomads were able to settle into villages. By 1776, when the first Europeans arrived, Southern Paiutes were occupying the region. Eventually, Mormon pioneers, miners, and lumbermen settled on the arid land.

Archaeologists have found a rich collection of prehistoric sites in the monument, including burials, farms, caves, trails, rock shelters, camps, watchtowers, villages, quarries, and rock art images. Because they are difficult to reach even today, many of these places have escaped the vandalism so common to those more accessible and well known.

Nampaweap, "Foot Canyon" in Paiute, is one of the largest petroglyph sites in Parashant National Monument, created by ancestors of the Pueblo and Paiute peoples who passed through this ancient travel corridor. Using a stone, they pecked flakes from the surface of large basalt boulders to reveal the lighter colored rock underneath. Humanlike figures, animals, and geometric designs are all represented.

Nampaweap is northeast of Toroweap, near the Grand Canyon and Mt. Trumbull. For travel information and a topographical map, contact the *Interagency Visitor Center* in St. George, Utah. To reach the office, from I-15, take exit 6 (Bluff Street) and turn southeast onto Riverside Drive for one-third of a mile.

The other recently created national monument in northern Arizona is **Vermilion Cliffs National Monument**, which borders Glen Canyon National Recreation Area to the east and Kaibab National Forest to the west and extends north into Utah. The land in Vermilion Cliffs is as remote and unspoiled as that in Parashant, and includes almost 300,000 acres of slickrock, desert grasslands, sandy plateaus, and sandstone. The cliffs themselves jut three thousand spectacular feet above the southern edge of the Paria Plateau, revealing layer after layer of brilliant red sandstone and dark shale. Archaeologists have found evidence of human habitation thousands of years old, with Ancestral Puebloan sites especially abundant. Intact walls, field houses, trails, granaries, burials, and camps, as well as some of the Southwest's earliest known rock art, have all been preserved here in the dry desert air. In the stunning Paria Canyon, you can hike to petroglyphs and campsites seven hundred years old. This is one of the most popular hikes in the monument.

For more information on Paria Canyon, see Chapter 23, Southern Utah, page 436. For maps and more information on Vermilion Cliffs National Monument, contact the BLM Arizona Strip Field Office in Fredonia.

Remember that Parashant and Vermilion Cliffs National Monuments are rugged wilderness. No paved roads or visitor services exist inside the monuments. Be sure to plan accordingly.

The **Kaibab Paiute Indian Reservation**, 50 miles north of the Grand Canyon on US 89A to AZ389, is in the remote plateau and desert grasslands of northwestern Arizona. It is home to around two hundred members of the Kaibab Paiute band, and the economy centers around tourism and livestock. Noteworthy tribal crafts include traditional leather beadwork and coiled wedding baskets. AZ389 crosses the reservation from east to west.

To learn more about the Kaibab Paiutes, stop at **Pipe Spring National Monument**, 15 miles southwest of the town of Fredonia and just off AZ389. Pipe Spring is an oasis that was known to Indians, Spanish explorers, and early settlers as the only reliable source of water for miles. Over one thousand years ago, the life-giving spring attracted people from the Basketmaker culture. The nomadic Paiutes, whose descendants now live on the surrounding reservation, came here later.

Mormons discovered Pipe Spring in 1858, but hostile Navajos drove them away in the late 1860s. When a treaty was signed several years later at Ft. Defiance, Arizona, Mormons returned with more ambitious plans. Construction was begun—but only partially completed—on a fort (Winsor Castle) to claim the water supply and to protect what was to be a cattle-tithing center for animals donated to the church.

The Kaibab Paiute tribe and the National Park Service jointly operate the monument's *visitor center/museum*. Exhibits in the cultural museum cover the tribe's history and culture and Mormon settlement. In the morning, Paiute women are here demonstrating traditional Paiute crafts such as the art of beadwork. During the summer, candle dipping and other living history demonstrations are also presented. You can visit the grounds on a self-guided tour or with a ranger. The gift shop sells books on the region and on Southwestern Indian arts and crafts. A year-round campground with tent sites, RV hookups, and restrooms is nearby. For reservations at the campground, call tribal headquarters.

The *Mu'uputs (Owl) Canyon Trail* is near the museum and only accessible with a native guide. The hike is a round-trip of about 1 mile, and it leads past petroglyphs and a rich variety of plants and animals. Make reservations in advance by calling the tribal office.

North of Pipe Spring on AZ389 is **Colorado City**. You can visit two excavated *prehistoric sites* here: just south of the Carling Reservoir on a dirt road are several pithouses, and at the north end of town on Academy Avenue (across from the community center) is a pit structure believed to have been a kiva surrounded by pueblo rooms.

See South of St. George in Chapter 23, Southern Utah for information on Little Black Mountain Petroglyph Site.

EAST OF GRAND CANYON NATIONAL PARK

See Chapter 7, The Navajo, pages 104 and 105, for Cameron and Little Colorado River Navajo Tribal Park.

HAVASUPAI RESERVATION
Map #2

Sites: Beaver Falls, Havasu Canyon, Havasu Falls, Havasupai Lodge, Mooney Falls, Navajo Falls, Supai, tribal museum

Havasu Canyon is an enclosed side gorge of the Grand Canyon characterized by towering cliffs, torrential waterfalls, and lush vegetation. Havasu Creek defines the picturesque canyon as it rushes past the town of Supai, then cascades to meet the Colorado River. Traditionally, the Havasupai farmed their fields here during the spring, summer, and early autumn, spending the winter gathering food on the plateaus.

About 450 Havasupai (*H vasúa Baaja*, "People of the Blue-Green Water") live on 188,077 acres in the canyon, isolated by the same imposing cliff walls that kept out Spanish conquistadors, American settlers, and other Indian tribes. The Havasupai speak the Havasu language, which has only been a written language for about twenty years, and exhibit great pride in their traditional culture.

The center of the reservation is the village of **Supai**. The only way to get there is down an 8-mile trail or by helicopter, and an entrance fee is charged. For those not up to the steep, dusty hike, local families hire out horses or mules. Reservations should be made at least six weeks in advance through the Havasupai Tourist Office, and some restrictions apply. Check the day before your arrival to ensure your animal is available. You can also provide your own horse and feed and pay a trail fee. Be sure to bring food and water for yourself, too, and start early to avoid the midday heat. Also leave all liquor, drugs, weapons, and pets at home.

The trail to Supai begins at Hualapai Hilltop, a remote access point at the end of a partly paved 70-mile road. This road is accessed from AZ66 about 7 miles east of Peach Springs (to reach AZ66, take I-40 west of Flagstaff). Once you arrive in Supai, you must check in with the Village Office unless you are staying in the lodge.

The *tribal museum* in Supai has cultural displays, including the basketry and beadwork for which the tribe is noted. Crafts can also be purchased here. The museum is in the Tribal Arts Enterprise building.

Havasupai Lodge has twenty-four basic rooms with air-conditioning and private baths, but without phones, TV, or rollaway beds. The alternative is to stay at the pleasant campground along Havasu Creek. Fires are not allowed, and the only shower available here is a swim in the water below Havasu Falls, but the campground does have picnic tables, spring water, and pit toilets. Be aware that thefts have been reported at the campground.

Visitors must first obtain a tribal permit and advance reservations to camp or stay in the lodge by contacting the Havasupai Tourist Office. Make your reservations at least six months in advance if you plan to stay during March through October.

The town café serves breakfast, lunch, and dinner, and the general store sells groceries. Both operate on a cash-only basis. The post office is next to the store, and a health clinic offers emergency care.

About 1.5 miles downstream from Supai is the first of a series of four **waterfalls** of crystal clear blue-green water. *Navajo Falls* plummets seventy-five feet over travertine, moss, and vines into a pool of seventy-degree water that provides a refreshing swim. It was named in honor of a nineteenth-century Havasupai chief who was kidnapped by Navajos when an infant. The often-photographed *Havasu Falls* drops one hundred feet into a shimmering turquoise pool. *Mooney Falls* ("Mother of Waters" to the Havasu) is the most dramatic of the four. It plunges 196 feet into travertine pools of iridescent emerald green. The trail to the bottom of the waterfall passes two tunnels; chains are rigged through iron stakes to help hikers navigate the steepest part. *Beaver Falls* is a series of cascades 4 miles downstream from Mooney.

To reach Hualapai Hilltop, take I-40 east of Flagstaff to Seligman. Go northwest on AZ66 for 28 miles, and turn right onto Indian Road 18 for 63 miles to Hualapai Hilltop. From the west, take AZ66 northeast out of Kingman for 60 miles, and turn left onto IR18 for 63 miles. No services are available after leaving AZ66.

HUALAPAI NATION
Map #3

Sites: Diamond Creek Road, Grand Canyon West, Hualapai Lodge, Peach Springs

The Hualapai or Hwal'bay, "People of the Tall Pines," consider themselves to be descendants of the prehistoric Cerbat people, who once populated northwest Arizona. Historically, they are part of the Yuman-speaking family of tribes who made their homes on or near the Colorado River. Because of conflict with Anglo settlers over land, the Hualapai (*WALL-uh-pie*) were exiled south to the Colorado River Reservation. Many died there, and most of the survivors fled back to their traditional lands. In 1883, they secured a reservation along the lower 108 miles of the Grand Canyon.

Capt. McGee (left) and Wes Synella (right), two Hualapai men, sit in front of a Navajo rug circa 1930.

The road to Grand Canyon West travels through a Joshua tree forest.

The million acres of the Hualapai Reservation now range from rolling grassland to forest to rugged Colorado River canyons. The population of the reservation is 1,353, and enrolled tribal members are 2,156. Much of the tribal revenue comes from crafts (basketry and the manufacturing of dolls), farming, timber sales, cattle, and tourism. Fishing, hunting, and river rafting are popular tourist activities.

The village of **Peach Springs**, 54 miles northeast of Kingman on AZ66, is the only town on the reservation.

Permits are required for recreation, back road use, trophy game hunting in September and October, and raft trips through the lower Grand Canyon. Inquire at the Hualapai Wildlife Conservation Department or at *Hualapai Tribal River Runners* on the corner of AZ66 and Diamond Creek Road. This outdoor guide company leads the only one-day and two-day raft trips on the Colorado River available in the canyon. Trips begin at Hualapai Lodge from spring through autumn.

Hualapai Lodge in town is AAA approved and has sixty rooms decorated in Southwestern décor. The lobby displays tribal art, and the restaurant serves a full menu that includes traditional Hualapai food. Authentic Native American crafts, souvenirs, snacks, and necessities such as film and sunscreen are sold in the gift shop. The lodge also offers package deals with Hualapai Tribal River Runners for guided tours to sites on the reservation, including Grand Canyon West and Diamond Creek Road.

The primitive gravel **Diamond Creek Road**, off AZ66 beside the River Runners office in town, travels 21 miles north of town to the Colorado River and Diamond Creek. This is the only auto road in the Grand Canyon that reaches the river. Tourists first used it in 1883, and a hotel was located here between 1884 and 1889. Today, the road is passable in dry weather by cars with good clearance. During the rainy season in July and August, high clearance vehicles are recommended. Near the sandy beach by the river are a few picnic tables, an outhouse, and boat launch.

A steady stream of small planes, tour buses, and helicopters converge daily at the busy terminal at **Grand Canyon West**, where visitors are then loaded onto buses to drive to observation points on the west rim of the canyon. *Guano Point* offers a remarkable view of the Colorado River and has a café that sells barbecue. *Eagle Point* has a view of sacred Eagle Rock, believed to carry prayers to the Great Spirit; a Hualapai-guided tour of an Indian village with dwellings of various tribes; and traditional dancers. However, the main attraction is not for the faint of heart. Perched at the edge of the canyon is a seventy-foot, horseshoe-shaped, transparent walkway that juts out into thin air, allowing those unafraid of heights to look to the bottom of the Grand Canyon four thousand feet below. The **Skywalk** has received mixed reviews since its 2007 opening, mainly because of the cost to visitors (a minimum of $85 once you add the required tour, reservation, and admission fees) and the fact that no cameras are allowed. The Skywalk is part of a facility that, when completed, will include a visitor center, museum, movie theater, gift shop, restaurants, and wedding/event center.

Hualapai Ranch is a recreated Old West town with wagon rides, cowboy demonstrations, and a cookout. Call the tribally owned Grand Canyon Resort Corporation for details.

From Kingman, take US93 north about 30 miles to the turnoff for Dolan Springs (Pierce Ferry Road). Travel north about 28 miles and through a Joshua tree forest to Diamond Bar Road. Turn right onto a maintained but rough dirt road that winds through BLM land for 14 miles. Once you enter the Hualapai Reservation, the road becomes wide open and paved for the last 7 miles to Grand Canyon West.

PAGE
Map #4

Around Town: Blair Trading Post Museum, hiking/biking trails, John Wesley Powell Memorial Museum

Nearby: Antelope Canyon, Glen Canyon N. R. A. (Antelope Point Marina, Carl Hayden Visitor Center, dam, Wahweap Marina), Lees Ferry, Marble Canyon, Navajo Bridge, Navajo Village Heritage Center

Page, the largest community in far northern Arizona, sits on a mesa overlooking the southern shores of Lake Powell. The small town began in 1957 with Glen Canyon Dam, when construction workers moved here to work on the giant hydroelectric project. Today, it provides a convenient base for exploring not just the neighboring Lake Powell but also the adjoining Navajo Nation and the various nearby national parks and monuments.

The **John Wesley Powell Memorial Museum** displays artifacts from John Wesley Powell's expedition through the Grand Canyon. Native American items include prehistoric pottery, jewelry, and tools used by Southwestern tribes. The museum's visitor guide covers attractions, lodging, maps, and transportation options. The museum also acts as a reservation agent for guided boat tours, scenic flights, and raft trips, as well as boat and houseboat rentals on Lake Powell. It is located on the corner of Lake Powell Boulevard and North Navajo Drive.

Navajo Village Heritage Center in southwest Page, at the junction of AZ98 and Copper Mine Road, has cultural demonstrations, food, and traditional dancing and music.

As you might expect, outdoor recreation is popular in Page. The town and its environs have miles of urban *trails* that provide hikers and bikers with awe-inspiring views of Lake Powell's crystal blue water, the stunning red rock cliffs of Glen Canyon, and the Navajo Reservation. Rimview Trail circles the top of the mesa. Look for the trailhead at the parking lot at the end of North Navajo Drive (near Lake View Elementary School). Horseshoe Bend trail, 2 miles south of town off US89, leads to a superlative view of the Colorado River.

You can also book a guided trip on land, air, or water from one of the outfitters in town. Page is the embarkation point for numerous raft trips on the Colorado River, and neighboring Lake Powell offers just about any water sport you want, including fishing, skiing, powerboating, swimming, and houseboating, which is the most popular way to see the lake. See Chapter 23, Southern Utah, page 433 for more information on Lake Powell.

For a more leisurely pastime, stop at one of the trading posts in town to browse their beautiful and authentic Native American artwork. *Blair Trading Post* in the Dam Plaza also has a museum of Indian art and artifacts. The *Page-Lake Powell Tourism Bureau,* located in the shopping center between Navajo and Elm streets, has tourist information. You can also book a boat or raft trip here and find out more about scenic flights. Popular tours to nearby Antelope Canyon are also available.

NORTH OF PAGE

See Chapter 23, Southern Utah, page 433 for Glen Canyon National Recreation Area and Rainbow Bridge.

SOUTH OF PAGE

Fifteen miles downstream of Glen Canyon Dam on the Colorado River is **Lees Ferry**, which is the official start of the Grand Canyon.

In 1871, Mormon John D. Lee and his seventeen wives settled here after he was exiled for his role in the massacre of emigrants near St. George, Utah, an act for which he was eventually executed. For nearly six decades, the ferry he established was the only way to cross the Colorado River for hundreds of miles around. Pioneers, Indians, miners, and tourists all used it before Navajo Bridge was built several miles downstream. Today, Lees Ferry is one of the few places in Canyon Country where you can drive to the Colorado River.

Lees Ferry, 42 miles from Page on Hwy 89A, is part of Glen Canyon National Recreation Area and is administered by the National Park Service.

Next to Lees Ferry Junction and the park entrance are a gas station, restaurant, store, and motel at Marble Canyon. From here, a side road leads 6 miles to the river, where there is a boat launch popular with river runners, a ranger station, and a National Park Service campground.

A 1-mile walking tour leads upstream from the launch ramp to the site of the original ferry crossing and several historic buildings, including an old fort. Longer hikes, such as the one to Paria Canyon, can also be accessed from here, as well as world-class trout fishing further upstream.

Navajo Bridge, just east of Lees Ferry Junction on Hwy 89A, leads across the Colorado River to the Navajo Nation. The interpretive center at the west end of the bridge has exhibits on Navajo life and about the 1927–28 construction of the historic bridge that eventually replaced the ferryboat crossing. This bridge was in turn replaced in 1995, but the old bridge remains as a pedestrian walkway over the Colorado River.

From here, Hwy 89A travels southwest about 40 miles to Jacob Lake, following along the foot of the spectacular Vermilion Cliffs, to the Kaibab Plateau.

Although the **San Juan Southern Paiutes** have lived in northern Arizona for several hundred years, the tribe was not recognized by the United States government until 1989. Today, tribal enrollment is around 260 members, with many of them living in distinct communities on the Navajo Reservation. The largest of these is at Hidden Springs about 10 miles north of Tuba City. Another community is at Paiute Canyon/Navajo Mountain on the Arizona/Utah border. The San Juan Southern Paiute Yingup Weavers Association was formed to preserve the basketry skills of community weavers.

EAST OF PAGE

See Chapter 7, The Navajo, page 104, for Antelope Canyon.

EVENTS

APRIL *Unity Powwow* held at the Page High School football field. Call 928-645-2741.

JUNE *San Juan Southern Paiute Powwow:* Outdoor powwow that includes dancing and the crowning of SJSP princess.

SEPTEMBER *Kaibab Paiute Heritage Days:* Drum and dance contests, juried art show, and vendors. Kaibab-Paiute Reservation.

CONTACT INFORMATION

Arizona State Parks
1300 W. Washington, Phoenix, AZ 85007
602-542-4174 • www.pr.state.az.us

Blair's Trading Post
626 N. Navajo, Page, AZ 86040
800-644-3008 • www.blairstradingpost.com

Bureau of Land Management
www.blm.gov/az/st/en.html
Arizona Strip Field Office
(Vermilion Cliffs National Monument)
430 Main Street, Fredonia, AZ 84790
435-688-3246
Interagency Office
345 E. Riverside Drive, St. George, UT 84790
435-688-3200

Carl Hayden Visitor Center
Glen Canyon Dam, Page, AZ 86040
928-645-6404

Grand Canyon Chamber of Commerce
PO Box 3007, Grand Canyon, AZ 86023
928-638-2901
www.grandcanyonchamber.org

Grand Canyon National Park
PO Box 129, Grand Canyon, AZ 86023
928-638-7888
www.nps.gov/grca/index.htm
Backcountry Information Center
Box 129, Grand Canyon, AZ 86023-0129
928-638-7875 (Mon-Fri, 1-5pm) *or*
928-638-7888 (recording)
928-638-2125 (fax)
www.nps.gov/grca/planyourvisit/
backcountry.htm
Daily 8am-noon & 1pm-5pm
Grand Canyon Field Institute
www.grandcanyon.org/fieldinstitute
**Grand Canyon N.P. Lodges/Xanterra
Parks and Resorts**
PO Box 699, Grand Canyon N. P., Grand
Canyon, AZ 86023
888-297-2757 *or* 928-638-2631
www.grandcanyonlodges.com
www.xanterra.com
Grand Canyon National Park River Unit
Box 129, Grand Canyon, AZ 86023
800-959-9114 *or* 928-638-7843

Grand Canyon National Park *(continued)*
National Park Service Campground and
Tour Reservations
877-444-6777
www.recreation.gov
South Rim
www.nps.gov/grca/index.htm
  Canyon View Information Plaza
  (Mather Point)
  Daily 8am-5pm (hours vary seasonally)
  Desert View Information Center
  (at East Entrance)
  Daily 9am-5pm; winter hours as staffing
    permits
  Phantom Ranch
  303-297-2757 *or* 888-297-2757
  Trailer Village
  888-297-2757 *or* 928-638-2631 (same-
    day reservations)
  Tusayan Ruin and Museum
  928-638-2305
  Daily 9am-5pm (weather permitting)
  Yavapai Observation Station
  Daily 8am-6pm in summer; 9am-5pm
    in winter
North Rim
www.nps.gov/grca/index.html
  Grand Canyon Lodge
  928-638-2631
  www.grandcanyonnorthrim.com
  Kaibab National Forest/DeMotte
  Campground
  www.fs.fed.us/r3/kai/recreation/
    campgrounds
  Park Service Information Desk
  928-638-7864
  Daily 8am-6pm

Grand Canyon-Parashant National Monument
www.nps/gov/para
  NPS Monument Headquarters
  601 Nevada Highway, Boulder City, NV 89005
  702-293-8907
  BLM Monument Headquarters/
  Arizona Strip Field Office
  345 E. Riverside Drive, St. George, UT 84790
  435-688-3200

Grand Canyon Railway
800-843-8724 *or* 928-773-1976
www.thetrain.com

Havasupai Tribal Council
PO Box 10, Supai, AZ 86435
928-448-2731 • www.havasupaitribe.com
Entrance fee required
  Havasupai Lodge
  PO Box 159, Supai, AZ 86435
  928-448-2111 *or* 928-448-2201
  Lobby hours: daily 7am-7pm Apr-Oct;
    daily 8am-5pm Nov-Mar
  Havasupai Tourist Office/Camping
  Reservations
  PO Box 160 Supai, AZ 86435
  928-448-2121, -2141, -2174, *or* -2180
  Daily 7am-7pm, Apr-Oct; daily 8am-5pm,
    Nov-Mar
  Havasupai Tribal Museum
  928-448-2611

Hualapai Tribal Council
PO Box 179, Peach Springs, AZ 86434
928-769-2216
  Grand Canyon West
  877-716-9378 *or* 702-787-9378
  www.destinationgrandcanyon.com
  Terminal and Gift Shop: daily 7am-
    6:30pm; last tour 5:30pm; fee
  Hualapai Lodge
  900 Rte 66, Peach Spring, AZ 86434-0538
  888-255-9550 *or* 928-769-2230
  www.grandcanyonresort.com
  Hualapai River Runners
  887 Route 66, Peach Springs, AZ 86434
  888-255-9550 *or* 928-769-2219
  Wildlife Conservation Department
  PO Box 249, Peach Springs, AZ 86434
  602-769-2227

John Wesley Powell Memorial Museum
6 N. Lake Powell Blvd, PO Box 547, Page, AZ 86040
888-597-6873 *or* 928-645-9496
www.powellmuseum.org
Mon-Sat 9am-5pm, May-Sept; Mon-Fri 9am-
  5pm, Oct and Apr; closed mid Dec-mid
  Feb; fee

Kaibab-Paiute Tribe
Tribal Affairs Building
HC65 Box 2, Fredonia, AZ 86022
928-643-7245
www.kaibabpaiutetribal.com
  Pipe Spring National Monument
  HC 65, Box 5, Fredonia, AZ 86022
  928-643-7105 • www.nps.gov/pisp
  Daily 7am-5pm, Jun-Aug; daily 8am-5pm,
    Sep-May; fee

Kaibab Visitor Center
Jacob Lake, AZ 86022
928-643-7298
Daily 8am-5pm

Lees Ferry Ranger Station
928-355-2234 • www.nps.gov/glca/lferry.htm

National Geographic Visitor Center and IMAX Theater
PO Box 3309, Tusayan, AZ 86023-3309
888-355-0550 *or* 928-638-2468
www.explorethecanyon.com
Showtimes: daily 8:30am-8:30pm, March-Oct; daily 10:30am-6:30pm, Nov-Feb; fee

Navajo Bridge Interpretive Center
928-355-2319
Daily 9am-5pm, April-Nov; no fee
Or contact: **Cameron Visitor Center**
PO Box 459, Cameron, AZ 86020
928-679-2303

Navajo Village Heritage Center
PO Box 2464, 1253 Coppermine Road, Page, AZ 86040
928-660-0304 • www.navajovillage.com
Mon-Sat, late afternoon/evening tours, dinner, dancing; fee

Page-Lake Powell Tourism Bureau
647A Elm Street, PO Box 332, Page, AZ 86040
888-261-7243 *or* 928-660-3405 (cell)
www.pagelakepowellchamber.org
www.pagelakepowelltourism.com

Pipe Spring National Monument
HC65 Box 5, 406 North Pipe Spring Road, Fredonia, AZ 86022
928-643-7105 • www.nps.gov/pisp
Monument/Museum: daily 7am-5pm, June-Aug; daily 8am-5pm, Sept-May; fee
Winsor Castle: tours begin every half hour: daily 8am-4:30pm, June-Aug; daily 9am-4pm, Sept-May
Interpretive Programs: daily in the morning hours, June-Aug

San Juan Southern Paiute Tribe
PO Box 1989, Tuba City, AZ 86045
928-283-5761

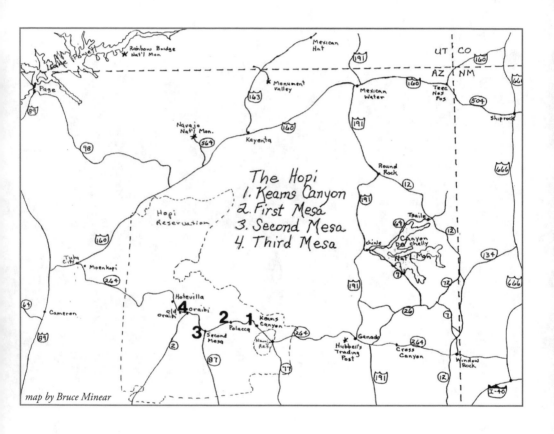

The Hopi
1. Keams Canyon
2. First Mesa
3. Second Mesa
4. Third Mesa

map by Bruce Minear

CHAPTER 6

THE HOPI

THE HOPI RESERVATION, established in 1882, is surrounded on all sides by the Navajo Nation. From east to west, the 1.5 million acres of the reservation consist of three mesas that splay out like fingers from the sacred Black Mesa and the surrounding land. The mesas are connected by AZ264, which travels between Window Rock and Tuba City on the Navajo Reservation.

Most of the ten to twelve thousand Hopi tribal members live in one of the twelve villages near or on the mesas. The separate villages have always been relatively autonomous, and they remain so today. The Hopi Tribal Council acts primarily as a liaison between villages and agencies of federal and state governments. The tribe has voted against gaming but has leased land on Black Mesa for mining, farming, and ranching, albeit controversially.

The Hopi are friendly but private people, and all photography, sketching, and recording are prohibited at ceremonies and in the villages. In addition, molesting shrines, entering kivas, or removing sacred stones is forbidden. Some villages require a guide to visit, while others are closed on particular dates. In general, look for local rules posted at the entrance of each village, and confine your visits to between 8am and 5pm. Visiting archaeological sites requires a tour guide, and visiting the petroglyphs at Pumpkin Seed Hill and Dawa Park requires a permit issued by the Cultural Preservation Office.

The Hopi are famous for the artistry of their crafts. Superb silverwork includes jewelry, silverware, combs, and other personal and household items. Fine textiles are produced by Hopi men and popular with other Puebloans. Baskets made on Second Mesa are expertly woven from Hilaria grass and yucca leaves. On First Mesa, the sturdy and relatively inexpensive pottery is dark brown and red on light brown and is based on a style made popular by potter Rachel Nampeyo at the turn of the century. Third Mesa carvers create katsina figures that are intricately carved from the dried roots of cottonwood trees and then painted and decorated.

These and other arts and crafts can be purchased at various stores throughout the mesas, as well as directly from artisans in their homes in the villages. Look for window signs that advertise crafts for sale. A complete listing of arts-and-crafts outlets is posted on the tribal Web site under visitor information.

KATSINAS

Katsinas are unique to Pueblo cultures. For both the Hopi and the Zuni, they are supernatural beings that bring gifts and messages from the spirit world and can influence the natural world. Over three hundred katsinas have been identified, both male and female. Katsina dancers participate in a variety of ceremonies that begin with their arrival in December and end with their departure in July. Some of these dances are open to respectful visitors.

A katsina doll is also a representation of these spirits. They are carved out of cottonwood roots by Hopi men and out of pine by Zuni men, then adorned with the unique features, colors, and regalia of the beings. They are not toys but are given to women and children to use as a fetish and as a teaching tool. Some are also carved to be sold.

For part of the year, the katsinas stay with the people. The rest of the time, they return to their homeland. For the Hopi katsinas, it is the sacred San Francisco Peaks, Kisiau and Waynemai. From

there, the spirits ascend to the stars, carrying the prayers of the people with them. The mythical lake where the Zuni katsinas reside is reached through Listening Spring Lake, which is at the confluence of the Little Colorado River and the Zuni River. The most important katsinas are called wuya.

A variety of katsinas surround a Sun Katsina at the Desert Cabelleros Western Museum

Camping on the reservation is permitted in several places. Call the tribal offices for information. You can find food and lodging in Keams Canyon and on Second Mesa but make your reservations early. In addition, village cooperatives and privately owned stores sell snacks, and some families serve food from their homes.

One of the best times to visit is during one of the unique public ceremonies held in village plazas. Although the most sacred of these ceremonies are closed to the public, others are not. Many of these begin at sunrise on Saturday or Sunday and continue intermittently throughout the day. Katsina Dances are held from January to July (many are closed to the public), Social Dances are held August through February (most are open to the public), and Snake Dances are held August through December (usually closed to the public).

KEAMS CANYON
Map #6

Villages: Keams Canyon, Yu Weh Loo Pah Ki
Other Sites: Awatovi, Inscription Rock

Keams Canyon, at the base of First Mesa on the eastern edge of the reservation, is the Indian Agency headquarters. The village was named after Thomas Keam, who built a trading post at the mouth of the canyon in 1875. A few miles up the canyon, northeast of town, you can visit a picnic area and **Inscription Rock**, where Kit Carson carved his name.

Keams Canyon Motel has modest accommodations, a popular café (closed Sundays and after lunch on Saturdays), and a gift shop selling Hopi and Navajo crafts. This and the motel at the Hopi Cultural Center are the only two on the reservation, so be sure to make your reservations early, especially for public ceremony weekends. *Keams Canyon Shopping Center* has a café, art gallery, and one of the three gas stations on the reservations. Picnic areas are located next to the shopping center and at Beaver Dam in a wash north of town.

South of town are the ruins of **Awatovi** (*ah-WHAT-o-vee*). Begun as a small village in the twelfth century, and eventually growing to cover twenty-three acres, Franciscan friars came to Awatovi in 1629 and built a church using forced Indian labor. During the 1680 Pueblo Revolt, the church was destroyed, but the Spanish reestablished the mission in 1700. Enraged by the Spanish and their relentless destruction of Indian culture, the Hopi destroyed the mission again. Although many of the Awatovians accepted Spanish dominance, other Hopi did not. The men of Awatovi were killed and their women and children moved to other villages. For the permit and guide needed to visit this and other local prehistoric sites, ask at the Cultural Preservations Office.

McGee's Indian Art Gallery in Keams Canyon began as a trading post in 1874 and still stocks high-quality Native American art created by local artisans. You will find traditional and contemporary designs, including Navajo rugs and jewelry, and items from Zuni and other Pueblo artists. The gallery's specialty is Hopi katsinas, jewelry, and pottery.

The newest Hopi community is 2 miles east of Keams Canyon at **Yu Weh Loo Pah Ki**, "Spider Mound." The village was established as a result of the long-standing Hopi-Navajo land dispute. When the U.S. Supreme Court finally decreed that Hopi families living in the Jeddito Wash area must move from there to designated Hopi Partitioned

*Walpi on the Hopi's First Mesa commands a view of the surrounding land.
Note the stone corrals at the base. (1912)*

Lands, some of them settled at Yu Weh Loo Pah Ki. It is now the only charter community on the reservation.

An estimated eighty-five people live here in an undeveloped community of home-steads connected by dirt roads. Running water has reached all the homes, but some do not have electricity, and there are no phone lines or public facilities. Funds are being raised for community development through sales at the Spider Mound Gallery and Gift Shop in the Hopi Cultural Center on Second Mesa (see below).

FIRST MESA
Map #2

Villages: Hano (*HAH-no*), Polacca (*po-LAH-kah*), Sichomovi (*see-CHO-mo-vee*), Walpi (*WALL-pea*)

First Mesa is about 11 miles west of Keams Canyon on AZ264. At the base of the mesa is the town of **Polacca**, founded by a man from Hano in the early 1900s. Many Hopi have moved here from the mesas for convenience.

Hano (Hanoki) is a settlement of Tewa people who fled from the Rio Grande pueb-los of New Mexico after the 1680 Pueblo revolt against the Spanish. In exchange for set-tling here, they agreed to act as guardians of the access path to the mesa. Many have kept their own language and ceremonies, and they continue to develop their excellent pottery-making skills. The famed potter Nampeyo was a Tewa from Hano.

Although **Sichomovi** (*or Sitsomovi,* meaning "Place of the mound where the wild cur-rants grow") seems to be a part of Hano, it is a separate community founded in 1750 as a colony of **Walpi** (or *Waalpi,* meaning "Place of the gap"). The village of Walpi is a short distance away at the tip of the mesa. You can park on the mesa and walk to Walpi.

Walpi, one of the most picturesque of the Hopi villages, is well worth the walk and is exotic as any village found in the Near East. It sits perched high above the desert floor, hugging the edge of sheer cliffs in a series of terraces since 1690. The path that circles around Walpi is often precariously close to the six-hundred-foot precipice, with ceremonial kivas only a stone's throw away from the edge. A covered passage (*kiska*) connects the plaza to other parts of town.

The handful of people who still live in Walpi do so without electricity or running water. Instead, they collect rainwater in bowl-shaped depressions on the far side of Walpi in much the same way as their ancestors did. The community is known for the quality of its ceremonial dances and crafts, with the men carving katsina dolls and the women fashioning pottery. Signs direct visitors to the houses of individual artisans.

To visit the village, you must join one of the guided tours that leave from either Ponsi Hall in Sichomovi or from the tourist booth in the Walpi parking lot. Tours leave daily every 40 minutes, between 7:00am and 6:00pm in summer and from 8:00am to 5:00pm the rest of the year. A fee is charged. Ponsi Hall and the tourist booth also have the dance schedule for First Mesa.

Between First and Second Mesas is the *Hopi Market,* which has a large variety of local Hopi and Navajo crafts. Follow the blue signs to the market.

SECOND MESA
Map #3

Villages: Mishongnovi (*muh-SHONG-no-vee*), Shongopavi (*shung-AH-po-vee*),
 Shipaulovi (*shuh-PAW-lo-vee*)
Other Sites: Second Mesa Cultural Center

Second Mesa is 8 miles west of First Mesa. At the foot of the mesa is *Hopi Fine Arts,* where you can shop for Hopi baskets and katsina dolls.

The villages of **Mishongnovi** (*Musungnuvi*) and **Shipaulovi** (*Supawlavi*) are reached by a short paved road climbing from AZ264 about a half mile west of its junction with AZ87. Mishongnovi was named for the leader of the Crow clan who brought his people here from the San Francisco Peaks in A.D. 1200. *Supaulovi* means "the Mosquitoes," referring to the reason the Hopi left their previous home in Winslow. Both villages frequently host ceremonies. Showers are available for a small fee at the community center in Mishongnovi, as long as you can bring your own soap and towels. Hilda Burger serves food, and Supaulovi has village tours; call the community center for times and cost.

Shongopavi (*Songoopavi*) has a population of around 740. Although it was established in the 1100s, it has not always been in the same place, having moved here sometime after 1680 from its original site below the mesa rim (where it was called Maseeba*).*

Between Shungopavi and the Second Mesa Cultural Center is a Korean takeout in a private residence. *Tsakurshovi* is a small shop with a surprisingly large selection of jewelry and katsina dolls.

The hub of Second Mesa is the **Hopi Cultural Center.** The *museum* includes exhibits on Hopi culture and history, early photographs of the pueblos, information on handicrafts, and approximate dates of ceremonies in the various villages. Arrangements can also be made here for a Hopi-guided tour to various sites on the reservation. *Spider Mound Gallery and Gifts* sells arts and crafts from Hopi youth. Some of the proceeds are earmarked for community development at the new village of Spider Mound.

The *Hopi Cultural Center Motel* has basic rooms that are moderately priced. Since it is one of the few places to stay in Hopiland, it is important to make reservations at least three months in advance. The motel's restaurant offers inexpensive Indian and American fare, including piki bread, blue corn pancakes, *ba-duf-su-ki* (pinto bean and hominy soup), and *nok-qui-vi* (corn and lamb stew). Shops here also carry an excellent selection of Hopi arts and crafts. A small primitive campground and picnic area are available on a first-come basis. Campers may sometimes use shower facilities at the motel for a small fee.

Just west of the center is the *Hopi Silvercraft Cooperative Guild*, a crafts cooperative and retail store dedicated to perpetuating the excellence and authenticity of Hopi art/craft. A large selection of Hopi overlay jewelry, katsina dolls, pottery, paintings, baskets, and weavings is offered. Tours to watch Hopi artisans are available with advance arrangements.

Food is also available at the junction of AZ264 and AZ87 at LKD's, a small restaurant, and Sekakuku, a store with a deli takeout.

THIRD MESA
Map #4

Villages: Bacavi (*BAH-ko-vee*), Hotevilla (*HOTE-vil-lah*), Kykotsmovi (*kee-KOT-smo-vee*), Moenkopi (*MUN-koh-pea*), Oraibi (oh-RYE-vee)

Third Mesa is 5 miles west of Second Mesa. **Kykotsmovi** (*Kiqotsmovi*), at the base of the mesa, means "Mound of ruined houses." The village was also once called New Oraibi because its founders were former Oraibi residents who had adopted Christianity and other aspects of European culture. It is now headquarters for the Hopi Tribal Coun-

Young Hopi women with side-whorled hairstyles show their unmarried status. (Between 1911 and 1920, H.S.Poley)

cil and is the location for the *Office of Public Relations*, which provides visitor information. The office is near the tribal council building 1 mile south of AZ264. Gas is sold 24 hours a day at the *Village Store*, and picnic areas are on the east side of Oraibi Wash Pumpkin Seed Hill. Browse through one of the largest selections of katsinas in the area at *Monongya Gallery*, or through the items at *Hamana So-o's Arts & Crafts* that are based on katsina images.

Two miles west on AZ234 is **Old Oraibi** (*Orayvi*), a village of kivas and terraced pueblos built of stones and logs. Founded around A.D. 1150, it is one of the oldest continuously inhabited settlements in the United States. You can obtain permission to visit at the village leader's home just outside the main village. Several galleries in and near the village make this one of the best places in Hopiland to shop for fine handcrafted items.

Four miles northwest on AZ264 is **Hotevilla** (*Hoatvela*), known for the beauty of its dances, basketry, and other crafts. The name means "skinned back," a reference to the village spring that is reached by leaning under a rock overhang. Gas is sold here at the co-op store. The village was settled in 1906 as the result of a dispute among the residents of Old Oraibi, with those on the losing side of the argument moving here. When federal authorities insisted they move back to Old Oraibi, some refused and were jailed. Those who did return were resented, and once again, tension built between Hopis. Finally, the dissenting faction packed up and moved to **Bacavi** (*Paaqavi*), which is now on the opposite side of the highway from Hoatvela.

Coal Mine Canyon is a strikingly beautiful canyon of jagged rock, colored white and red and streaked with black coal. The canyon, called Honoo Ji' in Navajo, is a favorite place for Navajo medicine men to gather sands and shales for sandpaintings. A picturesque overlook on the rim has picnic tables. Fossil shells can also often be found along the rim. A permit is needed for hiking. The site was once part of the western boundary of the Navajo Nation, but a recent court settlement concerning the Hopi-Navajo land dispute transferred it to the Hopi Nation.

The village of **Moenkopi**, "Place of running water," is 2 miles southeast of the Navajo town of Tuba City, and although it is 40 miles west of Third Mesa, it is considered a Third Mesa village because it is a satellite of Oraibi. The land around Moenkopi was traditionally used to grow crops by Oraibi farmers, who would run the forty-five miles from Third Mesa to tend their fields here. The village was settled in the 1870s by Chief T'Ivi and other residents of Old Oraibi, and it is now the most modern of the Hopi villages. Near town you can still see prehistoric villages that were abandoned before A.D. 1300.

OTHER ARIZONA LOCATIONS

If you plan on spending time around Oak Creek and Sedona, the Hopi tribe owns and operates the forty-two-room *Kokopelli Inn*. The Hopi tribe also owns and operates the *26 Bar Ranch*, a bed-and-breakfast in the town of Eager in the White Mountains.

EVENTS

Information about Hopi dances can be obtained from the Office of Public Relations in Kykotsmovi. Katsina dances are held at times between the winter solstice to just after the summer solstice. Precise dates are set according to the position of the sun and not usually announced ahead of time. Sometimes the easiest way to find a ceremony is to drive through the mesas and look for a crowd of people standing on the housetops.

JANUARY-JULY *Katsina Dances:* These masked dances are now often closed to the public because of past disrespect from visitors. However, some public dances are still held on weekends from May through mid-July. Visitors are encouraged to bring folding chairs and protection from the sun. No photography is allowed.

JULY *Rodeo:* Held in early July in Polacca.

AUGUST-DECEMBER *Snake Dance:* A sixteen-day ceremony that culminates in a dramatic event where Hopi men dance with poisonous snakes in their mouths. The dance is held every other year in Mishongnovi and Gray Spring to pray for the blessing of rain to ensure a good harvest. It is now closed to the public.

AUGUST-FEBRUARY *Social Dances:* These weekend dances are usually open to the public.

CONTACT INFORMATION

Community Development Offices
Bacavi
928-734-9360
Hotevilla
928-734-2420
Kykotsmovi
928-734-2474
Mishongnovi
928-737-2520
Moenkopi (Lower)
928-283-5212
Moenkopi (Upper)
928-283-8054
Shipaulovi
928-737-2570
Shungopavi
928-734-7135
Sichomovi
928-737-2670
Walpi
928-737-9556

Guided Tours
Ancient Pathways
Bertram Tsavadawa
928-306-7849
First Mesa Consolidated Tours of Walpi
928-737-2262 • http://hopibiz.com
Mon-Fri 9:30am-4pm; fee
Left-Handed Hunter Tour Company
Gary Tso
928-734-2567

Hamana So-o's Arts & Crafts
Oraibi, AZ
928-607-0176

Hopi Cultural Preservation Office
PO Box 123, Kykotsmovi, AZ 86039
928-734-3612 • www.nau.edu/~hcpo-p

Hopi Fine Arts
928-737-2222

Hopi Market
PO Box 303, Indian Route 2, MP 45,
Kykotsmovi, AZ 86039
928-309-7027 • www.hopimarket.com

Hopi Office of Public Relations
PO Box 123, Kykotsmovi, AZ 86039

Hopi Second Mesa Cultural Center
Cultural Center Restaurant and Inn
PO Box 67, Second Mesa, AZ 86043
928-734-2401
www.hopiculturalcenter.com
Museum
928-734-6650
Mon-Fri 8am-5pm & Sat-Sun 9am-4pm,
summer only; fee

Hopi Silvercraft Cooperative Guild
928-734-2463

Hopi Tribe Administrative Offices
928-734-3000

Hopi Tutuveni
PO Box 123, Kykotsmovi, AZ 86039

Keams Canyon Motel
AZ264, Milepost 403, Keams Canyon, AZ
86034
928-738-2297

Kokopelli Inn
Contact information: 6465 Highway 179,
    Sedona, AZ, 86351
888-733-5656 *or* 928-284-1100

McGees Indian Art Gallery
PO Box 607, Keams Canyon, AZ 86034
928-738-2295 • www.hopiart.com

Monongya Gallery
Oraibi, AZ
928-734-2344

Polacca Hall Visitor Center
Sichomovi
928-737-2262
9:30am-4pm, summer; call for winter hours

Tsakurshovi
Second Mesa
928-734-2344

Walpi (Guided Tours)
Ponsi Hall Visitor Center
928-737-2262
Daily 9am-5pm summer; daily 9:30am-4pm
    winter; fee

Village of Walpi Tour Services
Daily 8am-6pm, Apr-Sept; daily 8am-5pm,
    Oct-March; fee

26 Bar Ranch
26 Bar Ranch Road, Eager, AZ, 85925.
928-333-2102 • www.26barranch.com

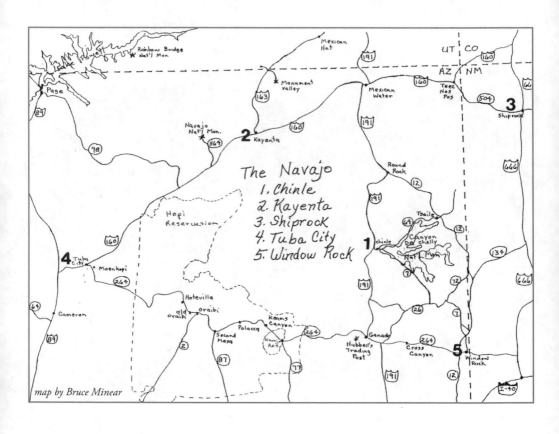

map by Bruce Minear

CHAPTER 7

THE NAVAJO

THE NAVAJO NATION has around 225,000 members, making it the largest Indian group in the United States. About 180,000 of them live in Navajoland (*Diné Bikeyah*), a vast area of 25,000 square miles that is larger than the state of West Virginia, taking up most of northeastern Arizona and spilling into northwestern New Mexico and southeastern Utah. Three smaller communities are located a distance away from the main reservation at Alamo, To'hajiilee, and Ramah. (See Chapter 19, New Mexico's I-40 Corridor.)

The Navajo (Diné) has been one of the most successful Native groups in learning how to incorporate their traditional way of life with modern times. In the 1920s, the discovery of oil on the reservation provided a base of financial stability for the tribe. This, along with coal, uranium, and tourism, provides the main sources of tribal income today. Allowing casinos in Navajoland is currently a controversial issue that is being discussed among the Diné.

Along with over a dozen national monuments, tribal parks, and historic sites, the Navajo Nation encompasses some of the most spectacular scenery in the Southwest. The towns are small and widely scattered throughout the reservation. Main towns for tourists include Kayenta, Tuba City, Chinle, and the Navajo capital of Window Rock. The *Navajo Nation Tourism Office* in Window Rock has information and a free visitor guide for tourists.

The Navajo arts-and-crafts industry is thriving, and artists are famous for the high quality of their silver and turquoise jewelry and their weavings. Other notable items include baskets, distinctive brown pottery, and women's velveteen blouses and long skirts with styles patterned after the clothing of the army wives at Fort Sumner. Trading posts and galleries in Navajoland are good places to purchase these and other arts and crafts. For more information, contact the tribally owned *Navajo Nation Arts and Crafts* stores. The unique Navajo sandpaintings continue to be created primarily as a ceremonial art. Those offered for sale recreate only a small portion of a complete ceremonial painting.

Opportunities for outdoor recreation abound in Navajoland. Lakes, reservoirs, and mountain streams in the Chuska Mountains offer excellent fishing. Popular spots include Asaayi Lake in Bowl Canyon Recreation Area, Berland Lake, Wheatfields Lake, and Tsaile Lake. Hikers enjoy the beauty of Antelope Creek Canyon and Marble Canyon adjoining the Grand Canyon. Several campgrounds offer camping for a small fee.

For information and fishing and hunting permits, contact the *Navajo Nation Department of Fish and Wildlife*. For permits for hiking, camping, and backcountry use, contact the *Navajo Nation Parks and Recreation Department* in Window Rock, Antelope Canyon Tribal Park, Monument Valley Tribal Park, or Cameron Visitor Center. Be advised that much of the terrain is rugged, trails can be strenuous, and unimproved roads are often impassable when wet. Also be on the alert for rapid weather changes and flash floods.

Tour companies owned and operated by Navajos provide excursions with guides who bring an authentic cultural perspective and intimate knowledge of the land. Contact the visitor centers, motels, or the Navajo Nation Tourism Office for more information.

As part of an effort to preserve their cultural heritage, the Navajo emphasize the use of their own language in daily interactions, and it is still used exclusively during religious ceremonies. For an experience of the Navajo language, tune to radio station KTNN at 660 AM. This same complex language was famously used during World War II by the Navajo code talkers, radio operators who created an unbreakable code that helped the United States win the war with Japan.

Many Navajo continue to practice their traditional rituals, particularly the Fire Dance, the Enemy Way Dances in summer, and the Yei-bi-chei ceremony in winter. Other healing ceremonies are also an active part of Navajo spiritual practices. Many of these ceremonies are open to visitors who obtain permission to attend. Traders and tribal rangers are good resources for where to find local dances. In addition, the *Navajo Nation Fair Office* has information on special events such as intertribal powwows and song and dance contests that are held throughout the year to preserve cultural heritage. Weekend events and current news are also listed in the tribal newspaper, *Navajo Times*.

When planning a visit, remember that although the rest of Arizona elected to stay on Mountain Standard Time year-round, the Navajo Nation is on Mountain Daylight time. For example, when it is 5pm in Tuba City during the summer, it is 4pm at Grand Canyon National Park. Also keep in mind the rules of the reservation. In particular, know that no alcoholic beverages are permitted. Individuals do not own the land, but families hold the use rights, so straying off established roads is considered trespassing.

We have divided the sites into four major sections centered on core cities that provide lodging and dining options for visitors: Southeast/Chinle and Window Rock, Southwest/Tuba City, Northwest/Kayenta, and Northeast/Shiprock.

SOUTHEAST NAVAJOLAND

CHINLE
Map #1

Around Town: Canyon de Chelly National Monument
Nearby: Tsaile

Chinle is the largest town in central Navajoland. Located on US191 about 37 miles north of Ganado and 97 miles southeast of Monument Valley, the town provides tourists an alternative to Window Rock and Kayenta for lodging and dining.

Canyon de Chelly is still home to Navajo families.

The main attraction at Chinle is **Canyon de Chelly National Monument**. Dramatically sculpted red sandstone, a scenic canyon stream edged with stately cottonwoods, hundreds of prehistoric ruins and pictographs, red-roofed hogans, and tidy contemporary Navajo farms all combine to make this a unique and stunning place to visit.

The area has been inhabited for at least five thousand years, making it the longest uninterrupted place of habitation on the Colorado Plateau, and one of the longest in North America. At one time, nomadic tribes collected wild foods and hunted here. Around A.D. 350, prehistoric Indians made the canyons their home, living in winter caves and summer brush shelters. The inhabitants learned to build pithouses—partially underground dwellings roofed with sticks and mud—and to plant corn, squash, and beans in fields on the valley floor. Eventually, they moved into aboveground stone masonry dwellings and then between A.D. 1100 and 1300 into cliff houses.

For about four hundred years after the Anasazi abandoned the canyons, Hopi farmers visited sporadically, cultivating crop fields in the summer, then returning to their mesa homelands after the harvest. By the 1700s, the Navajo had moved to the canyon. They prospered here until Colonel Kit Carson led the United States Army against them in 1863–64, destroying their homes, livestock, fruit trees, and food stores and starving them into submission.

Today around fifty Navajo families live at Canyon de Chelly (*de-SHAY*), cultivating orchards and grazing sheep on the flat canyon floors in summer, and then moving to the rims in winter. The land belongs to the Navajo Nation, while the National Park Service administers their over one hundred prehistoric sites.

Canyon de Chelly National Monument extends for twenty-six miles and contains sixty major ruins. The heart of the monument is a trio of giant gorges (Canyon de Chelly, Canyon del Muerto, and Monument Canyon) sliced into the red sandstone plateau by the Rio de Chelly River and its tributaries. With sheer sandstone walls rising as high as one thousand feet, the views of the canyons are dramatic, and it is especially spectacular to visit after an afternoon thunderstorm has sent thousands of waterfalls plummeting over the rims. Be aware, flash floods can close the canyon floor to motorized tours, especially in the spring and late summer.

The *visitor center*, 3 miles east of Chinle on Navajo Route 7, features a gift shop, a traditional hogan, an audiovisual program, and an archaeological museum with informative exhibits on local cultures from the Archaic period to the present. In summer, rangers demonstrate prehistoric skills such as flint knapping and tool making, and Navajos demonstrate more modern skills such as weaving and silversmithing. In addition, rangers lead daily cultural programs, lectures, and hikes during the summer. Backcountry permits are also available here.

Nearby *Cottonwood Campground* is refreshingly situated in a grove of cottonwood trees and has picnic tables, fireplaces (bring your own fuel), toilets with running water, and evening ranger programs May through September. The free campground is open year-round, but no water is available from November to March. No reservations are taken except for group sites.

Both Canyon de Chelly and Canyon del Muerto have paved rim drives that provide viewpoints into the gorges. Ask at the visitor center for a detailed guidebook. Allow 1.5 to 2 hours for each drive.

North Rim Drive (Navajo Route 64) follows Canyon del Muerto for several miles and then continues on to the town of Tsaile. Overlooks on the road include Lodge Ruin, *Antelope House* cliff dwellings, Massacre Cave, and *Mummy Cave*. Canyon del Muerto (Spanish for "Canyon of the Dead") also contains the best rock art, and many think it is the more impressive canyon of the two.

In an alcove across from Antelope House is the *Tomb of the Weaver*, where the well-preserved mummy of an old man was discovered wrapped in a blanket of golden eagle feathers and accompanied by a thick bow, baskets of food, and over two miles of cotton yarn. At Mummy Cave many well-preserved early burials and artifacts have been found. In the cliff nearby are eroded hand- and toeholds that ancient inhabitants used to climb to and from their fields. Massacre Cave was named for an 1805 Spanish punitive expedition led by Antonio de Narbona. One hundred and fifteen Navajos were killed as the Spanish fired down on them from the rim overlooking the cave.

South Rim Drive (Navajo Route 7) follows the old Fort Defiance Trail. It has several overlooks to the floor of the Canyon de Chelly. Two of the most famous are Spider Rock—home of the Navajo's legendary Spider Woman, who taught the people how to weave—and White House Ruins, named for the white plaster on the cliffs above it.

For a closer look at the nine-hundred-year-old *White House Ruins*, take the self-guided trail 1.25 miles to the sandy canyon floor. The dwelling was easily defended from enemies by drawing up the ladders. The trail is a moderate two-hour hike, but bring water and be

White House Ruins in Canyon de Chelly were left by the Anasazi.

prepared for a wade across Chinle Wash on the canyon bottom. A trail guide is available at the visitor center. Free guided tours can also be arranged during the summer at the visitor center, but reservations are recommended.

All other entry into the canyon requires a Navajo guide and a park permit, which is available at the visitor center. Access is by hiking, horseback, or four-wheel drive (including driving your own vehicle). National Park Service guides and park-certified guides are available for hiking or four-wheel-drive tours. Fees start at $15 an hour. Overnight trips are also possible. Tsegi Guide Association leads private tours either hiking or using your own vehicle. Contact them at the visitor center. Some of the other tour companies include Thunderbird Lodge Jeep Tours, Canyon de Chelly Tours, DeChelly Tours, Moki Treks, and Antelope House Tours. Horseback tours are offered by Justin's Horse Rental, Twin Trail Tours, and Totsonii Ranch, 17 miles east of the visitor center.

The only lodging actually in the monument is at *Thunderbird Lodge*, a half-mile southwest of the visitor center. This historic motel began in 1902 as a trading post and grew into a place for early tourists to get a hot meal, spend the night, and take an organized tour of the canyon. In addition to lodging, Thunderbird has a restaurant, gift shop, exhibits, and horse rentals.

At the entrance to Canyon de Chelley is a *Navajo Arts and Crafts Enterprise,* one of five locations. Other restaurants and gift shops are available in the nearby town of Chinle. Additional lodging is available at Best Western Canyon de Chelly Inn, Holiday Inn Chinle, and Many Farms Inn.

EAST OF CHINLE

The town of **Tsaile** is about 23 miles east of Canyon de Chelly Visitor Center and 54 miles north of Window Rock on Navajo Route 12.

In town is Diné College, created in 1969 as a community college focusing on preparing its students to become contributing members of Navajo society. On campus is the hogan-shaped Ned Hatathli Cultural Center, which houses the *Hatathli Museum and Gallery.* Exhibits at the museum cover Navajo culture and history, as well as Anasazi pottery and a Plains Indian collection. In addition, authentic Navajo arts and crafts are for sale. The museum is on the third and fourth floors of the six-story center. Also in the center is the *Diné College Bookstore*, which sells publications covering Navajo and other Native American topics.

Just south of the college is *Tsaile Lake*, where you can fish (permit required) and enjoy peaceful scenery.

Ten miles south of Tsaile is *Wheatfields Lake*, a large mountain lake popular for trout fishing, boating, picnics, and camping. Tribal permits are available at the lakeside store, which also sells groceries and fishing supplies.

For an experience of cultural immersion, spend the night at *Coyote Pass Hospitality*, a Navajo bed-and-breakfast that provides lodging in a one-room hogan with wood stoves and electricity, but no running water. The breakfast menu includes blue corn pancakes, Navajo burritos filled with potatoes and cheese, and blue corn cereal. Your host, Will Tsosie Jr., enjoys sharing with you insights into his culture. He is also available to guide you to scenic sites, including some that are off the beaten track. Coyote Pass Hospitality is 30 minutes northeast of Chinle near Tsaile. Reservations are required.

HOGAN

Hogan (hooghan) means "the place home." It is the traditional dwelling of the Navajo, who learned how to make it soon after their emergence into this, the Fourth World. As described in the Blessingway ceremony, the builder of the first hogan was either Talking God or Coyote, depending on which version of the story you hear. Its building site, materials, and design elements were all carefully chosen to be in harmony and balance with nature. All subsequent hogans echo these elements and are also considered sacred. The dirt floor provides a direct connection to the Earth Mother and the shape of the roof mirrors that of the Sky Father. The walls echo the upward thrust of the mountains and trees, and the door faces the rising sun. Turquoise, obsidian, jet, abalone shell, and white shell beads, all with symbolic importance to the Navajo, are some of the other incorporated elements. During construction, a medicine man blesses the hogan, praying that it will become a place where the family grows in love for each other and where its members are protected from hardship and discord. When the home is complete, sacred ceremonial objects are placed inside it.

Although the first hogan had a fork-stick frame with five sides and a fire in the center, new styles have emerged since the early 1900s, some with six or eight sides. Nontraditional construction materials, such as plywood and asphalt shingles, are also now incorporated. And although hogans are still used for dwellings in isolated rural areas, today most of them are used only for ceremonial purposes.

Traditional hogans are still used by the Navajo.

WINDOW ROCK
Map #5

Around Town: Chi' Hoo Tso Indian Market, Council Chambers, Fort Defiance, Good Shepherd Mission, Navajo Arts and Crafts Enterprise, Navajo Nation Museum, Library and Visitor Center, Navajo Nation Zoological and Botanical Park, St. Michael's Mission, Tse Bonito Park, Window Rock Monument, and Navajo Veteran's Memorial Park
Nearby: Bowl Canyon Recreation Area, Church Rock, Hubbell Trading Post National Historic Site, Lake Asaayi, Lupton Tea Pot

Window Rock has been an important Navajo community since A.D. 1300 and the capital of the Navajo Nation since 1935. The main streets in town are AZ264, which runs east/west, and Navajo Route 12, which travels north from its intersection with AZ264.

The extensive exhibits at the modern **Navajo Nation Museum, Library, and Visitor Center** on AZ264 cover Anasazi culture and Navajo tribal history and culture. Included are displays of jewelry, textiles, pottery, historical trade items, and an authentic hogan. The gift shop stocks Indian-made arts and crafts and regional texts about the tribe's history and culture. The library has an in-depth research collection, and the center hosts a variety of educational and cultural programs in its conference rooms, auditorium, and outdoor amphitheater. Travelers can find pertinent information on local sites, lodging, and dining at the tourist information kiosk.

The tribally owned **Navajo Arts and Crafts Enterprise** on AZ264 is one of this organization's five locations on the reservation. Here you can buy authentic works by Navajo artists such as silver jewelry, baskets, and rugs, as well as handcrafted items from other Southwestern tribes. You can also arrange for an English/Navajo-speaking tour guide.

For a more eclectic shopping experience and an opportunity to meet some of the locals, visit **Chi' Hoo Tso Indian Market**, located at the intersection of AZ264 and Navajo Route 12. A variety of vendors here sell merchandise that ranges from home furnishings to Navajo-crafted jewelry. Food booths offer squash stew, pinyon nuts, mutton stew, fry bread (round dough patty fried in oil), Navajo tacos (fry bread topped with hamburger, lettuce, tomato, and salsa), Kneel Down bread (a dense cornbread wrapped in corn husks), and other traditional favorites.

Tse Bonito Park is a half-mile east of the market on AZ264. In 1864 it was used by Kit Carson as a stopping place during the infamous Long Walk, when the Navajo were forced to relocate from Ft. Defiance to New Mexico. The large sandstone monoliths in the park are called the Haystacks. Tse Bonito has shaded picnic tables, a campground, and the **Navajo Nation Zoological and Botanical Park**, which exhibits plants and animals that are important to Navajo in their natural habitats. A sampling of the thirty species of wild and the handful of domestic animals represented includes golden eagles, cougars, elk, coyotes, black bears, and double-fleeced, four-horned Churro sheep. Many of the animals were found orphaned or injured in the wild and subsequently donated to the zoo.

The administrative center for the tribe sits in the northeast part of town off Navajo Route 12. Of particular interest is the circular-shaped **council chambers**, where the eighty-eight delegates to the tribal council meet and enact legislation. Each delegate is elected by a chapter, which is based on population and similar to a county. Visitors can arrange to tour

*Navajo Code Talker
statue at Window Rock
honors Navajo veterans.*

the building to learn more about the Navajo's sophisticated government, to see the colorful wall murals depicting Navajo history, and to observe the legislature when it is in session.

The council chambers looks out on **Window Rock Monument and Navajo Veteran's Memorial Park.** Window Rock (*Tse'gha'hoodzani* in Navajo, meaning "perforated rock") is a graceful forty-seven-foot sandstone arch that has inspired the name for the town. The wind-scoured arch also plays an important role in the Navajo Water-Way ceremony. Loose stones just below Window Rock mark the site of a prehistoric Indian pueblo. More recently, a Veteran's Memorial has been built at its base to commemorate the Navajo code talkers of World War II and other veterans. Picnic tables, water, and restrooms are available for day use. To reach the park, take Navajo Route 12 north of AZ264 at the light and follow the signs.

If you continue north on Navajo Route 12 you will come to **Fort Defiance**, begun as a fort in September of 1851 by Colonel Edwin Vose in "defiance" of the Indians. Kit Carson later used it as his headquarters during his harshly punitive campaign, and in 1868, it became the first Navajo Indian Agency, issuing sheep and supplies when the Navajo returned from exile in Fort Sumner. Today, it is an administrative center with a hospital, school, and Bureau of Indian Affairs offices. **Good Shepherd Mission** was established here in 1908 by Episcopalians. The current church was built in 1955 and incorporates Navajo symbolism. The forty-eight-acre compound includes a retreat house, greenhouse and gardening program, and the Hummingbird Gallery, which sells native-made arts and crafts and provides demonstrations of traditional arts.

St. Michael's Mission is 3 miles west of Window Rock on AZ264 from its intersection with Navajo Route 12. The original adobe chapel, built in 1898 by Franciscan missionaries, was replaced by this large stone church in 1937. A small historical museum in the mission building now has displays on early-twentieth-century Navajo culture and the life of the Franciscan friars who lived here. The mission is still active in daily Navajo life today.

Accommodations are available in Window Rock at the *Quality Inn Navajo Nation*

Capital. In addition to motel rooms with Southwestern decor, the motel has a swimming pool and a gift shop that sells Indian arts and crafts. The moderately priced restaurant serves traditional native dishes and Mexican and American food and is your best choice in town. Individual and group tours can also be arranged from here. The motel is located on AZ264 about a half-mile east of the intersection with Navajo Route 12.

Another lodging option is *Navajoland Days Inn* in St. Michaels, 4 miles west of Window Rock on AZ264. Lodgers here receive a free continental breakfast and use of the swimming pool. The motel also has a restaurant and gift shop.

NORTH OF WINDOW ROCK

Bowl Canyon Recreation Area in the Chuska Mountains attracts fishing enthusiasts, hikers, campers, and picnickers who also come here to enjoy the beautiful mountain scenery and cooler temperatures. *Camp Asaayi (Ah-SY-yeh)* has sixteen cabins and a dining hall that can be rented by large groups in the summer. West of the camp is *Lake Asaayi*, which is open to the public for trout fishing, camping, and picnicking. Private boats and canoes are allowed on the lake with a permit, but no motor boats are allowed.

EAST OF WINDOW ROCK

Church Rock is a 5,500-foot-tall steeple of sandstone that is 35 miles from Window Rock and visible from the town of Gallup, New Mexico. The town of Church Rock is less than 2 miles from Red Rock State Park, where popular native ceremonial events are held throughout the year, so locals sometimes organize arts, crafts, and food vendors to coincide with these events. See Chapter 19, New Mexico's I-40 Corridor, page 358, for information on Red Rock State Park.

Chaco Culture National Historical Park is east of Window Rock in New Mexico. See Chapter 17, Northwest New Mexico, page 318, for information.

WEST OF WINDOW ROCK

An interesting rock formation is *Lupton Tea Pot*, southwest of Gallup on I-40 near Lupton. This is a rock that looks like a teapot standing ready to pour a steaming cup off the rock ledge where it sits.

The town of Ganado, 30 miles west of Window Rock on AZ264, was named after Ganado Mucho, leader of the western Navajo until his death in 1892. One mile west of Ganado on AZ264 is **Hubbell Trading Post National Historic Site**. Customers have been coming to Hubbell Trading Post since 1878, making it the oldest continuously operating trading post in the United States, and it continues today much as it did in the days when Navajo families rode here in covered wagons to trade. The post is stuffed with merchandise, old and new, as well as with priceless paintings and Indian artifacts accumulated by the Hubbell family.

As a National Historic Site, Hubbell Trading Post also has a bookstore, a small museum, artists who demonstrate traditional skills such as weaving and silversmithing, and picnic tables. Visitors can take a free guided tour of the Hubbell home and/or a self-guided tour of the grounds, where gardens of flowers and vegetables traditionally grown in the Southwest bloom in summer.

TRADING POSTS

Since the Civil War, trading posts have acted as centers for buying, selling, socializing, and catching up on the latest gossip, as well as served as points of direct contact between Indians and Anglos. Hard cash was scarce, so the medium of exchange was often tokens that belonged to each individual post. The Indians also traded crafts and raw goods such as wool. Anything left to spend could be kept in the form of a credit with the post. The system depended on the honesty of the trader, for when language was a barrier, the Native Americans simply pointed to what they wanted until the change on the counter was gone.

Many traders were friends to the American Indians, helping not only with food and supplies but also with legal and medical advice, emergency help, and credit. In addition, it was through the traders that the American public gained its initial awareness of the richness of native cultures.

John Lorenzo Hubbell, the founder of Hubbell's Trading Post, was such a trader. Not only was he one of the first to recognize the value of Navajo silverwork and weaving, but he also encouraged design changes he believed would sell.

Outbuildings at Hubbell Trading Post remind visitors of its historic past.

SOUTHWEST NAVAJOLAND

TUBA CITY
Map #4

Around Town: Tuba City Trading Post
Nearby: Antelope Canyon, Antelope Point Marina, Cameron, dinosaur tracks, Elephant Feet, Grand
 Falls of the Little Colorado River, Little Colorado River Navajo Tribal Park, Navajo Bridge

Tuba City (population around 8,000 people) is the largest community in the western portion of the reservation. Although named after a famous Hopi leader, Chief T'Ivi (pronounced *Tuba*), and once the Hopi's domain, the town was actually settled in 1877 by Mormon pioneers. Later, in 1903, it became the site of the United States Indian Agency.

Near the center of town at Main Street and Moenave is the hogan-shaped **Tuba City Trading Post**, established in the 1870s. By the early 1900s, the post had become a social and commercial hub for Navajos living on the western reservation. Many famous Americans, including Zane Grey and Theodore Roosevelt, also enjoyed a visit here. Today the trading post has been restored and operates much as it did historically. In addition to groceries, you can find authentically made Indian jewelry, sandpaintings, rugs, and other arts and crafts.

Behind the trading post is **Explore Navajo Interactive Museum**, which looks at the culture and historic contributions of the Navajo using their own words. Exhibits in a separate building focus on the code talkers.

Adjacent to the trading post is the *Quality Inn Tuba City*, with motel rooms in Southwestern décor, a full-service restaurant, and a gift shop. The RV park has full hookups, laundry facilities, and a convenience store. Also on-site is an example of a traditional hogan. Both the motel and trading post have information on dances and events on the Navajo and Hopi reservations. Several fast food restaurants are nearby.

A more modest option is *Diné Inn Motel* at US160 and Peslakai Avenue. The motel offers AAA and AARP discounts.

Another lodging possibility is the *Greyhills Inn*, which offers simple and inexpensive lodging in what was once an Indian boarding school. The rooms are private, but the bathrooms are shared. From the intersection of US160 and AZ264, take US160 about a half-mile northeast to Warrior Drive.

The town's shopping center has Basha's Diné Markets supermarket, two restaurants, and other shops. Tuuvi Travel Center is at the edge of town at the junction of US160 and AZ264.

NORTH OF TUBA CITY

Near the settlement of Tonalea north of Tuba City on US160 are two isolated sandstone towers called **Elephant Feet**. Stop your car on the side of the road, walk to the base of the formations, stand between the rocks, and have a friend take your photo. You will look like you are standing between the feet of a giant elephant.

Navajo Bridge spans eight hundred feet across the Colorado River from Arizona into

Navajoland. The *visitor center* has exhibits about Navajo life and construction of the bridge. You can walk across the bridge to enjoy a scenic view of Marble Canyon and of the river 470 feet below you and to browse the Navajo arts and crafts vendors. The bridge is east of Lees Ferry on Hwy 89A. See Chapter 5, Grand Canyon Country, page 77, for more information.

For an unforgettable experience, travel 5 miles on AZ98 from Page to **Antelope Canyon**, one of the most stunning slot canyons in the Southwest. It is actually two canyons, Upper and Lower Antelope, both of which drain into Lake Powell.

You may have seen the famous Southwestern photograph of a narrow passageway through walls of swirled sandstone that are lit by the sun into translucent shades of yellow, orange, and red. This is Upper Antelope Canyon. The Navajo call it *Tse' bighanilini*, meaning "the place where water runs through rocks." Lower Antelope Canyon (*Hasdestwazi*, meaning "spiral rock arches") is longer and deeper than Upper Antelope and involves descending a series of ladders to the bottom of the gorge.

To enjoy the mystery and haunting beauty of **Upper Antelope Canyon**, you will need a permit and an authorized guide, available from tour operators in Page or at the entrance to the canyon. From Page, take Coppermine Road south to AZ98. Turn east and go 2 miles to the Navajo Tribal Park and parking lot. From here it is a 3.5-mile dusty, bumpy ride to the canyon. The walk through the canyon is not strenuous. For the best photos, bring a tripod.

Lower Antelope Canyon is just across AZ98 on N22B. Permits are sold on site. Although the entrance stations are closed November through February both canyons are open.

Antelope Point Marina is an $80 million, upscale project on the shores of Lake Powell being developed in cooperation with the Navajo Nation. The state-of-the-art marina is now open and offers rentals of luxury houseboats and other watercraft. Marina Village has the Market Place, live entertainment, and dining facilities. Ja'di' To'oh is the only restaurant on the water at Lake Powell. Also planned are a luxury resort, RV park, campground, Navajo cultural center, and artist studios where visitors can view demonstrations.

Navajo once grazed their sheep near Antelope Point. To take their herds to the river, they carved steps into the side of Navajo Canyon, which can still be seen today. The marina is 7 miles east of Page, Arizona, via AZ98 and N22B and 10 miles upstream from Wahweap marina.

SOUTH OF TUBA CITY

Cameron is conveniently located at the junction of US89 and AZ64, about 1 hour from Flagstaff, 1 hour from the South Rim of the Grand Canyon, and 1.5 hours from Lake Powell.

Cameron Visitor Center, at the junction of US89 and AZ64, has information about visiting the Navajo Nation, the Grand Canyon, and other places of interest. In particular, ask here for permits for trails to the Colorado River, Marble Canyon, Coal Mine Canyon, Rainbow Bridge, and other sites on the western portion of the Navajo Nation. Also at the highway junction is a *Navajo Arts and Crafts Enterprise*.

Founded in 1916 by Hubert and C. D. Richardson, the Navajo-operated *Cameron Trading Post* is one of the few authentic trading posts left in Arizona. The barter system is still active at Cameron, as Navajos and Hopis swap art, crafts, wool, and pinyon nuts for merchandise and groceries. The trading post is an excellent place for both the beginning and serious collector looking for either contemporary or antique Indian art. The *Collector's Gallery* displays and sells museum-quality work such as antique Plains Indian beadwork, antique Navajo rugs, historic baskets, Pueblo pottery, and jewelry. The gift shop has an extensive inventory of Navajo rugs, Hopi katsinas, Pueblo pottery, Navajo sandpaintings, baskets, sculpture, jewelry, and other Southwestern and Native American art. Southwestern-themed domestic items are also on sale.

Cameron Trading Post Indian Lodge provides comfortable accommodations in an Indian lodge landscaped with native stone. The modern rooms are furnished with carved-oak furniture and some come with a balcony overlooking the Colorado River. The restaurant serves Navajo tacos, fry bread, and a homemade green chili that gets rave reviews from customers. A delightful garden planted in the 1930s is still flourishing today and provides an enjoyable respite for travelers. Behind the lodge are a lovely view and the suspension bridge that leads across the Little Colorado River Gorge to the Grand Canyon.

Cameron Trading Post also has a basic RV park, convenience store, and gas station. Be sure to make your lodging reservations early for this popular place.

From Cameron, AZ69 travels west to the Grand Canyon. Along the way you can stop for a view deep into the gorge of the Little Colorado River at **Little Colorado River Navajo Tribal Park**. This river, known as "Little C" or "LCR" for short, begins in the White Mountains, flows through Winslow and Wupatki National Monument, and eventually joins the Colorado River in the Grand Canyon. The overlook has a picnic area and lines of booths where Navajo vendors sell inexpensive Indian arts and crafts.

Upstream toward Flagstaff, the LCR flows along the southwestern edge of the Painted Desert, where in early spring and again briefly during the summer monsoons it creates the **Grand Falls of the Little Colorado River**. The falls are a 600-foot wide torrent of chocolate brown water that thunders over a 185-foot precipice into the canyon below. During full flow, Grand Falls are said to be larger than Niagara Falls, but at other times of the year, the amount of water dwindles to a trickle. To reach Grand Falls, you will need a four-wheel-drive vehicle. Take US89 north of Flagstaff 1.8 miles and turn right onto Camp Townsend–Winona Road. Turn left at Leupp Road and follow it for 13 miles to the unmarked Navajo Route 6910 (between milepost 5 and 6). Turn left and drive on this rough road for 9.4 miles to a turnoff on the left that leads to the falls. You can also access Leupp Road from I-40 at Winona exit 211, which is 17 miles east of Flagstaff. Follow Townsend-Winona Road for 2 miles to Leupp Road. Be aware that Navajo Route 6910 can be impassable during wet weather. March and April are the best times to visit.

WEST OF TUBA CITY

Just off US160, a few miles west of town, are Jurassic-era **dinosaur tracks** preserved in sandstone. Take the unpaved road north (right) at the small sign to Moenave (between mileposts 316 and 317). The 200-million-year-old footprints that are most visible today are those of a three-toed dinosaur, which was probably a carnivorous biped about ten feet tall. The tracks are most vivid after a rain when they fill with water. Colorful Navajo arts and crafts vendors ply their wares a short distance from the tracks.

NORTHWEST NAVAJOLAND

KAYENTA

Map #2

Around Town: Kayenta Visitor Center Museum, Navajo code talkers exhibit
Nearby: Monument Valley Navajo Tribal Park, Navajo Arts and Crafts Enterprise, Navajo National Monument

Merril L. Sandoval from Tuba City was a Navajo Code Talker during World War II.

Two large pools of water have made the town of Kayenta an oasis for centuries. Because it is one of the few settlements in this part of Navajoland, the town makes a good hub for visiting the amazing and unique landscape of Monument Valley, which is about 20 miles northeast of town, and the prehistoric ruins of Navajo National Monument southwest of town. Kayenta has several motels, restaurants, and a shopping center. Stop at the Burger King near the center of town to see a display on the **World War II Navajo code talkers** that includes Japanese and American items collected by one of the code talkers on the battlefield.

For an introduction to the Navajo culture, stop at the hogan-shaped **Kayenta Cultural Center/Visitor Center**. This cultural center provides travel information, including names of local tour guides; a museum that features examples of male and female hogans, a sweat lodge, a shade house, and other cultural exhibits; Navajo historical artifacts; arts-and-crafts demonstrations; a gift shop; and evening dances in an outdoor amphitheater. The center is on US160 near the intersection with US163.

The newest area lodging is the *Hampton Inn-Navajo Nation*, located on US160 in the center of town adjacent to the visitor center. The three-story adobe motel has Native American décor and offers a free continental breakfast to lodgers. The restaurant serves Native American and Southwestern food, and the gift shop sells handcrafted Indian items.

Holiday Inn-Kayenta is also in the center of town and is a popular stop for tour groups. The menu at the restaurant includes Navajo and American dishes.

Best Western Wetherill Inn has modest but comfortable rooms and a café serving Navajo and American food. It is 1 mile north of the junction of US163 and US160.

The *Anasazi Inn* is at the mouth of Tsegi Canyon 10 miles west of Kayenta on US160. The motel has a full-service restaurant and a gift shop.

NORTH OF KAYENTA

Monument Valley Navajo Tribal Park, 23 miles northeast of Kayenta on US160 to US163 (visitor center), is the geographic center of the Colorado Plateau and one of the most photographed landscapes in the world. Imagine a flat, sagebrush-dotted plain punctuated by towering monoliths, stately mesas, fragile arches, delicate spires, and fanciful figures in stone, all cast in hues of red, pink, and purple. Then come here to see beyond your imaginings. Sunset is an especially gorgeous time as the colors and shapes of the land mystically change with the deepening shadows.

Near the entrance to the valley is the 1,500-foot *Agathla Peak* (*Aghaa'la* in Navajo), the center of the world according to Navajo legend. Most of Monument Valley's landmarks are remnants of weathered sandstone, while a few, such as Agathla Peak (also known as El Capitan), were left by ancient volcanoes. People have lived in the shadow of these monoliths for centuries. Petroglyphs and Anasazi ruins dating earlier than A.D. 1300 have been found in the park. Generations of Navajo have also called the valley home, and around one hundred Navajos still live here. In 1863–64 it was a refuge for a Navajo chief and his followers, who hid from Kit Carson among the intricacies of stone. Hoskinini Mesa is named after him.

The small *visitor center* is 4 miles east of US163. It has information, a few displays, a gift shop, and a picnic area. The View Restaurant offers meals with a spectacular view of the valley. Mitten View Campground has ninety-nine sites and is open year-round, but no facilities or running water are available October to March. Reservations are accepted for groups of ten or more.

The 17-mile loop *Valley Drive* travels through the heart of the park and can be followed with a self-guided brochure available at the visitor center. Allow 1.5 hours for the drive. Water and restrooms are available only at the visitor center.

Monument Valley evokes a mysterious past and timeless present.

Valley Drive is a rough dirt road, especially at the beginning. To save the wear and tear on your car, to visit areas that are closed to the general public, and to learn more about native lore, take a guided tour. To book a vehicle or horseback tour, contact Goulding's Tours or one of the other tour operators listed under the contact information at the end of this chapter. In addition, the visitor center has an up-to-date list of tour operators.

Hiking in Monument Valley is also restricted, except for the 3.2 mile *Wildcat Trail*, which circles West Mitten Butte. Pick up a brochure at the visitor center for this memorable self-guided hike. For guided hikes, contact Sacred Monument Tours or Keyah Hozhoni Tours.

The only place to stay in Monument Valley is the historic *Goulding's Lodge*, 6 miles west of the visitor center. The lodge has a small indoor pool, a laundromat, and the Stagecoach Dining Room, serving American and Navajo food. If you plan to stay here, be sure to make your reservations early as it is often full. Goulding's also offers guided tours of Monument Valley and has a gift shop that sells Indian crafts. There is also a nearby store selling groceries and fuel, and a KOA Campground.

Goulding's Museum and Trading Post began as a trading post in 1924, and a museum is now housed in a re-creation of the post from the late 1920s and early 1930s. Displays include photographs and historical Navajo artifacts, items from the Goulding family, and memorabilia from films made in Monument Valley, such as John Ford's *Stagecoach,* shot in 1939.

To avoid the crowds at Goulding's, continue on the paved road about 10 miles to *Oljato Trading Post*, a combination of historic trading post and museum. In operation since 1921, the mercantile still sells a diversity of goods, from corn grinders to canned goods, in a building only slightly changed since its inception. The customer next to you may well speak more Navajo than English. A small museum displays Navajo craft work and artifacts from the last 150 years. Navajo rugs, a special collection of dolls, and other local arts and crafts are available to buy, and Navajo Country Guided Trail Rides provides tours to Monument Valley.

In addition to motels in Kayenta, other lodging options are *Navajo Trails Motel*, north on US160 in Teec Nos Pos, and motels in the Utah towns of Mexican Hat and Bluff. Navajo cheeseburgers, Navajo tea, and other native dishes are sold by various vendors who operate out of rustic huts situated along the road to the Tribal Park.

A *Navajo Arts and Crafts Enterprise* is at the gateway to Monument Valley on US160 and AZ163.

SOUTH OF KAYENTA

Navajo National Monument contains three Kayenta Anasazi cliff dwellings that are some of the largest and best preserved in the Southwest. *Betatakin* and *Keet Seel* can still be visited, but *Inscription House* is now closed to the public.

The *visitor center* has exhibits that detail what life was like for the early inhabitants here, a movie about the Anasazi, a short slide show, books and maps for sale, and a gift shop that sells jewelry and other Navajo arts and crafts. Behind the visitor center is a replica of a traditional Navajo forked-stick hogan and sweat lodge.

Betatakin (Navajo for "ledge house"), the most accessible of the three ruins and in an excellent state of preservation, nestles in a huge alcove in Tsegi Canyon. It was built around A.D. 1250 and then abandoned only fifty years later, possibly because of annual floods. At one time, as many as 125 people may have lived here. The Hopi believe this 135-room ruin was the ancestral home to their Fire Clan. The paved, self-guided Sandal Trail, which starts from behind the visitor center, is a 1-mile round-trip to Betatakin Overlook and back. Visiting the ruins requires a more demanding guided tour, which is a 5-hour, 5-mile hike with a strenuous climb. Tours leave at 8:30am and 11am (if enough interest) daily from mid-May to mid-September and sporadically during other months. Register at the visitor center desk up to a day ahead for this free hike, and be aware that space is limited.

The remote Keet Seel (Navajo for "broken pieces of pottery") is the largest cliff dwelling in Arizona, and its 160 rooms and five kivas are some of the best preserved. It was occupied from about A.D. 950 until about 1300. An aura of peace pervades this magnificent setting, where the Ancient Ones, upon leaving their homes here, sealed many of the doorways as if they planned to return. A guided hike leaves daily mid-May to mid-September; during other months, hikes are scheduled sporadically. Since the hike is a strenuous 17 miles round-trip, most people spend the night at the primitive campground at the ruins during the summer. Reservations can be made up to five months in advance.

A slightly easier way to visit is on horseback. A commercial tour with a Navajo guide leaves the visitor center every morning in summer, returning the same day. Make your reservations early.

Inscription House Ruins, the smallest of the cliff dwellings, is 30 miles from head-quarters and not open to the public.

There is no charge for staying at the campground near the visitor center, open year-round with water and restrooms available. Campfire talks on the history, archeology, and the natural history of the area are often offered.

The visitor center and overlook trail are open year-round, but trails to the ruins may close in winter. The turnoff to the monument is 54 miles northeast of Tuba City or 22 miles southwest of Kayenta on US160 to Black Mesa Junction, and then 9 miles west on AZ564.

Thirty miles west of Kayenta and north on US160 is a Navajo Arts and Crafts Enterprise.

NORTHEAST NAVAJOLAND

SHIPROCK
Map #3

Around Town: Shiprock Trading Post
Nearby: Four Corners Monument and Navajo Tribal Park

Shiprock, 28 miles west of Farmington on US64, is the largest Navajo community in Navajoland. It is named for a massive volcanic upthrust that rises 1,700 feet from the desert floor about 13 miles southwest of the town. Its outer core has eroded away and only the inner core and walls (dikes) remain, giving the structure the appearance of a sailing ship or a winged bird. In Navajo, it is called *Tse' Bit'a'i*, "Rock with Wings." One legend tells about giant birds that lived on the rock and terrorized the people. The Diné asked the Warrior Twins for help, and the twins were successful in killing the monster birds. Since Shiprock is a sacred site for the Navajo, climbing it is prohibited.

Shiprock Trading Post specializes in Navajo textiles between 1890 and 1930 and in antique Pueblo jewelry.

Four Corners Monument and Navajo Tribal Park is the only place in the United States where four states touch—Arizona, Colorado, New Mexico, and Utah. The spot is marked by a granite and brass monument and dozens of stalls of Navajo vendors selling traditional food and handmade arts and crafts. In addition, a small center has cultural demonstrations, a picnic area, and portable restrooms. No water is available. The monument is west of Teec Nos Pos off US160.

OTHER LOCATIONS

Rainbow Bridge National Monument is in Glen Canyon National Recreation Area. (See Chapter 23, Southern Utah, page 433.)

Although ancestors of the **San Juan Southern Paiute** have lived in northern Arizona for years, the tribe was not recognized by the United States government until 1989. Today tribal enrollment is around 254 members who live in several communities on the Navajo Reservation. The San Juan Southern Paiute Yingup Weavers Association has been formed to preserve the basketry skills of community weavers.

EVENTS

For information about Navajo Nation events, call 928-871-6436 or visit www.DiscoverNavajo.com. Navajo Nation fairs are held at different communities throughout the year. Events usually include a rodeo, arts and crafts, dance performances, and other entertainment. The largest of these fairs is held at Window Rock in September. Information is at 928-871-6478 or 928-871-6647 or www.navajonationfair.com.

MONTHLY *Crownpoint Rug Auction:* Navajo rug auction held monthly on the second or third Friday at Crownpoint Elementary School. A public auction of 300 to 400 rugs each month. Viewing is 4-6pm, auction begins 7pm. Call 505-786-7386 (Christina Ellsworth, co-manager) or 505-786-5302 (Ena Chavez, manager), or visit www.crownpointrugauction.com.

JANUARY *Shiprock Balloon Festival:* Small balloon festival in Shiprock, NM.

MAY *Native American Arts Auction:* Art auction, arts and crafts vendors, and food. Hubbell Trading Post NHS, Ganado, AZ. Information at 928-755-3475 or visit www.nps.gov/hutr or www.friendsofhubbell.org.

Marathon Relay & Half Marathon Walk: The only marathon event on the Navajo Nation. Held in Shiprock, NM. Information at www.shiprockmarathon.com.

Ralph Johnson Memorial Rodeo: Rodeo events and parade. Ganado, AZ. Call E. Bedonie at 928-386-5294 for information.

JUNE *Eastern Navajo Arts and Crafts Festival:* Dancing, arts and crafts vendors and demonstrations, food booths, rug auction, entertainment, and cultural talks. Torreon/Star Lake Chapter House. Call 505-731-2422 or 505-731-2336.

Music Festival: Entertainment, arts and crafts vendors, and book signings. Navajo Nation Museum, Window Rock, AZ, phone 928-871-7941 or visit http://ggsc.wnmu.edu/mcf/museums/nnm.html.

JULY *Eastern Agency Navajo Fair:* Regional Navajo fair held in Crownpoint, NM.

Navajo Nation Fourth of July Celebration/PRCA Rodeo: One of the largest events in the Navajo Nation. Rodeo, carnival, dances, concerts, youth days, powwow, sports, fireworks, exhibits, and arts/crafts booths. Held July 4th weekend at Navajo Nation Fairgrounds in Window Rock, AZ. Call 928-871-6478 for information.

AUGUST *Central Navajo Fair:* Carnival, powwow, rodeo, Miss Central Navajo, parade. Chinle, AZ. *Native American Arts Auction:* Art auction, arts/crafts vendors, and food. Hubbell Trading Post NHS, Ganado, AZ. Call 928-755-3475 or visit www.nps.gov/hutr or www.friendsofhubbell.org.

Sheep Is Life Celebration: An opportunity to buy direct from the weaver at an all-day rug auction designed to promote hand-processed and Navajo churro rugs. Diné College, Tsaile, AZ. Information at www.navajolifeway.org.

SEPTEMBER *Navajo Nation Fair:* Billed as the largest Indian fair and rodeo in the U.S. Traditional song and dance, all-Indian rodeo, intertribal powwow, Miss Navajo Nation pageant, prize-winning arts/crafts for sale, parade, carnival, concerts, contests, wild-horse race, traditional food, and agricultural & livestock exhibits. Around 200,000 people usually attend. Wed-Sun after Labor Day weekend, Navajo Nation Fairgrounds, Window Rock, AZ. Contact 928-871-6478 or visit www.navajonationfair.com.

Southwestern Navajo Fair: Regional Navajo fair held in Dilkon, AZ.

Utah Navajo Fair: Regional Navajo fair held in Bluff, UT.

OCTOBER *Northern Navajo Fair and Nightway Chant (Yei-Be-Chei Healing Ceremony):* Regional Navajo fair and ceremony. Held early October in Shiprock, NM.

Western Navajo Fair: Regional Navajo fair held in Tuba City, AZ.

NOVEMBER *Keshmish Festival:* Cultural events, entertainment, and fine art in jewelry, pottery, weaving, and other art forms. Navajo Nation Museum, Window Rock, AZ, phone 928-871-7941 or visit http://ggsc.wnmu.edu/mcf/museums/nnm.html.

Todineeshzee Fourth of July Rodeo and Fair: Includes an all-Indian rodeo, carnival, powwow, Indian arts/crafts vendors, parade, fireworks, and fun run.

CONTACT INFORMATION

Camp Asaayi
Daily, April-October, depending on weather

Anasazi Inn – Tsegi Canyon
PO Box 1543, Kayenta, AZ 86033
928-697-3793 • www.anasaziinn.com

Antelope Canyon-Lake Powell Navajo Tribal Park Office
Navajo Parks and Recreation, PO Box 4803,
    Page, AZ 86040
928-698-2808
www.navajonationparks.org/htm/antelope
    canyon.htm
Entrance stations are open daily 8am-5pm,
    Mar-Oct; fee

Antelope Point Marina
PO Box 4180, Page, AZ 86040
928-645-5900
www.antelopepointlakepowell.com

Best Western Canyon de Chelly Inn
100 Main Street (Rte 7), PO Box 295, Chinle,
    AZ 86503
800-327-0354 *or* 928-674-5874
www.canyondechelly.com

Best Western Wetherill Inn
1000 Main Street, PO Box 175, Kayenta, AZ 86033
800-937-8376 *or* 928-697-3231
www.bestwestern.com/wetherillinn

Cameron Trading Post
PO Box 339, Cameron, AZ 86020
800-338-7385 *or* 928-679-2231 ext. 415 (gallery)
www.camerontradingpost.com

Cameron Visitor Center
PO Box 459, Cameron, AZ 86020
928-679-2303
www.navajonationparks.org/htm/littlecolorado.htm

Canyon de Chelly National Monument
PO Box 588, Chinle, AZ 86503
928-674-5500 • www.nps.gov/cach
    Visitor Center: Daily 8am-5pm; no fee
    928-674-5500
    Weather conditions: 928-674-5500 ext.222

Chi' Hoo Tso Indian Market
Intersection AZ264 & Navajo Route 12,
    Window Rock, AZ 86515

Coal Mine Canyon
Contact: Cameron Visitor Center, PO Box
459, Cameron, AZ 86020
928-679-2303

Council Chambers (tours)
PO Box 1400, Window Rock, AZ 86515
928-871-6417

Coyote Pass Hospitality
PO Box 91-B, Tsaile, AZ 86556
928-724-3383 *or* 928-724-3258
http://navajocentral.org/cppage.htm

De Chelly Tours
928-674-3772

Diné Inn Motel
PO Box 1669, Tuba City, AZ 86045
928-283-6107

Explore Navajo Interactive Museum
PO Box 247 Main St. and Moenave Rd., Tuba
City, AZ 86045
928-640-0684 • www.explorenavajo.com
Mon-Sat 10am-8pm; Sun 12 noon-8pm; fee

Four Corners Monument
PO Box 2520, Window Rock, AZ 86515
928-871-6647
www.navajonatioparks.org/htm/fourcorners.htm
Daily 8am-5pm, Sept-May; daily 7am-8pm,
May-Sept; fee

Good Shepherd Mission
PO Box 618, Kit Carson Drive, Fort Defiance,
AZ 86504
928-729-2322
www.goodshepherdmission.org

Goulding's Monument Valley Lodge
1000 Main Street, PO Box 360001,
Monument Valley, UT 84536
435-727-3231 • www.gouldings.com

Greyhills Inn
PO Box 160, Tuba City, AZ 86045
928-283-4450

Hampton Inn – Navajo Nation
Highway 160, PO Box 1217, Kayenta, AZ 86033
800-426-7866 *or* 928-697-3170
www.hampton-inn.com
www.monumentvalleyonline.com

Hatathli Museum and Gallery
PO Box 37, Tsaile, AZ 86556
928-724-6654

Holiday Inn – Chinle
PO Box 1889, Chinle, AZ 86503
800-465-4329 *or* 928-674-5000
www.holiday-inn.com

Holiday Inn – Kayenta
US160 and US163, PO Box 307, Kayenta, AZ
86033
800-465-4329 *or* 928-697-3221
www.holiday-inn.com

Hubbell Trading Post National Historic Site
Hwy 264, PO Box 150, Ganado, AZ 86505
928-755-3475 • www.nps.gov/hutr
Daily 8am-6pm, summer; daily 8am-5pm,
winter; no fee

Justin's Horse Rental
928-674-5678

Kayenta (visitor information)
928-697-8451 • www.kayentatownship.com

Little Colorado Gorge Navajo Tribal Park
c/o Cameron Visitor Center, PO Box 459,
Cameron, AZ 86020
928-679-2303
www.navajonationparks.org/htm/littlecolorado.htm

Many Farms Inn
PO Box 307, Many Farms, AZ 86033
928-781-6362

Moki Treks
866-352-6654 • www.mokitreks.com

Monument Valley Navajo Tribal Park
Monument Valley, AZ 84536
435-727-5870-5874 *or* 435-727-5875
www.navajonationparks.org
Scenic Drive: Daily 6am-8:30pm, May-Sept;
daily 8am-4:30pm, Oct-Apr; fee
   Visitor Center
   4 miles SE of Hwy 163
   Campgrounds
      Goulding's Campground
      435-727-3231 • www.gouldings.com
      Mitten View Campground
      435-727-5870
   Tour Operators
      Bennett Tours
      800-862-8270
      Crawley's Monument Valley Tours, Inc.
      Kayenta, AZ 86033
      928-697-3734 • www.crawleytours.com
      Daniel's Guided Tours
      800-596-8427
      Goulding's Tours
      435-727-3231

Hozhoni Tours
Kayenta, AZ 86033
928-697-8198
www.hol-biz.com/hozhonitours

Keyah Hozhoni Tours
PO Box 1695, Kayenta, AZ 86033
928-309-7440
www.monumentvalley.com

Navajo Country Guided Trail Rides
Oljato Trading Post
435-727-3210

Roland's Navajo Land Tours
N. Hwy 163, Kayenta, AZ 86033
928-697-8198

Sacred Monument Tours
435-727-3218 *or* 928-380-4527
www.monumentvalley.net

Totem Pole Tours
800-345-8687

Navajo Times
PO Box 310, Window Rock, AZ 86515-0310
http://navajotimes.com

Navajo Arts and Crafts Enterprises
PO Box 160, Window Rock, AZ 86515
866-871-4095 *or* 928-871-4090
www.gonavajo.com
Mon-Fri 9am-6pm (Mountain Time)

Alamo
Hwy 169 at Mile Marker 30
505-854-2987

Cameron
US89 and AZ64
928-679-2244

Chinle
Hwy 191 and Route 7
928-674-5338

Grants
1100 West Santa Fe Ave, Grants, NM
505-285-3910

Kayenta
Hwy 160 and Route 163
928-697-8611

Navajo National Monument
North of Hwy 160 on Hwy 564
928-672-2600

Window Rock
Hwy 264 and Route 12
928-871-4090

Navajo Bridge Visitor Center
928-355-2319
Daily 9am-5pm, April-Nov
Or contact: Cameron Visitor Center
PO Box 459, Cameron, AZ 86020
928-679-2303

Navajo Nation Department of Fish and Wildlife
PO Box 1480, Window Rock, AZ 86515
928-871-6451 *or* 928-871-6452
www.navajofishandwildlife.org

Navajo Nation Museum, Library, and Visitor's Center
PO Box 1840, Hwy 264 and Loop Road, Window Rock, AZ 86515
928-871-7941
http://ggsc.wnmu.edu/mcf/museums/nnm.html
Tues-Fri 8am-8pm and Mon & Sat 8am-5pm; donation

Navajo Nation Parks and Recreation Department
PO Box 2520, Bldg. 36A, E. Hwy 264 at Rt. 12, Window Rock, AZ 86515
928-871-6647
www.navajonationparks.org

Navajo Nation Tourism Department
PO Box 663, Window Rock, AZ 86515
928-871-6436 *or* 928-871-7371
www.explorenavajo.com
www.discovernavajo.com

Navajo Nation Zoological and Botanical Park
Tse Bonito Tribal Park, Hwy 264, Bldg. 36A, PO Box 1480, Window Rock, AZ 86515
928-871-6574
www.navajofishandwildlife.org/nnzoo.htm
Daily 10am-5pm; no fee

Navajo National Monument
HC-71, Box 3, Tonalea, AZ 86044
928-672-2700 • www.nps.gov/nava
Daily 8am-5pm

Navajo Trails (tour company)
PO Box 1190, Pinon, AZ 86510
719-588-1884 • http://gonavajotrails.com

Navajo Trails Motel
HRC 6106, Box 62, Teec No Pos, AZ 86514
928-674-3618

Navajo Transit System
Bus service to Navajo and Hopi lands
928-729-4002

Navajoland Days Inn
PO Box 905, St. Michaels, AZ 86511
928-871-5690

Oljato Trading Post
PO Box 360416, Monument Valley, UT 84536
435-727-3210
Daily 8am-8pm

Quality Inn – Navajo Nation Capital
48 West Highway 264, PO Box 2340,
   Window Rock, AZ 86515
800-662-6189 *or* 928-871-4108
www.choicehotels.com

Quality Inn – Tuba City
Main Street & Moenave Ave., PO Box 247,
   Tuba City, AZ 86045
800-644-8383 *or* 928-283-4545
www.qualityinntubacity.com

Shiprock
PO Box 3810, Shiprock, NM 87420
505-368-1081

St. Michaels Historical Museum
PO Box 680, St. Michaels, AZ 86511
928-871-4171
Mon-Fri 9am-5pm, Memorial Day-Labor Day;
   no fee

Thunderbird Lodge
Hwy 191 and Rte 7, PO Box 548, Chinle, AZ
   86503
800-679-2473 or 928-674-5841 *or* -5842
www.tbirdlodge.com

Thunderbird Lodge Jeep Tours
Tours of Canyon de Chelly
800-679-2473 *or* 928-674-5841
www.tbirdlodge.com

Totsonii Ranch
928-755-6209
www.totsoniiranch.com

Tsegi Guide Association
c/o Canyon de Chelly Visitor Center
928-674-5500

Tuba City Trading Post
Main Street and Moenave Avenue, Tuba City, AZ
928-283-5441

Twin Trail Tours
928-674-8425

Veterans Affairs
PO Box 430, Window Rock, AZ 86515
928-871-6413

**Window Rock Monument & Navajo Veteran's
   Memorial Park**
c/o Navajo Nation Parks & Recreation, PO
   Box 9000, Window Rock, AZ 86515
928-871-6647 • www.navajonationparks.org
Daily 8am-5pm

Yei-bi-chei Footpath Journeys
Tours of Canyon de Chelly
www.footpathjourneys.com

ARIZONA'S WEST RIVER COAST

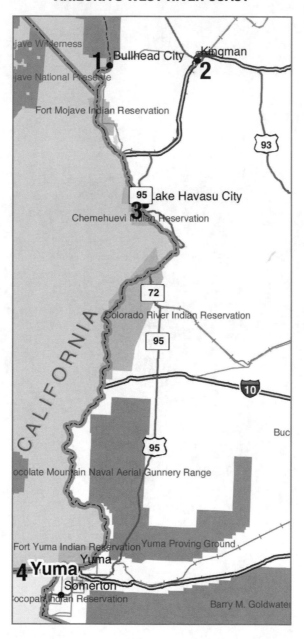

1. Bullhead City   3. Lake Havasu City
2. Kingman   4. Yuma

CHAPTER 8

ARIZONA'S WEST RIVER COAST

THE BANKS OF THE LOWER Colorado River from Bullhead City to Mexico provided a homeland to a group of Yuman-speaking Indians who share a common culture. These peoples produced pottery that resembled the pots of the Hohokam and relied on dreams as an important source of power. From their neighbors, they learned to weave cotton blankets and record events on calendar sticks that were passed down through generations. Today, the remaining groups—the Mojave, Yuma, Cocopah, and Maricopa—still live in or near their traditional homelands. Some of their ancestral curing rites and dances also survive.

The Mojave call themselves *Pipa a'ha macave*, meaning "People who live along the water." Their homes were once brushwood and sand-covered huts scattered along the river bottomlands. The river also provided them with fish for food, reeds for rafts, and mesquite trees for food and fuel. With a strong sense of nationalism, Mojaves often fought with their neighbors and other groups farther afield. At one time they produced pottery, but the craft has since died out among them. However, elaborate beaded capes and other beadwork is still produced.

The Yuma refer to themselves as the *Quechan* in reference to the trail they followed after emerging into this world at Spirit Mountain. They cultivated beans, squashes, melons, pumpkins, and cotton in their ancestral homeland, which lay along the river between those of the Cocopah and Mojave. A reservation was established for them in 1883, but after years of losing land to changing government policies, the tribe now owns about 25,000 acres of less-than-ideal land and no water rights. Their only craft that survives today is beadwork.

BULLHEAD CITY
Map #1

Around Town: Colorado River Historical Society Museum
Nearby: Fort Mojave Indian Reservation, Grapevine Canyon, Havasu-Topock National Wildlife
   Refuge, Oatman

Bullhead City is on the banks of the Colorado River where Arizona, California, and Nevada meet. It began as the construction camp for Davis Dam and now attracts summer vacationers who enjoy the diverse opportunities for water recreation provided by the calm warm water of Lake Mohave and the rushing cold water of the Colorado River. A Colorado River tour leaves from here and travels round-trip to Lake Havasu and back.

The **Colorado River Historical Society Museum** has historical photographs, descriptions of the nearby California intaglios (immense ancient figures outlined in the earth), an exhibit of an Indian village, metates, and Mojave pottery. Displays detailing an Indian attack on emigrants traveling to California and the Apache capture of a white girl demonstrate the precarious relationship between Indians and Euro-Americans at that time. The small museum is on AZ95 just north of the Laughlin Bridge at Davis Camp.

NORTH OF BULLHEAD CITY

Grapevine Canyon is one of the canyons that surround Spirit Mountain, sacred to the lower Colorado River Indian tribes as their spiritual birthplace. In light of the significance of the mountain and canyons to the Yavapai, Hualapai, Pai pai, Havasupai, Mojave, and Maricopa, the area has been listed on the National Register of Historic Places and named a Traditional Cultural Property. Grapevine Canyon itself is a desert oasis that has been frequented by people since as early as A.D. 1100. Some of the earliest who camped here were members of the Amacava culture, ancestors of the Mojave people, and possibly the Southern Paiute.

Visitors today can see the large concentration of rock art in the isolated canyon. A quarter-mile gravel and sand trail leads from the parking lot to the mouth of the canyon, where petroglyphs are etched on large boulders. Interpretive signs help to explain the site. For a closer view of some of the petroglyphs, bring binoculars.

Grapevine Canyon is off AZ163 on the dirt Christmas Tree Pass Road, which is a right turn at mile marker 13, 6 miles west of Davis Dam. After about 2 miles of following Christmas Tree Pass Road, turn left onto a short spur road that leads to parking. For more information, contact Katherine's Landing Ranger Station in Lake Mead National Recreation Area or the Bullhead Chamber of Commerce.

SOUTH OF BULLHEAD CITY

Fort Mojave Indian Reservation stretches along the Colorado River into Arizona, Nevada, and California, with tribal headquarters located in Needles, California. Much of the 23,000 acres in Arizona exists in one-mile checkerboard squares. The reservation is home to about 1,100 Mojave (Hamakhava) Indians. Visitors can fish, hunt for game birds, picnic, camp, and enjoy water sports. The riverbanks are dotted with campsites, most of them primitive. For permits, contact the tribal police.

Fort Mojave Mini-Museum and Cultural Center displays tribal beadwork and jewelry, and you can sometimes watch the artists at work. In Mohave Valley, a convenience store sells gas and supplies and an RV park offers full service hookup spaces. The small *Spirit Mountain Casino* along US95 has slot machines. Just across the Colorado River in Nevada is the large *Avi Resort and Casino*, with a beach, marina, hotel, spa, golf course, restaurants, movie theater, and casino.

Spirit Mountain, sacred to the Mojave, is 5 miles northwest of the reservation. Mojaves believe it was their home when all people were one tribe. Because of conflict though, Mutavela—the Creator—divided the land into north, south, east, and west. The other people moved away (some of whom told lies and were turned white), but the Mojave were granted the land along the Colorado River stretching from Bill Williams River to Black Canyon.

South of Fort Mojave is **Havasu-Topock National Wildlife Refuge**, which protects three hundred miles of shoreline along the Colorado River where visitors can fish and camp. *Topock Gorge*, created by the Colorado River winding through ancient volcanic rock, has ancient petroglyphs at Picture Rock.

The refuge runs along the Colorado River north of Lake Havasu to *Topock Marsh* about 15 miles south of Bullhead City. Camping and boat launching facilities are in the marsh, and boating and fishing are allowed in Topock Gorge. To reach the refuge from I-40, take exit 1 (Havasu NWR) near the California/Arizona border and follow the signs. To reach Topock Marsh from Mohave Valley in Arizona, follow AZ95 south to Courtwright Road and turn left. Watch for the sign.

The U.S. Fish and Wildlife offices, in Needles, California, just across the state border, has fishing and camping permits and detailed information about the refuge. To reach it, from I-40, take the J street exit and travel southwest .6 mile to headquarters.

SOUTHEAST OF BULLHEAD CITY

Oatman, named for a family killed by Apaches in 1851, was a flourishing gold mining center until 1942. The small town now provides visitors with an immersion into the Old West, with gunfights staged on weekends, wild burros (descended from burros turned loose by miners) wandering the streets, historic buildings, stagecoach rides, a museum, galleries, shops, and a walking tour through old mining tunnels. Oatman is on historic Route 66 about 25 miles southeast of Bullhead City.

KINGMAN
Map #2

Around Town: Fort Beale Springs, Mohave Museum of History and Art, Powerhouse Visitor Center and Museum
Nearby: Hualapai Mountain Park, Hualapai Reservation (see Chapter 5, Grand Canyon Country, page 74), Havasupai Reservation (see Chapter 5, Grand Canyon Country, page 73), Lake Havasu State Park

In 1857, the U.S. War Department sent Lt. Edward F. Beale to the Kingman area to build a wagon road and to study the use of camels as pack animals in the American Southwest. The route he chose for the road passed a series of springs that provided a reliable source of water; one of them came to be called Beale's Springs.

*A display of Mohave
items at the Mohave
Museum of History
and Arts in Kingman.*

As traffic along the Fort Mohave–Prescott Toll Road increased, so did tensions with the local Hualapai. In 1871, a U.S. infantry company from Fort Whipple was sent there to establish *Camp Beale's Springs* for the protection of travelers on the road and settlers. The fort also distributed supplies to the Hualapai and for a brief period acted as a temporary reservation. In 1874, Indians were forced to relocate to the Colorado River Indian Tribes Reservation, and the place was abandoned. The site of the fort can still be visited, although not much remains. Go west on Beale Street to Ft. Beale Drive, and turn right.

Today Kingman is the Mohave County seat. It sits at the junction of I-40 and AZ93 and at the heart of historic Route 66. Nearby is year-round water recreation at lakes Havasu, Mead, and Mohave.

The **Mohave Museum of History and Art** has several rooms of exhibits that interpret the history and culture of the Hualapai and Mojave. The varied collection includes carved objects made from local turquoise, as well as murals and dioramas depicting the settlement of the region. In the Indian Room a full-sized wickiup is displayed, along with baskets, pottery, a cradleboard, and other artifacts. Browse through the nineteenth- and early twentieth-century photographs of local Indians for a flavor of that bygone era, and read the wall text to better understand their view of the world. Look for other items such as Navajo weavings scattered throughout the rest of the museum. You can also visit the library for more in-depth information or the gift shop to purchase contemporary Native American crafts. The museum is just off historic Route 66 on Beale Street.

Also on Route 66 is the *Powerhouse Visitor Center*, which has a map of the Beale Street Historic District and information on Hualapai Mountain Park 14 miles southeast of town, where visitors can camp, hike, hunt, fish, river raft, and picnic in the ancestral home of the Hualapai. The center also has shops and a museum dedicated to Route 66.

LAKE HAVASU CITY
Map #3

Around Town: Lake Havasu Museum of History, Lake Havasu State Park
Nearby: Colorado River Indian Reservation ('Ahakhav Tribal Preserve, Blue Water Resort and Casino, California Desert Intaglios, CRIT Arts and Crafts Center and Museum, La Paz Town-site, Old Mohave Presbyterian Mission, Poston Memorial Monument)

The first settlers in the area were Mojave Indians, who were followed by the Cheme-huevis (the Paiutes of southeastern California). The town itself began as a planned com-munity in 1963 and is now famous as the resting place of London Bridge, which in 1968 was bought from England by American entrepreneur Robert McCulloch. The bridge was subsequently disassembled and much of it transported to Lake Havasu, where McCulloch had it reconstructed as a tourist attraction. Next to Lake Havasu Convention and Visitors Bureau is the **Lake Havasu Museum of History,** which has Chemehuevi baskets, histori-cal photos, grinding tools, and a cradleboard among its exhibits. To reach the museum from AZ95 turn right onto London Bridge Road, and then take a quick left into the shop-ping center. The front of the museum faces AZ95.

Lake Havasu State Park, which preserves lowland desert terrain and a diversity of plants and animals, features an interpretive garden. In winter and early spring, it showcases plants the Indians grew and used. The *Mohave Sunset Trail* winds easily for 1.5 miles past the habitat of cottontail rabbits, birds, and lizards. Boating, watersports, and forty-two campsites are available with shower facilities, hookups, and a dump station. Be aware that during summer and holiday weekends, this popular park often reaches capacity. Lake Havasu State Park is off AZ95 and Industrial Boulevard.

SOUTH OF LAKE HAVASU CITY

The 268,000 acres of the **Colorado River Indian Reservation (CRIT)** includes ninety miles of river frontage in Arizona and California. There are about 3,400 tribal members; tribal offices are in Parker. The reservation was established in 1865 for the Mojave and Chemehuevi, who have lived around here for centuries. After World War II, members of the Hopi and Navajo tribes were allotted land here and joined them. The four feathers on the tribal seal represent these distinct groups.

The Mojave and Chemehuevi are traditionally an agricultural society, and with sen-ior water rights to the Colorado River, their modern economy still centers on crops like cot-ton, wheat, lettuce, and melons. Recreation, government, and light industry also supply jobs.

Ancient trails, rock art, and intaglios are still visible today. A place called *Topock Maze* (off I-40 about 12 miles south of Needles, California) consists of long, roughly parallel rows of dirt and pebbles that create geometric patterns on the earth. The Mojave people consider this a sacred place and the portal for their dead to enter into the afterlife. The *California Desert Intaglios*—giant drawings on the desert floor of unknown origin—are 15 miles north of Blythe, California. These enigmatic figures of animals and hunters stretch between 85 and 167 feet and were brought to the attention of the modern world in 1931, when a pilot flew over them. Call the *CRIT Cultural Tourism Office* at the Blue

Water Resort for more information on the maze, intaglios, and places of interest on the reservation.

Outdoor enthusiasts can enjoy recreation on the Colorado River and Lakes Moovalya and Havasu. Purchase permits from the *CRIT Fish and Game Department* for hunting (dove, quail, waterfowl, rabbit, and predator), fishing (trout, bass, catfish, crappie, and bluegill), and boating.

CRIT Arts and Crafts Center and Museum is in the library building at the Tribal Administrative Center off US95 at 2nd Avenue and Mohave Road in Parker. Displays include artifacts of the Ancestral Pueblo, Hohokam, and Patayan cultures. Models of traditional shelters, a large collection of baskets and other crafts, old photos and memorabilia from early reservation life, and exhibits about Camp Poston (see below) are also exhibited. A research library contains historical books, manuscripts, photographs, and tapes, and the gift shop sells local crafts. The center oversees the *Old Mohave Presbyterian Mission* in the historic townsite of *La Paz*, which is about 2 miles southwest of Parker on 2nd Avenue. Both are on the National Register of Historic Places.

'Ahakhav Tribal Preserve, near the Tribal Administration Center off Mohave Road on Rodeo Drive, protects over 1,200 acres along the Colorado River. By 1955, the river's natural flow had been changed by dams, and non-native species were endangering the indigenous plants and animals. The preserve was established to replant and revive this backwater along the lower Colorado River basin and to learn lessons that could be applied to other threatened areas. A 4.6-mile trail leads through the preserve. Wildlife observation, canoeing (rentals available), fishing with a tribal permit, swimming, picnicking, and day camps are available.

In 1999, CRIT opened the *Bluewater Resort and Casino* in Parker with dining, an indoor water park, and live entertainment. The hotel has 200 rooms, a spa with a fifteen-foot waterfall, an exercise center, a banquet and conference center, and a theater. Miniature golf, a 160-dock marina, and retail shops are nearby.

Native Americans and others on a boat on the Colorado River in the early 1900s.

Ironically, given the forced relocation of so many Indian groups in the past, one of the tourist attractions on the reservation is the site of a Japanese American internment camp from World War II. In Poston, 18 miles south of Parker, the *Poston Memorial Monument* marks where 17,867 people were confined, between May 1942 and November 1945, because of wartime hysteria and prejudice. The tarpaper barracks did not survive, but a stone memorial has been erected near the site of the original Camp 1, and a kiosk provides information about the internment camps.

To reach the CRIT reservation, travel west on I-10 to exit 19 near the California border. Turn north on AZ295 for the 2.5-hour trip to Parker, a town of 3,140 people that is completely surrounded by the reservation. Parker is a trade center for CRIT and nearby communities. Contact the *Parker Chamber of Commerce* for local food and lodging information.

YUMA
Map #4

Around Town: Arizona Historical Society Sanguinetti House (Century House) Museum and Garden, Yuma Art Center, Yuma Quartermaster Depot State Historic Park
Nearby: Cocopah Indian Tribe (Cocopah Casino, Cocopah Museum, and Cultural Center, Cocopah Resort and Conference Center, Cocopah Bend RV and Golf Park, Cocopah Rio Colorado Golf Course), Ft. Yuma–Quechan Tribe (Ft. Yuma Quechan Museum, Paradise Casino)

Yuma was built on the only natural Colorado River crossing for miles in either direction. Many tribal trails converged here, where the Colorado and Gila rivers meet. For years, the Quechuan people farmed the floodplains in the winter and escaped to the cooler land of the coastal mountains during summer's heat. They also acted as trade brokers by exchanging shells and fishhooks from the Pacific Coast tribes for baskets and pottery arriving from eastern cultures.

The first European to come here was Captain Hernando de Alarcon, a member of Coronado's 1540 expedition. The tribes he found living on the lower Colorado River were the Quechan, Cocopah, and Mojave.

In 1774, a treaty with Quechan leader Palm was drafted to allow Spanish colonists free access to the river crossing and the California missions. After the Spanish broke their part of the bargain in 1781, the Indians revolted, destroying the Spanish missions and killing the settlers. For the next forty years, Yuma Crossing was inaccessible to the Spanish.

In 1849, the Quechan operated a flourishing ferry business here for American prospectors on their way to the California goldfields. When American John Glanton and his men started their own ferry operation and began abusing the Indians and robbing the immigrants, the Quechan retaliated by killing Glanton and his gang and hiding his treasure of gold. Three survivors fled to California, where they complained to authorities about an Indian uprising, adding the story about the hidden treasure. By the end of the year, U.S. soldiers had established Fort Yuma. In 1852, an army war of attrition against the Quechan left many homeless and starving as their crops and villages were burned. By the end of the year, most had surrendered.

Information and maps for the Yuma and the surrounding area's heritage and historical sites are available at the *Yuma Chamber of Commerce.*

Yuma Quartermaster Depot State Historic Park now marks the site of the traditional crossing point on the Colorado River, where two granite outcroppings shorten the distance across the river. The 1865 Quartermaster Depot has been restored, and exhibits tell about some of the people who have lived here at Yuma Crossing. The Quechan-narrated film provides insight into life here in earlier times.

Public and private interests have recently begun a collaboration with the goal of conserving and interpreting the community's natural and cultural resources. **Yuma West Wetlands Park** now has willow-shaded walkways through burrowing owl and osprey habitat where mile-wide trash mounds used to be. A boat ramp, picnic areas, and paths make this a popular destination for residents. The Quechan Indian nation and private landowners also plan to restore the Colorado River to some of its original appearance by planting native trees and vegetation on 1,400 acres along the river in the **East Wetlands District** near the Ocean-to-Ocean Bridge.

The **Arizona Historical Society Sanguinetti House (Century House) Museum and Garden** is dedicated to the history and cultures of Yuma Crossing. Housed in one of the oldest territorial buildings in town, peacocks, parrots, and parakeets vie with bougainvillas for the most colorful display in the garden. Indian artifacts include pottery, basketry, arrowheads, and beadwork of the Seri, Quechan, Cocopah, and other area tribes. The gift shop sells local Indian crafts, and the Garden Café serves breakfast and lunch seasonally.

The downtown **Yuma Art Center** is a gallery with quality artwork of contemporary Arizona artists, including Native Americans. The museum's "Expressions of Indigenous Cultures" exhibit is a collaborative effort with the Cocopah (also spelled *Cocopa*) Indian tribe.

A Pullman coach pulled by a vintage engine leaves most weekends from the *Yuma Valley Railway* station behind city hall for an afternoon trip 12 miles along the banks of the Colorado River. A narrator provides information about the Cocopah lands, as well as the local lore. Another unique way to pass through the history of the area is by boat. *Yuma River Tours* offer excursions which pass ruins and petroglyphs, historical sites, and the Imperial National Wildlife Refuge.

SOUTH OF YUMA

Protected in the **Imperial National Wildlife Refuge** is the last unchanneled section of the Colorado River before it enters Mexico. Work to restore the cottonwood and willow forests that once sustained the endangered southwestern willow flycatcher and other wildlife is bringing back an ecosystem devastated by woodcutting, dam building, wildfires, land clearing for agriculture, and the encroachment of exotic plants. Eventually, the over 15,000 acres of this thirty-mile stretch along the river in Arizona and California (now a federally designated wilderness) may return to what it was before European contact.

At the *visitor center*, a wildlife video, native plant garden, and other exhibits tell the story of the refuge. The *Painted Desert Trail* is a 1.3-mile self-guided trip through a landscape punctuated with colorful geology and offering a view over the Colorado River valley. The shade at *Meers Point* makes it a pleasant place to launch a canoe, rest, or picnic.

The refuge is north of Yuma 25 miles on US95, then west on Martinez Lake Road for 13 miles. Signs direct you to the visitor center.

EAST OF YUMA

The Quechuan (*Kwuh-tsan*), a Yuman-speaking group, live on both sides of the Colorado River, with much of their land, most of the 2,475 tribal members, and tribal headquarters in California. The portion of their land in Arizona is about 3 miles east of Yuma. The **Fort Yuma-Quechan Tribe** operates Paradise Casinos, five RV camping facilities, and a museum. Fishing is also popular; call the administrative offices for details and permits.

Originally built by Spaniards, the Fort Yuma settlement included a military post and St. Thomas Mission, which was founded by Franciscan Padre Garces, a tireless explorer who helped to blaze the overland trail to San Francisco. The fort itself was established in 1855 to station U.S. troops fighting the Quechan and later the Apache. It is now headquarters for the Quechan tribe. An *artist's marketplace* on the hill above the fort is open daily.

Fort Yuma-Quechan Museum has displays depicting the history and culture of the tribe, including examples of their beadwork and clay figurines, relics from the days of the Catholic mission and the army, models illustrating Indian dress, and historic photos. Outside is a reconstruction of a traditional home. Museum staff can also provide directions to the petroglyphs and other places of interest on the reservation.

Slots, bingo, blackjack, and poker, as well as the Seahorse Restaurant and scheduled stage entertainment, are offered at the *Paradise Casinos.*

SOUTH OF YUMA

Near the border with Mexico, about 13 miles southwest of Yuma off US95, is the **Cocopah Indian Reservation**. The Cocopah is a small agricultural group (880 people) related to the Quechan, who migrated here from Baja California. The 6,500-acre reservation, established in 1917, is divided into East, West, and North Cocopah, with tribal offices in West Cocopah. Most of the reservation land is leased to non-Indians for agriculture.

When the Spaniard Captain Alarcon first saw the Cocopah in 1540, he described them as tall and powerful with painted faces, feather adornments, and pierced noses decorated with seashells. He also remarked on their ability to carry hundred-pound loads on their heads.

The Cocopah are known for their beadwork, skilled traditional singers, and costumes of ribbon dresses and shirts. They once used the lower Colorado River and delta to fish for salmon and shellfish and as a highway for poling log rafts to reach the wild wheat and other plants growing along the shore. In the late nineteenth century, they added "steamboat pilot" to their list of skills. Dams and diversion projects have changed the flow of the river and the way of life of the Cocopah. Now the tribe leases river bottomland for agriculture and promotes tourism.

The *Cocopah Museum and Cultural Center* is on the West Reservation County Road 15 north of Somerton and is dedicated to the history, traditions, and culture of the Cocopah people. Museum displays, art, and crafts provide an insight into their daily and ceremonial life. Desert willow bark skirts, arrowed baskets, clan tattoo designs, weapons, musical instruments, and games are all included. An outdoor heritage park surrounds the museum and showcases indigenous plants. A gift shop sells tribal arts and crafts and Native American music. The museum is at the tribal headquarters on the West Reservation. To reach the museum, from I-8 take US95 past the Cocopah Casino. Continue 1 mile past Somerton and turn north (right) onto Avenue G. Turn west (left) onto CR15 for 2 miles and past the railroad tracks, then follow the signs to the building with the tribal seal.

The new *Cocopah Resort and Conference Center* in Somerton offers lodging, a fitness center, cultural display area, and gift shop. Adjoining it is the *Cocopah Casino*, which has gambling and a small gift shop featuring Cocopah jewelry among its items. You can enjoy live entertainment in the casino's lounge and dine at the Artisan Restaurant or River Edge Sports Bar. A food court is planned for the corridor connecting the casino and hotel. *Cocopah Korner* convenience store is next door to the resort.

Cocopah Rio Colorado Golf Course (formerly Dove Creek Golf Course) is also a new tribal enterprise with an eighteen-hole golf course, pro shop, driving range, and grill. The *Cocopah Bend RV and Golf Park* has 805 RV hookups, a large swimming pool, a convenience store, and an eighteen-hole golf course. Tennis, pitching horseshoes, and archery are other activities at the facility.

Hunting permits can be purchased from the tribal offices.

EVENTS

Speed boat races are held periodically on Lake Moovala, Colorado River Indian Reservation.

FEBRUARY *Fort Mojave Powwow:* Powwow held at the Avi Hotel and Casino at Fort Mojave Reservation.

Yuma Crossing Day: Commemoration of the historic Yuma Crossing includes cultural demonstrations by Native Americans, arts and crafts, food booths, and living history demonstrations. Held at the end of February at the Quechan Museum and other historic sites in the town of Yuma.

MARCH *CRIT Establishment Days:* Mojave elders provide traditional dances, food, and games for the children. Held at the Colorado River Indian Tribes Reservation.

San Pasqual Annual Powwow: Intertribal powwow that includes dancing and vendors. Held at Fort Yuma–Quechan Reservation.

JULY *CRIT 4th of July Celebration:* Fireworks, crafts and food vendors, and games for the children. Held at Colorado River Indian Tribes Reservation.

Fort Yuma–Quechan Indian Tribe Powwow: On July 4, the tribe sponsors a powwow with dancing and singing events and art/craft and food vendors.

SEPTEMBER *National Indian Days Celebration:* Includes a powwow, traditional singing and dancing, a parade, beauty pageants, games, an all-Indian rodeo, and arts-and-crafts booths. Held at Manataba Park, Colorado River Indian Reservation.

Native American Cultural Fair: Native American arts and crafts and food vendors. Locomotive Park in Kingman, 602-753-1433.

OCTOBER *Annual National Indian Days:* Powwow and Miss Colorado River Indian Tribes, Junior Miss, and Little Miss pageants. Held at CRIT Reservation.

Cocopah Cultural Celebration: Traditional Bird Singing and Dancing performances, free buffet lunch, arts and crafts vendors, cultural booths, and children's entertainment. Western Cocopah Indian Reservation.

Fort Mojave Indian Days Celebration: Includes a parade, Mojave tribal dances, games, art/craft show, food booths, raffles, and the Miss Mojave Pageant. Tribal Gym and Park in Bullhead City.

Quechan Days: Features dancing, arts and crafts, food booths, Miss Quechan pageant. Fort Yuma–Quechan Indian Tribe.

NOVEMBER *Fall Gathering of the Four Tribes:* Tribal dances and booths selling Native American art, crafts, and food. Held at CRIT Reservation.

CONTACT INFORMATION

Arizona Historical Society Museums
www.historicalsociety.org
    **Sanguinetti House (Century House),
    Museum, and Garden**
    240 and 248 S. Madison Avenue, Yuma,
    AZ 85364
    928-782-1841
    Tue-Sat 10am-4pm; fee

Arizona State Parks
1300 W. Washington, Phoenix, AZ 85007
602-542-4174 • www.pr.state.az.us

Bullhead City (Chamber of Commerce)
1251 Highway 95, Bullhead City, AZ 86429
800-987-7457 *or* 928-754-4121
www.bullheadchamber.com

Bullhead City (City)
1255 Marina Blvd, Bullhead City, AZ 86442
928-763-9400 • www.bullheadcity.com

Cocopah Indian Reservation
Tribal Headquarters: County 15th & Avenue G,
Somerton, AZ 85350
928-627-2102 • www.cocopa.com
    Cocopah Bend RV and Golf Park
    6800 Strand Avenue, Yuma, AZ 85366
    928-343-9300 *or* 800-537-7901 (reservations)
    www.cocoparrv.com/about.html
    Cocopah Casino
    15318 South Ave. B, Somerton, AZ 85350
    800-237-5687
    www.cocoparesort.com
    Cocopah Resort and Conference Center
    15268 South Ave. B, Somerton, AZ 85350
    928-722-6677
    Cocopah Rio Colorado Golf Course
    220 North Marshall Loop Road, Somerton,
    AZ 85350
    928-627-0057
    Cocopah Museum and Culture Center
    County 15th & Avenue G, Somerton, AZ
    85350
    928-627-1992
    Mon-Fri 9am-4pm, early closure noon last
    Fri of month; no fee

Colorado River Historical Society Museum
355 Hwy 95, Bullhead City, AZ 86429
928-754-3399
www.bullheadcity.com/tourism/Hismuseum.asp
Tue-Sun 10am-4pm, Sept-June (closed July
and August)

Colorado River Indian Tribes (CRIT)
Route 1, Box 23-B, Parker, AZ 85344
928-669-9211 • http://critonline.com
    'Ahakhav Tribal Preserve
    25401 Rodeo Dr, Parker, AZ 85344
    928-669-2664 ext. O (operator)
    www.ahakhav.com
    Blue Water Resort and Casino
    11300 Resort Drive, Parker, AZ 85344
    888-243-3360 *or* 928-669-7000
    www.bluewaterfun.com
    CRIT Arts and Crafts Center/Museum
    Rt. 1, Box 23-B, Parker, AZ 85344
    Mon-Fri 8am-5pm & Sat 10am-3pm
    (closed during lunch)
    928-669-1335 museum
    928-669-1272 administration
    CRIT Cultural Tourism Office
    at Blue Water Resort/Casino, 11300 Resort
    Drive, Parker, AZ 85344
    928-669-7037
    rcharles@bluewaterfun.com
    CRIT Fish and Game Department
    PO Box 777, Parker, AZ 85344
    928-669-9285
    Poston Memorial Monument
    Mohave Road, Poston, AZ

Colorado River Tours
Bullhead City, AZ 86442
800-327-2386 *or* 702-298-8363

Fort Mojave Indian Tribe
500 Merriman Ave., Needles, CA 92363
760-629-4591 • www.fortmojave.com
    Avi Resort and Casino
    10000 Aha Macav Parkway, Laughlin, NV
    89029
    800-284-2946 • www.avicasino.com
    Fort Mojave Indian Days
    619-326-4810
    **Fort Mojave Mini-Museum and
    Cultural Center**
    1599 Plantation Road, Mohave Valley, AZ
    86440
    928-346-1636
    Mon-Fri 8am-4pm
    Spirit Mountain RV Park
    8545 S. Highway 95, Mohave Valley, AZ
    86440
    928-346-1225 • www.smrv.com
    Tribal Police
    602-346-1521

Fort Yuma–Quechan Tribe
Fort Yuma-Quechan Indian Museum
350 Ticaho Road, Fort Yuma, AZ
760-572-0661
Daily, Mon-Fri 8am-noon & 1pm-5pm; fee
Paradise Casinos
450 Quechan Drive, Yuma, AZ 85364
888-777-4946 *or* 760-572-7777
www.paradise-casinos.com
Tribal Administration Building
350 Picacho Road, Winterhaven, CA 92283
760-572-0201
Tribal Council
PO Box 1899, Yuma, AZ 85366
760-572-0213

Grapevine Canyon
Katherine's Landing Ranger Station, Katherine's
Landing, AZ 86430
928-754-3272 *or* 928-754-3030
www.nps.gov/lame/hikegvine.htm
Daily 8am-4pm

Havasu-Topock National Wildlife Refuge
PO Box 3009, 317 Mesquite Ave, Needles, CA
92363
760-326-3853
www.fws.gov/southwest/refuges/arizona/havasu
Mon-Fri 8am-4pm

Imperial National Wildlife Refuge
PO Box 72217, Yuma AZ 85365
928-783-0652
www.fws.gov/southwest/refuges/arizona/
imperial.html
Mon-Fri 7:30am-4pm & Sat-Sun 9am-4pm,
mid Nov-Mar

Kingman Department of Tourism/Powerhouse
Visitor Center
120 W. Route 66, Kingman, AZ 86401
866-427-7866 or 928-753-6106
www.kingmantourism.org
Daily 9am-6pm (closes at 5pm Dec-Feb)

Kofa Inn
1700 S, California Ave, Parker, AZ 85344
800-742-6072 *or* 928-669-2101

Lake Havasu City Convention/Visitors Bureau
314 London Bridge Road, Lake Havasu City,
AZ 86403
928-453-3444 • www.golakehavasu.com

Lake Havasu Museum of History
320 London Bridge Road, Lake Havasu, AZ
86403
928-854-493 • http://havasumuseum.com
Tue-Sat 1pm-4pm; fee

Lake Havasu State Park
699 London Bridge Road, Lake Havasu, AZ
86403
928-855-2784
www.pr.state.az.us/Parks/parkhtml/havasu.html
Daily sunrise-10pm (closes when park reaches
capacity)

Lake Mead National Recreation Area
601 Nevada Way, Boulder City, NV 89005
702-293-8907
www.nps.gov/lame/home.html

Mohave Museum of History and Art
400 West Beale Street, Kingman, AZ 86401
Mon-Fri 9am-5pm & Sat 1pm-5pm
928-753-3195 • www.mohavemuseum.org

Oatman/Goldroad Chamber of Commerce
Box 423, Oatman, AZ 86433
928-768-6222

Parker Chamber of Commerce
1217 California Ave., Parker, AZ 85344
928-669-2174
www.coloradoriverinfo.com/parker

Yuma Art Center/Museum
254 South Main, Yuma AZ 85366
928-329-6607 (Exhibits) *or*
928/373-5202 (Theater)
www.yumafinearts.com
Tue-Th 10am-5pm, Fri 10am-7pm & Sun
1pm-5pm; fee

Yuma County Chamber of Commerce
180 W. 1st Street, Suite A, Yuma, AZ 85364
887-782-0438 *or* 928-782-2567
www.ci.yuma.az.us (city)
www.yumachamber.org (county)

Yuma Convention and Visitors Bureau
377 S. Main, Yuma AZ 85366
800-293-0071 *or* 928-783-0071
www.visityuma.com
Mon-Fri 9am-6pm & Sat 9am-4pm & Sun
10am-1pm, Nov-Apr; Mon-Fri 9am-5pm
& Sat 9am-2pm, May-Oct

Yuma Quarermaster Depot State Historic Park
201 N. 4th Avenue, Yuma, AZ 85364
928-329-0471
www.pr.state.az.us/Parks/parkhtml/
  yumacross.html
Daily 9am-5pm; fee

Yuma River Tours
1920 Arizona Ave, Yuma, AZ 85364
928-783-4400
www.yumarivertours.com

Yuma Valley Railway
PO Box 10305, 100 N. Second Street, Yuma,
  AZ 85366
928-783-3456
Sat & Sun at 1pm (cooler months); fee

CENTRAL ARIZONA

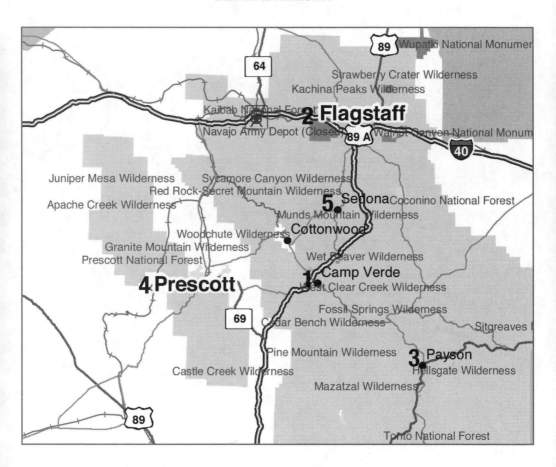

1. Camp Verde
2. Flagstaff
3. Payson

4. Prescott
5. Sedona

CHAPTER 9

ЛЛЛЛЛЛ

CENTRAL ARIZONA

CAMP VERDE
Map #1

Around Town: Fort Verde State Historical Park
Nearby: Montezuma Castle and Well National Monument, Yavapai Apache Nation (Cliff Castle
Casino, Lodge at Cliff Castle, Native Visions Tours, Stargazer Pavilion)

Camp Verde, 60 miles south of Flagstaff on I-17, is the oldest settlement in Verde Valley. The small town's heritage is one of ranching, military influence, and indigenous cultures.

Fort Verde State Historical Park is off I-17 at exit 285 in Camp Verde. The Tonto Apache and Yavapai people who farmed near the Verde River resisted settlers who tried to take their land. In 1866, the army heeded the settlers' call for help and established a military post here called Camp Lincoln. The name was changed to Fort Verde when the camp was moved to its present location. Occupied from 1865–90, the fort was the base of operations for General George Crook during the tumultuous time when Indians in the Southwest were being forced onto reservations. It remains the best preserved example of an Arizona fort from this "Indian Wars" period. The park has exhibits and reenactments of frontier army life plus information about the Apache army scouts. The museum includes a few Native American artifacts.

NORTHEAST OF CAMP VERDE

Montezuma Castle and Well National Monument protects the well-preserved and significant ruins of the prehistoric Sinagua culture. Montezuma Castle was named in the mistaken belief that Aztecs built this five-story, twenty-room dwelling pocketed in the mouth of a cave about one hundred feet high on a sheer cliff. Even though Aztecs were not the masons, Mesoamerican traders no doubt visited. Rather, Sinagua Indians were the residents from A.D. 1100–1450. It was a formidable fortress for its fifteen to twenty residents, with windowless walls almost twelve feet thick that were constructed from limestone and mud. The simple task of pulling up the ladders eliminated enemy access.

Well-preserved walls at Montezuma Castle National Monument

The shady, self-guiding *Sycamore Trail* leads one-third mile along Beaver Creek to views of the ruins. A larger pueblo at the base of the cliff, once six stories high with about forty-five rooms, has almost disappeared. The *visitor center* displays depict the everyday life of the Sinagua, as well as local ecology and geology. Books, videos, and maps are sold in the center, and a picnic area is beside the river.

Montezuma Castle is a few miles outside of Camp Verde. From I-17 north of town take exit 289 and follow the signs.

The other part of the national monument is *Montezuma Well*, 11 miles northeast of Montezuma Castle. According to legend, this is where the Yavapai people emerged into this world. After a global flood inundated the area, a girl, Kamalapukwia, is said to have survived and settled in Oak Creek Canyon to repopulate the land.

Montezuma Well is a fifty-five-foot-deep limestone sinkhole filled with water a constant 76 degrees Fahrenheit. The unique pond is fed by underground springs that pump about 1.9 million gallons into it daily. The green water is high in carbon dioxide, making it impossible for fish to live here. Turtles, on the other hand, thrive.

Between A.D. 1125 and 1400, about 150 to 200 Sinaguans built homes overlooking the pond. A self-guiding *nature trail* travels a short distance past the pond and cave ruins. Other trails lead to remnants of the irrigation system, where water still flows into ancient canals. Look beside the road about a half-mile before reaching the pond for evidence of a prehistoric canal and a quarter-mile further along for the outline of a Hohokam pithouse built around A.D. 1100.

Montezuma Well is 5 miles off I-17 from exit 293. There is no visitor center at Montezuma Well.

The **Yavapai-Apache Nation** (Camp Verde Reservation) has about 1,550 Tonto Apache (*Dil zhee*) and Yavapai (*Wipukyipai*) members who live in four separate communities: Camp Verde, Clarkdale, Middle Verde, and Rimrock.

In 1873, Apache chief Chat-ly-pah surrendered to the United States Army. In spite of being promised an eight-hundred-square-mile reservation along the Verde River, he and his followers, along with local Yavapai, were marched through winter-flooded rivers and mountain passes to the San Carlos Indian Agency. Although 1,500 people were forced to walk this "March of Tears," only around 200 Yavapai and Apache were still alive when they returned to their homeland twenty-five years later. Each year on Exodus Day weekend, the exile and return are remembered with ceremony, dancing, singing, and food.

Today, the soil deposits on the Verde Valley's rich river floodplain support an agricultural enterprise, which is the basis of the tribe's economy. Retirees and tourists also contribute.

Cliff Castle Casino, at exit 289 off I-17 near Montezuma Castle National Monument, is owned by the tribe. Gaming, dining, nightly entertainment, bowling, an arcade, and horseback riding are offered here. Next door is the *Lodge at Cliff Castle*, an eighty-room lodge and conference center, and the *Stargazer Pavilion*, which sponsors outdoor entertainment and powwows. The lodge also arranges trail rides and hiking trips.

Distant Drums RV Resort is near the casino and features RV hookups, a general store, heated swimming pool, and RV supplies.

Native Vision Tours uses vans and horses on its scenic tours. Native arts and crafts are for sale in its gift shop in Camp Verde.

Look for copies of the monthly tribal newspaper, *Gah'nahvah/Ya Ti' News*, for more information about the community. It is also available on the tribal Web site.

The Yavapai and Apache are noted for their basketry, which can be purchased from individual artisans. Call the tribal offices for dates of public dance performances.

FLAGSTAFF
Map #2

Around Town: Arizona Historical Society/Pioneer Historical Museum, Coconino Center for the Arts, Museum of Northern Arizona
Nearby: Arizona Snowbowl Ski Area, Elden Pueblo Ruin, Lamar Haines Memorial Wildlife Area, Old Caves Crater, Spirit Mountain Ranch, Sunset Crater National Monument, Walnut Canyon National Monument, Wupatki National Monument

Fresh spring water no doubt encouraged prehistoric Indians to build their homes in the area. Thousands of ruins attest to how attractive they found it. By the time American settlers arrived, the indigenous people living here were Apaches, Navajos, Yavapais, and Paiutes. They all discouraged the newcomers from staying, but eventually the various cultures learned to live together, and the city now takes pride in its cultural diversity.

Flagstaff is the hub of the region and a good place to stay, eat, and shop for Indian arts and crafts. In addition to the Museum of Northern Arizona and the Coconino Center for the Arts/Art Barn (see below), there are several other galleries in town. For maps, dates of festivals and special events, and information on other local attractions such as Riordan Mansion State Historic Park and Lowell Observatory, visit the *Flagstaff Chamber of Commerce* in the railroad depot.

The main office of the *Coconino National Forest* is on the west side of town off US66 and Thompson Street. Obtain information here about visiting some of the over nine thousand prehistoric sites in the national forest.

The **Coconino Center for the Arts/Art Barn** celebrates the arts in northern Arizona with performances, events, exhibits, and works for sale by local artists, including Native Americans. On the same grounds is the **Arizona Historical Society/Pioneer Historical Museum**, which depicts the history of the area from the arrival of the conquistadors in 1540 to the present. The center and museum are 2 miles northwest of downtown on US180.

One mile farther north on US180 is the internationally famous **Museum of Northern Arizona**, which has exhibits dedicated to the anthropology, biology, geology, history, archaeology, and art of the Colorado Plateau. The museum campus has fifty-two buildings, including a research center, retreat center, Historic Colton House, Discover Center, charter high school, and residential communities. Housed in the museum are over 5 million pieces, including archaeology and ethnographic artifacts ranging from baskets to katsinas. One of the unique displays includes a full-size kiva from a Hopi village that includes a digital touch screen interpreting the wall murals.

The gift shop has a diverse selection of authentic Navajo blankets, Hopi katsinas, Hopi and Pueblo pottery, and Navajo and Hopi jewelry. Crafts demonstrations are sometimes held in summer, and the extensive bookstore stocks information on regional Indian cultures and archaeology. Educational programs emphasize Native cultures, including festivals and marketplaces through the Heritage Programs and Ventures trips. Exhibitions of work by exceptional Navajo, Hopi, and Zuni artists are also held. The museum library is open for research.

NORTH OF FLAGSTAFF ON US180

Flagstaff sits at the base of the towering San Francisco Peaks, legendary home of the Hopi katsinas and one of the Navajo's four sacred mountains. The peaks are volcanic in origin and topped with tundra and ancient bristlecone pines.

Both the Navajo and Hopi protested the opening of **Arizona Snowbowl Ski Area** on the peaks, but to no avail. The area now has skiing in the winter and a scenic skyride on summer weekends and holidays to the top of Mt. Agassiz (11,200 feet), which affords a sweeping view of the Grand Canyon and northern Arizona. You will also find picnic facilities and a snack shop. To reach the ski area, take US180 (Humphreys Street) north of town about 7 miles to Snowbowl Road and follow the signs.

Also on Snowbowl Road is **Lamar Haines Memorial Wildlife Area** where a trail leads .7 mile to the remains of a cabin and stone shed built in 1892 by German immigrant Ludwig Veit. Near the small pond are petroglyphs. The trailhead leaves from the parking lot near milepost 4.5. For information on current hiking conditions, maps, and other trails, contact the Peaks Ranger Station.

Twenty-one miles north of Flagstaff on US180 is **Spirit Mountain Ranch**, home to seven rare white buffalo. An estimated one in 10 million animals is born this color, and they are considered sacred by many Native Americans. One Sioux story tells of how White Buffalo Calf Woman brought the sacred pipe bundle and taught the people to pray using ceremony and ritual. When she left, she promised to return and usher in an age of harmony and spirituality.

NORTH OF FLAGSTAFF ON US89

Elden Pueblo Ruin is a few miles north of Flagstaff off US89. When prehistoric Pueblo people lived here, the masonry walls enclosed over sixty-five rooms. Three small houses, as well as a kiva, were situated around the main building. Ongoing excavation and stabilization work continues, and archaeological programs allow you to experience hands-on investigation under professional supervision. The ruin is past the Peaks Ranger Station in the Coconino National Forest. Stop at the ranger station for a self-guiding leaflet and information.

Another ruin is at the end of a moderate 1.2-mile hike that leads to the rim of **Old Caves Crater**. Between A.D. 1250 and 1300, a group of Sinagua lived high on the summit of this extinct volcano, possibly because the view over the surrounding countryside made surprise attack unlikely. After living here for a short time, the Sinagua migrated out of the area. Their pueblo once had seventy to eighty rooms built over chambers (called "bubbles") that were formed when lava cooled. The people carved these cavities into storerooms and connected them by tunnels. A ball court and burials have also been found nearby. The pueblo and artifacts that remain are fragile; please do not disturb them.

To reach the pueblo, travel north on US89 to Silver Saddle Road (between mileposts 422 and 423), and turn right about a half mile to the trailhead. Take the right fork at the trail junction on the summit, and be ready for a 430-foot elevation gain.

Farther north is **Sunset Crater National Monument**, which preserves a dramatic landscape created by violent earthly forces. The terrain was born around nine hundred years ago amidst powerful earthquakes and roaring volcanic explosions that spewed chunks of fire and ash into the air. For the next two hundred years, periodic flare-ups continued to disturb the silence.

Sunset Crater was created by a series of volcanic eruptions over hundreds of years.

When the volcano first erupted, the surrounding land was inhabited by prehistoric people; the burned remains of their houses have since been found. The cataclysm drove them away, but it also brought a blessing. For eight hundred miles in all directions a fine layer of ash blanketed the land, and when it cooled, it acted as garden mulch, trapping precious moisture and adding nutrients to the arid ground at a time of increased rainfall. Miraculously, corn grew where once it had shriveled and died.

Sinagua Indians settled here after the volcano quieted down, and other groups like the Hohokam probably did as well. More people may have lived around Sunset Crater after the eruption than before it, and for almost two hundred years they prospered, until the west wind piled the ash into erratic drifts, and once again the land was exposed to the moisture-robbing sun. By A.D. 1300, the residents had relocated to more attractive sites.

The desolate gray-black slopes of Sunset Crater are now skirted at the bottom by trees and rimmed at the top by a fiery-red stain created by chemicals once deep within the earth. To protect its soft slopes, hiking to the top is not allowed, but at the base, a self-guiding, easy nature trail loops 1 mile across the intriguing formations of the *Bonito Lava Flow*.

For a climb to the top of a different cinder cone, follow the half-mile *Lenox Crater Trail*. This path is steep enough that, although it takes about thirty minutes to walk up it, it only takes about fifteen minutes to walk down.

The *visitor center* for Sunset Crater, 2 miles from the entrance, has exhibits, summer interpretive activities, and information about the monument. Picnic areas are located near the visitor center, by Lava Flow Trail, and at Painted Desert Vista between Sunset Crater and Wupatki.

Bonito Campground, a Coconino National Forest facility just west of the park boundary, has forty-four sites available between mid-April and mid-October. The campground has drinking water and restrooms, but no showers. Contact the Peaks Ranger Station.

The narrow, winding *Sunset Crater–Wupatki Loop Road* travels about 20 miles northeast of Sunset Crater to **Wupatki National Monument**, which has over two thousand ruins dating from about A.D. 500 to 1400. Wupatki can also be reached by returning to US89 and continuing north from Sunset Crater.

The Sinagua settled at Wupatki (Hopi for "Tall House") around A.D. 500. They left when Sunset Crater erupted in A.D. 1064–65 but returned about forty-five years later, along with Kayenta Ancestral Puebloans from the northeast and Cohoninas from the west. The cultures shared their knowledge with each other, with the Ancestral Puebloans teaching their neighbors how to build multilevel masonry villages and Cohoninas sharing innovative ways to make pottery.

Wupatki became one of the Sinagua's most important villages and trade centers, with about one hundred people living in town and several thousand more in pithouses and smaller pueblos close by. Their trade network expanded until it brought to them exotic items like turquoise, shell jewelry, copper bells, and the feathers of tropical parrots and macaw from as far away as Mesoamerica.

During a drought in the 1200s, the Indians migrated again, possibly relocating south to the Verde Valley or northeast to the Hopi Mesas. Hopi legends trace the ancestors of their Parrot Clan to Wupatki and their Snake Clan to nearby Wukoki.

The *visitor center* has artifacts and hands-on exhibits about the twelfth- and thirteenth-

An artist's rendition of Wupatki in its heyday.

century inhabitants, along with cultural demonstrations such as pottery making, stick-figure making, and weaving. The bookstore sells books, posters, maps, and videos.

The center also has information on self-guided visits to Wukoki, Lomaki, and other easily accessed ruins. In April and October, rangers lead a backpacking trip to *Crack-in-the-Rock*, a dramatic ruin atop a mesa that affords sweeping views of the Little Colorado River. This strenuous 16-mile round-trip passes numerous petroglyphs and other pueblo sites. Make reservations at least two months ahead. A fee is charged and participants are chosen by lottery.

Behind the center is the short, self-guiding *Wupatki Ruin Trail*. On one side of the ruins, which rise three stories high from the black lava, is an open-air amphitheater where village meetings and ceremonies probably took place. Features to look for include a rare ball court and a blowhole that circulates air between the surface and narrow underground cracks.

The 36-mile loop road through Sunset Crater and Wupatki rejoins US89 about 15 miles north of its starting point.

EAST OF FLAGSTAFF

Sinagua Indians flourished in what is now **Walnut Canyon National Monument**. Between about A.D. 1125 and 1250, they farmed these canyon rims and maintained an active trade stretching to the Gulf of Mexico and Central America. Eventually, they moved away to become the ancestors of some of the modern Hopi clans. Cleverly hidden among the limestone overhangs and outcroppings, over three hundred of their well-preserved cliff homes still remain camouflaged by nature.

The *visitor center* has a small museum with an exhibit depicting the three stages of excavation and a map showing the Sinagua trade routes with neighboring cultures. Other displays center on farming techniques and the use of natural materials to fashion sandals, soap, medicine, and baskets. In addition, the center shows videos on request, sells books, and provides ranger-led programs and hikes to some of the ruins. Picnic areas are also nearby.

Island Trail, a three-quarter-mile self-guided trail, begins behind the visitor center and travels past twenty-five cliff dwellings. The steep trail descends 185 feet with 240 steps and paved paths to the canyon below. Remember that coming back up this trail will be harder than going down it. The easier *Rim Trail* has two scenic viewpoints and passes two surface dwellings. It is a half-mile loop that takes twenty to thirty minutes.

Walnut Canyon is 7.5 miles east of Flagstaff off I-40 at exit 204.

PAYSON
Map #3

Around Town: Museum of Rim Country Archaeology, Rim Country Museum
Nearby: Pine-Strawberry Museum, Tonto Apache Reservation (Mazatzal Casino), Shoofly Village
   Ruins

Payson is higher and cooler than Phoenix, as the many retirees in town will tell you. The most popular local site is Tonto Natural Bridge State Park, about 10 miles northwest of town. The first white man to see this "world's largest travertine bridge" was prospector David Gowan, who was chased there by Apaches.

Museum of Rim Country Archaeology (MRCA) is the first museum in Arizona to be dedicated solely to archaeology. Displays with archaeological artifacts, murals, and information about Mogollon (*mug-ee-on*) Rim cultures and the historical and modern applications of archaeology make up the collection. Hands-on exhibits are included, and a gift shop sells local crafts. The other important components of the museum are its research and educational programs, including excavations through the auspices of Pima Community College. The museum is housed in what was once the town library, located on Main Street a few blocks west of AZ87.

The **Rim Country Museum** complex has historical buildings (including the cabin of Western author Zane Grey) and displays that cover the prehistory and history of Arizona's Rim Country. The complex is in Green Valley Park in town.

NORTH OF PAYSON
Shoofly Village Ruins, occupied from A.D. 1000 to 1250, was a two-story pueblo with about eighty rooms and courtyards once surrounded by a stone wall. The outlines of many of the walls are still visible. The people who lived at this 3.75-acre site were hunters and farmers and might have been related to the Hohokam. A quarter-mile, self-guided trail provides easy access from the parking lot, and there is a picnic area. Shoofly Village is managed by the Tonto National Forest. It is 5 miles northeast of Payson on Houston Mesa Road.

The **Pine-Strawberry Museum** looks back at the homestead era of the late nineteeth century, as well as the prehistory of the region. The Archaeology Room displays pottery from the Strawberry II excavation, fossils and arrowheads found near Pine and Strawberry, and Hopi katsinas. The museum is on Route 87 (Beeline Highway) in the town of Pine and is housed in a former Mormon Church.

SOUTH OF PAYSON

Half a mile south of Payson on AZ87 is the **Tonto Apache Indian Reservation**; at eighty-five acres, it is the smallest in Arizona. Established in 1972, it is now home to many of the 111 enrolled Yavapai and Apache. Beadwork and basketry can be purchased on the reservation. Dancers from the tribe participate in the Fourth of July celebration at the Coconino Center for the Arts in Flagstaff.

On AZ87, near the south end of Payson, is *Mazatzal Casino*, with gaming, a restaurant, entertainment, a meeting center, and a shop selling native crafts. Across the highway from the casino, the Tonto Apache Market often sells crafts in addition to groceries, beer, and gasoline.

PRESCOTT
Map #4

Around Town: Phippen Museum, Sharlot Hall Museum, Smoki Museum
Nearby: Lynx Creek Ruin, Yavapai-Prescott Indian Tribe

Prescott Valley was once home to people of the Desert Archaic culture. Their spear points, found in valley camps and caves, have been dated back ten thousand years. These nomadic hunters and gatherers learned to make pottery and settled in villages after corn arrived from Mexico, sometime between A.D. 500 and 800. What is known as the Prescott culture (a branch of the Patayan prehistoric group) evolved over the next six hundred years, during which time farming and trading became increasingly important.

Since the twentieth century, population in the valley has exploded, fueling the growth of the towns of Prescott, Prescott Valley, and Chino Valley. Prescott, once the territorial capital, is the largest of these. Here you will find plenty of restaurants and accommodations, as well as museums, galleries, six golf courses, boutiques, five lakes, and some gorgeous scenery.

Prescott is also a mecca for those who love the outdoors. Mountain bikers, hikers, and horseback riders travel the numerous trails, fishermen and boaters enjoy the lakes, miners pan for gold in the streams, and campers rest in temperatures that are considerably cooler than those found 85 miles south in Phoenix.

An irreplaceable collection of Southwest Indian artifacts ranging from pre-Columbian through contemporary is housed in the Pueblo-style building of the **Smoki Museum of American Indian Art and Culture**. Emphasis of the exhibits is on the indigenous peoples of Northern Arizona and Prescott Valley. Included is a kiva duplicating the floor plan of one at Oraibi on the Hopi Mesas, prehistoric pottery and stone tools, split-twig figures over three thousand years old, a large collection of jewelry and baskets, and paintings of the turn-of-the-century Hopi Reservation done by Kate Cory. Plains Indian items are also on display, including clothing and beadwork. A bookstore and gift shop selling Native American items are on site, and the museum sponsors special events, lectures, and performances. The museum is one block north of E. Gurley Street (AZ69) on N. Arizona Street.

The state-funded **Sharlot Hall Museum**, located near downtown, comprises several historic buildings, including the Territorial Governor's Mansion. Its room of Indian displays includes pottery, basketry, jewelry, and artifacts from both prehistoric and historic Southwest cultures. A small living-history program in summer focuses on life in the nineteenth century. They also have extensive research and archival resources. The museum includes *Fort Whipple Museum*, the former officer's quarters of the fort. The museum, located on the Veteran's Administration campus on North AZ89, focuses on U.S. military history during territorial days and hosts periodic historic re-enactments.

The **Phippen Museum** showcases Western artists in permanent and temporary exhibits that include works by Native Americans. Native artifacts and jewelry date back to the late nineteenth century. The gift store sells books, fine art, and Indian crafts. The museum is 7 miles north of downtown on AZ89.

NORTHEAST OF PRESCOTT

About 150 Yavapai (YAHV-uh-pie) live in the Prescott area, most of them on the **Yavapai-Prescott Indian Reservation**, which is 1395 acres bordered on three sides by the town. Basketry is the tribe's most noted craft. Traditionally, the Yavapai ranged from here west to the Colorado River, where they lived on *rancherias*. Today, there are three main groups, at Fort McDowell, Camp Verde, and Prescott.

When Euro-American settlers first came here in the 1860s, they found about two thousand "People of the Sun" already living here. Although a Yuman-speaking tribe, the Yavapai were mistaken for hostile Apaches and relentlessly attacked by the newcomers. When General Crook ordered all "roving Apache" rounded up in 1871 and sent to reservations, the Yavapai were included. Later, they were forced on the "March of Tears" to San Carlos. In the early 1900s, eight families were allowed to return to the Prescott area. Their leader, Sam Jimulla, and his wife, Viola, were instrumental in securing a reservation for their people. In 1956, another 1,320 acres were added to the original 75.

Contemporary Yavapai economic development is closely tied to the greater Prescott economy. *Frontier Village Shopping Center*, approximately 250 acres along AZ69 and the largest retail center in Arizona north of Phoenix, is leased from the tribe.

Statue of a Native American woman and child at the Yavapai Prescott Resort

Prescott Resort, Conference Center, and Casino (formerly Sheraton Resort and Conference Center) is located on the reservation just northeast of the junction of US89 and AZ69. The resort sits atop a hill overlooking town and offers luxury accommodations, dining, a heated pool, and salon. A full-service health club with tennis and racquetball courts is also on site. Over a million dollars of artwork created by local artists is for sale in the lobby. Bucky's Casino, adjoining the resort, has gambling, dining, and a children's arcade. Across the street, Yavapai Bingo and Gaming

Center at the same address also has slots, poker, and blackjack, and scheduled non-smoking times.

During part of November and December, Arizona's largest gingerbread village comes to life at the hotel. Chefs, schools, corporations, and other individuals buy a "lot" to fill with their creations. Local children submit gingerbread people, and if you are visiting then, you can create one yourself with a cookie and supplies donated by the hotel. A model railroad circles the town, and the money raised goes to support the Yavapai Big Brothers and Big Sisters. At the same time, Prescott goes all out with holiday decorations, earning itself the nickname of "Arizona's Christmas City."

Frontier Days, several days of celebration around July 4th, is another popular community event.

EAST OF PRESCOTT

A three-quarter-mile trail (fairly steep) leads to **Lynx Creek Ruin**, once home to members of the Prescott culture. The interpretive area at the ruin focuses on the plants used by the prehistoric residents, and hikers can enjoy a spectacular panoramic view of Prescott Valley from the platform there. To reach the ruin, which is near Lynx Lake Recreation Area, take AZ69 to Walker Road and turn south. Look for the dirt road to the ruin on your left. Parking, picnic tables, and trail brochures are available at the trailhead; the trail to the ruin is Trail 301. For more information, contact the Prescott National Forest office in Prescott.

SEDONA
Map #5

Around Town: Boynton Canyon, vortexes
Nearby: Clemenceau Heritage Museum, Honanki-Bear House Ruins, Oak Creek Canyon, Palatki Ruins, Tuzigoot National Monument, V-Bar-V Ranch Petroglyphs

Stunning red-rock scenery, prehistoric Indian ruins, mystical energy vortexes, trendy art galleries, and spas are the attractions in Sedona. Set amidst towering, vibrant-red buttes that seem to light on fire during sunsets, the beautiful canyons, fresh water, and mild climate of Sedona once provided a comfortable home for many Native groups, including the Nizhoni, Ancestral Puebloans, Apache, and Yavapai. At Sinagua Plaza, a life-sized bronze sculpture has story panels that tell the history of the Sinagua, who lived in the area between A.D. 700 and 1400.

The land around Sedona holds particular importance for the Yavapai. According to their legends, either Great Earth Mother or Grandmother Spirit lives in **Boynton Canyon**. You can follow Boynton Canyon Trail up the canyon through woods and past several small Sinagua cliff ruins along the way. To reach the trailhead, turn north onto Dry Creek Road from AZ89A in west Sedona and follow the signs. A small parking lot is on the right a quarter-mile before the entrance to Enchantment Resort; it requires a Red Rocks Pass, available from the Sedona Visitor Center. This moderate hike can be crowded, and parts of the canyon have been subject to vandalism.

Boynton Canyon is also one of Sedona's **vortexes**, which are believed to be spots of potent earth energy and which were considered sacred power places by local Indians. Many people visit today to test the forces for themselves. Another vortex is *Bell Rock*, located on AZ179 toward Oak Creek. The National Forest Vista Point offers a view of the rock across the road. *Cathedral Rock*, at Red Rock Crossing along the banks of Oak Creek, and *Airport Mesa* are two other easily accessible vortexes.

Sedona is a center for fine contemporary Western and Native American art. Some say that its fifty or so art galleries rival the shopping in Santa Fe. *Tlaquepaque* (*Tla-keh-pah-keh*; "the best of everything" in the ancient Aztec language) is an arts and crafts shopping center named after a village near Guadalajara, Mexico. Built to resemble an Old Mexico market square with fountains, gardens, and courtyards, it is a pleasant place to browse for Native American and other items. To get there, take AZ179 south of AZ89A in town for about .3 mile and turn right at the cobblestone driveway. Other galleries are located on AZ179 just south of the Y intersection and in Old Town, which is the first half-mile of AZ89A north of the intersection. Other shopping is in uptown, the corridor along AZ179, the Old Marketplace in West Sedona, and the Village at Oak Creek (factory outlet stores).

The main *visitor center* is one block north of the Y intersection at the corner of north AZ89A and Forest Road in uptown Sedona. Ask here for a list of companies providing jeep tours of Sedona, the vortexes, the Hopi Mesas, the Navajo Nation, and ancient ruins. Airplane and helicopter rides, horseback rides, and chuckwagon suppers are other options to ask about. Also, inquire about a Red Rocks Pass—a hiking and parking fee needed to visit many of the popular sites around Sedona. The pass can also be purchased at the Coconino Ranger Stations (see below) and from machines at some of the sites. The Sedona SuperPass, which provides discounts to attractions and meals, can be purchased at the visitor center as well.

Among the lodging options is the Radisson Poco Diablo Resort, operated by the Fort McDowell Yavapai Nation. (See Chapter 11, Metropolitan Phoenix/Valley of the Sun, page 174.)

Coconino National Forest contains several archaeological sites of prehistoric and historic cultures. A Red Rocks Pass (or displayed America the Beautiful Pass) is required to park and hike in the National Forest. The *Red Rock Ranger Station*, at the first left past the intersection of AZ89A and AZ179A, has information on the pass and the Heritage Sites of Palatki Ruins, Honanki Ruins, and V-Bar-V Ranch petroglyphs.

NORTH OF SEDONA

Oak Creek Canyon is north of town toward Flagstaff on AZ89A. In addition to outstanding scenery, a keep-you-on-your-toes drive of steep switchbacks, and an opportunity to waterslide through natural red rock sluices at Slide Rock State Park, you may find Native American vendors selling their crafts at the scenic overlook.

SOUTH OF SEDONA

Built between A.D. 1150 and 1300, the pueblo at **Palatki Ruins Heritage Site** once housed thirty to fifty people in a series of alcoves. The Red Cliffs of Supai sandstone display excellent examples of pictographs left by them and by earlier and later residents such as the Yavapai and Apache. There is a small museum and bookstore and two interpretive trails leading to the rock art and cliff dwelling. Volunteers interpret the site and answer questions. Reservations timed for 9:30am, 11:30am, and 1:30pm are required to visit.

The ruins at Tuzigoot National Monument seem to spill down the hillside.

To reach Palatki (Hopi for "Red House") from Sedona, travel south on AZ89A from the Y (away from Oak Creek Canyon) to a group of mailboxes about a half-mile south of mile marker 365, and then turn right onto Forest Road 525 at a group of mailboxes. Travel to Forest Road 795 and turn north. Be sure to check with the Red Rocks Ranger District for road conditions before you go; the site is only open when the 8-mile dirt road is dry and passable to passenger cars.

Honanki-Bear House, another pictograph site and cliff dwelling occupied at about the same time as Palatki, is 2.5 miles away. Honanki was one of the Verde Valley's largest population centers from 1130 to 1280. To reach it, take Forest Road 525 for 10.2 miles from AZ89A. Ask at the forest service offices in town for alternate directions via an especially scenic high-clearance road.

If you continue south on AZ89A, you will come to the town of Cottonwood. **Clemenceau Heritage Museum** has a few arrowheads and pottery in their displays. Changing exhibits often include Native American items.

Perched above the Verde Valley, northwest of Cottonwood, **Tuzigoot National Monument** began around A.D. 1225 as a small village of about fifty people. In the 1200s, it grew into a prehistoric refugee camp as farmers from the north fled a severe drought. At one time, several hundred Sinaguans farmed here, using natural springs for irrigation water.

Tuzigoot is on a hillside that rises 120 feet above the valley floor, and, unlike many Southwestern ruins, it provides an expansive view. Most of the 110 rooms had no doors and were entered by ladders through ceilings of pine and sycamore beams, willow branches, and mud. The inhabitants probably lived short lives. Of the excavated burials, 42 percent were children under the age of nine. The oldest adult found was around forty-five.

The *visitor center* has a museum displaying turquoise mosaics, shell jewelry, pottery, and a replica of a living space, as well as exhibits explaining Sinagua agriculture, weaving, building techniques, and burials. There is also a bookstore.

A one-third-mile, self-guiding trail leads through the restored, walk-in ruins that trace three hundred years of Sinagua development. To reach the sites, take Main Street from Cottonwood toward Clarkdale.

At the **V-Bar-V Ranch Heritage Site**, a cliff face with 1,032 individual petroglyphs holds the largest collection of its kind in the Verde Valley. A volunteer is on duty to explain the Beaver Creek petroglyph style found here, etched between A.D. 1150 and 1400 by the southern Sinagua. The site, open on a limited basis, is about a half-mile past the Beaver Creek Campground, reached by traveling 2.8 miles east of the I-17 junction and AZ179 on Forest Road 618. Contact the Red Rocks Ranger District for current information.

EVENTS

VARIES *Yavapai-Apache Tribe:* Members sponsor Sunrise Dances throughout the year. Contact tribal headquarters for specifics.

FEBRUARY *Exodus Days:* Yavapai-Apache tribe commemorates the 1875 "March of Tears" into exile at San Carlos. It includes a reenactment, powwow, and arts/crafts booths.

MARCH *Spring Powwow:* Powwow on Northern Arizona University campus in Flagstaff. Call the university for information.

MAY *Southwest Indian Arts Festival:* Performances by Indian dancers and musicians, arts/crafts booths, children's activity area, fry bread, and Navajo tacos. Smoki Museum in Prescott.

Zuni Festival of Arts and Culture: Dancing, cultural interpreters and demonstrations, music, food, arts/crafts, and storytelling. Museum of Northern Arizona in Flagstaff, 928-774-5213 or www.musnaz.org.

SUMMER *Festival of Native American Arts:* Music, dance performances, and arts and crafts demonstrations and sales, with a focus on groups from the Four Corners area. Held June, July, and August in Flagstaff, sponsored by Coconino Center for the Arts, 928-779-2300.

Hopi, Zuni, and Navajo Artists Exhibition: Noted artists from the Hopi, Zuni, and Navajo tribes exhibit their works during the summer at the Museum of Northern Arizona.

JUNE *Yavapai-Prescott All-Indian Powwow:* Competitive and powwow dancing, food booth, and a princess pageant. Third weekend in June in Prescott.

JULY *Flagstaff Indian Days:* Powwow, rodeo, vendors, and beauty pageant. Held at Ft. Tuthill, Coconino County Fairgrounds, near Flagstaff airport about 2 miles south of AZ89 or I-17. For information, contact Pam Singer: 928-522-7001 or email singer_ella@hotmail.com.

Hopi Festival of Arts and Culture: Weekend of fine arts/crafts, cultural presentations, music, dancing, storytelling, traditional food, and educational events, all pertaining to the Hopi people. Museum of Northern Arizona in Flagstaff, 928-774-5213 or www.musnaz.org.

July 4th Yavapai-Apache Powwow: Singing, dancing, food vendors, and arts and crafts booths. Held at Camp Verde.

Navajo Rug and Indian Art Auction: Hundreds of items are offered at this annual auction, including Indian baskets, jewelry, carvings, pottery, and Navajo weavings. Smoki Museum in Prescott.

Prescott Indian Market: Juried art show and distinctive jewelry, ceramics, blankets, katsinas, and other high-quality items for sale at one of the premier Native American art markets in the Southwest. Also entertainment and demonstrations of silversmithing, weaving, basketry, katsina carving, and other arts. Sharlot Hall Museum, 928-445-3122.

AUGUST *Navajo Festival of Arts and Culture:* Weekend of artists, storytellers, cultural interpreters and demonstrations, hoop and traditional dancing, music, and educational events, all pertaining to the Navajo people. Museum of Northern Arizona in Flagstaff, 928-774-5213 or www.musnaz.org.

Phippen Museum Western Art Show and Sale: Art by a variety of artists from the American West. Memorial Day Weekend in Prescott.

DECEMBER *Christmas Indian Art Market:* Indian arts/crafts sale, Native American food and music, gift shop discounts. Smoki Museum in Prescott.

CONTACT INFORMATION

Arizona Historical Society/Pioneer Historical Museum
2340 North Valley Road, Flagstaff, AZ 86001
928-774-6272
Mon-Sat 9am-5pm

Arizona Ski Bowl
PO Box 40, Flagstaff, AZ 86002
928-779-1951
www.arizonasnowbowl.com

Arizona State Parks
1300 W. Washington, Phoenix, AZ 85007
602-542-4174 • www.pr.state.az.us

Art Barn (*see* Coconino Center for the Arts)

Bureau of Land Management
www.blm.gov/az/st/en.html
　Phoenix District
　21605 N. 7th Avenue, Phoenix, AZ 85027
　623-580-5500

Camp Verde Chamber of Commerce
385 Main Street, Camp Verde, AZ 86322
Mon-Fr 9am-4pm, Sat-Sun 10am-3pm
928-567-9294
www.campverde.org
www.visitcampverde.com

Camp Verde Reservation (*see* Yavapai-Apache tribe)

Clemenceau Heritage Museum
1 North Willard Street, Cottonwood, AZ
928-634-2868
www.clemenceaumuseum.org
Wed 9am-noon; Fri-Sun 11am-3pm; donation

Coconino Center for the Arts/Art Barn
2300 North Fort Valley Road, Flagstaff, AZ 86001
928-774-0822 Art Barn
928-779-2300 Coconino Center
www.culturalpartners.org
Tues-Sat 11am-5pm

Coconino National Forest (*see* U.S. National Forest)

Elden Pueblo Ruin (see also Coconino National Forest)
www.fs.fed.us/r3/coconino/about/districts/peaks/elden-pueblo-project.shtml

Flagstaff Visitor Center
1 E. Route 66, Flagstaff, AZ 86001
800-842-7293 *or* 928-774-9541, -4505
www.flagstaffarizona.org
Mon-Sat 8am-5pm; Sun 9am-4pm

Fort Whipple Museum
550 N Hwy 89, Bldg 11, Veteran's Administration Campus, Prescott, AZ 86301
928-445-3122 • www.sharlot.org
Thurs-Sat 10am-4pm

Fort Verde State Historical Park
125 E. Holloman, PO Box 397, Camp Verde, AZ 86322
928-567-3275
www.pr.state.az.us/Parks/parkhtml/fortverde.html
Daily 8am-5pm; fee

Honanki Heritage Site
Red Rock Ranger District, PO Box 20249, Sedona AZ 86341
928-282-4119 *or* 928-282-3854 (Palatki)
www.fs.fed.us/r3/coconino/recreation/red_rock/honanki-ruins.shtml
Daily with reservations; fee

Montezuma Castle/Well National Monument
Montezuma Castle Road, Camp Verde, AZ 86322
928-567-3322 • www.nps.gov/moca
Daily 8am-6pm, summer; daily 8am-5pm, winter; fee

Museum of Northern Arizona
3101 North Fort Valley Road, Flagstaff, AZ 86001
928-774-5213 • www.musnaz.org
Daily 9am-5pm; fee

Museum of Rim Country Archaeology
PO Box 935, Pine, AZ 85544 (mailing address)
510 W. Main Street, Payson, AZ 85541
928-468-1128
www.rimcountrymuseums.com/rimcountry archaeology.htm
Wed-Sun 10am-4pm; fee

Northern Arizona University
South San Francisco Street, Flagstaff, Arizona 86011
602-523-9011, -3182 • http://home.nau.edu

Painted Desert (*See* Petrified Forest)

Palatki Heritage Site
Reservations: 928-282-3854 or 928-282-4119
(Red Rocks Ranger District)
www.fs.fed.us/r3/coconino/recreation/red
rock/palatki-ruins.shtml
9:30am-3pm (daily depending on weather); fee

**Payson/Rim Country Regional Chamber of
Commerce**
100 West Main, Payson, AZ 85547
800-672-9766 *or* 928-474-4515
www.rimcountrychamber.com

Peaks Ranger Station
5075 N. Highway 89, Flagstaff, AZ 86004
928-526-0866
Mon-Fri 7:30am-4:30pm
Bonito Campground
928-527-1474
Daily mid Apr-mid Oct

Phippen Museum
4701 Highway 89 North, Prescott, AZ 86301
928-778-1385 • www.phippinartmuseum.org
Mon-Sat 10am-4pm & Sun 1pm-4pm; fee

Pine-Strawberry Museum
PO Box 564, Pine, AZ 85544
928-476-3547 • www.pinestrawhs.org
Mon-Thurs 10am-4pm, Fri-Sun 10am-4pm,
mid May-mid Oct; Mon-Sat 10am-2pm,
Mid Oct-mid May

Pioneer Historical Museum
2340 N. Ft. Balley Road, Flagstaff, AZ 86001
928-774-6272
www.arizonahistoricalsociety.org
Mon-Sat 9am-5pm

Prescott Chamber of Commerce
117 W. Goodwin Street, Prescott, AZ 86302
800-266-7534 *or* 928-445-2000
www.prescott.org • www.yavapai-tourism.org

Prescott National Forest (*see* U.S. National Forest)

Radisson Poco Diablo Resort
1752 S. Highway 179, Sedona, AZ 86336
800-333-3333 *or* 928-282-7333
www.radisson.com/sedonaaz

Rim Country Museum
PO Box 2532, Payson, AZ 85547
928-474-3483
www.rimcountrymuseums.com
Wed-Mon 12noon-4pm; fee

Sedona Chamber of Commerce
PO Box 478, Sedona, AZ 86339
Visitor Centers:
331 Forest Road, Sedona AZ 86339
Tequa Plaza, Oak Creek, AZ 86339
800-288-7336 *or* 928-282-7722
www.visitsedona.com
Mon-Sat 8:30am-5pm & Sun 9am-3pm, Apr-
Oct; Mon-Sat 9am-5pm, Nov-Mar

Sharlot Hall Museum
415 W. Gurley Street, Prescott, AZ 86301
928-445-3122 • www.sharlot.org
Museum: Mon-Sat 10am-5pm & Sun 1pm-
4pm; fee
Archives/Library: Tues-Fri Noon-4pm & Sat
10am-2pm

Smoki Museum
147 North Arizona Street, Prescott, AZ 86301
928-445-1230 • www.smokimuseum.org
Tues-Sat 10am-4pm & Sun 1pm-4pm; fee

Spirit Mountain Ranch
PO Box 31106, Flagstaff, AZ 86003
928-606-2779 • www.sacredwhitebuffalo.org
Daily 9am-4pm summer; call rest of the year

Sunset Crater Volcano National Monument
2717 N. Steves Boulevard, Suite 3, Flagstaff,
AZ 86004
www.nps.gov/sucr
Visitor Center: Daily 8am-5pm, May-Oct;
daily 9am-5pm, Nov-Apr
Scenic drive and trails: Daily sunrise-sunset; fee

Tlaquepaque
336 Hwy 179, Sedona, AZ 86339
928-282-4838 • www.tlaq.com
Shops open daily 10am-5pm; restaurant hours
vary

Tonto Apache Reservation
Reservation 30, Payson, AZ 85541
928-474-5000
Mazatzal Casino
800-777-PLAY • www.777play.com

Tuzigoot National Monument
PO Box 219, Camp Verde, AZ 86322
928-634-5564 • www.nps.gov/tuzi
Daily 8am-6pm, Memorial Day–Labor Day; daily
8am-5pm Labor Day-Memorial Day; fee

United States National Forest Service
  Coconino National Forest
  www.fs.fed.us/r3/coconino
    Main Office
    1824 South Thompson, Flagstaff, AZ 86001
    928-527-3600
    Mon-Fri 8am-4:30pm
    Peaks Ranger Station
    5075 N. Hwy 89, Flagstaff, AZ 86004
    928-526-0866
    Mon-Fri 7:30am-4:30pm
    Red Rocks Ranger District
    250 Brewer Road, Sedona, AZ 86339
    928-282-4119
    Mon-Fri 8am-4:30pm
  Prescott National Forest
  344 S. Cortez, Prescott, AZ 86303
  928-443-8000
  www.fs.fed.us/r3/prescott
  Office: Mon-Fri 8am-4:30pm
  Tonto National Forest
    Payson Ranger District
    1009 E. Hwy 260, Payson, AZ 85541
    928-474-7900

V-Bar-B Ranch Petroglyphs
Contact Red Rock Rock Ranger District
PO Box 20429, Sedona, AZ 86341
928-282-4119
Fri-Mon 9:30am-3:30pm

Yavapai-Apache Tribal Headquarters
PO Box 1188, 2400 W. Datsi Street, Camp
  Verde, AZ 86322
928-567-3649 • www.yavapai-apache.org
  Cliff Castle Casino
  555 Middle Verde Rd., Camp Verde, AZ
    86322
  800-381-7568 *or* 928-567-7900
  www.cliffcastlecasino.net
  Distant Drums RV Resort
  583 West Middle Verde Road, Camp Verde,
    AZ 86322
  877-577-5507 *or* 928-554-0444
  www.distantdrumsrvresort.com
  Native Visions Tourism
  928-567-3035
  The Lodge at Cliff Castle
  800-524-6343 *or* 928-567-6611
  Stargazer Pavilion
  928-567-7999
  Yavapai Apache Cultural Department
  928-649-6959

Yavapai-Prescott Reservation
530 E. Meritt, Prescott, AZ 86301
928-445-8790 • www.ypit.com
  Bucky's Casino
  1505 East Highway 69, Prescott, AZ 86302
  800-756-8744 • buckyscasino.com
  Open 24 hours
  Prescott Resort and Conference Center
    and Casino
  1505 East Highway 69, Prescott, AZ 86301
  800-967-4637 *or* 928-776-1666
  prescottresort.com
  Yavapai Bingo and Gaming Center
  800-756-8744

Walnut Canyon National Monument
Walnut Canyon Road, Flagstaff, AZ 86004
928-526-3367 • www.nps.gov/waca
Daily 8am-5pm, May-Oct; daily 9am-5pm,
  Nov-Apr; fee

Wupatki National Monument
2717 N. Steves Boulevard, Suite 3, Flagstaff,
  AZ 86004
928-670-2365 *or* 928-526-1157 (headquarters)
www.nps.gov/wupa
Email MaryBlasing@nps.gov for information
  about Crack-in-the-Rock backpacking trip.
Visitor Center: Daily 8am-5pm, May-Oct;
  daily 9am-5pm, Nov-Apr
Scenic drives, trails, and pueblos: Daily sunrise
  to sunset; fee

EAST CENTRAL ARIZONA

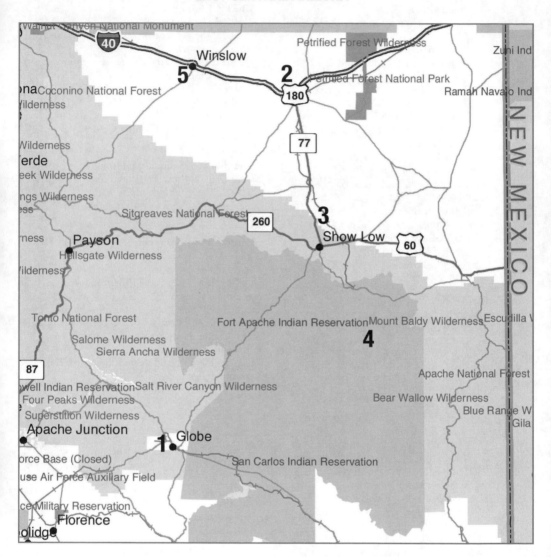

1. Globe
2. Holbrook
3. Pinetop/Lakeside

4. White Mountain Apache
   Reservation (Fort Apache)
5. Winslow

CHAPTER 10

EAST CENTRAL ARIZONA

GLOBE
Map #1

Around Town: Gila County Historical Museum

Nearby: Apache Trail Scenic Byway, Besh-Ba-Gowah Archaeological Park, Gila Pueblo, San Carlos Apache Reservation (Apache Gold Casino and Resort, Apache Stronghold Golf Club, San Carlos Apache Cultural Center, San Carlos Lake, Seneca Lake Recreational Park), Tonto National Monument

Globe sits at the eastern end of the Apache Trail on a 12-mile strip carved from the San Carlos Indian Reservation after silver was found there. Copper eventually replaced silver in importance, and mining is still important to the local economy. The town has also become a trading center for the San Carlos Reservation.

Gila County Historical Museum, housed in what was once Old Dominion Mine's fire and rescue station, has prehistoric and Apache artifacts among its items. The museum is 1 mile north of Globe on US60.

For information and a historic walking tour map, visit the *Globe/Miami Chamber of Commerce* on Broad Street. Information on the nearby Tonto National Forest is available at the *Globe Ranger Station*, about 2 miles southeast of downtown Globe.

NORTH OF GLOBE

The Tonto Basin, a river valley of rich soil and abundant small game that attracted people from the surrounding semi-arid mesas as early as 5000 B.C., is the site for **Tonto National Monument**. Permanent settlers arrived here around A.D. 100, but they abandoned the place around A.D. 600. By A.D. 750, Hohokam from the lower Gila and Salt River valleys had moved into the area. Over the years, their culture evolved into a new one, the Salado.

By A.D. 1100, people of the Salado (Spanish for "salt") culture were living in pueblo villages near irrigated fields of corn, beans, pumpkins, amaranth, and cotton. This continued until the thirteenth century, when they moved to cliff homes. They also gathered

A trail leads to the ruins at Tonto National Monument.

cactus and mesquite, hunted small game, and traded as far away as Colorado, Mexico, and the Gulf of California. Their crafts included distinctive polychrome pottery (red, white, and black) and intricately woven cotton cloth. For unknown reasons, somewhere between 1400 and 1450, the people abandoned the Tonto Basin.

Tonto National Monument contains the remains of three fourteenth-century Salado villages nestled in natural rock shelters and shallow alcoves. The *visitor center museum* has an audiovisual show on the Salado culture and displays ceremonial objects, pottery, cotton cloth, ancient bows and arrows, and many perishable artifacts like pot rests, reed cigarettes, and grass hairbrushes.

The ruins are some of the most well-preserved in Arizona. A steep half-mile, self-guided trail takes about 1 hour to complete and leads to Lower Cliff Dwelling, where nineteen small rooms were built of quartzite and mud. Many of the wood and mud roofs remain. The forty rooms of Upper Cliff Dwelling can be visited by guided tour only, November to April. This strenuous hike has an elevation gain of six hundred feet on a 3-mile round-trip and takes about three hours.

Tonto National Monument is west of Globe on US60 to AZ188 (Apache Trail Scenic Byway) and then northwest for 30 miles.

Continue on AZ188 to the junction of AZ88, and turn left for **Apache Trail Scenic Byway**. The Apache Trail was a shortcut once used by Indians to cross the Superstition Mountains, which hold prehistoric ruins thousands of years old. The scenic byway now leads 78 miles to Apache Junction through the rugged terrain, following the trail and passing geologic wonders and sites of historic interest. Theodore Roosevelt called the views it accesses "the most sublimely beautiful panorama nature ever created." As the road twists through rugged mountains covered with cactus forests and along the precipitous walls of Fish Creek Canyon, it passes several popular lakes, including Theodore Roosevelt Lake and Canyon Lake, where Yavapai and U.S. soldiers clashed at Skeleton Cave in 1872. Plan a day for the trip, and be advised that part of the road is well-graded gravel that is passable to cars but not recommended for RVs or trailers. More information is available from Tonto National Forest Headquarters in Phoenix or NFS district offices (Tonto Basin Office in

Roosevelt on the eastern end of Apache Trail and Mesa Ranger District Office on the western edge).

SOUTH OF GLOBE

Besh-Ba-Gowah Archaeological Park preserves Salado ruins, dating from roughly A.D. 1225 to the early 1400s, which were built on the site of abandoned Hohokam pithouses. The ruins overlook Pinal Creek, which the Salado used to irrigate fields of corn, beans, cotton, and squash.

At its peak, Besh-Ba-Gowah (Apache for "Place of Metal") was home to an estimated four hundred people. Aligned to the winter and summer solstice, the large pueblo was constructed mainly of rounded river cobbles and mud and contained three central plazas and over two hundred rooms. The residents exported powder pigments, pottery, cotton cloth, turquoise, and beads along the ancient trade corridor that led from Casas Grandes in Mexico to the Salado River. Items left behind when they moved away were woven baskets and mats, shell jewelry, and numerous types of ceramics, including the widely traded and distinctive polychrome with black and white designs on red clay.

Part of the village site has been bulldozed, but a self-guided trail leads through the remaining ruins, which are partially reconstructed. Ladders climb to rooms containing pottery, a loom, and other items used by the Salado.

In the museum are artifacts and exhibits recreating the Salado lifestyle, and an ethnobotanical garden displays the native and cultivated plants used by the Salado. There are also a gift shop, small research library, special programs, and guided tours.

Besh-Ba-Gowah is about 1.5 miles from downtown Globe. Take South Broad Street to Jesse Hayes Road.

At **Gila Pueblo** about a mile upstream from Besh-Ba-Gowah, the neighboring Salado built over two hundred rooms in a complex that was occupied between A.D. 1225 and 1400. After being excavated, the pueblo was rebuilt in 1928 by archaeologists Harold and Winifred Gladwin. The pueblo is now the site of Eastern Arizona College, and further excavation has been done by its students. Plaques at the rebuilt pueblo interpret the history of the site. For information, contact the college or the Greater Globe–Miami Chamber of Commerce.

EAST OF GLOBE

The **San Carlos Apache Indian Reservation** was established in 1871, and many of the tribe's over ten thousand enrolled members now live here. The Black and Salt rivers form natural boundaries between San Carlos and the Fort Apache Reservation to the north. Tribal enterprises include timber operations, cattle ranching, mining, and recreation. Governmental agencies on the reservation employ many San Carlos Apaches, and a shopping complex has been completed.

In addition to basketry, beadwork, and carving, San Carlos artisans make peridot jewelry. Named "Heart of the Earth" and "Stone of the Sun," peridot crystals have been collected in the area for thousands of years from the world's largest gem deposit of the mineral.

The reservation has over 1.8 million acres of varied climate and landscape that ranges from cool pine forests to grasslands to cactus desert. Opportunities for outdoor recreation are plentiful. Big game includes deer, bear, elk, javelina, and mountain lion; small game includes quail, waterfowl, and squirrel. The reservation is also a mecca for wildlife photographers and bird watchers. Hiking, picnicking, boating, and camping are also popular.

San Carlos Lake, south of the village of San Carlos, is one of the hottest bass fishing spots in the state. Twenty-three miles long, two miles wide and with 158 miles of shoreline, it is the largest lake completely within Arizona. When Coolidge Dam created San Carlos Lake, the water covered the site of the original Indian Agency. A tribal burial ground was also inundated, but the Apaches convinced the U.S. government to protect it with a concrete slab. The lake is well-stocked with bass, crappie, and bluegill and is open year-round. *San Carlos Lake Marina*, 2 miles north of the dam, has information and permits for recreation activities or for travel to other areas of the reservation. It also sells fishing supplies, groceries, snacks, and gasoline. Several campgrounds are near the lake, and next to the marina is a trailer park with hookups.

Seneca Lake Recreational Park is about 30 miles northeast of Globe off US60. The lake has boat fishing, developed campsites, a picnic area, and a small store selling permits. Other places for fishing and hiking include Black River and Salt River recreation areas, plus scores of remote lakes and small ponds that are home to trout and catfish.

Fishing and hunting permits can be obtained from stores on the reservation, from the *San Carlos Recreation and Wildlife Division Office* on the corner of Moon Base Road and AZ170 in Peridot, or downloaded from their Web site.

Tribal offices are in the small community of San Carlos, east of Globe on US70, then north on CR6. The town's visitor services include a post office, convenience store, groceries, gas, dry goods, and the *Apache Nation Chamber of Commerce*, whose Web site also lists the local native-owned businesses. Vendors sell traditional food daily in the center of town, and Apache and other Native American arts and crafts are occasionally available at the Community Center's Saturday morning garage sale.

Agave stalks fitted with a single string form an Apache violin like this one. (1883–1888 A. Frank Randall)

On US70 near San Carlos is the *San Carlos Apache Cultural Center* (near milepost 272). The artists' guild outlet here is one of the best reservation sources for authentic arts and crafts, including peridot jewelry.

Dioramas and displays in the museum provide information about contemporary Apache people, and artifacts provide testimony to their traditional lifestyle and history. Look for the Apache violins on display, and ask about hearing a tape of one being played.

Apache Gold Casino Resort, 5 miles east of Globe on US70, features two restaurants, casino-style gambling, nightly entertainment, a gift shop selling baskets and beadwork, and a nearby convenience store. The Best Western hotel offers lodging and a pool, steam room

< 152 >

and workout area, and a conference center with full catering. Shows, concerts, and pow-wows are scheduled throughout the year in the Pavilion. The RV park has hookups, showers, a pool, and satellite TV. Sprawling through the mesquite and sage covered hills and valleys is the eighteen-hole *Apache Stronghold Golf Club* with a pro shop, golf school, putting green, driving range, and practice area. A grill provides food.

HOLBROOK
Map #2

Around Town: Navajo County Museum
Nearby: Painted Desert, Petrified Forest National Park

Centuries before the railroad station was established in 1882, the vicinity around Holbrook had been occupied, beginning with prehistoric Indians and continuing to the modern-day Hopi and Navajo. On summer weeknights, Native American dancers now perform on the lawn next to the Old County Courthouse. The **Navajo County Museum** in the courthouse is open at the same time, with the historical exhibits including a few miscellaneous Indian items. The *Holbrook Chamber of Commerce* has more information on the area.

EAST OF HOLBROOK

The land in **Petrified Forest National Park/Painted Desert** was inhabited by Desert Archaic, Basketmaker, and Ancestral Pueblo people from as early as A.D. 300 to around 1400, and the central section of the Petrified Forest contains numerous prehistoric sites. During the time they lived here, the residents transitioned from semi-nomadic hunters to farmers living in pueblos.

Legend claims that the Petrified Forest was turned to stone by an Indian goddess, enraged when the wood was too wet to start her fire. Scientists, speaking in terms of geologic time, claim that about 225 million years ago an ancient forest grew here in a stream-crossed valley. Repeated flooding toppled the trees and then blanketed them with dirt that was saturated with silicon-rich water. Sealed in a sediment tomb, the logs decayed so slowly that silicon had time to combine with oxygen and form quartz crystals in the plant tissue, sometimes even replacing it. Other trace minerals interacted with the plant residue as well, and the trees were transformed into objects looking like petrified rainbows.

North of the petrified wood sites is the spectacular *Painted Desert*, consisting of colorful bands of eroded shale and sandstone that stretch all the way to the Grand Canyon. With the right amount of heat, light, and desert dust, even the air here seems to shimmer with color. Early morning or evening and following a rain are times when the hues are most vivid.

The *Painted Desert Visitor Center* has a film showing the process of wood petrification and exhibits on the human history, geology, ecology, and fossils in the park. It also provides information on camping and hiking trails, maps, and a bookstore.

Painted Desert Inn Museum and Bookstore at Kachina Point was originally built with Indian labor so tourists in the 1920s would have a place to stay. Later, in 1948, the inn served as the park's northern headquarters. Hopi artist Fred Kabotie painted six murals on the walls using traditional themes, including the story of a journey through the Petrified

Forest to Zuni Salt Lake to collect salt and a Buffalo Dance mural that depicts a January ceremony performed to ensure good hunting and snow. A similar dance may have taken place in the plaza at the ancient Puerco pueblo (see below). After a recent rehabilitation and restoration of the Kabotie murals, the Desert Inn now functions as a museum and bookstore specializing in Native American books, posters, and crafts. Guided tours are also offered, but no lodging or food service is available.

The trail to *Painted Desert Wilderness*, which contains numerous Indian sites and petroglyphs, begins near Kachina Point behind the inn. Directions, a hiking guide, and the required free permit for overnight use are available at the visitor center.

The 27-mile *scenic drive* through Petrified Forest National Park travels along the rim overlooking the Painted Desert and then crosses I-40 into the Petrified Forest. Stop at *Puerco Indian Ruin*, left behind by twelfth-, and later fourteenth-century farmers who depended on the reliable water of the Puerco River and the rich soil of its floodplain. The one-story pueblo contained about seventy-five rooms, and at least two kivas centered on a rectangular plaza. You can still see room foundations and one of the kivas. Petroglyphs decorate the boulders below the village, one of them marking the summer solstice. Ranger demonstrations, held here between June 10 and June 30, discuss the fourteen sites in the park that contain solar markings.

From Puerco Ruin the road continues to *Newspaper Rock*, a huge sandstone boulder pecked with petroglyph messages from the past. The impressive collection here includes pictures of hands, spirals, and frogs.

Blue Mesa Trail leads through a colorful canyon in Petrified Forest National Park.

Agate House is accessible at the Long Logs area, where a short self-guiding trail leads through the intensely colored petrified wood to a partially restored pueblo. People occupied Agate House about seven hundred years ago, using colorful blocks of petrified wood for building. Two of the original seven rooms have been reconstructed.

Other stops in the park lead to bizarre landscapes and a breathtaking kaleidoscope of petrified wood. At the opposite end of the park is the *Rainbow Forest Museum*, which features geological and historical exhibits including artifacts from the prehistoric residents. Behind the museum is a path through a mosaic of colors and massive logs of petrified wood. The center also has a gift shop and bookstore and issues permits for hiking in *Rainbow Forest Wilderness*, which has traces of Indian inhabitants. Trails begin in the southern half of the park at Flattops Trailhead.

Be aware that taking petrified wood, even a tiny sample, from the park is illegal. Souvenirs can be bought from one of the rock shops just outside the park and in Holbrook.

Petrified Forest National Park can be entered from I-40 at the north entrance (Painted Desert Visitor Center) or from US180 at the south entrance (Rainbow Forest Museum). The park is sometimes closed by snow in winter.

PINETOP/LAKESIDE
Map #3

Nearby: Apache County Museum, Butterfly Lodge and Museum, Casa Malpais Archaeological Park, Lyman Lake State Park
Nearby Indian Reservations: White Mountain Apache Indian Reservation

Most people visit the family-friendly towns of Pinetop and Lakeside to enjoy outdoor recreation in the pristine Apache-Sitgrave National Forest and White Mountain Apache Indian Reservation. Winter brings skiers and snowmobilers, while summer attracts hikers, mountain bikers, horseback riders, golfers, birdwatchers, and fishing enthusiasts. Over the years, Pinetop and Lakeside have merged together into one larger community. Between the two of them, you will find dozens of places to stay.

EAST OF PINETOP/LAKESIDE
The **Butterfly Lodge Museum** preserves the mountain home of author James Willard Schultz and his son Lone Wolf (Hart Merriam), who was a prolific painter and sculptor. The name of the cabin is *Apuni Oyis* in the Blackfeet language. Lone Wolf's mother was Natahki, a Blackfeet Indian, and he was raised on a reservation in Montana. James Schultz's adventure stories about the West were serialized in popular adult and children's magazines. The restored lodge is near the tiny town of Greer on AZ373 south of AZ260.

In the town of Springerville is an important archaeological site at **Casa Malpais Archaeological Park**. Casa Malpais ("House of the Badlands") is an ancient Mogollon pueblo thought to have been a major trade and ceremonial center with astronomically aligned features. The fifteen-acre site overlooks Round Valley and was occupied for about two hundred years in the thirteenth and fourteenth centuries. The pueblo, two or three stories high and with over 120 rooms, was built on a series of basalt terraces at the edge of the White Mountain Volcanic Field. Underneath are over one hundred giant cracks forming catacombs that were possibly once used as ceremonial and burial chambers. At 62 by 55 feet, the square kiva is one of the largest ever found in the United States.

The museum displays a variety of artifacts from the excavation, including a basalt stone bowl with frogs carved on the sides. The pueblo can only be visited on a 1.5-hour guided tour that leaves from the museum in downtown Springerville at 9am, 11am, and 2pm, weather permitting. The trail circles the pueblo and rectangular kiva before climbing 250 feet up a masonry staircase and past numerous petroglyphs to a scenic overlook.

The Hopi and Zuni claim a connection with Casa Malpais and are acting as consultants to the staff's archaeologists to help interpret the site. Some places are still considered sacred and remain closed.

Some prehistoric sites in **Lyman Lake State Park** are also still considered sacred ancestral homes by the Hopi people. *Rattlesnake Pointe Pueblo*, occupied by fifteen families between 1325 and 1390, once had between eighty and ninety rooms. It sits on a long ridge overlooking the rich floodplain of the Little Colorado River. The *visitor center* offers a trail guide for the short hike to the ruin, as well as seasonal ranger-led tours.

The quarter-mile *Peninsula Petroglyph Trail* leaves from the campground and passes rocks etched with ancient symbols. It requires a slight climb. The longer, steeper *Ultimate Petroglyph Trail*, on the east side of the lake, is only accessible by boat. The half-mile trail ends at a large boulder covered with petroglyphs. Seasonal ranger-led tours are available.

The park has two picnic areas, log cabin and yurt rentals, camping units with beach access, showers, RV hookup sites, paved boat ramps, and a seasonal camper supply/boat rental store. It is between Springerville and St. Johns on US180.

The **Apache County Museum** in St. Johns, 26 miles north of Springerville, has prehistoric and historic artifacts of Indian cultures, particularly those of the Little Colorado River Valley, along with other exhibits that highlight the area's past. The museum is located in the center of town.

Rattlesnakes are one of the hazards in the Southwest.

Rattlesnake

WHITE MOUNTAIN APACHE INDIAN RESERVATION
Map #4

Sites: Alchesay and Williams Creek hatcheries, Cibecue, Fort Apache Historic Park, Hawley Lake, Hon-Dah Resort and Casino, Horseshoe Lake, Kinishba Pueblo Ruins, Reservation Lake, Salt River Canyon, Sunrise Park Resort, Sunrise Lake, Whiteriver

Established in 1897 on part of the ancestral homelands of *Ndee*, "The People," the White Mountain Apache Reservation is home to many of its 12,600 enrolled members. Here tribal members have been able to successfully blend their environmental concerns with economic development. Timber operations, tourism, and livestock management generate much of the community's income.

This internationally famous sportsman's paradise of scenic mountains, savannahs, and woodlands has opportunities for camping, skiing, hiking, rafting, canyoneering, boating, and hunting small and big game, particularly elk. The 1.6-million-acre reservation has four hundred miles of mountain streams and over twenty-five stocked lakes, so fishing is also popular—some say the best in the West. Horseshoe and Hawley lakes are two of the more popular spots.

Before exploring the back roads, be aware that some places are closed to tourists. This includes the summit of sacred Mt. Baldy, where tribal members, old and young, still make spiritual pilgrimages. For an up-to-date list of available outdoor activities, and to obtain the necessary permits and licenses, contact the *Wildlife and Outdoor Recreation Division* in Whiteriver next to the White Mountain Apache Motel. Fishing permits and native guides are also available at some stores and service stations around the reservation, in particular Hon-Dah Ski & Outdoor Sports and Hon-Dah Service Station at AZ260 and AZ73, and Hawley Lake Store between Hon-Dah and Sunrise south of AZ260.

The *White Mountain Independent* newspaper and KNNB Apache Radio Broadcasting Corp at 88.1, 89.9, and 99.1 FM are sources of local news.

EAST OF US60

Three miles south of Pinetop/Lakeside at the intersection of AZ73 and AZ260 is **Hon-Dah ("Be My Guest") Resort and Casino.** The resort has a pool, hot tub, sauna, retail shops, conference center, restaurant, and 128 hotel rooms. The casino has slots, table games, and live entertainment most nights. Hon-Dah R.V. Park is across the street. A gift shop and convenience store selling permits are nearby. Hon-Dah Ski and Outdoor Sport Store is a good place to purchase permits and supplies, make arrangements for guided trips, and obtain recreation information.

East of the resort off AZ260 is **Horseshoe Lake**, a 121-acre lake open mid-May to mid-September and again in the winter for ice fishing. Facilities here sell permits and camping and fishing supplies and also rent boats.

Hawley Lake is a remote but popular spot with cabins, a small hotel and café, grocery store, boat rentals, and a marina. This is a place to get back to nature: the cabins are fully equipped with dishes, pans, and toasters but offer no phones, microwaves, or TVs. The campground has RV hookups, a dump station, and a laundromat. The 260-acre lake is open mid-May to mid-October, and fishing permits are sold here. It is past the village of McNary on AZ260, then south on AZ473.

Tribal headquarters, Fort Apache Cultural Center, Ft. Apache History Park, and Kinishba Ruins are near the town of **Whiteriver,** northeast of Pinetop/Lakeside on AZ73. Services in town include a trading post that sells Apache crafts, a motel, a restaurant, a hospital, and a shopping center. During summer months, Apache vendors erect booths along the main street to sell their beadwork, basketry, woodcarvings of the Mountain Spirits, dolls, and cradleboards. A few Apache artists also still make the unique Apache violin.

About 4 miles south of Whiteriver is **Fort Apache Historic Park**, originally established in the spring of 1870 as Camp Ord. The fort's history includes the contributions of White Mountain Apache scouts like Alchesay, who were recruited from bands of peaceful farmers to work with United States soldiers against warring Apache leaders like Geronimo and Cochise. Partly because of the scouts' service to the government, the tribe was able to keep a portion of its homeland. Over twenty buildings from the 1870s are on the self-guided tour, and guided tours can also be arranged.

Also on the fort grounds is the *Apache Cultural Center and Museum (Nohwike'Bagowa,* "House of Our Footprints"). The small museum has changing exhibits highlighting Apache history and lifestyles. Displays include military artifacts, historical photographs, and crafts, as well as tapes of early life, ancient Apache legends, and chants. The gift shop sells baskets, Crown Dance figures, beadwork, and other Apache art. Ask about guided walks through the Apache Village located just outside the museum and summer nature tours along the river. A visit to Nohwike'Bagowa also entitles you to enter the rest of the historic park and Kinishba Ruins National Historic Landmark (see below).

A short walk from the museum, in the log cabin that was once General Crook's headquarters, is the *Apache Office of Tourism.* On a hill just off the highway is a small *military*

cemetery where Apache scouts lie next to white soldiers and civilians. On January 30, 1988, Julius Colelay, the last remaining scout, was buried here.

Four miles west of Fort Apache is **Kinishba Pueblo Ruins National Historic Landmark**, once one of the largest Mogollon settlements in Arizona. Kinishba (Apache for "Brown House") was occupied from about A.D. 1232 until 1350, at which time it was abandoned, possibly because of drought. Coronado visited this two-story pueblo with between four hundred and five hundred ground floor rooms when he passed through the area. Get a leaflet and directions, check on road conditions, or arrange for a guide at the Apache Cultural Center and Museum. The pueblo is off AZ73 on gravel roads.

Apache items are displayed in the Desert Caballeros Western Museum.

Both **Alchesay and Williams Creek hatcheries**, north of Whiteriver off AZ73, have exhibits and a self-guided tour. These two fish hatcheries are used to stock the streams and lakes on the Apache reservations and those on other federally funded Arizona lands. The hatchery story starts with the arrival of eggs from as far away as Massachusetts and ends with loading the eight-inch-long fish onto specially designed trucks that inject oxygen into the cold water for the journey to the stocking point.

Further east on AZ260 is the turnoff to AZ273 south and the **Sunrise Park Resort**, the largest ski resort in Arizona. Here you'll find winter activities, as well as summer horseback riding, mountain biking, lift rides, cookouts, and RV camping. The ski area offers downhill and cross-country skiing, snowboarding, snowshoeing, snow tubing, ski tours, and snowmobiling. The resort, visited by over 250,000 skiers a year, has three peaks with over sixty-five runs geared to family skiing. Lessons, childcare services and equipment sales, rental, and repair are also available. With the resort's snowmaking abilities, the season usually runs from late November to early April, although mild winters can make this schedule slightly unreliable. The ski lift also operates during the summer for hikers.

Three miles north of the ski area is **Sunrise Lake**, 920 acres of water brimming with large rainbow trout. The marina rents boats and sells fishing permits. The 106-unit *Sunrise Park Lodge* is the closest lodge to Sunrise Park Resort. About half of its rooms overlook the lake, and its two on-site restaurants provide your best dining options in the area. *Sunrise Sports Center*, a half-mile south of the lodge, has groceries, gas, supplies, and permits. You can also rent mountain bikes and cross-country skis or sign up for snowmobile tours here.

Reservation Lake has camping, cabins, boats, groceries, tackle, gas, and permits. It is open April to November and reached off AZ260 on AZ273.

ALONG US60

North of the town of Globe, US60 and AZ77 lead along the edge of the reservation and across the **Salt River Canyon,** called by some the mini Grand Canyon. This incredible place of chasms and towering cliffs is three miles wide and 1,410 feet deep in some places. Recreation includes hiking, boating, fishing, primitive camping, and a short but dangerous raft and kayak season for experienced river-runners only. Contact the Globe Ranger Station for the required permits and information.

About 30 miles northeast of Globe and near the highway bridge crossing the Salt River is *Salt River Canyon Trading Post*. It sells supplies, gas, arts and crafts, and permits for fishing and traveling on reservation roads past the post. The nearby Salt Banks, where algae and mineral deposits from a series of salt springs have colored the rocks orange, red, and dark green, is sacred to the Apache and closed to the public.

WEST OF US60

West of US60 on CR12 is **Cibecue** ("Reddish Bottomland"), a small settlement that is home to the Cibecue Apache. The shopping center in town sells gas, food, and supplies. Two and a half miles south of town is Cibecue Creek Battlefield. In the winter of 1880–81, a Cibecue medicine man, Noch-ay-del-klinne, began preaching about a new religion, which predicted the expulsion of the whites and foreshadowed the Ghost Dance. He was killed here in 1882 by U.S. soldiers, an act that led to a general Apache uprising.

In 2003, two separate wildfires north of town combined into the Rodeo-Chediski fire to become the largest fire in Arizona history, eventually burning 467,000 acres of Fort Apache Reservation, national forest, and private land, along with hundreds of homes. Reclamation efforts have been underway since then but are still not complete.

To reach Cibecue, travel 20 miles northeast of Salt River Canyon on US60, and turn northwest onto County Road 12. Cabin and boat rentals, groceries, gas, permits, and tackle are available 8 miles north of the Cibecue turnoff from US60.

WINSLOW
Map #5

Nearby: Homolovi State Park

Mormons tried to call this place home, but they had the bad luck to settle in a spot that was prone to annual flooding. The *Winslow Visitor Center*, adjacent to I-40 off exit 253, has maps and information about the area, including Meteor Crater National Landmark, west of town off I-40. Exhibits in the center introduce the people of northeastern Arizona, and behind the building to the east is what is left of the Mormon town of Brigham City, built in 1876 and occupied for only four short years.

NORTHEAST OF WINSLOW

Homolovi State Park preserves what was once a major trade site for ancestors of the Hopi. Homolovi ("Place of the Little Hills") is still important to contemporary Hopis, and they return periodically on pilgrimages to maintain their ancestral ties to it. They also believe that the land here, including each ruin, potsherd, and petroglyph, is sacred and should be respected. Research here is ongoing, and archaeologists are cooperating with the Hopi to learn more about this ancient site and how to protect it.

Occupation of Homolovi (*ho-MOL-o-vi*) ranged between A.D. 630 and 1400, beginning with pithouse hamlets and ending with large pueblos. Four major and over three hundred other sites have been found in the park. Two of these are easily accessible to visitors. *Homolovi I* is a pueblo on a rise by the river and was possibly built on the site of an earlier pithouse. *Homolovi II* is the largest of the park's pueblos. A half-mile paved trail (wheelchair accessible) leads along the top of the mesa to the ruins. Signs interpret the rock art and describe the village of 1,200 to 2,000 rooms arranged around three plazas. Thousands of people once lived at this major trade center, which was constructed around A.D. 1330. Most of the site has not been extensively excavated, so you will be able to see what a site looks like before archaeologists reconstruct it.

Homolovi IV, on the other side of the Little Colorado River, was occupied between A.D. 1260 and 1400. It is currently closed to the public because of earthquake damage. The nearby ruins of *Homolovi III* have been buried for protection from erosion.

The *visitor center* has exhibits and information on other trails in the park. The gift shop sells traditional artwork by local Native Americans and books pertaining to the prehistory and history of the Four Corners. The shop is run by the *Arizona Archaeological Society* in Winslow, which also cooperates with the state park to provide special programs and activities that are open to the public. A sign in the parking lot directs visitors to a .8-mile round-

Ancestral Puebloans left behind pieces of pottery at Homolovi Ruins State Park

trip walk to *Sunset Cemetery*. Sunset was a Mormon settlement built here in 1876, with rocks taken from Homolovi I used for some of the construction.

A campground, open from mid-April thru mid-October, has over fifty spaces, hookups, showers, picnic tables, and grills.

Homolovi State Park is about 3 miles northeast of Winslow. Take exit 257 off I-40 onto AZ87 and follow it north 1.3 miles to the park entrance. AZ87 continues past the state park 67 miles to the Hopi Reservation through the surrealistic Little Painted Desert.

EVENTS

VARIES The White Mountain Apache Reservation has celebrations and ceremonies that are open to the public. Many of the Apache celebrations include *Mountain Spirit Dancing*, a colorful nighttime ceremony with participants dressed in splendid headdresses, skirts, and moccasins dancing to the rhythm of stick rattles and drums. Ask at motels or the tribal offices for dates of the dances, which are held frequently on summer weekends. Also look in the Fort Apache Scout newspaper. *Rodeos* are held on many weekends in the warmer months, such as the Canyon Day Rodeo. Call 928-338-4346 or 877-338-9628 (toll free) for information.

APRIL *Spring Roundup All-Indian Rodeo:* Rodeo and powwow held at Bylas, San Carlos Apache Indian Reservation.

SUMMER *Sunrise Ceremony:* Held on many summer weekends at White Mountain Apache Reservation. Contact tribal offices for specific dates and places.

JUNE *Elderfest:* Held to honor tribal elders, who come from all over Arizona to attend. Called *Shiwoye* by the Apache, it includes a barbecue, dancing, entertainment, and arts-and-crafts displays. In Whiteriver, White Mountain Apache Reservation.

Hon-Dah Powwow: Contestants come from U.S. and Canada for Fancy Dance and Grass Dance contest. Also arts/crafts and Apache Crown Dance. Held at Hon-Dah Resort in Whiteriver. Info at 928-369-7568 or www.hon-dah.com or www.azwhitemountains.net.

JULY *July 4th Celebration:* Includes a rodeo, Mountain Spirit dancing, fireworks, races, and Western dance and music. In conjunction, the Sunrise Hotel sponsors a three-day archery shoot. White Mountain Apache Reservation.

White Mountain Native American Art Festival and Indian Market: This festival brings together many of the finest artists, dancers, singers, and storytellers from numerous Southwestern tribes. Held in Pinetop/Lakeside. Call 602-367-4290 for information.

SEPTEMBER *White Mountain Apache Tribal Fair and Rodeo:* Includes Mountain Spirit Dancing and Sunrise dances, a parade, singing, dancing, queen and princess pageants, arts and crafts, a carnival, and a rodeo. Held in Whiteriver, White Mountain Apache Reservation on Labor Day weekend.

OCTOBER *Apache Days:* Celebration with dances, folk art, and food. Members of various tribes set up booths to sell their crafts and food. In Globe.

NOVEMBER *San Carlos Apache Tribal Fair:* Dances, crafts, and food are included in this fair. San Carlos Apache Indian Reservation.

Veteran's Day Fair: All-Indian rodeo, powwow, Miss San Carlos Apache Pageant, a parade, food, arts and crafts, music, and drumming. Members of tribes come from around North America to attend. In San Carlos, San Carlos Apache Indian Reservation. Call 602-475-2361 for information.

CONTACT INFORMATION

Apache County Historical Museum
180 W. Cleveland, PO Box 146, St. Johns, AZ 85936
928-337-4737
Mon-Fri 8am-4pm; no fee

Apache Trail Scenic Bryway
www.byways.org/explore_byways/2058

Arizona Archaeological Society (Homolovi Chapter)
HC63 Box 6, Winslow, AZ 86047
www.homolovi.com

Arizona State Parks
1300 W. Washington, Phoenix, AZ 85007
602-542-4174 • www.pr.state.az.us

Besh-Ba-Gowah Archaeological Park
1100 Jess Hayes Road, Globe, AZ 85501
928-425-0320
Daily 9am-5pm; fee

Bureau of Land Management
www.blm.gov/az/st/en.html
Arizona State Office
One North Central Avenue, Suite 800, Phoenix, AZ 85004
602-417-9200
Phoenix Office
21605 North Seventh Avenue, Phoenix, AZ 85027
623-580-5500
www.blm.gov/az/pfo/index.htm

Butterfly Lodge Museum
PO Box 76, Greer, AZ 85927
928-735-7514
www.wmonline.com/butterflylodge.htm
Thu-Sun 10am-5pm, Memorial Day-Labor Day; Fri-Sun 10am-5pm, Labor Day-Memorial Day; fee

Casa Malpais Archaeological Park
318 E. Main Street, Po Box 807, Springerville, AZ 85938
928-333-5375
www.centerfordesertarchaeology.org/visit/casa_malpais.php
Daily 8am-4pm museum; tours leave at 9am, 11am, and 2pm; fee

Eastern Arizona College (Gila Pueblo)
www.universities.com/On-Campus
www.Eastern_Arizona_College.html

Fort Apache Reservation (*see* White Mountain Apache Reservation)

Gila Pueblo (*See* Eastern Arizona College)

Gila County Historical Museum
1360 N. Broad Street, Globe, AZ 85501
928-425-7385
Mon-Fri 10am-4pm and Sat 11am-3pm; no fee

Globe/Miami Chamber of Commerce
1360 N. Broad St., Globe, AZ 85501
800-804-5623 or 928-425-4495
www.globemiamichamber.com
Mon-Fri 8am-5pm; Sat, Sun 10am-4pm Oct-Apr

Holbrook Chamber of Commerce
100 East Arizona St. Holbrook, AZ 86025
800-524-2459 *or* 928-524-6558
www.ci.holbrook.az.us
Mon-Fri 8am-5pm

Homolovi Ruins State Park
HCR63-Box 5, Winslow, AZ 86047
928-289-4106
www.pr.state.az.us/Parks/parkhtml/homolovi.html
Park: daily sunrise to sunset; fee
Visitor Center: daily 8:30am-5pm

Lyman Lake State Park
PO Box 1428, St. Johns, AZ 85936
928-337-4441
www.pr.state.az.us/Parks/parkhtml/lyman.html
Quiet hours 10pm-7am

Navajo County Museum
100 E. Arizona Street, Holbrook, AZ 86025
800-524-2459 *or* 928-524-6558
Mon-Fri 8am-5pm and summer Sat-Sun 8am-
4pm; donation

Petrified Forest National Park/Painted Desert
PO Box 217, Petrified Forest, AZ 86028
928-524-6228 • www.nps.gov/pefo
Daily 8am-5pm, winter; extended summer
hours; some side roads close earlier; fee

Pinetop-Lakeside Chamber of Commerce
102C West White Mountain Blvd, Lakeside, AZ
85929 *or* PO Box 4220, Pinetop, AZ 85935
800-573-4031 *or* 928-367-4290
www.pinetoplakesidechamber.com

San Carlos Apache Reservation
PO Box O, San Carlos, AZ 85550
928-475-2361
www.sancarlosapache.com/home.htm
   Apache Gold Casino Resort
   PO Box 1210, San Carlos, AZ 85550
   800-272-2438 *or* 928-475-7800
   www.apachegoldcasinoresort.com
   Apache Nation Chamber of Commerce
   PO Box 1240, San Carlos, AZ 85550
   928-475-2579
   www.sancarloapache.com/Native_Businesses.htm
   Apache Stronghold Golf Club
   PO Box 1210 San Carlos, AZ 85550
   928-475-4653
   San Carlos Apache Cultural Center
   PO Box 760, Peridot, AZ 85542
   928-475-2894
   www.sancarlosapache.com/San_Carlos_
      Culture_Center.htm
   Mon-Fri 9am-5pm

San Carlos Lake Marina
928-475-2756
San Carlos Recreation and Wildlife Division
Hwy 70, Box 97, San Carlos, AZ 85550
  888-475-2344 *or* 928-475-2343
www.sancarlosrecreationandwildlife.com
Mon-Fri 8am-4:30pm and Sat 7am-3pm

Springerville Chamber of Commerce
418 East Main, Springerville, AZ 85938
928-333-2656 • www.springerville.com

Tonto National Monument
PO Box 707 Roosevelt, AZ 85545
928-467-2241 • www.nps.gov/tont
Daily 8am-5pm (extended hours in summer),
  Lower Ruin Trail closes one hour earlier; fee

United States National Forest Service
  Tonto National Forest
  2324 East McDowell Road, Phoenix AZ
    85006
  602-225-5200 • www.fs.fed.us/r3/tonto
  Mon-Fri 8am-4:30pm
     Globe Ranger District
     7680 South Six Shooter Canyon Road,
       Globe AZ 85501
     928-402-6200
     Mesa Ranger District
     5140 East Ingram, Mesa AZ 85205
     480-610-3300
     Mon-Fri 8am-4:30pm
     Tonto Basin Ranger District
     HCO2, Box 4800, Roosevelt, AZ 85545
     928-467-3200
     Daily 7:45am-4:30pm

White Mountain Apache Tribe (Fort Apache
  Reservation)
PO Box 700, Whiteriver, AZ 85941
877-338-9628 *or* 928-338-4346
www.wmat.nsn.us
  Alchesay/Williams Creek hatcheries
  Mon-Fri 7:30-3:30
  Alchesay National Fish Hatchery
  928-338-4901
  Williams Creek National Fish Hatchery
  928-334-2346
  Apache Culture Center and Museum
    (Nohwike'Bagowa)
  PO Box 507, Fort Apache AZ 85926
  928-338-4625
  www.wmat.nsn.us/wmaculture.shtml
  www.wmat.us/wmaculture.shtml
  Mon-Sat 8am-5pm June-Aug; Mon-Fri
    8am-5pm, Sept-May; fee

Apache Office of Tourism
PO Box 710, Fort Apache, AZ85926
928-338-1230
www.wmat.nsn.us/tourism.shtml
Fort Apache Historic Park
PO Box 628, Fort Apache, AZ 85926
928-338-4625 (museum); 928-338-4525
    (recorded information)
www.wmonline.com/attract/ftapache.htm
Hawley Lake
PO Box 550, McNary, AZ 85930
928-369-1753 (Community Development
    Corporation)
928-335-7511 (store at the lake)
www.wmat.nsn.us/hawleycabins2.html
Hon-Dah Resort and Casino
777 Highway 260, Pinetop, AZ
800-929-8744 *or* 928-369-0299
RV Park: 928-369-7400
www.hon-dah.com
Hon-Dah Ski and Outdoor Sport
877-226-4868 *or* 928-369-7669
www.hon-dah.com/ski_shop.html
Horseshoe Lake
928-521-1534
Kinishba Ruins National Historic Landmark
www.cr.nps.gov/nr/travel/amsw/sw12.htm

Reservation Lake
602-338-4417
Salt River Canyon Trading Post
602-367-5126, ext. 8573
Sunrise Park Resort
PO Box 117, Greer, AZ 85927
800-772-7669 *or* 928-735-7669
www.sunriseskipark.com
White Mountain Apache Enterprises
PO Box 26, Whiteriver, AZ 85941
928-338-4967
http://wmat.us/enterprises.shtml
Wildlife and Outdoor Recreation Division
PO Box 220 Whiteriver, AZ 85941
928-338-4385
http://wmatoutdoors.org
Mon-Fri 8am-5pm (closed during lunch),
    Sat hours in summer

Winslow Visitor Center
300 West North Street, Winslow, AZ 86047
928-289-2434
www.winslowarizona.org/visiting.html
Mon-Fri 8am-5pm

METROPOLITAN PHOENIX/VALLEY OF THE SUN

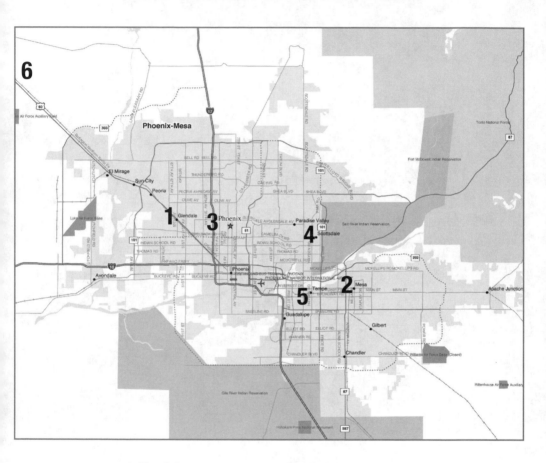

1. Glendale
2. Mesa
3. Phoenix

4. Scottsdale
5. Tempe
6. Wickenberg

CHAPTER 11

![decorative wave pattern]

METROPOLITAN PHOENIX:
VALLEY OF THE SUN

THE PHOENIX METROPOLITAN AREA is also called the "Valley of the Sun." In prehistoric times, thousands of Hohokam people farmed here, and in 1867, the remnants of their vast irrigation system inspired Jack Swilling to promote the area to homesteaders. Because the legendary Phoenix bird also rose from the ashes of its former self, the new city was named after it.

From its modest beginnings, metropolitan Phoenix has sprawled to cover four hundred square miles and include almost 4 million people. Years ago, population outgrew the local water supplies, and it is now piped to town 150 miles from the Colorado River.

Native American influence in Phoenix is broad and deep, from modern Indian communities to ancient ruins. Indian art and artifacts fill galleries and museums, and the valley is dotted with reminders of native contributions, such as the statue honoring the Navajo code talkers on the northeast corner of Central Avenue and Thomas Road or the Pima-inspired Blue Coyote Wrap available at local spas.

Learn more about Arizona territorial and state history at the Arizona State Capitol Museum, Pioneer Living History Museum, or Heritage Square. Explore the twenty-first-century at the Arizona Science Center or soak in the luxury of a world-class resort. No matter what you choose to do, your visit will almost certainly be accompanied by plenty of blue sky and sunshine.

GLENDALE & THE WEST VALLEY
Map #1

Around Town: The Bead Museum, Drumbeat Indian Arts, the Mercado
Nearby: White Tank Mountain Regional Park

The town of Glendale, northwest of downtown Phoenix, has numerous historic buildings and is one of the best places in the valley to buy antiques. **Drumbeat Indian Arts** on Clarendon Avenue has one of the largest selections of Native American tapes and records in the United States. Styles range from traditional to contemporary rock music. The store also sells Indian arts-and-crafts supplies, beaded items, musical instruments, and books. It also has a mail-order catalog. Other shopping is at the **Mercado**, a two-block area on Van Buren Street between 5th and 7th streets, which is patterned on a traditional Mexican village. Some of its specialty shops carry Native American arts and crafts.

Since as early as 30,000 B.C., beads have been used for religious expression, currency, and personal adornment. At **The Bead Museum** exhibits, educational programs, and publications tell the story of their use in cultures around the world, including in the Americas. The museum is also a source of beads and supplies for the collector and beadworker. To reach it, go west from the Glendale exit off I-17 to 58th and then drive north.

WEST OF GLENDALE

West of Glendale is **White Tank Mountain Regional Park**, where flash floods have plunged over cliffs and out of chutes to scour out depressions—called tanks—in the white granite rocks below. Water that collected in the resulting basins was probably an enticement for Hohokam people to settle here between A.D. 500 and 1100. At least seven villages were built, and petroglyphs are scattered throughout the thirty thousand acres of desert, canyons, and mountains that compose the park. You can hike, horseback ride, and enjoy the seasonal waterfall. A *visitor center* at the entrance has a few exhibits and a gift shop, as well as information about places to see *rock art*, like Petroglyph Plaza about a half-mile down Waterfall Trail. None of the forty campsites have hookups. The mountain park is west of Glendale on I-10 to AZ303 (exit 124), north on AZ303 to Olive Avenue, and west to the end of Olive Ave.

MESA
Map #2

Around Town: Mesa Southwest Museum, Park of the Canals
Nearby: Apache Trail Scenic Byway, Superstition Mountain Lost Dutchman Museum

The suburb of Mesa is just east of Phoenix. Permanent and changing exhibits at the excellent **Mesa Southwest Museum** chronicle the natural and cultural history of the area with a variety of well-presented exhibits, including animated dinosaurs (particularly popular with children), an indoor waterfall, mining displays, and a replica of a Spanish mission. The Native People's Gallery includes a Salado cliff dwelling, authentic petroglyphs, and a Hohokam village. The museum is one block north of Main in downtown Mesa. Also part of the museum is the nearby Mesa Grande, a platform mound used from about A.D. 1000 to 1400 by the Hohokam.

Park of the Canals preserves visible remnants of Hohokam canals which were later used by Mormon settlers. One fragment is by the playground, and you can walk through another near the back of the small botanical garden.

EAST OF MESA

East of Mesa is the small town of Apache Junction. Three and a half miles northeast of town is the **Superstition Mountain Lost Dutchman Museum**, dedicated to the legends of treasure hidden in the nearby Superstition Mountains. One of the most famous legends—of the Lost Dutchman Mine—claims that Spanish gold was hidden by Apache raiders and later discovered by an old German prospector named Jacob Waltz who periodically braved the local warriors to trade portions of it. The museum also has a collection of Hohokam and Salado tools, pitchers, turquoise pieces, and shell pendants.

East of Apache Junction AZ88 is the **Apache Trail Scenic Byway**. The Apache Trail was a shortcut once used by Indians to cross the Superstition Mountains. See Chapter 10, East Central Arizona, page 150, for more information.

PHOENIX
Map #3

Around Town: Deer Valley Rock Art Center, Desert Botanical Garden, Fry Bread House, Heard
Museum of Anthropology, Phoenix Art Museum, Phoenix Museum of History, Pueblo Grande
Museum and Archaeological Park, South Mountain Park, Steele Indian School Park
Nearby: Agua Fria National Monument

The *Greater Phoenix Convention and Visitors Center* in downtown Phoenix and the *Arizona Office of Tourism* on Washington Street have a wide selection of information on the entire state and a combined pass for Greater Phoenix. The *BLM office* on North 7th Avenue oversees numerous prehistoric sites around the region and also has visitor information.

Protecting over 1,500 petroglyphs etched on six hundred boulders, **Deer Valley Rock Art Center** is an educational and research facility operated by Arizona State University. An easy quarter-mile trail through volcanic rocks leads to the *Hedgepath Hills Petroglyph Site*, where over a span of thousands of years, people from the Archaic, Hohokam, and Patayan cultures etched over 1,500 petroglyphs that are still considered sacred by their descendants. The complete meaning of the glyphs may never be known. Although their design is simple, with pictures of such things as astronomical objects, humanlike figures with large fingers, spirals, and animals, among others, their meaning is considerably more complex. Some may have marked tribal migrations, while others related to traditional stories. Still others probably had spiritual significance, such as those the local Yavapai have identified as signifying the journey of the soul.

The trail to the petroglyphs is an easy well-marked quarter-mile path. Indoor exhibits include videos and an interactive computer program, while special programs provide more in-depth insight into the process of producing, preserving, and understanding the ancient images. A gift shop is on-site, and on Saturday mornings guided tours are conducted from October through April. From downtown, travel north on I-17 to Deer Valley Road (exit 217B). Take Deer Valley Road about 2.5 miles west to 35th Avenue. Continue west another half-mile, and bear right at the fork in the road to the parking lot.

A walk in the **Desert Botanical Garden** through the red-rock desert terrain that flanks the streams in Papago Park is a good way to learn more about the unique ways life has adapted to the heat and aridity of the desert. Peaceful trails here lead past over twenty thousand plants native to deserts throughout the world, and three acres are devoted exclusively to local Sonoran Desert flora and fauna. Stations to hear, smell, touch, and taste the desert plants are located along the many wheelchair-accessible paths. The paths are lit after sunset, providing an opportunity to view the night-blooming flowers. The place was

AGAVE

Agave, also called mescal or century plant, is a common plant in the Southwest with succulent or semi-succulent leaves that form rosettes. It was a major food crop for the Hohokam, and the Mescalero Apache were also highly dependent on it as a source of food, drink, and fiber.

Mescal fruit can be eaten fresh or dried, or juice extracted from it can be fermented into an agave-based liquor. Mature agaves (10 to 30 years old) are gathered for food by cutting the leaves off near their bases. This leaves a "head," which resembles a giant pineapple. The Mescalero cooked these heads in a 10- to 12-foot diameter pit oven, a hole in the ground filled with wood and flat rocks. The wood was burned, and when all that was left was hot coals, a foot or more of moist grass and twigs was laid in the pit with the mescal on top. This was then covered with a foot of earth and a fire on top of that. After baking for 12 to 24 hours, the roasted mescal was black on the outside with a pulpy white center. This center was then spread out to dry, or the roasted heads could be saved for several months as a food source. Alternatively, the heads could be further cooked to make an intoxicating beverage. Burned rock middens used in prehistoric times to prepare agave can still be found on the plateaus and in the canyons.

Agave was an important plant for the native inhabitants.

once an Indian townsite, and the one-third-mile *Plants and People of the Sonoran Desert Trail* shows how these earlier desert dwellers used the resources around them. It includes examples of Native American dwellings and gives visitors a chance to try activities like twisting agave fibers into twine and pounding mesquite beans into flour.

The *Center for Desert Living* research facility demonstrates ways to live harmoniously with the desert. Desert House shows how modern amenities make living here more comfortable, and a trail connects examples of successful landscaping and gardening in the extreme conditions of the desert. A garden shop offers plants, gifts, and books inspired by the Southwestern deserts, and an outdoor café lets you dine on a patio while enjoying the desert views. Seminars and demonstrations are scheduled periodically, so check the calendar when you visit.

Desert Botanical Garden is located on the eastern edge of Phoenix in Papago Park (Galvin Parkway and Van Buren Street) and adjacent to the popular Phoenix Zoo. March and April, when the desert blooms, are excellent times to visit.

The internationally acclaimed **Heard Museum**, housed in three locations, is one of the best in the West. Holding a collection of around 39,000 artifacts and works of art from prehistoric through modern times, this world-famous museum is an excellent place to learn about Native peoples and to purchase their traditional and contemporary art. Emphasis is on southwestern cultures.

At the main museum in downtown Phoenix, ten galleries and courtyards display stunning examples of native art. The permanent exhibit *Home: Native People in the Southwest* defines the importance of land, community, family, and language to the Indian people. It weaves the museum's most prized masterpieces, reproductions of native structures and gardens, a thirty-foot-long fence made of glass and clay, and examples of Indian poetry and thought into a tapestry of understanding. An education center, four-hundred-seat auditorium, Arcadia Farms Café, and museum shop are also on site. Permanent and changing exhibits are often interactive, and the addition of frequent arts and crafts demonstrations, weekend entertainment, and guided tours make a visit here unforgettable.

The *Heard Museum North*, in a new facility in north Scottsdale, features "Our Voices, Our Land," an audiovisual program with photography, native music, and narration by native people. Two exhibit galleries display items from the museum's vast collection, and a Native American interpretive garden showcases plants used by the indigenous people. Textiles, pottery, jewelry, and other authentic native art can be purchased at the museum shop, and Southwestern dishes can be sampled at the garden café.

At the *Heard Museum West,* "Our Stories" uses items from the Heard collections to enable members of Arizona's various Indian groups to reflect on the history and lifestyle of their people. Permanent and traveling displays, activities and educational programs, tours, and a shop selling authentic Native American jewelry and artwork are also here. It is at the intersection of Civic Center Plaza and Paradise Lane just east of the stadium in the City of Surprise.

The **Phoenix Art Museum** is one of the largest in the Southwest and covers artistic movements from the Renaissance to the present. Among its seventeen thousand pieces of art are those in the Western American Art Collection, which focuses on the history and landscape of the American West with works by famous artists such as Bierstadt, Remington, and Russell. It is located at Central Avenue and McDowell Road.

Exhibits in the **Phoenix Museum of History** span two thousand years of life in the Salt River valley and draw from a collection of nearly forty thousand items, prehistoric to modern, including Indian crafts such as baskets, pottery, and Hopi katsinas. Permanent and changing exhibits, a library, archives, and a museum shop are located in Heritage and Science Park in downtown Phoenix.

Pueblo Grande Museum and Archaeological Park is 102 acres at the site of a 1,500-year-old Hohokam ruin. Homes, storage rooms, outdoor cooking, activity areas, cemeteries, and several ball courts were all once part of the settlement here. Today, you can see a large platform mound with partially restored eight-hundred-year-old ruins on top (which may have been a ceremonial or administrative center), an excavated ball court 85 feet by 41 feet, irrigation canals, and replicas of Hohokam houses. A walk along *Ruin Trail*, a two-thirds-mile interpretive trail, leads to the top of the mound and enters *Doorways to the Past*, an authentic recreation of a prehistoric adobe compound with early pithouses and coursed-adobe homes furnished with replicas of Hohokam artifacts.

Hohokam life is highlighted with interactive exhibits and a changing gallery in the museum, which is decorated with designs from Hohokam pottery. One popular exhibit, *Dig It*, allows visitors to experience methods used by archaeologists to excavate, analyze, and use what they find. The staff tends a garden with plants the Hohokam cultivated, and the gift shop sells Native American crafts, books, and tapes. Regular educational programs and weekend guided tours are also offered. Take I-10 to AZ143, travel north to Washington Street, and turn left. The Archaeological Park is on the southeast corner of 44th Street and Washington.

Abundant evidence of native cultures has been found on the sixteen thousand acres of **South Mountain Park/Preserve**, claimed to be the largest metropolitan park in the world. You can explore this ancient hunting ground on its fifty-eight miles of hiking, biking, and riding trails. Hohokam petroglyphs can be seen on Mormon Trail, Javelina Trail, Beverly Canyon Trail, and others. Exhibits and rangers at the Environmental Education Center off the Central Avenue entrance provide information and maps. The main entrance to the park is south of downtown on Central Avenue.

Nine hundred students once attended the Phoenix Indian School, which was known for its marching bands and athletic program. After operating for ninety-nine years, it closed in 1990, graduating nineteen students in its final class. **Steele Indian School Park** preserves some of the old buildings, along with new fountains and gardens. Entering from the South Entry Garden, a spiral walkway descends through native desert plants to a tranquil fountain. At the other end of the garden, the path crosses a bridge into the "Circle of Life," a walkway that encloses the school buildings and marks the four directions with special exhibits. Poetry written by Native Americans, informative signs, a waterfall fed from a 2.5-acre bird-shaped lake, meandering walkways through desert flora, and shady ramadas make this an enjoyable place to visit. The park is at 3rd Street and Indian School Road near downtown Phoenix.

The Steele Indian School in Phoenix educated Indian students for almost a century.

When you are ready to take a break from sightseeing, stop at **Fry Bread House** on North 7th Avenue for an authentic and delectable sample of that traditional Indian mainstay. You can even order chocolate buttered fry bread for desert.

NORTH OF PHOENIX

Agua Fria National Monument contains a significant system of late prehistoric sites (at least 450 sites and four major settlement areas) dating from A.D. 1250 to 1450. Multiroomed structures, plazas, compound walls, petroglyphs, and rock alignments created to retain water runoff can all be found in this 71,000-acre monument. Other sites relate to early Euro-American settlement. A rich diversity of native plants and wildlife also reside here in the canyons, mesas, and riparian landscape, from small reptiles such as Gila monsters to large animals such as mountain lions, javelina, elk, and black bears.

Access to most of the monument is limited, and no visitor facilities exist. A four-wheel-drive vehicle is recommended. Unfortunately, even though few roads go into this undeveloped place, proximity to the Phoenix metropolitan area has meant vandals have found it. Please report any you see to the BLM Phoenix District, which is also the place to get information on visiting the remote archaeological sites, camping, hiking, and bird watching in the area. Another option is to book a day with *Archaeological Adventures* to document unexplored prehistoric sites.

Agua Fria National Monument is about 40 miles north of Phoenix off I-17. From I-17, take the dirt road at exit 256 (Badger Springs Road) to the parking area. Be sure to sign the register.

SCOTTSDALE
Map #4

Around Town: Artwalk, Heard Museum North, Native American and Environmental Learning Center, Native Trails

Nearby: Cave Creek, Fort McDowell Yavapai Nation (Asah Gweh Oou-o Eagle View RV Resort, Ft. McDowell Adventures, Radisson Fort McDowell Resort and Casino, Radisson Poco Diablo Resort, We-Ko-Pa Golf Club), River of Time Museum, Salt River Pima-Maricopa Indian Community (Casino Arizona at Salt River, Casino Arizona at Talking Stick, Cyprus Golf Course, Hoo-Hoogam Ki Museum, Salt River Recreation Area, Talking Stick Golf Club, The Pavilions), Sears-Kay Ruin

This upscale shopping mecca has over 125 *galleries and museums* and is one of the best places in the valley to find fine art. Fans of cutting-edge contemporary art can enjoy the well-regarded Scottsdale Museum of Contemporary Art, adjacent to the Scottsdale Center for the Arts. Those who admire the visionary architecture of Frank Lloyd Wright can visit Taliesin West, once his winter camp and now headquarters to the Frank Lloyd Wright Foundation and School of Architecture.

Both the novice and experienced collector of Native American fine art will find an astonishing variety of quality pieces that range from antique to contemporary. Well-known galleries include Bischoff's at the Park, John C. Hill Antique Indian Art, Old Territorial Shop, Faust Gallery, Gilbert Ortega Museum Gallery, Turkey Mountain Traders, and River Trading Post.

The Scottsdale Gallery Association sponsors a regular Thursday evening **Artwalk** that includes gallery receptions and opportunities to meet the artists. Look on their Web site for a map of galleries. Information is also available at the *Scottsdale Convention and Visitor's Bureau* in the Galleria Corporate Center.

El Pedregal Festival Marketplace, on the northern edge of Scottsdale at the corner of Scottsdale Road and Carefree Highway (adjacent to the exclusive Boulders resort in Carefree), is an exclusive shopping center of boutiques and galleries. It is also the home of the **Heard Museum North**. See the Heard Museum in Phoenix for more information.

At the Scottsdale Civic Center Mall, Native Americans from several tribes join together for musical performances that include traditional instruments and dances ranging from the intricate hoop dance to the energetic fancy dance. Native foods and arts and crafts are also available for sale. Called **Native Trails**, the shows are held January through March on most Tuesdays, Thursdays, and Saturdays from 12 noon to 1:15pm. Native Trails is sponsored by the Fort McDowell Yavapai Nation, produced by the Scottsdale Center for the Performing Arts, and is part of the town's "Culture Quest Scottsdale."

The **Native American and Environmental Learning Center** at the Hyatt Regency Scottsdale Resort has a friendly staff of native artists and educators participating in ongoing demonstrations. A sample of activities includes learning about traditional tools and weapons, sampling piki bread, or weaving. Native dancing is held on Friday evenings at 5:00pm.

NORTH OF SCOTTSDALE

The town of **Cave Creek** still maintains some of the Wild West character from its days as a gold-mining camp in the 1870s. A main attraction in town is the family-oriented Frontier Town, and several shops sell Indian crafts.

Cave Creek Museum has more about local history. The archaeology wing displays a small selection of pottery, rugs, and tools, along with trade goods and items from nearby digs. Examples from Hohokam, Yavapai, and Apache cultures are included. The reproduction of a Hohokam dwelling echoes the buildings found at nearby Sears-Kay Ruin. Ask at the desk for a brochure for visiting this ruin. In addition, the museum store sells books, gifts, and Indian arts. To reach Cave Creek Museum, take I-17 north of Phoenix to Carefree Highway (exit 223) and turn east to Cave Creek. The museum is at the corner of Basin and Skyline.

Sears-Kay Ruin is east of Cave Creek in Tonto National Forest. This forty-room Hohokam village was built around A.D. 1200, and for a century and a half it thrived as home for one hundred people. The well-preserved ruin includes five walled units, with the largest building situated on a hill and encircled by a massive stone wall. Interpretive signs provide information about the Hohokam, and the panoramic views are impressive. A fairly easy 1-mile loop trail starts from the parking lot. Facilities include toilets, picnic tables, and grills.

To reach the ruins from Cave Creek, take Cave Creek Road east from Carefree about 6 miles. At the junction with Bartlett Dam Road, bear north (left) for 2.8 miles to Sears-Kay Ruin Road. Turn east for a quarter-mile to the parking lot.

SOUTH OF SCOTTSDALE

Just south of Scottsdale is the **Salt River Pima-Maricopa Indian Community**, established in 1879 as home for the Pima (*Akimel O'odham*, meaning "River People") and Mari-

The ribs of saguaro cactus are included in the Hoo-Hoogam Ki Museum's walls at the Salt River Pima-Maricopa Indian Community.

copa (*Xalychidom Piipaash*, meaning "People who live toward the water"; also called Pee Posh). The two groups originally banded together for protection against the Yuma and Apache.

Tribal enrollment now exceeds six thousand. The community includes 53,600 acres, with 35 percent in a natural preserve and over 20 percent used for farmland and grazing of livestock. The Akimel O'odham tribal emblem is the "Man in the Maze," which symbolizes how the choices each person makes on his or her journey through life affect that person's ultimate destination.

A good place to start your visit is the *Hoo-Hoogam Ki Museum* ("House of the Ancestors") dedicated to the community's armed forces veterans. It was constructed by layering adobe and desert plants in the "sandwich" style of building, which traditionally involved a framework of cactus ribs covered with arrow weeds and adobe plaster. Museum displays include baskets, pottery, native foods, historical photographs, and other artifacts of the Akimel O'odham and Pee Posh. The museum also has authentic Akimel O'odham baskets and Pee Posh pottery for sale, as well as traditional food for breakfast and lunch. Craft demonstrations are sometimes scheduled. The museum is in the tribal complex on Osborn Road east of AZ101.

Tribal enterprises include leasing land to the *Pavilions* in Mesa, which covers 140 acres and is one of the largest shopping malls in the Southwest. They also own *Cyprus Golf Course,* with two nine-hole courses, a putting green, and driving range, and *Talking Stick Golf Club,* with thirty-six pro-designed holes and the Golf Digest Instructional School. A clubhouse, golf shop, and restaurant are also on-site. *Casino Arizona at Salt River* (Loop 101

Fields of Pima cotton are grown on the reservation.

and McKellips) and *Casino Arizona at Talking Stick* (Loop 101 and Indian Bend next to the Pavilions Shopping Center) both include restaurants, gaming, and entertainment. The complex at Talking Stick has Arizona's largest sports' bar. McKellips highlights the Show-stoppers Live, which is a musical tribute to American performers and shows a fine collection of Maricopa pottery. Native American items are for sale in the gift shop, and complementary limousine service is available.

Salt River Recreation Area provides opportunities for hiking, fishing, shoreline camping, and picnicking. Tubing is also popular on both the Salt and the Verde rivers. To reach the recreation area, take AZ87 to Fort McDowell Road, then travel south 3 miles to turnoffs leading to the Verde River.

The tribe also owns communications, light industry, and retail businesses on and off the reservation.

EAST OF SCOTTSDALE

At the **River of Time Museum** in Fountain Hills, an orientation video narrated by a modern Yavapai and shown on a water wall starts your visit to the local history displays. Exhibits focus on the geology, archaeology, and modern story of the Lower Verde Valley. There is also a gift shop. The museum is in the Fountain Hills library on the southeast corner of Avenue of the Fountains and La Montana Blvd.

Fort McDowell Yavapai Nation, formerly Fort McDowell Mojave/Apache Nation, was named for the military post founded here in 1865. It became an Indian reservation in 1890 and a community of Yavapai, Mojave, and Apache Indians in 1903. Today many of the nine hundred enrolled members live on these 24,680 acres straddling the Verde River. In addition to agriculture and construction enterprises, tourism provides employment for members of the community.

The panorama from the *Radisson Fort McDowell Resort and Casino* includes the Superstition Mountains, the Four Peaks, and Red Mountain. Native cultural heritage is emphasized throughout this four-diamond luxury resort, which has 247 rooms, a conference center, grand ballroom, water play area, large swimming pool, fitness center, and wireless Internet access. The restaurant features Native American and other Southwestern dishes, many of which are made with pecans, citrus fruit, and herbs grown at the community's Fort McDowell Farm and grilled over locally grown mesquite. The casino has live entertainment, 24-hour gambling, a restaurant, and deli. Take Beeline Highway (AZ87) to Fort McDowell Road. "Old West" programs are provided by *Fort McDowell Adventures* at the resort. Trail rides, river rides, and hayrides, as well as cattle drives and jeep tours, are conducted. Outdoor dining, cowboy games, old-fashioned photos, line dancing, and a private professional rodeo complete the experience.

Golfers rave about the award-winning *We-Ko-Pa Golf Club*, with its lush fairways and dramatic views of the surrounding desert and mountains (We-Ko-Pa means "Four Peaks"). Representations of water and fire, symbols important to the Yavapai, are incorporated into the clubhouse, which also has a golf shop, full-service restaurant, and outdoor patio. A practice facility is also available. This public golf course is next to the Radisson Resort.

Another tribally owned hotel is located off the reservation, along the banks of Oak Creek with scenic views of the red rocks of Sedona. The *Radisson Poco Diablo Resort* boasts award-winning dining, luxury rooms, a swimming pool, tennis courts, fitness center, spa, large meeting space, and a nine-hole golf course. This lush oasis is sheltered by cotton-woods and weeping willows and is located about a mile from the heart of town.

If you are traveling by recreation vehicle, you can stay at the *Asah Gweh Oou-o (Eagle View) RV Resort*, with water, hookups, cable TV, phone jacks, and Internet access for its 150 spaces. The park offers a complementary continental breakfast, a swimming pool, spa, clubhouse, library, and a free shuttle to the casino, golf club, and Fort McDowell Adventures.

Fort McDowell Yavapai reservation is about 23 miles northeast of Phoenix.

TEMPE
Map #5

Around Town: Arizona State University Museum of Anthropology, Tempe Historical Museum
Nearby: Ak-Chin Indian Community (Harrah's Ak-Chin Casino, Him-Dak Eco-Museum), Casa
Grande Ruins National Monument, Chandler Historical Museum, Gila River Indian Community (Firebird International Raceway, Gila River Indian Center and Museum, Gila River Casinos, HuHugam Heritage Center, Sheraton Wild Horse Pass Resort/Spa/Convention Center)

The town of Tempe is near the site of Pueblo de Los Muertos, a large Hohokam set-tlement more than five miles long and close to one mile wide. When Mormons founded Tempe in 1883, they used ancient Hohokam canals to irrigate their own fields.

Using items from the university's anthropology department and Deer Valley Rock Art Center, the **Arizona State University (ASU) Museum of Anthropology** explores how human beings have adapted to a changing world and expressed themselves over time. Docent-led tours are available with advance notice. The museum is on the ASU campus in the Anthropology building at the intersection of Cady Mall and Tyler Mall in Tempe. There is limited metered parking around the perimeter of the campus and a few parking garages, so be prepared to walk.

The **Tempe Historical Museum** uses artifacts and interactive exhibits to cover the prehistory and history of Tempe, beginning with the Hohokam. The museum is north of US60 on Rural Road in the Tempe Library Complex.

SOUTH OF TEMPE

Focusing on the history of central Arizona, the **Chandler Historical Museum** includes some exhibits on the Hohokam, particularly their red on buff pottery, stonework, and shell jewelry. The museum is in historic downtown Chandler. Take Chandler Blvd from I-10 east to Arizona Ave. then south to Buffalo. The museum is south of the parking garage.

The 387,000 acres of the **Gila River Indian Community**, which was established in February 1859 as the first reservation in Arizona, is home to about twelve thousand Pima (Akimel O'odham) and Maricopa (Pee Posh), a Yuman-speaking group who moved here from the Colorado River to escape warfare with the Quechan in 1825. Although the two groups speak different languages, they share many of the same customs.

Akimel O'odham women excel in making baskets, and Pee Posh women are known for pottery that is traditionally made of red clay, coiled and smoothed with wooden pad-dles, polished with a stone, blackened with mesquite pitch, and fired. Ida Red Bird, one of the most famous Pee Posh potters, was from Gila River.

Echoing the shape of a buried pot, a rounded mound of earth arcs over the HuHugam Heritage Center.

The *HuHugam Heritage Center* is dedicated to the history, culture, and language of the Akimel O'odham and Pee Posh through archaeological and ethnographical preservation and research, as well as community education. Among their artifacts is a noteworthy collection of baskets. The center complex itself is striking, built into a massive earth berm so that it resembles a giant buried pot. The heritage center also has an exhibit gallery, museum store, library and archives, ethno-botanical garden, and a ballcourt/amphitheater that is patterned after a Hohokam ball court. HuHugam is 1 mile west of I-10 off Maricopa Road (exit 164).

Twenty miles south of Phoenix at the Casa Blanca interchange (exit 175) off I-10, the *Gila River Indian Center and Museum* interprets the history and art of the Akimel O'odham and Pee Posh. Exhibits cover the history and culture of both groups and include Hohokam artifacts and a traditional Akimel O'odham dwelling. The gift shop sells outstanding Pee Posh pottery, Akimel O'odham basketry, Jemez Pueblo pottery, Zuni fetishes, and other fine arts and crafts made by native artisans from the United States and Mexico. Outside in Gila Heritage Park are examples of traditional native dwellings. The full-service restaurant has an unusual menu of Indian and American food, and weekend crafts demonstrations and performances are occasionally held. Gila River Farms, which harvests melons, vegetables, cotton, grains, and citrus on sixteen thousand acres of tribal lands, sometimes has a booth selling community-grown produce at the small museum.

The Gila River Indian Community owns several business and industrial parks, including Wild Horse Business Park next to I-10. The park features the *Sheraton Wild Horse Pass Resort/Spa/Convention Center,* which is surrounded by the Sonoran Desert, where wild horses still roam. The resort has five hundred luxury rooms with decor representing the Gila River Indian cultures. It also includes the Whirlwind Golf Club with two eighteen-hole courses, Aji Spa with a fitness center and pool, and Koli Equestrian Center, which offers riding lessons and trail rides on tribal land. Rawhide Western Town and Steakhouse is a large Western-themed attraction that stages gunfights, cookouts, and stagecoach rides. There are several dining options, including the award-winning Kai, which blends indigenous and contemporary recipes into unique dishes (reservations recommended). Water features include four pools, a waterslide inspired by the Casa Grande Ruins, and a 2.5-mile replica of the Gila River complete with boat rides ferrying guests to the golf club and nearby Wild Horse Pass Casino.

Flowers and desert plants edge the curved path to a quiet courtyard at the Gila River Indian Center and Museum.

Three *Gila River Casinos* are owned by the tribe: the 24-hour Lone Butte is 1 mile south of Chandler Blvd on 56th Street, Vee Quiva is 15 miles south of I-10 on 51st Ave, and Wild Horse Pass is next to the Sheraton Resort.

Firebird International Raceway is a motor-sport park that hosts a variety of race competitions on four race circuits, a quarter-mile drag strip, and a lake for powerboat races. A professional driving school is also here. The facility is off I-10 between exits 152 and 164.

Headquarters for the Gila River Indian Community is in Sacaton south of Phoenix off I-10 at exit 175. In the center of town is a monument honoring Mathew B. Juan, the first Arizonan and the first Native American to die in World War I.

Around 645 Tohono O'odham and Akimel O'odham make their home in the 28,848-acre **Ak-Chin Indian Community**. The name means "place where the wash loses itself in the sand or ground" and refers to traditional planting at the base of a slope to receive runoff from seasonal rain and melting snow. Farming is still a major source of tribal income, with fifteen thousand acres devoted to growing cotton and other crops. Look for copies of the tribal newspaper, the *Ak-Chin O'odham Runner*, or listen to KOHN 91.9 FM, called the voice of the Tohono O'odham Nation, for a greater understanding of their modern lifestyle.

By promoting communication between the generations, the *Him-Dak* ["way of life"] *Eco-Museum* seeks to pass on the old ways and to protect archaeological resources on the reservation. This nontraditional museum encourages community members to contribute items and ideas for exhibits, so the eclectic displays can range from T-shirts commemorating past celebrations to children's artwork. Displays of local art and tribal history are also included.

In addition to gambling, *Harrah's Ak-Chin Casino* offers entertainment and dining options. Adjacent to the casino is a conference center with lodging, a garden courtyard enclosing a large pool, a fitness center, and a gift shop offering Native American and Southwestern art. Golf packages enable guests to use the nearby Duke at Rancho El Dorado course.

The Ak-Chin community is about 35 miles south of Phoenix in the Sonoran Desert. Take AZ347 from I-10 at exit 164.

Massive portions of a Hohokam complex rising three stories high are protected at Casa Grande National Monument.

Casa Grande Ruins National Monument, the nation's first archaeological preserve, protects a large Hohokam complex inhabited from about 1200 to the mid-1400s. Partly because its caliche (*cuh-LEE-chee*) mud walls hardened like concrete, it contains some of the best-preserved prehistoric ruins in southern Arizona.

The monument has over sixty sites, including a walled ball court and the three-story Casa Grande, which once looked out over terraced fields and an extensive canal system covering over eighty-five miles. At thirty-five feet tall, this is the largest known Hohokam building. Questions remain over what it was used for and why it was abandoned, but one theory is that the "great house" was an astronomical observatory. Look in the upper left of the west wall for the circular window that on the summer solstice aligns with the setting sun.

You can easily explore the Casa Grande compound along a three-hundred-yard self-guided trail. The other compounds and buildings in this community of three to five thousand people covered a full square mile. You can view the ball court and platform mounds from the picnic area in front of the museum. The museum has excellent displays about Hohokam lifestyle, farming techniques, and trade networks.

Casa Grande is at the north edge of Coolidge at the junction of AZ287 and AZ87. Signs lead to the entrance.

WICKENBURG
Map #6

Around Town: Desert Caballeros Western Museum
Nearby: Hassayampa River Preserve

North of Phoenix on US60 is the town of Wickenburg, which has preserved its image as a Wild West town since it was founded in 1863. Several historic buildings can be seen on the town's walking tour. Next to the only traffic light in the town is the **Desert Caballeros Western Museum**, with an extensive collection of Western art and well-done period rooms and historic street scenes. Albert Bierstadt, Charles Russell, Maynard Dixon, and Frederick Remington are some of the more famous of the "cowboy" artists represented. The Native American Room has thoughtfully arranged displays of Hopi katsinas and weavings, Gan Dancer dolls, Maria Martinez pottery, Akimel O'odham and Apache baskets, Mogollon shell inlay, and other items from pre-Columbian to modern Southwestern Indian cultures. Books, art prints, and other items are for sale in the gift shop.

SOUTHEAST OF WICKENBERG

One of Arizona's most important bird-watching sites is 3 miles southeast of town at the Nature Conservancy's **Hassayampa River Preserve**. Here a five-mile section of the Hassayampa River (Apache for "river that runs upside down") reemerges from its hundred-mile journey under the desert floor to create a unique desert oasis. It is one of the few places where you can still see the Sonoran Desert's riparian life-zone that once supported thousands of indigenous people. Experiencing the spring-fed marshes of Palm Lake, lush riverbanks, dense mesquite bosques, and cottonwood-willow forests makes it easier to imagine the bounty this life-zone offered to native people.

Nature trails wind through the 660-acre preserve, which protects javelina, peccary, bobcat, mule deer, and over 280 species of birds that nest or rest here during their migrations. In the 1860s ranch house, the *visitor center* has interactive displays that interpret the unique plants and animals living here. Guided walks are also scheduled. The entrance to Hassayampa Nature Preserve is 3 miles southeast of Wickenburg on the west side of US60 just north of mile marker 114.

At the Hassayampa River Preserve, a riparian oasis is created where the river's channel emerges briefly from under the desert floor.

EVENTS

For a current listing of area events, check *Phoenix Metro* magazine, available at newsstands. Also check for special events at places like the Heard Museum and Deer Valley Rock Art Center.

The *Pima/Maricopa Basket Dancers* perform social dances and spiritual rituals throughout the year. For information about these and other events open to the public, contact their community relations department at 480-850-8056.

MONTHLY *Native American Jewelry Show:* Held at the Radisson Fort McDowell Resort on the third weekend of each month.

JANUARY-MARCH *Native Trails:* Traditional music and dancing, cultural talks, and arts/crafts sale. Sponsored by Ft. McDowell Yavapai Nation and produced by Scottsdale Center for the Performing Arts. Held most Tuesdays, Thursdays, and Saturdays from 12 noon to 1:15 pm at Scottsdale Civic Center Mall. Contact 480-421-1004, or visit www.culturequestscottsdale.com or www.sccarts.org/culture_quest.php.

JANUARY *Gila River Mul-Chu-Tha (Gathering of the People) Fair:* Rodeo, parade, art exhibits and sales, Basket and Rain dances, crafts demonstrations, and food. Held in late January or early February in Sacaton, Gila River Indian Community.

Indian Artists of America: Live and silent auctions of Indian art, from traditional to avant-garde. Held at Rawhide Western Town and Steakhouse at Wild Horse Pass, Gila River Indian Community.

Spring Round-Up Rodeo: Bull riding, roping, barrel racing, and other rodeo events. Fort McDowell Yavapai Reservation.

FEBRUARY *O'odham Tash:* One of the largest intertribal events in the country, this celebration consists of four days of dancing, an all-Indian rodeo, parade, barbeque, beauty pageant, and arts/crafts exhibits and sales. Chicken scratch dancing, a modern dance performed by the Tohono O'odham, can be seen, as well as "taka," traditional Indian field hockey, played between O'odhams and Paiutes. Held on President's Day weekend. Call 520-836-4723 or Casa Grande Chamber of Commerce at 520-836-2125.

World Championship Hoop Dance Contest: Top dancers from around the U.S. and Canada compete in this colorful event of precision and skill. Call the Heard Museum at 602-252-8848 or visit www.heard.org.

MARCH *Gila River Arts and Crafts Center Celebration:* Indian dances and arts and crafts demonstrations and sales. Third weekend in March at Gila River Indian Center.

Heard Museum Guild Indian Fair and Market: Traditional and contemporary Native American entertainment and dancing, demonstrations, Indian food, and extensive selection of authentic art and crafts. Hundreds of the finest Native American artists exhibit at Arizona's largest Indian market. First weekend in March at the Heard Museum in Phoenix, 602-252-8840, www.heard.org.

Morningstar Celebration of the American Indian: Includes the annual World Dance Championships and Arts Festival, a powwow, fine art gallery and sale, cultural dance and artist demonstrations, children's activities, storytelling, and Indian food. Held at Arizona Veteran's Memorial Coliseum in Phoenix, sponsored by Amerindian. Call 602-396-3333.

Native American Fine Arts Show: Juried art show and sale. Held at the Radisson Fort McDowell Resort.

St. John's Indian Fair: Dance performances, handcrafted items, and an Indian barbeque. First Sunday in March at Indian Mission School, Gila River Indian Community. Call 602-550-2400.

APRIL *Scottsdale All-Indian Days Annual Powwow:* Members from over fifty United States and Canadian tribes gather to dance and sell their arts/crafts. Call 602-230-3399.

MAY *Sovereignty Day:* Commemorates the three-week standoff between the Fort McDowell Yavapai and the state of Arizona over the tribe's gaming operation. Includes a four-mile walk to the casino from the Recreation Center, lunch, and public presentation. Held at Fort McDowell.

AUGUST *Gathering of the Pais:* Yuman-speaking people join for a pageant of Pai women demonstrating traditional talents and with traditional dress. Includes Ft. McDowell Yavapai, Yavapai-Prescott, Yavapai-Apache, Havasuapai, Hualapai, Pai-Pai (Mexico). Held in Supai.

OCTOBER *Arizona State Fair:* Headline entertainment, midway and carnival, concerts, 4-H exhibits, all-Indian rodeo, ethnic food, and cooking contests. Held mid-October through mid-November at State Fairgrounds in Phoenix. 602-252-6771, www.azstatefair.com.

St. Francis Church Feast Day: Honors St. Francis with traditional dancing and Indian food, such as chili, tortillas, and fry bread. Held on October 4 at the Ak-Chin Reservation.

NOVEMBER *Arizona State Fair:* See October listing.

Gila River Artists Market: Artwork for sale by tribal artists. Held at the Sheraton Wild Horse Pass Resort.

Gila River Christmas Sale and Fair: Arts and crafts sale, dance performances, children's activities, and a raffle. Late November at Gila River Indian Community Arts and Crafts Center.

Orme Dam Celebration: All-Indian rodeo, parade, and cultural performances to commemorate the defeat of a proposed dam that would have flooded the Fort McDowell Yavapai tribal homelands. Held at Yavapai Village on Fort McDowell Yavapai Reservation.

Pima Maricopa Arts Festival: Sale of works by Pima and Maricopa artists. Held first Saturday in November at Gila Indian Center, Gila River Indian Community.

DECEMBER *Fiesta Bowl Parade:* The parade for the annual Fiesta Bowl football game is sponsored by the Ft. McDowell Yavapai Nation. Hundreds of thousands of people line the streets of Phoenix to watch the parade, making it the largest single-day spectator event in Arizona.

Pueblo Grande Museum Indian Market: Rated one of the ten best markets in the U.S. Authentic art and jewelry can be bought directly from the over 450 artisans from dozens of tribes. Traditional dances, music, and food. Held second weekend in December at Steele Indian School in Phoenix, sponsored by Park Pueblo Grande Museum. Call 877-706-4408 or 602-495-0901 or visit www.pmarket.org or www.pueblogrande.com.

CONTACT INFORMATION

Agua Fria National Monument
(*see* BLM Phoenix Office)
www.blm.gov/az/aguafria/pmesa.htm

Ak-Chin Indian Community
42507 W. Peters and Nall Road, Maricopa, AZ 85239
520-568-2227
www.ak-chin.nsn.us/main.html
  Harrah's Ak-Chin Casino
  15406 Maricopa Road, Maricopa, AZ 85239
  800-427-7247 *or* 480-802-5000
  888-302-2765 for golf getaway
  www.harrahs.com/our_casinos/akc/index.html
  Him-Dak Eco Museum and Archive
  47685 N. Eco Museum Road, Maricopa, AZ 85239
  520-568-1350 *or* 520-568-9480
  Mon-Fri 9am-5pm; Sat by appointment

Archaeological Adventures
623-465-1981
www.archaeologicadventures.com

Arizona Office of Tourism
1110 W. Washington Street, Suite 155, Phoenix, Arizona 85007
866-275-5816 *or* 602-364-3700 (administration)
www.arizonaguide.com
www.ArizonaVacationValues.com (special discounts)
Mon-Fri 8am-5pm

Arizona State Fairgrounds
1826 W. McDowell, Phoenix, AZ 85007
602-252-6771 • www.azstatefair.com

Arizona State Parks
1300 W. Washington, Phoenix, AZ 85007
602-542-4174 • www.pr.state.az.us

Arizona State University (ASU) Museum of Anthropology
ASU Museum of Anthropology, Tempe, AZ 85287
480-965-6224
www.asu.edu/clas/shesc/asuma
Mon-Fri 11am-3pm during school year; appt only summer/winter sessions; no fee

Bead Museum
5754 W. Glen Drive, Glendale, AZ 85301
623-931-2737 *or* 623-930-7395
www.beadmuseumaz.org
Mon-Sat 10am-5pm; Thur 10am-8pm; Sun
11am-4pm; fee

Bureau of Land Management
www.blm.gov/az/st/en.html
   Arizona State Office
   One North Central Avenue, Suite 800,
      Phoenix, AZ 85004
   602-417-9200
   Mon-Fri, 9am-4pm
   Phoenix Field Office
   21605 North 7th Avenue, Phoenix 85027
   623-580-5500

Casa Grande Ruins National Monument
1100 Ruins Drive, Coolidge, AZ 85228
520-723-3172 • www.nps.gov/cagr
Daily 8am-5pm, hourly tours begin 9:15am; fee

Cave Creek Museum
6140 Skyline Road, Cave Creek, AZ 85327
480-488-2764 • www.cavecreekmuseum.org
Wed-Sun 1pm-4:30pm, opens at 10am on Fri,
Oct-May; fee

Chandler Historical Museum
178 E. Commonwealth Ave. Chandler, AZ 85225
480-782-2717 • www.chandlermuseum.org
Mon-Sat 11am-4pm; no fee

Deer Valley Rock Art Center
3711 West Deer Valley Road, Phoenix, AZ 85308
623-582-8007
www.asu.edu/clas/shesc/dvrac
Tue-Sat 9am-5pm & Sun 12pm-5pm, Oct-
Apr; Tue-Fri 8am-2pm, Sat 9am-5pm &
Sun 12pm-5pm, May-Sep; fee

Desert Botanical Garden
1201 N. Galvin Parkway (at Papago Park),
Phoenix, AZ 85008
480-941-1225
recorded information 480-481-8190
www.dbg.org
Daily 7am-8pm, May-Sept; daily 8am-8pm,
Oct-Apr (some early closings in Sept, Nov
& Dec); fee

Desert Caballeros Western Museum
21 N. Frontier St, Wickenburg, AZ 85390
928-684-2272 • www.westernmuseum.org
Mon-Sat 10am-5pm; Sun noon-4pm; fee

Drumbeat Indian Arts
4143 North Sixteenth Street, Glendale, AZ 85311
800-895-4859 *or* 602-266-4823
www.drumbeatindianarts.com

**Fort McDowell Yavapai Nation (formerly Fort
McDowell Mojave-Apache Nation)**
PO Box 17779, Fountain Hills, AZ 85269
480-837-5121 • www.ftmcdowell.org
   Asah Gweh Oou-o (Eagle View) RV Resort
   9605 N. Fort McDowell Road, Fort
      McDowell, AZ 85264
   480-836-5310
   www.eagleviewrvresort.com
   Fort McDowell Adventures
   14803 Hiawatha Hood Road, Fountain
      Hills, AZ 85269-7597
   480-816-6465
   www.fortmcdowelladventures.com
   Fort McDowell Casino
   Fort McDowell Road, Fountain Hills, AZ
      85304
   800-843-3678 *or* 480-837-1424
   www.fortmcdowellcasino.com
   Fort McDowell Farm
   18002 North Mustang Way, Fort
      McDowell, AZ 85264
   480-837-2585
   Radisson Poco Diablo Resort
   1752 S. Highway 179, Sedona, AZ 86336
   800-333-3333 *or* 928-282-7333
   www.radisson.com/sedonaaz
   **Radisson Resort and Casino at Fort
      McDowell**
   10438 N. Fort McDowell Rd.,
      Scottsdale/Fountain Hills, AZ 85264
   800-715-0328 or 480-789-5300 (direct
      hotel reservations)
   www.radissonfortmcdowellresort.com
   800-333-3333 (Radisson reservations)
   www.radisson.com/ftmcdowellaz
   Tourism Office
   480-816-7108
   We-Ko-Pa Golf Club
   18200 East Toh Vee Circle, Fort
      McDowell, AZ 85264
   480-836-9000 • www.wekopa.com

Fry Bread House
4140 N. Seventh Avenue, Phoenix, AZ 85013
602-351-2345
Mon-Thurs 10am-7pm & Fri-Sat 10am-8pm

Gila River Indian Community
315 West Casa Blanca Road, Sacaton, 85247
520-562-6030
www.gric.nsn.us/newdirection
www.gilarivertourism.com
    Firebird International Raceway
    20000 Maricopa Road, Chandler, AZ 85226
    602-268-0200 • www.firebirdraceway.com
    Gila River Casinos
    5550 Wild Horse Pass Road, Chandler, AZ
      85246
    800-946-4452 • www.wingilariver.com
    Gila River Indian Center and Museum
    PO Box 457, Sacaton, AZ 85247
    480-963-3981
    Daily 8am-5pm; no fee
    Huhugam Heritage Center
    4759 N. Maricopa Road, Chandler, AZ
      85226
    520-796-3500 • www.huhugam.com
    Wed-Fri 10am-4pm; fee
    Koli Equestrian Center
    6940 North Broken Ear Road, Chandler,
      AZ 85226
    602-565-4422 *or* 602-361-6102
    www.chuckstrailriding.com
    Rawhide Western Town and Steakhouse
    5700 West North Loop Road, Chandler,
      AZ 85226
    800-527-1880 *or* 480-502-5600
    www.rawhide.com
    Sun-Thurs 5-9pm, Fri-Sat 5-10pm, June-
      Sept; Mon-Thur 5-10pm, Fri-Sun
      11am-10pm, rest of year; no fee
    Sheraton Wild Horse Pass Resort and Spa
    5594 West Wild Horse Pass Boulevard,
      Chandler, AZ 85226
    602-225-0100
    www.wildhorsepassresort.com
        Aji Spa
        602-385-5759
        www.wildhorsepassresort.com/
          spa-wild-horse-pass.html
        Kai Restaurant
        602-225-0100 (reservations)
    Whirlwind Golf Club
    5692 North Loop Road, Chandler, AZ 85226
    480-940-1500
    www.wildhorsepassresort.com/golf.html

Glendale Visitor Center
5800 W Glendale Drive, Suite 140, Glendale,
    AZ 85301
877-800-2601 (toll free) *or* 623-930-4500
www.visitglendale.com
Mon-Sat 10am-5pm

Greater Phoenix Convention and Visitors Bureau
www.visitphoenix.com
    Downtown Visitor Information Center
    50 N. Second Street (Second & Adams
      Streets), Phoenix, AZ 85004
    602-254-6500
    Mon-Fri 8am-5pm
    Biltmore Visitor Information Center
    2404 E. Camelback Road, #100E (Camel
      back Rd & 24th Street)
    877-225-5749

Hassayampa River Preserve
49614 Hwy 60, Wickenburg, AZ 85390
928-684-2772 • http://nature.org/arizona
Fri-Sun 8am-5pm (trails close at 4:30am), mid
    May-mid Sept; Wed-Sun 8am-5pm (trails
    close at 4:30), rest of the year; fee

Heard Museum
2301 N. Central Avenue, Phoenix, AZ 85004
602-252-8848; 602-252-8840 (administra-
    tion); 602-252-8344 (shop/bookstore)
www.heard.org
Daily 9:30am-5pm; fee
    Heard Museum North
    32633 N. Scottsdale Road, Scottsdale, AZ
      85262
    480-488-9817
    Mon-Sat 10am-5pm and Sun noon-
      5pm; fee
    Heard Museum West
    16126 N. Civic Center Plaza, Surprise, AZ
      85374
    623-344-2200
    Thurs-Sat 10am-5pm, May-Sept.; Tues-
      Sun, 9:30am-5pm, Oct-Apr; fee

Mesa Convention and Visitor Bureau
120 N Center Street, Mesa, AZ 85201
480-827-4700 • www.mesacvb.com

Mesa Southwest Museum
53 North MacDonald Street, Mesa, AZ 85201
480-644-2230
www.city ofmesa.org/swmuseum
Tue-Fri 10am-3pm, Sat 11am-5pm, Sun 1pm-
    5pm; fee

**Native American and Environmental Learning
    Center**
Hyatt Regency Scottsdale Resort and Spa at
    Gainey Ranch
7500 E. Doubletree Ranch Road, Scottsdale,
    AZ, 85258
480-444-1234, ext 5806
http://scottsdale.hyatt.com/hyatt/hotels/index.jsp

Native Trails
480-421-1004 (culture quest)
www.culturequestscottsdale.com
Tues, Thurs, & Sat 1:30pm, Jan-March

Park of the Canals
1710 N. Home Road, Mesa, AZ 85203
480-644-4705 (Mesa Parks and Recreation)
Sunrise to sunset

Phoenix Art Museum
1625 N Central Avenue, Phoenix, AZ 85004
602-257-1222 (recording) • www.phxart.org
Tues 10am-9pm, Wed-Sun 10am-5pm; fee

Phoenix Museum of History
105 North 5th Street, Phoenix, Arizona 85004
602-253-2734 ext 221 • www.pmoh.org
Tue-Sat 10am-5pm; fee

**Pueblo Grande Museum and Archaeological
  Park**
4619 E. Washington, Phoenix, AZ 85034
877-706-4408 or 602-495-0901;
   602-495-0900 (recording)
www.pueblogrande.com
Mon-Sat 9am-4:45pm, Sun 1pm-4:45pm; fee

Radisson Poco Diablo Resort
1752 S. Highway 179, Sedona, AZ 86336
800-333-3333 or 928-282-7333
www.radisson.com/sedonaaz

River of Time Museum
12901 N. La Montana Blvd, Fountain Hills,
  AZ 852612
480-837-2612 • www.riveroftimemuseum.org
Wed-Sun 1pm-4pm, Sept-May; Fri-Sun 1pm-
  4pm, June-Aug; fee

Salt River Pima-Maricopa Indian Community
10005 E. Osborn Rd, Scottsdale, AZ 85256
480-850-8000
www.saltriver.pima-maricopa.nsn.us
   Casino Arizona
   480-850-7734 • www.casinoaz.com
      Casino Arizona at Salt River
      524 North 92nd, Scottsdale, AZ 85256
      480-850-7777
      Showstoppers Live: 480-850-7734
      Casino Arizona at Talking Stick
      9700 East Indian Bend Road,
      Scottsdale, AZ 85256
      480-850-7777
      Limousine service
      480-850-7790

Community Relations Department
480-850-8056
Cyprus Golf Course
10801 East McDowell Road, Scottsdale,
  AZ 85256
480-946-5155
Hoo-Hoogam Ki Museum
10005 East Osborn Road, Scottsdale AZ
  85256
480-850-8190
Mon-Fri 9:30am-4:30pm, Sat 10am-1pm
(Oct-May only); no fee
Talking Stick Golf Course
9998 East Indian Bend Road, Scottsdale,
  AZ 85256
480-860-2221
www.talkingstickgolfclub.com

Scottsdale Convention and Visitors Bureau
4343 N. Scottsdale Road, Suite 170, Scottsdale, AZ 85251
800-782-1117 or 480-421-1004
www.scottsdalecvb.com, www.culture
  questscottsdale.com
Mon-Fri 8am-5pm

Scottsdale Gallery Association
7145 E. 1st Street, Scottsdale, AZ 85251
480-990-3939 recording
www.scottsdalegalleries.com

Sears-Kay Ruin (See Tonto National
  Forest/Cave Creek Ranger Station)

Show Up Now
Online pass for admission to fifteen museums
  in the greater Phoenix area
www.showupnowpass.com

South Mountain Park/Preserve
10919 South Central Avenue, Phoenix, AZ 85042
www.ci.phoenix.az.us/PARKS/hikesoth.html
   Environmental Education Center
   602-534-6324
   Wed-Sat 8am-2pm & Sun 8am-1pm, May-
      Sept; Wed-Sat 9am-3pm & Sun 9am-
      2pm, Oct-Apr

Steele Indian School Park
300 E. Indian School Road, Phoenix, AZ 85012
602-495-0739
http://phoenix.gov/PARKS/sisp.html
Daily 6am-10pm; no fee

Superstition Mountain Lost Dutchman Museum
4087 North Apache Trail, Apache Junction, AZ 85219
480-983-4888
www.superstitionmountainmuseum.org
Daily 9am-4pm; fee

Tempe Historical Museum
809 E. Southern Ave, Tempe, AZ 85282
480-350-5100 • www.tempe.gov/museum
Mon-Thurs 10am-5pm, Sat 10am-5pm, Sun 1-5pm; no fee

Tempe Convention and Visitors Bureau
51 W 3rd Street, #105, Tempe, AZ 85281
480-894-8158 • www.tempecvb.com

Tonto National Monument
PO Box 707, Roosevelt, AZ 85545
928-467-2241 • www.nps.gov/tont
Daily 8am-5pm (extended summer hours); Lower Ruin Trail closes one hour earlier; fee

United States National Forest Service
Tonto National Forest
2324 East McDowell Road, Phoenix AZ 85006
602-225-5200 • www.fs.fed.us/r3/tonto
Mon-Fri 8am-4:30pm
Cave Creek Ranger District (Sears Kay Ruin)
40202 N. Cave Creek, Scottsdale, AZ 85262
480-595-3300
Mesa Ranger District
5140 East Ingram, Mesa AZ 85205
480-610-3300
Mon-Fri 8am-4:30pm
Tonto Basin Ranger District
HCO2, Box 4800, Roosevelt, AZ 85545
928-467-3200
Daily 7:45am-4:30pm

White Tank Mountain Regional Park
13025 N. White Tank Mountain Road, Waddell, AZ 85355
623-935-2505
www.maricopa.gov/parks/white_tank
Sun-Thu 6am-8pm, Fri-Sat 6am-10pm; fee

Wickenburg Chamber of Commerce
216 N. Frontier Street, Wickenburg, AZ 85390
928-684-5479
www.outwickenburgway.com
Mon-Fri 9am-5pm & Sat-Sun 10am-3pm

SOUTHERN ARIZONA

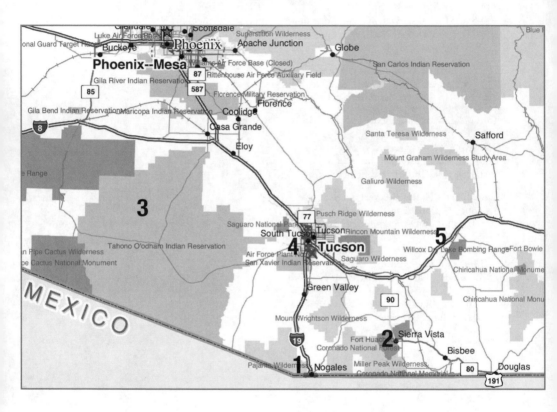

1. Nogales
2. Sierra Vista
3. Tohono O'odham Nation

4. Tucson
5. Willcox

CHAPTER 12

‍〰〰〰〰〰‍

SOUTHERN ARIZONA

NOGALES
MAP #1

Around Town: Pimeria Alta Historical Society Museum
Nearby: Tubac, Tubac Presidio State Historic Park, Tumacacori National Historical Park

Nogales, Arizona, is a pleasant city that sits in Nogales Pass at the southern end of I-19 and just across the border from the Mexican town of Nogales. The name is Spanish and refers to the numerous walnut trees that once grew in the mountain pass.

The O'odham refer to Nogales as "No-wa:l." They and other indigenous peoples used Nogales Pass as a trade and migration route and for access to the Gulf of California. In the late seventeenth and early eighteenth centuries, Father Eusebio Kino followed the pass between what is now northern Sonora in Mexico and southern Arizona to establish a string of Jesuit missions. He called the area *Pimeria Alta*, referring to the Indians who lived here.

Pimeria Alta Historical Society Museum, in the former city hall, focuses on southern Arizona and northern Mexico from the Hohokam to modern times. The small museum has Native American artifacts, early household items, historical photographs, and a research library with numerous publications about regional history.

The *Nogales/Santa Cruz County Chamber of Commerce* can help with accommodations if you wish to further explore the area once defended by the Apache or if you want to cross the border to visit Mexico.

NORTH OF NOGALES

Tumacacori National Historical Park is off I-19 at exit 29. This was once the hub of Pimeria Alta during Spanish colonial days. The remains of three missions (Tumacacori, Calabazas, and Guevavi) are preserved here, although only the church at Tumacacori is currently open to the public on a regular basis. Its massive adobe walls, bell tower, and domed sanctuary remain essentially intact.

Some of the 90,000 adobe bricks used to build the early 19th century mission are still in place at Tumacacori National Historical Park.

A self-guided walk leads through the well-preserved ruins of the church and adjoining *convento* where the priests lived. The garden is planted with herbs, flowers, and trees typically found at Spanish missions in Arizona, and exhibits and dioramas at the *visitor center* tell the story of life at the mission for the Indians and Spaniards. Books and videos are for sale, and on weekends local Native Americans and Mexicans provide crafts demonstrations. The other two mission units can be visited during a reserved monthly tour.

Three miles north of Tumacacori is the town of **Tubac**, a well-known artist colony. The *Village* shopping area has galleries and working art studios, some of which offer quality Native American arts and crafts.

People have lived in the vicinity of **Tubac Presidio State Historic Park** for thousands of years. The Hohokam may have been here as early as 300 B.C. They were followed by the Akimel O'odham and Tohono O'odham in the 1500s. A small Akimel O'odham village existed at this site in 1691, when Father Eusebio Francisco Kino established nearby Tumacacori Mission and Tubac became a Spanish mission farm/ranch (*visita*). During the 1751 Great Pima Revolt, the Indians destroyed the Tubac settlement, but in 1752 the Spanish returned to establish a presidio. The military abandoned the presidio in 1776, and the settlement again collapsed under the force of Apache raids. Subsequent resettlement and abandonment continued into the nineteenth century.

Today the park protects the ruins of the presidio. The original adobe foundation, walls, and plaza floor can be seen in an underground exhibit. Interpretive exhibits also tell the story of the area's Native Americans, and Spanish colonial living history enactments occur from October to March on Sunday afternoons. The park is off I-19 at exit 34.

Tumacacori was a hub of activity during the time when Spanish padres came to Pimeria Alta to establish missions among Indians they called "Pima."

SIERRA VISTA
MAP #2

Nearby: Amerind Foundation Museum, Chiricahua National Monument, Cochise Stronghold, Coronado National Memorial, Fort Huachuca, San Pedro Riparian National Conservation Area

The small city of Sierra Vista sits at the junction of AZ90 and AZ92 at an elevation of 4,650 feet, which provides it with one of the most comfortable climates you'll find in southern Arizona. The nearby San Pedro National Conservation Area and Ramsey Canyon Preserve make this a popular place for birders. The town is also a good base for exploring the popular Kartchner Caverns State Park about 25 miles north of town and the Wild West and mining histories of nearby Tombstone and Bisbee. For more information, contact the *Sierra Vista Convention and Visitors Bureau*, off Coronado Drive on Tacoma Street in the northeast part of town. The center also sells books and maps of southern Arizona.

SOUTH OF SIERRA VISTA

Close to the border with Mexico is **Coronado National Memorial**, near where Francisco Vasquez de Coronado passed on his quest for the legendary Seven Cities of Gold. The goal of the five-thousand-acre memorial is not to preserve artifacts from his expedition but to encourage contemplation about the cultural interactions and changes to the land that resulted from his sixteenth-century journey. The *visitor center* has a video, artwork, photographs, and interpretive text, plus examples of Spanish colonial armor and clothing to try on. A short hike outside the center leads three-quarters of a mile to *Coronado Cave*, which you can explore with a permit. A drive up *Memorial Pass* will reward you with an expansive view of the mountains (including Baboquivari Peak on the O'odham Reservation 80 miles away), valleys, the San Pedro River, and Sonora, Mexico. The memorial has other hiking trails and picnic tables, but no camping is allowed. The memorial is 20 miles south of town on AZ92, and then about 5 miles to the visitor center.

EAST OF SIERRA VISTA

Apache and Clovis people once lived in what is now the BLM's **San Pedro Riparian National Conservation Area.** Willow, cottonwood, and other river vegetation still grow here along one of the last free-flowing rivers in the Southwest. The conservation area, which is one of the richest wildlife areas in the country, stretches about forty miles south to the Mexican border in a one-to-three mile swath, providing support for over four hundred bird, eighty mammal, and forty-five reptile and amphibian species. Day-use and primitive backcountry camping are allowed.

The valley also holds evidence of ancient cultures, including *Murray Springs Clovis Site*, where hunters from the Clovis culture killed and butchered now-extinct bison and mammoth over ten thousand years ago. A one-third-mile long trail at the site interprets Clovis hunting techniques and describes medicinal uses of some of the plants along the way. This largely undisturbed campsite yielded a bone tool resembling a wrench, which was found in a mammoth footprint and thought to have been used to straighten spear shafts. The site is about 6 miles east of town on AZ90 to Moson Road, and then north (left) for about 1 mile to the entrance road on the right. Visitor information is available at the BLM office in Sierra Vista, or at the *San Pedro House* visitor center and bookstore 9 miles east of Sierra Vista on AZ90.

Although the ruins of *Presidio Santa Cruz de Terranate* consist only of a few adobe walls from the chapel and commandants quarters, and weathering foundations and walls of other buildings, they are the most intact example left of the region's presidios. An interpretive trail tells of life in this isolated outpost, which was established in 1775 to protect New Spain's frontier from Indian attacks. The Apache vigorously objected to its construction, and their raids forced the Spanish to abandon the fortress less than five years later. The only access is via a well-marked trail across the desert. To reach it, take AZ90 north of Sierra Vista to AZ82 and turn toward the ghost town of Fairbank. About 2 miles west of Fairbank, turn north onto Kellar Ranch Road, and travel about 3 miles to the trailhead. The 2-mile hiking trail leads to the site.

WEST OF SIERRA VISTA

Fort Huachuca (*wah-CHOO-kah*) was founded in 1877 to protect San Pedro Valley settlers and travelers from hostile Apache raiders and to block Apache escape routes into Mexico. U.S. soldiers and their wives, friendly Apache scouts, and buffalo soldiers (Black U.S. infantry, so named because their courage and curly hair reminded Indians of a buffalo's hide and bravery) were once stationed here. Since 1954, the fort has been used for the testing of electronic and communication equipment and is now a headquarters for military intelligence. *Fort Huachuca Museum* is in two turn-of-the-century buildings on the "Old Post." It displays military artifacts, dioramas, and memorabilia from the fort, as well as items concerning the Indian wars.

Fort Huachuca is just west of town at the mouth of Huachuca Canyon. The fort is an active military installation. Visitors must present proper identification and register at the gate to ask for directions to the museum.

After having been closed to the public for many years, Garden Canyon has recently been reopened. As well as the canyon being a popular spot for bird watching, the *Garden Canyon Pictograph Site* has Apache paintings of a golden eagle, Crown Dancer, and other designs. Follow the main road through the entrance to the base to the well-marked left turn, and take this road to the pictograph site.

TOHONO O'ODHAM NATION
Map #3

Sites: Baboquivari Mountain Park, Desert Diamond Casinos, Fortaleza Village, Kitt Peak National Observatory, San Xavier Mission del Bac, Sells

Labeled the Papago by Spanish conquistadors, the Tohono O'odham tribe has since reclaimed their traditional name, which means "People of the Desert." Related linguistically and culturally to the Akimel O'odham (which means "People of the River," and who were named "Pima" by the Spanish), the semi-nomadic Tohono O'odham once had a "two village" way of life, meaning they moved yearly between summer camps located near crop fields and winter villages set beside reliable mountain springs.

As farmers, they took advantage of seasonal rains to cultivate grains, tepary beans, corn, melons, and squash. In addition, wild food sources, such as small game, mesquite beans, agave, acorns, and the fruit of the Creas Giganteus (*petayah*), were utilized, and the Saguaro cactus was a staple.

Basketweaving (*hohata*) was a highly developed skill among Tohono O'odham women. Saguaro, yucca, mesquite, devil's claw, desert spoon, beargrass, ocotillo, and willow are some of the desert plants they used to weave baskets (*hoha*), trays, hats, sleeping mats, cradleboards, traps, doors for brush shelters, and many other household necessities. Today both men and women are basketweavers, and the skill has become an art form.

Birds nest in saguaro cactus and use them as platforms to survey their hunting territory, animals and humans eat the fruit, and people have fashioned their strong ribs into building materials.

The Tohono O'odham Nation has over 25,000 tribal members in southern Arizona and several thousand more in Sonora, Mexico. Their reservation, which is about the size of Connecticut, is located on traditional homelands in the Sonoran Desert and is exceeded in area only by that of the Navajo. The main reservation, which is west of Tucson, is centered in the town of Sells. Three parts of the reservation are noncontiguous to this main section: the Gila Bend Indian Reservation/San Lucy District northwest of Tucson near the town of Gila Bend, the twenty-acre Florence Village west of Sells, and San Xavier south of Tucson.

Major rebellions against the Spanish in the 1660s and 1750s allowed the Tohono O'odham to retain their traditional way of life for many years. Not until Euro-Americans arrived in large numbers did the people begin to lose much of their culture. Although still struggling to reclaim the parts of their heritage that were lost, progress has been made as the Tohono O'odham have worked to revitalize their language, basketweaving skills, games, and desert foods. TOCA (Tohono O'odham Community Action) is a group that has been instrumental in cultural renewal. You can visit this nonprofit organization's store in the Tohono O'odham's new **Cultural Center and Museum**, 7 miles south of Sells in Topawa. Geared to helping visitors learn more about the culture and understand its people, the facility has exhibits, artist's studios, galleries, a gift shop, and an outdoor storytelling circle.

One of their traditional dances is the "skipping" or "scraping" dance; they call it *chelkona*. This distinctive dance is performed by young women in flowing white dresses and young men in white shirts and pants. During the dance, participants display symbols of clouds and sea gulls above their heads. Photographs are not generally permitted. Contact the tribal office for performance information.

Most of the tribal income comes from its three *Desert Diamond Casinos*. You can find one of the tribe's casinos at the San Xavier Business Park, at the intersection of I-19 and Pima Mine Road south of Tucson. This location also features the Agave Restaurant, a sport's bar, and a 2,400-seat performing arts center. Gambling and food are also offered at the original Desert Diamond Casino in Nogales. The Golden Ha:san, on the way to Organ Pipe Cactus National Monument near the town of Why, has slots, a grill, and convenience store/gas station. A free shuttle services the Pima Mine and Nogales casinos.

There are no hotels and few places to eat on the reservation. For touring or camping in the backcountry, where gravel roads lead through the parched desert to widely scattered settlements such as Si:l Naggia (Saddle Hanging), you need permission from each district you visit (there are eleven). Call tribal headquarters for information.

GILA BEND DISTRICT

This part of the reservation is northwest of Tucson near the town of Gila Bend. **Fortaleza Village** is the ruins of a pre-Columbian fortified village with about fifty stone houses and three large ceremonial chambers that were constructed by the Hohokam. Built on a high volcanic outcrop that affords unobstructed views of the Gila River, the site was eventually abandoned, and then resettled in 1200 by migrants from the Tucson area. The site still has spiritual importance to the O'odham. Ask at the museum in Gila Bend or contact tribal headquarters to see if it is open to visit.

MAIN

The tribal headquarters is located in **Sells,** the nation's capital. With a population of about 2,800 people, it is the largest town on the reservation. Sells also has two small cafés and a small gift shop where baskets and jewelry can be purchased.

Quinlan/Baboquivari Mountains include the sacred Baboquivari Peak and **Kitt Peak National Observatory,** which leases land from the O'odham. With eight astronomical research institutions, the observatory holds the world's largest collection of telescopes. A self-guided tour leads to three of the larger telescopes, and guided tours are also available. The *visitor center* has astronomy exhibits, a picnic ground, and a museum shop that sells astronomy items, as well as Indian basketry. Evening programs allow visitors to view the night sky through the telescopes; reservations are required well in advance. To reach Kitt Peak, take AZ86 southwest of Tucson about 56 miles.

SAN XAVIER DISTRICT

The 71,000 acres of the San Xavier section is just south of Tucson. Its major tourist attraction is **San Xavier Mission Del Bac,** established in 1700 by Father Eusebio Kino as the first Spanish mission in the area. He built the mission where a Tohono O'odham settlement once stood, in a place where the Santa Cruz River reappears after flowing underground. Its Indian name was Wa:k, which means "place where the water appears" or "underground spring."

It was reported that Father Kino was respected by the Indians for his kindness, sensitivity, and humility. When not teaching them about animal husbandry and new farming methods, he spent his time traveling along ancient native pathways between Sonoran Desert settlements. After he left the mission, it was abandoned several times, until the Franciscans revitalized it in 1778.

Today San Xavier is still an active Catholic church and one of the most photographed missions in the world. Called the "White Dove of the Desert," this stunning white adobe church lends a quiet beauty to the brown of the surrounding desert. In the last ten years, the elaborate interior of the church has been extensively renovated to renew some of its original beauty. Walking through the thick mesquite doors is reminiscent of an earlier time, when the wooden pews were new and lined with worshippers gazing at the same ornate carvings and painted frescoes that are lit by sacramental candles today.

The mission also has a small museum with historical exhibits and a gift shop. Across the square and under ramadas in San Xavier Plaza, vendors sell Tohono O'odham baskets, as well as Zuni, Navajo, and Hopi arts and crafts. On some days, particularly religious holidays, they also sell Indian fry bread and other food.

Nearby is **Baboquivari Mountain Park**, which has picnic facilities and a campground.

San Xavier Mission is 9 miles south of Tucson off I-19. Take exit 92 and follow the signs. The facility can be toured daily and Sunday after mass.

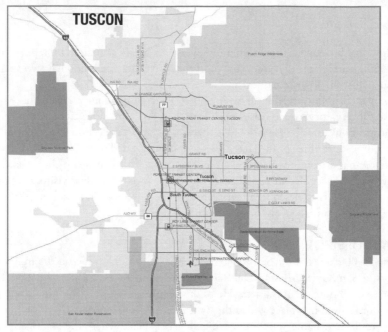

TUCSON
Map #4

Around Town: Arizona State Museum, Arizona–Sonora Desert Museum, Fort Lowell Museum, Fremont House Museum, Ironwood Forest National Monument, Second Street Museum, Saguaro National Park, Tohono Chul Park, Tucson Botanical Garden, Tucson Museum of Art
Nearby: Catalina State Park, Colossal Cave, Gila Bend, Sonoran Desert National Monument, Painted Rocks Petroglyph Site, Organ Pipe Cactus National Monument, Pascua Yaqui Tribe

In Tucson (*TOO-sahn*), you can spend the morning in the prehistoric past viewing exhibits at the Arizona State Museum, and in the afternoon fast-forward to the twenty-first century at the Pima Air and Space Museum or Biosphere 2. In between, you can enjoy the city's cosmopolitan flavor and unique setting in the Sonoran Desert.

The colorful desert and mountains surrounding Tucson have a long history of native habitation. As early as A.D. 100, Hohokam Indians farmed the banks of the Santa Cruz River, which flows through town. Akimel O'odham Indians moved here later, and it was their village of Stjuk-shon for which Tucson was named.

In 1762, the Spanish government moved Sobaipuri Indians here from the San Pedro Valley in the east. The unintended result was an increase of Apache raids on Spanish settlements, since the Sobaipuri had been blocking Apache access to the Santa Cruz Valley. To protect against the raids, construction on a presidio began in 1775. Twenty-eight years and several Indian attacks later, it was completed. In the 1790s, members of the Apache tribe, called the "Apaches de Paz," settled peacefully in town and joined Spanish soldiers in fighting their more warlike relatives.

The *Tucson Convention and Visitors Bureau* has information on reconstruction plans

*The Hohokam crafted
large pots for storage.*

for the presidio and San Augustine Mission Complex, as well as a guide to reputable Native American art dealers. You can also purchase the "Tucson Attractions Passport" here for a nominal fee. It includes two-for-one offers and discounts to fifty popular sites in southern Arizona. The center is off Broadway in downtown Tucson.

The **Arizona Historical Society** has three museums of Native American interest. *Fremont House Museum* in the Community Center Complex is a restored 1880 adobe house that was the home of John C. Fremont's daughter when he was territorial governor. It covers Spanish colonial and U.S. army days. The museum also sponsors special programs and historic walking tours. The *Second Street Museum, Library, and Archives* covers state history from the arrival of the Spanish to the present. *Fort Lowell County Park and Museum* encompasses part of the Hardy Site, a large Hohokam pithouse village inhabited around A.D. 1000. Although the village was once four or five times as large as Fort Lowell Park, only a small portion has been excavated. Fort Lowell itself was established as a supply depot in 1862 and later became a key post for operations against the Apache. The restored remains of the fort now house a museum with artifacts from the Hohokam village, the Apache Wars, and the military. The park is 7 miles northeast of downtown. Take I-10 to exit 256, go east on Grant Road to Craycroft, and then turn north.

Exhibits at the **Tucson Museum of Art** include art and artifacts from the different cultures that have lived in the area, from pre-Columbian to contemporary times. The museum also has a gift shop, café, and six-thousand-volume research library. It is housed in six historical buildings that are part of El Presidio Historic District, which was once the site of the Spanish colonial military garrison and is now a marketplace of galleries and restaurants.

Arizona State Museum has extensive exhibits covering the native peoples of the Southwest from prehistoric times to the present. This Smithsonian affiliate excels in research and is the Southwest's oldest and largest anthropology museum. Included with their Navajo textiles is one of the biggest rugs ever woven, and the museum's collection of whole Southwestern Indian pottery vessels is the largest in the world. The "Paths of Life" exhibit was created in collaboration with representatives from ten Arizona and Mexico tribes. Using video, artifacts, and art, it spans from creation stories to modern lifestyles to foster an understanding of each unique culture. Special events and lectures on Native American historical and contemporary topics are offered frequently, and the gift shop highlights Indian crafts and books.

The museum is on the University of Arizona campus, east of the main gate at the corner of University Boulevard and N. Park Avenue. Take Speedway Blvd. east from I-10 to Euclid, then turn south to the parking area. Also of interest at the University of Arizona are its extensive art museum, photography museum, mineral museum, and science center.

Among the pleasant gardens at the 5.5-acre **Tucson Botanical Gardens** are a Native American Crops Garden and a Tohono O'odham path with a ramada and plants used by the people for food, clothing, shelter, and medicine. The botanical garden also has a greenhouse, gift shop, and picnic area. Tours and special events are offered. The Tucson Botanical Gardens are in midtown. Take exit 256 from I-10 and turn east onto Grant Road. At Alvernon Way, turn left to the gardens.

Tohono Chul Park provides a home for over four hundred species of desert plants and an abundance of wildlife native to the American Southwest and Mexico on its thirty-seven acres. In the ethno-botanical garden, native crops are grown using traditional cultivation methods. Programs and exhibits are designed to further an appreciation of the desert environment and to reflect the interaction between it and the people who have called the area home. Native American works of art are displayed in the Desert Discovery Education Center. There is a museum shop and tea room on site. Take exit 248 from I-10, drive east on Ina Road to Paseo del Norte, and then turn left.

Encompassing twenty-one acres of desert in Tucson Mountain Park, the **Arizona–Sonora Desert Museum** is considered one of the best zoos in the world. An extensive collection of Sonoran Desert plants and animals, all displayed in natural settings, make this an enjoyable place to learn about the land and inhabitants of southern Arizona. The underground earth sciences center provides an interior look at the geology that supports it all. To reach the museum, travel west from I-10 on Speedway, and then turn right on Kinney for 2.5 miles.

The Arizona–Sonora Desert Museum also has a comprehensive guide to **Ironwood Forest National Monument**, which is 129,000 acres twenty-five miles northwest of Tucson that preserves a rich stand of Ironwood trees. These ecologically important trees are found only in the Sonoran Desert and can grow up to forty-five feet in height and live as long as 1,500 years. The monument also preserves evidence of over five thousand years of human activity, including two hundred Hohokam cultural sites dated from 600 B.C. to A.D. 1450. Included in the monument are the Lost Robles Archeological District, the Cocoraque Butte Archeological District (which has ancestral ties to both the Tohono O'odham and the Hopi), and the Mission of Santa Ana del Chiquiburitac. Contact the Tucson BLM office for more information.

SAGUARO NATIONAL PARK

The giant saguaro cacti in Saguaro National Park are some of the oldest and most massive specimens around, standing fifty feet tall and weighing ten tons. The park was created to protect them from development. Its two segments are on opposite sides of Tucson. The eastern unit (Rincon Mountain District) contains a mature forest with cactus as

SAGUARO CACTUS

The saguaro (sah-WAH-ro) cactus dwarfs all other plants in the Sonoran Desert, the only place it occurs naturally. These giant cacti can weigh up to 6 tons (mostly water) and live over 150 years. The first branches do not appear for 50–100 years. The cactus serves as a nesting home for gilded flickers and screech owls and provides flower nectar for Mexican white-winged doves and long-nosed bats. The saguaro also nurtured the Tohono O'od-ham people, who gathered the ripe fruit (bahidaj) in July by knocking it off the mother plant with long poles. They then used the cactus fruit for food, jam, syrup, and ceremonial wine. Shelters and fences came from the plant's woody ribs, and the seeds were eaten or dried and saved. The harvest was so important to Indians that it marked the beginning of the new year.

old as 150 years, while the western unit (Tucson Mountain District) preserves a younger growth.

Saguaro West is a few miles west of the Arizona–Sonora Desert Museum. The district has a *visitor center* with exhibits, slide show, bookstore, naturalist talks, and maps to nature trails and hikes. Picnic areas, a campground with hookups and a dump station, and an equestrian center are also in Saguaro West. The 6-mile *Bajada Loop Drive* travels past a short quarter-mile trail to dozens of Hohokam petroglyphs at *Signal Hill*.

Saguaro West is about 16 miles west of downtown Tucson on Speedway (which becomes Gates Pass Road). When the road ends at Kinney, turn right to the park entrance. Alternately, take I-10 north of Tucson to exit 242 (Avra Valley Road) and follow the signs.

The more popular **Saguaro East**, or Rincon Mountain Unit, is east of Tucson in the foothills of the Rincon Mountains. The *visitor center* features an audiovisual program, museum exhibits, a bookstore, and guided nature walks (winter only). The 8-mile paved scenic drive through the old-growth saguaro forest, as well as several hiking trails, allow a closer look at the abundant wildlife and the yuccas, agaves, paloverde trees, and other desert plants that grow here. Picnic areas are available, and backcountry camping is allowed with a permit.

Saguaro East is about 15 miles from downtown Tucson. Travel east on Broadway or Speedway to Freeman Road and turn right. At Old Spanish Trail, turn left and look for signs to the park entrance.

NORTH OF TUCSON

In **Catalina State Park** the *Romero Ruin Interpretive Trail* meanders past pithouses and a ball court built by prehistoric Hohokam who once farmed here. There is also picnicking, hiking, horseback riding, and camping in this 5,500-acre desert preserve. The park is in the foothills of the Santa Catalina Mountains several miles north of Tucson on AZ77 (Oracle Road).

SOUTH OF TUCSON

For information on **San Xavier del Bac**, see the Tohono O'odham Nation, above.

EAST OF TUCSON

The running surface water and a constant 70-degree temperature in **Colossal Cave** attracted prehistoric people, including the Hohokam, who came 950 years ago, and the Sobaipuri, who moved into the vicinity in the fifteenth century. Because this large cavern is a dry cave, unusual artifacts such as wooden arrow shafts bound with sinew and an adhesive—made from either a plant or insect—have survived the centuries. Some of them are on display in the small *La Posta Quemada Ranch Museum*, along with the Prehistoric Cave Shrine and Ancient Weavers exhibits. The one-hour guided tour of the cave (the only access) covers its history, legends, and geology. You can also enjoy horseback riding, stagecoach rides, and hayrides.

Colossal Cave Mountain Park is privately owned. To reach it, take I-10 19 miles southeast of Tucson to exit 279 at the town of Vail, and follow the signs for 7 miles to the cave.

WEST OF TUCSON

The town of **Gila Bend** is west of Tucson on I-8 near a sharp westward bend in the Gila (*Hee-la*) River. Early residents of the fertile riverbanks here were the Opas, and later the Hohokam. Father Eusebio Kino founded a village on the river's bend in 1699, and indigenous people were still here when California prospectors came through in 1850.

The *Gila Bend Tourist Information Center and Historical Museum*, on the business loop from I-8, presents an overview of the area. Exhibits in the museum include Native American baskets, tools, pottery, and arrowheads, as well as artifacts from *Gatlin Archaeological Park*, the site of a large Hohokam ceremonial platform and village built around A.D. 800. The stone mirrors, copper bells, macaw feathers, and marine shells give evidence of a wide

The venomous Gila monster lurks in holes and under rocks and shrubs in the Southwestern deserts.

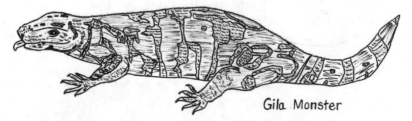

Gila Monster

< 200 >

trading area for the five hundred or so people who lived here. The archaeological park is still being excavated, with future plans to open it to visitors and include a traditional O'odham dwelling.

Sonoran Desert National Monument protects 496,000 acres of prehistoric cultural resources and diverse desert plants, including a large forest of saguaro cactus. Desert bighorn sheep, mountain lions, and javelina share the biological resources with many amphibians and reptiles such as the desert tortoise. Ancient trails lead towards sources of salt and shells in the Gulf of California, and a twenty-three-mile long corridor still preserves parts of the historic Juan Bautista de Anza, Mormon Battalion, and Butterfield stage trails. Ruined villages along the base of the slopes in the Table Top Mountains were home to ancestors of modern O'odham, Quechan, Maricopa, and Cocopah people, and rock art, stone quarries, and early campsites are scattered throughout the area.

Rough roads lead into the wilderness off I-8 at exits 144 and 140, and AZ238 from Maricopa to Gila Bend provides access to the Butterfield Overland Stage Route and the North Maricopa Mountains. There are no facilities, and a four-wheel-drive vehicle is recommended. Contact the BLM Office in Phoenix for information, maps, and the necessary permit to visit the Sand Tank Mountains.

Painted Rocks Petroglyph Site, also administered by the Phoenix Field Office of the BLM, may once have been a natural boundary between the Maricopa and their Quechan enemies. Today this impressive site has some of the best examples of Hohokam rock art in the state, including pictures of snakes, lizards, glyphs marking the winter and summer solstice, and geometric and human figures. Historic renderings from Juan Bautista de Anza's expedition to California and glyphs made by later travelers with the Mormon Battalion and the Butterfield Overland Mail are also present. Primitive camping and picnic tables are available, but there is no potable water. A campground host is on-site October through April.

To reach Painted Rocks, take I-8 west of Gila Bend about 12.5 miles to exit 102, and then turn north onto Painted Rocks Dam Road for 10.7 miles to Rocky Point Road. Take this unpaved road west for .6 mile to the site. Please note that Painted Rocks Petroglyph Site may be shown on your map as "Painted Rocks State Park." However, due to toxic pollution from pesticides in the reservoir, access to Painted Rocks Dam and the Lake Unit of the state park (about 4.5 miles north of the petroglyphs) has been closed since 1989.

Organ Pipe Cactus National Monument preserves the rare organ pipe cactus in 516 square miles of the Sonoran Desert. Other desert plants used by native inhabitants, such as mesquite, saguaro, cholla, and ocotillo, also thrive here. Two self-guided scenic drives (gravel) plus several hiking trails provide the visitor a closer view of the land. The *visitor center* has exhibits and other information and provides guided tours in the winter.

To reach Organ Pipe, take AZ86 west of Tucson through the Tohono O'odham reservation to AZ85 and turn south. Be sure to fill your gas tank and your water jugs before you leave Tucson. Other than the two campgrounds in the monument, the handful of basic motels and the Guest House Inn Bed and Breakfast in Ajo provide the nearest lodging. This small town is also one of the only places to get gas for miles around.

The people of the **Pascua Yaqui Community** call themselves *Yoeme*, meaning "Human Beings." Originally a Uto-Aztecan people from Mexico, they fought long wars against the Spanish and the Mexican governments. After siding with Pancho Villa in his campaign against Mexico, many sought refuge in the United States, where they settled in Old Pascua Yaqui Village in the early 1900s. The city of Tucson later grew up around them, and when they were designated an official United States tribe in 1978, the government established an 895-acre reservation for them south of Tucson at New Pascua. The Pascua Yaqui have since devised a tribal constitution and a written form of their language.

Casino Del Sol is built like a Tuscan resort, with soaring ceilings and 22,500 square feet of gaming. It includes Arizona's largest outdoor amphitheater, the *Anselmo Balencia Tori Amphitheater (AVA)*, which brings in national acts. The casino is west on Valencia off I-19.

Casino of the Sun is a 40,000-square-foot casino with three restaurants. It is about 5 miles off I-19, west on Valencia to Camino de Oeste, and then left about a half-mile.

The tribe also owns *Del Sol Marketplace* offering fuel, food, and other items, as well as the *AAA Pet Lodge* offering 24-hour supervision and boarding for dogs and cats in temperature-controlled kennels with large yards, a landscape nursery, a charcoal packing plant, and radio station.

About 12,700 Yaqui are enrolled members of the tribe, and around 30,000 of their relatives still reside in Mexico. Their songs and stories reflect their roots in Sonora, and artisans craft Deer Dance statues, carved *pascola* (clown) masks, and flutes.

The Yaqui maintain a passionate religious life that is a unique blend of Catholicism and traditional beliefs. Visitors can enjoy their colorful and distinctive ceremonies during many Catholic holidays, particularly at Easter time. One of the most impressive ceremonies incorporates the *Deer Dance*, when men, adorned with rectangular pieces of black woven cloth, leg rattles made from giant moth cocoons filled with pebbles, and headdresses with attached deer heads, move to the accompaniment of drums and raspers. Holding two gourd rattles, they dance to become a vehicle for the spirit of the deer, Maaso, to visit the people. In the morning Maaso returns to his flower-enchanted wilderness, but for one night he comes to bless his brothers and sisters and to cleanse the world.

To reach the reservation, take I-19 south to exit 95 (Valencia Road). Turn west to Camino de Oeste, and then turn south. For dates and locations of dances, contact the Tucson Visitors Bureau or the tribal offices.

WILLCOX
Map #5

Around Town: Chiricahua Regional Museum/Museum of the Southwest, Willcox Commercial Store

Nearby: Amerind Foundation Museum, Aravaipa Canyon, Cochise Stronghold, Chiricahua National Monument, Dankworth Village, Eastern Arizona Museum, Fort Bowie National Historic Site, Gila Box Riparian Natural Conservation Area, Graham County Historical Society Museum, Museum of Anthropology

The town of Willcox was built in the homeland of the Chiricahua Apaches in 1880 as a construction camp for the railroad. You can still shop at the **Willcox Commercial Store**, once frequented by Geronimo to purchase supplies. This small town (about 3,100 people) is 90 miles east of Tucson on I-10 and serves as a tourist center for Cochise County. One of the most popular pastimes in Willcox is bird watching, encouraged by the northern limit of the colorful trogon in Cave Creek Canyon and the annual wintering of about thirty thousand sandhill cranes in Sulphur Springs Valley. The museum dedicated to hometown singing cowboy legend Rex Allen is also a favorite.

The **Chiricahua Regional Museum and Research Center/Museum of the Southwest** on Maley Street highlights the history of the Apaches, U.S. cavalry, and miners. Featured are a bust of Cochise, Indian artifacts, historical exhibits, a gift shop, and art gallery.

The *Willcox Chamber and Cochise Information Center* can provide more information about the area, including the Circle of Cochise, an auto route that provides insight into the local geology and history. Part of the route retraces that of the Overland Mail stagecoach route. The information center is off I-10 at exit 340 (AZ186) and then north on Circle I Road.

NORTH OF WILLCOX

Prehistoric sites in the Gila River valley date from A.D. 300 to 1200 and include the Hohokam, Mogollon, and Ancestral Puebloan cultures. Directions to **Gila Box Riparian Natural Conservation Area**, which preserves the plants and animals living along four stream channels and the cliff dwellings along Bonita Creek, can be obtained from the Bureau of Land Management offices in Safford.

For a wilderness experience of what the land was like before Anglo settlement, visit **Aravaipa Canyon**, in the Galiuro Mountains west of Safford. Over 230 species of birds and an abundance of wildlife, some rare or endangered, now live here. Only fifty people per day are allowed to use the area, and permits must be obtained in advance from the BLM in Safford.

Roper Lake State Park is south of Safford and has Dankworth Ponds and **Dankworth Village**, a multicultural archaeological village covering the time period from 9000 B.C. to the 1600s. The sites and dwellings have been recreated by the Arizona State Parks Department and the BLM. The Dankworth Ponds site is 2 miles south of the state park, which is about 6 miles south of Safford on US191.

For information on lodging and services, visit the *Graham County Chamber of Commerce* just west of downtown Safford on US70. Dioramas and exhibits here include Native American history.

Just north of Safford in the town of Thatcher, the **Museum of Anthropology** showcases the prehistory of the Gila Valley with the significant Mills Collection covering the Salado period (A.D. 1250–1450). A diorama depicts the late Ice Age, while a hands-on area has activities such as chiseling an arrowhead, grinding corn, and rubbing sticks together to make fire. Extensive exhibits include Indian pottery, axes, arrowheads, and jewelry. The library has texts covering Southwestern archaeology and anthropology. The museum is in the Eastern Arizona College's Student Services Building near the corner of Main Street (US70) and College Avenue.

Also in Thatcher, the **Graham County Historical Society Museum** has one room of Indian pottery, baskets, tools, photographs, and other artifacts of the Salado, Apache, and Hohokam cultures. The museum is in the historic high school on 4th and US70.

Further north on US70 in the town of Pima is the **Eastern Arizona Museum**, which has a small collection of pottery, blankets, arrowheads, and other Indian relics. The museum is on US70 at Main Street.

Chiricahua Apaches and U.S. cavalry troops once clashed near Ft. Bowie National Historic Site.

SOUTHEAST OF WILLCOX

South of Willcox near Apache Pass is **Fort Bowie National Historic Site**. Called Puerto del Dado ("Pass of Chance") by the Spanish, Apache Pass was traveled by Apaches, Spanish, and American prospectors crossing between the foothills of the Dos Cabezas and Chiricahua mountains. Fort Bowie was established here in 1862 to protect the Butterfield Stage Trail, and it later became a center for General George Crook's army. His operations against the Apache ended with the end of the Indian Wars in 1886, when Geronimo surrendered and the Chiricahua were forced to move to Alabama and Florida. The fort was officially abandoned in 1894.

The stabilized adobe ruins of Fort Bowie still remain, at the end of a fairly flat 1.5-mile foot trail that parallels the military wagon road and passes the foundations of the Butterfield Overland Stage Station, an Apache wickiup, the Chiricahua Apache Indian Agency, Apache Pass Spring, and a cemetery. Plan two hours for the round-trip hike, which will give you a sense of the isolation of the soldiers stationed here. The small *ranger station/museum* has interpretive exhibits, Apache crafts, information, and a bookstore. Ranger talks can be arranged with advance reservations. Picnic tables are at each end of the trailhead, but no camping is allowed.

To reach Fort Bowie, take AZ186 about 20 miles southeast to Apache Pass Road, then turn east 8 miles to the parking lot and trailhead. This unpaved road is not recommended in bad weather. The site can also be reached from Bowie off I-10 at exit 362 or 366, and then south about 13 miles on the paved and gravel Apache Pass Road.

Chiricahua National Monument is in a remote, forested region of the Chiricahua Mountains once frequented by the fiercely independent Chiricahua (*Cheer-a-CAH-wah*) Apache. They called this place "Land of the Standing-Up Rocks," referring to the giant rock formations that have been naturally sculpted into unusual and intriguing shapes. Cochise Head peak, which is said to resemble the profile of that famous Apache, is there, along with Duck on a Rock, China Boy, and others. An 8-mile scenic drive travels to *Massai Point Overlook*, where geological displays interpret the origin of this picturesque land. Other scenic overlooks are on Bonita Canyon Road, which leads to the monument.

Wildlife habitats in the monument range from mountain forest to desert grassland, and many animals common to the Southwest and Mexico can be seen from the 17 miles of hiking trails. The *visitor center* has a trail guide and exhibits covering Chiricahua lifestyle, early ranching activity, wildlife, and geology.

Bonita Canyon Campground has twenty-six campsites and a picnic area, and campfire programs are offered from mid-March to mid-September. Trailers are limited to twenty-six feet.

To reach the monument, take AZ186 32 miles southeast of Willcox, and turn east for 3 miles on AZ181.

SOUTHWEST OF WILLCOX

Founded in 1937 by archaeologist William Fulton, the **Amerind Foundation Museum** and research facility is dedicated to Native American cultures, particularly those of the American Southwest and Mexico. This outstanding private collection includes over 25,000 archaeological and cultural items such as beadwork, costumes, ritual masks, and weapons, spanning the time period from the end of the last ice age to the present. One entire room is dedicated to ceremonial dancing. Paintings and sculptures of contemporary Native American artists are displayed in the gallery, and artists demonstrate their skills in the main gallery during Native Arts Weekends.

The museum shop sells high-quality arts and crafts of the Southwest native peoples, as well as books on the prehistory, history, and culture of Native Americans. The picnic area provides a lovely setting to enjoy the flora, fauna, and spectacular rock formations of Texas Canyon.

The museum is off I-10 at exit 318 just past the town of Benson, then 1 mile east on Dragoon Road and left at the sign.

Cochise Stronghold is a rugged rock fortress in a canyon on the western slopes of the Dragoon Mountains in Coronado National Forest. This scenic woodland, surrounded by sheer cliffs and granite domes, was named after Apache leader Cochise (from *chies*, Apache for wood), who used it as a hideout in the late nineteenth century. Seeking revenge for the murder of his relatives by a U.S. army officer, he and his warriors rode out to attack Butterfield stagecoaches, isolated ranches, and travelers who came within a hundred miles of the area. Then the Indians retreated to the safety of their protected home. Cochise was never defeated in battle, but in 1874 he met with General O. O. Howard and signed a final peace treaty with the United States. After he died on the Chiricahua Reservation, he was supposedly buried somewhere deep within Cochise Stronghold.

Self-guided trails at Cochise Stronghold now interpret the life of the Apache. Look for the tall bluffs at the entrance to the campground that once served as lookout towers to warn of approaching cavalry. Another lodging option is the privately owned *Cochise Stronghold Bed and Breakfast*. The owners of this passive solar inn can provide you with a wealth of information on Cochise Stronghold and the desert environment, plus a breakfast that includes mesquite-cornmeal pancakes and other Southwestern fare.

Cochise Stronghold is southwest of Willcox on I-10 at exit 331, and then south on AZ191. In Sunsites, take Ironwood Road (which becomes Forest Rt. 84) west about 9 miles to the campground entrance. Note that Ironwood Road is rocky and rough, and it includes several stream crossings that are impassable in wet weather. RVs longer than twenty-two feet are not recommended.

EVENTS

A complete listing of area events is available from the Tucson Visitor Center. Call 800-638-8350 or 520-624-1817.

VARIES *Arizona Archaeological and Historical Society:* Lectures on the ancient ruins, art, and artifacts of the Southwest, as well as tours and field studies of Arizona archaeological sites. In Tucson. Call 520-885-6283.

FEBRUARY *American Indian Exposition:* Artist demonstrations, arts/crafts for sale, and music and dance performances. Tucson Expo Center, 520-622-4900.

Cocopah Powwow: Includes traditional singing, Gourd and Bird dancing, arts and crafts, and food booths. Tumacacori area in mid-February.

Sells Rodeo and Parade: Annual Tohono O'odham event for eighty years. Held at Sells, AZ, first weekend in February.

Southwest Indian Arts Fair: Features around two hundred artists from the Southwest with high-quality art for sale, also music. Arizona State Museum, 520-626-8381.

University of Arizona Wildcats Powwow: Includes a powwow, Miss Indian University of Arizona pageant, fun run, and arts and crafts. Held in Arizona Stadium in Tucson, 520-621-3835.

MARCH/APRIL *Archaeology Expo:* Displays and booths from museums, Native American tribes, government agencies, and archaeological and historical organizations, with an emphasis on visitor participation. Also includes living history reenactments, entertainment, and tours of local sites. Part of Arizona Archaeology and Heritage Awareness Month. Held at Tubac Presidio State Historic Park. Call 602-542-7138.

Cocopah Festivities Day: Rabbit and Round dances, singing, Miss Cocopah contest, games, and sports. Indian food such as fry bread, beans, and Indian tacos are also sold, as well as beadwork, fine gourd rattles, and other arts and crafts. Near Tumacacori.

Cultural Fair: Celebration of pioneer, Hispanic, and Native American contributions to the culture of the Safford/Thatcher area. Indian dancing, crafts, and food are included.

Wa:k Powwow: Intertribal dancing and arts/crafts vendors. San Xavier del Bac, 602-294-5727.

Yaqui Easter Ceremonies: Also known as the Easter Celebration, this pageant is held during Easter Week and includes the Deer Dance. Other dances depict the battle between good and evil and the crucifixion. Near Tucson, call 520-883-2838.

MAY *Waila Festival:* Celebration of the Tohono O'odham traditional "chicken scratch" dance music. Arizona Historical Society, 520-628-5774.

JULY *Ha:San Bak: Saguaro Harvest Celebration:* A celebration of the summer saguaro harvest. La Posta Quemada Ranch at Colossal Cave Mountain Park, 520-647-7121.

Native American Arts Festival: Juried art show that includes rugs, jewelry, and paintings. Food vendors included. Festival is in Pinetop, and pre-show is held at Hon-Dah Casino.

SEPTEMBER *Indian Days Celebration:* To foster understanding and appreciation of Native American cultures. It includes a competition powwow, arts festival, and job fair. Held in late September at the Convention Center. Call the Tucson Indian Center for information, 520-884-7131.

OCTOBER *Tucson Meet Yourself Festival:* Celebrates the diversity of the people who live and have lived in Tucson with food, dancing, and folk art. Held in Presidio Park on the 2nd weekend in October. Call 520-792-4806 or visit www.tucsonmeetyourself.org.

NOVEMBER *Native American Heritage Month Powwow:* Includes over three hundred dancers and an arts-and-crafts market. Amigos Indoor Complex in Tucson on Thanksgiving weekend. Other powwows are also held at the complex throughout the year. 520-622-4900.

Tohono O'odham All-Indian Fair and Rodeo: Rodeo, art/craft and food booths, powwow, and beauty pageant. Held in Sells.

DECEMBER *Tumacacori Fiesta:* Indian dancing, crafts vendors, and food booths. It is held in early December at Tumacacori Museum.

CONTACT INFORMATION

Amerind Foundation Museum
2100 N. Amerind Road, Dragoon, AZ 85609
520-586-3666 • www.amerind.org
Tue-Sun 10am-4pm; fee

Arizona Historical Society
    Fort Lowell County Park and Museum
    2900 North Craycroft Road, Tucson, AZ 85712
    520-885-3832
    Wed-Sat 10am-4pm; no fee
    Fremont House Museum
    151 S. Grande Ave, Tucson, AZ 85701
    520-622-0956
    Mon-Fri 10am-4pm; fee
    Second Street Museum, Library, and Archives
    949 E. 2nd Street, Tucson, AZ 85719
    520-628-5774
    Mon-Sat 10am-4pm & Sun afternoon;
      donation

Arizona–Sonora Desert Museum
2021 N. Kinney Road, Tucson, AZ 85743
520-883-2702 • www.desertmuseum.org
Daily 7:30am-5pm (no entry after 4:15 pm),
    Mar, Apr, May, & Sept; daily 7:30am-
    10pm, June-Aug, daily 8:30-5pm (no entry
    after 4:15 pm), Oct-Feb; fee

Arizona State Museum
PO Box 210026, 1013 E. University (University
    Blvd & N. Park Ave), Tucson, AZ 85721
520-621-6302
www.statemuseum.arizona.edu
Mon-Sat 10am-5pm & Sun noon-5pm; fee

Arizona State Parks
1300 W. Washington, Phoenix, AZ 85007
602-542-4174 • www.pr.state.az.us

Bureau of Land Management
www.blm.gov/az/st/en.html
    Phoenix
    21605 N.7th Avenue, Phoenix, Arizona 85027
    623-580-5500
    Safford
    711 14th Avenue, Safford, AZ 85546
    928-348-4400
    Mon-Fri 7:45am-4:15pm
    Sierra Vista
    1763 Paseo San Luis, Sierra Vista, AZ 85635
    520-439-6400
    Mon-Fri 8am-4pm
    Tucson
    12661 East Broadway, Tucson, AZ 85748
    520-258-7200

Catalina State Park
11570 N. Oracle Rd, PO Box 36986, Tucson,
    AZ 85740
520-628-5798
www.pr.state.az.us/Parks/parkhtml/catalina.html
Visitor Center: Daily 8am-5pm

Chiricahua National Monument
Superintendent, HCR #2, Box 6500, Willcox,
    AZ 85643
520-824-3560 • www.nps.gov/chir
Daily 8am-4:30pm; fee

**Chiricahua Regional Museum and Research
    Center/Museum of the Southwest**
127 E. Maley St., Willcox, AZ 85643
520-384-3971
Mon-Sat 10am-4pm (as volunteer staff permits); fee

Cochise Stronghold
Contact: Coronado National Forest Douglas
    Ranger District
3081 N. Leslie Canyon Road, Douglas, AZ 85607
520-364-3468
www.forestcamping.com/dow/southwest/
    corocmp.htm#cochise%20stronghold

Cochise Stronghold Bed & Breakfast
21126 W. Windaneer Trail, PO Box 232,
    Pearce, AZ 85625
877-426-4141 *or* 520-826-4141
www.cochisestronghold.com

Colossal Cave Mountain Park
16721 E. Old Spanish Trail, Vail, AZ 85641
Cave tours: 520-647-7275
La Posta Quemada Ranch: 520-647-7121
La Posta Quemada Ranch Stables: 520-647-3450
www.colossalcave.com
Mon-Sat 8am-6pm & Sun 8am-7pm, mid
    Mar-mid Sept; Mon-Sat 9am-5pm & Sun
    9am-6pm, mid Sept-mid Mar; fee

Coronado National Memorial
4101 East Montezuma Canyon Road,
    Hereford, AZ 85615
520-366-5515 • www.nps.gov/coro
Daily 9am-5pm; no fee

Dankworth Village (*See* Roper Lake State Park)
www.blm.gov/az/sfo/dankworth.htm

Eastern Arizona Historical Museum
2 North Main Street, Pima, AZ 85543
928-485-9400
Wed-Fri 2pm-4pm & Sat 1pm-5pm or by ap-
    pointment; no fee

Fremont House Museum (*See* Arizona Historical Society)

Fort Bowie National Historic Site
3203 South Old Fort Bowie Road, Bowie, AZ 85605
520-847-2500 • www.nps.gov/fobo
Visitor Center: daily 8am-4:30pm
Trails: daily sunrise-sunset; no fee

Fort Huachuca
PO Box 766, Boyd & Grierson Streets, Bldg 4140, Ft. Huachuca, AZ 85613
520-533-5736 *or* 520-533-3898
www.huachuca-usaic.army.mil
http://huachuca-www.army.mil/HISTORY/museum.htm
Mon-Fri 9am-4pm & Sat-Sun 1pm-4pm; no fee

Fort Lowell County Park and Museum (*See* Arizona Historical Society)

Gila Bend (town)
644 W. Pima Street, PO Box A, Gila Bend, AZ 85337
928-683-2255 • www.gilabendaz.org

Gila Box Riparian Natural Conservation Area
928-348-4400 (BLM Safford)
www.blm.gov/az/nca/gila_box/gila.htm

Graham County Chamber of Commerce
111l Thatcher Blvd, Safford, AZ 85546
888-837-1841 *or* 928-428-2511
www.visitgrahamcounty.com/index.html
Mon-Fri 8am-5pm & Sat 10am-2pm

Graham County Historical Society Museum
4th & Main, Thatcher, AZ
520-348-0470
Mon 12noon-8pm, Tues & Sat 10am-5pm; no fee

Guest House Inn
700 Guest House Road, Ajo, AZ 85321
520-387-6133 • www.guesthouseinn.biz

Ironwood Forest National Monument
(*See* BLM Tucson Field Office)
www.blm.gov/az/ironwood/ironwood.htm

Kitt Peak National Observatory
602-325-9200 *or* 520-318-8726; for reservations, call 9am-4pm
www.noao.edu/kpno
Daily 9am-4pm; Visitor Center, 9am-3:45pm; guided tours, 10am, 11:30am, & 1:30pm; viewing from telescope dome in evening with reservations

Murray Springs
www.blm.gov/az/nca/spnca/murray.htm

Museum of Anthropology at Eastern Arizona College (Mills Collection)
615 N. Stadium Avenue, Thatcher, AZ 85552
800-678-3808 *or* 928-428-8320
www.eac.edu/About_EAC/Mills_Collection
Mon-Fri 8am-5pm during the school year

Museum of the Southwest
1500 North Circle I Road, Willcox, AZ 85643
520-384-2272
Mon-Sat 9am-5pm & Sun 1pm-5pm

Nogales/Santa Cruz County Chamber of Commerce
123 W. Kino Park, Nogales, AZ 85621
520-287-3685 • www.nogaleschamber.com
Mon-Fri 8am-5pm

Organ Pipe Cactus National Monument
Superintendent, Rte 1, Box 100, Ajo, AZ 85321
520-387-6849 • www.nps.gov/orpi
Monument: daily 24-hours; fee
Visitor Center: daily 8am-5pm

Painted Rocks Petroglyph Site
BLM Phoenix Field Office, 21605 N. 7th Ave, Phoenix, AZ 85027
623-580-5500
www.az.blom.gov/pfo/paint.htm

Pascua Yaqui Community
7474 South Camino de Oeste, Tucson, AZ 85746
520-883-5000 • www.pascuayaquitribe.org
  AAA Pet Lodge
  6391 South Mark Road, Tucson AZ 85746
  520-883-6445
  Anselmo Valencia Tori (AVA) Amphitheater
  5655 W. Valencia Blvd., Tucson, AZ 85746
  800-344-9435 (tickets)
  Casino del Sol
  5655 W. Valencia Road, Tucson, AZ 85746
  520-838-6506 • www.casinodelsol.com
  Casino of the Sun
  7406 S. Camino de Oeste, Tucson, AZ 85746
  800-344-9435 ext 5450 *or* 520-879-5450
  www.casinosun.com
  Del Sol Marketplace
  5405 W. Valencia Blvd, Tucson, AZ 85757
  520-838-7000

Pimeria Alta Historical Society Museum
136 N. Grand Ave, Nogales, AZ 85628
520-287-4621
Tues-Fri 10am-noon & 1:30pm-5pm; Sat 10am-4pm; no fee

Roper Lake State Park (Dankworth Ponds)
101 E. Roper Lake Road, Safford, Arizona 85546
928-428-6760
www.pr.state.az.us/Parks/parkhtml/roper.html

Saguaro National Park
Superintendent, 3693 South Old Spanish Trail,
    Tucson, AZ 85730
www.nps.gov/sagu
    Park: Daily 7am-sunset (open to hikers 24 hours)
    Visitor Centers: Daily 9am-5pm
    Tucson Mountain Unit (Saguaro West),
    2700 N. Kinney Road
    520-733-5158
    Rincon Mountain Unit (Saguaro East),
    3693 S. Old Spanish
    Trail, 520-733-5153

San Pedro Riparian National Conservation
    Area (*see* BLM Sierra Vista)
www.blm.gov/az/nca/spnca/spnca-info.htm
    San Pedro House
    520-508-4445 • 9:30-4:30 pm

(Mission) San Xavier del Bac
1950 West San Xavier Road, Tucson, AZ 85746
520-294-2624 • www.sanxaviermission.org
Daily 7am-5pm; no fee

Second Street Museum, Library, and Archives
(*See* Arizona Historical Society)

Sierra Vista Convention and Visitors Bureau
1011 N. Coronado Drive, Sierra Vista, AZ 85635
800-288-3681 *or* 520-417-6960
www.visitsierravista.com
Mon-Fri 8am-5pm, Sat 9am-4pm

Sonoran Desert National Monument
(*See* BLM Phoenix Field Office)
www.blm.gov/az/sonoran/sondes_main.htm

Tohono Chul Park
7366 N. Paseo del Norte, Tucson, AZ 85704
520-742-6455 or 602-575-8468 (recording)
www.tohonochulpark.org
Daily 7am-sunset, Exhibit House 9am-5pm; fee
    (must be paid by 5pm to stay until sunset)

Tohono O'odham Nation
PO Box 837, Sells, Arizona 85634
520-383-2028
    Baboquivari Mountain Park
    520-383-2236
    Cultural Center and Museum
    PO Box 431, Sells, AZ 85634
    530-383-0201
    8am-5pm, Mon-Fri

Desert Diamond Casino
I-19 and Pima Mine Road
    Agave Restaurant
    520-393-2720 • Daily 11am-9pm
    Casino
    866-332-9457 *or* 520-294-7777
    Mon-Fri 9am-4am; Sat-Sun 24 hours
    Shuttle
    866-332-9467 *or* 520-393-2749
    reservations; 520-323-7777
Golden Ha:san Casino/Store Casino
866-332-9467 *or* 520-362-2746
    Convenience Store
    520-362-3395
Kitt Peak National Observatory
602-325-9200 or 520-318-8726;
    for reservations call 9am-4pm
www.noao.edu/kpno
Daily 9am-4pm; Visitor Center 9am-3:45pm;
    guided tours 10am, 11:30am & 1:30pm
(Mission) San Xavier del Bac
1950 West San Xavier Road, Tucson, AZ
    85746
520-294-2624 • www.sanxaviermission.org
Daily 7am-5pm; no fee

TOCA (Tohono O'odham Community Action)
State Route 86, Sells, AZ 85634
520-383-4966 • www.tocaonline.org
Mon-Fri 10am-5pm

Tombstone Chamber of Commerce
PO Box995, Tombstone, AZ 85638
888-457-3929 • www.tombstone.org

Tubac Chamber of Commerce
PO Box 1866, Tubac AZ 85646
520-398-2704 • www.tubacaz.com

Tubac Presidio State Historic Park
PO Box 1296, One Presidio Drive, Tubac, AZ
    85646
520-398-2252
www.pr.state.az.us/Parks/parkhtml/tubac.html
Daily 8am-5pm; fee

Tucson Botanical Gardens
2150 North Alvernon Way, Tucson, AZ 85712
520-326-9686 • www.tucsonbotanical.org
Daily 8:30am-4:30pm; fee

(Metropolitan) Tucson Convention & Visitors
    Bureau
100 S. Church Ave #7199, Tucson, Arizona 85701
800-638-8350 *or* 520-624-1817
www.visittucson.org
Mon-Fri 8am-5pm & Sat-Sun 9am-4pm

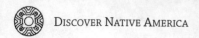

Tucson Museum of Art
140 N. Main Avenue, Tucson, AZ 85701
520-624-2333 • www.tucsonarts.com
Mon-Sat 10am-4pm, Sun noon-4pm; closed
    Mon in summer; fee (no fee Sun)

Tumacacori National Historical Park
PO Box 67, 1891 E. Frontage Road,
    Tumacacori, AZ 85640
520-398-2341 • www.nps.gov/tuma
Daily 9am-5pm; fee

Willcox Chamber of Commerce and Visitors
    Center
1500 North Circle I Rd, Willcox, AZ 85643
800-200-2272 *or* 520-384-2272
www.willcoxchamber.com
Mon-Sat 9am-5pm, Sun 10am-2pm

NORTHWEST COLORADO

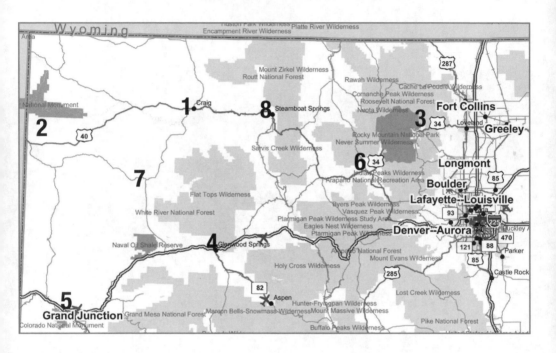

1. Craig
2. Dinosaur National Monument
3. Estes Park
4. Glenwood Springs

5. Grand Junction
6. Granby
7. Meeker
8. Steamboat Springs

CHAPTER 13

NORTHWEST COLORADO

MUCH OF NORTHWEST COLORADO is wilderness. Many even claim that the modern concept of "wilderness" was born here, when in 1920 a Forest Service architect by the name of Arthur Carhart recommended the land around Trapper's Lake be left wild rather than turned into housing developments. Although ski slopes, towns, and other developments have sprung up in the region since then, the spaces are still wide open more often than not. And whether it is the magnificent high mountain landscape of Rocky Mountain National Park or the jagged canyon country of Dinosaur National Monument, the scenery is still spectacular.

In an earlier age, Fremont Indians left their mark here in the form of rock art and abandoned settlements. When the settlers arrived centuries later in the 1800s, the people who greeted them were the nomadic Utes, who marked many of the sites they passed on their travels as sacred. You can still enjoy some of the healing hot springs they did, or trace sections of the Ute Trail, the route they used to move between winter and summer camps and to follow game animals.

CRAIG
Map #1

Around Town: Museum of Northwest Colorado, Sandrocks Nature Trail
Nearby: Brown's Park National Wildlife Refuge, Irish Canyon

In the far northwestern corner of Colorado, you can still experience the flavor of life in the West when the only people here were Native Americans. Moffat County itself has 1.7 million acres of colorful badlands, mountain peaks and valleys, rolling hills covered with sagebrush, and rugged sandstone canyons administered by the BLM (over half the land in the county is public domain). In addition, the county has only 2.56 residents per square mile, which meets the federal definition of "frontier" (six persons or fewer per square mile).

Craig, located at the junction of US40 and CO13, is the seat of Moffat County and its economic center. The area is replete with elk, deer, mountain lions, bear, antelope, and bighorn sheep, making it a popular destination for wildlife viewing and big-game hunting. For more information on this and other outdoor recreation, contact the *Craig Chamber of Commerce/Moffat County Visitor Center* or one of the tour operators located in town. Also ask at the chamber for a guide for **Sandrocks Nature Trail**, which passes 250 petroglyphs etched by cultures as early as the Archaic and as late as the Shoshone. Along the trail, look for designs of hands, paw prints, animals, and lightning bolts, and for spots where axes may have been sharpened and arrowheads fashioned.

The **Museum of Northwest Colorado**, in the former Colorado State Armory, displays historical photos, a famous collection of cowboy and gunfighter gear dating back to the 1800s, and railroad memorabilia. The bookstore stocks books covering Ute history.

You can also spend time in town shopping for Western collectibles.

WEST OF CRAIG

About 90 miles northwest of Craig is **Brown's Park National Wildlife Refuge**, a nesting and resting place for migratory waterfowl along the Green River now managed by the U.S. Fish and Wildlife Service. Evidence of prehistoric settlement in the area dates back to 1500 B.C. The thirty-mile long valley was also once a favorite Ute and Shoshone winter camp, rich with game animals, tall grass, water, and shelter from the harsh elements. In 1830, Baptiste Brown settled here at Brown's Hole and organized a rendezvous of mountain men and Indians. The place was later called Ft. Misery and abandoned because it never prospered. A spectacular 100-mile drive will take you there and back. From Craig, take US40 west to Maybell, and turn northwest onto CO318.

Groves of aspen contrast with the pine forests of Colorado.

On the way, take a detour on the maintained gravel CR10N to the colorful and highly scenic **Irish Canyon,** where you can view Fremont petroglyphs on the walls of the canyon, along with an interpretive exhibit of the rock art. Unmarked cultural sites can also be found in and around the canyon. Part of the canyon has been designated an "Area of Critical Environmental Concern" based on its outstanding scenery, rare plants, and geology. A small campground is at the site.

A self-guided brochure for the rock art, maps, and information about Irish Canyon and other sites on the Brown's Park route are available at the Craig Chamber of Commerce/Moffat County Visitor Center or the BLM Little Snake Field Office in Craig. Be aware that services are limited in this part of Colorado and cell phone coverage is extremely limited; be sure to take adequate food, water, and gasoline with you.

DINOSAUR NATIONAL MONUMENT
Map #2

This national monument preserves the fossilized remains of dinosaurs, as well as evidence of the prehistoric people who hunted and built their shelters here in the rugged mountains, canyons, and along the rivers.

Headquarters Visitor Center is on US40 near the town of Dinosaur, Colorado (3 miles east of the Utah border). This small center features a slide show, exhibits, maps, and information about the features of the park. No entrance fee is charged here.

The main visitor center and dinosaur quarry is accessed from Vernal, Utah. See Chapter 21, Northern Utah, page 401, for more information on the monument and its Fremont sites.

ESTES PARK
Map #3

Around Town: Estes Park Area Historical Museum
Nearby: Rocky Mountain National Park, Eagle Plume's Trading Post

At over 7,500 feet elevation, Estes Park boasts stunning mountain scenery and world-class outdoor recreation. Wildlife is so abundant here that during the winter, the town has three times as many elk as nearby Rocky Mountain National Park. A hike along the paved path around Lake Estes often reveals a herd of them dining on the golf course grass.

Estes Park is also a tourist town filled with shops, restaurants, galleries, and entertainment. As such, it can be jam-packed with people in the summer. In a less crowded era, Indians may also have used this place as a summer resort. You can see a display of archaeological evidence for this theory at **Estes Park Area Historical Museum,** which also displays pioneer artifacts.

The most imposing building in Estes Park is the historic Stanley Hotel, built on a hill overlooking the town. It was the inspiration for Stephen King's novel *The Shining* and was used as a set for the ABC television adaptation. For a more sweeping panorama of Rocky Mountain National Park and the Continental Divide, ride to the summit of Prospect Mountain on Estes Park Aerial Tramway.

A free shuttle leaves from the visitor center to points around town and also to connect with shuttles for hikers in Rocky Mountain National Park.

NORTH OF ESTES PARK

People have visited the mountains above Estes Park for over eleven thousand years, moving to these higher elevations when summer temperatures enticed them to the lush meadows and cool forests. Hunting animals and gathering plants on both sides of the Continental Divide, they followed trails still accessible today. Although most signs of their summer camps have disappeared, Utes, Shoshones, Arapahos, and Comanches all once roamed the area. In particular, the Ute controlled the mountains until the late 1700s, when the Arapaho moved west from the plains.

The east entrance to **Rocky Mountain National Park** is accessible from Estes Park via US34 or US36. The west entrance to the national park is 1.5 miles north of the town of Grand Lake on US34. If you want to avoid the crowds, this is a better access point.

Rocky Mountain National Park is a spectacular mountain wilderness of 416 square miles, most of it still in a pristine state, partly because mining was never a successful venture here and commercial activity is now strictly limited in the park. If you are an outdoor enthusiast, you will no doubt love it here.

Wildlife is abundant in the park today. Black bears, moose, cougars, elk, mule deer, eagles, bighorn sheep, and coyote all roam freely. Bird watching is a popular pastime for visitors, and at least 280 different species reside here, making it a Globally Important Bird Area.

The park's high mountain peaks (at least sixty of them exceed 12,000 feet) were sacred to the Indians and considered to be steeped in power. On top of Old Man Mountain you can still see heavy river boulders carried there by warriors on Vision Quests. Long's Peak and Mt. Meeker were the "two guides," and their prominences used as beacons from the plains. Long's Peak was also a place to harvest eagle feathers. A hunter would hide under a stone platform roofed with brush and baited with a coyote or wolf carcass, waiting to grasp the legs of the eagle lured to the traps.

Spearheads and scrapers used by mammoth hunters have been found discarded along ancient trails, along with substantial rock walls and hunting blinds used to ambush elk, deer, and bighorn sheep. Above timberline throughout the larger Arapaho-Roosevelt National Forest, forty-two game drive systems have been found, ranging from the relatively recent ones of five hundred years ago to those constructed by Paleo-Indians nine thousand years ago.

One ancient trail now leads hikers across Flattop Mountain. Another, *Taieonbaa*, meaning "Child's Trail," crosses the Continental Divide through a less rocky place. Now called **Trail Ridge Road**, it is the highest continuous paved road in the United States and one of the most popular in the park. For 48 spectacular miles, it winds through forests, alpine tundra, and over the Continental Divide at twelve thousand feet high, connecting Estes Park on the eastern slope of the Rocky Mountains with Grand Lake on the western slope. Breathtaking vistas reveal meandering rivers, quiet beaver ponds, and deep wilderness valleys shaped by glaciers and now blanketed by trees. The road is open from Memorial Day through October, depending on snow. Plan at least half a day for the drive.

The original **Ute Trail** intersects Trail Ridge Road at Ute Crossing and then crosses

Hikers can still follow portions of the Ute Trail from Trail Ridge Road.

and re-crosses the road in several places. Ute Trail can be hiked through Windy Gulch from the trailhead in Upper Beaver Meadow. The Indians often used the valley here as a campsite.

Indians once traveled the route of **Fall River Road** to reach the abundant game in the mountain meadows. The one-way gravel road winds leisurely for 11 miles over the alpine tundra and connects to Trail Ridge Road at the Alpine Visitor Center.

The Arapaho called the bowl of Fish Creek Valley *Tah-kah-aanon,* meaning "The Circle," and often erected summer villages here. The valley is visible from the lower end of the parking lot at Lily Lake Visitor Center. The popular **Bear Lake Road** accesses areas favored by these early visitors, who often camped and grazed their horses in the flat green pastures of Tuxedo and Hallowell Park. At a place by the parking lot near Big Thompson River in Moraine Park, they brought stone from across the Divide to carve their pipes, calling it *Haatja-noont-neechee,* "Where the Pipes Are Made."

The park has *six visitor centers*: Alpine Visitor Center atop Fall River Pass; Beaver Meadows Visitor Center/Park Headquarters on US36 near Estes Park; Fall River Visitor Center on US34 about 5 miles west of Estes Park; Kawuneeche Visitor Center at the western entrance to the park near the town of Grand Lake; Lily Lake Visitor Center on CO7 south of Estes Park; and Moraine Park Museum 2.5 miles southwest of park headquarters. They all have exhibits and provide information on backcountry travel, camping, and places of interest in the park. The park also provides a free shuttle for hikers.

Be aware that no lodging and no service stations exist within the park. The closest places to stay are in the towns of Estes Park on the eastern edge of the park and Grand Lake on the western edge. Also be prepared for changeable and extreme weather. Temperatures can drop over 40 degrees in less than twenty-four hours, and at higher elevations, snow in July is possible. The park is all above 7,500 feet, so protect yourself from the sun, and drink plenty of water to counteract the effects of the high altitude.

Bear Lake glistens serenely under snow-capped peaks in Rocky Mountain National Park.

SOUTH OF ESTES PARK

Eagle Plume's Trading Post, established in 1917, specializes in historic and contemporary Indian arts and crafts, and it is a good place to buy authentic jewelry, textiles, basketry, and other items. While here, take the time to view Charles Eagle Plume's extensive art collection of over one thousand historic and prehistoric pieces. The trading post is 10 miles south of Estes Park on CO7.

GLENWOOD SPRINGS
Map #4

Around Town: Frontier Historical Museum, Glenwood Hot Springs Pool, Glenwood Caverns
Adventure Park and Iron Mountain Tramway, Yampah Spa, and Vapor Caves
Nearby: Dotsero-Ute Trail, Rifle Creek Museum

Glenwood Springs is known today for its healing hot springs, just as it was in the time of the Utes, who considered the place holy and the heart of their homeland. Each year they traveled here to partake of the fifty or so hot springs that once lined both sides of the river. They soaked in the geothermal mineral water to heal their ailments and wounds, they rejuvenated with steam baths in the 122-degree vapor caves, and they scooped out holes in the warm earth, covered themselves with pine boughs, and relaxed with purifying mud baths. Even after they were forced to a reservation, Utes returned as often as possible to the springs they called *Yampah*, "Big Medicine."

Yampah Hot Springs now feeds **Glenwood Hot Springs Pool**, the largest outdoor hot springs pool in the United States. It extends for three city blocks and includes a waterslide, a 104-degree therapy pool, and a 90-degree main pool for swimming and diving. The pleasant Glenwood Hot Springs Lodge is conveniently situated next door to the pool, and lodgers are given unlimited pool access. Look in the lobby of the lodge for paintings and stories of Ute Indians by local artist Jack Roberts. The pool and lodge are located at exit 116 on I-70.

Next door to the lodge is the historic Hotel Colorado. This elegant Victorian hotel originated as a mountain resort in the late 1800s and has attracted many notable visitors since then. In addition to lodging and fine dining here, you will find outdoor recreation guides and equipment rental.

Just east of the pool is **Yampah Spa and Vapor Caves**, with the only known natural steam vapor caves in North America. This collection of underground cave chambers was once used by Utes for purification in preparation for vision quests. The caves remain important to them today, and they still visit occasionally to conduct ceremonial "sweats."

Frontier Historical Museum is dedicated to preserving the history of Glenwood Springs and Garfield County through museum exhibits, photographs, educational programs, and historical archives. Among its Native American items are an extensive arrowhead collection, a mano and metate that visitors can use to grind corn, a gourd dipper, historical photos of local Indians, and carved sections of Ute message trees, which were used as a communication device.

For a panoramic view of the mountains and town, take the Iron Mountain Tramway to Exclamation Point at the top of Iron Mountain. The tram is part of Glenwood Caverns Adventure Park.

More information is available at *Glenwood Springs Chamber Resort Association* on Grand Avenue. In addition to the main office that is open during business hours, a small area with literature is open twenty-four hours.

NORTH OF GLENWOOD SPRINGS

A century ago, the Ute Trail crossed throughout the mountains of Colorado. Today fragments of it are still visible.

Outside the town of Dotsero, a portion of the trail climbs from the Colorado River Basin across the Flat Tops to the White River Basin, leading through panoramic scenery and areas of abundant wildlife. It was later used as a wagon road by prospectors in the early 1900s to access the town of Carbonate. **Dotsero-Ute Trail** hiking trail follows the route for 4 miles. The trailhead is north of Dotsero off the Colorado River Road. For more information, contact the White River National Forest office in Glenwood Springs.

WEST OF GLENWOOD SPRINGS

The town of Rifle is 28 miles west of Glenwood Springs on I-70. *Rifle Visitor Information Center* has maps and information on the numerous outdoor recreational opportunities in the nearby White River National Forest and state parks.

Rifle Creek Museum, in the former city hall, has twenty rooms of exhibits that range from Native American artifacts to a frontier dentist's office.

UTE LEADERS

Ouray, who had an Apache father and was adopted into the Ute tribe after marrying a Tabeguache girl, was one of the most famous Ute leaders of the 19th century. He worked to save as much Ute homeland as possible through peaceful negotiation with the United States government, which designated him the representative for the entire Ute tribe. Ouray died from Bright's disease on August 2, 1880, at the age of forty.

Chipeta, Ouray's second wife, was a Tabeguache Ute and a diplomat in her own right. She attended numerous treaty negotiations in both Colorado and Washington, D.C. She outlived her husband by many years, dying in 1924 at the age of eighty.

Colorow, a member of the White River Band, was leader of the Northern Utes and a fierce protector of his people. In contrast to Ouray, he lacked the skills of a diplomat. The United States government considered him a threat.

GRAND JUNCTION
Map #5

Around Town: Museum of Western Colorado, Western Colorado Center for the Arts

Nearby: Colorado National Monument, Dinosaur Diamond Prehistoric Scenic Byway (McDonald Creek Canyon, Rim Rock Drive), Dominguez Canyon, Grand Mesa Scenic Byway (Grand Mesa National Forest, Land's End, Pioneer Town), Rangely (Canyon Pintado, Rangely Outdoor Museum)

Grand Junction lies in Grand Valley, which was part of the Ute Reservation until 1881, when the Indians were "removed" to Utah. Three months later a town was founded here called simply "Ute." The town was later renamed West Denver, and finally Grand Junction, after its location at the confluence of the Gunnison River and the Grand River (which is now called the Colorado River). Today Grand Junction is the largest town in the region and a hub of activity. Visitors and residents alike enjoy hiking, biking, sampling fresh fruit from the nearby orchards, and touring the wineries.

The historic downtown district has preserved some of the character of the town's past. The **Museum of Western Colorado** on 5th Street and Ute Avenue consists of several museums, outdoor sites, a research library, and an education center. The *History Museum and Smith Tower* in downtown Grand Junction is the main museum. Among its collections are an audio station that teaches the Navajo language and an adobe dwelling with an excellent collection of Mimbres and other Southwestern pottery.

Other branches of the museum include Cross Orchards Historic Farm, dedicated to recreating pioneer life in the early 1900s, and Dinosaur Journey Museum (exit 19 on I-70 in the nearby town of Fruita), focusing on paleontology.

Mesas rise above orchards and wineries near Grand Junction.

The **Western Colorado Center for the Arts** devotes a portion of its permanent collection to Native American artifacts. Included are excellent Navajo weavings that date from the early 1900s to modern times, as well as pottery from the Hopi, Casa Grandes, Ancestral Puebloan, Tusayan, Jeddito, and Salado cultures. The pottery is always on display, but the rugs are only occasionally available to view.

The *Grand Junction Visitor Center*, on the south side of I-70 at Horizon Drive, has more information.

NORTH OF GRAND JUNCTION

The town of *Rangely* began as a Ute trading post in the late 1800s. *Rangely Outdoor Museum*, at the west end of town, now displays Ute and Comanche artifacts, along with Fremont points and Ancestral Puebloan pots. The museum is housed in the Wolf Canyon historic schoolhouse.

Numerous **rock art sites** can be seen near Rangely, including those in Canyon Pintado ("Painted Canyon") and along Dragon Road. Ask at the museum or the *Rangely Chamber of Commerce* for a free descriptive brochure and map to the petroglyphs. One is also available on the museum's Web site, the BLM White River Field Office in Meeker, or visitor centers in Fruita and Grand Junction. The milepost markings on the map are useful since signs for areas of interest are sometimes hard to see from the road.

Canyon Pintado National Historic District is south of Rangely on CO139 in Douglas Creek Valley (and 35 miles north of Grand Junction). The canyon has eight marked, well-preserved rock art sites depicting both humans and animals. The pictographs and petroglyphs were drawn and carved on the sandstone cliffs by Fremont Indians, who migrated here from the Great Basin in Utah looking for food, and by Utes, who roamed the area from about A.D. 1500 to 1800. Among the 1,500 images are wedge-shaped people, bison, hands, bear paws, horses, birds, and reptiles. Look for the large Kokopelli figure at mile 56 that is visible from your car and the Sun Dagger site marking the summer solstice at milepost 67.6.

An auto tour of Canyon Pintado takes about one hour. Allot an additional hour to hike the East Four Mile Trail. Several of the sites along the trail are marked as wheelchair accessible, but access is not always easy. More information is available from the BLM White River Field Office in Meeker.

EAST OF GRAND JUNCTION

Grand Mesa is a 53-square mile, flat-topped mountain where you can fish, hike, camp, and enjoy awe-inspiring scenery. The mesa is dotted with lakes and covered with dense alpine forest, and it provides views from the top that are nothing short of spectacular.

For at least eight thousand years, Grand Mesa has been a place of seasonal settlements and prime summer hunting grounds. The Folsom, Fremont, and Ancestral Pueblo peoples may all have visited, as well as those from a culture some archaeologists call the Uncompahgre People, which populated the area from A.D. 1 to 1300.

At various times, the Ute called the mesa "Thunder Mountain" and *Thigunawat*, *meaning* "Home of Departed Spirits." In 1776, a group of them guided Dominguez and Escalante to an encampment here. Grand Mesa was the ancestral hunting grounds where Chief Douglas and the Utes involved with the Meeker incident brought their Anglo captives. The hostages were eventually released unharmed in response to an emissary sent by Chief Ouray.

To reach Grand Mesa with its unusual beauty and soaring views, take I-70 about 25 miles northeast of Grand Junction to CO65, and turn east to the mesa. At the top of the mesa is *Grand Mesa Visitor Center*. Stop here for interpretive exhibits, a high-altitude native garden, and visitor information.

The **Grand Mesa Scenic Byway** is the section of CO65 that runs from I-70 south through the town of Mesa to the town of Cedaredge. For part of the time, the road follows the trail once used by Uintah Utes from White River, and Tabeguache Utes from the Uncompahgre and Gunnison valleys, for tribal visits. *Pioneer Town* in Cedaredge is designed

Hidden in the rugged lands of Colorado National Monument is ancient rock art left by people who hunted, farmed, and gathered here.

LEGEND OF GRAND MESA

Eagle

In times past, three pairs of great eagles lived along the north rim of the mesa. Debris from their giant nests spilled over the edge of the cliffs and created thunderous slides off the white rocks.

Called Bahaa-Nieche, these huge Thunderbirds sometimes carried off Indian children. When one of then took Sehiwaq's son, the chieftain angrily climbed to the top of the mesa, found a nest, and hurled the young eaglets over the cliff. Living below the cliffs was the serpent Batiqtuba, who devoured the baby birds.

The furious Thunderbirds attacked Batiqtuba, carried the snake into the air, and tore it apart. Fire and thunder streamed from the Bahaa-Nieche as they threw what was left of Batiqtuba down to the ground. The fight tore huge open pits into the ground and created great torrents of rain that filled the pits with water. Today you can still see the many lakes they created.

to recreate the frontier life of the early settlers. The displays in its Sutherland Indian Museum include an extensive arrowhead collection.

The Scenic Byway also leads across the top of Grand Mesa along Forest Service Road 122 to *Land's End Observatory and Trail*, where you can enjoy an impressive panoramic view of Grand Valley over 1 mile below, the La Sal Mountains 60 miles west in Utah, and the San Juan Mountains 90 miles south. Once one of the steeper and more hazardous Indian trails in the area, this is now a well-maintained gravel road that can also be accessed from US50 south of Grand Junction. The Grand Junction Forest Ranger District has more information on Grand Mesa.

WEST OF GRAND JUNCTION

Colorado National Monument preserves a bold and colorful Western landscape of rugged canyons, sculpted rocks, and soaring plateaus. Archaic Indians left behind hide scrapers 5,600 years ago in No Thoroughfare Canyon. Later, Fremont Indians used the canyon for growing corn, hunting, and gathering pinyon nuts and other wild foods. The culture disappeared between 1,200 and 1,350 years ago, to be replaced more recently by the Ute. Rock art in this remote canyon still attests to these earlier people. An 8.5-mile hiking trail leads modern-day visitors into the canyon.

Rim Rock Drive follows 23 miles from the Grand Valley through the monument's high country. As it winds along the edge of the Uncompahgre Uplift over two thousand feet above the valley, it offers magnificent panoramic views. The drive, which takes about one hour, begins at the *visitor center*. Here you can obtain a booklet and map of the drive and its wayside exhibits that provide information on the natural and human history of the park. The center also has exhibits, a slide show, and bookstore.

The west entrance to Colorado National Monument is accessed from exit 19 off I-70 in Fruita; the east entrance is accessed from exit 31 off I-70 in Grand Junction. Take bug spray to fend off the gnats if you are visiting from mid-May through mid-June.

The *Fruita Colorado Welcome Center* is also at exit 19 off I-70. It is a good place to find information on the monument and northwestern Colorado. Ask here for a brochure covering the **Dinosaur Diamond Prehistoric Scenic Byway**, which leads through some breathtaking Colorado and Utah scenery. In addition to paleontology sites, the road travels past archaeological resources and through the Uintah-Ouray Ute Indian Reservation.

McInnis Canyons National Conservation Area was created to preserve a wilderness of breathtaking scenery, outstanding opportunities for outdoor recreation, and varied archaeological sites and paleontology resources. No paved roads or visitor centers exist in the Conservation Area.

Of archaeological interest is *McDonald Creek Canyon*, now a Cultural Resource Management Area near the Colorado/Utah border where camping and fires are not permitted. Fremont Indians lived here a thousand years ago, no doubt attracted by the creek water, abundant plants and small game animals, and the sheltering cliffs. A short hiking trail up the east side of the canyon leads past four panels of rock art; an interpretive sign at the trailhead gives directions to the panels. Southwest of Grand Junction is *Dominguez Canyon*, which also has a trail past rock art. For directions to these and other sites, inquire at the BLM office in Grand Junction.

GRANBY
Map #6

Nearby: Hot Sulphur Springs Resort, Pioneer Village Complex

Granby nestles in an alpine valley that boasts soaring views of Rocky Mountain National Park and the Continental Divide. The town is conveniently situated near the intersections of US34 to Estes Park, US40 to Steamboat Springs, and CO125 north to Wyoming. You will find plenty of opportunities for summer and winter outdoor recreation here, as well as places to stay and eat while exploring this part of Colorado's mountains. The *Granby Chamber of Commerce* and the *Grand County Colorado Tourism Board* have more information.

WEST OF GRANBY

Hot Sulphur Springs is a small, quaint town located at 7,600 feet in a wide mountain valley called Middle Park. Large animal herds once took advantage of the abundant grazing opportunities here, and Native Americans followed them. Since Ute and Arapaho hunters often vied for the same territory, fighting among them was common.

The Ute also favored this place for a campsite because of the hot springs and the natural shelter of the bluffs that enclose Byers Canyon. When they bathed in the mineral water, they did so in a specific order: men, horses, dogs, children, and women.

The seven springs at Hot Sulphur Springs have flowed from deep below the earth for countless years. Two Ute legends speak of their origin. In one, an ailing chief stayed behind to die when his tribe moved to another camp. He built a huge fire within one of the springs

In autumn, mountain valleys as here in Estes Park are filled with the drama of bull elks bugling, fighting, and gathering their herds.

and prayed to the Great Spirit for a return to health. His prayers were answered with a cure, and he returned to his band with gratitude and news of the healing waters.

In another legend, a wise Ute shaman tried to convince his people to make peace with the Plains tribes. The young warriors, however, chose to fight, and thus began a tradition that continued until the Europeans came. In despair, the shaman sought solitude by the river. His campfire, still burning to this day, warms the waters of the hot springs.

Today, you can enjoy the hot springs at *Hot Sulphur Springs Resort and Spa*. Having been in continuous operation for over 140 years, this hot springs resort is one of the oldest in the nation. William Byers, the first white man to own the springs, used deceptive tactics—as was often the case—to transfer ownership of the hot springs from the Utes to himself in the mid-1800s.

In 1997, the resort was renovated and reopened with a ceremony that included a special blessing by a Ute tribal spiritual leader. Along with lodging, the facility now has over twenty mineral pools and private baths. Motel guests receive free use of the pool for two days. The complex is situated at the north edge of town across the Colorado River.

The Grand County Historical Society has three museums in its complex—a historic log cabin in the Heritage Park Museum, Cozens Ranch and Stage Stop Museum, and *Pioneer Village Complex*. The Pioneer Village Complex has a few historical Indian artifacts, as well as 8,500-year-old artifacts from the Windy Gap archaeology site, which was occupied seasonally for perhaps 3,500 years. The museum is at the east end of town on US40.

MEEKER
Map #7

Around Town: White River Museum
Nearby: Ute Agency site, Thornburg Historical Site

Major John Wesley Powell lived in White River Valley with the Indians during his 1868–69 expedition. Powell Park, which was named for him, became the site of the White River Indian Agency.

In 1878 Nathan Meeker arrived at the Indian Agency. He brought his family with him, as well as a plan to "civilize" the Utes by plowing into farmland the pastures they used for their prize horses. Since the Utes considered farming to be "women's work," and since a horse was a Ute's most prized possession, conflict between the two was inevitable. On September 20, 1879, angry Utes killed Meeker and his employees, and the agency was burned. Meeker's wife and daughter were taken hostage, along with a woman named Mrs. Price and her two children. After twenty-four days and the intercession of other Utes, they were released unharmed. The U.S. Army was called to the area, and the Indians were banished to a reservation in eastern Utah.

The parade ground of the army post established in 1880 after the Meeker incident is now the town park around the courthouse. At the north end of the park are three log cabins once used as barracks by the troops.

Soldiers built the log cabin that now houses the **White River Museum**, a folk museum that displays historical photographs, potsherds, arrowheads, and Ute items, including Ute Chief Colorow's pipe and rifle. One item of interest is the plow Meeker used to dig up the Indians' pony racetrack, thus precipitating the Meeker uprising. The museum also has information about the Battle of Milk Creek of 1887, a.k.a. the Thornburg Battle, which involved the Utes and the U.S. cavalry, and is considered one of the last major Indian uprisings in the United States.

For visitors who want to explore the surrounding mountains, the Flat Tops Wilderness is the second largest wilderness area in Colorado. During the summer, you can enjoy a scenic drive along the 82 miles of the Flat Tops Trail Scenic Byway from Meeker to Yampa (take CO64 east of town to CR8). Be advised this is a fair-weather road.

NORTHEAST OF MEEKER

Thornburg Historical Site has one historical marker in honor of the soldiers killed in the Thornburg Battle and two to commemorate the fallen Indian warriors. The site is northeast of Meeker. Take CO13 to CR15, turn, and follow the road 17 miles to the site.

WEST OF MEEKER

Three miles west of town on CO64 is a marker and arrow pointing to the site of the **White River Ute Agency**. To the right of the monument is the wide shallow area called Josephine Basin, where Meeker's daughter unsuccessfully tried to hide.

STEAMBOAT SPRINGS
Map #7

Around Town: Tread of Pioneers Museum, mineral swimming pools
Nearby: Strawberry Park Hot Springs, Windy Ridge archaeological site

As early as the 1300s, Yampatika Utes summered here and enjoyed some of the 150 mineral springs in the area. For food, they dug up the potato-like yampa root that grows along the banks of the Yampa River flowing through town.

Although now a major ski resort, the town still retains some of its flavor as a Western ranching town. The **Tread of Pioneers Museum** preserves the history of local pioneer life. Native American displays include Ute beadwork and basketry, Hopi pottery, and historical photographs by Edward Curtis.

Steamboat Springs Health and Recreation Association runs a recreational complex with three spring-fed hot **mineral swimming pools** and a waterslide.

Rocky Mountain Ventures, operating with special use permits from the U.S. Forest Service, leads snowshoe and hiking tours to a buffalo ranch in the Mt. Harris area, which is also home to deer, elk, coyotes, and eagles.

NORTH OF STEAMBOAT SPRINGS

To enjoy the same healing waters the Indians did, visit **Strawberry Park Natural Hot Springs**. Masonry has been used here to build unique, rock-lined pools in the creek where a series of hot springs flow down into it. This controls the water temperature and provides a lovely natural setting for the hot springs. If you have time, book a massage or spend the night in one of the rustic cabins or in your own tent at the site. Bathing suits are required in the hot springs during daylight hours. To reach the hot springs, follow CR36 (Strawberry Park Road) 7 miles north of town.

SOUTH OF STEAMBOAT SPRINGS

The **Windy Ridge archaeological site**, at the top of Rabbit Ears pass, was once an extensive tool quarry for ancient peoples. A trail passes through a mile-wide lithic procurement area, where even today the ground is littered with quartzite flakes and tools left from thousands of years of use. A fired mud structure built 8,500 years ago has also been found here. Utes also traveled through here on their way between Middle and North Parks, and sites in the area held religious significance for them. From the top of the main quarry ridge, you can enjoy an expansive view of Rabbit Ears Peak and Whiteley Peak. Interpretive tours with an archaeologist are sometimes available from the *Yampatika Nature Center* in town.

EVENTS

MAY *Glenwood Springs Ute Powwow:* Dancing, arts, crafts, and food. Held in mid-May.
Grand Olde West Days: Traditional activities such as a carnival, music, parades, rodeo, and vendors. Held at Moffat County Fairgrounds in Craig on Memorial Day weekend. Call Craig Chamber of Commerce or visit www.grandoldewestdays.com for events schedule.

JULY *Michael Martin Murphy's West Fest:* Tribute to the traditions and spirit of the American West. Music, artist exhibits, and three camps—Cowboy, Mountain Man, and Native American. Included are Indian dancers, storytellers, and traditional native activities such as flute making and tipi painting. Held in Snowmass, July 4th weekend, www.westfest.net.
Range Call Rodeo: Reenactment of Meeker incident by townspeople on July 4th weekend. Call Meeker Chamber of Commerce.

CONTACT INFORMATION

Brown's Park National Wildlife Refuge
1318 Highway 318, Maybell, CO 81640
800-344-9453 *or* 970-365-3613
http://brownspark.fws.gov

Bureau of Land Management
www.blm.gov/co/st/en.html
  Colorado State Office
  2850 Youngfield Street, Lakewood, CO 80215
  303-239-3600
  Craig Field Office
  455 Emerson Street, Craig, CO 81625
  970-826-5000
  Glenwood Springs Field Office
  50629 Hwy 6 & 24, PO Box 1009, Glen wood Springs, CO 81602
  970-947-2800
  Grand Junction Field Office
  2815 H Road, Grand Junction, CO 81506
  970-244-3000
  Little Snake Field Office
  455 Emerson Street, Craig, CO 81625
  970-826-5000
  White River Field Office
  73544 Hwy 64, Meeker, CO 81641
  970-878-3601

Eagle Plume's Trading Post
9853 Hwy 7, Allenspark, CO 80510
303-747-2861 • www.eagleplume.com

Canyon Pintado
www.co.blm.gov/wrra/c_pintado1.html

Colorado National Monument
Fruita, CO 81521-0001
970-858-3617 • www.nps.gov/colm
Visitor Center: Daily 8am-6pm, Memorial Day-Labor Day; daily 9am-5pm, Labor Day-Memorial Day

Colorado State Parks
303-866-3437
Reservations: 800-678-2267, 303-470-1144, *or* http://parks.state.co.us

Colorado Welcome Center
340 Hwy 340, Fruita, CO 81521
970-858-9335
www.colorado.com/getting36

Craig Chamber of Commerce
360 E. Victory Way, Craig, CO 81625
800-864-4405 *or* 970-824-5689
www.craig-chamber.com
www.colorado-go-west.com

Dinosaur Chamber of Commerce
PO Box 202, Dinosaur, CO 81610
800-864-4405
www.colorado-go-west.com

Dinosaur Diamond Scenic Byway
www.dinosaurdiamond.org

Dinosaur National Monument, Headquarters Visitor Center
4545 E. Hwy 40, PO Box 210, Dinosaur, CO 81610-9724
970-374-3000 • www.nps.gov/dino
Daily 8:30am-4:30pm, May 28-Sept 6; Mon-Fri 8am-4:30pm, Sept 7-May 26; no fee

Dominguez Canyon
www.co.blm.gov/gjra/dominguezwsa.html

Estes Park (town)
PO Box 1200, 170 MacGregor Avenue, Estes Park, CO 80517
970-577-3800
www.estesparkcvb.com • www.estesnet.com

Estes Park Convention and Visitors Bureau
500 Big Thompson Avenue, Estes Park, CO 80517
970-577-9900 *or* 800-44-ESTES

Estes Park Area Historical Museum
PO Box 1691, 200 Fourth Street, Estes Park,
CO 80517
970-586-6256 • www.estesnet.com/museum
Mon-Sat 10am-5pm, Sun 1pm-5pm, May-
Oct; Fri-Sat 10am-5pm & Sun 1pm-5pm,
Nov-Apr; no fee

Frontier Historical Museum
1001 Colorado Avenue, Glenwood Springs,
CO 81601
970-945-4448
www.frontierhistoricalsociety.com
Mon-Sat 11am-4pm, May-Sept; Mon &
Thurs-Sat 1pm-4pm, Oct-Apr; fee

Fruita Chamber of Commerce
432 East Aspen Avenue, Fruita, CO 81521
970-858-3894 • www.fruita.org

Glenwood Caverns Adventure Park
51000 Two Rivers Plaza Road, Glenwood
Springs, CO 81601
800-530-1635 *or* 970-945-4228
www.glenwoodcaverns.com

Glenwood Hot Springs Lodge and Pool
401 N. River Street, PO Box 308, Glenwood
Springs, CO 81602
970-945-6571 *or* 800-537-7946
www.hotspringspool.com
Pool: daily 7:30am-10pm daily, summer; daily
9am-10pm, winter; fee

**Glenwood Springs Chamber of Commerce/
Visitor Center**
1102 Grand Avenue, Glenwood Springs, CO 81601
888-445-3696 *or* 970-945-6589
www.glenwoodchamber.com

Granby Chamber of Commerce
PO Box 35, Granby, CO 80446
800-325-1661 *or* 970-887-2311
www.granbychamber.com

Grand County Historical Society
110 E. Byers Avenue, PO Box 165, Hot
Sulphur Springs, CO 80452
970-725-3939 • www.grandcountymuseum.com
Pioneer Village Complex
U.S. Hwy 40, Hot Sulphur Springs, CO 80452
970-725-3939
Tues-Sat 10am-5pm & Sun 1-5pm, sum
mer; Wed-Sat 10am-4pm, winter; fee

Grand County Colorado Tourism Board
PO Box 131, Granby, CO 80446
800-729-5821
www.grand-county.com/Towns_Map.aspx

**Grand Junction Visitor Center and
Convention Bureau**
740 Horizon Drive, Grand Junction, CO
81508
800-962-2547 • www.visitgrandjunction.com

Grand Lake
Chamber of Commerce
PO Box 429, Grand Lake, CO 80447-0057
970-627-3372; 800-531-1019 (free
vacation planner)
www.grandlakechamber.com
Visitor Center
14700 US Hwy 34, Grand Lake, CO 80447
970-627-3402

Grand Mesa Scenic Byway
www.grandmesabyway.org

Grand Mesa
Visitor Center
CO65 on top of Grand Mesa
970-856-4153
Daily 9am-5pm, June-Sept; most weekends
9am-5pm, Oct-May; no fee
Land's End Observatory and Trail
Forest Service Rd 122 on Grand Mesa

Hot Sulphur Springs Resort and Spa
PO Box 275, Hot Sulphur Springs, CO 80451
800-510-6235 *or* 970-725-3306
http://hotsulphursprings.com

**McInnis Canyon National Conservation
Area/McDonald Creek**
www.co.blm.gov/mcnca/mcdonald.htm

Meeker Chamber of Commerce
710 Market Street, PO Box 869, Meeker, CO
81641
970-878-5510 • www.meekerchamber.com

**Museum of Northwest Colorado/Cowboy and
Gunfighter Museum**
590 Yampa Avenue, Craig, CO 81625
970-824-6360 • www.museumnwco.org
Mon-Fri 9am-5pm & Sat 10am-4pm; no fee

Museum of Western Colorado
462 Ute Ave, Grand Junction, CO 81501
888-488-3466 *or* 970-242-0971
www.wcmuseum.org
Cross Orchards Historic Farm
3073 F Road, Grand Junction, CO 81504
970-434-9814
www.wcmuseum.org/crossorchards.htm
Tues-Sat 9am-4pm, May-mid Oct; fee
Dinosaur Journey Museum
550 Jurassic Court, Fruita, CO 81521
970-858-7282 • www.dinosaurjourney.org
Daily 9am-5pm, May-Sept; Mon-Sat 10am-
    4pm, Sun noon-4pm, Oct-Apr; fee
History Museum and Smith Tower
462 Ute Avenue, Grand Junction, CO 81501
970-242-0971 • www.wcmuseum.org
Mon-Sat 9am-5pm & Sun Noon-4pm,
    May-Sept; Tues-Sat 10am-3pm, Oct-
    Apr; fee

Pioneer Town
PO Box 906, Cedaredge, CO 81413
970-856-7554 • www.cedaredgecolorado.com
Mon-Sat 9am-4pm & Sun 1-4pm, Memorial
    Day-late Sept; fee

Pioneer Village Complex (*See* Grand County
    Historical Society)

Rangely Chamber of Commerce
209 E Main St, Rangely, CO 81648-3048
970-675-5290 • www.rangely.com

Rangely Outdoor Museum
150 Kennedy Drive, PO Box 131, Rangely,
    CO 81648
970-675-2612
www.rangely.com/museum.html
Mon-Sat 10am-4pm, June-Aug; Fri-Sat 10am-
    4pm, Apr-May & Sept-Oct; no fee

Rifle Chamber of Commerce
200 Lions Park Circle, PO Box 809, Rifle, CO
    81650
970-625-2085 *or* 800-842-2085
www.riflechamber.org

Rifle Creek Museum
331 East Avenue, Rifle, CO 81650
970-625-4862
Mon-Fri 10am-4pm, May-Oct; fee

Rocky Mountain National Park
1000 Highway 36, Estes Park, CO 80517
800-378-3798 or 970-586-1206
www.nps.gov/romo
Daily 24 hours; fee
Recorded information: 970-586-1333
Backcountry: 970-586-1242
Camping reservations: 877-444-6777
Road and weather conditions: 970-586-1333
Visitor Centers:
Alpine
Daily, early May-early Oct
Beaver Meadows-Park Headquarters
Daily 9am-5pm, with extended summer
    hours
Fall River
Daily 9am-5pm, with extended summer
    hours
Kawuneeche
Daily 9am-5pm, with extended summer
    hours
970-627-3471
Lily Lake Visitor Center
Daily, early May-early Oct
Moraine Park Museum
Daily, early May-early Oct

Rocky Mountain Ventures
8829 Pine Grove Road, Steamboat Springs,
    CO 80488
970-870-8440 • www.verticalgrip.com

Steamboat Springs Chamber Resort
    Association
1225 S. Lincoln Avenue, PO Box 774408,
    Steamboat Springs, CO 80477
970-879-0880
www.steamboat-chamber.com

Steamboat Springs Health and Recreation
    Association
136 Lincoln Avenue, Steamboat Springs, CO
    80477
970-879-1828 • www.sshra.org

Strawberry Park Hot Springs
44200 County Road #36, Steamboat Springs,
    CO 80487
970-879-0342
www.strawberryhotsprings.com
Sun-Thurs 10am-10:30pm (no entry after
    9:30pm); Fri-Sat 10am-12 midnight (no
    entry after 10:30pm); fee

Tread of Pioneers Museum
8th and Oak Streets, PO Box 772372, Steamboat Springs, CO 80477
970-879-2214
www.yampavalley.info/history0074.asp
Tues-Sat 10am-5pm; fee

U.S. Fish and Wildlife Service
www.fws.gov

U.S. National Forest Service; Rocky Mountain Region
740 Simms Street, Golden, CO 80401
mailing address: PO Box 25127, Lakewood, CO 80225-0127
303-275-5350
hearing impaired: 303-275-5367
www.fs.fed.us/r2
   Arapaho & Roosevelt National Forests-Pawnee National Grassland
   2150 Centre Avenue, Building E, Fort Collins, CO 80526-8119
   970-295-6600
   hearing impaired: 970-295-6794
   www.fs.fed.us/r2/arnf
   Grand Junction Ranger District
   764 Horizon Drive, Grand Junction, CO 81506
   970-242-8211; TYY 970-242-8411
   Grand Mesa, Uncompahgre, and Gunnison National Forests
   2250 Hwy 50, Delta, CO 81416
   970-874-6600; TYY 970-874-6660
   www.fs.fed.us/r2/gmug
   Medicine Bow-Routt National Forests, Thunder Basin National Grassland
   2468 Jackson Street, Laramie, WY 82070
   307-745-2300
   hearing impaired: 307-745-2307
   www.fs.fed.us/r2/mbr
   White River National Forest
   900 Grand Ave., PO Box 948, Glenwood Springs, CO 81602
   970-945-2521
   hearing impaired: 970-945-3255
   www.fs.fed.us/r2/whiteriver

Western Colorado Center for the Arts
1803 N. Seventh Street, Grand Junction, CO 81501
970-243-7337 • www.gjartcenter.org
Tues-Sat 9am-4pm; fee (no fee Tues)

White River Museum
565 Park Street, PO Box 413, Meeker, CO 81641
970-878-9982
www.meekercolorado.com/museum/htm
Mon-Fri 9am-5pm & Sat-Sun 10am-5pm, mid Apr-mid Nov; Fri-Sat 11am-4pm, mid Nov-mid Apr; no fee

Yampah Spa and Vapor Caves
709 E. Sixth Street, Glenwood Springs, CO 81601
970-945-0667 • www.yampahspa.com
Daily 9am-9pm; fee

Yampatika Nature Center
925 Weiss Drive, Steamboat Springs, CO 80477
970-871-9151 • www.yampatika.org
Mon-Fri 8am-5pm

COLORADO'S FRONT RANGE/HIGH PLAINS

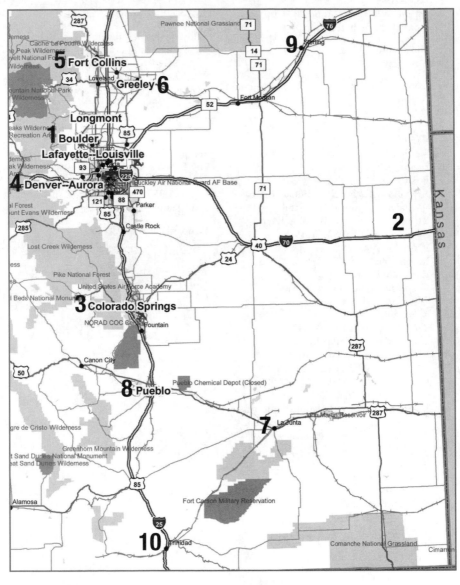

1. Boulder
2. Burlington
3. Colorado Springs
4. Denver
5. Fort Collins

6. Greeley
7. La Junta
8. Pueblo
9. Sterling
10. Trinidad

CHAPTER 14

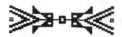

COLORADO'S FRONT RANGE
AND HIGH PLAINS

ALTHOUGH INDIGENOUS PEOPLES traveled and camped on the Colorado plains for centuries past, most of the physical evidence of their presence has long since disappeared. During the 1930s, "dust blowouts" uncovered abandoned campsites and stone circles often referred to as "tipi rings." Many artifacts were looted, but some evidence found its way into museums. The majority of what remains is on private land, where knowledgeable farmers and ranchers still catch an occasional glimpse of a fire-ring or camp remnants.

BOULDER
Map #1

Around Town: Boulder History Museum, University of Colorado Henderson Museum
Nearby: Leanin' Tree Gallery of Western Art, Longmont Museum

Captain Thomas Aikens and a party of prospectors first met Arapaho Chief Niwot (a.k.a. Left Hand) here near Boulder Creek. The intruders promised to stay for only one winter, so Chief Niwot helped to restrain some of his more aggressive warriors from attacking them. Niwot then told Aikens about a prophetic dream in which Boulder Creek flooded and engulfed the Indians but spared the prospectors.

Contrary to Aikens's promise, the prospectors did not leave in the springtime, and within two years the tide of settlers had forced the Arapaho out of the area. In 1864, Niwot and Aikens met again, this time during the Sand Creek Massacre. Niwot, refusing to fight his white friends, stood with arms folded in the middle of the shooting and was mortally wounded.

Today, the town of Boulder is set strikingly next to the tilted red rock sentinels of the Flatirons. People come to ski in the nearby mountains, climb rocks in Eldorado Canyon, and enjoy the tens of thousands of acres of protected open space in and around town. In places once used for hunting or planting by Cheyenne, Apache, and Ute people, a system of trails now provides access. Some, like those in Gregory Canyon and Bear Canyon, are

The cottonwood tree was used in many ways by the Plains Indians. In scarce times, they even scraped the stringy inner bark to use for food.

likely to follow ancient routes. To explore them, obtain information through the *City of Boulder Open Space and Mountain Parks* or *Boulder County Parks and Open Space*.

In addition to varying anthropological exhibits, the **University of Colorado Henderson Museum** permanently displays some of the pottery, tools, sandals, and other artifacts excavated on the university's archaeological digs. A Natural History Hall, Paleontology Hall, and hands-on Discovery Corner round out the exhibits. The museum is off Broadway, just north of the University Memorial Center (UMC). The parking garage next to the UMC is often full, so be prepared to walk; consider public transportation, or join the ubiquitous bicycle riders.

Located in an old mansion near the university at 12th and Euclid, the **Boulder History Museum** includes *The Storymakers' Gallery* with a section about Chief Niwot and the Cheyenne and Arapaho Indians that includes a print of a buffalo hide painting depicting the Sand Creek Massacre. An interactive display challenges visitors to match traditional items made from buffalo parts with their current counterparts (e.g., buffalo bladder to water bottle).

As home to the University of Colorado, the National Center for Atmospheric Research, and the National Institute of Standards and Technology, Boulder is a cultural hub boasting a vibrant arts scene. To experience the unique flavor of the community, visit the Pearl Street Mall and its shops and restaurants. One of the more historic places to stay in town, the Hotel Boulderado is near the open-air mall.

"Indian Voices" is a Native American program broadcast on KGNU Boulder 88.5 FM, KGNU Denver 1390 AM, and online at www.kgnu.org on Sundays, 3-4pm.

NORTH OF BOULDER

Leanin' Tree Gallery Museum of Western Art has a large private collection of works by important twentieth-century Western and Indian artists, including the Native American expressionist Fritz Scholder. Native themes are also seen in many works in the galleries and sculpture garden. Leanin' Tree Gallery is north of Boulder on CO119.

A permanent gallery in the **Longmont Museum and Cultural Center** tells the story of the people who lived where the Front Range and northern plains meet. The survey begins with artifacts left twelve thousand years ago by Clovis hunters and continues to the early 1800s, when Cheyenne and Arapaho people formed a symbiotic trade link with the traders at the forts just being built. A recreated section of Fort St. Vrain, which was built nearby in 1837 by the Bent Brothers and Ceran St. Vrain, stands beside a Cheyenne-style tipi to show the peaceful interdependence of the two groups. Indians exchanged horses, buffalo meat, and buffalo robes for European guns, metal items, beads, blankets, and canvas. The multimedia exhibit continues with the discovery of gold near Denver in 1858, after which tensions rose between the groups, leading to the infamous Sand Creek Massacre in November of 1864 and the final battle at Summit Springs in 1869. The museum also has a small gift shop which sells some Native American books.

BURLINGTON
Map #2

Around Town: Burlington Old Town
Nearby: Beecher Island Battlefield, Wray Museum, Sand Creek Massacre Site, Genoa Tower and Museum, Limon Heritage Museum

The town of Burlington is one of the few places to find a room along I-70 in eastern Colorado. Several motels are located within a mile of exit 437. You won't find anything fancy here, just basic lodging. The Colorado Welcome Center, a quarter-mile west of exit 438, provides travel information for the area and the rest of the state.

A few Native American artifacts and a tipi are in **Burlington Old Town Museum and Emporium**, the re-creation of an early 1900s village complete with an old-time carousel, gunfights, and melodramas. Burlington's *visitor center* is in the same location.

NORTH OF BURLINGTON

In September of 1868, Major George Forsyth and fifty scouts camped at what is now **Beecher Island Battlefield** on a mission to find whites taken captive by Indians. Roman Nose, a famous Northern Cheyenne leader, and six hundred Cheyenne, Northern Arapaho, and Sioux warriors attacked the scouts, who took refuge on a sandbar in the Arikaree River and dug trenches for protection. For nine days, the battle raged, until the scouts were rescued by reinforcements. A monument commemorates the soldiers who were killed, and trails lead to the river and the top of the bluff where the Indians regrouped between attacks. Most years in September, a re-enactment of the battle is staged by the Colorado Cavalry. Beecher Island is about 50 miles north of Burlington off US385. Call the Wray Museum for more detailed directions.

To see a diorama and artifacts from the battlefield, visit the **Wray Museum**. The museum also has a collection of prehistoric artifacts from the Jones-Miller Paleo-Indian bison kill site, excavated south of town by archaeologists from the Smithsonian Institution. The display of the site was designed by Smithsonian experts and includes a re-creation of the bone bed.

The life-sized model of a ten-thousand-year-old bison was sculpted by a local artist in honor of the sacred white buffalo. It is interesting to compare the head size of the seven-foot tall ancient bison with that of the much smaller modern one on the wall. In addition, a timeline uses photos and artifacts to tell the story of archaeological preservation efforts. Other rooms and buildings at the 13,500-square-foot museum interpret the history of Yuma County. The museum is on US34 in town.

SOUTH OF BURLINGTON

One of the darkest days for the Cheyenne and Arapaho people occurred at what is now **Sand Creek Massacre National Historic Site**. By the summer of 1864, hostilities between Anglos and Indians had disrupted the flow of supplies along the overland trails. In August, Colorado governor John Evans created a volunteer militia to deal with the problem, placing Colonel John Chivington, a former Methodist minister who had gained glory during the Civil War, in charge.

On the morning of November 29, 1864, over one hundred lodges of Southern Cheyenne under Chief Black Kettle and eight lodges of Arapaho under Chief Niwot slept peacefully along the dry bed of Sand Creek. Army officers at Fort Lyon had earlier assured them of protection. Chivington chose to ignore that promise and the white flag that Black Kettle raised. He gave his men free rein to attack the village. As many as two hundred men, women, and children were subsequently slaughtered and their bodies mutilated by the soldiers, many of whom were drunk.

Black Kettle miraculously survived the massacre, only to be killed almost four years later, when, on November 27, 1868, troops again ignored the white flag of truce flying from his tipi. This time, the army commander was George Armstrong Custer.

To reach Sand Creek National Historic Site, travel 1 mile east of the town of Chivington on CO96, and turn north onto CR54 for about 8 miles. Turn right at the T-intersection with CRW. In about 1 mile follow the sign on the left leading to the site. Sand Creek became a National Historic Site on August 2, 2005. The site is not open in severe weather, and visitors are admonished to stay on the trail and advised to dress for biting insects.

EAST OF BURLINGTON

The twenty-room **Genoa Tower and Museum** (a.k.a World's Wonderview Museum) and store is a mixture of the fascinating and the bizarre. Owner Jerry Chubbuck is an avid collector of arrowheads, and he displays twenty thousand of them that were found within a hundred-mile radius of the tower. During a 1957 collection trip southeast of the town of Kit Carson, Chubbuck discovered the site of an 8,500-year-old bison kill, which became known as the Olsen-Chubbuck archaeological site. The museum now displays some of the artifacts from its excavation. On the more kitschy side are the two-headed calf and the one thousand pictures painted on the rock walls in the early 1900s by a Sioux Indian called Princess Ravenwing. The museum is 1 mile west of Genoa on the frontage road (exit 371 off I-70).

Further west on I-70 is the town of Limon. The **Limon Heritage Museum** at Railroad Park has a Cheyenne-style tipi furnished with lazy-backs, shields, spear points, and grinding stones, as well as a room for the Dan Houtz Native American Artifact Collection. The museum is also a good place to ask about sites along the Smoky Hill Trail, once the shortest route between the Missouri River and the gold fields. Today, CO86 from Limon to Franktown follows the trail through the scenic Bijou Basin.

The skyline of Colorado Springs is set against the backdrop of Pikes Peak.

COLORADO SPRINGS
Map #3

Around Town: Colorado Springs Fine Arts Center-Taylor Museum of Southwest Studies, Colorado Springs Pioneers History Museum, Garden of the Gods, Rock Ledge Ranch Historic Site
Nearby: Manitou Cliff Dwellings Museum, Manitou Springs mineral springs, Old Colorado City, Pikes Peak, Seven Falls, Ute Pass Historical Society Museum, Ute Pass Trail, Will Rogers Shrine of the Sun

When white settlers arrived here in the mid-1800s, they were greeted by Ute Indians who frequented the area for hunting, religious ceremonies, and winter quarters. The Ute knew Pikes Peak as "Great Shining Peak," and they followed Ute Pass Trail for access between the mountains and plains. Today, "Great Shining Peak" still dominates the skyline, and US24 now follows part of the Ute's seasonal trail. You can visit both, along with places like the Cave of the Winds, the U.S. Air Force Academy, the U.S. Olympic Training Center, Pro Rodeo Hall of Fame and Museum of the American Cowboy, and the Cheyenne Mountain Zoo.

In addition to significant works of American art, the Colorado Springs Fine Arts Center's **Taylor Museum of Southwest Studies** has an excellent collection of Spanish colonial and Native American arts that focus on the Navajo, Pueblo, and Apache from around 1850 to the present. State-of-the-art galleries showcase world-renowned permanent collections and international traveling exhibitions in the new museum addition to the Fine Arts Center. A performing arts theater, art education center, and satellite facility displaying modern art are also part of the center.

Garden of the Gods, a city park off Gateway Road, preserves 1,364 acres of stunning red and white sandstone formations. Ute Pass Trail crossed here near Balanced Rock, and various groups camped, worshiped, and held intertribal meetings in the sheltered places. Petroglyphs, arrowheads, grinding stones, and other artifacts have been found around Gateway Rocks and in Cathedral Canyon. There are 8 miles of hiking trails providing easy access to the geological wonders of the park, including the famous Kissing Camels. Sunrises and sunsets are truly spectacular here.

Garden of the Gods Trading Post, built in the 1920s in the Pueblo style, sits in the southwest corner of the park near Balanced Rock. It is the largest trading post in Colorado that sells native arts and crafts as well as souvenirs. The gallery displays Santa Clara pottery, Hopi katsinas, and other Indian art, and a small café, open for summer lunches and early suppers, sells buffalo burgers.

The privately owned *visitor and nature center* at Gateway Road off 30th Street has a few displays covering the local Indian history, educational films, two gift shops, maps, and a café with lunch and snacks. Talks, tours, and guided walks are also offered.

Rock Ledge Ranch Historic Site is a living-history museum featuring life along the Central Front Range of Colorado from 1775 to 1907. Staff and docents in period clothing demonstrate activities and explain the living conditions at various interpretive areas, including a pioneer homestead, farm, blacksmith shop, and orchard. The American Indian interpretive area depicts the life of local Ute and Plains Indians during 1775 to 1835. Rock Ledge Ranch is across from the Garden of the Gods Visitor Center on 30th Street and is open seasonally. The entrance to the site is on Gateway Road. Tickets can be purchased at Garden of the Gods Visitor Center or a kiosk at the ranch.

Downtown in a historic building that was once the county courthouse, **Colorado Springs Pioneers Museum** contains an elegant 1900 Sioux dress covered with beadwork from neck to hem. Displayed in a side room on the main floor of the museum, it is said to have been made by an Indian girl who was part of Buffalo Bill's Wild West Show when they visited England to entertain Queen Victoria. The room also contains other beaded items, as well as Ancestral Puebloan pottery and a large White Mountain Apache grain basket. Among the items in the small third-floor Indian room are a Cheyenne headdress and leggings and a Ute cradleboard, riding quirt, and hobbles made for their beloved horses. In the same hall are three reconstructed rooms from the home of Helen Hunt Jackson, writer and tireless advocate of Indian rights. Her most famous work, the novel *Ramona*, decried the treatment of the mission Indians.

WEST OF COLORADO SPRINGS

Just west of town is the **Broadmoor-Cheyenne Mountain area**, which is anchored by the historic and luxuriant Broadmoor resort. Behind the hotel at the west end of Cheyenne Boulevard is South Cheyenne Cañon, one of the favorite hunting places of the Ute. This box canyon forms a natural corral that was ideal for trapping wild horses and buffalo. A 1-mile drive leads through the canyon to the base of *Seven Falls*, where the water plunges 181 feet down seven separate granite terraces. An elevator or walk up 264 steps leads to a trail with dramatic views of the city. During the summer Native Americans perform public dances during the day, and computerized lighting illuminates the falls at night.

Nearby is the *Will Rogers Shrine of the Sun*. Rogers was a Cherokee Indian, and the shrine has mementos of the famed humorist's life, along with murals of Native American life in the Pikes Peak region. To reach the shrine, take exit 138 from I-25 and follow the signs to the Cheyenne Mountain Zoo. Access to the shrine is included with zoo admission.

Utes, Arapahos, Kiowas, and Cheyenne often drank from the mineral springs at *Manitou Springs,* which are fed by melting snows from Pikes Peak. *Manitou* is a Native American word for "spirit," and the place was considered a neutral ground where all could come to heal in peace. When the British adventurer George Ruxton visited in 1847, he found beads and leather pieces marking the sanctuary. The Utes continued to visit here until 1879, when they were relegated to reservations.

The town is 4 miles west of Colorado Springs on US24. The *mineral springs* are still active today, and public taps are available to fill bottles with the cool, healing waters that gave the town its nickname of "Saratoga of the West." Memorial Park at Manitou and Deer Path avenues center around Seven Minute Springs. Maps pinpointing the locations of other springs are available at the chamber of commerce on Manitou and Mayfair avenues.

A boulder marking the *Old Ute Trail* is in the center of town near Soda Springs Park. In 1912, Chief Buckskin Charley and some of his Ute tribesmen commemorated the trail with ceremonial dances and the placement of a box of offerings underneath the stone.

Old Ute Trail can still be followed for 3 miles by starting at the trailhead near Mt. Manitou Incline on Ruxton Avenue. It climbs in easy grades to US24 near the town of Cascade. Other sections exist and more are being recovered, with the hope of eventually restoring the trail between Manitou Springs and the lush grasses of South Park where buffalo once roamed.

Some of Manitou Springs' merchants sell authentic Native American arts and crafts. Other stores can be found in the renovated historic district of *Old Colorado City*, 1 mile east of Manitou Springs on US24. The Flute Player Gallery in town has a varied selection of fine Indian art that includes miniature horsehair baskets woven by Tohono O'odham and Akimel O'odham artists.

In the early 1900s, W. S. Crosby moved massive portions of an Ancestral Puebloan cliff dwelling from southern Colorado to Cliff Canon, where it became **Manitou Cliff Dwellings Museum**. Visitors can explore the cliff dwellings and reproductions of a mesa top building and view the native plants along the nature walk. The museum contains dioramas, videos, and Crosby's collection of Ancestral Puebloan artifacts. A gift shop sells native crafts, and in the summer Santa Clara Pueblo Indians dance for the public. The cliff dwellings are west of Colorado Springs on the US24 bypass in Phantom Cliff Canon.

US24 continues west to the turnoff for the 19-mile road to the top of 14,110-foot **Pikes Peak**. It is usually passable in summer (depending on weather), but the last half is unpaved and has no guardrails. Other ways to visit the top are by hiking (eight hours and strenuous) or the Pikes Peak Cog Railway, by far the easiest route.

The town of **Woodland Park**, further west of Colorado Springs on US24, accesses another portion of the Ute Trail at *Centennial Trailhead*. A cabin at the trailhead displays arrowheads and spearheads and has information about the Native American inhabitants. Another site operated by the Ute Pass Historical Society is the *Pikes Peak Museum*, which has a few artifacts from the Southern Ute and a small display of clothing and beadwork. The museum and a gift shop are located in the Cultural Center. The Historical Society also has other historical exhibits in buildings scattered throughout town, including at Rampart Library.

DENVER

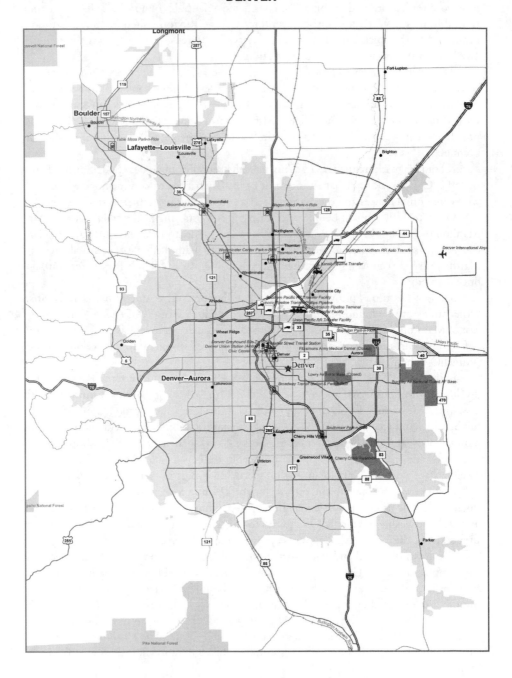

DENVER
Map #4

Around Town: Colorado History Museum, Colorado State Capitol Building, Confluence Park, Denver Art Museum, Denver Museum of Nature and Science, Denver Public Library
Nearby: Buffalo Bill's Grave and Museum, Denver International Airport, Genesee Park Buffalo Herd, Golden Pioneer Museum, Roxborough State Park

In the spring of 1858, William Green Russell and his prospector friends traveled to the confluence of the South Platte River and Cherry Creek searching for gold. Russell, married to a Cherokee woman, had heard about the gold from her kinsmen who prospected in the area the year before. Russell did not find much gold, but he did meet a band of Southern Arapaho camping by the river. Since the Treaty of Fort Laramie had given this land to the Arapahos in 1851, the Indians did not seem alarmed by the intruders. Chief Little Raven pledged that his people would maintain peace, although he did admit he hoped the white men would not stay long.

The Arapaho warned the newcomers that building a settlement at the confluence of the two rivers was "bad medicine." The prospectors ignored the advice, and the bad medicine hit in May of 1864, when a flood killed twenty people and swept away the ramshackle frame buildings of the burgeoning new town. **Confluence Park** now marks the site of Denver's beginnings. It is near downtown just off 15th Street and I-25.

Also downtown, the *Denver Metro Convention and Visitor's Bureau* on 16th and California can give you information on visiting the city. A free shuttle travels through the central shopping district of the tree-lined 16th Street pedestrian mall, and the city is served by numerous city buses and a light rail system. Theater, music and art, the aquarium, Denver Zoo, U.S. Mint, Ocean Journey, Forney Museum of Transportation, Elitch Gardens, and Denver Botanic Gardens are some of the other attractions people come to visit. The city also maintains a connection to its historical past at the landmark Brown Palace Hotel, the "Unsinkable" Molly Brown House Museum, and the restored Byers-Evans House Museum.

It is easy to find the golden dome of the opulent **Colorado State Capitol**, where one of the sixteen stained glass windows under the rotunda honors Chief Ouray for his diplomacy. For a spectacular view of the city and the Rocky Mountains, climb the stairs to the top of the dome. A good time to visit is in the morning before the tour groups arrive.

The **Colorado History Museum** next to the capitol traces the history of Colorado's residents with permanent and changing exhibits. The collection includes artifacts, clothing, original documents, and photographs of Native Americans, as well as interactive exhibits like "Ancient Voices: Stories of Colorado's Distant Past." Items highlight Ancestral Puebloan, Apishapa, and Paleo-Indian people. A life-sized video invites visitors to witness the slow unfolding of a day in an Indian camp by a stream in the San Luis Valley. Other exhibits compare European and Native cultures and use detailed dioramas to show scenes of such activities as a Pawnee buffalo hunt and Ancestral Pueblo daily life. Native American art, crafts, and books are sold in the gift shop.

The **Denver Art Museum**, which holds one of the most extensive collections of North American native arts and crafts in the world, is easy to find. Look for the dramatic build-

A golden dome commemorating the gold rush that brought thousands to Indian homelands tops the Colorado State Capital.

ing to the west of the Colorado History Museum. The American Indian art collection is in the North Building on Levels 2 and 3. Items are also sometimes displayed in the South Building.

The over eighteen thousand objects in this excellent collection are displayed to draw attention to their artistic qualities. Objects come from tribes across the United States and Canada and span from prehistoric times to the present. Included are clothing, baskets, jewelry, Pueblo pottery, beadwork, Hopi katsinas, Navajo textiles, and other items used in everyday life, plus a representation of the interior of a Plains Indian tipi. Although it is not always on display, one notable item is the Two Grey Hills–style rug by Daisy Taugelchee, perhaps the most talented Navajo weaver ever. Woven in the 1940s in the Two Grey Hills style, this rug took six miles of yarn to complete.

Outside the north entrance to the museum is *The Wheel*, a sculpture inspired by Native American circular stone structures that were built for spiritual purposes and called medicine wheels. It is aligned with the four directions and the summer solstice and is used as a civic gathering place.

Also downtown in Civic Center is the **Denver Public Library**, the largest library in the Rocky Mountain region. Its celebrated Western History collection houses hundreds of thousands of books, manuscripts, historical photos, and Western fine art & prints.

The North American Indian collection in the **Denver Museum of Nature and Science** shows how diverse materials and environments have resulted in distinctive Indian cultures. In addition to numerous artifacts, it includes a full-sized replica of part of a Pueblo village, dioramas of a Plains Indian encampment, an Eskimo snow house, and a Northwest Coast clan house. A Navajo hogan is also recreated and can be entered. The museum also has an extensive natural history collection covering four continents, gems and minerals, an IMAX theater, planetarium, gift shop, and café. It is in City Park, east of downtown Denver.

Denver is a major metropolitan city with several good places to shop for native arts and crafts. *Native American Trading Company*, across the street from the Denver Art Museum, is a leading source of Native American and Southwestern art. Another IACA member is *West Southwest Gallery* in Cherry Creek North, which specializes in Indian jewelry and pottery. *David Cook Fine American Art*, in lower downtown Denver, focuses on historic Native American pieces, including old pawn jewelry. *The Mudhead Gallery* in the Grand Hyatt Hotel sells museum quality art by recognized Native American artists, as well as pawn jewelry.

In addition to the variety of restaurants you would expect to find in a city the size of Denver, two places to eat offer a unique experience. One is west of town (see *The Fort,* under West of Denver below) and one is in town. Reservations are recommended for both. *Buckhorn Exchange* was founded in 1895 and is the oldest restaurant in Denver. The mounted animal heads that line the walls give the place an Old West ambience. For a taste of the type of food the Plains Indians enjoyed, order the buffalo or elk. The restaurant is south of downtown Denver across the street from the light rail station.

SOUTH OF DENVER

South of Denver is **Roxborough State Park**, where the year-round availability of game animals, a variety of vegetation, and an abundance of water created an attractive place for the indigenous people. Within the park, prehistoric and historic Indian sites and artifacts have been discovered. Today, hiking is a popular activity in the tranquil setting. Ask about periodic tours of the nearby Lamb Springs prehistoric site. Take Santa Fe Drive (CO85) south to Titan Road, turn right (west) and travel 3 miles. Continue as the road curves south and becomes North Rampart Range Road to the intersection with Roxborough Park Road (3.5 miles) and the park entrance.

EAST OF DENVER

Spirit of the People at **Denver International Airport** is a collaboration of artwork by thirteen tribes from around Colorado. Murals and paintings, historical and contemporary photographs, and audio presentations tell the story from Paleo-Indian times into the present. Displays are in two parts of the airport. A photo gallery is located near the secured area for international passenger arrivals, and an audio presentation is on the bridge to Concourse A. An information center for the city of Denver is on the east side of the 5th floor. The airport is northeast of Denver on Peña Boulevard.

WEST OF DENVER

When schoolteacher Lois Elhers used her summer vacations to live with and learn about Indian tribes, she asked their members to make dolls dressed in authentic tribal clothing. Her collection from thirty-nine different Native American groups is displayed at the **Golden Pioneer Museum** on the north bank of Clear Creek in downtown Golden. Also on permanent display are stone tools, arrowheads, baskets, and pottery from various tribes, as well as displays which tell the rest of Jefferson County's history. There is a heritage garden walk, reading room, outdoor patio, and bookstore/gift shop.

William "Buffalo Bill" Cody, whose Indian name was *Pahaska*, meaning "Long Hair," was an Iowa farmer turned frontier scout, buffalo hunter, and showman. **Buffalo Bill's Grave** and **Museum** has original posters advertising his Wild West Show, which brought Native Americans to the eastern United States as performers. For the show's reenactment of the Battle of Little Big Horn, about half of the Indians actually had fought in the battle. His always dramatic, sometimes exaggerated productions were advertised to show historical events and became part of the mythic lore of the Wild West. The museum has Indian artifacts, Buffalo Bill mementos, and Western art. There is a gift shop and snack bar selling buffalo burgers, and Cody's grave is nearby. It is off I-70 at exit 256 on Lookout Mountain.

Also off I-70 west of Denver is the **Genesee Park Buffalo Herd**, which can sometimes be seen from the highway. The viewing area is off exit 254.

The Fort restaurant is housed in a reproduction of Bent's Fort, a historic trading post on the Santa Fe Trail (see Chapter 14, Colorado's Front Range and High Plains). The staff dresses in frontier costumes, and the menu includes slightly updated frontier recipes using buffalo, quail, and elk. On most Friday and Saturday evenings, Native American flute music accompanies the experience, and special events often recreate the bygone time. The trade lodge in the tent outside sells authentic Native American art and reproductions of fur-trade era items. It is southwest of Denver off CO8 near the town of Morrison and the stunning outdoor Red Rocks Park and Amphitheater. Reservations are advised.

FORT COLLINS
Map #5

Around Town: Duhesa Lounge, Fort Collins Museum
Nearby: Lindenmeier Site

Camp Collins was established in the 1860s as a small military post to protect travelers on the Overland Trail. On I-25 north of town near the Wyoming border are the remnants of a natural stone fort used by Indians and later immigrants for protection from hostile groups. Of note was a battle fought between Crow and Blackfeet warriors in 1831.

The town is now headquarters for the Roosevelt and Arapaho national forests and the site of Colorado State University.

In the foothills northeast of town is the *Lindenmeier Archaeological Site*, which revealed 10,500-year-old information about the Folsom culture and became one of the most famous archaeological discoveries in the United States. The **Fort Collins Museum** in the library park has one small section that tells the story of the dig and includes a Folsom tool box. An eight-foot column of soil layers illustrates how archaeologists find relative dates for sites. As you look up, imagine four more feet, because that is the distance archaeologists dug to find Lindenmeier material. The city is in the process of creating a long-term exhibit at the museum covering the cultural heritage of the Soapstone Prairie Natural Areas, which includes the Lindenmeier site, now a National Historic Landmark. Trails and signage for Soapstone Prairie are also being developed.

Duhesa Lounge, in the Lory Student Center at Colorado State University, is dedicated to Native Americans. The lounge showcases changing exhibits of contemporary and historical Indian artists, with an accent on Colorado and Southwestern artists. Look for the Navajo rugs at the head of the stairs, a carved wooden totem pole, and photos of petroglyphs in the lounge. Powwows are sometimes held at the Student Center.

GREELEY
Map #6

Around Town: Greeley History Museum, Meeker Home
Nearby: Fort Vasquez, Pawnee Buttes National Grassland

Clovis hunters stalked mammoths in the Greeley area about 11,500 years ago. Later Indians hunted the smaller game animals that survived the end of the Ice Age, and by 1200 B.C. early farmers had arrived. Eventually, the Apache, Arapaho, Comanche, and Cheyenne moved into the South Platte region, while Lakota, Utes, and Pawnee sometimes hunted here. White diseases, the demise of the buffalo, and pressure from gold seekers after 1858 caused the Indians to eventually give up their land. By 1865, they were mostly gone from here, to be replaced by cattle drives and the railroad.

Settlers, inspired by the "Go West Young Man" attitude of Horace Greeley and led by his employee Nathaniel Meeker, came in 1869 to start a utopian agricultural settlement called Union Colony. Meeker built a two-story adobe house for his family, and the nineteenth-century **Meeker Home** is now open seasonally. Look for the story of Josephine—who had a better relationship with the Ute Indians than her father did—and a small changing variety of Indian items.

The **Greeley History Museum** downtown has a few displays about the earliest local settlers, including the jacket and skirt Josephine Meeker made from a blanket during her time as a Ute captive. One of the historical photos is of Shawsheen, Chief Ouray's sister, who was captured by an Arapaho band and later freed from near Island Grove Park by a cavalry unit from Camp Collins. A diagram shows the parts of a Great Plains tepee, which includes a liner that prevented shadows from being cast on the walls at night.

Another popular tourist stop is Centennial Village Museum in Island Grove Regional Park, where Cheyenne tree burials, beads, and artifacts were once found. The museum preserves buildings and artifacts used on the High Plains between 1860 and 1920. Almost half a million modern visitors also come to Greeley for the annual Independence Day Stampede, a ten- to twelve-day 4th of July celebration with Western rodeos, food, parade, concerts, and a carnival. Find out more about visiting here at the *Greeley Convention and Visitors Center* downtown in the historic Union Pacific Station.

SOUTH OF GREELEY

South of town on US85 near Platteville is **Fort Vasquez Historic Site and Museum**. Fort Vasquez was a 100-square-foot adobe fort established around 1835 by Louis Vasquez and Andrew Sublette as part of the Rocky Mountain Fur Company. These mountain men traded black silk handkerchiefs, ivory combs, blankets, brass kettles, and liquor to the Indians for buffalo robes. You can visit a reconstruction of the fort and small museum displaying Plains Indian artifacts. Books about Native Americans are sold in the bookstore, and reenactments are sometimes held.

EAST OF GREELEY

At **Pawnee National Grassland** you can experience the majesty and peace of an ancient short-grass prairie. Spreading for miles, this vast expanse is sparsely dotted with

THE BUFFALO

Buffalo were central to the lifestyle of the Plains Indians, providing them with a means of survival and inspiring ceremonies and stories. Every part of the animal was used, from the flesh, tongue, and organs for food to the sinews for thread. Bedding, clothing, saddles, shields, drums, and bags were all made from the hide. Horns became cups and powder horns, and bones were fashioned into scrapers, shovels, awls, and weapons. Brains were used to tan hides, chips became fuel, and even toys were made by stuffing leather balls with hair. In some instances, the Indians even imitated the behavior of a herd, which gathers around wounded or ill members and moves by placing cows and calves in the middle protected by mature adults.

ranches, deserted homesteads, and a few tiny towns, so only a handful of scattered lights compete with the vivid stars at night. You might see a pronghorn antelope almost blending into the buff and brown prairie, or a coyote or fox furtively crossing your path. You will almost certainly find a prairie dog town or two and possibly a road blocked by cows since much of the land is open range. Expect flowers to punctuate the short prairie grasses from early summer to autumn and a variety of bird songs to break the silence in every season. This is an internationally famous birding site.

The most visible landmarks are the twin towers of Pawnee Buttes, which rise like sentinels 250 feet above the prairie sea. The buttes were once lookout posts for local Indians, and archaeologists continue to excavate their campsites. Hikers also find their arrowheads and artifacts, but do be aware that it is illegal to remove them.

A trail from the Pawnee Buttes Overlook leads 1.5 miles down the bluff and through the badlands to the West Butte (the East Butte is on private land). Note that it is closed March 1 to June 30 to protect nesting hawks and falcons. The one equipped campground, Crow Valley, is north of Briggsdale and has information posted about the grassland. It is closed in the winter, but primitive camping is allowed anywhere on public land in the preserve.

Pawnee National Grassland is 35 miles east of Ft. Collins and 25 miles northeast of Greeley. One way to reach the buttes is to travel 15 miles north of Briggsdale on CR77 to CR120. Turn east for 6 miles to Grover, and then take CR390 southeast for 6 miles to CR112. Turn east for 8 miles and follow the signs. Be sure to fill up your gas tank, take water, and dress for weather changes. Roads in the grassland are often impassable when wet, and in many places public land is mixed with private, so a useful first stop is the Arapaho and Roosevelt National Forest office in Greeley to purchase an area map. It is located north of town on O Street and can be tricky to find, so call them for directions.

The twin towers of Pawnee Buttes can be seen here in the distance.

LA JUNTA
Map #7

Around Town: Koshare Indian Kiva Museum
Nearby: Bent's Old Fort National Historic Site, Comanche National Grassland, John Martin
    Reservoir, Las Animas

Many of the sites near La Junta are connected with the Santa Fe Trail, which came through here. US350 from here to Trinidad now follows the old route. Get more information from the Otero Museum at the corner of 3rd and Anderson.

Managed by Boy Scouts, the **Koshare Indian Kiva Museum** has a rare collection of native art and artifacts that includes katsinas and works by renowned artists, including potters Maria Martinez and the Nampayo family. A lot more controversial are the troop's interpretations of Plains and Pueblo tribal dances, which they perform each summer in their kiva-shaped ceremonial room. The museum store sells some Native American arts and crafts.

SOUTH OF LA JUNTA

The 400,000 acres of **Comanche National Grassland** reveal glimpses of the land the Indians knew. Although it might seem to be a stark and empty landscape, the prairie and branching canyons and arroyos of the Purgatoire and Cimarron provide homes for a diversity of plants and animals. Prehistoric people also lived here, evidenced by their rock art. *National Forest Service stations* in La Junta and Springfield have directions to some of the sites, as well as maps and more information. Vandalism has been extensive on the grasslands, so please respect the irreplaceable rock art you find.

The Timpas Unit is reached from La Junta. At *Vogel Canyon*, two permanent springs still support a variety of wildlife where people lived three to eight hundred years ago. Look for rock art on the east side of Canyon Trail (1.75 easy miles) and on Mesa Trail, which also leads to ruins. To reach Vogel Canyon, take CO109 south of La Junta for 13 miles and turn right (west) at the Vogel Canyon sign (CR802). Follow CR802 for 1.5 miles, and then turn left onto Forest Service Road 505A. Follow this road for 1.5 miles to the parking lot. Primitive camping is allowed in the parking area. There is a picnic area and restroom, but no water.

Although the main attraction on the full-day hike to remote *Picketwire Canyon* is the 1,300 visible dinosaur footprints, you can also see petroglyphs along the way. The sites are not identified, but a little careful detective work will reveal to you the animal figures and abstract designs. An estimation of their age ranges from 375 to 4,500 years. You will want to be well prepared with information and water for this strenuous trek. No facilities are available in the canyonlands, although primitive camping is allowed at the trailhead. Horseback riding, non-motorized biking and guided auto tours—which take place April through June and September through October using your own high-clearance four-wheel-drive vehicle—are other ways to get there.

The Forest Service office in La Junta has information on the necessary gear and current conditions, as well as directions to the trailhead. Picketwire is about 25 miles south of La Junta.

The Carrizo Unit is most easily accessed from the Springfield area. A 2.5-mile loop trail at *Picture Canyon* leads to a unique, isolated place that once attracted nomadic tribes with available shelter, water, and food. Several campsites have been found under the rock overhangs, and the foundations of a substantial village remain on the northern rim. Blue Horse and Spotted Woman are two of the red and black pictographs drawn there by seventeenth- and eighteenth-century Plains Indians. Although you can take a self-guided tour here, some of the images have astronomical significance that is explained on guided tours during the spring and fall equinoxes.

Picture Canyon is on the Colorado/Oklahoma border. From La Junta, take CO109 south for 58 miles to US160. Turn east (left) for 25 miles to County Road 10. Turn south (right) for 9 miles to County Road M. Follow County Road M 8 miles to County Road 18, and then turn south (right) for 8 miles. Turn south (right) at the sign (Forest Service Road 533) and continue 1 mile to the parking lot.

Carrizo Picnic Ground also has rock art. The short loop trail passes images of mountain sheep, deer, and elk with branching horns. Carrizo also has picnic tables and restrooms. From the intersection of County Roads M and 10, travel west on County Road M for 5.5 miles to Forest Service Road 539. Turn south (left) for 1.9 miles to the parking area.

EAST OF LA JUNTA

Bent's Old Fort National Historic Site may look quiet today, but the adobe structure recreates what was once bustling with trade between Arapaho, Cheyenne, Kiowa, and Comanche Indians and white traders and trappers. At times the lodges of visiting tribes would surround the post for miles.

The fort was built in 1833–34 by the Bent Brothers, William and Charles, and Ceran St. Vrain. It soon became the most important stop along the mountain branch of the Santa Fe Trail, a trade route connecting Missouri and Mexico. Inside the thick walls were warehouses, a billiard room, a trade room, and numerous living areas for visitors and residents.

In 1837, William Bent married Owl Woman, daughter of prominent Cheyenne leader Yellow Wolf. One of their five children was George, who later lived with the Cheyenne and married the daughter of Chief Black Kettle. His accounts eventually helped to preserve the history of the tribe.

During the Mexican War in the 1840s, Colonel Stephen Kearny's Army of the West used the trading post as a military storehouse and hospital. The government horses decimated the grasslands, so the Indians and buffalo moved elsewhere. It was the beginning of the end of Bent's Old Fort. When the United States demanded to buy it in 1849, William was so outraged by the low purchase offer that he destroyed it. He subsequently built Bent's New Fort about thirty miles downriver.

Bent's Old Fort has been reconstructed as a living history museum. A blacksmith's hammer often rings out from the forge across the plaza, and guides in nineteenth-century garb are available to answer questions and man the counter in the restored trading room. A separate museum store sells authentic reproductions of the trade goods exchanged at the fort. Consider visiting during one of the reenactments of fort life held throughout the year, such as the Indian Encampment in September. A shuttle is available for the quarter-mile trip from the parking lot to the fort, which is northeast of La Junta. Take US50 to CO109 and travel north 1 mile to CO194. Turn east 6 miles to the fort.

Two miles south of **Las Animas** on CO101 is *Boggsville*, built in the 1860s as the first Anglo settlement and the last home of Kit Carson, Colorado's superintendent of Indian Affairs in 1867. Boggsville was born when rancher Thomas Boggs and his wife, Rumalda (Charles Bent's stepdaughter and niece of Kit Carson's wife), were joined by several other settlers, including John and Amache Prowers. Amache was the daughter of a Cheyenne leader killed at Sand Creek. In repayment for his and other relatives' deaths, she received government land that her husband used to run his cattle. Amache led a cross-cultural life. She was trilingual, rode a bike and skated, added sugar to buffalo meat to make candy, and put up prickly pear pickles. Her Indian relatives often visited the settlement in the early days.

In the 19th century, the plaza at Bent's Fort was filled with the sounds of trading.

A self-guided trail leads beside the river and around the site to the restored Boggs and Prowers houses, and there are volunteer guides on site during the season. A small trade room sells books and souvenirs. Across the road from the entrance is the cemetery where William Bent is buried.

Across the tracks in Las Animas is *Kit Carson Museum*, housed in an old German prisoner of war barracks. Displays include Sioux, Comanche, and Kiowa arrowheads, blankets, and clothing. Also look for the black and white portraits of William Bent and his Cheyenne Wife, Owl Woman.

John Martin Reservoir, a popular spot for water sports and home to a variety of wildlife, is east of town on US50. It is believed that Caddoa Indians, a semi-agricultural people from the southern plains, once lived here. Numerous petroglyphs are visible below the reservoir on Rule Creek in a place now managed by the Army Corp of Engineers. Stop at their office for directions and to ask for an available guide.

Colorado State Parks manages a campground at the lake that accommodates 213 RVs, campers, and tents. Their *visitor center* is south of Hasty on CR24. To reach the Corps of Engineers' office, continue past the visitor center, state park campground, and dam.

PUEBLO
Map #8

Around Town: El Pueblo History Museum

Pueblo is situated along the Arkansas River at an early crossroads for Arapaho, Cheyenne, Comanche, Ute, and Kiowa Indians and later trappers, traders, and settlers. Before 1848, the river created the U.S. border with Mexico, and in the seventeenth and eighteenth centuries, Indians often fled across it to escape the Spanish and enslavement. In 1842, James Beckwourth and other fur traders built an adobe trading post at the junction of Fountain Creek and the Arkansas River. By early 1855 the post had been abandoned.

People now come to Pueblo to see Rosemount Mansion, take the Historic Arkansas River Walk, or shop in the Union Avenue Historic District. Many also follow US50 west into the mountains to Cañon City and to where the world's highest suspension bridge spans the Royal Gorge.

On the grounds of **El Pueblo History Museum** is a plaza built in the style of the old trading post. The rooms are furnished to represent different activities that would have occurred in the 1842 settlement. Next to the plaza is an archaeological pavilion protecting what was uncovered when the original structures were excavated. Inside the museum, artifacts range from the Ancestral Pueblo to twentieth-century Colorado Indian groups. Permanent and changing galleries round out the story of the people who settled here. The museum shop has a section devoted to Native American books. The museum is three blocks from I-25 off exit 98B.

BATTLE OF GREENHORN MEADOWS PARK

In 1777, Juan Bautista de Anza, Governor of New Mexico, launched an expedition of six hundred soldiers against the local Comanches. He was joined by two hundred Apaches and Utes. The expedition crossed the Rocky Mountains at Ute Pass and overtook Comanche Chief Cuerno Verde near present-day Pueblo.

Cuerno Verde, "Green Horn," was young and daring, and on September 2, 1779, with only fifty men, he attacked the Spanish contingent. During the ensuing battle he was killed. A bronze plaque by the creek in Greenhorn Meadows Park in Colorado City (25 miles south of Pueblo) commemorates the fight.

The Comanche battled on, but by 1789 the Spanish had convinced them to settle on the San Carlos de los Jupes reservation, nine miles east of Pueblo and close to where the St. Charles River empties into the Arkansas. Their reservation has since been moved to Oklahoma.

STERLING
Map #9

Around Town: Overland Trail Museum

Nearby: Julesburg, Fort Morgan Museum, Fort Sedgwick Historical Museum, Summit Springs Battlefield

Indians, trappers, traders, gold seekers, and settlers once traveled along the Overland Trail through here. Established as a mail and passenger route in 1862 to avoid more hostile regions further north, the Overland Trail was the only emigrant route the government kept open during the violent Plains wars from 1864–66.

Although dedicated primarily to the settlers who came in the westward migration, including a recreation of a late nineteenth-century prairie town, the **Overland Trail Museum** has a display of arrowheads, beadwork, and pottery by local Plains Indians. Native American dancers perform at the annual July 4th celebration at the museum.

Get directions here or at the Logan County–Sterling Chamber of Commerce in the old depot in town for a self-guided auto tour of nine Overland Trail sites.

SOUTH OF STERLING

Overlooking the Platte River where the Overland Trail left the river to head toward Denver, **Fort Morgan** provided the only military presence between Julesburg and the burgeoning population along the Front Range. After Sand Creek inflamed the Indians toward revenge, wagon trains were not allowed to leave here until thirty armed men could travel with them. Twenty sod and adobe buildings surrounded by a parade ground once stood on Railroad Avenue, where modern residents now play tennis or enjoy the skate park.

On Main Street in City Park, the *Fort Morgan Museum* has glass-covered drawers of Native American pendants, points, knives, and scrapers from a wide time frame. The exhibit of a fictional archaeological dig along the Platte River shows how the layers and artifacts found in situ help archaeologists interpret sites. There are also scale models of the old sod fort, along with a soldier's kit, saber, and military saddle and an exhibit showing a few artifacts from the battle of Summit Springs.

EAST OF STERLING

Camp Ranking, later called Ft. Sedgwick, was established on May 19, 1864, where the Overland Trail branched away from the Oregon Trail. Near present-day **Julesburg**, this post was one of many attacked by Cheyenne, Arapahos, and Sioux after the Sand Creek Massacre. In response to these incidents, Brigadier General Robert Mitchell ordered the prairies burned from Nebraska to Denver with the hope of driving away the buffalo and the Indians with them. His plan backfired when the Indians retaliated by attacking every ranch from Ft. Sedgwick to Ft. Morgan (100 miles southwest) and killing most of the settlers in between. In February, they also burned the town of Julesburg while residents watched from the safety of the army post.

The *Ft. Sedgwick Historical Society Museum* interprets the history of the fort and the Julesburg settlements. You can also see items like Plains Indian grinding stones, tools, and pottery. Look for a beaded headband and baby moccasins and a replica of pictures from the Cheyenne Dog Soldier ledger book about Julesburg and the fort. Inquire here for a map of the South Platte River Trail, an auto tour that passes many of the nearby historical sites.

You can also shop in the small gift shop. The trail guide and pictures of the ledger pages are also available at the Colorado Welcome Center at the US385 exit off I-76.

On July 11, 1869, the last battle in Colorado between the United States Cavalry and the Plains Indians took place at *Summit Springs Battlefield*. The fighting was between a band of Northern Cheyenne warriors called Dog Soldiers led by Tall Bull and army forces commanded by Major Eugene Carr, including Buffalo Bill and 150 Pawnee scouts. Tall Bull and over fifty of his followers were killed, and a Cheyenne village burned. The only white casualty was a woman being held captive by the Cheyenne. A few plaques and a granite monument mark the battleground, which is in a small, isolated hollow nestled in the prairie hills.

The Arapaho used feathers and buckskin to fashion clothing.

Take CO63 about 5 miles south of Atwood to Washington County Line Road (Road 60), and turn east for 4 miles. Turn right for 1 mile on a gravel road to the battlefield. It is on private land, but there is hiking access.

TRINIDAD
Map #10

Around Town: A. R. Mitchell Museum of Western Art, Louden-Henritze Archaeology Museum
Nearby: Trinidad Lake State Recreation Area

Northwest of town rise the majestic Spanish Peaks, called *Huajatolla,* or "Breasts of the World," by Indians and considered sacred by many tribes. Legends of the peaks abound, including one about a race of ancient sun worshipers who lived there. The *Colorado Welcome Center* off exit 14 from I-25 and the *Trinidad-Las Animas County Chamber of Commerce* on the second floor in the same building can give you information on visiting.

The town of Trinidad was built in 1859 on the mountain branch of the Santa Fe Trail. A bronze tablet on the Columbian Hotel on Main Street is one of the places in town marking the route. The Baca House and Bloom House, nineteenth-century homes of wealthy residents, still provide a glimpse into that bygone era.

In addition to Western art and Hispanic religious folk art, the **A. R. Mitchell Museum of Western Art** displays a collection of Indian artifacts that includes pottery and clothing. The museum is housed downtown in a 1900s department store building.

At Trinidad State Junior College, the **Louden-Henritze Archaeology Museum** exhibits a replica and artifacts from Trinchera Shelter, a dry cave east of town where ancient perishable items such as braided ropes and yucca sandals were found. Other artifacts in the museum have come from excavations done by students and staff. The museum is in Freudenthal Library on campus.

WEST OF TRINIDAD

Carpios Ridge picnic area at **Trinidad Lake State Recreation Area** has an interpretive exhibit about the stone circles found here. Once called "tipi rings," they are now known to mark the site of Jicarilla Apache dwellings. Today fishing, boating, and hiking are popular activities, and there is a campground with electricity and a dump station. The recreation area is 3 miles west of town on CO12.

EVENTS

Colorado State University sponsors powwows at the Student Center, 970-491-8946. For a list of regional events, visit www.alternativevoices.org or Rocky Mountain Indian Chamber of Commerce, 924 W. Colfax Ave., Suite 104F, Denver, CO 80204, telephone 303-629-0102, Web site www.rmicc.org (click on community events).

JANUARY *Colorado Indian Art Market:* Native and non–Native Americans sell their crafts, fine arts, and fashions. Call 303-447-9967 for information.

MARCH *Denver March Powwow:* One of the largest powwows in the U.S. Indians from around the country come to perform in traditional and fancy dance contests and to sell their arts and crafts. Held at the Denver Coliseum. Call 303-936-4826 for information.

APRIL *Oyate-AISES Spring Powwow:* Powwow on the campus of the University of Colorado. Call Oyate at CU for information, 303-492-8874.

MAY *Fort Vasquez Fur Trappers Rendezvous:* Includes Native American crafts and dances. Held at Fort Vasquez.

AUGUST-SEPTEMBER *Colorado State Fair:* Exhibits in the Cultural Heritage Center at the State Fair focus on Native Americans. Held for seventeen days, beginning late August and ending Labor Day weekend. Call 719-561-8484 or 800-444-3247 for information.

SEPTEMBER *Crossroads at the Council Tree Native American Music Festival:* Includes music, food, and art. Held at Fort Collins Museum in early September.

Fort Vasquez Fur Trappers Rendezvous: Includes Native American crafts and dances. Held at Fort Vasquez.

OCTOBER *Denver Art Museum's Friendship Powwow:* Features traditionally dressed dancers from western tribes, native arts and crafts, and traditional food. Held at the museum in early October.

NOVEMBER *Northern Cheyenne's Annual Sand Creek Spiritual Healing Run:* Three-day run to commemorate the victims and survivors of the Sand Creek Massacre. Begins at Sand Creek and ends at the State Capitol in Denver. Also includes ceremonies and candlelight vigil. Call Otto Braided Hair, 406-477-8026, Darius Smith 720-913-8459, or Bill Tall Bull 303-329-7390 for information.

CONTACT INFORMATION

A.R. Mitchell Museum of Western Art
150 East Main Street, Trinidad, CO 81082
719-846-4224
www.santafetrailscenicandhistoricbyway.org/
  mitch.html
Tue-Sun 10am-5pm summer; no fee

Bent's Old Fort National Historic Site
35110 Highway 194 East, La Junta, CO 81050
719-383-5010 • www.nps.gov/beol
Fort: Daily 8am-5:30pm summer, 9am-4pm
  winter; fee
Tour: Daily 9:30am-11am and 1pm-2:30pm,
  June-Aug; Daily 10:30am-1pm, Sept-May
Living History Program: summer only

Boggsville
Las Animas, CO 81054
719-456-1358
Open seasonally; fee

Boulder Convention and Visitors Bureau
2440 Pearl Street, Boulder, CO 80302
800-444-0447 *or* 303-442-2911
www.bouldercvb.com
www.bouldercoloradousa.com
Mon-Thu 8:30am-5pm, Fri 8:30am-4pm

Boulder County Parks and Open Space
5201 St. Vrain Road, Longmont, CO 80503
303-678-6200
www.co.boulder.co.us/openspace
Mon-Fri 8am-4:30pm; no fee

Boulder History Museum
1206 Euclid, Boulder, CO 80302
303-449-3464
www.boulderhistorymuseum.org
Tue-Fri 10am-5pm, Sat-Sun noon-4pm; fee

Buckhorn Exchange
1000 Osage Street, Denver, CO 80204
303-534-9505 • www.buckhorn.com
Lunch: Mon-Fri 11am-2pm; Dinner: Mon-
Thu 5:30pm-9pm, Fri-Sat 5pm-10pm, Sun
5pm-9pm

Buffalo Bill's Grave and Museum
987½ Lookout Mountain Road, Golden, CO
80401
303-526-0747 • www.buffalobill.org
Daily 9am-5pm, May-Oct; daily 9am-4pm,
Nov-Apr; fee

Burlington Old Town
420 South 14th, Burlington, CO 80807
800-288-1334 *or* 719-346-7382
www.burlingtoncolo.com/oldtown.htm
Mon-Sat 9am-5pm, Sun noon-5pm (last tour
4pm); fee

**Burlington Visitor's Center-Chamber of
Commerce**
420 South 14th, Burlington, CO 80807
719-346-8070 • www.burlingtoncolo.com
Mon-Fri 9am-5pm

Centennial Village
1475 A Street, Greeley, CO 80631
970-350-9220 • www.greeleygov.com
Tue-Sat 10am-4pm, mid Apr-mid Oct; fee

**City of Boulder Open Space and Mountain
Parks**
66 South Cherryvale Road, Boulder, CO 80303
303-441-3440
www.ci.boulder.co.us/openspace
Mon-Fri 8am-5pm; no fee

Colorado History Museum
1300 Broadway, Denver, CO 80203
303-866-3682
www.coloradohistory.org/hist_sites/CHM/
Colorado_History_Museum.htm
Mon-Sat 10am-5pm, Sun noon-5pm; fee

**Colorado Springs Convention and Visitor's
Center**
515 South Cascade Ave, Colorado Springs, CO
80903
877-745-3773 *or* 719-635-7506
www.experiencecoloradosprings.com
Mon-Fri 8:30am-5pm (extended hours June-
Aug)

**Colorado Springs Fine Arts Center/Taylor
Museum of Southwest Studies**
30 W. Dale, Colorado Springs, CO 80903
719-634-5581; 719-634-5583 (box office)
www.csfineartscenter.org
Tues-Wed 10am-5pm, Th-Sat 10am-8pm, Sun
10am-5pm; fee

Colorado Springs Pioneers Museum
215 South Tejon, Colorado Springs, CO
80903
719-385-5990 • www.cspm.org
Tue-Sat 10am-5pm, Sun 1-5pm (June-Aug
only); no fee

Colorado State Capitol Building
200 East Colfax, Denver, CO 80203
303-866-2604 (tours/information)
303-866-4747 (visitor services)
www.colorado.gov/dpa/doit/archives/cap/con-
tents.htm virtual tour
Mon-Fri 7am-5:30pm; no fee

Colorado State Parks
303-866-3437 • http://parks.state.co.us
Reservations: 800-678-2267, 303-470-1144,
or online

Colorado Welcome Center
www.colorado.com/getting36
Daily 8am-6pm, summer; daily 8am-5pm, rest
of year
I-70 between exits 437 and 438, Burlington, CO 80807 • 719-346-5554
3745 E. Prospect Rd., I-25 exit 268, Fort
Collins, CO 80525 • 970-491-3583
20934 CR 28, Julesburg, CO 80737 •
907-474-2054
309 Nevada, Trinidad CO 81082 •
719-846-9512

Comanche National Grassland (See U.S. National Forest Service)

David Cook Fine American Art
1637 Wazee, Denver, CO 80202
303-623-8181
www.davidcookfineamericanart.com
Mon-Sat 10:30am-6pm and by appt

Denver Art Museum
100 West 14th Avenue Parkway, Denver, CO
80204 (mailing address)
720-865-5000 • www.denverartmuseum.org
Tue-Thu 10am-5pm, Wed-Fri 10am-10pm,
Sat-Sun 9am-5pm; fee

Denver International Airport
8500 Peña Blvd, Denver, CO 80249
800-247-2336 or 303-342-2000
www.flydenver.com

Denver Metro Convention and Visitor Bureau
www.denver.org • www.denver365.com •
www.visitdenver.com
    1600 California Street, Unit 6, Denver, CO
        80202
    800-233-6837 or 303-892-1505
    Mon-Fri 9am-6pm, Sat 9am-5pm
    DIA East Metro airport
    303-317-0629

Denver Museum of Nature and Science
2001 Colorado Blvd, Denver, CO 80205
800-925-2250 or 303-322-7009
www.dmns.org
Daily 9am-5pm; fee

Denver Public Library
10 W. 14th Avenue Parkway, Denver, CO 80204
720-865-1111 • http://denverlibrary.org
Mon-Tues 10am-8pm, Wed-Fri 10am-6pm,
    Sat 9am-5pm, Sun 1-5pm

Duhesa Lounge-Lory Student Center
Colorado State University, Ft. Collins, CO
    80523
970-491-6444 • welcome.colostate.edu
Mon-Thu 6am-11pm, Fri 6am-midnight, Sat
    7am-midnight, Sun 11am-11pm

El Pueblo History Museum
301 North Union, Pueblo, CO 81003
719-583-0453
www.coloradohistory.org/hist_sites/
    Pueblo/Pueblo.htm
Tue-Sat 10am-4pm; fee

The Fort
19192 Highway 8, Morrison, CO 80465
303-697-4771 • www.thefort.com
Mon-Fri 5:30pm-10pm, Sat 5pm-10pm, Sun
    5pm-9pm

Ft. Collins Museum
200 Matthews Street, Ft. Collins, CO 80524
970-221-6738 • www.fcgov.com-museum
Tue-Sat 10am-5pm, Sun noon-5pm; no fee

Ft. Collins Convention and Visitors Bureau
19 Old Town Square, Suite 137, Ft. Collins,
    CO 80524
800-274-3678 or 970-232-3840
www.ftcollins.com

Ft. Collins Visitor Center/Colorado Welcome Center
3745 East Prospect Rd.#200, Fort Collins,
    CO 80525
800-274-3678 or 970-491-3583
www.colorado.com/city43

Ft. Morgan Chamber of Commerce
300 Main Street, Ft. Morgan, CO 80701
800-354-8660 or 970-867-6702
www.fortmorganchamber.org

Ft. Morgan Museum
414 Main Street, Ft. Morgan, CO 80701
970-542-4010, ext 8 • www.ftmorganmus.org
Mon & Fri 10am-5pm, Tue-Thu 10am-8pm,
    Sat 11am-5pm, summer; Mon-Fri 10am-
    5pm, Sat 11am-5pm, Tues & Thurs ex-
    tended evening hours 8pm, winter; no fee

Ft. Sedgwick Historical Society and Museum
114 East 1st Steet, Julesburg, CO 80737
970-474-2061
Hours vary

Ft. Vasquez Historic Site and Museum
13412 US85, Platteville, CO 80651
970-785-2832
www.coloradohistory.org/hist_sites/ft_vasquez/
    ft_vasquez.htm
Mon-Sat 9:30am-4:30pm, Sun 1pm-4:30pm,
    summer; Wed-Sat 9:30am-4:30pm, Sun
    1pm-4:30pm, rest of year; no fee

Garden of the Gods
1805 North 30th Street, Colorado Springs,
    CO 80904
719-219-0108
Daily 5am-9pm Nov-Apr; 5am-11pm May-
    Oct; no fee
    Visitor Center
    1805 North 30th Street, Colorado Springs,
        CO 80904
    719-634-6666; 719-219-0107 (gift shop)
    www.gardenofgods.com
    Daily 8am-8pm Memorial-Labor Day;
        9am-5pm winter
    Trading Post
    324 Beckers Lane, Manitou Springs, CO
        80829
    800-874-4515 or 719-685-9045
    www.co-trading-post.com
    Daily 8am-8pm, summer; Daily 9am-5:30,
        rest of the year

Genoa Tower and Museum (World's Wonder View Tower)
30121 Frontage Road, Genoa, CO 80818
719-763-2309
Daily 8am-8pm, Mar-Sept; reduced winter hours

Golden Pioneer Museum
923 10th Street, Golden, CO 80403
303-278-7151
www.goldenpioneermuseum.com
Mon-Sat 10am-4:30pm, Sun 1pm-4pm, summer; fee

Greater Pueblo Chamber of Commerce
302 North Santa Fe, Pueblo, CO 81003
800-233-3446 *or* 719-542-1704
www.pueblochamber.org
Mon-Fri 8am-5pm

Greeley Convention and Visitors
902 7th Avenue, Greeley, CO 80631
800-449-3866 *or* 970-352-3567
www.greeleycvb.com
Mon-Fri 8am-5pm

Greeley History Museum
714 8th Street, Greeley, CO 80631
970-350-9220
www.greeleygov.com/Museums/Greeley
HistoryMuseum.aspx
Mon-Fri 8:30am-4:30pm, Sat 10am-4pm, Sun noon-4pm; no fee

John Martin Reservoir
Colorado State Park Visitor Center
30703 Road 24, Hasty, CO 81044
719-829-1801 • http://parks.state.co.us
Daily 8am-5pm Sept-Apr, 8am-8pm May-Labor Day
U.S. Army Corp of Engineers Office
CR 2995, Hasty, CO 81044
719-336-3476
www.spa.usace.army.mil/recreation/jm
/index.htm
Mon-Fri 7:30am-4:30pm

Kit Carson Museum
9th and Bent Las Animas, CO 81054
719-456-2507
Daily 1pm-5pm, Memorial-Labor Day; by appt rest of the year

Koshare Indian Kiva Museum
115 West 18th Street, La Junta, CO 81050
719-384-4411 • www.koshare.org
Daily noon-5pm; until 9pm on show nights; fee

La Junta Chamber of Commerce
110 Santa Fe Ave, La Junta, CO 81050
719-384-7411 • www.lajuntachamber.com

Leanin' Tree Gallery Museum of Western Art
6055 Longbow Drive, Boulder, CO 80301
800-777-8716 *or* 303-530-1442
www.leanintreemuseum.com
Mon-Fri 8am-5pm; Sat, Sun 10am-5pm; no fee

Limon Heritage Museum and Railroad Park
899 First Street, Limon CO 80828
719-775-0430
Mon-Sat 1pm-8pm, summer; no fee

Longmont Museum and Cultural Center
400 Quail Road, Longmont, CO 80501
303-651-8374
www.ci.longmont.co.us/museum
Tue-Sat 9am-5pm, Wed 9am-8pm, Sun 1am-5pm; no fee

Logan County/Sterling Chamber of Commerce
109 N. Front Street, Sterling, CO 80751
866-522-5070 *or* 970-522-5070
www.logancountychamber.com
Daily 9am-4pm

Louden-Henritze Archaeology Museum
Trinidad State Junior College
719-846-5508
www.trinidadstate.edu/museum
Mon-Thu 10am-3pm most of the year, winter by appt; no fee

Manitou Cliff Dwellings
Phantom Cliff Canon, Manitou Springs, CO 80829
800-354-9971 *or* 719-685-5242
www.cliffdwellingsmuseum.com
Daily 9am-6pm May-Sept; 10am-4pm Dec-Feb; 9am-5pm Mar-Apr and Oct-Nov; fee

Manitou Springs Chamber of Commerce
354 Manitou Ave, Manitou Springs, CO 80829
800-642-2567 *or* 719-685-5089
www.manitousprings.org
Mon-Fri 8:30am-7pm, Sat-Sun 9am-6pm

Meeker Home Museum
1324 9th Ave, Greeley, CO 80631
970-350-9220
www.greeleygov.com/Museums/
MeekerHome.aspx
Wed-Fri 1pm-4pm May-Sep or by appointment; fee

Mudhead Gallery
555 17th Street, Denver, CO 80202
303-293-0007
www.mudheadgallery.net
Mon-Fri 9am-5pm and by appt

Native American Trading Company
213 West 13th Street, Denver, CO 80204
303-534-0771
www.nativeamericantradingco.com
Tue-Fri 10am-5pm, Sat 11am-4pm, 1st Fri
5pm-9pm

Old Colorado City
2400 block of Colorado Avenue, Colorado
Springs, CO 80904
719-577-4112 • www.oldcoloradocity.com

Overland Trail Museum
21053 CR 25 5/10, Sterling, CO 80751
970-522-3895
www.sterlingcolo.com/dept/pir/vtour/
overlandtrail.php
Mon-Sat 9am-5pm, Sun 1pm-5pm, Apr-Oct;
Tue-Sat 10am-4pm, Nov-Mar; no fee

Pikes Peak Cog Railway
515 Ruxton Road, PO Box 351, Manitou
Springs, CO 80829
Daily 8am-5:20pm, mid June-mid Aug; vari-
able schedule rest of year; fee
719-685-5401
www.cograilway.com

Pueblo Visitor Center (see Greater Pueblo
Chamber of Commerce)

Rock Ledge Ranch Historic Site
1401 Recreation Way, Colorado Springs, CO
80905
719-578-6777 • www.rockledgeranch.com
Wed-Sun 10am-5pm, early June-Labor Day; fee

Roxborough State Park
4751 Roxborough Drive, Littleton, CO 80125
303-973-3959
www.parks.state.co.us/Parks/roxborough

Sand Creek Massacre National Historic Site
910 Wansted, PO Box 249, Eads, CO 81036
or 35110 Hwy 194 East, La Junta, CO 81050
719-438-5916; 719-383-5051, ex 118; *or* 719-
729-3003 • www.nps.gov-sand
Fri-Sun 9am-4pm; no fee

Seven Falls
2850 S. Cheyenne Canyon Road, Colorado
Springs, CO 80906
719-632-0765 • www.sevenfalls.com
Daily 8:30am-10:30pm, summer; Daily 9am-
4:15pm, winter; fee

The Flute Player Gallery
2511 W. Colorado Avenue, Colorado Springs,
CO 80904
888-632-7702 *or* 719-632-7702
www.fluteplayergallery.com

**Trinidad-Las Animas County Chamber of
Commerce**
309 Nevada Ave 2nd floor, Trinidad, CO
81082
866-480-4750 *or* 719-846-9285
www.trinidadco.com
Mon-Fri 9am-5pm

Trinidad Lake State Park
32610 Highway 12, Trinidad, CO 81082
719-846-6951
http://parks.state.co.us/parks/trinidadlake
Visitor Center: Sun-Thu 8am-8pm, Fri 8am-
10pm, Sat 8am-9pm; fee

United States National Forest Service
Arapaho and Roosevelt National Forests
2150 Centre Ave, Bldg E, Ft. Collins, CO
80526
970-295-6600
www.fs.fed.us/r2/arnf/index.shtml *(click on
Greeley)*
Mon-Fri 8am-5pm
Pawnee National Grassland
660 O Street, Greeley, CO 80631
970-346-5000
Mon-Fri 8am-4:30pm
**Pike and San Isabel N. F., Cimarron and
Comanche National Grassland**
2840 Kachina Drive, Pueblo, CO 81008
719-553-1400; TDD 719-553-1404
www.fs.fed.us/r2/psicc/coma
Comanche National Grassland (offices)
Carrizo Unit
27204 US287, PO Box 127,
Springfield, CO 81073
Mon-Fri 8am-5pm
719-523-6591
Timpas Unit
1420 E. 3rd, La Junta, CO 81050
719-384-2181
Mon-Fri 8am-5pm, closed 12-1 for
lunch

University of Colorado Henderson Museum
Henderson Building, CU campus, 15th Street
& Broadway, Boulder, CO 80309
303-492-6892
http://cumuseum.colorado.edu
Mon-Fri 9am-5pm, Sat 9am-4pm, Sun 10am-
4pm; fee

Ute Pass Historical Society
222 East Midland, PO Box 6875, Woodland
Park, CO 80866
719-686-7512
www.utepasshistoricalsociety.org
> **Centennial Trailhead**
> 710 W. Midland Ave., Woodland Park, CO
> 80866
> Dawn to dusk
> **Pikes Peak Museum**
> 210 East Midland, Woodland Park, CO
> 80866
> 719-686-1125
> Tue & Wed 9am-4pm (extended hours as
> volunteers permit); no fee
> **Rampart Library**
> 218 East Midland, Woodland, Park 80866
> 719-687-9281
> Tue-Thu 10am-8pm, Fri 10am-6pm, Sat
> 10am-4pm, Sun 1pm-4pm, summer;
> Tue-Thu 10am-7pm, winter; no fee

Ute Pass Trails
www.trailsandopenspaces.org/trails/
Ute-Pass.pdf

West Southwest Gallery
257 Fillmore, Denver, CO 80206
866-770-7069 *or* 303-321-4139
www.westsouthwest.com
Mon-Sat 10am-5:30pm, Sun noon-4pm

Will Rogers Shrine of the Sun
4250 Cheyenne Mountain Zoo Road, Colorado Springs, CO 80906
719-578-5367 • www.cmzoo.org/shrine.html
Daily 9am-5pm, summer; 9am-4pm, winter; fee

Wray Museum
205 East 3rd, Wray, CO 80758
970-332-5063
www.wrayco.net/museum_homepage.html
Tue-Sat noon-4pm; fee

SOUTHWEST COLORADO

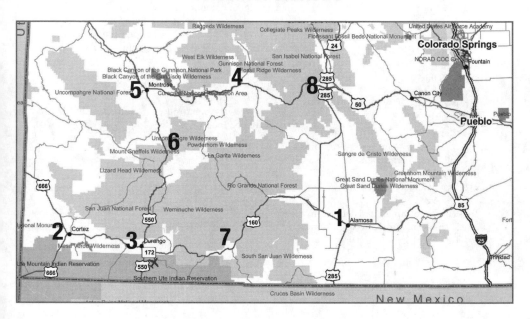

1. Alamosa
2. Cortez
3. Durango
4. Gunnison

5. Montrose
6. Ouray
7. Pagosa Springs
8. Salida

CHAPTER 15

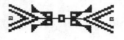

SOUTHWEST COLORADO

ALAMOSA
Map #1

Around Town: Luther E. Bean Museum
Nearby: Alamosa/Monte Vista National Wildlife Refuges, Fort Garland, Great Sand Dunes National Park, Rio Grande County Museum, San Luis Museum and Cultural Center

The town of Alamosa nestles in San Luis Valley, also home to small game, elk, deer, coyote, porcupine, and beaver. Around 125 miles long and surrounded on all sides by mountains, the valley has been a spiritual home, hunting ground, and travel route between the high plains and mountains for millennia.

Stone-age spear and dart points give evidence nomadic hunter/gatherers lived here as early as eleven thousand years ago. They probably moved elsewhere during times of drought and then returned in times of plenty to gather wild plants for food and medicine and to hunt the herds of mammoths and prehistoric bison that grazed on the abundant grasses.

Later, Utes camped in the valley, where on most days the sky is a vivid azure color. When you see it, you will understand why they were called the "Blue Sky People."

The **Luther E. Bean Museum** in Richardson Hall on the campus of Adams State College devotes the second floor to native groups of the region. Displays include rugs, art, pottery, weavings, and baskets. The college is on US160.

EAST OF ALAMOSA

Great Sand Dunes National Park sits at the northern end of San Luis Valley. To reach it, follow US160/285 east of Alamosa for 15 miles, and turn left onto CO150. Alternately, take CO17 north of Alamosa, turn right onto CR6 (toward San Luis Lakes SWA), and then left on CO150.

The Great Sand Dunes were formed as wind blew grains of sand into the barrier of the Sangre de Cristo Mountains. After thousands of years, trillions of tons of it have piled up to create ever-changing dunes that are the tallest in North America, over seven hundred feet high.

Mountains of shifting sand collect at the base of the Sangre de Cristo Mountains to form the Great Sand Dunes.

Called *sowapophe-uvehe,* or "the land that moves back and forth," by the Ute, *ei-anyedi,* or "it goes up and down," by the Jicarilla Apache, and "singing sands" by others, the dunes are ever-changing and create haunting sounds when the wind blows just right. Jicarillas still come here to collect sand for ceremonial paintings, Tewa/Tiwa-speaking people believe their ancestors emerged into this world through a nearby lake, and Blanca Peak, which rises southeast of the dunes, is considered by the Navajo to be one of their four sacred mountains. They call it *Sisnaajini,* "White Shell Mountain."

The national park preserves a home for various plants and animals with diverse habitats that include 13,000-foot-high mountain tundra, ancient spruce and pine forests, marshes and lakes, cottonwood and aspen groves, and the constantly shifting dunes. The *visitor center* has interpretive programs, exhibits, and a bookstore. Ask to see *Sacred Trees,* a video featuring Utes relating traditional uses of the ponderosa pine. Backcountry permits are also available here.

Pinyon Flats Campground, 1 mile north of the visitor center, has eighty-eight campsites available on a first-come basis. There are no hookups, and rigs over thirty-two feet will find it difficult to turn around. The privately owned Oasis Campground outside the monument has larger sites and hookups.

Fort Garland, 26 miles east of Alamosa off US160, was built in 1858 to defend settlers against Ute and Apache raiders in New Mexico territory. The fort now houses a re-creation of the headquarters of controversial fort commander Kit Carson, whose one-year stay here in 1866 improved relations with local Indians. You can also view photographs and artifacts used by the buffalo soldiers garrisoned here during the Indian wars and Hispanic folk art from around the valley.

Sixteen miles south of Fort Garland on CO159 is the small village of **San Luis**, built by the Spanish in 1851 as the first permanent European settlement in the valley. *San Luis Museum and Cultural Center* highlights the culture of the settlers and also includes Indian artifacts. Indian artists are sometimes featured in the murals and artwork.

For unknown eons, the spring and autumn silence of San Luis Valley has been broken by the haunting cries of sandhill and whooping cranes on their annual migrations. Snow melting in the surrounding mountains feeds the Rio Grande, surface ponds, and underground aquifers that are now part of the **Alamosa/Monte Vista National Wildlife Refuges**, making it an oasis in an otherwise arid valley. Thousands of northern pintails, Canada geese, and cranes still use this marshy place as a migratory rest stop. Bald eagles, hawks, and short-eared owls winter here, too, protected by the two refuges, one east and one west of Alamosa.

To reach *Alamosa National Wildlife Refuge*, travel east of town on US160 about 3 miles to El Rancho Lane, and then turn south to the visitors' facilities. A hiking trail here leads along the Rio Grande to Bluff Overlook, providing an overview of the wetlands.

WEST OF ALAMOSA

Monte Vista National Wildlife Refuge is west of Alamosa on US160-285 and 5 miles south on CO15. A self-guided auto tour starts at the small information station, which is open as volunteers permit.

The drama of the ancient bird migrations is documented in rock art at the **Rio Grande County Museum**, 31 miles northwest of Alamosa on US160 in the town of Del Norte. The museum also displays other prehistoric artifacts and provides information on the Old Spanish Trail that traversed the area.

CORTEZ
Map #2

Around Town: Cortez Center Museum and Cultural Park, Mesa Indian Trading Company and Gallery/Mesa Verde Pottery, Notah Dineh Trading Company and Museum, trading posts

Nearby: Anasazi Heritage Center, Canyon of the Ancients National Monument, Crow Canyon Archaeological Center, Hovenweep National Monument, Mesa Verde National Park, Ute Mountain Ute Reservation (casino, Sleeping Ute Pottery Factory, Ute Mountain Tribal Park), Yucca House National Monument

The Indians who enjoyed the spring water near Cortez called the place *Tsaya-toh,* or "Rock Water." Southwest of town you can see one of their most visible landmarks, Sleeping Ute Mountain. From certain angles, the outline of a sleeping Indian is easily distinguished, with feathered headdress in the north and arms folded across his chest to form the high point. Legend claims the mountain was once a great warrior god who fought against evil beings. As they battled, their feet pushed in valleys and raised mountains. Although the great warrior god was wounded and entered a deep slumber, one day he will rise to fight the enemies of the Ute People.

The small Cortez Center Museum and Cultural Park, partnered with the University of Colorado, has interpretive exhibits on the prehistoric Basketmaker and Pueblo periods, as well as Ute and other Indian groups. The center is also a working lab for the excavation north of town at Yellow Jacket, an archaeological site that was once a large Ancestral Puebloan ceremonial center. Native Americans and noted archaeologists provide cultural and historical programs at the center on most summer weeknights. Guided tours of archaeological sites, movies, events, workshops, and special programs with Indian dancers, musicians, artists, code talkers, and storytellers are also offered.

After the town of Cortez was founded in 1886, Ute and Navajo artisans began visiting to exchange their handmade arts and crafts at local trading posts. Some of these posts are still active today, making Cortez a good place to buy items made by artisans living on the nearby Ute and Navajo reservations and at the New Mexico Pueblos. The Mesa Verde Country Web site and the *Cortez Chamber of Commerce* have a list of stores that sell authentic Indian items. The chamber also displays Ancestral Puebloan artifacts and crafts by Indian artisans.

Notah Dineh Trading Company and Museum stocks a large inventory of handcrafted items in both traditional and contemporary styles, including the largest selection of Navajo rugs in the Four Corners. In addition, the museum displays historic art and artifacts collected by the trading post over the years.

Mesa Indian Trading Company and Gallery/Mesa Verde Pottery, 1 mile east of town on US160, sells Navajo and Ute pottery and other Native American arts and crafts. Local artists often provide demonstrations on weaving and pottery painting, and in the summer traditional dancers perform.

NORTH OF CORTEZ

The Dolores Archaeological Program was the largest archaeological contract ever awarded in the United States. The project surveyed 1,600 prehistoric sites and excavated 120 of them, all the while working ahead of the equipment that built McPhee Reservoir. Most of the recovered artifacts represent the Northern San Juan Ancestral Puebloan tradition from A.D. 1 to 1300; some of these are exhibited at the **Anasazi Heritage Center** 10 miles north of Cortez on CO145, and then left on CO184.

A "please touch" attitude is carried out in interactive exhibits that include learning the technique of tree-ring dating, grinding corn on a metate, weaving, playing computer games, and viewing Ancestral Puebloan seeds through a microscope. A full-sized replica of an A.D. 800 pithouse depicts Ancestral Puebloan daily life, and a model of a test trench conveys the idea of how modern archaeologists work.

You can follow a short trail in front of the museum to the twelfth-century *Dominguez Ruin*, thought to be the first recorded archaeological site in Colorado and mentioned by the 1776 Dominguez-Escalante Expedition. At one time, this was a Chacoan trade outpost where timber, deer hides, and farm produce were swapped for luxury items such as turquoise, parrot feathers, and shell ornaments from the southern California and Gulf coasts. A self-guiding trail brochure tells about the ruins, as well as the local natural history. Arrangements for guided tours can be made by calling in advance.

The center's gift shop sells books on archaeology and replicas of Ancestral Puebloan pottery. You can also obtain information here on the *Trail of the Ancients National Scenic Byway* (see Chapter 23, Southern Utah, page 428) and find maps to more remote sites in the *Canyon of the Ancients National Monument* (west of Cortez).

Crow Canyon Archaeological Center offers a unique opportunity for amateurs to participate in field seminars, archaeological digs, and education programs lasting from three days to five weeks. Crow Canyon also conducts hands-on Native American cultural seminars, workshops, and field trips led by Pueblo Indian scholars and noted Southwestern archaeologists. Call for reservations.

SOUTH OF CORTEZ

Ute Mountain Ute Reservation (597,288 acres) was established in 1897 for the Weeminuche Utes. Today it is home to about two thousand people. The majority of the land is in Colorado, with small portions in New Mexico and Utah. Much of the tribal income stems from gas and oil deposits on the reservation and tourism.

The town of Towaoc, 11 miles south of Cortez on US491, is the center of the reservation. Just outside of town is the tribally owned *Ute Mountain Ute Casino*, which has gambling, Kuchu's Restaurant, and a gift shop. For lodging, try either the ninety-room hotel with pool, hot tub, sauna, and exercise room, or the RV park with tent, tipi, and full-service RV sites. A 24-hour shuttle transports employees and visitors between the casino and other sites of interest.

Sleeping Ute Pottery Factory Outlet/Ute Mountain Indian Pottery Factory manufactures pottery decorated with designs adapted from the Ancestral Puebloans and modified by the Ute. A walking tour through the plant shows a modern pottery-making process that includes mold casting, hand-painting, hand-carving, hand-glazing, and firing in kilns. Pieces are sold in the showroom or through a catalog. The plant is 8 miles south of Cortez on US491.

Ute Mountain Tribal Park is 125,000 acres set aside to preserve hundreds of minimally reconstructed Anasazi cliff and surface dwellings. Although twice the size of Mesa Verde, this primitive area receives far fewer tourists, so the isolation can add to your sense of adventure and discovery. Another plus is having an Indian tour guide to provide a unique perspective on Anasazi and Ute history and culture. The backcountry ruins are accessible by guided tour only, either in your own vehicle or one provided for you for an additional fee. Full- and half-day tours begin from the Ute Mountain Visitor Center, 20 miles south of Cortez on US491. Be prepared for primitive conditions by bringing drinking water, lunch, and a full gas tank if you plan to use your own car, and make your reservations at least twenty-four hours in advance.

Hiking, mountain biking, and backpacking are available year-round in some parts of the reservation, weather permitting. Contact Ute Mountain Tribal Headquarters for the necessary permits and reservations.

In June, the Ute Mountain Utes celebrate the Bear Dance, which is open to visitors. This is a traditional healing ceremony that involves Utes dressing and dancing as bears to bring blessings to those present and healing to the world.

Yucca House National Monument was an important Ancestral Puebloan community center from A.D. 1150 to 1300. Located between Cortez and Towaoc, it is one of southwest Colorado's largest archaeological sites. The site is still unexcavated, so what you will see when you visit are two large mounds made of rubble and covered with vegetation. No facilities are available. Directions and a downloadable visitor guide for the monument are available at www.nps.gov.

EAST OF CORTEZ

Richard Wetherill and his brother-in-law Charley Mason were looking for lost cows one winter morning in 1888; what they found was unexpected and far more exotic. As they peered across a canyon through the blowing snow, an ancient stone city came slowly into view. Speechless with wonder, the two men stared in disbelief at the majestic, 217-room Cliff Palace resting in silence in a cave alcove.

It was an extraordinary archaeological find. The ruins, along with those of other dwellings built on this high plateau cut with canyons and green with juniper and pinyon pine, would become part of a World Heritage Site and **Mesa Verde National Park**.

Around the beginning of the first millennium, ancestors of the modern-day Pueblos drifted here. They farmed and created excellent baskets, but they left no evidence of permanent houses. That changed around A.D. 400, when they began to produce pottery and to build pithouses covered with logs and mud plaster in alcoves and on mesa tops. For several hundred years, their civilization progressed, until eventually they were farming scattered plots atop the mesas and building magnificent apartments perched in the canyon walls. At one time, as many as five thousand people may have lived here.

Mesa Verde civilization flourished until the late 1200s, when the people turned their backs on the homes of their ancestors and most likely migrated to the south. Their cliff dwellings had been occupied for less than one hundred years.

From the entrance gate to Mesa Verde, it is 21 twisting miles to the park headquarters, museum, and major ruins on Chapin Mesa. *Morefield Campground* is 4 miles from the park entrance and a refreshing place to stay. Over 425 private campsites are hidden in the oak and pinyon-juniper trees. If you stay here, your neighbors will likely include wild turkey and deer. The campground also has showers, an RV dumping station, and some utility hookup sites. Evening campfire programs are conducted daily from early June to Labor Day. Reservations are taken through ARAMARK; the campground is not usually full, although there is sometimes a wait for the hookups.

Visitor services in *Morefield Village* include a snack bar, grocery store, Native American crafts shop, service station, laundry, and guided tours. A pancake breakfast and evening barbecue are available daily. The campground and village are open from mid-April to October.

Far View Visitor Center, on the main road 15 miles from the entrance, is the best place to start your tour during the main tourist season. The center features contemporary Southwestern Indian exhibits, a bookstore, and an overview of the park, including information on the two driving routes to ruins. It also sells the timed-entry tickets you will need to visit the ruins of Cliff House, Balcony House, and Long House. Arrive early in the day, as space is limited. Also note that visitors are restricted from touring both Cliff Palace and Balcony House on the same day.

Between mid-October and mid-April, Far View Visitor Center and most cliff ruins are closed, but Chapin Mesa Archaeological Museum (see below) is open during off-season with information on what to visit at that time.

Between mid-April and mid-October, lodging and guided tours of the park can be arranged at *Far View Motor Lodge*. The lodge is AAA approved, and each of the 150 rooms has a private balcony. Perched on the edge of the mesa the vistas are spectacular, so if you spend the night, be sure to ask for a room with a view. You can also sample Southwestern

Although named Square Tower House (in Mesa Verde), the most visible part of this ruin was actually a 3-storied room block in the back of the cliff dwelling. The original front of the dwelling has since fallen away.

fare in the dining room, watch an Indian crafts demonstration, shop for Native American crafts, or attend the evening multimedia programs on Ancestral Puebloan and contemporary Indian cultures. Contact ARAMARK for reservations and information on programs and tours.

Two roads lead from Far View to park ruins. The route to the top of *Wetherill Mesa* follows a mountain road that is 12 miles of sharp curves (vehicles over 8,000 pounds gross vehicle weight and/or 25 feet long are prohibited). The road is open 8am-4:30pm from Memorial Day to Labor Day. A free tram also runs to these mesa ruins.

A car tour of Wetherill Mesa takes between three and four hours, depending on the number of pullouts you stop at to see the outstanding views of the park and landmarks in the Four Corners states. Trails on ruins on the mesa include a steep, half-mile round-trip trail to Step House, which has pithouses, petroglyphs, a masonry structure, and prehistoric stairs; a level, three-quarter-mile self-guided trail to the Badger House Community of four mesa top ruins; and a half-mile ticketed and ranger-guided tour to *Long House*, the second largest ruin in the park. The trail to Long House includes a two-hundred-foot vertical descent and a walk into a cave where prehistoric Indians once lived. The large central plaza here was probably used for ceremonies.

The main road from Fair View continues 6 miles to *Chapin Mesa*, where Spruce Tree House, Cliff Palace, and Balcony House are located. Along the way is a self-guided trail you can take to *Far View Ruins*.

All of the major ruins on Chapin Mesa can be viewed from overlooks, but hiking is restricted to designated trails. Most are self-guiding, but a few can be taken only with ranger guides.

With some of the finest prehistoric artifacts found in the Southwest, many of them excavated at Mesa Verde, *Chapin Mesa Archaeological Museum* presents a comprehensive overview of the life of the Ancestral Puebloans who lived here. The museum also lists the schedule for ranger-conducted tours and has a bookstore. A Diné weaver, Doris Tsosie, weaves rugs on her loom in the gift shop, and her daughter sells turquoise, coral, and silver jewelry on the patio. On the terrace, Diné and Hopi potters sell their wares.

The most easily accessible of the major cliff dwellings in the park is *Spruce Tree House*, named for the tree Wetherill and Mason climbed to reach the ruin when they discovered it. It is the third-largest cliff dwelling in the park, with around 114 rooms and eight kivas. The half-mile, paved, self-guided trail begins near the museum, and takes between forty-five minutes and one hour, round-trip. It includes an optional climb down a ladder into a roofed kiva. The trail is open 8:30am-6:30pm in summer, and rangers are on duty to answer questions. In winter, it is often the only cliff ruin open, and then only by guided tours that leave two or three times a day from the museum.

Two trails leading into Spruce Canyon begin on the Spruce Tree Trail. *Petroglyph Point Trail* is 2.8 miles to one of the few displays of rock art in the park. It ends at the parking lot near the museum. The trail is fairly flat except for a scramble up the rocks to the top of the mesa for the return. *Spruce Canyon Trail*, 2.1 miles round-trip to the canyon bottoms, is a bit more strenuous and not as scenic. Register at the ranger office to take either of these trails.

Ruins Road Drive on Chapin Mesa is open 8am to sunset but is often closed in winter because of snow. It consists of two 6-mile loops that provide a closer look at many of the ruins.

To gain a full understanding of the sequence of architectural development at Mesa Verde, take the right fork first, past mesa top pithouses and ruins. Wayside exhibits and viewpoints highlight the changes, beginning with the earliest pithouses dating back to the sixth century A.D.

The right fork road also passes *Sun Temple*, a multistoried D-shaped structure with tiny enclosed rooms that was probably used for ceremonies. The Park Service has topped the ruins with concrete to protect them from water, and visitors are asked to stay off the low walls. From Sun Temple, you can look across the canyon to Cliff Palace.

The left fork of Ruins Road leads to Cliff Palace and Balcony House. *Cliff Palace* is the largest cliff dwelling in the Four Corners states, with 217 rooms and twenty-three

Cliff Palace is the largest ruin at Mesa Verde National Park

kivas. Nestled in a canyon wall and hidden from the plateau above, its brown hues blend into the surrounding cliffs. The half-mile trail that now leads to the ruin includes descending stone stairs. Climbing back, four ten-foot ladders parallel the ancient hand-and-toe-hold trail to the top of the mesa.

A favorite for the adventurous is a visit to *Balcony House*, which includes climbing a thirty-two-foot ladder and crawling through a ten-foot long tunnel. The trail is a half mile and takes about an hour.

WEST OF CORTEZ

You can visit several prehistoric places, mostly undeveloped, in the **Canyon of the Ancients National Monument**, a 164,000-acre monument estimated to have over twenty thousand archaeological sites, including villages, fields, petroglyphs, sweat lodges, sacred springs, check dams, reservoirs, great kivas, cliff dwellings, and shrines.

Lowry Ruins, the most developed of the sites in the monument, was once an Ancestral Puebloan religious or trade center. A pueblo constructed here in A.D. 1090 contained about forty rooms and eight small kivas, one of which was decorated with murals. The Great Kiva, forty-five feet in diameter, is especially impressive. Influences from both Chaco Canyon and the later Mesa Verde tradition make this a unique site.

A wheelchair-accessible trail will lead you through fields to the partially excavated surface dwellings. Once there, the self-guided trail gives information about the main ruin and affords spacious views. Picnic facilities and restrooms are on-site, but no camping is allowed.

The most reliable approach to Lowry Ruins is northwest of Cortez on US491 (formerly US666) for about 18 miles to Pleasant View, then west for 9 miles on a gravel road (County Road CC).

A 6.5-mile trail connects *Sand and East Rock Canyons*, which contain small Ancestral Puebloan cliff dwellings and self-guided hikes. The trail passes ancient ruins that remain largely undisturbed and the types of plants, animals, and scenery seen by the early inhabitants.

The trail is accessed from US491 (formerly US666) north of Cortez, and then west about 8.5 miles on County Roads P and N. An alternate route is to follow US491 south of town to the signs for the airport and Hovenweep National Monument and turn west onto County Road G (McElmo Road) for 12 miles. The trail is sometimes marked with rock cairns and can be steep and rugged. Get a good map, carry sufficient water, tell someone where you are going, and wear a hat, sensible shoes, and clothing for harsh terrain. Rattlesnakes, biting insects, scorpions, and mountain lions have been encountered at Hovenweep.

Sand Canyon Pueblo at the northern trailhead dates to the late thirteenth century. Built inside a masonry wall and around a spring at the head of a canyon, it was probably a major community and ritual center, containing 420 rooms, fourteen towers, and ninety kivas, including a great kiva. The site has self-guided interpretation.

Near the parking lot at the southern terminus of the trail (McElmo Road) is a large butte with Castle Rock Pueblo at the base. Several more small cliff dwellings are nearby.

In the thirteenth century, Ancestral Puebloans also built *Painted Hand Pueblo*, which gets its name from a nearby pictograph. The masonry tower perched on a boulder is thought to be part of a communication network that conveyed messages using firelight at night and pyrite and mica mirrors during the day. The site is in rugged backcountry, and a high-clearance vehicle is recommended.

You can obtain more information about visiting sites in Canyon of the Ancients National Monument from the Anasazi Heritage Center near Dolores.

Hovenweep National Monument contains the ruins of six Ancestral Puebloan villages hidden in twenty miles of canyons and mesas along the Utah-Colorado border. Of particular interest are the multistoried square, oval, circular, and D-shaped towers found here. No one knows for sure their purpose, but speculation includes use as forts, food storage bins, lookout towers, astronomical observatories, signal towers, temples for religious rites, or a combination of all of these.

Over ten thousand years ago, Paleo-Indians seasonally visited the mesas of Hovenweep to hunt game and gather food. By around A.D. 900, people had established permanent settlements and were farming the rich mesa-top soil.

The residents of Hovenweep excelled as potters and masons. They also developed farming techniques that included planting crops in the flat lands to the north with the aid of astronomical features built to predict the solstices and equinoxes.

Life was not easy at Hovenweep, and the difficulties were compounded by cyclical drought and competition for natural resources. By the end of the thirteenth century, the people had begun their exodus out of the canyons.

The six clusters of ruins in the monument include large towers, houses, kivas, storage shelters, and check dams. The most accessible are the *Square Tower Group*. A *visitor center* here has exhibits, a bookstore, and an interpretive trail through the best-preserved and most easily accessed buildings. The small campground, open all year, is designed for tents, but a few spaces can accommodate RVs up to twenty-five feet. The campground also has

Holly Ruins is built at the edge of the canyon in Hovenweep National Park.

restrooms, drinking water, picnic tables, and cooking grills, but the nearest supplies, wood, and gasoline are at Hatch Trading Post, 16 miles west in Utah, or Ismay Trading Post, 14 miles southeast in Colorado. You can download a map from the monument's Web site.

Other ruins in Hovenweep include Horseshoe, Holly, Hackberry, Cajon, Cutthroat Castle, and Goodman Point.

Hovenweep National Monument is still undeveloped, and since it is off the beaten track, visiting here can be a welcome respite from the crowds at Mesa Verde and other more accessible ruins. You can reach the visitor center and Square Tower Group on paved roads from either Utah or Colorado. From Cortez, take US491 south to County Road G (McElmo Canyon Road), and turn west to the visitor center. In Utah, take UT191 from White Mesa (about 15 miles south of Blanding), and turn east onto UT262.

To access most of the outlying units in Colorado, take Route 10 (a dirt road) from US491 near Pleasant View. Be aware that high-clearance vehicles are recommended for visiting the outlying ruins, and after heavy rains the dirt roads in the monument may be impassable. If in doubt about conditions, call ahead.

DURANGO
Map #3

Around Town: Center of Southwest Studies
Nearby: Navajo State Recreation Area, Southern Ute Reservation (Lake Capote, Sky Ute Casino/Lodge, Sky Ute Downs, Sky Ute Museum/Cultural Center)

Utes, attracted by the relatively mild climate, the rich meadows of Animas Valley where elk grazed, and easy access to both the desert and the mountains, were here years before the Denver and Rio Grande Railroad established the town of Durango. Today, Durango is a hub of activity for southwestern Colorado, including the departure point for the popular narrow-gauge train ride to Silverton. During the height of tourist season, it is wise to make your lodging reservations in advance.

Fort Lewis College's **Center of Southwest Studies** displays Indian artifacts in a building at the north end of campus adjacent to the concert hall. Changing displays, juried art shows, and gallery talks and lectures are offered. The permanent collection of one-of-a-kind Navajo, Pueblo, and Hispanic textiles representing eight hundred years of weaving is a highlight. The campus is on a hill east of town, and affords an expansive view of the Animas Valley.

SOUTH OF DURANGO

The **Southern Ute Reservation**, established in 1868, is home to about twelve hundred members of the Mouache and Capote bands of the Southern Ute Indians. The 313,288 acres of the reservation hold oil, gas, sand, and gravel deposits, as well as timbered mountains, mesas, and seven rivers providing recreational opportunities that include big-game hunting and fishing.

Tribal headquarters and a memorial park honoring Ute leaders and U.S. military veterans are in the town of Ignacio on CO172. *Sky Ute Lodge and Casino*, just north of Ignacio on US172, has the Rolling Thunder Café and Pino Nuche Restaurant, meeting rooms, 24-hour gambling, and a hotel with swimming pool, hot tub, and 24-hour desk service where you can also get information on a free scheduled shuttle to the Durango, Pagosa Springs, and Farmington areas. Early reservations are advised at the lodge during the times of the spring Bear Dance and other special events.

Steps away from the casino/lodge is *Southern Ute Museum and Cultural Center*, with displays of Ute bead and leatherwork, historical photographs, and an audiovisual program in a replica of a tipi that chronicles Ute history. You can also purchase arts and crafts in the gallery or arrange to see crafts demonstrations.

Sky Ute Downs/Sky Ute Event Center and RV Park has facilities for rodeos, horse shows, horse clinics, and powwows with a heated indoor arena, large outdoor arena, campsites, and RV park.

Spring-fed *Lake Capote*, at the junction of US160 and CO151 near Chimney Rock, is well stocked with trout, and the campground tent and RV sites have hookups. The general store sells camping and fishing permits and rents fishing gear and rowboats. The lake is open daily, March through October.

Plans are underway to open more of the reservation for outside use. Contact the Southern Ute Division of Wildlife, Department of Parks and Recreation for up-to-date information.

Navajo Lake, east of Ignacio on CO151, feeds the Navajo Irrigation Project and consists of four developed recreation sites. Three are in northern New Mexico, but **Navajo State Park** at the upper end of the reservoir is in Colorado. The park has a marina, restaurant, store, boat rentals, modern campgrounds, picnic areas, and a nature trail. A few motels and restaurants are in the town of Arboles 2 miles away. The *visitor center* has displays of the dam and Ancestral Puebloan artifacts excavated before the land was submerged under the reservoir.

GUNNISON
Map #4

Nearby: Curecanti National Recreation Area

Buffalo and deer were plentiful when the Ute hunted here in the early seventeenth century. After the Los Piños Indian Agency was established in 1868, the Utes moved west of the valley until San Juan gold strikes attracted miners to their land. In 1873, the Brunot Treaty forced the Indians even farther west.

Today, the Western-style town of Gunnison is a scenic and relaxed place to stay while you explore the surrounding Rocky Mountains.

WEST OF GUNNISON

Curecanti National Recreation Area is named for Ute leader Curecata, who hunted here with his people along the Gunnison River. When the dam was built, archaeological surveys found hearth sites from seven thousand years ago. One is recreated at the *visitor center* off US50.

A five-thousand-acre archaeological preserve and six-thousand-year-old dwellings are in the area, which also encompasses three reservoirs, including Blue Mesa, the largest body of water in Colorado, and Morrow Point, which is at the beginning of the Black Canyon of the Gunnison River.

The three visitor centers and campgrounds are only open in the summer: Elk Creek 16 miles west of Gunnison with programs in the campground Friday and Saturday nights; Lake Fork 25 miles west of Gunnison near the Blue Mesa Dam with a campground near the marina; and Cimarron and its adjoining campground 35 miles west of Gunnison.

MONTROSE
Map #5

Nearby: Black Canyon of the Gunnison National Park, Ute Indian Museum; Delta (Ft. Uncompahgre, Ute Council Tree)

The town of Montrose sits at an elevation of 5,764 feet on the western slope of the Rocky Mountains in the Uncompahgre Valley. Utes hunted here long before the 1881 treaty established it as part of a reservation. The ruins of Fort Crawford, built in 1880 to pacify the Utes after the Meeker uprising, are about 8 miles from town on the west bank of the Uncompahgre River. The valley was opened to white settlement in 1881, and most Utes were forced to leave by 1884.

Several inexpensive places to stay and eat make Montrose a good base camp for enjoying the abundant outdoor recreation opportunities and the outstanding beauty of the surrounding mountains.

NORTH OF MONTROSE

In the early 1800s, Antoine Robidoux built a trading post northwest of the current town of **Delta**. Indians came to trade with the trappers at the post until Utes burned it down in 1844.

Just north of the bridge in Delta is a small sign marking the *Ute Council Tree*, a cottonwood tree over two hundred years old and now a Colorado landmark. Once a famous Ute meeting place, it was here that Chief Ouray and his wife, Chipeta, met with U.S. soldiers to talk peace.

Across the river is Confluence Park, at one time a Ute winter campsite. Next to the park is Fort Uncompahgre, a living history museum where the staff is adorned with beards and buckskins similar to those worn by mountain men. Tall wooden gates and sod-roofed huts recreate the trading fort originally built by Robidoux.

SOUTH OF MONTROSE

Ute Indian Museum was once part of the four-hundred-acre farm of Ute Chief Ouray and his Tabeguache Ute wife, Chipeta. Photographs plus traditional and ceremonial items that once belonged to Ouray, Ignacio, and other Utes are displayed in what is the most complete Ute collection in the state. Dioramas highlight the Ute lifestyle, and the grave of Chipeta, who died in 1924, is also here.

In addition, the museum includes the site where Dominguez and Escalante, led by Ute guide Atanasio, camped by the Uncompahgre River in August of 1776. It is marked by a cross-shaped ramada.

In late September the museum sponsors the Native American Lifeways Festival, which includes lectures, demonstrations, and special exhibits by local Utes.

The museum is 3 miles south of Montrose on US550. The Montrose Visitor's Center is also here.

EAST OF MONTROSE

Black Canyon is a dramatic gorge fifty miles long, a half-mile deep, and edged with near-vertical walls of 2-billion-year-old dark volcanic and metamorphic rocks. **Black Canyon of the Gunnison National Park** preserves twelve of the canyon's most scenic miles.

Folsom hunters used the rim, and later Utes chased deer and buffalo on the canyon's edge, but they believed anyone entering the canyon would never be seen alive again. Today most of the canyon is wilderness suitable for camping and hiking, with the Gunnison River at the bottom providing excellent fishing for those willing to make the strenuous trek.

Both the South Rim and North Rim provide outstanding overlooks into the canyon. *Gunnison Point Visitor Center,* on the South Rim, has exhibits, interpretive programs, and a campground. Permits must be obtained here for backcountry climbing, hiking, and kayaking. The South Rim is accessed from CO347 off US50 east of Montrose. There is limited access in winter.

Pontoon boat tours through the upper Black Canyon are scheduled during the summer from Morrow Point. For reservations, contact the Elk Creek Visitor Center in Curecanti National Recreation Area.

OURAY
Map #6

Around Town: Ouray Historical Museum, Ouray Hot Springs Pool, Weisbaden Hot Springs Spa and Lodgings

Ute leader Ouray and his people loved this picturesque alpine valley, surrounded as it is by a dramatic 13,000-foot, multicolored amphitheater of rock. In spring, they could

watch the red, gray, and orange mountains cascade with waterfalls flowing from the melting high-country snowfields. In summer, they hunted the elk, deer, and Rocky Mountain sheep that roamed freely through the luxuriant valley. Throughout the year, they soaked their bodies and rested their spirits in the healing waters of the hot springs.

Ouray Hot Springs Pool uses the odorless water of the mineral springs to fill the two swimming pools in the park at the north end of town. The large pool is 250 feet long by 150 feet wide, with the water in its three sections cooled to varying temperatures. A fitness center is also on site.

The San Juan Mountains around Ouray are some of the most beautiful in Colorado.

Several motels in town tap into the hot springs, too. One of the oldest of these is **Weisbaden Hot Springs Spa and Lodgings**, which has subterranean natural grottoes and an outdoor pool filled with hot springs water. If you don't want to spend the night, you can still bathe in the hot springs and enjoy the full range of spa treatments.

Housed in a hospital built in 1887, **Ouray Historical Museum** displays artifacts and photographs of the Utes including the town's namesake, Ouray, and his wife, Chipeta. Evening lectures in summer highlight local history.

For outdoor enthusiasts, hiking, mountain biking, fishing, backpacking, and jeep touring opportunities are abundant in the spectacular San Juan Mountains that surround the town.

PAGOSA SPRINGS
Map #7

Around Town: Pagosa Spring, The Springs Resort
Nearby: Chimney Rock Ruin, Lake Capote

Pagosa means "healing waters," and according to Ute legend, the hot springs appeared here one night when a fire was built to carry prayers to the Great Spirit asking for an end to a terrible plague. The prayers were answered when the fire became a boiling pool of healing water.

At one time, both the Ute and Navajo claimed exclusive right to the waters of Pagosa. In 1866, the two groups decided to settle their conflict with a fight to the death between a representative from each of them. Lieutenant Colonel Albert Pfeiffer, an adopted member of the Utes, agreed to champion them. He chose bowie knives as the weapons for battle. When the fight began, instead of rushing in for close combat, "Tata" (as Pfeiffer was known in Ute) hurled his knife through the air, killing his Navajo opponent and winning the hot springs for his adopted people.

General William Ashley of the Rocky Mountain Fur Company organized the first rendezvous here in 1823. It soon became a yearly opportunity for fur trappers to meet other trappers and Indian friends for business and socializing. Today, the Mountain Man Rendezvous held annually at the base of Reservoir Hill overlooks the campsite used by Southern Utes on their visits to the hot springs.

The original **Pagosa Spring** is near downtown, south over the bridge on 4th Street and along what was once Navajo Trail. It is billed as the world's hottest and largest hot springs, pumping out 1 million gallons of 153-degree water daily.

Several other places in town also use hot springs water to fill swimming pools or hot tubs. One of them is **The Springs Resort,** where terraced deposits of pink, green, and white hold pools of mineral-rich water that then flows into a central pond by the San Juan River. A full-service spa and resort hotel, it has eighteen different mineral pools, including one that can be used by non-guests.

The **Spa at Pagosa Springs** also provides mineral pools where you can soak away your troubles. The spa offers massages, and the facility includes motel rooms and a seasonal RV park.

The *Pagosa Springs U.S. Forest Service District Ranger* office on 2nd and Pagosa streets (US160) has information about hiking, fishing, and camping in the surrounding national forest, as well as about tours to Chimney Rock Ruins (see below) and other archaeological sites in San Juan National Forest.

WEST OF PAGOSA SPRINGS

Just west of town on the right side of US160-84 is a *historical marker* indicating the site of the fight between "Tata" Pfeiffer and his Navajo opponent for rights to use the hot springs.

The ruins of the **Chimney Rock** archaeological area perch atop a mesa a thousand feet above the valley floor. Speculation is that it was an Ancestral Puebloan religious, trading, timber shipping, or astronomy center. The two rock pinnacles were probably used as a shrine to the Twin War gods, and some Pueblos still come here for ceremonies to maintain a link to their ancestors.

The site shows heavy influence from Chaco Canyon culture and was connected to it by an ancient road. A Chacoan great house, pithouse, guardhouse, and great kiva have been excavated, and there are also over two hundred backfilled or undisturbed structures in the six-square-mile area.

Living at the top of the mesa posed unique challenges for the residents. Water was scarce, so it was probably transported daily from the Piedra River valley below, a round-trip of over a mile. The masons, who left palm and fingerprints in the clay fragments, needed tons of rock and dirt carried up the cliffs for their building. In addition, the poor soil on the mesa meant at least some individuals farmed and lived in temporary camps on the valley floor.

One theory is that the inhabitants of Chimney Rock were an elite class supported by workers in the valley. Another theory speculates the elevation of the mesa aided in defense or in sending messages to Chaco Canyon. Strong evidence also points to the use of Chimney Rock as an astronomical observatory—every 18.6 years the moon is framed between the twin towers in a major lunar standstill, and a line of sight across a circular stone basin can be used to mark important solar cycles.

Chimney Rock was an outlier of the Chaco culture. Signal fires from here could be seen as far away as Chaco Canyon.

The only way to visit Chimney Rock is with a two-hour guided tour, available May 15 through September 15, weather permitting. Tours leave from the parking lot by the visitor center cabin 3 miles south of US160 on CO151. Contact Chimney Rock or the National Forest Service's Pagosa Springs office for information and reservations.

For visiting nearby **Lake Capote**, see the Southern Ute Reservation, page 271.

SALIDA
Map #8

Around Town: Salida Hot Springs, Salida Museum
Nearby: Mount Princeton Hot Springs, Saguache County Museum, South Park

The Ute occupied semipermanent villages in the Upper Arkansas Valley until they obtained the horse and the ability to travel to other hunting grounds. In 1806, Zebulon Pike found the remains of a village here that he believed once sheltered three thousand people.

Salida Hot Springs in Centennial Park has Colorado's largest indoor hot springs pool, as well as private tubs filled by hot mineral water piped from eight miles away at Old Poncha Springs, once enjoyed by the Ute.

Next to the pool is **Salida Museum**, with some Ute pottery, arrowheads, and artifacts. It is open as volunteers permit.

NORTH OF SALIDA

Mt. Princeton Hot Springs Resort was built at a place where Utes once wintered in warm thermal caves along the creek. The resort now has a hotel, swimming pools, private tubs, and rock-lined hot springs pools in the creek. Other springs are nearby, including the hottest one in Colorado, 165–183 degrees. Inquire at the resort, which is north of Salida on US285 to Nathrop, and then west for 4.5 miles on CR162.

If you continue north and east on US285, you will pass through **South Park**, 1,200 square miles of expansive grasslands ringed by stunning mountains. The abundant game attracted members of various Indian groups, and because its reserves were considered worth a fight, many skirmishes took place here. One of the fiercest was a three-day battle in the spring of 1852. Facing each other across a stream, Utes and Comanches agreed the winner would be the group that could force the other one to a nearby ridge. Under the rules for combat, rest and food breaks were agreed to. The Comanches emerged victorious, but the Utes still continued to come to these rich hunting grounds.

In the early nineteenth century, South Park was a gathering place for fur trappers and their Indian wives. *Bayou Salado Rendezvous and Burro Days* near Fairplay and *Rocky Mountain College Rendezvous* at Lost Park re-create their encampments. See Events below for more information.

SOUTH OF SALIDA

The name of the town of Saguache comes from the Ute word *Sa-qua—qua-chi-pa*, meaning "Water at the Blue Earth." **Saguache County Museum** houses a large Indian arrowhead collection, as well as displays of Indian rugs, pottery, spear points, and baskets.

EVENTS

Sky Ute Downs is an equestrian center and racetrack in Ignacio that hosts Indian dances, horse shows, and rodeos. Call 970-563-4502 for current schedule.

VARIES *Council Tree Powwow:* American Indian artists, dancers, and vendors, as well as tipi village tours. Confluence Park in Delta. Visit www.counciltreepowwow.org/history.

Pagosa Rendezvous: A Mountain Man Rendezvous. Tents and tipis erected to relive the trading, eating, and black powder shooting contests of an earlier time. East on Spring Street along the base of Reservoir Hill in Pagosa Springs.

Southern Ute Sun Dance: Traditional religious dance held twice a year. Southern Ute Reservation. 800-772-1236, ext. 300

MAY *Indian Arts and Western Culture Festival:* Juried Indian art market, rug auction, Indian dances, archaeological tours, and fiddle contest. Throughout Montezuma County (Cortez, Dolores, Manucs, Towaoc). Call 800-530-2998.

Rendezvous of Cultures: Includes stories, songs, and dances from the local cultures, including Ute, Hispanic, and mountain man. Memorial Day weekend at Fort Garland.

Southern Ute Bear Dance: Traditional Bear Dance and feast honoring the bear's special relationship with the Utes. Memorial Day weekend, call 800-772-1236, ext. 300.

JUNE-AUGUST *Cortez City Park:* Traditional native dancing on summer evenings, Monday-Thursday, at 7pm Call 970-565-8227.

Ute Mountain Bear Dance: To mark the time when bears awaken from winter hibernation. Five days of games, food, arts and crafts, dancing, and singing. Ute Mountain Ute Reservation, the first weekend in June.

Ute Mountain Round-Up Rodeo: Includes a rodeo, carnival, barbecue, dancing, and parade. Held in June at the Legion Arena at Ute Mountain Ute Reservation. Call 970-565-8151.

JUNE-SEPTEMBER *Ute Heritage Dancers and BBQ:* Every Wednesday evening, June through September, Sky Ute Lodge hosts a barbecue, tour of the Cultural Center and performances by the Southern Ute Heritage Dancers. A fee is charged.

JULY *Mesa Verde Arts and Crafts Show and Sale:* Native American and Western artists sell their arts and crafts. Held at end of July at Morefield Campground in Mesa Verde National Park.

Thunder Mountain Lives Tonight: History as drama in the outdoor theater in Confluence Park in Delta. Begins with the Ute myth of the Thunderbird and tells the story of the people of Delta County. July 4 through Labor Day, Tuesday-Saturday. Contact the Delta Chamber of Commerce.

Bayou Salado Rendezvous and Burro Days: Rendezvous is a historic reenactment of pre-twentieth-century frontier gathering, with shooting and storytelling contests, trader's row, Council Fire, and parade. You must be in primitive dress to attend evening activities. It is held in Hartsel. Burro Days are in Fairplay and include burro and llama races, barn dance, auction, entertainment, food, and more. Contact South Park Chamber of Commerce or visit www.burrodays.com/pages/rendezvous.htm.

AUGUST *Heritage Fair:* Flint-knapping demonstrations, archaeology talks, Indian dancing and a celebration of the early nineteenth-century mountain men. Early August at the Rio Grande County Museum in Del Norte.

Rocky Mountain Rendezvous: Recreation of mountain man encampment. This teaching rendezvous includes free classes on nineteenth-century skills such as quilling, tanning, and flint-knapping. Second week in August at Lost Park outside of Jefferson. Take Lost Park Road (FS #56) off 285 about 1 mile northeast of Jefferson. Contact Harley McKlacken (970-340-3066), http://cap-n-ball.com/college, or South Park Chamber of Commerce.

SEPTEMBER *Native American Lifeways Festival:* Demonstrations, lectures, and special exhibits by local Utes. Late September at the Ute Indian Museum outside of Montrose. 970-249-3098.

Southern Ute Fair and Powwow: Parade, footraces, games dancing, arts and crafts booths, and food vendors. Second weekend in September.

OCTOBER *October Festival:* Autumn heritage celebration at Cortez Center dedicated to various cultures in the area. Includes Native American events such as storytelling and dancing.

DECEMBER *Christmas Season:* December evening open house at Spruce Tree House in Mesa Verde National Park. The cliff dwelling is decorated with luminaries. Call the park for details.

CONTACT INFORMATION

Alamosa Chamber of Commerce
Cole Park, Alamosa, CO 81101
800-258-7597 *or* 719-589-3681
www.alamosa.org

Alamosa/Monte Vista National Wildlife Refuges
8249 Emperius Road, Alamosa, CO 81101
800-344-9453 *or* 719-589-4021
http://alamosa.fws.gov
> **Visitor Center**
> 9383 El Rancho Lane, Alamosa, CO 81101
> 719-589-4705
> Mon-Fri 10am-4pm, Mar-Nov; Nov-Feb closed
> **Monte Vista Center**
> 6140 Hwy 15, Monte Vista, CO 81101
> Open seasonally with volunteers

Anasazi Heritage Center
27501 Highway 184, Dolores, CO 81323
970-882-5600; TDD 970-882-4825
www.co.blm.gov/ahc
Daily 9am-5pm, Mar-Oct; daily 9am-4pm, Nov-Feb; fee

ARAMARK
Box 277, Mancos, CO 81328
970-529-4421

Black Canyon of the Gunnison National Park
102 Elk Street, Gunnison, CO 81230
970-641-2337
> **Visitor Center, South Rim**
> Daily 8am-6pm, summer; 8:30am-4pm. Fall-spring
> 970-249-1914, ext 423
> www.nps.gov/blca

Bureau of Land Management
www.blm.gov/co/st/en.html
> **San Juan Resource Area**
> 15 Burnett Court, Durango, CO 81301
> 970-247-4874; TDD 970-385-1257

Canyon of the Ancients National Monument
27501 Hwy 184, Dolores, CO 81323
970-882-5600 • www.co.blm.gov/canm

Center of Southwest Studies
Fort Lewis College
1000 Rim Drive, Durango, CO 81301-3999
970-247-7456 • http://swcenter.fortlewis.edu
Mon-Fri 1pm-4pm or by appointment

Chimney Rock Archaeological Area
Interpretive Program, PO Box 1662, Pagosa Springs, CO 81147
www.chimneyrockco.org
> **Visitor Center**: daily 9am-4:30pm in season 970-883-5359; call 970-264-2287 in off-season to leave message
> **Daily tours**: 9:30am, 10:30am, 1pm and 2pm mid May-Sept

Colorado State Parks
303-866-3437
Reservations: 800-678-2267, 303-470-1144, or online • http://parks.state.co.us

Colorado Welcome Center
928 East Main, Cortez, CO 81321-3325
970-565-3414
Daily year-round

Cortez Center Museum and Cultural Park
25 N Market Street, Cortez, CO 81321
970-565-1151
Mon-Sat 10am-10pm, Memorial Day-Labor Day; Mon-Sat 10am-5pm, rest of the year; no fee

Cortez Chamber of Commerce
928 East Main, PO Box 958, Cortez, CO 81321
970-565-3414 • www.cortezchamber.com

Crow Canyon Archaeological Center
23390 County Road K, Cortez, CO 81321
800-422-8975 *or* 970-565-8975
www.crowcanyon.org

Curecanti National Recreation Area
970-641-2337 • www.nps.gov/cure
> **Visitor Centers**
> Cimarron: intermittently 9am-4pm, mid May-Sept30; 970-249-4074
> Elk Creek: daily 8am-6pm, summer; Mon-Fri 8:30am-4:30pm rest of year; 970-641-2337 ext 205
> Lake Fork: open on limited basis, mid May-Sept 30; 970-641-3129

Delta Chamber of Commerce
301 Main Street, Delta, CO 81416
970-874-8616 • www.deltacolorado.org

Durango Chamber Resort Association
111 S. Camino Del Rio, Durango, CO 81302
800-525-8855 *or* 970-247-0312;
Lodging 800-463-8726 • www.durango.org

Fort Garland
29477 Highway 159, Fort Garland, CO 81133
719-379-3512
www.coloradohistory.org/hist_sites/ft_
    Garland/ft_garland.htm
Daily 9am-5pm, Apr-Oct; Thu-Mon 8am-
    4pm, Nov-Mar; fee

Fort Uncompahgre
205 Gunnison River Drive, Delta, CO 81416
970-874-1718 • www.delta-fort.org
Mon-Fri 9am-3pm, Apr-Sept; 1800s Christmas
    celebration, Dec; fee

Great Sand Dunes National Monument
11500 Hwy 150, Mosca, CO 81146
719-378-6300 • www.nps.gov/grsa
    Visitor Center
    11999 Hwy 150, Mosca, CO 81146
    719-378-6399
    Daily 9am-4:30pm in winter; daily 9am-
        5pm rest of year, with extended hours
        as staffing permits
    Oasis Campground
    719-378-2222

Gunnison Chamber of Commerce
500 E. Tomichi Ave, Gunnison, CO 81230
970-641-1501 • www.gunnison-co.com

Hovenweep National Monument
McElmo Route, Cortez, CO 81321
970-562-4282 • www.nps.gov/hove
Daily 8am-5pm

Luther E. Bean Museum
208 Edgemont Blvd, Adams State College,
    Richardson Hall Room 256, Alamosa, CO
    81101
719-587-7609 • www.adams.edu/lutheran
Weekdays 1pm-4:30pm or by appointment;
    no fee

**Mesa Indian Trading Company/Mesa Verde
    Pottery**
27601 East Hwy 160, Cortez, CO 81321
800-441-9908 *or* 970-565-4492
www.mesaverdepottery.com

Mesa Verde Company (See Aramark)

Mesa Verde Country Information Bureau
PO Box HH, Cortez, CO 82321
800-253-1616
www.mesaverdecountry.com/tourism/tourism.html

Mesa Verde National Park
PO Box 8, Mesa Verde, CO 81330
970-529-4465 • www.nps.gov/meve
Year-round, but no services in winter: Fee
    ARAMARK
    Mesa Verde Company
    PO Box 277, Mancos, CO 81328
    800-449-2288 *or* 970-564-4300
    http://visitmesaverde.com
    Chapin Mesa Archaeological Museum
    Daily 8am-6:30pm, mid Apr-mid Oct;
        8am-5pm rest of the year
    Far View Lodge
    One Navajo Hill, Box 277, Mesa Verde
        National Park, CO 81330
    Reservations: 866-875-8456
    Far View Visitor Center
    Daily 8am-5pm, mid Apr-mid Oct
    970-529-4465

Monte Vista National Wildlife Refuge (*See*
    Alamosa National Wildlife Refuge)

Montrose Visitors and Convention Bureau
1519 E. Main, PO Box 335, Montrose, CO
    81402
800-873-0244 *or* 970-252-0505
www.visitmontrose.net

Mt. Princeton Hot Springs Resort
15870 CR 162, Nathrop, CO 81236
888-395-7799 *or* 719-395-2447
www.mtprinceton.com

Navajo State Park
1526 CR982, Arboles, CO 81121
Camping & cabin reservations: 800-678-2267
    or 303-470-1144
Marina: 970-883-2628
Visitor Center & office: 970-883-2208
http://parks.state.co.us/Parks/Navajo

Notah Dineh Trading Company and Museum
345 West Main, Cortez, CO 81321
800-444-2024 *or* 970-565-9607
www.notahdineh.com

Ouray Historical Museum
420 6th Avenue, PO Box 151, Ouray, CO 81427
970-325-4576
www.ouraycountyhistoricalsociety.org
Mon-Sat 10am-4pm & Sun noon-4pm, sum-
    mer; hours vary with volunteers, spring &
    fall; fee

Ouray Hot Springs Pool
1200 Main, PO Box 468, Ouray, CO 81427
970-325-7073 or -7076
www.ouraycolorado.com/fitness
Daily 10am-10pm summer; Mon-Fri 12 noon-
    8:45pm & Sat-Sun 11am-8:45pm, winter; fee

Ouray Visitor Center
Ouray, CO 81427
800-228-1876 *or* 970-325-4746
www.ouraycolorado.com

Pagosa Springs Chamber of Commerce
402 San Juan Street, PO Box 787, Pagosa
    Springs, CO 81147
800-252-2204 *or* 970-264-2360
www.pagosaspringschamber.com

Rio Grande County Museum
580 Oak, Del Norte, CO 81132-2210
719-657-2847
Mon Sat 10am 5pm, summer; Tue, Fri, Sat
    noon-5pm, winter; fee

Saguache County Museum
Hwy 285, PO Box 243, Saguache, CO 81149
719-655-2557 *or* -2805
Daily 10am-5pm, summer; fee

Salida Chamber of Commerce
406 W. Hwy 50, Salida, CO 81201
877-772-5432 *or* 719-539-2068
www.salidachamber.org

Salida Hot Springs
410 W. Hwy 50, Salida, CO 81201
719-539-6738 • www.salidapool.com

Salida Museum
406 W. Rainbow Boulevard (Hwy 50 at I St.),
    Salida, CO 81201
719-539-7483
Daily 11am-7pm, summer; fee

San Luis Museum and Cultural Center
401 Church Street, San Luis, CO 81152
719-672-3611
www.museumtrail.org/SanLuisMuseum.asp
Daily 10am-4pm summer; daily Mon-Fri 9am-
    4pm winter; fee

San Luis Valley Historical Museum
306 Hunt Avenue, PO Box 1593, Alamosa,
    CO 81101
719-587-0667
www.museumtrail.org/SanLuisValleyHistory-
    Museum.asp
Daily 10am-4pm, June-Sept, or by appoint-
    ment; no fee

South Park Chamber of Commerce
PO Box 312, Fairplay, CO 80440
719-836-3410
www.parkchamberofcomerce.org

Southern Ute Reservation
Southern Ute Tribe, PO Box 737, Ignacio, CO
    81137
970-563-0100 • www.southern-ute.nsn.us
  Lake Capote
  970-883-2273
  Sky Ute Event Center/RV Park
  200 E. Hwy 151, PO Box 550, Ignacio,
      CO 81137
  970-563-4502
  Sky Ute Lodge and Casino
  14826 Hwy 172 North, Ignacio 81137
  888-842-4180 *or* 970-563-3000
  Reservations: 800-876-7017
  Shuttle: 888-842-4180 *or* 970-563-3000
  www.skyutecasino.com
  Southern Ute Division of Wildlife
  970-563-0130
  Parks and Recreation, ext. 2412
  Southern Ute Museum and Cultural Center
  970-563-9583; gift shop 970-563-4649
  www.southernutemuseum.org
  Mon-Fri 10am-6pm, Sat-Sun 11am-3pm;
      closed Sun in winter

The Spa at Pagosa Springs
317 Hot Springs Blvd., Pagosa Springs, CO
    81147
800-832-5523 *or* 970-264-5910
www.pshotsprings.com

The Springs Resort
165 Hot Springs Boulevard, Pagosa Springs,
    CO 81147
Bathhouse: daily 7am-11pm (970-264-2284)
800-225-0934 *or* 970-264-4168
www.VisitPagosaHotSprings.com

Toh-Atin Gallery
145 West Ninth Street, PO Box 2329,
    Durango, CO 81302
800-332-5799 in state; 800-525-0384 out of
    state • www.toh-atin.com

U.S. Forest Service
  Gunnison Ranger District
  216 N. Colorado, Gunnison, CO 81230
  970-641-0471
  Pagosa Springs Ranger District
  180 Pagosa Street, Box 310, Pagosa Springs,
      CO 81147
  970-264-2268

Ute Indian Museum
17253 Chipeta Drive, Montrose, CO 81401
970-249-3098
www.coloradohistory.org/hist_sites/
    UteIndian/Ute_indian.htm
Mon-Sat 9am-4:30pm & Sun 11am-4:30pm,
    mid May-Oct; Mon-Sat 8:30am-5pm,
    Nov-Dec; Tues-Sat 8:30am-5pm, Jan-mid
    May; fee

Ute Mountain Ute Reservation
Box 52, Towaoc, CO 81334
970-565-3751 • www.utemountainute.com
    Sleeping Ute Pottery Factory Outlet/
        Ute Mountain Pottery Factory
    Hwy 160-491, Cortez, CO 81334
    800-896-8548 *or* 970-565-8548
    Summer hours, Mon-Sat 9am-6pm & Sun
        12 noon-6pm, summer hours
    Sleeping Ute RV Park
    800-889-5072 *or* 970-565-6544
    Towaoc Library
    970-565-3751
    Ute Mountain Casino-Hotel
    #3 Weeminuche Dr., Towaoc, CO 81334
    www.utemountaincasino.com
    Casino: 800-258-8007 *or* 970-565-8800
    Hotel: 888-565-8837 *or* 970-565-8837
    Shuttle: 970-565-8800
    Ute Mountain Tribal Park
    Towaoc, CO 81334
    970-565-9653 *or* 800-847-5485
    Visitor Center: 970-749-1452

Wiesbaden Hot Springs Spa and Lodgings
625 5th Street, PO Box 349, Ouray, CO 81427
888-846-5191 *or* 970-325-4347

Yucca House National Monument
c/o Mesa Verde National Park , PO Box 8,
    Mesa Verde, Colorado 81330
Online Visitor Guide and directions:
    www.nps.gov/yuho

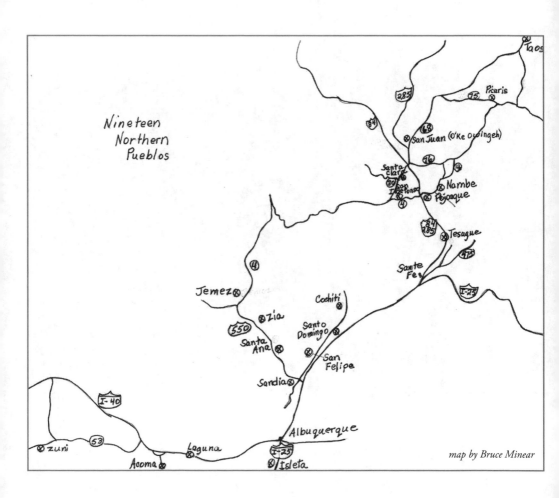

Nineteen
Northern
Pueblos

Taos

285 · Picuris · 75

84 · 68 · San Juan (O'Ke Owingeh)

74

Santa Clara · 30 · 72

San Ildefonso · Nambe

4 · Pojoaque

84 · 285 · Tesuque

475

Santa Fe

4 · I-25

Jemez

Zia · Cochiti

550 · Santo Domingo

Santa Ana

San Felipe

Sandia

I-40

zuni · 53 · Laguna · Albuquerque

Acoma · I-25 · Isleta

map by Bruce Minear

CHAPTER 16

THE PUEBLOS OF NEW MEXICO

VISITING THE NINETEEN INDIAN PUEBLOS

Visitors are welcome at most of the pueblos, as long as they are willing to abide by local rules. The pueblo's visitor center or tribal offices is a good place to start. Each pueblo hosts a Feast Day, a celebration of religious dances and sometimes processions, footraces, food vendors, and arts-and-crafts booths held on the same date each year. Many coincide with the Catholic Church's calendar that honors patron saints. Elaborate meals are part of Feast Days, but attending one requires an invitation from a Pueblo family. If you go, remember that seating may be limited, so allow dancers and elders to dine first, and don't linger at the table. Also know that a "thank you" is appropriate, but payment and tipping are not. Photography, sketching, cell phones, and recording devices are strictly prohibited on Feast Days unless otherwise noted. See Section II, Discovering Native America, for more details on visiting the pueblos.

A good source of information for the pueblos of Nambe, Ohkay Owingeh (formerly San Juan), Picuris Pojoaque, San Ildefonso, Santa Clara, Taos, and Tesuque is the Eight Northern Indian Pueblos Council. In addition to serving the members of the communities, this organization caters to tourists and lists up-to-date calendar information for pueblo events. Look for their guide at local places of lodging. The ENIPC also sponsors the popular summer Arts and Crafts Show, with hundreds of booths of talented Native American artists, colorful performances of traditional Pueblo dancing and music, and authentic Pueblo food.

Another good source is the Indian Pueblo Cultural Center, whose Web site takes you to thumbnail sketches of the pueblos and a calendar of events. *The Collector's Guide* by Wingspread Guides of New Mexico also lists events online.

ACOMA PUEBLO

Akome: native word for "People of the White Rock"
Hak'u: "To Prepare or Plan"

Acoma (*AH-koh-mah*) Pueblo's "Sky City" is perched almost 370 feet above the valley floor atop a sandstone mesa. The village was built at least one thousand years ago and vies with Taos and Old Oraibi for the title of the oldest continuously inhabited town in the United States. Once accessible only by ladders and toe- and finger-holds cut into the rock, it offered an ideal defense from enemies.

In 1598, the residents of Acoma rebelled against Spanish demands for tribute, hurling thirteen Spanish soldiers, including the nephew of Don Juan de Oñate, over the side of the cliff. The Spanish returned the next year with a vengeance, killing eight hundred of the Indians. They burned the village, sold many of the people into slavery, and cut off one foot of every man over the age of twenty-five before sending him to prison.

Today, about three thousand people make up this Keresan-speaking group. Only seven to ten families still live on the mesa, which has no running water or electricity. Many of the rest live in the nearby farming settlements of Acomita, McCartys, and Anzac, returning to Sky City for celebrations and feast days.

The new **Sky City Travel Complex** (exit 102 off I-40) offers services for tourists and truck drivers. Lodging with 150 rooms, a pool, Jacuzzi, and workout room is available at the *Sky City Hotel* with Southwestern décor that includes furniture built by woodcarvers from Acoma and a rotunda fountain that flows through a replica of traditional pots painted by Delores Aragon. Attached to the hotel is *Sky City Casino*, open every day, all day. The casino has several dining options, including *Huwak'a Restaurant,* serving posole, green chile stew, and other traditional food.

Acoma potters are known for their exquisite thin-walled pottery covered with a white slip. They then use yucca brushes to paint delicate black and red geometric designs, many of which are reminiscent of those used by the Ancestral Puebloans. You can purchase it and the bolder modern styles of pottery at the travel complex, the museum (see below), and from individuals along the Sky City tour route and at the top of the mesa.

Acoma artists are famous for their distinctive thin-walled pottery.

The Pueblo of Acoma spreads out on the top of a high mesa.

You can also buy pottery at the **Sky City Cultural Center and Haak'u Museum** at the base of the mesa. Look outside for the double-chambered pottery chimney, a courtyard, and ladders to the flat roof. Inside are wood-burning fireplaces and white-washed walls. The museum displays permanent and changing exhibits related to the Acoma people. The center also has the Ýaaká Café serving Acoma dishes, as well as a gift shop.

You can make arrangements here for an unforgettable guided tour to the **Sky City**, the only way the old pueblo can be visited. Daily hour-and-a-half tours are offered, as well as longer tours and tour packages that are held intermittently. A calendar/visitor guide is also available here, as well as by writing tribal headquarters. Be aware that to take a picture, you will need a permit. Filming or videotaping is not allowed.

Once on top of the mesa you will see adobe houses, with food stored on the first floor because it is cooler there, and smoke escaping from the top floor kitchen. *San Estevan del Rey Mission* was constructed between 1629 and 1640, with its forty-foot *vigas* (wooden roof beams) and every bit of the dirt used for the building hand-carried up the mesa from the desert below. A spectacular view of surrounding mountains, buttes, and valleys is a bonus.

Cyclists can join a 25, 50, or 100-mile race that winds across part of the Acoma and Laguna pueblos. Fishermen can try their luck with catfish and rainbow trout at *Acomita Lake* (just off exit 100). Call the tribal office to see if it has reopened, and if so, to obtain a permit. Also inquire here about big-game trophy elk hunts.

The pueblo is closed June 24 and 29 and the first and second weekend in October. Call ahead to confirm hours and to ask whether the pueblo is open to visitors when you plan to be there.

Acoma Pueblo is about 60 miles west of Albuquerque off I-40 at exit 102 for Sky City Hotel/Conference Center and Travel Center. From here, follow the signs onto Indian Route 32 past the tribal offices and the scenic overlook to Sky City Cultural Center. Signs also direct you to Sky City from exits 108 or 96.

COCHITI PUEBLO

Kotyete: "Stone Kiva"

Today, about fifteen hundred people make Cochiti (*KOH-chee-tee*) their home. The current pueblo was established around A.D. 1250, at the mouth of narrow White Rock Canyon along the Rio Grande with mountain views to the north, south, and west. Their oral history, however, tells of living in seven other places before settling here, including Frijoles Canyon in Bandelier National Monument.

This conservative Keresan community had limited European contact until Don Juan de Oñate's colonization in 1598. The pueblo was later abandoned during the 1680 Pueblo Revolt and resettled again in 1692 with the Spanish reconquest of the area, offering a refuge for Spanish colonists fleeing Navajo and Apache raids.

The central plaza, kiva, and a few original structures still stand. The mission church of **San Buenaventura**, built in 1628, has been restored to its nineteenth-century appearance. To tour the church and pueblo, contact the Governor's Office for permission. Photography, drawing, and recordings are not allowed.

Kasha-Katuwe Tent Rocks National Monument, managed by the Albuquerque BLM, is located along the western border of the pueblo's lands. This new national monument, formed by eruptions in the Jemez volcanic field 6 to 7 million years ago, is four thousand acres of cone-shaped tent rock formations as high as ninety feet, small canyons scooped and eroded by wind and water, and gray, pink, and beige layers of rock contrasting with the green and red of nearby plants and trees. Hoodoos, formed when soft rock underneath erodes more quickly than the harder rock on top, add to the uniqueness of the landscape. Soaring hawks, swallows, and bluebirds add their own distinctive flavor. Indians consider it a sacred place, and there is evidence of human use as long as four thousand years ago. You can explore the monument via a national recreation hiking trail with two loops. The trailhead is at the parking lot. Be advised that services here are limited, and the monument is open for day-use only. Also note that it is sometimes closed for tribal activities. To reach Tent Rocks from I-25 south of Santa Fe, take Cochiti exit 259, and follow NM22 and unpaved Forest Service Road 268 north.

Cochiti Lakes Recreation Area, created by one of the largest earth-filled dams in the United States, is on the Rio Grande in White Rock Canyon and is open for camping, swimming (no lifeguards are on duty), no-wake boating, picnicking, and fishing for catfish, trout, crappie, and bluegill. A tribal-owned marina and convenience store are located at the recreation area. Reservations for boat rentals are recommended. The Army Corps of Engineers runs a small *visitor center* overlooking the lake, with dioramas and exhibits describing the locale and life at Cochiti.

Just east of the lake at *Tetilla Peak Recreation Area* is a nature trail and *visitor center*. The lake is off I-25 about a half hour southwest of Santa Fe.

Cochiti Lakes Golf Course is rated in the top seventy-five courses in the country. In addition to the eighteen-hole course and driving range, Stone Kiva Bar and Grill serves breakfast and lunch daily and dinner Thursday through Saturday.

Cochiti crafts include the clay Storyteller figures, made famous in the 1960s by potter Helen Cordero, and traditional horsehide drums. Other clay figurines, black-on-cream pottery, jewelry, and masterfully crafted drums are popular as well.

To reach Cochiti, take I-25 south of Santa Fe about 25 miles. Turn left on NM16, then right onto NM22, and follow the signs.

ISLETA PUEBLO

Isleta: Spanish for "Little Island"
Shiewhibak: "Knife Laid on the Ground to Play With"

Isleta (*iz-LET-tah*) Pueblo is the largest Tiwa-speaking group, with about three thousand people. The current site was probably first occupied around A.D. 1250, but during the 1680 Pueblo Revolt, many of the residents were forced to flee south, and the pueblo was destroyed. In the early 1700s, a new village was built in the same place.

Today, the pueblo comprises several villages plus forested mountains, desert mesas, and land along the Rio Grande. Agriculture, ranching, and gaming profits are important to the pueblo, and Isleta artisans craft polychrome pots, black-on-white or red-on-white, along with jewelry and clothing.

Many of the original houses surround the plaza. The church was built in 1612 under the name of St. Anthony. After the people returned in the early 1700s, it was restored and renamed **St. Augustine Mission Church**. The church, with thick white-washed adobe walls varying between four and ten feet thick, is one of the oldest in the United States. The original clerestory window is still intact, and the inside walls are decorated with paintings of Catholic saints. The twin-towered church is open to visitors daily; a booklet inside gives the history of Isleta Pueblo.

Isleta Casino and Resort on NM47 includes restaurants, entertainment, and a gift shop and is one of the business enterprises operated by Isleta across the road. Next door to the casino is *Isleta Fun Connection*, with bowling alleys, billiards, an arcade, lounge, and café.

The tribe also operates the championship twenty-seven-hole **Isleta Eagle Golf Course** overlooking the Rio Grande, a convenience store, and **Isleta Lakes Recreational Complex**, where you can fish for trout and channel catfish, camp, and picnic.

To reach Isleta Lakes, take I-25 south of Albuquerque about 13 miles to exit 215. The pueblo is 3.5 miles southwest of Isleta Lakes.

The mission church at Isleta Pueblo is dedicated to St. Augustine, the Pueblo's patron saint

JEMEZ PUEBLO

Hemish: "The People"

Out of the ten groups of Towa-speaking people to greet Coronado, Jemez (*HAY-mez*) is the sole surviving one. Modern tribal economy is based on agricultural crops—corn and chilies in particular—the timber industry, and a thriving arts-and-crafts cottage industry. Many of the young men also work as firefighters during summer forest fires. Jemez Pueblo currently consists of about 3,400 tribal members, most of them residing in the village of Walatowa, "Village of the Canyon."

Jemez Indians arrived at the southern mouth of the red-walled Cañon de San Diego from the Four Corners area between A.D. 1275 and 1350. One of the villages they built was Guisewa, twenty miles north of the current village on NM4. In a militaristic fashion, the Jemez fiercely guarded their springs, trails, and important sites. When the Spanish gained dominion here, the Indians smashed all of their pottery so the invaders could not use it. For years, the Jemez people used Zia pots instead of making their own.

In the early 1700s, a Spanish mission was constructed at Guisewa and then rebuilt in the 1880s. You can visit the remains of San Diego de Jemez Mission and the abandoned village at **Jemez State Monument** (see Chapter 18, Northeast and North Central New Mexico, page 328).

Walatowa Visitor Center has a museum, information, and arts and crafts for sale. Exhibits focus on ancestral tribal lands and traditional arts. A nature walk outside winds through native flora, and the museum shop specializes in Jemez pottery. An online pottery catalogue is available at the visitor center Web site. Tours, dances, artist demonstrations, and traditional food can be arranged in advance for groups through Walatowa Ed-Ventures. A conference room seats up to one hundred people. Also ask here for information on the Jemez Mountain Trail National Scenic Byway, which travels 140 miles through gorgeous scenery and past interesting cultural resources. The visitor center is located in the Red Rocks Scenic area.

North of the pueblo along NM4, look for ramadas (brush shelters) providing shade for Jemez men and women who are selling traditional polychromatic pottery, other arts and crafts, freshly baked bread, and hot-out-of-the-pan frybread.

Holy Ghost Springs is open year-round for soaking in the hot springs and camping, and *Dragonfly Recreation Area* is open for camping and fishing for rainbow trout, channel catfish, and bass. Permits for elk hunting and bow hunting for turkey in the spring are available on a limited basis.

The nearby Santa Fe National Forest also offers numerous outdoor activities. Contact the National Forest Service representative stationed in the visitor center or the Santa Fe National Forest District office.

Traditional culture is valued highly in Jemez, and the village of **Walatowa** is open to visitors for various dances throughout the year. In 1838, the survivors from Pecos Pueblo moved to Jemez, so today, both tribes observe their ceremonials here. No photography, recording, or sketching are allowed.

To reach the visitor center, take I-25 north of Albuquerque to Bernalillo exit 242. Turn west onto US550 to San Ysidro and then right onto NM4 for 7 miles.

LAGUNA PUEBLO

Laguna: Spanish for "Lake"
Ka-waikah: "Lake People"

Six villages in the Rio San Jose Valley—Seama, Paraje, Mesita, Encinal, Paguate, and Old Laguna (the original village)—combine to create this community of 3,800 people on 425,000 acres of mountains, valleys, and grasslands. The largest Keresan-language pueblo, and the newest of New Mexico's pueblos, Laguna (*lah-GOO-nah*) was founded in the late 1600s by people from Cochiti, Santo Domingo, and Zia during the Spanish reconquest after the Pueblo Revolt. Later, members of other pueblos joined them.

The picturesque **San Jose de Laguna Mission Church** in Old Laguna was built in 1699. The interior is still decorated with original floor-to-ceiling religious murals and traditional Indian symbols on the altar. Its twin belfry towers and white-washed exterior create a familiar New Mexico landmark. Take exit 114 off I-40.

Mount Taylor Game Ranch offers its guests trout fishing, trophy elk hunting, and lodging.

One of the world's richest uranium mines once employed many of the Laguna men. A tribal reclamation project was subsequently instituted to restore the land. Laguna Industries, which manufactures components for the high-tech and communications industry, now employs many tribal members.

Traditional Laguna pottery was revived in the 1970s, with designs resembling the geometric, bird, and animal images found on Acoma ceramics. This, as well as other tribal arts and crafts such as jewelry, belts, moccasins, paintings, baskets, and traditional clothing, can be purchased from Laguna members in the village, as well as from stores at Casa Blanca Market Plaza, exit 108 off I-40. The shopping area also has **Dancing Eagle Casino**, an RV park, and tourist services, including a restaurant and family fun center.

Laguna, the newest of the pueblos, was founded in 1699

Fishing permits for **Paguate Reservoir** can be purchased at the Laguna Wildlife Conservation Office or Paguate village offices.

Laguna Pueblo also operates the **Route 66 Casino and Travel Center**. The center, I-40 exit 114, has travel services, and the casino offers Las Vegas–style gambling, a gift shop, entertainment, and restaurants. The new casino hotel has lodging, dining, an indoor pool, KXX nightclub, and children's activities.

Laguna Pueblo is west of Albuquerque off I-40 at exit 114.

NAMBE PUEBLO

Nambe: "Mound of Earth in the Corner"

Nambe (*nahm-BAY*) Pueblo is a Tewa community that has been occupied since about A.D. 1300. Tradition says that before the Spanish came, the Nambe people lived in eight villages in the surrounding hills. By the eighteenth century, the population had dwindled to about six or seven families. Today, that number has risen to over 1,700 people who live in Nambe at the base of the Sangre de Cristo Mountains surrounded by national forestland. Farming and ranching are done on pueblo lands, but most members work elsewhere.

The mission church was destroyed in the Pueblo Revolt, and then rebuilt in 1729. However, it collapsed in the early twentieth century, and the existing church was built in 1972. Most of the other pre-colonial buildings have also not survived to the present. Stop at the Governor's Office to register for a self-guided tour of the pueblo.

A highlight of a visit here is seeing the popular **Nambe Falls Recreation Area**, located a few miles east of the village center. *Nambe Lake* offers fishing for trout from March through November, RV sites, barbecue grills, water, and toilets. Permits for fishing, camping, boating, and picnicking are available at the ranger station on site. Below the dam and lake is a canyon sheltering waterfalls and deep pools that have spiritual significance to the people of Nambe. A twenty-minute hike through the cottonwoods at a moderate pace on rocky ground will take you to the base of *Nambe Falls*, which makes a striking three-tiered drop from a rock cleft. The site is frequently used for traditional Pueblo weddings. To reach Nambe Falls Recreation Area, take US285 about 20 miles north of Santa Fe. Turn east onto NM503 and follow the signs.

The tribe maintains a small herd of buffalo, which can often be seen on the 179 acres set aside for them. Ask at the Governor's Office to make arrangements.

Nambe arts and crafts, including micaceous clay and blackware pottery, sculpture, and channel inlay jewelry, are available from individual artisans and stores in the pueblo. Another important Nambe tradition is its dances, the most famous of which is the Elk Dance, danced every four to seven years on Nambe's Feast Day in October.

Nambe owns several environmentally sustainable businesses that include a water-bottling plant, a solar-generating station, and a biomass transfer station. A trout hatchery is currently in development.

OHKAY OWINGEH PUEBLO
(FORMERLY SAN JUAN PUEBLO)

San Juan: Spanish for "Saint John"
O'ke Owingeh: "Village of the Strong People"

Ohkay Owingeh, at the confluence of the Rio Grande and the Rio Chama River, was first occupied in the late twelfth century. Once the capital of a Pueblo province, its residents were the only ones who could declare war for the Pueblo peoples. When Juan de Oñate came in 1598, he was so impressed with the Ohkay Owingeh people's character that he made the village the site of his new capital. He reoccupied the ancestral site of Yunque Yungue, which he renamed San Gabriel. The settlement, which became the first capital, was abandoned in 1608 when Oñate moved his headquarters to Santa Fe. The ruins of the village and San Gabriel Catholic church are now indicated by a marker near the pueblo on the west side of the Rio Grande.

As forced labor, taxes, and the ban on traditional religious practices took their toll, Spanish rule became unbearable to many of the Indians. A medicine man from Ohkay Owingeh named Po'Pay ("Ripe Pumpkin") exercised the ancient power to declare war. With other Pueblo religious leaders, he planned and executed the 1680 revolt, which forced the Spanish out of the pueblos for the next twelve years. In 2007 a sculpture commemorating him was installed in the National Statuary Hall in the U.S. Capitol Building in Washington, D.C.

Today, Ohkay Owingeh is the largest of the Tewa-speaking pueblos, with about 6,700 members. It is also the main office for the Eight Northern Indian Pueblos Council (ENIPC), an organization dedicated to improving conditions for its members. The offices and a *visitor center* are located in a domed building behind the Ohkay Casino off NM68.

The busy town center is dominated by the brick Saint John the Baptist Catholic church and the smaller stone Our Lady of Lourdes shrine across the street from it. Although the two buildings were dedicated in 1913 and 1890, respectively, they give testament to Ohkay Owingeh as the site of the first parish in the United States, begun in 1598 by Franciscan priests traveling with Juan de Oñate. Traditional adobe homes and two square kivas surround the nearby dance plazas.

A man from Ohkay Owingeh Pueblo honors the spirit of the deer with a Deer Dance.

Ohkay Owingeh is known for skillfully made pottery, a distinctive brown and red decorated with carved symbols. Artisans also carve wood, weave clothing and willow baskets, craft drums, paint, embroider, and fashion coral and turquoise jewelry. The **Oke Oweenge Crafts Cooperative** sells arts and crafts made by them and other Pueblo artists. With advance notice, groups can arrange to see Indian dances and enjoy a meal of native foods. Also check here for the possibility of a tour to the village and San Gabriel site. The crafts cooperative is in the center of town next door to the church.

The Ohkay Owingeh own and operate the **Ohkay Casino Resort** on NM68 just north of Española. The resort includes a casino, café, snack bar, lounge with live local entertainment, and a hundred-room *Best Western Hotel* with a pool. The *Ohkay Travel Center* is next to the casino, and the nearby *Sporting Clays Club* has twelve stations for clay shooting. Nearing completion is the *Ohkay Owingeh General Aviation Airport* and a 35,000-square-foot *convention center.*

Tribal permits are sold for trout, bluegill, catfish, and bass fishing at the **tribal lakes** off NM68 at the north end of Española. The lakes are open year-round, weather permitting. Picnic sites, tent and RV campgrounds, river fishing, and a convenience store, which carries fishing supplies and permits, are also here.

Ohkay Owingeh is 1 mile north of Española on NM68, then left on NM74 at the sign.

PICURIS PUEBLO

Pikuri: Spanish for "Those Who Paint"
Piwwetha: "Pass in the Mountains"

This small, remote Tiwa pueblo was settled in the mid-1200s in the mountains near two major passes. Geography allowed it to become a prosperous trading center and a link between the Plains and Pueblo peoples. It eventually grew into one of the largest northern pueblos.

Picuris (*pea-kuhr-REESE*) reached its height in the 1500s, when over three thousand people lived here. It was the last pueblo to be discovered by the Spanish, and when they arrived in 1591, they described it as seven to eight stories high.

Picuris inhabitants played a major role in the 1680 Pueblo Revolt. To escape retaliation for this and subsequent revolts, they abandoned the pueblo in 1696 and went to live with their former trading partners, the Jicarilla Apache. In 1706 approximately three hundred people returned to Picuris.

Today, Picuris has around 1,800 members, although fewer than half of them live here. The tribe is the majority owner of **Hotel Santa Fe**, a four-star hotel in the heart of historic Santa Fe. The facility, which emphasizes Native American architecture and design, was recently voted one of the five hundred greatest hotels in the world by *Travel and Leisure* magazine. While staying at the hotel, you can learn more about Pueblo culture through hotel-sponsored events and shop for native arts and crafts in the gift shop.

Picuris pottery, some of the most durable around, sparkles from the golden-hued micaceous clay (clay with mica in it) from which it is fashioned. The bronze cooking pots made from it are said to enhance the flavor of food. The important cultural element of making micaceous clay pottery is being revived since the tribe's recent purchase of the mine that was their traditional source of clay.

At the pueblo, parts of the original plaza and village remain today, including an above-ground kiva. **San Lorenzo Mission**, a Spanish church completed in 1776, was recently restored using the original building methods and artifacts found during excavation. You can tour the pueblo and hilltop ruins for a small fee.

Picuris Pueblo Museum maintains the pueblo ruins, mission church, and restored kivas. It also displays prehistoric tribal artifacts, historical photos, and contemporary artwork. The gift shop sells weavings, pottery, and beadwork by local artists. Its traditional belts and kilts are also popular. You can make arrangements here for guided tours of the mission church, archaeological sites, and buffalo herd.

Visitors can fish for trout at **Pu-na** and **Tu-tah lakes**. Call Picuris Pueblo Fish & Game for information. Picuris also manufactures lumber, charcoal, and mushrooms for the retail trade.

Picuris is between Taos and Santa Fe on NM75, reached from both NM68 and NM76.

POJOAQUE PUEBLO

P'o Suwae Geh: "Place to Drink Water"

Pojoaque (*poh-HWAH-kay*), the smallest of the New Mexico pueblos, was established as early as A.D. 900 at a place where three rivers converge.

This Tewa pueblo was abandoned in the aftermath of the Pueblo Revolt but resettled in 1706. In the nineteenth century, Mexican encroachment, lack of water, and a smallpox epidemic further reduced the population until the pueblo was all but abandoned by 1915. It wasn't until 1946 that Pojoaque was officially recognized as a federal reservation.

Today, Pojoaque has around 2,700 members. About all that remains of the original pueblo buildings are a few stone walls north of the Catholic church. A new kiva has been built. Businesses along Cities of Gold Road paralleling US84/285 sell traditional crafts, including pottery, embroidery, beadwork, and silver.

Also on Cities of Gold Road is the award-winning **Poeh Cultural Center and Museum**, dedicated to the arts and cultures of the Pueblo peoples, with an emphasis on the six Tewa-speaking pueblos in Northern New Mexico (Nambe, Ohkay Ohwingeh, Pojoaque, San Ildefonso, Santa Clara, and Tesuque) and the Tiwa-speaking pueblos of Picuris and Taos. The museum's permanent exhibit *Nah Poeh Meng*, Tewa for "The Continuous Path," depicts Pueblo history through contemporary art, historic reproductions, and story. Collections feature art, archaeological artifacts, and historical items and photographs, while the building itself exemplifies traditional Pueblo architecture. A gift shop provides an outlet for the works of native artists in styles ranging from traditional to contemporary. The center also hosts traditional dances and cultural demonstrations on weekends and provides ongoing classes for Native Americans. In summer a popular farmer's market sells locally grown produce in front of the cultural center.

Across from Poeh Cultural Center is **O' Eating House**, which serves Pueblo cuisine and other regional foods. A few doors south of the center is the **Pueblo of Pojoaque Visi-**

tor Center and Gallery. Stop here for maps, tour referrals, brochures, and area information. Its gift shop has a varied selection of reasonably priced Indian arts and crafts.

The nearby **Cities of Gold Casino and Hotel** features a hotel, shopping, a sports bar, restaurants, a conference center, and gaming. A bowling alley adjacent to the casino and an RV park are scheduled to open soon. Also nearby is a wellness complex with workout rooms, pools, and racquetball courts and providing massage, acupuncture, herbal wraps, and chiropractic services.

The challenging twenty-seven-hole **Towa Golf Course** has a full-service restaurant in the clubhouse and meeting facilities. It will be one of the two golf courses at the **Buffalo Thunder Resort** when it opens in late 2008. This family-friendly resort will also include a 360-room hotel, Indian Cultural Center, pools, full-service spa, upscale Las Vegas–style casino, professional tennis club, restaurants, large meeting facilities, and outdoor recreation. Lodging is currently available at *Homewood Suites,* adjacent to the resort.

Pojoaque is 15 miles north of Santa Fe on US84-285.

SANDIA PUEBLO

Sandia: Spanish for "Watermelon"
T'uf Shur T'ia: "Green Reed Place"

This conservative Tiwa-speaking pueblo was founded around A.D. 1300 on the banks of the Rio Grande. When Coronado's expedition visited the site in 1539, he named it Sandia (*sahn-DEE-uh*) after the watermelon color of the eastern mountain cliffs during sunsets.

The village was abandoned after Governor Otermin sacked and burned it during the Spanish reconquest following the 1680 Pueblo Revolt. Many of the residents fled to Hopi country, but Puebloans returned with a few Hopis in the mid-1700s to resettle. The ruins of the old village still stand near the existing church, which was built in the late 1800s after an earlier church collapsed.

The pueblo has about 4,500 residents, and its landscape is still largely unchanged from earlier times. Grasslands, cottonwood forests along the river, irrigated fields of corn and alfalfa, and the edge of the Sandia Mountains are what you will find here. To visit, you will need permission from the Governor's Office. A small display of historical photographs is in the office.

The **Bien Mur Indian Market Center, Travel Center, and Gift Shop** is 7 miles north of downtown Albuquerque, off I-25 at exit 234 (Tramway Road). The Travel Center sells fuel and food. The Market Center has a kiva-shaped showroom selling quality, authentic Native American jewelry, katsinas, pottery, textiles, and

Pueblo pottery comes in a variety of shapes and designs.

other arts and crafts, such as Sandia's traditional redware pottery and willow and yucca baskets. Bien Mur, "Big Mountain" in Tiwa, is one of the largest Indian arts-and-crafts stores in the Southwest. It publishes a newsletter with tips on buying Native American art and hosts special events featuring Indian artists. An annual sale that coincides with the Albuquerque Balloon Festival features storewide discounts and visiting artists at the Market Center, plus Native American food vendors at the Travel Center.

Bien Mur is across from the casino. Look for the bison that live on the 107-acre *buffalo preserve* visible from a vantage point at the Market Center. Photography of the bison is allowed with no special permit needed.

Sandia Lakes Recreation Area offers trout fishing, picnicking, a nature trail, and small playground along the cottonwood-lined Rio Grande. The lakes are 1 mile north of NM556 off NM313.

The 24-hour **Sandia Casino and Resort** is housed in a Pueblo-style building built in the shape of a crescent. Panoramic windows rise forty feet to frame sweeping views. The hotel has 228 rooms and several options for meals, including rooftop dining at the Bien Shur Restaurant. The resort also boasts an eighteen-hole golf course and the Green Reed Spa, where you can be pampered with body treatments like a green reed clay wrap, facials, and massages. Big-name entertainment is booked for concerts in the outdoor amphitheater.

Sandia Pueblo is located 13 miles north of Albuquerque off I-25 on NM313.

SAN FELIPE PUEBLO

San Felipe: Spanish for "Saint Philip"
Katishtya: meaning unknown

San Felipe (*sahn fay-LEE-pay*), underneath Black Mesa in a sheltering valley on the banks of the Rio Grande, is the most conservative of the Keresan-speaking villages and is known for the beauty of its ceremonials. The Green Corn Dance, performed on Feast Day, is a dramatic event with hundreds of participants in traditional regalia.

Named for St. Philip by Spanish explorer Francisco Sanchez Chamuscado in 1581, San Felipe was abandoned during the Pueblo Revolt after the residents burned the church and retreated to the mountains. In 1692, Don Diego de Vargas persuaded the people of San Felipe to return and aid the Spanish in subduing other pueblos. They became loyal Spanish subjects, and their children born during the exile were baptized. The pueblo was eventually reestablished at its present site around 1700, with a new mission constructed in 1706. In the nineteenth century disease reduced the population to a few hundred, but today San Felipe has about three thousand members.

Tribal artisans craft *heishi* (handmade beads), embroidery, and turquoise and silver jewelry. Their traditional pottery, similar in style to that of Acoma, has disappeared, but other kinds are still made. During the Feast Day celebration, food and crafts booths are found near the San Felipe Church, built in the early eighteenth century. The rest of the year, Indian arts and crafts are available directly from a few artists' homes. Call the tribal offices for a list of artists.

At exit 252 off I-25 is **San Felipe Travel Center**, which includes a gift shop with a fine selection of regional Indian arts and crafts, a restaurant, and a trucker's lounge.

Casino Hollywood, which advertises a true Hollywood experience, is visible from I-25. A restaurant, arts-and-crafts shop, and gas station are nearby. Also at this exit is **Hollywood Hills Speedway**, a multipurpose sports and entertainment venue seating over ten thousand and offering powwows, rodeos, and dirt track auto and motorcycle racing. RV camping is also available.

Visitors are not encouraged at most areas of the pueblo except during public events and when booths appear with Pueblo arts and crafts for sale. Photography, recording, and sketching are strictly forbidden. Call the tribal offices for information on dates the pueblo is open.

San Felipe is located 10 miles north of Bernalillo at exit 252 off I-25.

SAN ILDEFONSO PUEBLO

San Ildefonso: Spanish for "Saint Ildefonsus"
Po-Who-Ge-Oweenge: "Where the Water Cuts Through"

The Tewa-speaking people of San Ildefonso trace their ancestors to Mesa Verdeans and Chacoans who came to the Pajarito Plateau around A.D. 1150. They settled at sites near Bandelier National Monument such as Tyuonyi and Tsankawi. The present-day pueblo along the banks of the Rio Grande was established sometime in the late 1500s. Losses during revolts against the Spanish plus smallpox and influenza epidemics reduced the population to less than a hundred at one time. Now, almost fifteen hundred people live in the pueblo.

San Ildefonso (*sahn ell-deh-FOHN-so*) warriors joined the 1680 Pueblo Revolt and rebelled again in 1696. General Don Diego de Vargas attacked the pueblo, whose residents, along with members of six other pueblos, fled to their sacred Black Mesa, where they successfully repelled the attacks.

The original Spanish church was erected in 1617 in honor of Patron Saint Ildefonso. It was destroyed in 1696, rebuilt in 1711, and then destroyed again. A church built in 1904 lasted until 1957, when it was demolished to make way for a replica of the first church. Many of the other buildings have been reconstructed while retaining their traditional architecture, and in the village plaza, a huge two-hundred-year-old cottonwood flourishes.

San Ildefonso has led the modern revival of Pueblo arts and crafts. Two of its most famous artisans were Maria Povenka Martinez and her husband, Julian, who in the 1920s developed burnished black-on-black pottery and popularized it by exhibiting Maria's work at the 1904 St. Louis World's Fair. Their son, Popovi Da, later created unique pottery glazes and revived the making of polychrome pottery. The tradition continues today with other artisans who fashion blackware, redware, and polychrome and incised pottery.

Today, many members rely on arts and crafts to make a living. The tribe opposes gaming and does not promote tourism, but over twenty thousand visit each year. Look for signs that indicate you are welcome to enter resident's homes to browse through their goods for sale and to meet the artists who created them.

The **San Ildefonso Visitor and Information Center** has brochures and information on guided and self-guided tours, craft demonstrations, and scheduled dances. It sells arts and crafts and permits to visit the pueblo, for photography, and to use the fishing pond and picnic areas along the Rio Grande.

Across the plaza to the northwest and adjoining the Governor's Office is **Maria Poveka Martinez Museum**. Displays here explain the traditional process of pottery making. Works by Maria Martinez and other Pueblo artists are featured, as well as other examples of arts and crafts.

Two gas stations, one with a convenience store, are located on the Jemez Mountain Trail Scenic Byway.

To reach San Ildefonso, follow US84-285 north of Santa Fe 19 miles. Turn west onto NM502 for 6 miles, and then turn north onto BIA401. An admission fee is charged, and the pueblo closes to visitors at 5pm.

SAN JUAN PUEBLO. *SEE* OHKAY OWINGEH PUEBLO

SANTA ANA PUEBLO

Santa Ana: Spanish for "Saint Anne"
Tamaya: meaning unknown

The oral history of the Keresan-speaking Pueblo of Santa Ana states that they migrated from the north, staying for a while in a place called White House, which may be in Mesa Verde. Conflict broke them into different groups; one of these groups came south in the sixteenth century to establish the village of Tamaya on the Jemez River.

In retaliation for Santa Ana's role in the Pueblo Revolt, Spanish soldiers attacked and burned the pueblo in 1687. It was re-occupied when the inhabitants acquiesced to Spanish rule, and they were periodically raided by Jemez Pueblo in retaliation for failing to resist Spanish rule. Most of the five hundred people of Santa Ana now live in Ranchitos, a newer village just north of Bernalillo, or on farms along the Rio Grande. The five-hundred-year-old pueblo of Tamaya is used as a ceremonial site and open to the public only a few days a year.

Santa Ana traditional pottery, a polychrome similar to that created at Zia Pueblo, was revived in the 1970s. It is available at the tribal center from the small **Ta-Ma-Ya Cooperative Association**, which also sells woven belts and other crafts.

Agriculture is still central to the life of the people of Santa Ana. Santa Ana Agricultural Enterprises (SAAE) grows blue corn for the domestic and international food and cosmetic markets, including museum gift shops, specialty food stores, and cruelty free products sold at The Body Shop. You can purchase their "Tamaya blue" corn, wild rice, frybread, and other Native American food, as well as cookbooks, online or by mail order from **The Cooking Post.**

Santa Ana Star Casino offers gaming, a three-thousand-seat concert arena, and bowling lanes. The casino is on the extension of Tamaya Boulevard, which becomes old Jemez Dam Road.

Golfers can play through high desert terrain interspersed with eight crystal blue lakes on the **Santa Ana Golf Course** on Tamaya Boulevard. The *New York Times* named it one of the three best true links-style courses in the United States. Reservations up to a week ahead are recommended. The *Prairie Star Restaurant*, nestled between large cottonwoods and evergreens in an old adobe mansion, offers unique dining in a setting with handmade kiva fireplaces, viga and latilla ceilings, and views of the golf course and nearby Sandia Mountains.

In addition to luxurious rooms, restaurants like the renowned Corn Maiden, pools including the kiva-shaped one, stables, tennis courts, and shops, the **Hyatt Regency Tamaya Resort and Spa** at Santa Ana Pueblo has the full-service Tamaya Mist Spa and Salon, a fitness/wellness center, and classes on yoga, fitness, and Tai Chi. This resort in partnership with the Hyatt Regency created 1,200 tourism jobs and management and leadership training. Many programs benefiting tribal members are funded from the profits.

In the lobby of the hotel, guests are greeted with the scent of cedar and warm glow from the kiva fireplace in winter. They can arrange for a tour of Santa Ana Pueblo, and during harvest season, of the Blue Corn Factory. They can also enjoy the upscale *Twin Warriors Golf Course*, a pro-designed eighteen-hole course that winds past waterfalls and is ranked among the top one hundred public golf courses in the United States. The *Tamaya Cultural Museum and Learning Center* has exhibits on the history and culture of the people of Santa Ana. Called *Srai-wi*, "to gather children together and share with them," the center offers classes for families on such things as Pueblo bread baking and pottery making. Members of Santa Ana guide walks and horseback rides along the bosque and provide storytelling under the stars.

The resort is on Tamaya Boulevard near Santa Ana Golf Course. Also near the resort is a **garden center** that sells a large selection of native and xeriscape plants, often using seed gathered and grown locally.

Picnic sites are available at *Jemez Canyon Reservoir*. Be sure to stop at the Jemez Canyon Overlook.

Santa Ana Pueblo is accessed from exit 242 off I-25 at Bernalillo, then on NM44-550.

SANTA CLARA PUEBLO

Santa Clara: Spanish for "Saint Claire"
Kha P'o: "Valley of the Wild Roses"
Ka-poo: "Singing Water"

Santa Clara Pueblo includes the current pueblo, founded in the fourteenth century, as well as **Puye** [*poo-yay*] **Cliff Dwellings**, considered one of the ancestral homes of the people of Santa Clara and other Tewa-speaking pueblos after they emerged from the underworld through a small lake near Alamosa.

Puye was occupied between A.D. 1250 and 1550 by immigrants from the Four Corners. Over fifteen hundred people made their homes here, originally building in caves hollowed out of the tuff cliffs and then moving to pueblos on the upper slopes and atop the mesa. Eventually, drought forced the people to move to the Rio Grande lowlands, where they established the village of Santa Clara at the place Santa Clara Creek enters the peaceful river.

In 1622, Franciscan missionaries built a Catholic church in the village. Anger at repressive policies grew until 1680, when Santa Clarans joined the Pueblo uprising against

Santa Clara and Nambe are two pueblos that traditionally perform the Buffalo Dance.

the Spanish occupiers. Domingo Naranjo, one of the rebellion's leaders, was from Santa Clara.

The cave rooms of Puye extend over a mile, and the stepping places and fingerholds used to climb between the mesa top and cavate rooms are still visible. Unfortunately, a fire in the year 2000 burned through the Santa Clara Canyon where the dwellings are. Both the dwellings and canyon are currently closed for reclamation. Call the Governor's Office to find out when they will reopen and to inquire about Santa Clara's lush pine forests and meadows with fishing lakes.

The pueblo itself consists of mostly modern structures. The old church collapsed in 1910, and the present mission was built around 1918. Arrangements for guided tours of the pueblo and church, pottery demonstrations, native dancing, and dining on native foods can be made through the tribal offices. Reservations should be made at least a week in advance.

Santa Clara is noted for its pottery, a carved and highly polished blackware and redware, often deeply incised, and for embroidery, woven textiles, jewelry, and beadwork. The wedding jar with two necks connected by a handle is distinctive to Santa Clara. Margaret Tafoya is one of the most famous of the potters. Other Santa Clara arts and crafts include sculpture, decorated gourds, willow baskets, and painting. Visitors are encouraged to wander the pueblo and visit the shops or homes with signs out front.

Black Mesa Golf Club, south of Española in Mesilla, is an award-winning twenty-seven-hole course that winds between sandstone ridges. Two-week advance tee times are available. A restaurant is also at the club.

Gambling and bowling are featured at the new **Big Rock Casino** and **Big Rock Bowl** in Big Rock Shopping Center in Española. A steakhouse and other restaurants provide dining options for visitors.

A *travel center* on NM30 sells gas and food, and *Dreamcatcher Cinema* provides movie entertainment.

Santa Clara Pueblo is 2 miles south of Española off NM30.

SANTO DOMINGO PUEBLO

Santo Domingo: Spanish for "Saint Dominic"
Khe-wa: "Pueblo"

This very conservative Keresan-speaking pueblo is one of the largest and oldest of the Rio Grande pueblos, with about 4,500 tribal members, including 3,600 who live at the pueblo. Although computers and modern conveniences have arrived at Santo Domingo, the people still highly value their traditional way of life.

The ancestors of Santo Domingo came from Mesa Verde and Chaco Canyon to settle on the Pajarito Plateau, eventually moving to the current village site in the fifteenth century. In 1598 Santo Domingo was designated the capital for all of the pueblos in what is now the state of New Mexico.

Nearby turquoise mines and a location along the route between Santa Fe and Albuquerque helped Santo Domingo to grow and inspired individuals to become traders and jewelry makers. Artisans here still make fine *heishi* (beads of bone, shell, or turquoise) jewelry, silver and turquoise jewelry, and pottery, including that of award-winning potter Robert Tenorio, who crafts black-and-cream-on-red ware.

Through the years, the village was abandoned several times to escape Spanish soldiers, including after the 1680 Revolt (one of the leaders of the revolt, Alonzo Catiti, was from Santo Domingo) and in 1692, when the pueblo was destroyed and some community members fled west. Later, they helped found Laguna Pueblo. The pueblo was also destroyed by recurrent floods, including in 1886, when most of the village and mission church were washed away. Rebuilding began shortly thereafter.

Santo Domingo still maintains itself as a farming community and emphasizes traditional religious practices, which include an extensive and colorful Green Corn Dance held on the August 4 Saint Dominic Feast Day and attended by thousands of spectators from around the world. The dance is held in the plaza, but activities begin and end at **Our Lady of Guadalupe Mission Church** on the east edge of the village. Every year the front of this picturesque church is painted with different colors and murals. It is open to visitors when religious services are not being held.

In an effort to preserve their traditional way of life, the tribal government does not promote tourism, but the talented artists who live here rely on visitors and are happy to welcome them. Look for signs to direct you to homes with crafts for sale. Two small stores in the village also sell snacks.

Kewa Gas Station and Convenience Store just off I-25 on NM22 sells gas and food. Crafts vendors often set up booths outside the store.

Santo Domingo is between Albuquerque and Santa Fe. Look for the Santo Domingo exit 259 from I-25, and then follow NM22 about 5 miles to the pueblo.

TAOS PUEBLO

Tua-Toh: "Place of the Red Willow"

The region around Taos (*TAH-ose*) Pueblo has been home to Tiwa people for perhaps 1,100 years. Legend has it they were led here by an eagle, which dropped a feather to indicate the spot for them to build. This chosen location near a major mountain pass helped the people of Taos become prosperous traders and meant they were influenced by Ute, Comanche, and Apache as they exchanged textiles and food for hides and meat. Some of this influence can be seen in Taos customs, physical makeup, and dress.

The Pueblo Revolt began at Taos Pueblo in 1680 when messengers ran from Taos Pueblo to the other pueblos with a knotted cord to show the number of days before the uprising. When de Vargas returned, he burned the village; reconstruction began around 1700. In 1847, the residents again revolted, and the pueblo became a refuge for Mexicans and Indians resisting the annexation of New Mexico by the United States. In one tragic in-

The external appearance of Taos Pueblo has changed very little over the centuries.

cident, the U.S. Army believed the mission church at Taos harbored the rebels, but when the soldiers burned it, only the women, children, and old men who had sought its refuge died.

Taos Pueblo has been designated both a World Heritage Site and National Historic Site. A visit to the village, one of the oldest continuously inhabited places in the United States, is like a trip back in time. Daily guided and self-guided tours and camera permits are available for a fee. As you amble from shop to shop through the dusty plaza, you may be greeted by the sound of barking dogs, the smell of home-baked bread for sale, and a view of the 1847 rebuilt San Geronimo Mission standing in quiet contemplation at one end of the plaza.

Electricity and indoor plumbing have still not made their mark at some parts of the impressive multistoried pueblo, and the primary source of water is still Rio Pueblo de Taos, which flows down from sacred Blue Lake in the mountains and divides the pueblo into two parts.

Artists' shops and studios surround the plaza and line the road leading to the pueblo. Taos Pueblo is noted for its log and hand ceremonial drums, leather and beadwork, and micaceous pottery. Flutes, jewelry, paintings, woodcarvings, and other arts and crafts are also for sale. Look for the signs by doorways indicating an artisan has work for sale inside or that a baker has bread. Taos also conducts some of the most colorful of the Pueblo dances and has contributed Round Dance music adapted by many other tribes for pow-wows.

Taos Pueblo owns a herd of 120 bison used for traditional purposes, and it can often be seen from afar. The pueblo also sponsors big horn sheep hunts on tribal lands.

To visit part of the reservation beyond the old village, stop at *Taos Indian Horse Ranch*, on Miller Road inside Taos Pueblo. They provide Indian-guided horseback rides of a few hours to overnight, wrangler cookouts, sleigh rides with large draft horses, storytellers, and music for a unique cultural experience.

To enjoy traditional and New Mexican cuisine, visit *Tiwa Kitchen* just outside the old village on the Taos Pueblo Road. The menu includes blue corn pancakes served with wild plum jelly, fresh bread baked from an horno, buffalo, and chile dishes.

The smoke-free *Taos Mountain Casino,* which is located on the main road into the village, has video slots, blackjack games, and a café. The casino provides free shuttle service from various locations around Taos. Some of the casino proceeds are dedicated to purchasing original tribal land around Blue Lake.

Of the approximately 4,400 members of Taos Pueblo, only about fifty people live in the historic village full-time. Many other families live in more modern residences elsewhere but return to homes they keep in the old district for feasts and ceremonies.

Taos Pueblo is about 2 miles from Taos. Visit their Web site for a walking tour map and a list of artists. To reach the pueblo, take Hwy 3/64 (Paseo de Pueblo Norte) north of Taos Plaza and bear right just past the Kachina Lodge. The parking lot is 2 miles north. Please note that the pueblo is closed to tourists in late winter or early spring for traditional observances.

TESUQUE PUEBLO

Te-Tsu-Geh: "Cottonwood Tree Place"

People arrived in Tesuque (*teh-SOO-kay*) Valley, possibly from Chaco Canyon, about A.D. 850. By 1200, scattered settlements dotted the land. The population eventually consolidated into six small villages, one of which was old Tesuque. Old Tesuque is close to Santa Fe, the Spanish capital, and its people played an important role in the 1680 Pueblo Revolt. August 10, the day Tesuque warriors struck the first blow of the rebellion, is still commemorated. Although hostilities ceased after the Spanish returned, the old village was abandoned for the current site on the banks of the Tesuque River farther from Santa Fe.

Over the next centuries, European diseases, loss of land, and lack of water severely affected Tesuque. By 1910 only seventy-five people remained in this Tewa pueblo. The population recovered during the twentieth century, partly by selling to tourists small, brightly painted figurines called "rain gods," which depict seated figures holding pots on their laps. By 2000, there were 806 people living on reservation lands.

The Tesuque people proudly observe their ancestral ceremonies and customs in a setting where the traditional feel has been retained with an enclosed plaza. The Catholic church, with room blocks two and three stories high, is listed on the Register of Historic Places. Potters have recently revived the traditional black-and-red-on-white micaceous clayware, and pueblo shops sell this and other arts and crafts, including embroidery, painting, and sculpture.

Tesuque has launched an economic development program that includes growing organic vegetables and herbs and the renovation of the area around Tesuque Plaza. On weekends, the tribe operates the **Tesuque Pueblo Flea Market**, also called the Santa Fe Flea

Market, 6 miles north of Santa Fe and near the Santa Fe Opera on US84-285. Vendors at this popular place sell an eclectic mix of items from as far away as Africa.

Camel Rock Casino and Travel Center on Hwy 48-285 is named for the distinctive sandstone formation just across the road. Gaming, live entertainment, and a café are offered here.

Camel Rock Suites in Santa Fe off I-25 at exit 282 is also tribally owned. It features reasonably priced rooms equipped for extended stay.

Tesuque Pueblo is off US285/84 a few miles north of Santa Fe.

ZIA PUEBLO

Tsiya: meaning uncertain

The design on the New Mexico flag, a sun with rays emanating to the four directions, is an ancient Zia (*TSEE-ah*) symbol traditionally considered an emblem of friendship. Occupied since A.D. 1250, this Keresan village was sacked by the Spanish in 1689 after the Indians resisted reconquest. Over six hundred of the rebels were killed and seventy more taken to El Paso as prisoners. Most of the survivors escaped to the surrounding mountains and then returned in 1692 to rebuild the pueblo on a hill overlooking the Jemez River. Today, some of the original buildings still stand, including **Our Lady of Assumption Mission**. Dedicated in 1612, the mission may be the oldest Catholic parish still operating in the United States. Damaged, but not destroyed in the Pueblo Revolt, the outside of the church is graced by murals of horses and tiny swallows. No pews stand on the packed earth floor inside, and the paintings are on wood.

War with the Spanish, nomadic raiders, disease, and the loss of territory almost led to the demise of Zia. In 1538, Spanish explorers estimated this was the largest of the pueblos with four thousand people living there; by the 1890s there were just ninety-eight. Today, the tribe has around 650 members. They are currently developing a community plaza in Bernalillo.

Zia Cultural Center sells the superb Zia pottery, made by painting geometric, plant, and animal designs on a white background. One well-known design is that of the Zia bird, with a big eye, a split tail, and outspread wings, often in an orange color outlined in black. The center also sells watercolor and oil paintings from noted Zia artists. Exhibits include modern Zia art and historic and prehistoric artifacts. Pottery demonstrations are held on the premises. To visit local artists, ask here for a map showing the location of studio/houses open to the public. The center is next to the Governor's Office on the village access road.

Zia Lake, open year-round for catfish, bass, and trout fishing, is 2 miles west of the pueblo along a gravel road. Picnic ramadas, restrooms, and rowboat rentals are available. Permits are sold at the pay station on the access road. To explore the mountains and plateaus along Indian Routes 78 and 79, you will need permission from the tribal office.

The pueblo, 19 miles northwest of Bernalillo, is off NM44.

ZUNI PUEBLO

She-we-na: "the Middle Place"

Although considered a Pueblo group, the Zuni (ZOO-nee) have a distinctive culture and language and seem to be a blend of at least two cultural groups. They also do not live along the Rio Grande but among towering mesas and plateaus above wide plains. When the Spaniard Fray Marcos de Niza saw the ancestral Zuni village of Hawikku in 1540, he is said to have mistaken the sun's reflection on the adobe for a city made of gold. Coronado soon followed. Expecting to find riches, he found a mud village instead.

During the 1680 Pueblo Revolt, the Zuni people took refuge on sacred Dowa Yallane Mountain, southeast of the present village. After they returned in 1692, the people consolidated their six ancestral villages at the ancient site of Halona Idiwan'a. This is where the pueblo is today.

Zuni farmers developed an elaborate system of check and diversionary dams to take advantage of the sudden, but infrequent, thunderstorms in the valley. This same system channeled water to act as erosion control in places of heavy runoff. They also built "waffle gardens," fields divided by low mud walls into small squares and rectangles that can be individually watered. With these methods, they had spectacular success, cultivating up to ten thousand acres at a time.

By the end of prehistoric times, the pueblo was a center of trade for a region ranging from the Colorado River to the Great Plains to northern Mexico. When the early white settlers came, the Indians continued in this role, supplying tons of corn to the military. The commander of Ft. Defiance at one time said the fort could not survive without Zuni corn.

Today the pueblo is a mixture of old and new, with horno ovens and red sandstone houses capped by tin roofs and television antennas. Inside the houses are microwaves and computers for many of the 7,700 residents.

A traditional Zuni lives a life filled with religious devotion and punctuated by ceremonial dances to give thanks for life's blessings. The masked Katsina Dances are the most sacred of the dances. They are held periodically throughout the spring and summer and culminate with the Shalako Ceremonial to bring the yearly cycle to a close by thanking the Creator for past blessings and praying for them to continue. To find the date of dances open to the public, call the tribal office sometime after September.

Also call here for directions, brochures on Zuni history and arts and crafts, information about guide services, and permits for photography or visiting the older villages, including the unrestored Hawikku.

Another place to register to visit Zuni and to obtain photo permits and a village map is at **A:shiwi A:wan Museum and Heritage Center**, across the bridge south of NM53 and west of the plaza at the intersection of Ojo Caliente and Pia Mesa roads. The center has artifacts and exhibits about Zuni history and a colorful mural of the Zuni creation story. Native plants are grown in the small patio, and occasionally feasts are prepared in the hornos and fire pits. To take a guided tour to watch artists at work, arrange a meal, or view historical and natural features on the reservation, call to make advance arrangements.

Our Lady of Guadalupe Mission has interior walls painted by Zuni artists Alex Seowtewa and his sons. The unique murals, still being created, combine images from Zuni culture with symbols and saints from Christianity. The mission was built in 1629 and restored by the National Park Service in the 1960s. Tours of the church, which is south of NM53 near the center of the old village, can be arranged in advance.

Farming, raising livestock, and wage work provide income for Zuni. Other tribal businesses include forest products, renovation of houses, electronic document conversion, and cellular phones.

Zuni artisans create a variety of fine arts and crafts. Look for traditional animal fetishes, unique katsina masks, and handsome silver jewelry. Frequently used techniques are channel inlay and needlepoint, which involves setting small polished stones, like turquoise, black jet, or lapis in silver. Often several family members will work on one piece, using designs that have been passed down from one generation to another.

The **Pueblo of Zuni Arts and Crafts Enterprise**, in the Zuni Tribal Building, sells these and other items. Their merchandise includes a variety of excellent arts and crafts produced by the members of the tribe, as well as native music and books about the Zuni. Another good place to purchase high-quality items is from individual Zuni artisans through the **Zuni Craftsmen Cooperative Association** off NM53. Some of the trading posts and shops along NM53, which is the main street in Zuni, are also operated and owned by Zuni people. In addition, Zuni artists have an open-air market in front of the tribal administration building on various days from mid-May to mid-October.

The only place to stay in the village is the **Inn at Halona Bed and Breakfast**, decorated with Pueblo art and offering modern amenities.

You can purchase permits for camping, hunting, and fishing at tribal lakes for northern pike, trout, large-mouthed bass, and channel catfish at the Fish and Wildlife Office.

Zuni is about 30 miles south of Gallup on NM602, then west on NM53.

EVENTS

Ancient Storytellers (505-747-6710, www.ancientstorytellers.com) is a native-owned tour company that offers customized tours of the pueblos of New Mexico and the Hopi and Navajo reservations in Arizona. Group and individual tours range from one to several days and include artist demonstrations, hands-on pottery workshops, bread baking, and feast meals. Tour packages are occasionally offered on Pueblo Feast Days.

Note: We recommend that before planning to attend the following events, you call ahead to confirm. Some dates and events change annually.

JANUARY 01: Turtle Dance at Taos Pueblo, Corn Dance at Santo Domingo Pueblo, Cloud, Basket Dance at Ohkay Owingeh Pueblo; various dances at other pueblos

06: Kings Day Celebration at Nambe, Picuris, Pojoaque, Ohkay Owingeh, Sandia, Santa Clara, and Taos Pueblos. Call for date at Tesuque Pueblo.

22: Vespers and Firelight Procession at San Ildefonso Pueblo, 505-455-3549

23: Annual Feast Day with Comanche, Buffalo, or Deer dances at San Ildefonso Pueblo

25: St. Paul Feast Day at Picuris Pueblo and Ohkay Owingeh Pueblo

Mid-January to late February: Basket, Game Animal, and Cloud dances at Santa Clara Pueblo

FEBRUARY 02: Candelaria Day Celebration at Picuris, San Felipe, and Taos Pueblos

1st or 2nd Weekend: Governor's Feast at Acoma Pueblo

2nd week TBA: Deer Dance at Ohkay Owingeh Pueblo

Taos Pueblo is closed annually for traditional observances in February and March. Call 505-758-1028 for exact dates.

MARCH Annual fishing derby at Ohkay Owingeh Pueblo Lakes. Call 505-753-5067 for date.
19: St. Joseph Feast Day at Laguna Pueblo
Easter Sunrise Mass for all denominations at the San Jose de Los Jemez Mission Church at Jemez State Monument. 505-829-3530
Easter Sunday dances at Cochiti, Nambe, San Ildefonso, Santo Domingo, and Zia Pueblos. Dances also on Monday at Cochiti, San Ildefonso, and Santo Domingo.
Taos Pueblo is closed annually for traditional observances in February and March. Call 505-758-1028 for exact dates.
APRIL Easter Sunday Dances: See MARCH.
Annual Tour de Acoma: 25, 50, and 100-mile Bike Challenge at Acoma Pueblo. Call 800-747-0181.
MAY 01: St. Phillip Feast Day with Corn Dance at San Felipe Pueblo
02: Santa Maria Feast with social dances at Acoma Pueblo (McCartys Village)
03: Santa Cruz Feast Day with footrace and Corn Dance at Taos Pueblo
Mother's Day & graduation arts market at Zuni Pueblo
Mother's Day powwow at Sky City Casino Hotel, Acoma Pueblo
Memorial Day Starfeather Powwow at Jemez Red Rocks
Memorial Day Red Rocks Arts & Crafts Show at Jemez Pueblo
Memorial Day carvers market at Zuni Pueblo
JUNE Butterfly Run-Walk at Pojoaque Pueblo, 505-455-3334
First Saturday: Corn Dance and blessing of the fields at Tesuque Pueblo
13: St. Anthony Feast Day with various dances at Santa Clara, Sandia, San Ildefonso, and Taos Pueblos; with Green Corn Dance at Ohkay Owingeh Pueblo; with children's footraces at Picuris Pueblo.
23-24: San Juan (St. John) Feast Day with Corn Dance or Comanche/Buffalo Dance at Ohkay Owingeh Pueblo
24: San Juan Feast Day with Traditional Corn Dance at Taos Pueblo
29: St. Peter Feast Day with Corn Dance at Santa Ana Pueblo
Zuni Pueblo is closed 4 days in June for *Deshkwi*, a fasting period. Call Zuni Visitors Center, 505-782-7238, for specific dates.
JULY Annual Eight Northern Indian Pueblos Artists and Craftsman Show at the Eight Northern Indian Pueblos Visitor Center at Ohkay Owingeh Pueblo. Contact 505-852-4265 or 800-793-4955.
Annual Intertribal Powwow at Taos Pueblo. For information call 505-758-1028 or www.taospueblopowwow.com.
1st weekend: Arts & Crafts Fair at Picuris Pueblo. Call to confirm.
04: Annual 4th of July Celebration of the Waterfall, Nambe Pueblo. Call 505-455-2036 to confirm.
14: St. Bonaventure Annual Feast Day at Cochiti Pueblo with Corn Dance.
25-26: Santiago Feast Day with Corn Dances at Taos and other pueblos.
26: Santa Ana (St. Ann) Annual Feast Day with Corn Dance at Santa Ana Pueblo; Harvest Dance and other dances at Laguna Pueblo (Seama Village) and Picuris Pueblo; Harvest Dances at Taos Pueblo.
AUGUST Expo at Zuni Pueblo
Sky City Balloon Rally at Acoma Pueblo. Call 1-888-Sky-City.
Tri-Cultural Arts and Crafts Fair at Picuris Pueblo Zuni Cultural Arts
Zuni Tribal Fair at Zuni Pueblo
Zuni Cultural Arts Expo at Zuni Pueblo. Call 505-782-7238 for information.
02: St. Persingula Feast Day with Corn Dance at Jemez Pueblo
04: St. Dominic Feast Day with Green Corn Dance at Santo Domingo Pueblo
09: San Lorenzo Sunset Dances at Picuris Pueblo
10: San Lorenzo Feast Day with footrace, pole climbing, dances, and art show at Picuris Pueblo; with dances at Acoma Pueblo (Acomita Village)
10: Pueblo Revolt celebration, with commemorative run from Tesuque Pueblo to Santa Fe Plaza, speeches, arts and crafts, food, traditional games, and dances

12: Santa Clara Feast Day with Buffalo, Harvest, or Corn Dance at Santa Clara Pueblo

14: Pueblo Independence Day commemorating the New Mexico Pueblo Revolt with a traditional relay footrace, and native food, music and dance at Jemez State Monument. Arts and crafts demonstration until 3pm. 505-829-3530

15: The Assumption of Our Blessed Mother Feast Day with Corn Dances at Zia Pueblo; Harvest and various Dances at Laguna Pueblo (Mesita Village)

28: St. Augustine Annual Feast Day at Isleta Pueblo

SEPTEMBER Sky City Powwow at Sky City Casino Hotel, Acoma Pueblo and 2nd Annual Fat Tire Event (off-road bike tour) at Acoma Pueblo. Call 1-888-SKY-CITY for dates.

Labor Day Weekend: Annual Arts and Crafts Fair at Santo Domingo Pueblo

02: San Estevan Annual Feast Day with Harvest Dance at Acoma Pueblo

04: St. Augustine Annual Feast Day with Harvest Dance at Isleta Pueblo

2nd Week: Harvest Dance at Ohkay Owingeh Pueblo

08: Nativity of the Blessed Virgin Mary's Feast Day with social dances at Laguna Pueblo (Encinal Village), with Corn Dance at San Ildefonso Pueblo

19: St. Joseph Annual Feast Day with Buffalo, Eagle, and social dances, parade, carnival, arts and crafts, baseball tournament, and fun runs at Old Laguna Pueblo

25: St. Elizabeth Feast Day at Laguna Pueblo (Paguate Village)

29: San Geronimo Eve: Vespers & Sundown Dance at Taos Pueblo

30: San Geronimo Annual Feast Day with Buffalo Dance, trade fair, traditional relay footrace, and pole climbing at Taos Pueblo

OCTOBER Ancient Way Festival along State Road 53 featuring local arts and crafts, food, and outdoor activities.

Bien Mur Art Fest at Sandia Pueblo

Open Air market and arts and crafts show at the Walatowa Visitor Center at Jemez Pueblo

Zuni Fall Festival and Arts Market at Zuni Pueblo

03: Evening Firelight Vespers at Nambe Pueblo

04: St. Francis of Assisi Annual Feast Day at Nambe Pueblo with Buffalo and Deer dances

17: St. Margaret Mary Feast Day with Harvest and social dances at Laguna Pueblo (Paraje Village)

24-27: Harvest Dance at Laguna Pueblo

NOVEMBER 12: San Diego Annual Feast Day at Tesuque and Jemez Pueblos, various dances

Thanksgiving Day: Christmas Lights Parade at Zuni Pueblo

Thanksgiving Weekend: Annual Arts and Crafts Show at Acoma Pueblo; Holiday Arts Market at Zuni Pueblo

DECEMBER Annual Christmas Bazaar and Arts and Crafts Show at Santa Clara Pueblo

Jemez Pueblo Holiday Bazaar and Arts And Crafts Show at the Walatowa Visitor Center in Jemez Pueblo

Farolito Tour Event at the San Jose de los Jemez Mission Church and ruins, Jemez State Monument, with music, Native American dances, and refreshments. 505-829-3530

11: Night dances at Pojoaque Pueblo. Vespers and procession usually held at 6pm (dusk)

12: Our Lady of Guadalupe Feast Day at Pojoaque and Jemez Pueblos

24: Christmas Eve Luminaria Tour at Acoma Pueblo.

24: Harvest, Arrow, Deer, and other Dances after Midnight Mass at Laguna Pueblo; Buffalo Dance following Christmas Eve Mass at Nambe Pueblo; Torchlight Procession of the Virgin Vespers and Matachine Dances at Picuris and Ohkay Owingeh Pueblos; various dances after Midnight Mass at San Felipe, Santa Ana, and Tesuque Pueblos; vespers, procession, various dances, and bonfires at Taos Pueblo

25: Christmas Day Dances at Tesuque, Santa Clara, and San Ildefonso Pueblos; Matachine Dance at Picuris Pueblo and Deer or Matachine Dance at Ohkay Owingeh and Taos Pueblos

25-29: Christmas Day Dances at San Felipe, Laguna, and Acoma Pueblos. Most pueblos have dances during the Christmas holiday.

26: Turtle Dance at Ohkay Owingeh Pueblo; various dances at Santo Domingo Pueblo

28: Holy Innocents Day, children's dances at Picuris and Santa Clara Pueblos

CONTACT INFORMATION

Acoma Pueblo
PO Box 309, Acoma, NM 87034
800-747-0181 *or* 505-552-6604
www.skycity.com
Daily April-October 8am-6pm; November-
March 8am-3:30pm; last tour leaves 1 hour
before closing; closed July 10-13; fee
Sky City Casino and Hotel
PO Box 310, Pueblo of Acoma, NM 87034
888-759-2489 *or* 505-552-6017
Sky City Cultural Center and Haak'u Museum
800-747-0181 *or* 505-552-7860
Daily 8am-6:30pm, Apr-Oct; daily 8am-4:30pm,
Nov-Mar; closed on days of some ceremonies
(call ahead); first tour begins as early as 8 am,
last tour is at 5pm; no fee for museum, fee for
Sky City tour
Sky City Travel Plaza
Exit 102 off I-40

Ancient Storytellers Tours
PO Box 2897, Española, NM 87532
505-747-6710 • www.ancientstorytellers.com

Cochiti Pueblo
PO Box 70, 255 Cochiti Street, Cochiti Pueblo,
NM 87072
505-465-2244 • www.pueblodecochiti.org
Cochiti Lake Recreation Area
505-465-2300
Store: 505-465-2682
US Army Corps of Engineers
Cochiti Lake Project Office
82 Dam Crest Road, Peña Blanca, NM
87041
505-465-0307
Visitor Center: Mon-Fri 8:30am-
3:30pm & Sat 10am-2pm
**Kasha-Katuwe Tent Rocks National
Monument**
BLM Rio Puerco Field Office, 435 Montano
Road, NE, Albuquerque, NM 87107
505-761-8700 *or* -8768
www.nm.blm.gov/recreation/albuquerque/
kasah-katuwe.htm
Daily, 8am-5pm Nov-mid Mar & 7am-
6pm mid March-Oct; fee
Pueblo de Cochiti Golf Course
5200 Cochiti Hwy, Cochiti Lake, NM 87083
505-465-2239
Stone Kiva Bar & Grill
5200 Cochiti Hwy, Cochiti Lake, NM
87083
505-465-2230

Eight Northern Indian Pueblos Council
PO Box 969, Ohkay Owingeh, NM 87566
800-793-4955 *or* 505-747-1593
www.puebloway.org
Arts and Crafts Show:
www.eightnorthernpueblos.com

Isleta Pueblo
PO Box 1270, Isleta Pueblo, NM 87022
505-869-3111 • www.isletapueblo.com
Isleta Casino and Resort
11000 Broadway SE, Albuquerque, NM
87105
877-747-5382 *or* 505-724-3800
www.isletacasinoresort.com
Mon-Wed 8am-4pm & Thurs-Sun 24 hours
Isleta Eagle Golf Course
4001 Hwy 47SE, Albuquerque, NM 87105
505-848-1900 *or* 866-475-3822
www.isletaeagle.com
Isleta Fun Connection
11000 Broadway SE, Albuquerque, NM
87105
505-724-3866
Isleta Lakes Recreational Complex
PO Box 383, Isleta, NM 87022
505-877-0370
Saint Augustine Mission Church
505-869-3398

Jemez Pueblo
7413 Hwy 4, PO Box 100, Jemez Pueblo, NM
87024
505-834-7359 • www.jemezpueblo.org
Holy Ghost and Dragonfly Lakes
505-834-7533
Walatowa Visitor Center
7413 Hwy 4, PO Box 100, Jemez Pueblo,
NM 87024
505-834-7235
Forest Service Representative: 505-834-7235
Daily 8am-5pm

Laguna Pueblo
PO Box 194 Laguna Pueblo, NM 87026
505-552-6654
Dancing Eagle Casino
I-40 exit 108, Casa Blanca, NM 87026
877-440-9966 *or* 505-552-7777
www.dancingeaglecasino.com
Daily 24 hours
Dancing Eagle Travel Center and RV Park
I-40 exit 108, Casa Blanca, NM 87026
505-552-7711

Mount Taylor Game Ranch
505-352-7877
Route 66 Travel Center and Casino
Exit 140 off I-40
Casino
505-352-7866 • www.rt66casino.com
Thurs-Sat, 24 hours; Fri-Sun, 8am-4pm
San Jose de Laguna Mission Church
505-552-9330
Mon-Fri 9am-3pm, Sunday services at
10am

Nambe Pueblo
Route 1, Box 117 BB, Santa Fe, NM 87506
505-455-2036
**Nambe Falls Recreation Area Ranger
Station**
505-455-2304
6am-9pm summer; 7am-7pm, winter;
closed Nov-Mar; fee

Ohkay Owingeh Pueblo *(formerly San Juan
Pueblo)*
PO Box 1099, Ohkay Owingeh Pueblo, NM
87566
505-852-4400
Bison Park
505-852-4400
Ohkay Casino Resort
PO Box 1270, Ohkay Owingeh Pueblo,
NM 87566
800-747-1668
Best Western Hotel
877-829-2865 *or* 505-747-1668
Ohkay Sporting Clays
505-747-0700
Ohkay Travel Center
505-753-5452
RV Park
505-753-5067 • www.ohkay.com
O'ke Oweenge Crafts Cooperative
Village center on NM 74, PO Box 1095,
Ohkay Owingeh Pueblo, NM 87566
505-852-2372 or 505-577-1469 (cell)
Mon-Fri 9am-5pm, summer; Mon-Fri
9am-4:30pm, fall-spring
San Juan Lakes and RV Park
North end of Española off NM68
505-753-5067

Picuris Pueblo
PO Box 127 Peñasco, NM 87553
505-587-2519
Hotel Santa Fe
1501 Paseo de Peralta, Santa Fe, NM
800-825-9876 *or* 505-243-2300
www.hotelsantafe.com
Picuris Pueblo Fish and Game
505-587-1601
Picuris Pueblo Museum Center
PO Box 487, Penasco, NM 87533
505-587-2957; guided tours 505-587-1099
www.nmculture.org/cgi-bin/
instview.cgi?_recordnum+PICU

Pojoaque Pueblo
Camino del Rincón, Ste. 6, Santa Fe, NM 87506
505-455-2278 • www.citiesofgold.com/Pueblo
Cities of Gold Casino and Hotel
10-B Cities of Gold Road, Santa Fe, NM
87506
Casino: 800-455-3313 *or* 505-455-3313
Pojoaque Gaming Center Visitor Center:
505-455-3460
Hotel: 877-455-0515 *or* 505-455-0515
www.citiesofgold.com
Casino: Thurs-Sat 24 hours & Sun-Wed
8am-4am
Homewood Suites by Hilton
800-225-54663 *or* 505-455-9100
www.homewoodsuites.com
O' Eating House
Reservations: 505-455-5065
Poeh Center and Museum
78 Cities of Gold Rd, Santa Fe, NM 87506
Cultural Center: 505-455-5041;
www.poehcenter.com
Museum: 505-455-3334;
www.poehmuseum.com
Pueblo of Pojoaque Visitor Center
96 Cities of Gold Road, Santa Fe NM 87506
505-455-3460
Mon-Sat 9am-6pm & Sun 10am-4pm,
Apr-Dec; Mon-Sat 9am-5:30pm & Sun
10am-4pm, Jan-Mar
**Pueblo of Pojoaque Wellness and Healing
Arts Center**
505-455-0515 (wellness) *or* 505-455-0320
(healing arts)
Towa Golf Resort
877-465-3489 *or* 505-455-9000
www.towagolf.com

Sandia Pueblo
481 Sandia Loop, Bernalillo, NM 87004
505-867-3317 • www.sandiapueblo.nsn.us
  Bien Mur Indian Market
  100 Bien Mur Drive NE (I-25 North and
    Tramway Road), Albuquerque, NM
    87113
  800-365-5400 *or* 505-821-5400
  www.bienmur.com
  Monday-Saturday 9am-5:30pm & Sunday
    11am-5pm
  Sandia Casino
  East side of I-25 off Tramway Boulevard
  800-526-9366 *or* 505-796-7500
  www.sandiacasino.com
  Sandia Lakes
  30 Rainbow Road NE, Albuquerque, NM
    87113
  800-357-3971 *or* 505-897-3971

San Felipe Pueblo
PO Box 4339 San Felipe Pueblo, NM 87001
505-867-3381
  Casino Hollywood
  Exit 252 off I-25
  877-529-2946 *or* 505-867-6700
  www.sanfelipecasino.com
  Mon-Thurs 8am-4pm & Fri-Sun 24 hours
  Hollywood Hills Speedway
  Exit 252 off I-25
  505-867-6700
  San Felipe Travel Center
  505-867-4706

San Ildefonso Pueblo
Rt. 5, Box 315-A, Santa Fe, NM 87501
505-455-2273 *or* 505-455-3549
  Maria Poveka Martinez Museum
  NW of plaza by the Governor's Office
  505-455-3549
  Weekdays 8am-4pm
  San Ildefonso Fishing Lake
  505-455-2273
  **San Ildefonso Visitor Center/Governor's
    Office**
  Pueblo Entrance Road
  505-455-3549
  Daily 8am-5pm; fee

San Juan Pueblo (*See* Ohkay Owingeh Pueblo)

Santa Ana Pueblo
2 Dove Road, Bernalillo, NM 87004
505-771-6700 • www.santaana.org
  Hyatt Regency Tamaya Resort and Spa
  1300 Tuyuna Trail Santa Ana Pueblo, NM
    87004
  800-554-9288 *or* 505-867-1234
  www.tamaya.hyatt.com
  email: dkupersc@tamaypo.hyatt.com
    **Tamaya Cultural Museum and
      Learning Center**
    800-554-9288 *or* 505-867-1234
  Jemez Canyon Reservoir
  82 Dam Crest Road, Peña Blanca, NM 87041
  **Santa Ana Agricultural Enterprises Native
    Plants, Tree Nursery, and Garden Center**
  157 Jemez Dam Road, Bernalillo, NM 87004
  505-867-1322
  www.santaana.org/garden.htm
  Santa Ana Golf Club
  288 Prairie Star Road, Santa Ana Pueblo,
    NM 87004
  505-867-9464 • www.santaanagolf.com
  Prairie Star Restaurant
  505-867-3327
  Santa Ana Star Casino
  54 Jemez Canyon Dam Rd, Santa Ana
    Pueblo, NM 87004
  505-867-0000 • www.santaanastar.com
  Ta-Ma-Ya Crafts Cooperative
  2 Dove Road, Bernalillo, NM 87004
  Tues & Thurs 10am-4pm, summer
  The Cooking Post
  2 Dove Road, Bernalillo, NM 87004
  888-867-5198 *or* 505-771-6752
  www.cookingpost.com
  Twin Warriors Golf Course
  505-771-6155
  www.twinwarriorsgolf.com

Santa Clara Pueblo
PO Box 580, Española, NM 87532
505-753-7326
  Big Rock Casino and Big Rock Bowl
  460 North Riverside Drive, Española, NM
    87532
  866-244-7625 *or* 505-367-4500
  www.bigrockcasino.com
  Mon-Thurs 8am-4am; Fri-Sun 24 hours
  Black Mesa Golf Club
  115 State Road 399, Española, NM 87532
  505-747-8946
  www.blackmesagolfclub.com
  Dreamcatcher Cinema
  33771 S Hwy 285, Española, NM 87532
  505-753-0087

Santa Fe National Forest
1474 Rodeo Road, Santa Fe, NM 87505
505-438-7840 • www.fs.fed.us/r3/sfe

Santo Domingo Pueblo
PO Box 99 Santo Domingo, NM 87502
505-465-2214 *or* -2215
    Kewa Gas Station and Convenience Store
    I-25 at exit 259
    505-465-2620

Taos Pueblo
PO Box 1846, Taos Pueblo, NM87571
505-758-1028 • www.taospueblo.com
Mon-Sat 8am-4:30pm & Sun 8:30am-
    4:30pm; closed mid Feb to early April, and
    during some ceremonies; fee
    Big Horn Sheep Hunts
    505-758-3883
    Taos Indian Horse Ranch
    PO Box 3019, 340 Little Deer Run Road,
      Taos Pueblo, NM 87571
    800-659-3210 *or* 505-758-3212
    www.taosindianhorseranch.com
    Taos Mountain Casino
    505-737-0777 *or* 888-946-8267
    www.taosmountaincasino.com
    Sun-Wed 8am-1am & Thurs-Sat 8am-2am
    Tiwa Kitchen
    Taos Pueblo Road, Taos, NM 87571
    505-751-1020
    Wed-Mon 11am-7pm, Apr-Oct; 11am-
      5pm, Nov-Mar call for arrangements

Tesuque Pueblo
Rt.42 Box 360-T, Santa Fe, NM 87506
505-983-2667
Call for days the pueblo is open
    Camel Rock Casino
    800-462-2635; 505-984-8414
    www.camelrockcasino.com
    Camel Rock Suites
    3007 S. St. Francis Drive, Santa Fe, NM
      87505
    877-989-3600 *or* 505-989-3600
    www.camelrocksuites.com
    Tesuque Pueblo Flea Market
    505-995-8626 *or* 505-983-2667
    Fri-Sun, mid March-mid Nov, weather
      permitting

Wingspread Guides of New Mexico, Inc.
116 Central Avenue SW, Suite 201, Albu-
    querque, NM 87102
505-245-4200
www.collectorsguide.com/wingwelc.html

Zia Pueblo
135 Capitol Square Drive, Zia Pueblo, NM
    87053-6013
505-867-3304
    Zia Cultural Center
    Weekdays 8am-noon and 1pm-5pm; no fee
    Zia Lakes
    505-867-3304

Zuni Pueblo
PO Box 339, 1203B State Hwy 53, Zuni
    Pueblo, NM 87327
505-782-7000 *or* 782-7238
www.ashiwi.org
    A:shiwi A:wan Museum and Heritage
      Center
    2 E. Ojo Caliente Road, PO Box 1009,
      Zuni, NM 87327
    505-782-4403
    www.ashiwi-museum.org/index.html
    Mon-Fri 9am-5:30pm, fall-spring; Mon-Sat
      9am-5:30pm, summer; donation
    Inn at Halona Bed and Breakfast
    800-752-3278 *or* 505-782-4547
    www.halona.com
    Our Lady of Guadalupe Mission Church
    505-782-7238
    Pueblo of Zuni Arts and Crafts
    1222 Hwy 53, Zuni, NM 87327
    505-782-5531
    Mon-Fri 9am-6pm, Sat 9am-5pm
    Pueblo of Zuni Fish and Wildlife Office
    505-782-5851
    Zuni Craftsman Cooperative Association
    1177 NM 53
    888-926-1842 *or* 505-782-4425
    Zuni Visitor Center at Tribal Headquarters
    PO Box 1009, Zuni, NM 87327
    505-782-7238

NORTHWEST NEW MEXICO

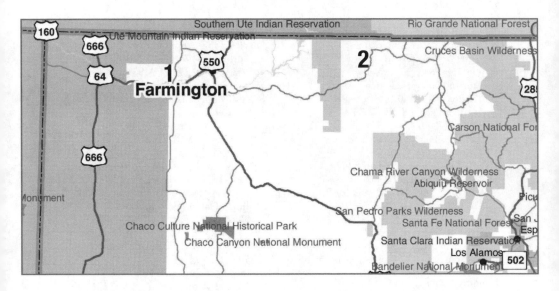

1. Farmington
2. Jicarilla Apache Nation

CHAPTER 17

NORTHWEST NEW MEXICO

FARMINGTON
Map #1

Around Town: Farmington Museum
Nearby: Angel Peak, Aztec Museum, Aztec Ruins National Monument, Bisti/De-Ná-Zin Wilderness Area, Chaco Culture National Historic Park, Jicarilla Apache Reservation, Navajo Lake State Park, Navajo Nation, Salmon Ruins and Heritage Park, Navajo Lake State Park

Farmington, with a population of 41,000, is the largest city in the Four Corners—the geographical region where Colorado, Utah, New Mexico, and Arizona meet. Located in the San Juan River valley near various major Ancestral Puebloan ruins, the town is also a leading trade center for the modern-day tribes of the region. You can see their influence at the many local trading posts, some of which were established over a hundred years ago. Today, in addition to selling locally produced arts and crafts, these stores provide food, gasoline, and other tourist necessities.

Farmington Museum and Visitors Center at Gateway Park explains the history, culture, and geology of the Four Corners. A simulated ride takes you on an underground search for oil and to exhibits on its extraction and use. Farmington: 100 Years of Change is a timeline covering early pioneer settlement to the present. In it the Three Waters Trading Post replicates a 1930s trading post with a pawn room and period goods and artifacts. Plans are to expand space for more Native American exhibits.

If you are in the market for authentic jewelry, pottery, rugs, and other arts and crafts from the Navajo and Hopi reservations and New Mexico pueblos, Farmington is a good place to shop. You can also watch demonstrations by local artists at some of the stores. A complete list of trading posts and pawnshops is available at the visitor center.

EAST OF FARMINGTON
East of town, on NM511 off US64, is **Navajo Lake State Park**, the principal source of water for the Navajo Indian Irrigation Project, which was developed to quench the thirst

of 110,000 acres of Navajo land. The dam, an embankment filled with millions of cubic yards of rocks and dirt, has created a thirty-five-mile-long reservoir that is now one of the best fishing holes in the state. Fed by melting snow-pack, the lake abounds in cold and warm water game fish, ranging from rainbow trout and kokanee salmon to bass and crappie. Hiking, picnicking, camping, hunting, and an array of water sports are also popular here.

The state park includes three recreation areas. *Pine River*, near the dam, and *Sims Mesa*, across the lake and accessible on NM527, both have a marina, boat rentals, developed campgrounds, interpretive displays, picnic area, and boat rentals. Pine River, the more developed of the two, has a visitor center with displays of ancient Puebloan life. The *San Juan River* section, below the dam and accessible by dirt road, is known for its excellent trout fishing. It has Cottonwood Campground, picnic areas, hiking trails, and fishing access, some of which is wheelchair-accessible.

Navajo Lake extends from New Mexico into Colorado. *Navajo State Recreation Area*, at the upper end of the reservoir, is on the Southern Ute Reservation near the town of Arboles, Colorado (see Chapter 15, Southwest Colorado, page 272).

About 11 miles east of Farmington toward Bloomfield on US64 is **Salmon Ruins and Heritage Park**. Built between A.D. 1088 and 1095, the pueblo here is one of the largest and most remarkably planned of the Chaco communities. It originally stood two stories high with around 250 rooms.

The small *museum* has a slide show and exhibits of some of the 1.5 million artifacts excavated from the ruin, as well as Ute, Apache, and Navajo items. The unique gift shop sells books, Native American arts and crafts, and archaeological reference materials. Before taking the short walk or drive from the museum to the ruins, ask for the booklet for the self-guiding trail.

A good place to learn more about the archaeology of San Juan County is the *research center and library*, where records and artifacts from the excavation are housed. For more in-depth study, you can join a *Journey into the Past* guided tour to Chaco Canyon, regional rock art, and sites on the Navajo homeland. All tours require advance reservations.

Outside the museum is *Heritage Park*, which depicts the lifestyles of various cultures in the San Juan Valley. Replicas of a furnished Navajo hogan, sweat lodge, wickiups, and a subterranean pithouse are highlights of the park.

Aztec Ruins National Monument is northeast of Farmington on NM516, and then north on NM550. The pioneers erroneously named the ruins here "Aztec," assuming the pueblo had been built by the Indians of Mexico. However, with over five hundred rooms, Aztec was one of the largest Ancestral Puebloan villages in the Southwest.

As an outlier of the Chaco Canyon culture centered 65 miles to the south, it was probably connected to it by a main road. At one time, the 2.5 acres of Aztec may have been a center for events and ceremonies. Construction began here around A.D. 1100, with hand-quarried sandstone blocks hauled from over a mile away and timber dragged from the mountains twenty miles north. Mysteriously, the Chacoans abandoned the town less than a hundred years after they built it.

In the early 1200s, a group of Ancestral Puebloans related to the Mesa Verdeans moved in, remodeled, and built additions. Then, in only fifty years or so, they too moved away, sealing the windows and doors and leaving everything in place, as if in preparation for

Chacoan architects designed attractive, patterned walls like this one at Aztec National Monument.

their return. Many archaeologists believe the emigrants eventually ended up in the Taos, San Juan, or Santo Domingo pueblos.

Over six hundred years later, Anglo settlers discovered Aztec and used it as a quarry for stones to build their own houses. Much valuable information was lost by the subsequent vandalism and stealing of artifacts.

Aztec's *visitor center* features a video about the Ancestral Puebloans, displays of pre-historic artifacts and pioneer items, and a bookstore. A self-guiding trail leads to the west pueblo through the room blocks and into the magnificent restored Great Kiva, where a tape of Indian chanting lends an aura of mystery. Great Kivas, built by the people of the Chaco culture, may have been used as social and administrative centers in addition to being used for the religious functions of kivas. One of the most distinguishing features at Aztec is the contrast between Chaco and Mesa Verde architectural styles; look for large sandstone blocks chinked with small stones for the Chacoan and T-shaped doorways for the Mesa Verdean.

In the adjacent town of Aztec is **Aztec Museum**. Although comprising mostly pioneer and mineral exhibits, it does display some prehistoric artifacts and Indian arts and crafts.

Southeast of Farmington is a 40-million-year-old geological formation surrounded by badlands and rising from what was once an ancient seabed. Called **Angel Peak** because from some angles it resembles a kneeling angel with one outstretched broken wing, the peak is believed by the Navajo to be the home of the "Sacred Ones." It remains a peaceful place to contemplate the silence, picnic, camp in primitive sites with no water or services, and hike. To reach this prominent landmark, take US64 east to Bloomfield, turn south onto NM44 for 15 miles, and then turn east at the sign onto a marked gravel road. The scenic overlook is 6 miles. Contact the BLM office in Farmington for more information on Angel Peak Recreation Area.

SOUTH OF FARMINGTON

The **Bisti/De-Na-Zin Wilderness Area** has changed little since the Navajo first named its features and made it part of their homeland. Two access points lead into this 45,000 acres of strange and desolate "badlands."

Bisti (meaning "a large area of shale hills" in Navajo) is a surreal landscape living up to its name, with acres of shale and sandstone sculpted by natural forces into weird formations, and with numerous fossil remains from the age of dinosaurs. Odds are that you won't have much company on your visit to Bisti. Even most animals avoid this stark place—that is, except for lizards, spiders, and snakes. If you feel particularly adventurous, visit at night when shadows cast by the moon add an even greater dimension of eeriness to the amazing scenery.

The turnoff to the Bisti parking lot is south of Farmington off NM371. Look for NCM (non-county-maintained) Road 7297, which is gravel for 2 miles.

De-Ná-Zin parking area is 8 miles south of the one for Bisti. De-Ná-Zin, which means "standing crane" in Navajo, was named after the large flocks of cranes that once rested here on their yearly migrations and inspired prehistoric people to peck their images into the rock. The land here remains remote and isolated, with little evidence of human encroachment. You can hike through the area's five habitat zones, including an upland pinyon-juniper community and sagebrush flat in the eastern portion of the wilderness, rolling grasslands in the south, scattered mesas, and a stand of ponderosa pine.

To reach De-Ná-Zin, take NM371 south of Farmington to County Road 7500 (8 miles past the Bisti access exit), and then turn east to the parking lot. Alternately, take NM44 south from Bloomfield to Huerfano Trading Post, and turn west onto CR7500. Note that CR7500 is a dry-weather dirt road that becomes slippery, rutted, and often impassable when wet.

For more information on both Bisti and De-Ná-Zin Wilderness Areas, contact the BLM office in Farmington.

Chaco Culture National Historical Park requires effort and planning to visit because

of its isolation and lack of services, but it is one of the jewels of the Southwest. Chaco Canyon was a magnificent center of Ancestral Pueblo culture from A.D. 850 to 1250. At its apex in the late eleventh and early twelfth centuries, it was the leader in Ancestral Pueblo religion, architecture, social organization, politics, and economics. At least 1,200 miles of roads, some over thirty feet wide, connected it with outlying communities across the Four Corners. This elaborate network of arrow-straight roads was a remarkable achievement for a culture that did not have carts, the use of the wheel, or large pack animals.

Rocks take on otherworldly shapes in Bisti/De-Ná-Zin Wilderness Area.

Pueblo Bonito is the largest of the ruins in Chaco Canyon

In addition to roads, Chacoan architects built distinctive multistoried pueblos using sandstone blocks chinked with small stones to create attractive designs. Another unique aspect of their masonry was that they would build two of these elaborate stonework walls beside each other and then fill the space between the walls with rubble.

Chacoan astronomers also made their mark on the culture. The walls and windows of pueblos were often aligned to the cardinal directions and to astronomical events such as the solstices and important moon rises. On Fajada Butte in the canyon, a shard of light bisects a carved nine-ringed symbol of the sun exactly at noon on the day of the summer solstice. Using devices such as these, they could predict the round of the seasons and direct the planting and harvest ceremonies.

As a center for administration, ceremony, and trade, life may have been bustling at Chaco, although recent theories postulate that few people actually lived here year-round. Still, the number of people probably ebbed and swelled as ceremonial and administrative events brought different groups to the canyon. Traders from exotic places may have been among them, coming with salt from the Zuni Lakes, turquoise from Galisteo Basin, seashells from the Pacific Ocean, and macaw feathers from Mexico to barter for Chacoan pottery, jewelry, and cornmeal.

Pueblo Bonito is the largest of the towns in the urban complex of stone at Chaco. At one time, around one thousand people may have lived here in over six hundred rooms. Room blocks bent into a crescent around the plaza, a long wall enclosed the front of the village, and dozens of kivas dominated the city.

Today Chaco Canyon has thirteen major excavated ruins that are open to explore. In addition, the place is not usually crowded because of the bone-jarring dirt road to the park entrance and limited services.

The *visitor center* is a good first stop for information, exhibits, a bookstore, a gift shop, and educational films. From here a 9-mile paved road loops through the canyon. Five self-guided trails wind from the road through the accessible ruins and petroglyphs, and four backcountry trails lead to more remote ruins. To gain a deeper understanding of the amazing culture that once flourished here, join a summer ranger-guided walk or listen to a summer evening campfire program.

A sixty-four-site campground without available water is about a mile from the visitor center. The campground is open year-round, but arrive early between April and October because it often fills by midday. No other lodging is available in the park.

The recommended way to reach Chaco Canyon is to travel south of Farmington on US550 to Nageezi Trading Post. Three miles past Nageezi, turn southwest onto CR7900, and then west onto CR7950. Follow the signs to the park. At least 13 miles of this route is fair-weather dirt road, which can be impassable when wet, so if in doubt, call ahead to inquire about conditions. The road is not recommended for RVs. The southern route from Highway 9 is very rough and often impassable.

Drinking water is available at the visitor center, but gas, showers, and food are not. Before visiting, fill the gas tank, pack the cooler with food and beverages, and bring your own firewood or charcoal if you plan to camp.

JICARILLA APACHE NATION
Map #2

Sites: Apache Nugget Casinos, Horse Lake Mesa Game Park, Jicarilla Apache Arts and Crafts Shop and Museum, Jicarilla Apache Historic District, Jicarilla Best Western Inn, La Jara archaeological site, prehistoric ruins

The Apache philosophy of life might be summed up in the phrase *Aba'achi migoya' meedasi nzho'go me ch'aa kai'i*, meaning "the Apache will lead forward by strong and beautiful thoughts." The Jicarilla (*hek-a-REH-ya*), like other Apaches, migrated to the Southwest from northwestern Canada. Primarily hunters and gatherers, they ranged and traded throughout northeastern New Mexico, southern Colorado, and into the Oklahoma panhandle before pressure from both white settlers and local Comanches pushed them out of these places.

In 1882, a reservation was established for them along the Rio Navajo. A year later the people were forced from there and sent to live with the Mescalero in southern New Mexico. On April 25, 1887, the Jicarilla began the long trek back from Mescalero to their earlier homelands around Cimarron, Taos, and Abiquiu, arriving over a month later. In 1987, they commemorated this return with a two-hundred-mile horse and wagon journey called the "Centennial Wagon Trek."

Today about 2,700 people live on the reservation, most of them in the small town of **Dulce**. The pristine land features mountain forests, rolling hills, and sagebrush flats edged by sandstone canyons. In places, you can still see traditional wickiups (houses of poles covered with grass and brush) blending with the landscape. The economy of the Jicarilla Nation stems mainly from mineral reserves on the reservation and tourism.

Jicarilla comes from a Mexican-Spanish word meaning "little basketmaker." At **Jicarilla Apache Arts and Crafts Shop** you can view examples of the superbly crafted Apache baskets, watch expert artisans at work, and buy baskets and other crafts the Jicarilla are famous for, such as beadwork, leatherwork, and jewelry. Displays on the history and culture of the Jicarilla Apache, as well as ancient pictographs, are in the **Jicarilla Cultural Center Museum** across the street from the Game and Fish Department. Both are good places to obtain information about visiting some of the **prehistoric sites** on the reservation, such as the cliff dwellings at *La Jara archaeological site*, the isolated pueblo ruins in *Cordova Canyon* on Tribal Road 13, or *Honolulu Ruins* on Road 63. The museum is on US64 just west of town center.

The only place to stay in town is the *Wild Horse Casino and Jicarilla Best Western Inn*, which has recently been renovated and expanded. In addition to gaming, the establishment offers lodging, full-service dining with Northern New Mexican and American food, a conference center, and a gift shop selling Jicarilla baskets, pottery, and beadwork along with traditional and contemporary Native American arts and crafts from other Indians. The facility also serves as a visitor center with maps, information, and package tours that include the Cumbres-Toltec train ride in Chama and a cultural presentation.

The *Apache Nugget Casino* is located on US550 between Bloomfield and Cuba on the southern end of the reservation. It has 210 slot machines, blackjack tables, a roulette wheel, a small restaurant, a gift shop, and a player's club.

The reservation is a paradise for outdoor enthusiasts, who delight in the abundant game, the seven lakes stocked with trout, the great variety of water birds, and the numerous backcountry trails. **Horse Lake Mesa Game Park** is a 14,500-acre reserve set aside for hunting trophy-quality elk, black bear, and predatory animals. Permits and guides are available for elk and deer hunts September through December, for waterfowl October through January, and for bear and turkey in the spring. Contact the Jicarilla Apache Department of Game and Fish for more information and maps.

The Game and Fish Department, as well as the tribal offices, also has maps that show the 119 acres of the **Jicarilla Apache Historic District**, which is the site of the original Indian agency.

Visitors to the reservation are asked to stay on main roads, J-roads, and state highways. Camera permits are not required, but remember it is always polite to ask before photographing an individual. However, no photos are permitted of the annual *Go-Jii-Yah* feast held at Stone Lake in mid-September.

The horse revolutionized the way of life of the Apache.

EVENTS

FEBRUARY *Jicarilla Day Powwow:* Traditional dress, dancing, drumming, and singing in Dulce.

APRIL *Apple Blossom Contest Powwow:* Annual powwow in Farmington, 800-448-1240.

JUNE *Aztec Fiesta Days:* Town festival with music, parade, carnival, contests, arts/crafts, and more. Native American events include dancing, Navajo weaving demonstrations, art show, arts/crafts, and food vendors. In Aztec, 505-334-9551 or 888-838-9551.

JULY *Little Beaver Celebration:* Powwow, rodeo, dances, parade, races, softball tournament, archery shoot, mudbog, pageantry, carnival, and car/truck show. Third weekend in July at Dulce, Jicarilla Apache reservation. Contact 505-759-3242 or http://jicarillaonline.com.

SEPTEMBER *Go-Jii-Yah Feast:* Traditional harvest festival with footraces, powwow, and rodeo. At Stone Lake, nineteen miles south of Dulce, Jicarilla Apache reservation. Contact 505-759-3242 or http://jicarillaonline.com.

Totah Festival: Art festival with juried art show and sale, powwow, and rug auction to foster understanding of Indian art and culture. Farmington Civic Center. Contact 800-448-1240 or www.farmingtonmuseum.org/totahfestival/totahfestival.html.

OCTOBER *Four Corners Storytelling Festival:* Celebration of the oral tradition of the Four Corners with national and local storytellers. At Berg Park and Lions Wilderness Amphitheater in Farmington. Call 505-599-1273.

Shiprock Fair (Northern Navajo Fair): Oldest Navajo traditional fair, with intertribal powwow, exhibits, traditional song/dance, beauty pageant, parade, all-Indian rodeo, Yei-Bei-Chei ceremony, and carnival. Usually the first weekend in October at Shiprock Fairgrounds. Contact 800-448-1240.

DECEMBER *Navajo Nativity:* Live nativity with participants in traditional Navajo dress. Presented by children of Four Corners Home for Children at Christmas time, 2103 W. Main in Farmington. Call 505-325-0255 or 800-448-1240.

Salmon Ruins Holiday Arts & Crafts Fair: Annual sale of arts/crafts by Four Corners artisans. McGee Park at Salmon Ruins NM, 505-632-2013 or 800-448-1240.

CONTACT INFORMATION

Aztec Museum and Pioneer Village
125 N. Main Street, Aztec, NM 87410
505-334-9829
Mon-Sat 9am-5pm, summer; Mon-Sat 9am-4pm, winter; fee

Aztec Ruins National Monument
84 CR 2900 (Ruins Road), PO Box 640, Aztec, NM 87410
505-334-6174 • www.nps.gov/azru
Daily 8am-6pm, summer; daily 8am-5pm, winter; fee

Aztec Visitor information Center
110 N. Ash, Aztec, NM 87410
888-838-9551 *or* 505-334-9551
www.aztecnm.com

Bisti/De-Ná-Zin Wilderness Area (*see* BLM Farmington Office)

Bureau of Land Management
www.blm.gov/nm/st/en.html
 Farmington Resource Area
 1235 La Plata Highway, Farmington, NM 87401
 505-599-8900

Chaco Culture National Historic Park
PO Box 280, Nageezi. NM 87037
505-786-7014 • www.nps.gov/chcu
Visitor Center: daily 8am-5pm
Ruins: open sunrise to sunset; fee

De-Ná-Zin Wilderness Area (*see* BLM Farmington Resource Area)

Farmington Civic Center
200 W. Arrington, Farmington, NM 87401-6239
800-448-1240

Farmington (town)
www.farmington.nm.us

Farmington Museum and Visitors Center at Gateway Park
3041 E. Main Street, Farmington, NM 87402
800-448-1240 *or* 505-599-1174
www.farmingtonmuseum.org
www.farmingtonnm.org
Mon-Sat 8am-5pm

Jicarilla Apache Nation
Tribal Headquarters
PO Box 507, Dulce, NM 87528
505-759-3242
www.jicarilla.net • http://jicarillaonline.com
  Apache Nugget Corporation
  Dulce, NM 87528
  505-759-3777 • www.apachenugget.com
  Arts and Crafts Shop
  505-759-4274
  Mon-Sat 8-5
  Department of Game and Fish
  PO Box 313, Dulce, NM 87528
  505-759-3255 • www.jicarillahunt.com
  Jicarilla Cultural Center and Museum
  PO Box 1367, Dulce, NM 87528
  505-759-1343
  Mon-Fri 8am-5pm
  **Wild Horse Casino and Jicarilla Best
      Western Inn**
  US64 (Jicarilla Blvd), Dulce, NM 87528
  Hotel: 800-637-5956 *or* 505-759-3663
  Casino: 800-294-2234

Navajo Lake State Park
1448 NM 511 #1, Navajo Dam, NM 87419
505-632-2278
www.emnrd.state.nm.us/PRD/Navajo.htm
  Pine Visitor Center:
  Daily 8am-4pm, Labor Day-mid May;
      Mon-Fri 7:30am-4:30pm & Sat-Sun
      6:30am-8:30pm, mid May-Labor
      Day
  Map of Navajo Lake
  www.nmparks.com

New Mexico State Parks
1220 South St. Francis Drive, Santa Fe, NM
    87505
888-667-2757 *or* 505-476-3355
www.emnrd.state.nm.us/PRD/index.htm

**Salmon Ruins, Museum, and Research Li-
    brary**
PO Box 125, Bloomfield, NM 87413
505-632-2013 • www.salmonruins.com
Mon-Fri 8am-5pm & Sat-Sun 9am-5pm, May-
    Oct; Mon-Fri 8am-5pm, Sat 9am-5pm,
    Sun noon-5pm, Nov-Apr; fee

NORTHEAST AND NORTH CENTRAL NEW MEXICO

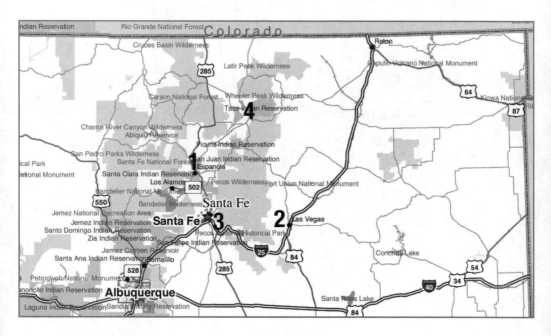

1. Espanola
2. Las Vegas
3. Santa Fe
4. Taos

CHAPTER 18

NORTHEAST AND NORTH CENTRAL NEW MEXICO

ESPAÑOLA
Map #1

Around Town: Chimayo Trading Post, Española Mission and Convento
Nearby: Abiquiu, Bandelier National Monument, Ojo Caliente Mineral Springs, Oñate Monument and Visitors Center, Orilla Verde Recreation Area
High Road to Taos: Chimayo, Fort Burgwin, Picuris Pueblo, Pot Creek Cultural Site
Jemez Mountain Trail: Bandelier National Monument, Jemez Pueblo, Jemez State Monument, Los Alamos County Historical Museum
Other Nearby Pueblos: Santa Clara Pueblo, San Ildefonso Pueblo, San Juan Pueblo, Taos Pueblo

Española lies between Santa Fe and Taos in the northern Rio Grande Valley. From town, several pueblos and sites of interest lie within easy driving distance. Although they are also easily accessed from either Santa Fe or Taos, the modest character of Española offers an economical alternative to the upscale ambience of its more famous neighbors. And along the scenic highways and back roads from town you can often find small roadside stands to buy fresh produce and strings of dried chilies called *ristras*.

In 1598, Don Juan de Oñate and his colonists arrived north of the town site, near the confluence of the Rio Grande and the Rio Chama rivers and at the Tewa-speaking Pueblo of *Ohkay Owingeh*, which consisted of five small villages. The Spanish built a church and an adobe complex and renamed the entire Pueblo *San Juan de los Caballeros*. From here, Oñate governed the new colony of *Nueva Mexico* (New Mexico) for several months, until the settlement was relocated to the village of *Yunque Yungue* on the west bank of the Rio Grande. The Spanish subsequently changed the name of Yunque Yungue to *San Gabriel*.

The **Mission/Convento complex** that once housed Governor Oñate's offices has been reconstructed on the present Plaza de Española. The plaza is off Paseo de Oñate (US84/285) in downtown Española.

The Paseo connects the plaza with the adobe **Chimayo Trading Post**. Once featured in a Smithsonian exhibit, this post was founded in the early 1900s by the Trujillo family and moved here from Chimayo in the 1930s. It is still operated by descendants of the founders and is said by some to be the last authentic trading post in the Santa Fe/Taos area. Also called the Marco Polo Shop, the small post sells Pueblo pottery, Navajo rugs, jewelry, and Chimayo weavings. A visit here is a bit like entering a living museum of the Old West.

Española Valley Chamber of Commerce on Paseo de Oñate has a free visitor guide and information on area lodging and dining options.

NORTH OF ESPAÑOLA

North of Española on US84 is the village of **Abiquiu**. The town was built in the 1740s on the site of a sixteenth-century Pueblo Indian ruin, although the area had been occupied for thousands of years. Shortly after settlement, the Spanish brought a group of *genizaros* to live with them. These were detribalized Indians (many of them Navajo and Apache) who had been pressed into domestic service and given Spanish surnames. Once they settled at Abiquiu, both Spaniards and Indians struggled to farm the barren land, raise cattle, and protect themselves from Ute raiding parties.

About 12 miles north of Abiquiu on US84 is Ghost Ranch, established in 1766. It is currently the setting for a Presbyterian church adult study, retreat, and research center. The conference center's **Florence Hawley Ellis Museum of Anthropology**, just west of the lower pavilion, has extensive displays covering twelve thousand years of culture in the Rio Grande, Chama, and Gallinas valleys. Contemporary works by Indian, Spanish, and Anglo artists are also displayed. A paleontology museum exhibits 250-million-year-old fossils, and the outdoor Living Museum is home to an assortment of native animals. The conference center offers classes and seminars that sometimes include Native American themes, and it is also the site of a variety of Elderhostel programs.

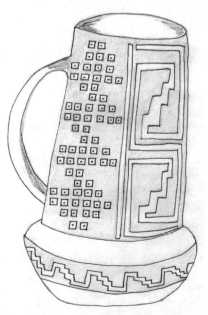

Five miles south of Abiquiu on US84 are **Poshouinge Ruins**. A steep, rocky, half-mile trail provides views of the Chama Valley and leads to the ruins, which encompass the remains of over seven hundred ground-floor rooms surrounding two plazas and with a large kiva. Interpretive signs enhance the experience.

Tesuque, Pojoaque, San Ildefonso, and Nambe pueblos are off US84/285 toward Santa Fe (see Chapter 16, The Pueblos of New Mexico).

About 25 miles north of Española on US285 is **Ojo Caliente Mineral Springs**, where four hot springs mingle to create a unique blend of geothermal waters said to exist no place else in the world. Early Puebloans and other Indians in the region visited the hot springs, and even Geronimo is said to have come here.

Anasazi potters decorated their utilitarian pottery with geometric designs.

On the ridge above the hot springs are the ruins of *Posi-ouinge* or *"green lush village,"* once a thriving Tewa village occupied between A.D. 1375 and 1550. According to legend, it was the sacred place where the Summer People and the Winter People reunited after being separated for many years. They lived here together until an epidemic forced them to relocate; some of the people subsequently founded a new village, *Oke'onwi*, also known as San Juan.

Although at one time Posi-ouinge may have been three-stories high, with storage and living space for seven thousand people, today about all you can see are ridges and mounds sprouting desert plants. The trail brochure available at the spa can help you decipher how these remnants relate to the original pueblo. The mile-long round-trip through the ruins is on an unpaved trail that is steep and rocky in places. It starts up the drainage from the hot springs.

After hiking the trail and enjoying the gorgeous views, take time to relax with the informal atmosphere and eclectic mix of people who visit Ojo Caliente. You can purchase a room in the historic hotel or in private suites and cottages, a breakfast at the small restaurant, a soak in one of the seven pools, and additional spa treatments. Classes in traditional Tewa pottery making and archaeological tours of the ruin are also offered through the spa.

North of Española on NM68 is the direct road to Taos. Known as the *Low Road*, or the *River Road*, it follows the Rio Grande for many miles and passes San Juan Pueblo. Seven miles north of Española, in Alcalde, look for the large bronze statue of Don Juan de Oñate on horseback marking the **Oñate Monument and Visitors Center**, which is devoted to the Spanish and Pueblo heritage of the Española Valley, including the influence of *El Camino Real*. Another stop on the Low Road is 16 miles from Taos at **Orilla Verde Recreation Area**, offering numerous recreational opportunities along the Rio Grande in the steep-walled Rio Grande Gorge. People have passed through the gorge since prehistoric times, as the petroglyphs along the Vista Verde Nature Trail attest. Speculation is that the enigmatic spirals and designs are a map of the canyon or that they are historical and spiritual records. For more information, contact the BLM's Taos Field Office.

EAST OF ESPAÑOLA

NM76 travels east of Española and links Santa Fe and Taos. The route is often called the *High Road* and is known as "the highway of the arts" because of the many artist studios, galleries, and trading posts beside it. Following the High Road is a picturesque journey past tiny adobe chapels, Hispanic villages little changed since they were created two hundred years ago, and several Indian pueblos (although starting from Española will eliminate the part of the route that passes Tesuque, Pojoaque, and Nambe pueblos).

Two miles east of Española in Santa Cruz is the *Historic Holy Cross Catholic Church*, built in 1733 and now containing Spanish colonial artifacts.

About 10 miles east of Española in the Sangre de Cristo Mountains, another stop on the High Road is the village of **Chimayo**, known for its small chapel and the weavings of eight generations of the Ortega and Trujillo families. Rancho de Chimayo is popular for its traditional New Mexican food and is one of the state's oldest restaurants.

From A.D. 1100 to 1400, ancestors of the Pueblo Indians lived in the area, and they named the sacred hill above the valley *Tsi Mayoh,* or "Flaking Stone of Superior Quality."

Like the Spanish who followed them, the Pueblos believed in the miraculous qualities of the mud at the base of the mountain. Today, samples of this holy earth are available at the town's Catholic chapel, *El Santuario de Chimayo*, which has become a mecca for pilgrims in search of healing. If you visit the small side chapel filled with discarded crutches and personal memorials left in gratitude for answered prayers, you will understand why Chimayo is also called "The Lourdes of America."

The *Chimayo Museum* on Plaza del Cerro highlights the history and culture of the village and its surrounding communities and supports the work of local artists.

After leaving Chimayo, the road continues past small hamlets where noted woodcarvers and weavers sell their creations from small family stores often located in their homes. The lovely *San Jose de Gracia Mission church* in Las Trampas is listed on the National Register of Historic Places. Near the village of Penasco is the Pueblo of Picuris. (See Chapter 16, The Pueblos of New Mexico, page 294, for more information.)

After Picuris, take the paved NM518 toward Ranchos de Taos. *Fort Burgwin*, originally a U.S. military post established to protect settlers from Apache and Comanche raiders, has since been reconstructed as the summer campus of Southern Methodist University's Center for Cultural and Natural Studies in New Mexico (SMU-IN-TAOS).

Also on campus is Pot Creek Pueblo, the largest prehistoric adobe village north of Santa Fe and once home to several hundred Ancestral Puebloans. Although the pueblo is not open to the public, you can visit **Pot Creek Cultural Site** adjacent to the campus. A 1-mile trail leads past a reconstructed dwelling plus the remnants of an irrigation system and ancient road that was part of the valley's extensive trade network.

NM68 continues to Ranchos de Taos. Turn right (north) onto NM68 to travel the few miles to Taos, or turn left (south) onto NM68 to return to Española.

WEST OF ESPAÑOLA

The *Jemez Mountain Trail* is one of the most scenic auto trips in the state. The route connects Española with NM44 at San Ysidro. Along the way it climbs onto the Pajarito Plateau, traverses an ancient caldera that is now a broad mountain park, and passes hot springs and geological formations. Sites with special connections to native groups include Santa Clara Pueblo, San Ildefonso Pueblo, Bandelier National Monument, Jemez State Monument, Jemez Pueblo, and San Ysidro. (For information on the several pueblos, see Chapter 16.)

To follow Jemez Mountain Trail, take NM30 south of Española past Santa Clara and San Ildefonso pueblos to NM502, and turn west toward **Los Alamos**. The birthplace of the atomic bomb, the Los Alamos National Laboratory now comprises a large scientific research center. Many of the ten thousand employees here are Native Americans who commute from nearby pueblos. The laboratory's Bradbury Museum tells about life in Los Alamos before and after the Manhatten Project.

Near downtown Los Alamos is the small *Los Alamos County Historical Museum*, which has a bookstore, a diorama of prehistoric societies on the Pajarito Plateau, local history exhibits, and World War II memorabilia. In the park north of the museum are Tewa ruins dating from around A.D. 1225.

To continue to **Bandelier National Monument**, take NM4 outside of Los Alamos and follow the signs to the monument. Beside the road into the monument is a self-guided

Ladders lead to cave dwellings at Bandelier.

nature trail to the large, unexcavated *Tsankawi Ruin*. Hand- and toeholds, faint petroglyphs, and dramatic views of the Sangre de Cristo Mountains and Rio Grande Valley are highlights of this 2-mile round-trip hike that includes several steep climbs.

The landscape at Bandelier is volcanic ash that has been compressed into a rock called tuff. You can see its shiny patina covering the cliffs in Frijoles Canyon. But underneath the tuff lies soft and crumbly rock that can easily be dug away with stone and wooden tools. In the late 1100s, Pueblo Indians did so to create cliff homes for about 550 people in the canyon, with more on the surrounding mesa. They lived here for centuries, but by the mid-1500s, a series of disasters had driven them away to resettle at Cochiti and other Keresan pueblos.

The *visitor center* features exhibits, audiovisual programs, a bookstore, a gift shop, a snack bar, and lists of local plants and animals. In addition, rangers conduct guided walks and campfire programs at the campground. The center has information on the monument's backcountry trails and camping possibilities (90 percent of Bandelier is wilderness), horseback riding in the summer, and cross-country skiing in the winter.

The easy, 1.5-mile trail into Frijoles Canyon leads to *Tyuonyi Ruin*, once a four-story circular pueblo that was home to about a hundred people. The trail then continues to dwellings where short ladders lead into darkened cave rooms that allow you to peer out the entrances to views of the canyon. A more demanding trail leads to *Ceremonial Cave*, where a series of stairs and steep ladders lead 140 feet up the cliff to a reconstructed kiva.

About 30 miles from Los Alamos on NM4 is **Jemez Springs**, an old resort with hot springs probably used hundreds of years ago by indigenous people. North of town is **Soda Dam**, built up over the centuries from the calcium deposits of Soda Spring. The dome under which the river flows is three hundred feet long and fifty feet high and is still building. Nearby is the Jemez Ranger Station, which has information on the campground and trails in the national forest.

The road continues to **Jemez State Monument**, containing the impressive ruins of the Jemez village of *Guisewa* (Gee-SAY-wah), and the mission church established by Spaniards in the 1620s. Before Juan de Oñate visited in the late sixteenth century, the people of Jemez Pueblo had lived in scattered villages in the surrounding mountains for at least two hundred years. The Franciscan priest assigned to the area convinced the Indians to unite into three villages, one of which was Guisewa, meaning "Place at the Boiling Waters." The villagers revolted several times against Spanish rule, each time abandoning Guisewa for the safety of the mountains. When they finally left the village for good, they constructed the new town of Walatowa, which is the site of the present-day Jemez Pueblo.

Guisewa is one of the places where ancestors of the Jemez Puebloans lived. It is now Jemez National Monument.

A self-guiding trail leads through the well-preserved ruins of the village and to *San Jose de los Jemez Mission* church. The small museum interprets the history of the old Jemez Pueblo from the viewpoint of the native inhabitants.

Galleries, some of which sell Native American artwork, line the main street of the small town of **Jemez Springs**. Visitors to the Bath House can soak in the naturally heated mineral water enjoyed by early inhabitants.

Past the village of Jemez Springs, the highway parallels the Jemez River, where you can fish, camp, and picnic. Stop at the *Walatowa Visitor Center* for information on Jemez Pueblo, on the left next to the Jemez Red Rocks (see Chapter 16, The Pueblos of New Mexico, page 290, for more information).

The Jemez Mountain Trail ends at San Ysidro and the junction with NM44.

LAS VEGAS
Map #2

Around Town: City of Las Vegas Museum/Rough Riders Memorial, Anthropology Laboratory
Nearby: Armand Hammer United World College of the West, Capulin Volcano, Folsom Man
Museum, Fort Union National Monument, Montezuma Hot Springs, Santa Fe Trail Museum,
Wagon Mound

The original inhabitants of Las Vegas Valley were Paleo-Indians. At a place north of town called Sapello (*Sah-PAY-o*), Clovis hunters camped over twelve thousand years ago. They used the surrounding hills to scout for game and then outflanked the herds and stampeded them into dead-ended grassy inlets surrounded by small hills. The raw material for their tools came from the back of the valley, where a long outcropping of gray andesite was quarried by flint-knappers for over six thousand years.

Later cultures also came to Sapello to harvest the buffalo herds—Archaic hunters using obsidian tools and Apaches with bows and arrows. By the 1750s, the dominant group was the Comanche.

The Spanish town of Las Vegas was built in 1835 with a central plaza to defend against Indians. It soon became a trade center for overland wagon trains on the Santa Fe Trail, and it was here that Colonel Kearney read the proclamation claiming New Mexico as a United States territory.

The **Las Vegas Museum/Rough Riders Memorial,** which commemorates the Rough Riders in the Spanish-American War of 1898, includes Indian weapons among its displays. For walking tours of the town past its 940 historical buildings, contact the Las Vegas Chamber of Commerce on Grand Avenue.

New Mexico Highlands University's Anthropology Laboratory is open to the public for research. It has collections from the Tinsley Site, Tecolote Pueblo Site, and two main instructional collections. The Native American Instructional Collection has language and cultural maps, tool replicas, reference books, and videos relating to North and Central American Indians. The Early Human Instructional Collection focuses on the rise of *Homo sapiens*.

NORTH OF LAS VEGAS

Pecos Pueblo Indians were enjoying the three thermal springs at **Montezuma Hot Springs** as early as A.D. 800, and according to legend, Montezuma II of the Aztecs visited here in the early sixteenth century. People still come today to enjoy a leisurely soak in the hot springs. The small, rustic springs are beside NM65 about 5 miles north of the town's central plaza.

Behind the hot springs is the massive Montezuma Castle, an old stone hotel built as a spa in 1888 by the Santa Fe Railroad. Today it houses **Armand Hammer United World College of the West,** a two-year college established to encourage multicultural harmony. Students have come here from over seventy countries, and the first graduating class included two Pueblo Indians, one from Zuni and one from Acoma. Each October the college sponsors International Days, when students invite the public to share food and dancing from other cultures. Throughout the year, tours are available by appointment.

About 29 miles northeast of Las Vegas, off I-25 at exit 366 in Watrous, is the access road to **Fort Union National Monument**. Originally built in 1851 to protect travelers along the Santa Fe Trail, Fort Union eventually grew into the largest military installation on the southwestern frontier. From here patrols were deployed into the prairie to escort wagon trains and to search for hostile Indians.

The original fort was only a crude collection of buildings. In 1861, these were replaced by massive earthwork fortifications that, although a marvel of engineering, washed away in less than two years. The final fort was an elaborate enterprise that included not only a military post and buildings but also a separate supply depot with warehouses, corrals, shops, offices, and quarters. When the Santa Fe Railroad replaced the Trail in 1879, Ft. Union gradually lost its importance. By 1891 it had been abandoned.

You can tour the ruins of Fort Union on a self-guided trail. Shallow, grass-covered ruts mark the route of the Santa Fe Trail as it fades into the distant prairie. From the foundations, empty rooms, freestanding chimneys, and recorded messages, you only need a little imagination to recreate the bustling life of the fort.

Ruins are all that is left today of Ft. Union, once the largest U.S. military installation in the Southwest.

The *visitor center* features artifacts from the ruins, a bookstore, tours, and living-history presentations in summer. No food or campsites are available, but there is a picnic area.

North from Watrous, I-25 passes Wagon Mound, an Indian and Santa Fe Trail landmark that resembles the top of a covered wagon. To learn more about the trail, continue north on I-25 to the town of Springer, where the Cimarron Branch once passed. The **Santa Fe Trail Museum**, in the restored Colfax County Courthouse, has Santa Fe Trail artifacts and historical photos.

Further north on I-25 is the turnoff for **Capulin Volcano National Monument**. Capulin Volcano, set in the Raton-Clayton volcanic field, is nearly a mile across at its base. Although earlier scientists believed that it was last active around eleven thousand years ago during the time of the Folsom culture, newer geological research suggests eruptions were approximately 56,000 to 62,000 years ago.

Capulin is a classic example of a large "cinder cone" volcano. When it erupted amid earthquakes, seething lava, and clouds of ash and debris, a towering cone of cinders spiked upward a thousand feet above the grasslands. Eventually, the lava cooled and plants returned, the hardy lichens breaking the rock into soil so that grasses, junipers, mountain mahogany, and gambel oaks could take root. When people finally did move into the area, they no doubt used the prominent volcano as a landmark for their travels.

The *visitor center* has exhibits, a short video, and summer ranger programs to help interpret the local geology and human and natural history. A bookstore is also on site. A self-guiding nature trail is next to the visitor center.

Capulin is the only volcano in North America that has a parking lot on the top. A narrow paved road winds around the volcano to the summit, where two short trails provide visitors with a closer look at the crater. A mile-long trail follows the rim and provides expansive views of snow-capped mountains, other volcanic cones, and rangelands in New Mexico, Oklahoma, Colorado, and Texas. The other trail descends into the crater, which is over three hundred feet deep.

Capulin is east of I-25 on US64/87, which passes through a valley dimpled with black rock and extinct volcanoes.

The Folsom archaeological site is where the first evidence for Paleo-Indians was discovered in the United States. George McJunkin, a former slave and local cowboy, stumbled upon it in an arroyo in 1908 after a flood, and he spent the next eighteen years trying to get the attention of archaeologists. The flint spear points he found embedded in some odd-looking bleached bones eventually revolutionized the anthropological theories about early man in North America. Since the bones belonged to an extinct species of giant bison that lived thousands of years ago, they provided proof that the individuals who made the spear points lived thousands of years ago, too.

Not much is at the site today except scrubby vegetation and arroyos, but some of the fossils and spear points that the hunters used can be seen at **Folsom Man Museum** in the town of Folsom, north of Capulin on NM325.

SANTA FE
Map #3

Around Town: Barrio de Analco Historic District, Institute of American Indian Arts Museum, Laboratory of Anthropology, Museum of Fine Arts, Museum of Indian Arts and Culture, Museum of New Mexico, Old Town, Palace of the Governors, San Miguel Mission, Santuario de Guadalupe, School of American Research, Wheelwright Museum of the American Indian
Nearby: Pecos National Historical Park
Nearby Pueblos: Cochiti Pueblo, Nambe Pueblo, Pojoaque Pueblo, Santo Domingo Pueblo, San Felipe Pueblo, Tesuque Pueblo

Santa Fe brings Old World charm to the present. Many of the buildings are "the oldest" this or that in the country, but before the Spanish built the city, an ancient Indian pueblo called *Kuapoge*, or "The Place of Shell Beads Near the Water," was located here, having been abandoned about a century before during the worst area drought in a thousand years.

The Spanish settlers adopted the building styles of the native inhabitants, so much of the city architecture is low and flat, with softly rounded lines and muted earth tones. Between the adobe buildings, streets that once served as ancient trails connecting pueblos, fields, and individual homes still wind in a pattern all their own. Now that the open spaces have been filled in with buildings, any logical pattern lies hidden from modern eyes.

During the Pueblo Revolt of 1680, Spanish immigrants sought refuge in the Palace of the Governors on the plaza in Old Town. Amidst the victory dances and war chants of the victorious Pueblo warriors, the frightened Spanish were allowed to retreat the three hundred miles to El Paso del Norte and safety. Until 1682, when the Spanish returned under de Vargas, the Indians used the palace for a pueblo. The Cross of the Martyrs, at 600 Paseo de Peralta, memorializes the twenty-one Franciscans killed in the revolt.

Santa Fe is also a mecca for artists and shoppers. The town has ten major museums and around two hundred world-class art galleries.

Old Town, at the heart of the city, is where the Santa Fe Trail once ended in what was described as a "sea of mud." Old Town is best seen on foot, even during times when the streets around the plaza are not closed to traffic. You can browse in the unique art galleries and shops, watch the other tourists, or just sit and try to figure out the city's street system.

The portico in front of the Governor's Palace in Santa Fe is a popular open-air market for Native American artisans.

You can also explore St. Francis Cathedral, Loretto Chapel, or some of the other historic buildings and their finely crafted interiors.

On the north side of the plaza is the adobe **Palace of the Governors**, the oldest public building in continuous use in the United States. Representatives of Spain, Mexico, the Confederate States (briefly), and the United States have all occupied it at various times. Before the Spanish reconquest, it even served as a pueblo. Today, Native Americans display their jewelry, ceramics, and freshly baked bread under the portal and on the plaza, creating an open-air market that provides an opportunity to buy arts and crafts directly from the artisans.

The Palace of the Governors now houses the state's history museum, which also includes a library and photographic archives. Exhibits cover the New Mexican past of the Indian, Spanish, Mexican, and American frontiers. In addition, the museum sponsors special events, lectures, and a native arts program.

The Palace of the Governors is part of the Museum of New Mexico, which also includes the Museum of Fine Arts, the Museum of International Folk Art, the Museum of Indian Arts and Culture, and five monuments statewide. A four-day reduced rate pass to visit these museums and the Museum of Spanish Colonial Art can be purchased at any of the museums in the system. One-day passes to Jemez and Coronado state monuments are also available here.

The Museum of Fine Arts, next door to the Palace of the Governors, features a permanent collection of over ten thousand pieces. Some Indian pieces are included among the works of Georgia O'Keeffe and the Taos Masters. In conjunction with the Museum of Fine Arts, the *Governor's Gallery*, which displays rotating works of New Mexico artists, sometimes features Native artists.

The Institute of American Indian Arts Museum across from St. Francis Cathedral is owned and operated by Native Americans and devoted to their fine arts. The Institute's collection of contemporary Native American art is one of the most comprehensive in the world. Exhibits include the works of students and alumni of the institute, as well as those pertaining to the history and significance of Indian art. Demonstrations by native artisans are scheduled periodically, and the bookstore sells literature on the art, history, and traditions of Native Americans. The institute itself is a congressionally chartered college where Native Americans study the culture of their people. It has provided training for many of the leading Indian artists of today.

The **School of American Research** is a center for anthropological studies that houses the Indian Arts Research Center. Its excellent collection of Southwestern Indian art contains over eleven thousand objects from forty Southwestern tribes. Included are textiles, katsinas, easel paintings, baskets, and ethnographic objects spanning the years from 1540 to the present. Tours are conducted every Friday by appointment only. The facility is several blocks south of Old Town on Garcia Street.

Four blocks south of the plaza, on the south side of the Santa Fe River, along the Old Santa Fe Trail (now the narrow East DeVargas Street), is *Barrio de Analco Historic District*, which means "district on the other side of the water." This is the oldest neighborhood in Santa Fe and was originally settled in the early 1600s by Tlaxcala Indians, who were segregated from the Spanish who brought them here from Mexico.

San Miguel Mission, one of the oldest Christian churches in continuous use in the country, sits along the trail at the corner of E. DeVargas and College streets. Churches have been on this spot since the early 1600s, when the first one was built by Tlaxcalan Indian servants under the direction of Franciscan friars. The original church was destroyed in the Pueblo Revolt and then rebuilt in 1710, partially on the old foundation. The remains of this first chapel can be seen through peepholes near the altar.

Across the street is a building made of puddled adobe and billed as the oldest house in the United States. The house itself is believed to predate the Spanish, and it was built on remnants of the Pueblo of Analco, which occupied the south side of the Santa Fe River seven hundred years ago.

At the corner of Agua Fria and Guadalupe streets is **Santuario de Guadalupe**, the oldest U.S. shrine to Our Lady of Guadalupe, patron saint of Mexico. The church, built with three-foot thick walls in the late 1700s by Franciscan missionaries, is now a nonprofit cultural center. Of note are the sanctuary's valuable art and artifacts, including a portrait of Our Lady of Guadalupe, dated 1783 and signed by renowned Mexican colonial painter Jose de Alzibar.

Further along the Old Santa Fe Trail, on Camino Lejo about ten minutes south of the plaza, is *Museum Hill*, a cultural complex that brings together artifacts and experiences from all over the world to create a mix unique to Santa Fe. Here, the Museum of Indian Arts and Culture, Laboratory of Anthropology, and Wheelwright Museum of the American Indian house items specific to the understanding of Native Americans in New Mexico. Milner Plaza, which is the location of the Museum of Indian Arts and Culture and the Laboratory of Anthropology, is also home to the Museum of International Folk Art and an outdoor labyrinth.

One of the world's finest collections of artifacts detailing the history and contemporary culture of Pueblo, Navajo, and Apache tribes is housed on Museum Hill at the **Museum of Indian Arts and Culture**. Exhibits include Clovis points, a hunting net that measures 151 feet long, clothing, the first pot fired by San Ildefonso artist Maria Martinez, and thousands of other items. One of its important collections is of Navajo weaving and silverwork. Contemporary life is also represented, with stories of The People told in their own voices.

Other items from the fifty thousand in the museum's collection are rotated into displays. Much of the material is from the next-door **Laboratory of Anthropology**, which is the official state archaeological repository. Its extensive library of fifteen thousand volumes is available for research.

The museum frequently hosts dances and demonstrations of skills such as weaving and making pottery. The Resource Center has touch displays for children, and the adjacent Museum Hill Café serves Native American dishes. Books and Indian arts and crafts can be purchased in the gift shop.

Also on Museum Hill is the privately owned **Wheelwright Museum of the American Indian**, founded in 1937 by Mary Cabot Wheelwright and Navajo medicine man Hastin Klah to help preserve Navajo traditions at a time when they were facing extinction. Originally called the House of Navajo Religion, its entrance still faces the rising sun, and five logs symbolize the five worlds of the Navajo.

Today, the eight-sided structure, shaped like a Navajo hogan, is dedicated to the changing Native American cultures, and exhibits range from historic to contemporary Native American arts. The museum's collection of Navajo sandpaintings comprises over six hundred reproductions of sand images created during healing ceremonies. Also included in the exhibits are Apache, Plains, and Pueblo Indian art and craft items.

The Case Trading Post, in the basement, is modeled after an early reservation store and stocks a large selection of books and high-quality native arts and crafts. The knowledgeable staff can help with information pertaining to purchases.

At various times, dances, demonstrations, and ceremonies are conducted at the museum. Storyteller Joe Hayes spins Indian tales at 7pm on July and August weekends near the tipi outside. The museum also offers guided tours to local pueblos, adult workshops, and lectures. The research library also includes historical notes and papers recording traditional ceremonies and the details of Navajo life.

Santa Fe is a prime place for anyone shopping for Native American arts and crafts. Many of the stores offer outstanding pieces, both contemporary and traditional, and some

The Santa Fe Indian Market draws thousands of shoppers each year to Santa Fe.

of the most famous artists have their work for sale here. Unfortunately, along with this thriving market in quality art is a considerable amount of tacky pastiche, as well as fake pieces labeled as authentic, so "buyer beware."

Most of the shops are clustered around the plaza or along **Canyon Road**, a few blocks southeast of the plaza and one of the oldest streets in Santa Fe. For example, *Medicine Man Gallery* has a large collection of Maria Martinez pottery for sale, as well as other antique Native American art.

Pueblo Indians and padres once walked Canyon Road to follow the Santa Fe River through the mountains to Pecos Pueblo. Today, art galleries, historical buildings, gardens, restaurants, and unusual shops cluster together, making it an excellent place to become immersed in the local arts scene. Good sources of information about buying Native American arts and crafts can be found in the annual *Wingspread Collector's Gallery Guide,* the Southwestern Association for Indian Arts (SWAIA), and the Santa Fe Gallery Association.

EAST OF SANTA FE

Pecos National Historical Park is east of Santa Fe off I-25 via NM63. The upper Pecos River valley was the frontier of Pueblo Indian civilization from the thirteenth to the nineteenth centuries. At an ideal location near the valley's farmlands, with fresh water from creeks and springs, and on a natural trade route between the Pueblo farmers and Plains nomads, the settlement of Pecos Pueblo grew steadily in size and activity until it became one of the largest pueblos in the Southwest. At one time it was four or five stories high, with 660 rooms and twenty kivas. Over two thousand people lived here, protected by walls and a view of intruders approaching from either the Rio Grande Valley or the Great Plains.

Although it was called Pecos by its Keres Indian neighbors, its Towa-speaking inhabitants called it Cicuye. When the Spanish passed through in 1540, the people of Cicuye welcomed them with the music of drums and bird-bone flutes and an abundance of food. The Franciscans soon came to stay, converting Indians, building a mission, and filling the kivas with sand. During the 1680 Pueblo Revolt, the Indians burned the original church

A ladder descends into an underground kiva at Pecos National Historical Park.

and built a kiva over the rubble. A subsequent church and convent where the priests lived was built in 1717.

Because of drought, famine, the decline of trade, marauding Comanches, and European diseases, the population of Pecos began to dwindle in the 1770s. In 1838, the last few residents left to join Jemez Pueblo, and the wagons rumbling by on the Santa Fe Trail soon passed only crumbling ruins. In 1999, descendants of its last residents revived Pecos. Over two thousand people walked the eighty miles from Jemez Pueblo back along the route of their ancestors to the site of the ancient city.

The well-organized interpretive museum at the *visitor center* features exhibits, an audiovisual program, a diorama, and a bookstore. The easy, self-guided trail winds through the *ruins* where two kivas have been reconstructed and can be accessed via ladders through the roofs. At the south end are the impressive ruins of *San Antonio de Padua* Catholic church.

The following pueblos are easily accessed from Santa Fe: Tesuque, Pojoaque, Nambe, Cochiti, Santo Domingo, and San Felipe (see Chapter 16, The Pueblos of New Mexico, for details).

TAOS
Map #4

Around Town: El Rincón, Governor Bent House and Museum, Kit Carson Home and Museum, Kit Carson Park, Martinez Hacienda, Old Town
Nearby: Hupobi Ruin, Millicent Rogers Museum, San Francisco de Asis Church
Nearby Pueblos: Picuris Pueblo, Taos Pueblo

Coronado arrived at the stacked adobe *Taos Pueblo* in 1540, and the Spanish established a mission and trade network here shortly thereafter. Comanche raids against the new Spanish settlement were frequent, so many homes were built with a rear wall joining them for protection. Animosities, however, were put aside once a year at the *Taos Trade Fair*, a community-wide event where Ute, Comanche, and Apache traders bartered their buckskins and buffalo hides for Spanish weapons and Pueblo vegetables. The release of captives, both Indian and Spanish, was often part of the bargain. The tradition continued into the nineteenth century, when mountain men and Santa Fe Trail merchants joined the swap meet.

Except for traffic-clogged Main Street, Taos today remains reminiscent of those earlier times, filled with adobe buildings, more horizontal than vertical, clustered around *placitas* (small, interior patios). Among them are almost eighty art galleries. Northeast of town, the multistoried Taos Pueblo is home to about 1,500 Pueblo Indians. (For more information on the pueblo, see Chapter 16, The Pueblos of New Mexico, page 302.)

The large, informative *Taos Visitor Center* lies at the intersection of Paseo del Pueblo Sur (NM68) and Paseo del Canon (US64). The center provides a guided walking tour of the town, information on the numerous Pueblo ceremonies and town festivals, and a pass to visit five Taos museums with a discounted ticket.

Downtown Taos is best seen on foot, with the car parked in one of the nearby municipal lots. **Old Town** centers around Taos Plaza, once the terminus of El Camino Real, the Royal Road from Mexico City to Northern New Mexico, and later an important stop on the Santa Fe Trail.

Trade goods from Mexico arrived along El Camino Real at Martinez Hacienda and were bartered to the Indians.

On Bent Street in Old Town, a half-block west of the Taos Inn and one block north of the plaza, is the **Governor Bent House and Museum**. Bent was trader, trapper, mountain man, co-builder of Bent's Fort, and first governor of the Territory of New Mexico. His political tenure lasted less than a year, from 1846 until January of 1847, when he was killed during the Taos Rebellion, a revolt against the United States by Taos Indians and Hispanic settlers. His old adobe home has a small museum, with a mishmash of frontier and Bent family artifacts ranging from the historical to the bizarre.

Kit Carson, who was loved by the Cheyenne but hated by the Navajo after he reluctantly led the army campaign against them that ended with the Long Walk to Bosque Redondo, once lived in Taos. The **Kit Carson Home and Historical Museum** preserves the house he bought in 1843 as a wedding present for his bride, Josefa Jaramillo. It is filled with Carson memorabilia and other artifacts from nineteenth century Taos and the Old West. The museum is near the plaza on Kit Carson Road.

The Old Indian Trail, used for years for travel between Taos Pueblo and the Spanish settlement, cuts through **Kit Carson Park**, which is north of the plaza on NM68. Carson and Josefa are buried in the cemetery beside other notable early Taos residents.

The Taos Trade Fair is still reenacted today at the **Martinez Hacienda** (*La Hacienda de los Martinez*), the large nineteenth-century home of one of the most successful local traders. In the old trade room on the front placita, you can see where Indians and Europeans once bartered for goods. The twenty-one-room hacienda is in the northwest part of town and can be toured throughout the year. It is 2 miles from the plaza on NM240.

A twenty-two-room, three-story adobe called the Big House was once home to Taos Pueblo Indian Tony Luhan and his eastern heiress wife, Mabel Dodge Luhan. Literary, artistic, and intellectual luminaries like Georgia O'Keeffe, Carl Jung, Willa Cather, Ansel Adams, Thornton Wilder, and D. H. Lawrence all visited here. The rambling **Mabel**

TAOS TRADE FAIR

At the Taos Fair, Comanche, Navajo, Kiowa, Ute, and Apache came to gamble, race and trade horses, and barter. Pueblo traders mingled with Plains Indians and Spanish and American trappers and traders in a colorful, noisy panoply. Indians brought salt, turquoise, hides, and minerals used in making paint. Captives were ransomed or traded south to become domestic servants or to work in the mines. Knives, tools, copper ports, cloth, blankets, and food such as hardtack and biscuits mixed with brightly colored exotic feathers and live macaws, copper bells, and shells to create a vibrant marketplace.

Dodge Luhan House, full of Pueblo-style architectural features, is now part of a lodging and conference center.

Shopping is a favorite pastime for visitors to Taos. You can see evidence of the town's popularity as an art colony in the many fine galleries and shops. One of the best places to buy authentic Native American handcrafts is at Taos Pueblo (see Chapter 16, The Pueblos of New Mexico, page 302).

The atmosphere in the centuries-old adobe building housing *El Rincón* trading post is like both museum and store: dark, cluttered and full of ambience. In 1909, Ralph Meyers opened the building as the first Indian curio shop in Taos. Taos and Navajo Indians worked in his shop making native crafts to sell to tourists. Meyers went on to become the model for the honest white trader in Frank Waters' book *The Man Who Killed the Deer*. The post now buys and sells items from the Pueblo and Plains Indians plus Spanish colonial and American Old West cultures. It offers contemporary silver and souvenirs as well. Artifacts from years of trading are displayed in the back room. The La Dona Luz Inn is also on the premises.

NORTH OF TAOS

The **Millicent Rogers Museum** has an excellent collection of Southwest Indian and Hispanic arts and crafts. Jewelry, textiles, katsinas, paintings, craftsmen's tools from the seventeenth and eighteenth centuries, agricultural implements, baskets, and changing exhibits are all included, as well as one of the most important collections of the lifework of Maria Martinez, famous potter from San Ildefonso Pueblo. The museum is in a historic adobe house with views of the Sangre de Cristo Mountains. The gift shop has an impressive selection of Native American crafts and Spanish woodcarvings. It is approximately 4 miles north of the plaza and a half mile south of US64.

SOUTH OF TAOS

Four miles south of Taos on NM68 is **Hupobi,** the ruins of a thousand-room adobe pueblo clustered around three plazas. The pueblo has ties to the Tewa Indians and was occupied from the mid-fourteenth to the mid-sixteenth centuries. One of the most unusual features of Hupobi is its extensive grid gardens that indicate the use of gravel mulch. To make arrangements to visit, contact the BLM Taos Resource Area.

A few miles south of Taos on NM68 is Ranchos de Taos. The small village's **San Francisco de Asis Church**, built by Franciscans in 1730 to convert the Taos Indians and as protection from Indian raids, is one of the most photographed churches in New Mexico. Notable artist Georgia O'Keeffe made it the subject of one of her most famous paintings.

EVENTS

FEBRUARY *American Indian Day:* Held at the New Mexico State Capitol in Santa Fe.

APRIL *Spring Contest Powwow:* Powwow sponsored by Institute of American Indian Arts (IAIA) in Santa Fe, 800-804-6423.

MAY *Jemez Red Rocks Arts and Crafts Show/Starfeather Powwow:* Annual arts/crafts show and powwow. At Jemez Red Rocks Memorial Day weekend.

AUGUST *Best of Santa Fe:* Live auctions for two days, with hundreds of antique American Indian items to bid on. Held at La Fonda Hotel. Call 888-314-0343, www.allardauction.com.

Historic Indian and World Tribal Arts Show: Around eighty-five dealers display and sell fine antique tribal art from America and the world. Proceeds partly benefit the Museum of Indian Arts and Cultures. Held at College of Santa Fe, 703-914-1268, www.b4time.com.

Invitational Antique Indian Art Show: Large art show for antique (pre-1935) Native American art. 201 W. Marcy, Santa Fe, NM 87501, 505-984-6760.

Mountain Man Rendezvous: Re-creation of a trade fair during the fur trade era. Reenactments, music, participants dressed in period gear, skill demonstrations, merchandise, and more. At Palace of the Governors in Santa Fe, 505-476 5100, www.palaceofthegovernors.org.

Pueblo Independence Day: Jemez State Monument commemorates the Pueblo Revolt of 1680 with traditional relay footrace, native food, music, dance, and arts/crafts demonstration. Call 505-829-3530.

Santa Fe Indian Market: Around a hundred thousand people from all over the world come to Santa Fe for this major event, which is one of the most prestigious Native American art shows in the world. Highlights include 1,200 artists displaying and selling their work in over six hundred booths, a juried art show, food and demonstration booths, entertainment, and youth market. Sponsored by the Southwestern Association of Indian Arts. 505-983-5220, www.swaia.org.

SEPTEMBER *Mountain Man Rendezvous and Living History Days:* Games, contests, food, demonstrations, participants in period dress, exhibitions, fur trade, and Indian encampments. In Angel Fire on Labor Day weekend. Call 800-446-8117 or contact Spirit Fire Muzzle Loaders, PO Box 1322, Angel Fire, NM 87710, www.angelfirenm.com/mountainman.

Taos Trade Fair: Celebrates Taos's past as a trade center, especially during Spanish colonial days. Music, entertainment, skill and craft demonstrations, and arts/crafts vendors. At Hacienda de los Martinez in Taos. Call 505-758-1000 or Taos Historic Museums at 505-758-0505.

LATE SEPTEMBER-EARLY OCTOBER *Taos Fall Arts Festival:* The town's major arts gathering highlights artists of Taos County, including Native Americans. Includes juried art show, arts/crafts fair, gallery openings, and other events, such as Taos Pueblo feast. Call 800-732-8267 or 505-758-3873 or websites, www.taoschamber.org or www.taosfallarts.com.

OCTOBER *Children's Powwow:* Only major children's powwow in country. At the Wheelwright Museum in Santa Fe, 505-982-4636, 800-607-4636 or www.wheelwright.org.

Sun Mountain Gathering: Arts/crafts demonstrations. Archaeological exhibits, dancers, drummers, and hands-on exhibits to educate the public about native people, culture, and history. Museum of Indian Arts and Culture, 505-476-1250, www.miaclab.org.

Taos Storytelling Festival: Hear master storytellers such as Joe Hayes and Cisco Guevara spin tales from Native American and other traditions. In Taos. Sponsored by SOMOS, the Society of the Muse of the Southwest, 800-732-8267.

DECEMBER *Farolito Tour:* Music, Native American dances, refreshments, tour of San Jose de los Jemez Mission church. Jemez State Monument, 505-829-3530.

CONTACT INFORMATION

Armand Hammer United World College of the West
PO Box 248, Montezuma, NM 87731
505-454-4200
www.uwcaw.uwc.org

Bandelier National Monument
15 Entrance Road, Los Alamos, NM 87544
505-672-3861, ext.517
505-672-0343 (recorded message)
www.nps.gov/band
Visitor Center: Daily 8am-6pm, summer;
    9am-4:30pm, winter; 9am-5:30pm, spring
    & fall
Monument: Daily 6:30am-sunset; fee

Bradbury Science Museum
15th and Central, Los Alamos, NM 87545
505-667-4444 • www.lanl.gov/museum
Tue-Sat 10am-5pm, Sun-Mon 1pm-5pm; no fee

Bureau of Land Management
www.blm.gov/nm/st/en.html
    Taos Resource Area
    226 Cruz Alta Road, PO Box 6168, Taos,
        NM 87571
    505-758-8851

Canyon Road
www.canyonroadarts.com

Capulin Volcano National Monument
PO Box 40, Capulin, NM 88414
505-278-2201 • www.nps.gov/cavo
Daily 7:30am-6:30pm summer; daily 8am-
    4pm, winter; fee

Chimayo Museum
13 Plaza del Cerro, Chimayo, NM 87522
505-351-0945 • http://chimayo.org

Chimayo Trading Post/Marco Polo Shop
110 Sandia Drive Española, NM 87532
505-753-9414

Cross of the Martyrs
600 Paseo de Peralta, Santa Fe, NM

El Rincón
114 Kit Carson Road, Taos, NM 87571
505-758-9188

El Santuario de Chimayo
Chimayo, NM 87522
505-351-4889
Daily, 9am-4pm

Española Valley Chamber of Commerce
710 North Paseo de Oñate, Española, NM
    87532
505-753-2831
www.espanolanmchamber.com

Florence Hawley Ellis Museum of Anthropology
HC77, Box 11, Abiquiu, NM 87510
877-804-4678 or 505-685-4333
www.ghostranch.org/museums
Tues-Sat 9am-5pm, with extended summer
    hours

Folsom Man Museum
PO Box 385, Main Street, Folsom, NM 88419
505-278-2122 (summer) or 505-278-3616
    (winter)
www.folsommuseum.netfirms.com
Daily 10am-5pm, summer; weekends 10am-
    5pm, May & Oct; fee

Fort Union National Monument
Watrous, NM 87753
505-425-8025 • www.nps.gov/foun
Daily 8am-6pm, summer; daily 8am-4pm,
    winter; fee

Fort Burgwin
SMU-IN-TAOS
Southern Methodist University, PO Box
    750145, Dallas, TX 75275
214-768-3657 • www.smu.edu/taos

Ghost Ranch
www.ghostranch.org
    Conference Center
    HC77 Box 11, Abiquiu, NM 87510
    505-685-4519
    Florence Hawley Ellis Museum of Anthropology
    Ghost Ranch Living Museum
    Ruth Hall Museum of Paleontology
    505-685-4333

Governor Bent House and Museum
117A Bent Street, PO Box 153, Taos, NM 87571
505-758-2376
www.laplaza.org/art/museums_bent.php3
Daily 9am-5pm, summer; daily 10am-4pm,
    winter; fee

Holy Cross Catholic Church
Santa Cruz, NM 87567
505-753-3345

Institute of American Indian Arts Museum
108 Cathedral Place, PO Box 20007 Santa Fe,
NM 87501
505-983-1777 • www.iaia.edu
Daily 9am-5pm June-Sept; Mon-Sat 10am-
5pm & Sun 12-5pm Oct-May; fee

Jemez Springs (town)
PO Box 269, Jemez Springs, NM 87025
505-829-3540 • www.jemezsprings.org

Jemez State Monument
PO Box 143, Jemez Springs, NM 87025
505-829-3530
www.nmmonuments.org/about.php?_instid=JEME
Wed-Mon 8:30am-5pm except closed Tuesday
in winter; fee

Kit Carson Home and Historical Museum
113 Kit Carson Road, Taos, NM 87571
505-758-0505 • www.taoshistoricmuseums.com
Daily 9am-5pm May-Oct; call for winter
hours; fee

Kit Carson Park
211 Paseo del Norte, Taos, NM 87571
505-758-8234

Laboratory of Anthropology (MIAC)
708 Camino Lejo, Santa Fe, NM 87505
505-476-1250 • www.miaclab.org
Daily 10am-5pm, summer; Tues-Sun 10am-
5pm, winter; fee

Las Vegas Chamber of Commerce
701 Grand Avenue, PO Box 128, Las Vegas
87701
800-832-5947 *or* 505-425-8631
http://lasvegasnm.org

**Las Vegas Museum & Rough Riders Memorial
Collection**
727 Grand Ave. Las Vegas, NM 87701
505-454-1401, ext. 283
www.lasvegasmuseum.org
Tues-Sun 10am-4pm, May-Sept; Tues-Sat
10am-4pm, Oct-Apr; donation

Los Alamos County Historical Museum
1921 Juniper St., PO Box 43, Los Alamos NM
87544
505-662-4493; 505-662-6272 for changing
exhibits
www.losalamos.com/historicalsociety
Mon-Sat 9:30am-4:30pm & Sun 11am-5pm,
summer; Mon-Sat 10am-4pm & Sun 1pm-
4pm, winter; no fee

Los Alamos Visitor Center
109 Central Park Square, Los Alamos, NM 87544
800-444-0707 • http://visit.losalamos.com

Mabel Dodge Luhan House
240 Morafo Lane, Taos, NM 87571
800-846-2235 *or* 505-751-9686
www.MabelDodgeLuhan.com

Marco Polo Shop (*See* Chimayo Trading Post)

Martinez Hacienda
708 Ranchitos Road, Taos, NM 87571
505-758-1000 • www.taoshistoricmuseums.com
Daily 9am-5pm, summer; winter hours vary; fee

Medicine Man Gallery
602A Canyon Road, Santa Fe, NM 87501
866-894-7451 • www.medicinemangallery.com

Millicent Rogers Museum
1504 Millicent Rogers Rd., PO Box A, Taos,
NM 87571
505-758-2462 • www.millicentrogers.org •
www.taosmuseums.org/mrm.php
Daily 10am-5pm, except closed Monday Nov-
March; fee

Montezuma Hot Springs
Las Vegas, NM 87701
Daily 6am-midnight; no fee

Museum of Fine Arts
107 W. Palace Avenue, Santa Fe, NM 87501
505-476-5072 • www.mfasantafe.org
Tue-Sun 10am-5pm; fee (no fee Friday evenings)

Museum of Indian Arts and Culture (MIAC)
710 Camino Lejo, PO Box 2087, Santa Fe,
NM 87504-2087
505-476-1269 *or* 505-476-1250
www.indianartsandculture.org
Daily 10am-5pm, summer; Tue-Sun 10am-
5pm, winter; fee

Museum of New Mexico Pass
505-827-6463
www.museumofnewmexico.org

**New Mexico Highlands University's Anthro-
pology Laboratory**
Hewett Hall, National Avenue & 12th Street,
New Mexico Highlands University, Las
Vegas, NM 87701
505-454-3321 *or* 505-454-3283 for
appointment
www.nmculture.org/cgi-bin/
instview.cgi?_recordnum=HAL

New Mexico State Parks
1220 South St. Francis Drive, Santa Fe, NM
 87505
888-667-2757 *or* 505-476-3355
www.emnrd.state.nm.us/PRD/index.htm

Ojo Caliente Mineral Springs
PO Box 68, 50 Los Banos Drive, Ojo Caliente
 NM 87549
800-222-9162 *or* 505-583-2233
www.ojocalientespa.com

Oñate Monument and Visitor's Center
State Road 68, Alcalde, NM 87511
505-852-4639
www.rioarribanm.com/resource.htm
Mon-Fri 8am-5pm

Orilla Verde Recreation Area (*See* BLM)

Palace of the Governors
105 E. Palace Avenue, Santa Fe, NM 87501
505-476-5100 • www.palaceofthegovernors.org
Daily 10am-5pm, summer; Tues-Sun 10am-5pm,
 winter; fee (except 5pm-8pm Fri, no fee)

**Palace of the Governors Native American Art
 Program**
505-476-5100 • www.newmexicoindianart.com
8am-dusk

Pecos National Historical Park
State Road 63, PO Box 418, Drawer 11, Pecos,
 NM 87552
505-757-6414, -6032 • www.nps.gov/peco
Daily 8am-6pm, summer; 8am-4:30pm,
 winter; fee

Poshouinge Ruins
Abiquiu, NM 87510

Posi-ouinge Pueblo (*See* Ojo Caliente)

Pot Creek Cultural Site
Carson National Forest, 208 Cruz Alta Road,
 Taos, NM 87571
505-758-6200
www.fs.fed.us/r3/carson/historic_site
Wed-Sun 9am-4pm, late June-early Sept

San Francisco de Asis Church
Ranchos de Taos, NM 87557
505-758-2754

San Miguel Mission (Santa Fe)
401 Old Santa Fe Trail, Santa Fe, NM 87501
505-983-3974
Mon-Sat 9am-5pm; Sun 10am-4pm; Mass Sun
 5pm

Santa Fe Convention and Visitors Bureau
Box 909, Santa Fe, NM 87504
800-777-2489 *or* 505-984-6760
www.santafe.org

Santa Fe Gallery Association
PO Box 9245, Santa Fe, NM 87504
800-359-9026 *or* 505-982-1648
www.santafegalleries.net

Santa Fe Trail Museum
614 Maxwell Avenue, PO Box 323, Springer,
 NM 87747
505-483-2682
Daily 9am-4pm, summer only; fee

Santa Fe Visitor Center
491 Old Santa Fe Trail, Santa Fe, NM 87503
505-827-7400

Santuario de Chimayo
PO Box 235, Chimayo, NM 87522
505-351-4889
www.archdiocesesantafe.org/AboutASF/
 Chimayo.html
Daily 9am-4pm, Oct-Apr; daily 9am-5pm,
 June-Sept

Santuario de Guadalupe
100 S. Guadalupe, Santa Fe, NM 87501
505-988-2027
Mon-Sat 9am-4pm, May-Oct; Mon-Fri 9am-
 4pm, Nov-Apr; no fee

**School of American Research/Indian Arts
 Research Center**
660 Garcia, PO Box 2188, Santa Fe, NM
 87504
505-954-7205 • www.sarweb.org

SMU-IN-TAOS/Fort Burgwin
6580 Hwy 518, Ranchos de Taos 87557
505-758-8322 • www.smu.edu/taos

**Southwestern Association for Indian Arts
 (SWAIA)**
PO Box 969, Santa Fe, NM 87504-0969
505-983-5220 • www.swaia.org

Taos Chamber of Commerce/Visitors Center
1139 Paseo del Pueblo Sur, Paseo del Pueblo
 Sur (Hwy 68) and Paseo del Canon (Hwy
 64), Taos, NM 87571
800-732-8267 *or* 505-758-3873
www.taoschamber.com

United States National Forest Service
Carson National Forest
208 Cruz Alta Road, Taos, NM 87571
505-758-6200 • www.fs.fed.us/r3/carson
Pot Creek Cultural Site
www.fs.fed.us/r3/carson/historic_site/
    adobe.shtml
Santa Fe National Forest
1474 Rodeo Road, Santa Fe, NM 87505
505-438-7840
www.fs.fed.us/r3/sfe/districts/jemez

Wheelwright Museum of the American Indian
704 Camino Lejo, PO Box 5153, Santa Fe,
    NM 87505
800-607-4636 *or* 505-982-4636
www.wheelwright.org
Mon-Sat 10am-5pm and Sun 1pm-5pm; no
    fee (donations welcome)

Wingspread Collector's Gallery Guide
116 Central Ave SW, Suite 201, Albuquerque,
    NM USA 87102
800-873-4278 *or* 505-245-4200
www.collectorsguide.com

NEW MEXICO'S I-40 CORRIDOR

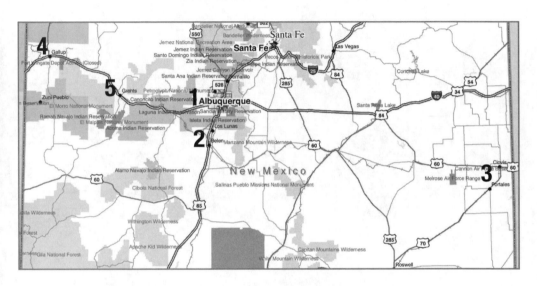

1. Albuquerque
2. Belén
3. Clovis/Portales

4. Gallop
5. Grants

CHAPTER 19

NEW MEXICO'S I-40 CORRIDOR

ALBUQUERQUE
Map #1

Around Town: Albuquerque Museum of Art and History, Old Town, Indian Pueblo Cultural
Center, Maxwell Museum of Anthropology, Petroglyph National Monument
Nearby: Alamo Navajo Chapter, Coronado State Monument, Jemez State Monument, Salinas
Pueblo Missions National Monument, To'hajiilee Navajo Chapter, Turquoise Trail (Tijeras
Pueblo, Museum of Archaeology and Material Culture, Sandia Cave, Cerrillos)
Nearby Pueblos: Laguna Pueblo, Isleta Pueblo, Jemez Pueblo, Santa Ana Pueblo, Zia Pueblo

Each night, the residents of Albuquerque go to bed atop the previous campsites of six
hundred generations. Of the seven thousand prehistoric sites that have been found in the
whole of Bernalillo County, well over half of them now lie beneath the city. One of the earliest of these sites—a Folsom shelter built eleven thousand years ago when the entire county
probably had fewer than a hundred people living in it—now lies in the populous suburb
of Rio Rancho.

After the appearance of the Folsom culture, the number of people in the area built
slowly over the next eight thousand years, so that by 1000 B.C. the estimated population
was somewhere between one thousand and fifteen hundred. Then, the people learned
about maize, and the population exploded, along with the quantity of pithouses they constructed for homes.

More than a millennium later, Pueblo settlements began to appear as local residents
learned to build four-story houses out of adobe composed of twigs, grass, and mud.
Along with maize, these farmers also learned to cultivate beans and squash. As the size
of their harvests grew, so did their villages, and the Rio Grande Valley soon became a
trade crossroads.

By A.D. 1050, the area was thriving, partly because it was located on the southeastern
boundary of the Chaco culture. When Chaco declined, the Indians moved from the valley into the rolling hills of the nearby Sandia and Manzano Mountains. By A.D. 1300,

ALBUQUERQUE

though, drought had forced them back again to the waters of the Rio Grande, where they set about constructing even larger pueblos.

Although Coronado and his entourage passed through the valley in 1540, Spaniards did not settle Albuquerque until 150 years later. In 1706, thirty families from Bernalillo moved to what is now Old Town, attracted by the cool waters and spreading cottonwood trees of the Rio Grande.

Albuquerque is now New Mexico's largest city, with a population of 450,000 and a wealth of economic and other opportunities that attract people from diverse cultures, including Indians from over 150 tribes. Attractions range from the National Hispanic Cultural Center to the Sandia Peak Tramway to the International Balloon Museum. The unique Rattlesnake Museum provides a close-up look at this indigenous snake, and native flora and fauna are showcased at the Rio Grande Botanic Garden.

The Rio Grande has since shifted its course to the west, but **Old Town**, off Rio Grande Boulevard NW, remains as a reminder of Spanish colonial times. An eighteenth-century Spanish adobe church, *San Felipe de Neri*, dominates the north end of the central plaza of Old Town. The church's interior mixes eighteenth- and nineteenth-century building traditions, including a stamped metal ceiling and plaster walls painted to resemble marble.

Dozens of quaint shops, galleries, and restaurants housed in earth-red adobe cluster around the plaza and give it a special ambience. Shoppers here can find everything from a belt made in Taiwan to a hundred-year-old Navajo rug. In summer under the east portico, local Indian artisans display their wares. You can learn more about the history, geology, and mythology of the turquoise so important to Native American arts and crafts at the *Museum of Turquoise,* located in a strip mall just west of Old Town. The museum's vast collection comes from sixty mines around the world.

The **Albuquerque Museum of Art and History,** in the museum complex on the northwest corner of Old Town, covers the history of the town and the Middle Rio Grande Valley from the arrival of the Spanish to the current day. The art of regional artists is highlighted, and the museum hosts traveling exhibits that often include American Indian art. An outdoor sculpture garden, café, and gift shop are also part of the facility.

Another part of the museum is *Casa San Ysidro,* in the village of Corrales north of Albuquerque. This large compound of historic and recreated buildings depicts architectural styles, beginning with Spanish Colonial New Mexican. The 1,300-item collection includes period furnishings, devotional art, and utilitarian goods. Native American textiles, pottery, and baskets are part of the collection. Visiting Casa San Ysidro requires joining a guided tour. It is 3.2 miles north on Corrales Road and then west on Old Church Road.

The **Indian Pueblo Cultural Center** one block north of I-40 on 12th Street provides an excellent introduction to Pueblo art, history, and culture. The center, owned and operated by the nineteen Pueblos of New Mexico, is housed in a building that resembles Pueblo Bonito in Chaco Canyon.

Pottery and crafts from each community are exhibited, as well as replicas of traditional homes. Historical photography by Edward S. Curtis, stone-tipped spears, Cochiti storyteller figures, instructions on how to bake bread in a horno, a video detailing the methods used by potter Maria Martinez, and Acoma pottery are some of the highlights.

A changing gallery showcases different Native American artists, and crafts are demonstrated on summer weekends. In the central courtyard, murals decorate the walls, and dancers in traditional regalia often perform to the beat of animal-skin drums. Photography is allowed.

The *Pueblo Harvest Café* serves Indian tacos (fry bread topped with pinto beans, tomato, lettuce, cheese, and salsa), green chili stew, blue corn pancakes, and other Pueblo food, much of it spiced with a healthy dose of chili pepper. The bookstore stocks an excellent selection of books on the Southwest and Native Americans, and the large gift shop sells souvenirs and quality Indian-made arts and crafts that range from clothing to sandpaintings. Visitors can also arrange for guided tours from the cultural center to Acoma and Zuni pueblos.

The research center, which is open to the public, has photos, books, and tapes about the Pueblos from the late 1800s to the present. The children's museum, open by appointment only, provides hands-on activities depicting Pueblo history and lifestyle. The adjacent *Four Winds Travel Center* has an Arby's restaurant, fuel, and convenience items for sale.

The large **Maxwell Museum of Anthropology**, on the campus of the University of New Mexico, chronicles the history of people around the world, with an emphasis on the Native Americans of the Southwest from Paleo-Indian times to the present. Some of the items from the collections of the university's renowned anthropology department are featured, as well as exhibits highlighting contemporary voices of the Southwest. Look for a recreation of a room at Chaco Canyon, hands-on activities for children, and prehistoric pottery from the Mimbres and Pueblo cultures.

In the basement, several rooms of ceramics, textiles, clothing, basketry, and other ethnological collections from around the world can be viewed by appointment. Over 230,000 images are in the photography archives, including many of the earliest photographs of the Pueblo and Navajo cultures, taken in the nineteenth century.

The museum also sponsors lectures, workshops, demonstrations, field trips, and music and dance performances. It is located on campus, between Martin Luther King Avenue and Las Lomas and east of University Boulevard on Redondo Drive. Limited parking is west of the museum between Las Lomas and MLK Avenue. Permits are available from the museum store.

Hidden in the jagged lava rocks of West Mesa, **Petroglyph National Monument** preserves one of the largest sites of rock art in North America (17 miles long and encompassing five extinct volcanoes). Etched into the igneous rock along the cliffs are over twenty thousand images of animals, people, and recognizable symbols, as well as those whose meanings are hidden in the mists of time. Most were left by native cultures between A.D. 1300 and 1680, but European immigrants are represented, too.

The *visitor center* has interpretive exhibits, a bookstore, summer cultural demonstrations, and guided hikes for groups. Three self-guided trails (wheelchair-accessible) in Boca Negra Canyon lead past the images. Picnic tables are also available.

To reach the visitor center, from I-40 take Unser Boulevard north 3 miles. The Boca Negra Unit is 5 miles north.

Albuquerque has numerous shopping opportunities at stores that stock excellent and authentic Native American arts and crafts, both historical and contemporary. Many of the most famous artists have their work in galleries here.

Laguna Pueblo, Isleta Pueblo, Santa Ana Pueblo, and Zia Pueblo are all near Albuquerque (see Chapter 16, The Pueblos of New Mexico, for information).

Thousands of rock art designs are readily visible at Petroglyph National Monument near Albuquerque.

THE TURQUOISE TRAIL FROM ALBUQUERQUE TO SANTA FE

The Turquoise Trail is a pleasant day-drive from Albuquerque to Santa Fe through the Sandia Mountains. The mountains retain their spiritual importance to the Sandia Pueblo people, who visit them regularly for ceremonies. Along the drive you can visit two ancient Indian sites, several small museums, a ski area, and towns that still retain their feel of the Old West.

Take I-40 east of Albuquerque to the NM536 exit near the small town of Tijeras, which is where the route begins. The ruins of **Tijeras Pueblo** are on the north side of the Sandia District Ranger Station. An interpretive trail leads through the pueblo that was once home to several hundred people.

Around A.D. 1313, people moved to Tijeras from the drought-stricken Rio Grande Valley. In this upland, they found a reliable water supply, and until about 1450 farmed corn and bartered with travelers on the well-used trade routes that passed by the pueblo. The ranger station interprets their lives with displays and Saturday afternoon programs consisting of music, lectures, and guided tours. Call in advance for special tours. The ruins can be visited at other times by following the self-guided trail.

This is also the place to ask about a tour to Sandia Cave (see below).

Cedar Crest, a few miles beyond Tijeras, is home to the **Museum of Archaeology and Material Culture**, where you can trace the timeline of local inhabitants, from Clovis hunters in the Ice Age to the victims of Wounded Knee.

Sandia Crest National Scenic Byway (NM536) beckons a few miles farther along the Turquoise Trail. As the road winds upward to Sandia Crest, it passes through four life zones and approximates the climate change between New Mexico and Canada's Hudson Bay. Before reaching the crest, the road passes Balsam Glade Picnic Ground. At this point a dirt-and-gravel road begins its 5-mile descent into Las Huertas Canyon and the trailhead for **Sandia Cave** on the northeast flank of the Sandia Mountains.

Deep in Sandia Cave, spear points, scrapers, and claws from a giant sloth extinct since 10,000 B.C. were discovered. The cave's stratigraphy is controversial, but this site was the first physical evidence of the Sandia culture, a contemporary of the Clovis.

Although this important archaeological site has been cleared of artifacts, you can still visit it. An easy trail leads a half-mile from the parking lot to a steep spiral staircase that climbs to the cave. Expansive views take in Mount Taylor in the distance, the Socorro Mountains to the southwest, and the Jemez range to the northwest.

Sandia Cave can also be reached from exit 242 on I-25 onto NM165. The cave is about 2 miles past the village of Placitas.

After passing Sandia Ski Area, the scenic byway ends at Sandia Crest, where you can eat at the restaurant, hike around the crest, and visit the observation deck for views of Mount Taylor (sacred to the Navajo), the Rio Grande (home to many Pueblo people), and the city of Albuquerque.

Back on the Turquoise Trail, the road follows the contours of the rolling high desert through a landscape dotted with pinyon pines and junipers. Nearby, Indians mined turquoise and lead for making jewelry and pottery in prehistoric times. When the Spanish came, they continued with the extraction of wealth from the mines, sending turquoise home to Spain to become part of the crown jewels.

In the small town of **Cerrillos**—once boasting twenty-one saloons and four hotels and a serious candidate for the capital of New Mexico—a turquoise mining museum testifies to the importance of this mineral. You will find it in the adobe *Casa Grande Trading Post*, which also has a petting zoo and sells antiques. Look in the town's *Historic Park* for a pit dug as a turquoise mine a thousand years ago, and note the nearby Cerrillos Hills that were long-used as a trail marker.

Miners brought their burros with them when they came to the Southwest searching for gold, silver, copper, and other minerals.

As you continue further on the Turquoise Trail, you will pass other towns that once sported saloons, prospectors, and other accoutrements of the mining boom, when the promise of wealth lured thousands to the region and changed it forever. Now the dusty streets house craft shops and artists, a unique assortment of museums and the occasional Hollywood crew, on location for a film shoot.

The Turquoise Trail ends at I-25 near Santa Fe.

NORTH OF ALBUQUERQUE

Coronado State Monument contains the partially reconstructed ruins of Kuaua or "Evergreen" Pueblo on the west bank of the Rio Grande. Kuaua, occupied between 1300 and 1650, was once a popular meeting ground for the Ancestral Puebloan and Mogollon cultures. In its heyday, the pueblo contained over one thousand rooms. It is possible that Coronado spent the winter of 1540 here with his entourage of 1,200 people and a stockyard of pigs, chickens, and cattle.

An interpretive trail winds through the ruins to a restored kiva, once used for religious ceremonies. You can enter the kiva via a ladder through the roof's smoke hole to see the walls decorated with reproductions of the original murals.

The *museum* chronicles the early settlement of the Rio Grande Valley. Some of the outstanding original paintings from the kiva are displayed, ranging from yellow-and-black masked katsinas to white rabbits and black fish. The children's wing has hands-on activities, and a video features Native American and Spanish lifestyles.

You can camp or picnic in the nearby *Coronado State Park*, which is also the headquarters for Bernalillo State Forest.

Coronado State Monument is located on US550 1 mile northwest of Bernalillo.

WEST OF ALBUQUERQUE

The small **To'hajiilee Chapter** is home to a portion of the Navajo tribe who settled at Cañoncito at the time of the Long Walk. Now considered a part of the Navajo Nation, about 740 members live here between two portions of the Laguna Pueblo. The chapter is west of Albuquerque, north of I-40.

Also at the time of the Long Walk, another portion of the Navajo Nation settled in the mountains southwest of Albuquerque where the isolated *Alamo Navajo Chapter* of the Navajo now live. Camping, fishing, hunting, and hiking are available by permit. The reservation is on NM169 off US60 at Magdalena. A *Navajo Arts and Crafts Enterprise* is at mile marker 30 on NM169.

BELÉN
Map #2

Nearby: Salinas Pueblo Missions National Monument, Tomé Hill

Taos isn't the only place in New Mexico that has attracted artists with the vibrant colors of its land and sky. Belén is home to the noted artist Judy Chicago and others who range from photographers to sculptors. The town also lies at the crossroads of two major highways and makes a convenient place to stay when exploring the area.

NORTH OF BELÉN

Tomé Hill rises north of Belén as a reminder of early volcanic activity in the area. Its prominence has attracted people for hundreds of years, who have used the hill as a landmark, lookout point, farmland, hunting territory, and for spiritual purposes. Most of the 1,800 petroglyphs found here were probably made by Pueblo people, but some of the circle designs might be as old as two thousand years. Kokopelli, shield bearers, spirals, horned serpents, geometric designs, and animal and human figures are all carved into the basalt boulders. El Camino Real skirted the base of El Tomé, and Spanish Penitentes later made it an important spiritual destination of their own.

Today, several trails lead to a summit shrine and Christian crosses, but the South Trail has been designated as the official route to the top. The quarter-mile climb is somewhat steep along a hard-packed trail. Two petroglyphs are off an unsigned trail near the top. Most of the rest of the petroglyphs are in rugged terrain and not accessible to the public. Tomé Hill is still used for spiritual pilgrimages, and visitors are asked to respect the sacred nature of the site.

SOUTHEAST OF BELÉN

A tour of **Salinas Pueblo Missions National Monument** starts south of Belén via I-25 and US60, or southeast of town on NM47 to US60, and then east toward the town of Mountainair. Salinas contains the ruins of three pueblos and Spanish missions and is an excellent place to gain an understanding of the cultural struggle between the Pueblo people and invading Spanish colonists.

In the tenth century, the inhabitants of the Salinas Valley were possibly part of the Mogollon culture. They gathered wild berries and nutritious pinyon nuts and hunted deer and antelope. In their irrigated fields they grew corn, beans, and squash. Family groups lived together in pithouses, which by A.D. 1100 were replaced by pole-and-thatch dwellings called *jacales*, which may have developed from Ancestral Puebloan influences. *Jacales*, in turn, gave way to apartment-style adobe buildings.

Between A.D. 1100 and 1500, Salinas grew as a populous trade center, and by the end of the sixteenth century, as many as ten thousand people lived in the area. Residents traded salt mined from lakes in the valley to the people of the Rio Grande pueblos and the Great Plains.

In 1598, the area came under Spanish rule. The Salinas residents, only lightly armed and described by the priests as mild and meek, were easily converted to Christianity, but heavy demands for tribute to the Crown and support of the Franciscan missions took their toll. In the 1660s and 1670s, epidemics and increased Apache raids, coupled with drought and famine, decimated the population of Salinas. By the late 1670s, the pueblos were deserted and were being called the "cities that died of fear."

Today, you can visit the ruins of three pueblos—Abo, Gran Quivira, and Quarai—all within a 25-mile radius of Mountainair. Each of the pueblos is administered as a separate unit, with interpretive information, a ranger on duty, self-guided trails, and picnic areas. Quarai and Gran Quivira also have archaeological displays.

A good place to start your tour is at the headquarters in Mountainair, on the corner of Ripley and Broadway (US60). Displays of the art and artifacts of Salinas and an audiovisual program introduce its culture and history.

Abo Ruins, now part of Salinas National Monument.
The pueblo was built beside a major trade route.

Abo Pueblo, at one time one of the largest Pueblo villages in the Southwest, is adjacent to what was once the major east-west trade route through Abo Pass. Tompiro Indians built the pueblo out of bright red sandstone near the gently flowing Abo River. They inhabited it from the 1300s to the 1670s, peacefully farming their fields.

By the late 1620s, Spaniards, using Indian labor, had built the church of San Gregorio beside the pueblo. They later erected a larger church and monastery, with two-foot-thick walls rising thirty feet high and supported by a sophisticated stone buttressing system. Much of the church can still be seen today, but only cactus-covered mounds mark the site of the dwellings.

Abo is 9 miles west of Mountainair off US60.

Gran Quivira Pueblo, on a hill majestically overlooking the Salinas Valley, has the most extensive of the pueblo ruins, with multiple levels of dwellings erected atop one another, each succession showing more sophisticated building skills. A lively trade was carried on from Gran Quivira with people in the Galisteo Basin, Acoma-Zuni region, and the Great Plains.

The earliest village began around A.D. 1200. By the time the Spanish came in 1598, Gran Quivira had around 1,500 inhabitants. The newcomers called it "Pueblo of the Striped Ones," because the Tompiro residents had the custom of painting stripes on their faces. Their pottery, too, was decorated with black and white stripes.

The Spanish erected two churches here, San Isidro in 1629 and San Buenaventura in 1659, with massive thirty-foot-high and six-foot-thick walls of blue-gray limestone. San Buenaventura was never completed, and the pueblo was abandoned in 1672.

Gran Quivira is on NM55 about 26 miles south of Mountainair.

Quarai Pueblo is the smallest of the three pueblos, built around A.D. 1300. About six hundred people lived here in what was once the southernmost of the Tiwa-speaking villages. The church of *Nuestra Senora de La Purisima Conception de Curac* was constructed by pueblo women and children under the direction of Spanish priests. It was finished in 1629, and even though the dirt roof has long since washed away, it remains the most complete of the large Salinas churches. A trail leads by the unexcavated pueblo dwellings to the mission. A grove of towering cottonwoods that once provided welcome shade for the Tiwas now protects several picnic tables.

Quarai is 8 miles north of Mountainair on NM55, then west of Punta de Agua on a gravel road.

CLOVIS/PORTALES
Map #3

Nearby: Blackwater Draw Archaeological Site and Museum, Eula Mae Edwards Museum and Art Gallery

Of special interest to archaeologists are the fluted Clovis points found near the town of Portales at what is now the **Blackwater Draw Archaeological Site and Museum.** These distinctive projectile points date back thirteen thousand years to the earliest known culture in New Mexico. Although there is now doubt that Clovis was the earliest culture in the New World, this important site was occupied for thousands of years and preserves a sequential record connecting the Paleo-Indian Clovis culture through Folsom and Portales to Archaic times.

Early Clovis people lived in small family bands, moving from camp to camp. They hunted now-extinct big game like mammoths and ancient bison and watched warily to protect themselves from saber-toothed tigers and dire wolves. As the regional climate changed, the lush vegetation that supported these large animals died. Over time, the people learned to hunt smaller animals and to utilize the plants that were left. By about 5000 B.C., their adaptation had given rise to the Archaic culture.

The site, found by a highway worker in 1932, is near a dried-up pond once fed by the Brazos River and used as a watering hole by Pleistocene animals and Paleo-Indians. Nearby depressions in the ground are thought to have been shafts they dug for water during times of drought.

The combination research facility and museum, operated by Eastern New Mexico University, has audiovisual presentations and displays of fossils and artifacts from the cultures found on site. Picnic and camping sites are nearby, and tours of the 160-acre site are available. The dirt south trail is a quarter-mile self-guided walk, and plans are in the works to create a self-guided north trail. The archaeological site, which is still being studied, is west of the museum on NM476. The museum is about 7 miles northeast of Portales and 8 miles south of Clovis on US70.

Eula Mae Edwards Museum and Art Gallery displays the novelist's prehistoric artifacts from local archaeological discoveries and hosts art shows. The museum is on the Clovis Community College campus east of Portales on NM 70 (south of CR10 on Schepps Boulevard).

Roosevelt County Chamber of Commerce in town has more information.

WEST OF CLOVIS/PORTALES
The forced relocation of the Mescalero Apache to what is now **Fort Sumner State Monument** began in late 1862 when Colonel Kit Carson, acting under orders from Brigadier General James H. Carleton, led a raid on a band of Mescalero in southern New

Mexico. After their defeat the Apache survivors were incarcerated here at the Bosque Redondo Indian Reservation.

Carson was then sent north to deal with the Navajo, where he burned their crops, killed their livestock, and starved thousands into submission. In 1863 and 1864, eight to nine thousand gaunt survivors were forcibly marched the 350 miles to Ft. Sumner to become farmers and to learn to live with their traditional enemies, the Apache. This tragic journey is still referred to as the "Long Walk" by the Navajo, who lost many of their ancestors along the way.

Apache and Navajo tried to coexist in this forbidding place and learn to farm, but a series of disasters doomed their attempts. In 1865, about 450 Mescalero, fed up with the hail, drought, cutworms, Comanche raids, alkaline water, and shortages of food and fuel, escaped from Bosque Redondo and returned to their spiritual home in the White and Sacramento mountains. By 1868, after years of deprivation, the Navajo had also departed, having been released by an army that finally admitted failure. Nearly one-third of the Indians had died during captivity.

You can see the thirty-five or so cottonwood trees that still survive out of the thousands planted by the Navajo and Mescalero. You can also hike the interpretive trail and visit the museum, which has artifacts from the old fort and exhibits depicting reservation life. Living history programs can be arranged for large groups.

Bosque Redondo Memorial honors the Navajo and Apache who died here or on the Long Walk, as well as the tribes' recovery. It was designed by a Navajo architectural firm and incorporates cultural symbols throughout, such as the clockwise path that winds through a cottonwood grove. The path leads to a doorway aligned with the winter solstice and a six-sided structure representing traditional shelter.

Fort Sumner State Monument is north of Roswell on US285 and NM20.

GALLUP
Map #4

Around Town: Gallup Cultural Center, Navajo Code Talkers Room, Red Rock Museum
Nearby: Red Rock State Park, Ramah Navajo Reservation
Nearby Reservations in Other Chapters: Acoma Pueblo, Laguna Pueblo, Hopi Reservation,
  Navajo Nation, Zuni Pueblo

The **Navajo Code Talkers Room** in the Gallup/McKinley Chamber of Commerce Building on historic Route 66 honors U.S. soldiers from the Navajo Nation in World War II. Using their native language, they developed a vital wartime code that Japanese intelligence was never able to crack. Photos and memorabilia commemorate the men.

The historic Santa Fe Railroad Depot houses the **Gallup Cultural Center**, operated by the Southwest Indian Foundation. Stories, songs, and exhibits relate the development of the art and life of local native peoples. A Gallery of the Masters features outstanding Native American art, the Kiva Cinema shows documentaries on the area, and nightly Indian dances are held on summer evenings at the outdoor pavilion just east of the center. You can shop for Indian art at the *Storyteller Gift Shop*. All proceeds go toward local education and programs promoting cultural preservation.

Gallup has traditionally been a crossroads for Indian trade, especially for nearby Hopis, Navajos, and Zunis. Over one hundred shops and galleries in town sell Indian-made goods, although they are not always authentic. Ask at the Chamber of Commerce for a list of shopping places.

Gallup also has a wealth of pawnshops. Many began as vehicles for local Indians to trade their goods for flour, sugar, and other food staples. Although the stores now work on a cash basis, they still often hold an item for a year and then declare it "dead pawn" and resell it. In the past, these items were often of exceptional quality, but today the vast majority of pawned items are inferior goods.

EAST OF GALLUP

Once home to the Anasazi from A.D. 300 to 1200, the massive red sandstone buttes at **Red Rock State Park** are now a center for contemporary tribes. The park has a trading post, rodeo arena, auditorium, convention center, historical museum, full-service camping facilities, and nature trails. Concerts, rodeos, and the popular Intertribal Indian Ceremonial are held in the large arena. The museum in downtown Gallup, on the corner of 3rd and W. Route 66, covers the history and present culture of the Pueblo, Navajo, Hopi, and Zuni. Works by local artists are included. In summer a demonstration "waffle garden" is planted with corn, beans, and squash.

The park is 1 mile north of I-40 (exit 33) and 4.5 miles east of Gallup on NM566.

SOUTH OF GALLUP

Zuni Pueblo is south of Gallup on NM602 (see Chapter 16, The Pueblos of New Mexico, page 306).

To visit the **Ramah Navajo Reservation**, about 40 miles south of the main Navajo lands, take NM602 south of Gallup and turn east onto NM53. A portion of the Navajo tribe settled here at the time of the Long Walk, and it is now one of the 109 chapters of the Navajo Nation. Most of the 1,700 Ramah Navajos still live in traditional hogans, and many maintain a semi-nomadic lifestyle. Near the town of Ramah (*Tlohchin* in the Navajo language, meaning "wild onion") you can see an interesting group of sandstone spires called Los Gigantes, "the giants," and the Zuni Mountains, where Navajos and Zunis still gather medicinal and ceremonial herbs.

GRANTS
Map #5

Around Town: New Mexico Mining Museum
Nearby: Casamero Ruin, El Malpais National Monument and Conservation Area, El Morro
National Monument

The town of Grants is just south of the 11,300-foot-high Mt. Taylor (*Tsoodzil*, or "Turquoise Mountain"), one of the Navajo's sacred mountains. A worthwhile stop in town is the **New Mexico Mining Museum**, where you can take a self-guided tour into an underground world created to simulate conditions in a uranium mine. Although the museum specializes in geology exhibits, it also displays Indian artifacts of pottery, baskets, and weavings from A.D. 700. It is located in the same building as the *Grants/Cibola County Chamber of Commerce*, where you can obtain more information.

A *Navajo Arts and Crafts Enterprise* is located on Historic Route 66 in town.

SOUTH OF GRANTS

El Malpais National Monument and Conservation Area preserves a landscape born in a series of eruptions ending about a millennium ago with an immense lava flow from some thirty volcanoes, destroying local villages and killing the residents. The surreal scenery fills an area half the size of Rhode Island with a jumble of cinder cones, ice caves, and extensive lava tubes. Gray-green lichens and spatter cones (piles of lava blobs in the shape of cones) blanket much of the flow.

Acoma, Laguna, Zuni, and Navajo people still visit to gather traditional plants and to honor their ancestral ties to this land. Each group has its own legend about the origin of Black Rock River, as the lava flows are called. One such legend claims it is the hardened blood of Kaubat, who was blinded by his sons, the Twins, to punish him for his gambling.

The monument/conservation area was established in 1987 and is administered jointly by the National Park Service and the BLM. The *Northwest New Mexico Visitor Center*, a multi-agency facility south of I-40 at exit 85 and onto NM53, has a bookstore, interpretive materials, and directions for driving and hiking through El Malpais (*Mal-Pie-EES*), as well as information on visiting other nearby places of interest. You can also ask here about primitive camping, caving, and backcountry hiking in the monument.

The *Zuni-Acoma Trail* (renamed the Zuni-Cibola Trail by the Spanish, and also called the *Ancient Way*) was the main trade and ceremonial route connecting these two pueblos. Part of the trail follows NM53 south of Grants. Seven miles of the trail travels through the northeast portion of the monument. It is strenuous—some would say formidable—and crosses four major lava flows. Rock cairns mark the trail across the dark igneous rock, and lava bridges have been built to span fissures in the hardened lava. If you don't want to hike the trail, you can still see an example of a lava bridge to the right of the exhibits at the trailhead on NM53, 16 miles south of I-40.

Continue south along NM53 for 23 miles from Grants to the National Park Service's *El Malpais Information Center*, which has geological exhibits, a bookstore, picnic tables, and ranger-guided activities during summer weekends.

Bandera Crater and Ice Caves, part of the El Malpais lava flow but privately owned, is a few miles further south on NM53. The trading post here has Indian artifacts and local Indian arts and crafts for sale.

An easy 1.5-mile trail behind the post leads to the eight-hundred-foot deep volcanic cone of Bandera Crater. From there, a short trail leads to seventy steps that descend to a viewing platform of Bandera Cave, the area's most accessible ice cave. An ice cave is created when rock outside a river of molten lava cools and hardens. When the lava finally drains out, a tunnel is left, which can later collapse and form an ice cave. Lava tubes have been found as long as several miles and as wide as fifty feet.

The temperature in Bandera Cave is a constant 31 degrees. The deepest ice in the cave, which is approximately twenty feet below the surface, dates back to 1100 B.C. Pueblo

Lava Tube at El Malpais

Indians and early settlers called the place Winter Lake and mined the ice. Hundreds of years ago, Coronado also visited this natural refrigerator, led here by Zuni guides.

Automobile access to the other side of El Malpais is from exit 89 off I-40 onto NM117, which forms the eastern boundary of the monument. Nine miles south of I-40 is the *Dittert Site*, the ruins of a small pueblo of about thirty rooms and a kiva. Currently, most of the ruins have been backfilled for protection. Ask at the nearby BLM ranger station for directions.

NM117 also leads past a spur road to *Sandstone Bluffs Overlook*, which affords a view of the distant cinder cones that stretch 20 miles from Cerro Brillante to Bandera Crater to form the "Chain of Craters." Further south on NM117 is a short trail to *La Ventana Arch*, one of the largest natural arches in New Mexico. The arch lies east of the highway in the forested rimrock country of the Cebolla Wilderness, which is rich in petroglyphs.

SOUTHWEST OF GRANTS

Southwest of Grants is Scenic Route 53, which follows the traditional route between Acoma and Zuni pueblos. The Spanish explorer Coronado, cavalry units, and settlers all followed this same Ancient Way.

The road leads to **El Morro National Monument**, a buff-colored bluff that remains a prominent local landmark. Ancestors of the Zuni Indians once lived on top of this two-hundred-foot-high mesa. They stayed there for less than two centuries before they abandoned their sprawling mesa-top homes for the more hospitable valley floor. You can still see some of the petroglyphs and pictographs they made.

El Morro was also a favorite resting spot for travelers along the Ancient Way (also called the Zuni-Acoma Trail). The first Europeans to use it were Spanish conquistadors in the seventeenth century, who found it to be a convenient place to pitch camp with a dependable source of water. They named the promontory "El Morro," and like the Indians before them etched messages into the sandstone mesa. You can still see the earliest one, the name of Don Juan de Oñate carved on Inscription Rock in 1605, which was fifteen years before the Pilgrims landed at Plymouth Rock. Since then, numerous others—Spanish, American, Mexican, Indian—have added to the record, leaving behind a cultural hodgepodge of graffiti that tells an abbreviated local history.

El Morro was an important landmark on the Zuni-Acoma Trail that connected these two pueblos.

The *visitor center* features a museum with interpretive displays of the seven hundred years of human history here, including some of the numerous artifacts excavated from the pueblo ruins. There is also a videotape, bookstore, and hands-on display.

The trail to *Inscription Rock*, a half-mile wheelchair-accessible loop, begins directly behind the visitor center and travels to the inscriptions at the base of the cliff. The steep Mesa Top Trail continues from here for 2 miles round-trip to the top of the mesa. The largest ruin is *Atsinna*, which is Zuni for "Writings on the Rock." Some archaeologists have estimated that it once contained as many as a thousand rooms.

The monument also has a picnic area, small campground, and RV sites, and several national forest campgrounds are nearby.

WEST OF GRANTS

Casamero, an outlier of the Chaco system built against the red sandstone of Ojo Tecolote Mesa, was occupied between about A.D. 1000 and 1125. In addition to the ruins of several small dwellings and parts of two prehistoric roads, the site consists of a characteristic Chacoan great house and great kiva, which are believed to have served as the religious and social centers for the community. The great house, which is considered Casamero Pueblo, once contained twenty-two ground-floor and possibly six second-story rooms. The unexcavated great kiva is about two hundred feet southeast of the pueblo. Casamero, along with Chaco Culture National Historical Site and six other outlying settlements, is a World Heritage Site.

To reach Casamero, travel west of Grants on I-40 about 19 miles to the Prewitt exit (63). Travel east on Route 66, and then north on CR19 toward Plains Escalante Generating Station. Follow the road about 4.3 miles to the parking area on the left, and then follow the short foot trail to the stabilized ruins. More information can be obtained from the BLM Albuquerque Field Office/Rio Puerco District.

EVENTS

VARIES *Indian Pueblo Cultural Center* sponsors a variety of traveling exhibits, dances, and symposiums throughout the year.

MONTHLY *Ceremonial Indian Arts Show:* Monthly show of high-quality art in Gallup, 10am-6pm. Contact Inter-Tribal Indian Ceremonial Office, 202 West Coal, 888-685-2564.

Coronado State Monument: Various workshops, such as Family Archaeology Day. 505-867-5351, www.nmstatemonuments.org

Crownpoint Rug Auction: Largest rug and craft sale on the Navajo Reservation. A good place to buy directly from the artist. Contact Gallup Inter-Tribal Ceremonial Offices for information, 505-863-3896, or www.mte.addr.com/rug-auction.

Fort Sumner State Monument: Variety of events such as living-history demonstrations, lectures, interpretive programs, arts shows, dinners of traditional Navajo and Mescalero Apache food, and more. Fort Sumner State Monument, 505-355-2573, www.nmstatemonuments.org.

APRIL *Earth Day:* Fabric of Life interpretive program on traditional Navajo textiles, including spinning and dying and weaving demonstrations; Navajo storytelling, children's hands-on activities, and arts/crafts sales. Fort Sumner State Monument, 505-355-2573.

Gathering of Nations Powwow: Powwow, Miss Indian World pageant and Indian Trader's Market. At University of New Mexico Arena, Albuquerque, 505-836-2810, www.gatheringofnations.com.

Indian Arts & Crafts Association Spring Market: One of the largest markets in the world offering exclusively authentic American Indian arts. Wholesale and retail markets are held on different days. Held at the New Mexico Expo in Albuquerque.

Pueblo Days Celebration: Dances and arts and crafts fair. Indian Pueblo Cultural Center, Albuquerque, 505-843-7270, www.indianpueblo.org.

MAY-SEPTEMBER *Indian Dances:* Native American dancing nightly from May-September at the Cultural Center in Gallup, 800-242-4282.

JUNE-AUGUST *Museum Feast Day:* Monthly event, with Indian dancing, farmer's market, Isleta bread-baking demonstration and food sale. Tucumcari Historical Museum, 505-461-4201 or www.nmculture.org/cgi-bin/instview.cgi?_recordnum=THM.

JUNE *Old Fort Days:* Rodeo, arts and crafts show, Diné Tah Navajo Dancers, Wild West shootout, parade, music, barbecue. Fort Sumner, 505-355-7705.

Summer Arts and Crafts Fair: Held at Indian Pueblo Cultural Center, Albuquerque, 505-843-7270, www.indianpueblo.org.

JULY/AUGUST *Gallup Inter-Tribal Indian Ceremonial:* Large intertribal gathering with representatives from over one hundred tribes throughout the U.S. Traditional song & dance, arts/crafts fair, parades, rodeo, food, educational programs. Red Rock State Park, Gallup, NM, 505-863-3896, www.gallupintertribal.com.

Ramah Navajo Community Fair: Powwow, Indian market, open show rodeo, carnival, and fireworks. At Pine Hill, 505-775-3230.

OCTOBER *Alamo Navajo Indian Day:* Traditional foods, song and dance, arts and crafts, and live music. Alamo Navajo Reservation, 505-854-2686.

Ancient Way Fall Festival: A variety of festivities are held at sites along the Ancient Way (NM53) between Grants and Gallup. Visit www.AncientWay-Route53.com for information.

IPCC Balloon Fiesta Week: Indian dances daily at 11am and 2pm, oven bread and artist demonstrations on weekdays, arts/crafts market on the weekend. At Indian Pueblo Cultural Center in Albuquerque, 505-843-7270, www.indianpueblo.org.

DECEMBER *Christmas at Kuaua:* Celebration with Native American and Spanish dancing, caroling, luminarias, and Santa Claus. Coronado State Monument, 505-867-5351.

Church Rock Indian Marketplace and Dances: Native artisans and craftspeople, Indian dance performances, and native food at the Outlaw Trading Post, Red Rock State Park. 505-488-5374

Winter Arts and Crafts Fair: At Indian pueblo Cultural Center in Albuquerque, 505-843-7270, www.indianpueblo.org.

CONTACT INFORMATION

Alamo Navajo Chapter
PO Box 827 Magdalena, NM 87825
505-854-2686 • http://alamo.nndes.org
   Navajo Arts and Crafts Enterprise
   505-854-2987

Albuquerque Convention and Visitors' Bureau
20 First Plaza NW Suite 601, PO Box 26866,
   Albuquerque NM 87102
800-284-2282 *or* 505-842-9918
www.abqcvb.org
Mon-Fri 8am-5pm

Albuquerque Museum of Art and History
2000 Mountain Road NW, Albuquerque, NM
   87104
800-659-8331 *or* 505-243-7255
www.cabq.gov/museum
Tues-Sun 9am-5pm; fee (no fee Sun 9am-1pm
   or 1st Wed of month)
   Casa San Ysidro
   973 Old Church Road, PO Box 1487,
      Corrales, NM 87048
   505-898-3915 or 505/897-8828
   Tour Times: Wed-Sun, varies with the
      season; closed Dec-Jan; fee

Ancient Way
Scenic Route 53
www.ancientway-route53.com

Bandera Crater and Ice Caves
12000 Ice Caves Road, Grants, NM 87020
888-423-2283 *or* 505-783-4303
www.icecaves.com
Daily 8am-one hour before sunset; fee

Blackwater Draw Archaeological Site and Museum
42987 Highway 70, Portales, NM 88130
www.enmu.edu/services/museums/
   blackwater-draw/museum.shtml
   Museum: 505-562-2202
   Mon-Sat 10am-5pm & Sun 12 noon-5pm,
      Memorial Day-Labor Day; Tue-Sat
      10am-5pm & Sun 12 noon-5pm, rest
      of the year; fee
   Site: 505-356-5235 (tours of site)
   Mon-Sat 10am-5pm & Sun 12 noon-5pm,
      Memorial Day-Labor Day; Sat 10am-
      5pm & Sun 12 noon-5pm, Labor Day-
      Oct & March-Memorial Day, weather
      permitting; closed Nov-Feb

Bureau of Land Management
www.blm.gov/nm/st/en.html
   Grants Field Station
   PO Box 846, Grants, NM 87020
   505-287-7911
   Rio Puerco Field Office
   435 Montano Road NE, Albuquerque, NM
      87107
   505-761-8700

Cañoncito Navajo Chapter (*See* To'hajiilee
   Navajo Chapter)

Casa Grande Trading Post
17 Waldo Street, Cerrillos, NM 87010
505-438-3008
Daily 8am-5pm; call ahead for unexpected closures

Casa San Ysidro (*See* Albuquerque Museum of
   Art and History)

Casamero Pueblo
Grants, NM 87020
505-287-7911
   or BLM, Rio Puerco Resource Area
   435 Montano Road NE, Albuquerque, NM
      87107-4935
   505-761-8700

Clovis Chamber of Commerce
105 E. Grand Street, Clovis, NM 88101
800-261-7656 *or* 505-763-3435

Coronado State Monument
485 Kuaua Road, PO Box 95, Bernalillo, NM
   87004
800-419-3738 *or* 505-867-5351
www.nmmonuments.org
Daily 8:30am-4:30pm daily, except closed
   Tuesday; fee

El Malpais National Monument
www.nps.gov/elma
   Headquarters
   PO Box 939, 123 E. Roosevelt Ave, Grants,
      NM 87020
   505-285-4641
   El Malpais Information Center
   505-783-4774
   Daily 8:30am-4:30pm
   El Malpais National Conservation Area
   Bureau of Land Management
   PO Box 846, Grants, NM 87020
   505-287-7911

El Malpais National Monument *(cont.)*
Northwest New Mexico Visitor Center
1900 E. Santa Fe, Grants, NM 87020
505-876-2783
www.nps.gov/archive/elma/NNMVC.htm
8am-5pm mountain standard time and
9am-6pm mountain daylight time

El Morro National Monument
Route 2, HC 61 Box 43 Ramah, NM 87321
505-783-4226 • www.nps.gov/elmo
Daily 9am-5pm with extended summer hours;
trails close half hour to 1 hour earlier

Eula Mae Edwards Museum/Art Gallery
417 Shepps Blvd, Clovis NM 88101
505-769-4115 • www.clovis.edu
Mon-Thu 8:30am-5pm & Fri 9am-1pm

Fort Sumner State Monument
Billy the Kid Road, Fort Sumner, NM 88119
800-426-7856 *or* 505-355-2573
www.nmmonuments.org
Wed-Mon 8:30am-5pm

Gallup/McKinley Chamber of Commerce
103 W. Historic Rt. 66, Gallup, NM
800-380-4989 *or* 505-863-3841 (visitor center)
www.gallupnm.org

Gallup Cultural Center
201 E. Historic Rt. 66, Gallup, NM
505-863-4131
Museum: Mon-Fri 9am-4pm

Grants/Cibola County Chamber of Commerce
100 N. Iron Ave, PO Box 297, Grants, NM 87020
800-748-2142 *or* 505-287-4802 • www.grants.org

Indian Pueblo Cultural Center
2401 12th Street NW, Albuquerque, NM 87104
866-855-7902 *or* 505-843-7270
www.indianpueblo.org
Museum: 9am-5pm; Gift Shop: 9am-5:30pm;
Restaurant: 8am-3pm weekdays, 8am-5pm
weekends; fee

Inter-Tribal Ceremonial Office
202 W. Coal Ave. Gallup, NM 87301
888-685-2564 *or* 505-863-3896
www.indianceremonial.com

Maxwell Museum of Anthropology
MSC01 1050, 1 University of New Mexico,
Albuquerque, NM 87131
505-277-5963 • www.unm.edu/~maxwell
Tue-Fri 9am-4pm & Sat 10am-4pm; no fee
(donations accepted)

Mount Taylor
505-287-8833 • www.fs.fed.us/r3/cibola

Museum of Archaeology and Material Culture
22 Calvary Road, PO Box 582, Cedar Crest,
NM 87008
505-281-2005 • www.museumarch.org
Daily 12 noon-7pm, May-Oct; fee

Museum of Turquoise
2107 Central Avenue NW, Albuquerque, NM
87104
505-247-8650
Mon-Sat 9:30am-4pm; fee

Navajo Arts and Crafts Enterprise
1100 West Santa Fe Avenue, Grants, NM
505-285-3910

Navajo Code Talkers Room
103 W. Hwy 66 Gallup, NM 87301
505-722-2228

New Mexico Mining Museum
100 N. Iron Street, Grants, NM 87020
800-748-2142 *or* 505-287-4802
www.grants.org.

New Mexico State Parks
1220 South St. Francis Drive, Santa Fe, NM
87505
888-667-2757 *or* 505-476-3355
www.emnrd.state.nm.us/PRD

Northwest NM Visitor Center (*See* El Malpais
National Monument)

Petroglyph National Monument
Visitor center: 6001 Unser Blvd NW,
Albuquerque, NM 87120
505-899-0205, ext. 331 • www.nps.gov/petr
Daily 8am-5pm; fee at Boca Negra Canyon

Portales Chamber of Commerce
100 South Ave. A, Portales, NM 88130
800-635-8036 *or* 505-356-8541
www.portales.com

Ramah Navajo Reservation
Route 2, Box 13, Ramah, NM 87321
505-775-7140 • http://ramah.nndes.org

Red Rock State Park
PO Box 10, Churchrock, New Mexico 87311
505-722-3839
www.ci.gallup.nm.us/rrsp/00182_redrock.html
www.gallup.nm.org

New Mexico's I-40 Corridor

Roosevelt County Chamber of Commerce
200 E. 7th Street, Portales, NM 88130
505-356-8541

Salinas Pueblo Missions National Monument
PO Box 517, Mountainair, NM 87036
505-847-2585 • www.nps.gov/sapu
Daily 9am-6pm, summer; 9am-5pm, rest of
the year; fee

To'hajiilee Navajo Chapter
Po Box 3398, To'hajiilee, NM 87026
505-836-4221 • www.tohajiilee.nndes.org

Tucumcari Chamber of Commerce
404 West Route 66, P.O. Drawer E, Tucumcari,
NM 88401
888-664-7255 *or* 505-461-1694
www.tucumcarinm.com

Tucumcari Historical Museum
416 South Adams, Tucumcari, NM 88401
505-461-4201 • www.cityoftucumcari.com •
www.tucumcarinm.com/visitors_guide
Mon-Sat 8am-6pm, summer; Mon-Fri 8am-
5pm, winter; fee

Turquoise Trail
Cibola National Forest Ranger Station
11776 Highway 337, Tijeras, NM 87059
505-281-3304
www.turquoisetrail.org/byway-area-
attractions.html

U.S. National Forest Service/Cibola National Forest
2113 Osuna Road NE, Suite A, Albuquerque,
NM 87113
505-346-3900 • www.fs.fed.us/r3/cibola
Mt. Taylor District
1800 Lobo Canyon Rd, Grants, NM 87020
505-287-8833
www.fs.fed.us/r3/cibola/districts/
mttaylor.shtml
Sandia District Ranger Station
11776 Hwy 337, Tijeras, NM 87059
505-281-3304
www.fs.fed.us/r3/cibola/districts/sandia.shtml
Mon-Fri 8am-5pm & Sat-Sun 8:30am-
5pm, summer; call for winter hours

Wingspread Collector's Gallery Guide
116 Central Ave SW, Suite 201, Albuquerque,
NM USA 87102
505-245-4200 • www.collectorsguide.com
Mon-Fri 8am-5pm

SOUTHERN NEW MEXICO

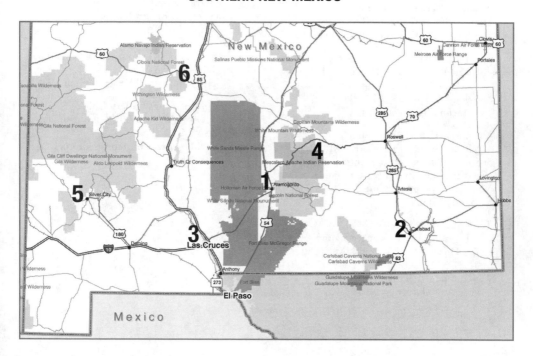

1. Alamogordo
2. Carlsbad
3. Las Cruces
4. Mescalero Apache Reservation
5. Silver City
6. Socorro

CHAPTER 20

SOUTHERN NEW MEXICO

ALAMOGORDO
Map #1

Around Town: Tularosa Basin Historical Museum
Nearby: Oliver Lee Memorial State Park, Three Rivers Petroglyph National Recreation Site, Valley of Fires Recreation Area, White Sands National Monument

Alamogordo has ties to both a space-age future and a Paleo-Indian past. Nearby White Sands Missile Range is the site of the first atomic bomb detonation and an important military facility linked to space exploration. You can learn more about the history of these modern developments at the New Mexico Museum of Space History.

In the distant past, people of prehistoric cultures made their homes in the desert and mountains that surround Alamogordo. Numerous sites have been discovered, including campsites of Folsom Man and a handful of early pueblos. Ancestors of the pueblo builders moved to the Tularosa Basin from the Rio Grande Valley sometime between 200 B.C. and A.D. 1. At first they lived in semipermanent dwellings and later erected pithouses. By A.D. 1000 they were building adobe pueblos, only to abandon them after a couple of hundred years, possibly because they were fleeing raids by Apache immigrants.

Centuries later, the U.S. government established Fort Tularosa to guard Apaches at what was then the Tularosa Southern Apache Reservation. Today, the Mescalero Apache Reservation is north of town, as well as Lincoln National Forest with its wealth of outdoor recreation opportunities. Alamogordo is a good place to stay while visiting either of them.

The **Tularosa Basin Historical Society Museum** has displays of prehistoric and Apache items that include moccasins, a cradleboard, and other artifacts. It is located next door to the *chamber of commerce*, which can provide you with visitor information.

NORTH OF ALAMOGORDO
One of the most extensive groupings of rock art in the Southwest is preserved at **Three Rivers Petroglyph National Recreation Site**. For about a mile along its rock walls, over twenty thousand petroglyphs have been pecked into the volcanic ridge.

Petroglyphs left by the Jornada Mogollon at Three Rivers Petroglyph Site give only vague clues about the people's beliefs.

Members of the Jornada Mogollon culture lived here between A.D. 900 and 1400, farming the Three Rivers Valley and establishing extensive trade networks with their neighbors. They stayed until drought forced them to move on.

An interpretive trail leads to their partially reconstructed village, where a pithouse, masonry house, and multiroom adobe structure show the progression of native architecture. Another trail leads to the top of the ridge, where hundreds of petroglyphs in the form of lizards, birds, trees, and geometric designs adorn the rock outcroppings. Goggle-eyed and horned beings also appear. Picnic shelters and RV camping are also available. Be aware that rattlesnakes are common in the area, and no dogs are allowed on the trails.

Three Rivers is off US54, about 27 miles north of Alamogordo. Unfortunately, since the site is so accessible, it has been subject to modern-day vandals who have scrawled their own graffiti across the ancient pictures and destroyed large pieces of some of the drawings. To report vandals, call the Bureau of Land Management.

Indian legend tells of a time when the **Valley of Fires Recreation Area** burned under a seething tongue of molten lava oozing from El Malpais, a small peak 44 miles to the north. (El Malpais National Monument can be visited near Grants.) Probably the youngest lava flow in the continental United States, it happened somewhere between 1,500 and 2,000 years ago. After the lava cooled, it cracked into fissures, pits, and collapses. Indentations around the edges of the flow provided shelter for local Mogollon people. When they moved on, they left behind petroglyphs, pictographs, and occasional bits of pottery.

A three-quarter-mile paved nature trail leads from the campground onto the flow. Although the region earned the nickname *Jornada del Muerto,* or "Journey of the Dead," from early travelers who found little water, firewood, or grazing as they crossed it, a surprising variety of plants and animals do survive here. Look for camouflaged rodents and reptiles, which have adapted their coloring to the dark lava, but try to explore in the morning before the temperature matches the area's name.

The *visitor center* is 4 miles northwest of Carrizozo on US380. It can also be reached from Socorro. The Bureau of Land Management's Roswell Resource Area administers it.

SOUTH OF ALAMOGORDO

The 180-acre **Oliver Lee Memorial State Park**, named for the prominent New Mexico rancher and state legislator who once lived here, was a campsite for many of the area's earliest inhabitants. For almost four thousand years people have traveled from the Sacramento Mountains to the Tularosa Basin on a well-worn trail through the oasis of Dog Canyon. They left behind over 170,000 stone artifacts, including scrapers, knives, and drills. Mortars, or "Indian wells," used to grind seeds, were also prevalent.

Around five hundred years ago, the Mescalero Apache arrived at Dog Canyon. A year-round stream and canyon springs, which support abundant wildlife in a lush riparian plant community unusual in this part of New Mexico, are undoubtedly why they chose the place as a sanctuary. Later they used it as a well-protected fortress against the pursuing U.S. Calvary. At least five major ballets between the two groups occurred here.

The *visitor center* has displays on the natural and human history of the park, including a few Apache artifacts, and conducts regular guided tours of the restored Lee ranch house. The state park also has developed picnic and campsites, some with RV hookups, and restrooms with showers. *Dog Canyon National Recreation Trail* leaves from the visitor center and follows an old Indian trail through the canyon to Joplin Ridge, affording panoramic views of the Tularosa Basin. The state park is 12 miles south of Alamogordo on US54, and then 4 miles on Dog Canyon Road.

WEST OF ALAMOGORDO

The remarkable **White Sands National Monument** preserves most of the world's largest gypsum dune field. Stop at the *visitor center* for the museum and bookstore. From here, you can take a round-trip 16-mile scenic drive (Dunes Drive) into the heart of the searing white dunes, where plants and animals have adapted to this harsh desert environment in amazing ways—like the soaptree yucca, which elongates its stem so the leaves will stay above the sand.

You can also hike the 1-mile, self-guided *Dune Life Nature Trail* or the backcountry *Alkali Flat Trail* for a more intimate experience of the dunes. Look for Apache wheat grass, which the natives harvested for food, labeled on the *Interdune Boardwalk Trail*.

The patterns of ripples on the dunes at White Sands National Monument change periodically with the shifting wind.

LEGEND OF THE WHITE SANDS

One of the most enduring Indian stories surrounding these brilliant shifting dunes is that of Pavla Blanca, the ghost of the Great White Sands. When Coronado and his party traveled here in 1540, Apache warriors attacked them. One valiant conquistador, Hernando de Luna, was mortally wounded and died somewhere in the dunes. Left behind to mourn him was his fiancée, Manuela. Not believing her betrothed could be dead, she set out from Mexico City to find him, but she disappeared along the way. Now she haunts the dunes looking for Hernando. If you look just after sunset on a breezy evening, you might see her ghostly form. Moderns claim what you are seeing is wind-swept dust eddying up from the dunes, but if you look with a different eye, you may see that the wraith-like figure is Manuela, come here to find her lost lover, with her white wedding gown swirling around her.

Folsom lance points left along ancient lake shores and lowlands in the Tularosa Basin are evidence that early people hunted here. Later people left scattered hearths throughout the dunes and gathered Indian ricegrass for food along the edges of the sands. Later agricultural villages appeared along the shores of Lake Lucero in the western part of the monument. Finally, the Apache came to the basin.

White Sand Dunes National Monument is 15 miles southwest of Alamogordo on US70. Be aware that Dunes Drive is sometimes closed owing to desert rains or missile testing on the adjacent White Sands Missile Range. You can call the day before for the testing schedule.

CARLSBAD
Map #2

Around Town: Carlsbad Museum and Fine Art Center, Living Desert Zoological and Botanical State Park

Nearby: Artesia Historical Museum, Carlsbad Caverns National Park, Lea County Cowboy Hall of Fame and Western Heritage Center

Although the major attraction is nearby at Carlsbad Caverns National Park (see below), the town of Carlsbad also has sites of interest.

Carlsbad Museum and Fine Art Center houses historic Apache artifacts such as buffalo-hunting spears and moccasins. Also included are stone tools from the Pleistocene era, Mimbres and Pueblo pottery, and the Burns Collection of Tarahumara artifacts from northern Mexico. The art center displays fine art from throughout the Southwest, and the gift shop sells books on the Southwest and Native American crafts such as Zuni fetishes, katsinas, drums, and silverwork.

On the northwest edge of town off US285, the **Living Desert Zoological and Botanical State Park** provides a glimpse into life on the Chihuahua Desert, which extends from southeastern New Mexico into Texas and Mexico. Exhibits cover human and natural history as well as environmental themes, and they include a desert arboretum, aviary, and nocturnal habitat. A self-guided, paved trail winds through sand dunes, where skinks and javelina live among the furniture chollo, sostol, and agave plants.

The *visitor center* features archaeological and historical exhibits. A statue in front called *Apache Way* depicts two Mescalero Apache women harvesting the spiked mescal agave plant. It is identical to the one at the Mescalero Apache Cultural Center. The museum sponsors a spring mescal harvest each May, at which time the plant is buried in a specially constructed pit and roasted for four days. At the end of that time, visitors are invited to partake of the mescal, which has a taste resembling sweet potato and smoky molasses. Native Americans also perform Mountain Spirit Dances at this time.

The park is also a haven for animals too sick or injured to survive on their own. After rehabilitation, they are returned to the wild.

NORTH OF CARLSBAD

In the Moore-Ward House in Artesia is the **Artesia Historical Museum and Art Center,** which has a large collection of arrowheads, as well as some Apache baskets and prehistoric tools.

SOUTH OF CARLSBAD

South of town on US62/180 is a World Heritage Site that remains one of the most remarkable caverns open to the public. **Carlsbad Caverns National Park** has over twenty-one miles of explored corridors filled with cave formations that are both stunning and bizarre. The earliest visitors to the cave were prehistoric Indians who took shelter under the overhang at the cave's entrance as early as twelve thousand years ago. They left behind faded pictographs and scattered cooking pits near the mouth of the cave, but they probably avoided the massive drop-off just beyond it that leads into the foreboding darkness of the interior.

Today, you can follow the lighted and paved *Natural Entrance Trail* on a 1-mile descent (sometimes steep) along the traditional route later explorers took into the heart of the cave. At the bottom is a restaurant, the fourteen-acre "Big Room" with features such as Rock of Ages, Bottomless Pit, and Painted Grotto. There is an elevator to transport you back to ground level. Plan about three hours for this self-guided tour. Another option is to ride the elevator down and take the hour-long walk around Big Room before taking the elevator back to the surface. Either way, take a sweater with you. The cave is a constant 56 degrees. Also note that strollers are not allowed in the cave.

The *visitor center* has interpretive activities, exhibits, an audiovisual program, a bookstore, a gift shop, a restaurant, a kennel, and a daycare center. Tours of the main caverns are available from here, as is information on back country caves and hikes along the fifty miles of trails through desert, canyons, and mountains in the national park. Outside the center is a 1-mile self-guided trail that showcases the plants of the desert.

The entrance to Carlsbad Caverns only hints at the massive underground chambers within the cave.

An estimated 400,000 Mexican free-tailed bats and at least fifteen other bat species make their homes in the recesses of the cave for part of the year. At dusk between May and October, you can watch the breathtaking spectacle of an enormous cloud of bats flying out of the cave to begin the nightly hunt for insects.

Slaughter Canyon Cave is 23 miles from the main cavern. In the winter, reservations can be made for a two-hour tour into this undeveloped cave. Be sure to bring your own flashlight and water and to wear sturdy hiking footwear for this strenuous trip. Also at the cave is a trail from the parking lot that leads past petroglyphs made by early Guadalupe Basketmakers.

EAST OF CARLSBAD

Although focusing on cowboys and pioneers, the **Lea County Cowboy Hall of Fame and Western Heritage Center** has recently added exhibits on local prehistoric and historic Native Americans. It is located on the northern outskirts of Hobbs just off NM18, between the campus of New Mexico Junior College and the hospital.

LAS CRUCES
Map #3

Around Town: Las Cruces Museum of Natural History, New Mexico State University Museum
Nearby: Chihuahuan Desert Nature Park, City of Rocks State Park, Deming Luna Mimbres
  Museum, Faywood Hot Springs, Fort Selden State Monument, Geronimo Springs Museum,
  Historic Hot Springs Mineral Baths, Las Cruces Natural History Museum, Mesilla (Gadsden
  Museum, Plaza), New Mexico Farm and Ranch Heritage Museum, Lordsburg-Hidalgo Museum

Las Cruces gets its name from an Indian attack on a group of travelers in 1830. The three crosses at N. Main and Solano memorialize those who were killed.

At the **New Mexico State University Museum** rotating exhibits often focus on Native

Americans from pre-Columbian to historic times. Its permanent exhibits spotlight the anthropology, history, and natural features of the Southwest. Pottery from prehistoric to modern times is displayed by type and area. Pueblo pieces displayed side by side, and pull-out drawers with a hundred types of prehistoric potsherds make it easy to compare. One case shows how pottery is made and includes materials used to make natural dyes and brushes. The museum is in Kent Hall at the intersection of University and Salano avenues.

To get safely close to some of the scarier residents of the Chihuahuan Desert, visit the **Las Cruces Museum of Natural History** just inside the southeast entrance to the Mesilla Valley Mall. Glass separates you from rattlesnakes, gila monsters, and large spiders, as well as from more benign turtles and other animals. The small museum also includes exhibits on native plants, astronomy, and dinosaurs.

NORTH OF LAS CRUCES

The **Chihuahuan Desert Nature Park** is 960 acres that protect archeological sites, geological formations, and desert plants and animals known and used by its ancient inhabitants. A self-guided tour booklet for the 1.2-mile *Desert Discovery Trail* includes write-ups about common plants along the trail. The half-mile *Desert Experience Mini-Trail* has interpretive signs with archaeology, anthropology, and desert information. Plans are underway to add a wickiup and hands-on displays to the mini-trail. The nonprofit nature park also sponsors educational programs throughout the year.

Chihuahuan Desert Nature Park is northeast of Las Cruces off US70. It has restrooms but no water, so be sure to bring your own. Take the Mesa Grande exit, make a U-turn under the highway, and travel west on the frontage road to Jornada Rd. Turn right (north) onto Jornada for 6.5 miles to the entrance, and turn left just before the entrance sign onto the road to the parking lot.

Fort Selden was established in 1865 along an ancient trade route to protect villages and wagon trains from raiding Apaches. Many of the adobe bricks used to construct it contain broken bits of Indian pottery. The fort stationed several companies of buffalo soldiers. General Douglas MacArthur grew up at the fort during the time his father was post commander. A walking tour through **Fort Selden State Monument** leads through the adobe ruins of the fort, and displays interpret its role in the history of Mesilla Valley. Staff recreations and nineteenth-century military encampments are held on some summer weekends. Fort Selden State Monument is at Radium Springs 13 miles north of Las Cruces at exit 19 off I-25.

Farther north along I-25 in the town of Truth or Consequences is **Historic Hot Springs Mineral Baths**. Native Americans took advantage of the curative powers of the mineral waters and considered the area a neutral ground. Legend has it that Geronimo himself often stopped here for rejuvenation. Bathhouses, saunas, and indoor tubs now utilize water from the town's huge, subterranean, 110-degree pool of mineral water.

Adjacent to the hot springs is **Geronimo Springs Museum and Geronimo Trail Visitors Center**, with a prehistoric collection that includes pottery canteens, dippers, jugs, and bowls marked by type and arranged geographically. Mogollon, Socorro, Tularosa, and Casas Grandes are some of the cultures represented. Tools to straighten arrows, stone effigies, and some items with unknown purpose are also in the room.

The Apache Room has exhibits on Apache leaders, including Geronimo, who was born in the area, and Lozen, the woman warrior described by her brother Victorio as his "right hand ... a shield to her people," because of her uncanny ability to find the enemy and to heal the wounded. This medicine woman eventually joined Geronimo and was one of the thirty-four people who surrendered with him in 1886 with the last significant guerrilla band of Apache. A gift shop sells Native American crafts and books on Indian lore. The interpretive center has displays and information on native plants and animals, as well as about festivals and sights you can visit.

SOUTH OF LAS CRUCES

The historic village of **Mesilla** (south off I-10 on NM28, exit 140) began as an Indian community. The Spanish subsequently settled on the site in 1848, and during the Civil War, it was briefly the Confederate capital of the Territory of Arizona. Today you will find galleries, museums, and restaurants, some occupying the original adobe buildings concentrated around the *plaza* to protect the Spanish from raiding Apaches. Stop at the visitor center on NM28 in the town hall for a map of the plaza and information on plans to make the area a New Mexico state monument.

EAST OF LAS CRUCES

Three thousand years of New Mexico agriculture are shown in the **New Mexico Farm and Ranch Heritage Museum.** It blends Indian, Anglo, and Spanish ways of working the land in permanent and temporary exhibits. The cutaway view of a Mogollon pithouse shows construction methods and typical furnishings in the homes of the first area farmers. A timeline leads visitors through interactive displays with artifacts, videos, and dioramas illustrating the development of agriculture. It includes ancient corn plants with tiny cobs, and a Tewa Indian and archaeologist explaining the irrigation systems used in Posi-ouinge Pueblo in northern New Mexico. In the outdoor working farm and ranch complex, look for Churro sheep favored by the Navajo because of the way their coarse wool takes on dye. Orchards, gardens, antique equipment, and demonstrations are also on site. Dickerson's Grill serves lunch, and there is a gift shop.

To reach the museum, take I-25 to exit 1 and turn east for 1.5 miles.

WEST OF LAS CRUCES

West of Las Cruces, on I-10 in the town of Deming is the **Deming Luna Mimbres Museum,** which has Mimbres pottery and baskets from A.D. 550 to 1150, as well as jewelry and pottery from other Southwestern tribes. The museum also has exhibits pertaining to frontier and military history. The gift shop sells Native American jewelry and books.

The rock walls at **City of Rocks State Park** rise as high as forty feet and create a unique type of landscape that can be seen in only a few other places in the world. Formed when a lava flow cooled several million years ago, the tufa has since been carved by wind and water into strange towering shapes. Concave smooth spots worn into the flat rocks in this maze of passageways show where native inhabitants once ground corn, and Mimbres arrowheads and pottery sherds can still be seen. The park has a *visitor center, Desert Botanical Garden*, and campground. The park is 30 miles northwest of Deming. Take US180 to NM61 and follow the signs.

Faywood Hot Springs is a rustic place to enjoy a mineral hot spring. These hot springs

*Massive rocks at City of Rocks State Park hide depressions
where prehistoric people once ground corn.*

rise out of a tufa dome next to the state park. Cabins, tent/RV camping, massage, and public/private mineral pools are available. The springs' healing properties were known to the Mimbres and Apache people who lived nearby.

The area around Lordsburg, at the western edge of New Mexico on I-10, is steeped in history. Nearby ghost towns are reminders of the time when the promise of wealth in the mountains drew miners into Indian Territory. The town itself was an internment camp during World War II. The **Lordsburg-Hidalgo Museum** has archaeology and history exhibits that include Indian culture from the region of New Mexico known as the boot heel.

MESCALERO APACHE RESERVATION
Map #4

On the Reservation: Casino Apache and Travel Center, Inn of the Mountain Gods Resort and
Casino, Mescalero Tribal Cultural Center and Museum, Ski Apache, St. Joseph's Apache Mission
Nearby: Fort Stanton Recreation Area (Fort Stanton, Rio Bonito Petroglyph Trail), Hubbard Museum of the American West, Lincoln

In the Sacramento Mountains, 720 scenic square miles make up the Mescalero Apache Reservation, home to over 3,300 Mescalero, Chiricahua, and Lipan Apaches. The Mescalero were so named because of their extensive use of the mescal agave plant for food. Before the arrival of the Spanish, they ranged across the Llano Estacado, or "Palisade Plains," from the Rio Grande and south into Chihuahua, Mexico.

The Mescalero became highly skilled horsemen who excelled in guerilla warfare. For years, they actively opposed the European newcomers, beginning with the Spanish and ending with the Americans. Eventually, in 1863, the Mescalero acknowledged defeat and surrendered to General James H. Carleton, who sent them to Fort Sumner, where they endured years of misery, disease, and starvation.

The Mescalero Reservation was established in 1873 near Fort Stanton, with the present location between the White and Sacramento mountains established in 1883. The Lipan joined the Mescalero here in 1903, coming from Chihuahua, Mexico, where the army had moved them earlier. In addition, about two hundred Chiricahua and Warm Springs Apaches came here after being released from prison in Fort Sill in 1913. In 1936, the Lipan and Chiricahua bands became members of the Mescalero.

Today, the Mescalero have built profitable industries in tourism, telecommunications, timber sales, and cattle ranching. There are over four thousand enrolled members and most residents live in frame cottages in the small town of Mescalero, lying along US70 between Tularosa and Ruidoso.

To view a video on Apache history and displays of traditional clothing, stop at the **Mescalero Tribal Cultural Center and Museum** in town. You can also ask here about ceremonials that may be open to the public. The most famous is the female puberty ceremony held over July 4.

It took twenty-three years to build the European-style **St. Joseph Apache Mission**, originally dedicated in 1939 and now on the National Register of Historic Places. This Romanesque church, constructed with native materials to replace a small adobe structure, was later re-dedicated as a memorial to the veterans of World Wars I and II. Over the years, local artists have contributed pictures of Apache leaders, a three-part mural of dancers at an Apache puberty ceremony, and background paintings of the Stations of the Cross. An Albuquerque artist, Robert Lentz, created the Apache Christ above the altar. An alcove is dedicated to *Kaia'tano':ron*, Kateri Tekakwitha, called the Lily of the Mohawks for her piety. She was beatified by Pope John Paul in 1980 and some consider her the patron saint of Indians. Native American items are sold in the gift shop.

One of the main attractions for visitors to the reservation is the luxury **Inn of the Mountain Gods Resort and Casino**, a five-star resort beautifully situated in a mountain meadow on the shores of Mescalero Lake, with sacred Sierra Blanca Peak (*Dzil gais' ání*, "Mountain with snow on top") towering above. Tall bronze sculptures of traditional Ga'an dancers and a smaller clown figure made by Apache artist Frederick Peso grace the fountain at the entrance. A winding staircase in the lobby leads to a large indoor fountain representing a medicine basket used in the puberty rites for Apache girls. Exhibits behind the fountain show the traditional contents of the medicine basket and tools of a medicine man. In addition to lodging, the inn has tennis courts, swimming pools, stables, restaurants, a health club, a convention center, and an eighteen-hole championship golf course that hosted the 2005 New Mexico Open. Other activities include cycling, horseback riding, archery, and trap and skeet shooting. The gift shop/fine arts gallery sells Apache arts and crafts. The Apache request that visitors do not come to the resort with certain animals or any part of those animals: a snake (snakeskin boots, belts, etc.) or owl, both of which are considered bad omens; or a bear, which is highly respected.

A good outlet for tribal art is the *Jordan T. Gallery* 1 mile south of the Inn of the Mountain Gods on Carrizo Canyon Road.

The tribe also owns **Casino Apache and Travel Center**, just off US70, which offers casino gambling in the form of slots, blackjack, table games, and video poker. It also has a full-service travel plaza with a convenience store and discount gas.

With clear air and breathtaking scenery, the Sacramento Mountains offer extensive

---

SUNRISE CEREMONY *(NA'II'EES)*

This four-day and four-night coming-of-age celebration honors the daughters of the Apache with one of the tribe's oldest and most important ceremonies. Amidst cattail pollen blessings, holy songs, feasting on chili stew and fried bread, gift giving, and community prayers and well wishes, girls who have reached puberty are ushered into womanhood.

Wearing specially made ceremonial dresses of fringed buckskin, the girls are believed to embody White Painted Woman (also known as Esdzanadehe, or Changing Woman) and to bring her healing power to the tribe. The ceremony emphasizes discipline and dignity, and the young women are admonished to listen carefully as they are guided and advised by an accompanying medicine woman. At night they dance the sacred songs in the ceremonial tipi erected by a medicine man and his male helpers and recount the time of creation and the history of the Apaches.

Another part of the ceremony is the nightly dances of the Mountain Spirits (or Ga'an, pronounced gah-IIAIIN), performed by black-hooded painted men to represent the Mountain Spirits, who taught the people how to live in balance with the earth. The Ga'an are accompanied by a clown, who points out people's shortcomings.

---

opportunities for outdoor recreation, and the high altitudes provide a refreshing retreat from the desert heat. Camping, fishing, and picnicking are available at Silver Lake, Eagle Creek Lake, Silver Springs, and Ruidoso Recreational Area. Lake Mescalero offers fishing, sailing, and boating, and Eagle Creek and Silver lakes have RV hookups. For permits and information, contact the *Mescalero Apache Conservation Office* or the Inn of the Mountain Gods. Hunting is another popular activity, and big-game hunts can be arranged through Mescalero Big Game Hunts.

Hugging the side of the 12,000-foot-high Sierra Blanca, and considered sacred by the Mescalero, is the 750-acre **Ski Apache,** which attracts nearly three hundred thousand skiers each season, as well as sightseers who ride the gondola to the top to enjoy the views. With an average snowfall of 180 inches augmented by a snowmaking system, and fifty-five runs and trails, this has become one of the most popular ski resorts in the Southwest.

NORTH OF THE MESCALERO APACHE RESERVATION

Just north of the reservation is the resort town of Ruidoso, where the horse, central to Apache culture, inspired the **Hubbard Museum of the American West,** located a quarter-mile east of the Ruidoso Downs racetrack off US70.

The museum has grown into a well-respected Western history museum and is affiliated with the Smithsonian. In addition to general interest items on the West, other displays include prehistoric stone artifacts and pottery, Cherokee dolls, modern katsinas and textiles, baskets, jewelry, and moccasins of the Plains Indians.

Fort Stanton National Recreation Area, operated by the Roswell Office of the BLM, contains the old Fort Stanton, Fort Stanton Cave, and sixty miles of trails. *Fort Stanton was* established in 1855 to protect settlers from Mescalero raiders. Other Indians traded and worked there. Many of the original buildings are still in use but are closed to the public. A small museum staffed by volunteers is open to tell the story of the fort, including its role in the Lincoln County and Civil Wars. Annual reenactments of fort life include Native American dances. Restoration plans in partnership with the Mescalero Apache Nation are underway. Fort Stanton is on Route 220 off US380 between Capitan and Lincoln.

A moderate 2.1-mile loop, *Rio Bonito Petroglyph National Recreation Trail* leads past a boulder in the river etched with messages left by the Jornada Mogollon. It is west of the Sierra Blanca Regional Airport off Route 220.

In the town of **Lincoln** on US380 stands a round stone tower built by early Hispanic settlers to defend themselves against the Apache. In the 1870s, the town became the focal point of the Lincoln County War.

Lincoln is still about a mile long and one street wide, the old buildings and bullet holes are preserved by the *Lincoln State Monument*, and the round stone tower still stands. The Anderson Freeman Visitor Center has a reproduction of a nearby prehistoric ceremonial cave, Apache baskets, cradleboards, and pottery. Other original buildings are preserved and open as museums. You can camp in Lincoln National Forest or call the monument for reservations to stay at the monument in a bed-and-breakfast hotel.

SILVER CITY
Map #5

Around Town: Silver City Museum, Western New Mexico University Museum
Nearby: Gila Cliff Dwellings National Monument, Gila Forest Wilderness, hot springs, Woodrow Ruin

The land around Silver City has a long history of human occupation. Mogollon people lived here from around A.D. 300 to 1450. The Apache also called this place "home," and in the late nineteenth century, the mountains here became the stronghold of Apache leaders Victorio and Geronimo.

Although most of the exhibits at the **Silver City Museum** cover pioneer and mining history, a small collection of Mimbres pottery, Casas Grandes, and Apache pieces are also included. In addition, the bookstore stocks books about the Mimbres and Apache.

Western New Mexico University Museum in Fleming Hall at the end of Tenth Street contains one of the world's largest permanently displayed collections of Mimbres pottery. In addition to prehistoric ceramics from the Mimbres and Casas Grandes cultures, there is pottery from the pueblos of San Ildefonso and Santa Clara. Prehistoric tools, jewelry, baskets, and historic Navajo rugs are in the collection, and traveling exhibits sometimes stop here. Inquire at the museum about prehistoric sites across the border in northern Mexico.

The *Chamber of Commerce* on Hudson Street has more information on other sites and outdoor recreation in the surrounding Gila National Forest.

NORTH OF SILVER CITY

The oldest dwellings at **Gila Cliff Dwellings National Monument** are pithouses built between A.D. 100 and 400. They were followed by rectangular homes, then pueblos and cliff houses inhabited from the late 1270s to the early 1300s.

The Mogollon who lived here used the bottomland to plant squash, maize, and beans. They were also skillful potters and weavers and fashioned yucca into clothing, sandals, and baskets.

Today you can see forty-two rooms of well-preserved cliff dwellings in five caves. A 1-mile loop trail (fairly steep in some sections) leads to the caves, which are 180 feet above the canyon floor. "Trail to the Past" leads to an earlier Mogollon pithouse and pictographs.

The small *visitor center* has an audiovisual presentation and baskets, pottery, tools, and displays about the lifestyle of the individuals who lived here. Camping is available in four campgrounds.

Two **hot springs** are in the nearby national forest.

Lightfeather Hot Spring is a half mile up Middle Fork Trail. The route passes through two river crossings along a trail used by the Apache. *Jordan Hot Springs* is 8 miles up the Middle Fork or 6 miles along Little Bear Canyon from Gila Cliff Dwellings Visitor Center. Information on the two hot springs can be obtained at the visitor center. They are popular, but you are cautioned not to immerse your head because of an organism that may cause meningitis when it contacts mucous membranes.

Gila Cliff Dwellings is 44 miles north of Silver City at the end of the narrow, winding NM15. Trailers are advised to take the slightly longer route via NM35. Pets are not allowed within the monument; kennels are available.

Gila National Forest Wilderness, which was once the province of Geronimo, Cochise, and Mangas Coloradas, is accessible on trails leaving from Gila Cliff Dwellings National Monument. Obtain information from the visitor center, or contact the Gila National Forest Wilderness.

Woodrow Ruin can be seen off NM293 overlooking the Gila River about 5 miles northeast of the town of Cliff. It was built by the Mimbres branch of the Mogollon culture, and at one time may have measured five hundred by nine hundred feet. Access to the ruin is granted through the *Gila National Forest Service office*. The office also has information on other prehistoric sites in the national forest.

The scenery in southern New Mexico blends mountain and desert.

*Snow geese gather
on a pond at
Bosque del Apache.*

SOCORRO
Map #6

Around Town: San Miguel Mission church
Nearby: Bosque del Apache Wildlife Refuge, El Camino Real International Heritage Center,
   Ft. Craig

Over seven hundred years ago, Piro-speaking Pueblo Indians settled the village of Tey-pana to farm, hunt, and raise turkeys. In 1598, when Don Juan de Oñate and Spanish colonists emerged starving and exhausted from the harsh Jornada del Muerto, the Indians supplied them with life-saving corn. In gratitude, the immigrants named the place So-corro, meaning "succor" or "assistance."

When the Oñate expedition continued north, two priests stayed behind to convert the peaceful Piro Indians and direct them to build a mission. Its windows were placed high in the walls to guard against attacks from unfriendly Indians, and its altar was decorated with solid silver pieces made from riches taken from nearby mines.

In the 1600s, the Piro were forced to abandon their pueblos because of European dis-eases and Apache raids. A few people remained, but with the 1680 Pueblo Revolt, they too fled south along with the Spanish.

Socorro was abandoned by the Spanish for over a hundred years. When settlers re-turned between 1819 and 1821, they used what was left of the massive walls and beams from the 17th century church to rebuild the mission. Legend has it that during a subsequent Apache raid, a winged man with shining sword appeared on the roof of the mission to scare off the attackers. In honor of their rescuer, the mission *Nuestra Señora de Perpétuo So-corro,* or "Our Lady of Perpetual Succor," was renamed **San Miguel Mission.**

The church is still used today and is open to visitors. A brochure describing its his-tory is available from the *Socorro Chamber of Commerce,* which also has information on tours to the Trinity site, Very Large Array (VLA) telescopes, and the Etscorn Observatory.

SOUTH OF SOCORRO

About 20 miles south of Socorro on NM1 is the **Bosque del Apache Wildlife Refuge**. The Spanish name translates as "Woods of the Apache," referring to the Apache who routinely camped in the forest by the river, but there is evidence of use by Puebloans as far back as A.D. 1100.

Birdwatchers are happy here year-round, but from November through February, they receive a special thrill when thousands of snow geese, ducks, and sandhill cranes stop at the refuge. The spectacle of a field coming to life at dawn with waking cranes is a sight and sound to remember.

A window in the *visitor center* overlooks a small stream and pipes in the sounds of the birds from outside. The gift shop sells pottery with Mimbres designs and a recorded auto tour of the refuge. Guided tours are offered on weekends.

Fort Craig, one of the largest western forts, was established to protect travelers on El Camino Real. From here, troops were sent to subdue Navajo and Apache raiders like Geronimo, Nana, and Victorio. During the Civil War, Union soldiers from Fort Craig defeated Confederate troops in the nearby Battle of Valverde Crossing. Some of the fort's stone and crumbling adobe walls remain and can be seen on a self-guided walk. Picnic tables, drinking water, a restroom, and a host to answer questions are also on-site. Living history events are sometimes held.

Take exit 115 from I-25 and turn north 5 miles to the entrance road. Then travel 4.5 miles to the site of the fort.

The **El Camino Real International Heritage Center** has artifacts and full-sized exhibits such as a colorful Taos marketplace, showcasing the road that from Spanish colonial times funneled the interchange of ideas, cultures, and products between northern New

---

DON JUAN DE OÑATE AND EL CAMINO REAL

In 1598, Don Juan de Oñate forged his way north from Mexico to the New Mexico province, taking with him settlers, soldiers, eight priests, two lay brothers, and Tlaxcalan Indians as servants. The caravan stretched for three miles, and progress was slow since they could only move as fast as the pigs. Spanish law required explorers and settlers to convert all the people they encountered, so the expedition stopped frequently while the missionaries tried to win over the native villages.

Oñate's route incorporated sections of ancient Indian paths and came to be called El Camino Real, the Royal Road, or King's Highway. Its 1,200 miles eventually connected Santa Fe/Taos to Mexico City and was soon well worn from traffic channeling supplies to and from the Spanish settlements. Much of the route followed the Rio Grande. However, a ninety-mile shortcut earned the name Jornada del Muerto, or "Deadman's Journey," because it led through a treeless, waterless territory guarded by hostile Indians and so harsh it was often crossed by starlight.

Mexico and Mexico. One of the results of this interaction was *mestizaje*, the blending of Indian-Hispano traditions. Mestizaje, an emphasis of the heritage center, can be witnessed in action in Matachines dances still performed by some Pueblos. Discovery drawers include Indian items, and there are also outdoor trails, an amphitheater with traditional performaces, and an overlook with a view toward the Jornada del Muerto and some of the early *parajes* (campsites) on El Camino Real.

To reach the center, take I-25 for 30 miles south of Socorro to exit 115. Travel south 1.4 miles on NM1 (Frontage Road), and turn east onto County Road 1598. The center is 2.7 miles down the road.

EVENTS

JANUARY *Red Paint Powwow:* Held in honor of the Chihene Apache of southwestern New Mexico. Powwow and competition, arts/crafts, and food vendors. Western New Mexico University, in Intramural Gym in Silver City. 505-538-3735, www.redpaintpowwow.net.

APRIL *American Indian Week:* Lectures, social gatherings, Pueblo Throw (recognition of community members and gratitude), arts/crafts expo, beauty pageant, and traditional dancing. New Mexico State University in Las Cruces. 505-646-4207, www.nmsu.edu/~aip.

Frontier Days: Living history demonstrations, period entertainments, and children's activities. Fort Selden State Monument, 505-526-8911.

MAY *Annual Mescal Roast:* Traditional roasting and eating of mescal at Living Desert Zoological and Botanical State Park in Carlsbad. 505-887-5516, www.nmparks.com.

Mother's Day Powwow: Dancing, singing, crafts, and food. Socorro, 505-881-8847.

JULY *Mescalero Apache Ceremonial and Rodeo:* Includes Sunrise ceremony (coming of age for girls), rodeo, powwow, arts and crafts booths, food vendors, traditional games, and parade. Visitors welcome, but no photography, recording, or note-taking allowed. Four days and nights, 4th of July weekend, Mescalero Feast Grounds on Mescalero Apache Reservation, 505-671-4494.

Mescalero Arts and Crafts Show: Artisans from throughout the West sell quality jewelry, sculptures, paintings, woodcarvings, and hand-painted clothing. Artist demonstrations also provided. Mescalero Apache Reservation, three days in late July, 505-671-4494.

AUGUST *Western Artists of America Annual Show, Hubbard Museum:* Art show of Western artists and art that often has a Native American theme. Hosted by Hubbard Museum. Contact Ed Holmes, 16745 E Saguaro Blvd #114, Fountain Hills, AZ 85268, or www.westernartistsofamerica.com.

SEPTEMBER *Mountain Spirits/Plains People:* Traditional skills demonstrations by Mescalero Apache Cultural Center at Fort Selden National Monument, 505-355-2573.

OCTOBER *Alamo Indian Days:* Fall celebration includes gourd dancing and food and craft vendors. US60 west of Socorro, 505-854-2635, ext. 1514.

DECEMBER *Our Lady of Guadalupe Fiesta:* Evening Indian dances, Catholic mass, fiesta, ascent of Mount Tortugas. In mid-December at Mesilla in Tortugas Village, 505-526-8171.

CONTACT INFORMATION

Alamogordo Chamber of Commerce/Visitor Center
1301 N White Sands Blvd, PO Box 518, Alamogordo, NM 88310
800-826-0294 *or* 505-437-6120
www.alamogordo.com

Artesia Historical Museum and Art Center
505 W. Richardson Ave, Artesia, NM 88210
505-748-2390
Tue-Sat 10am-noon & 1pm-5pm; No Fee

Bosque del Apache Wildlife Refuge
PO Box 1246, Socorro, NM 87801
505-835-1828 or 505-835-0424
Bookstore: 505-838-2120
www.fws.gov/southwest/refuges/newmex/bosque/index.html
Visitor Center: Mon-Fri 7:30am-4pm & Sat-Sun 8am-4:30pm
Refuge: one hour before sunrise-one hour after sunset

Bureau of Land Management
www.blm.gov/nm/st/en.html
   Las Cruces District Office
   1800 Marquess, Las Cruces, NM 88005
   505-525-4300
   Roswell Field Office
   2909 West Second, Roswell, NM 88201
   505-627-0272
   Socorro Field Office
   901 South Hwy 85, Socorro, NM 87801
   505-835-0412

Carlsbad Chamber of Commerce and Visitor Center
302 South Canal, Carlsbad, NM 88220
800-221-1224 *or* 505-887-6516
www.cnmchamber.com

Carlsbad Caverns National Park
3225 National Parks Highway, Carlsbad NM 88220
505-785-2232 • www.nps.gov/cave
   Cave
   Daily 8am—7pm summer (last entry via elevator 5pm & via Natural Entrance 3:30pm); daily 8am-5pm winter (last entry via elevator 3:30pm & via Natural Entrance 2pm); fee
   Tours
   877-444-6777 • www.recreation.gov

Carlsbad Museum and Fine Art Center
418 W. Fox, Carlsbad NM 88220
505-887-0276
Mon-Sat 10am-6pm, summer; Mon-Sat 10am-5pm, winter; fee

Chihuahuan Desert Nature Park
PO Box 891, Las Cruces, NM 88004
505-524-3334 • www.cdnp.org
Daily sunrise-sunset; no fee

City of Rocks State Park
PO Box 50, Faywood, NM 88034; fee
505-536-2800
www.enmrd.state.nm.us/PRD
Gate Hours: 7am-9pm

Deming Luna Mimbres Museum
301 S. Silver, Deming, NM 88030
505-546-2382
www.cityofdeming.org/museum.html
Mon-Sat 9am-4pm & Sun 1:30pm-4pm; donations accepted

El Camino Real International Heritage Center
PO Box 175, Socorro, NM 87801
505-854-3600 • www.caminorealheritage.org
Wed-Mon 8:30am-5pm, May-Oct; fee

Fort Craig (*See* BLM Socorro Field Office)
www.nm.blm.gov/sfo/fort_craig/fort_craig_home.htm

Faywood Hot Springs
165 Highway 61, HC 71 Box 1240, Faywood, NM 88034
505-536-9663 • www.faywood.com
Daily 10am-10pm; fee

Fort Selden State Monument
PO Box 58, Radium Springs, NM 88054
800-429-9488 *or* 505-526-8911
www.nmmonuments.org
Wed-Mon 8:30am-5pm; fee

Fort Stanton National Recreation Area
BLM Roswell Field Office
2909 W. Second Street, Roswell, NM 88201
505-627-0272
www.nm.blm.gov/recreation/roswell/fort_stanton_acec.htm
Mon-Fri 7:30am-4:30pm
   Fort Stanton
   www.fortstanton.com
   Thu-Mon 10am-4pm

Geronimo Springs Museum/Geronimo Trail Visitor Center
211 Main Street, Truth or Consequences, NM 87901
505-894-6600
www.geronimospringsmuseum.com
Mon-Sat 9am-5pm, Sun 11am-4pm; fee

Gila Cliff Dwellings National Monument
HC 68 Box 100, Silver City, NM 88061
505-536-9461 • www.nps.gov/gicl
Dwellings
Daily 8am-6pm Memorial Day-Labor Day; daily 9am-4pm rest of the year; fee
Visitor Center
Daily 8am-5pm Memorial Day-Labor Day; daily 8am-4:30pm rest of the year

Historic Hot Mineral Springs Baths and Spas
Downtown Palomas Hot Springs District, Truth or Consequences, NM 87901
800-831-9487 *or* 505-894-3536
Hot Springs Association
505-894-7154

Hobbs Chamber of Commerce
400 North Marland, Hobbs, NM 88240
800-658-6291 *or* 505-397-3202
www.hobbschamber.org

Hubbard Museum of the American West
841 Hwy 70 West, PO Box 40, Ruidoso Downs, NM 88346
505-378-4142 • www.hubbardmuseum.org
Daily 9am-5pm; fee

Las Cruces Convention and Visitor Bureau
211 N Water Street, Las Cruces, NM 88001
505-541-2444 • www.lascrucescvb.org

Las Cruces Museum of Natural History
700 S. Telshor #1608, Las Cruces, NM 88011
505-522-3120
www.las-cruces.org/publicservices/
museums/nhm.shtm • www.nmculture.org
Mon-Th 10am-5pm, Fri 10am-8pm, Sat 10am-5pm, Sun 1pm-5pm; no fee

Lea County Cowboy Hall of Fame and Western Heritage Center
5317 Lovington Highway, Hobbs, NM 82420
505-392-1275 *or* -5518
www.nmjc.edu/westernheritagemuseum
Museum: Tue-Sat 10am-5pm; fee
Office: Mon-Fri 8am-5pm

Lincoln State Monument
PO Box 36, Lincoln, NM 88338
800-434-6320 • www.nmmonuments.org
Daily 8:30am-4:30pm; no fee
Anderson Freeman Visitor Center
505-653-4025
Monument
505-653-4372

Living Desert Zoological and Botanical State Park
1504 Miehls Drive, Carlsbad, NM 88221
505-887-5516 • www.nmparks.com
Daily 8am-8pm, summer (last entry 6:30pm); daily 9am-5pm, winter (last entry 3:30); fee

Lordsburg Hidalgo Museum
710 E 2nd St., Lordsburg, NM 88045
505-542-9086

Mescalero Apache Reservation
Box 176 Mescalero, NM 88340
505-464-4494 or -4495
Casino Apache and Travel Center
25845 Hwy 70, Mescalero AN 88340
505-464-4960
Casino open Sun-Thurs 8am-4pm, Fri-Sat 24 hours
Inn of the Mountain Gods Resort and Casino
287 Carrizo Canyon Road, Box 269, Mescalero, NM 88340
800-545-9011 *or* 505-464-7777
Golf Shop: 505-464-7945
Mescalero Big Game Hunts: 505-464-7448
www.innofthemountaingods.com
Mescalero Apache Jordan T. Gallery
Carrizo Canyon Road, Mescalero, NM 88340
800-545-9011
Fri-Sun 10am-5pm
Mescalero Conservation Office and Recreation Office
PO Box 176, Mescalero, NM 88340
505-464-4427 *or* 505-671-4494
Mescalero Tribal Cultural Center and Museum
PO Box 176, Mescalero, NM 88340
505-464-4494, ext. 254 (or -4495)
Ski Apache
PO Box 220, Ruidoso, NM 88355
505-464-3600 • www.skiapache.com
24-hour snow report: 505-257-9001
St. Joseph Apache Mission
626 Mission Trail, Mescalero, NM 88340
505-464-4473 • www.stjosephmission.org
Daily during daylight hours (Sunday Mass 10:30am)

Mesilla
2340 Avenida de Mesilla, Mesilla, NM
505-647-9698
www.oldmesilla.org/html/mesilla_visitors_
center.html

**New Mexico Farm and Ranch Heritage
Museum**
4100 Dripping Springs Road, Las Cruces, NM
88011
505-522-4100 • www.frhm.org
Mon-Sat 9am-5pm, Sun noon-5pm; fee

New Mexico State Parks
1220 South St. Francis Drive, Santa Fe, NM
87505
888-667-2757 *or* 505-476-3355
www.emnrd.state.nm.us/PRD/index.htm

New Mexico State University Museum
New Mexico State University, Kent Hall, PO
Box 30001, Dept. 3564, Las Cruces, NM
88003
505-646-3739 • www.nmsu.edu/~museum
Tue-Sat noon-4pm; no fee

Oliver Lee Memorial State Park
409 Dog Canyon Road, Alamogordo, NM 88310
505-437-8284
www.emnrd.state.nm.us/PRD/oliverlee.htm
Daily 9am-5pm

San Miguel Mission
403 El Camino Real, Socorro, NM 87801
505-835-2891 • www.sdc.org/~smiguel

Silver City Chamber of Commerce
201 North Hudson, Silver City, NM 88061
800-548-9378 *or* 505-538-3785
www.silvercity.org

Silver City Museum
312 Broadway, Silver City, NM 88061
505-538-5921 • www.silvercitymuseum.org
Tue-Fri 9am-4:30pm, weekends 10am-4pm; fee

Socorro Chamber of Commerce
101 Plaza, Socorro, NM 87801
505/835-0424 • www.socorro-nm.com

**Three Rivers Petroglyph National Recreation
Site**
County Road B-30, Tularosa, NM 88352
505-438-7400
www.nm.blm.gov/recreation/las_cruces/
three_rivers.htm
(*see also* BLM Las Cruces District Office)

Truth or Consequences Chamber of Commerce
PO Drawer 31, Truth or Consequences, NM
87901
505-894-3536
www.truthorconsequencesnm.net

Tularosa Basin Historical Society Museum
1301 N. White Sands Blvd, Alamogordo, NM
88310
505-434-4438 • www.alamogordomuseum.org
Mon-Fri 10am-4pm, Sat 10am-3pm, Sun
noon-3pm; no fee

United States National Forest Service
www.fs.fed.us
Gila National Forest Service Office
3005 E. Camino del Bosque, Silver City,
NM 88061
505-388-8201
http://www2.srs.fs.fed.us/r3/gila
Mon-Fri 8am-4:30pm
**Gila National Forest Wilderness Ranger
Station**
HC 68, Box 50, Mimbres, NM 88049
505-536-2250
Lincoln National Forest
1101 New York Ave, Alamogordo, NM
88310
505-434-7200 • www.fs.fed.us/r3/lincoln
Mon-Fri 7:30-4:30

Valley of Fires Recreation Area
(*see also* BLM Roswell Field Office)
Campground: 505-648-2241
www.nm.blm.gov/recreation/roswell/valley_of_
fires.htm

Western New Mexico University Museum
Fleming Hall at 10th Street, Silver City NM
88062
505-538-6386
www.wnmu.edu/univ/museum.htm
Mon-Fri 9am-4:30pm (except Wed 1pm-
4:30pm), Sat & Sun 10am-4pm; no fee

White Sands National Monument
PO Box 1086, Holloman AFB, NM 88330
505-679-2599 • www.nps.gov/whsa
Dunes Drive
Daily 7am-sunset, Sept 5-May 25; daily
7am-9pm, May 26-Sept 4; fee
Visitor Center
Daily 8am-5pm, Nov 4-May 25; daily
8am-6pm, May 26-Nov 3

NORTHERN UTAH

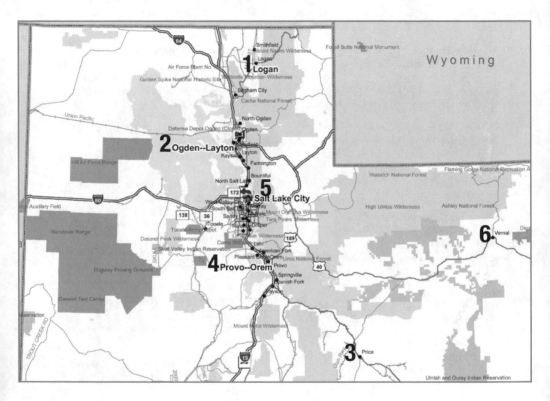

1. Logan
2. Ogden
3. Price

4. Provo
5. Salt Lake City
6. Vernal

CHAPTER 21

NORTHERN UTAH

UTAH HAS SOME OF THE MOST DIVERSE LANDSCAPE in the country, and at least five groups of native peoples continue to make it their home: Ute (for whom the state is named), Paiute, Goshute, Shoshone, and Navajo. The scenery in the northern part of the state ranges from stark, barren salt flats to mountains with lush alpine forests, and from world-class ski resorts to rugged canyons and fossil beds. In between is Utah's major metropolitan area where seventy percent of the state's population clusters around the I-15 corridor in Salt Lake City, Ogden, and Provo. But expect to find more than a megalopolis here. In northern Utah, the cosmopolitan is still surrounded by an abundance of wilderness, and much of the land that sustained the region's original inhabitants remains undeveloped and pristine.

LOGAN
Map #1

Around Town: Cache County DUP Museum, Nora Eccles Harrison Museum of Art, Utah State
University Museum of Anthropology
Nearby: American West Heritage Center, Bear Lake State Park, Bear River Battle Monument,
Crystal Hot Springs

The town of Logan, situated in the center of Cache Valley, was named for a trapper who hid his furs in the lush valley in the 1820s. The fort was built in the 1850s (along what is now Center Street) to open the area for settlers.

The **Museum of Anthropology** on the Utah State University campus is a teaching museum with exhibits on the early inhabitants of the Great Basin and other regions around the world. In the American West exhibit, you can try your hand at grinding corn on a mano and metate, view dioramas depicting life in the region before the white settlers came, and examine the museum's basketry collection. You can also learn about dendrochronology (tree-ring dating), the interpretation and protection of indigenous rock art, and the science of paleo-anthropology.

Also on campus is the **Nora Eccles Harrison Museum of Art**, which exhibits art from the American West, with an emphasis on modern and contemporary styles. Native Americans are among the featured artists.

For more information on the area and its abundant opportunities for outdoor recreation, as well as directions for a driving tour through thirty cities in Cache Valley, Utah, and Idaho, visit the *Cache Valley Tourist Information Center* in the Chamber of Commerce Building at 160 North Main. While there, stop across the street at **Cache County Daughters of Utah Pioneers (DUP) Museum** for historical accounts of Cache Valley Indians.

NORTH OF LOGAN

Bear River Heritage Area straddles the Utah-Idaho border. Here, where the Great Basin and the Rocky Mountains meet, the land is dotted with rendezvous and Shoshone cultural sites, as well as remnants of pioneer trails. Cache Valley, part of the heritage area, was a prime hunting ground for mountain Indians.

Near the Utah-Idaho border on US91, between Preston and Downey, Idaho, is the **Battle of Bear River Historical Marker,** designating the site of an 1863 raid against local Shoshones by Colonel Patrick E. Connor leading about 200 California Volunteers. Stationing men at both ends of Cache Valley to shoot anyone trying to escape, Connor and his men killed at least 225 Indians, many of them women and children. Only 27 soldiers lost their lives. Today Bear River is considered the largest single-day massacre of Indians in the United States. In-depth interpretive signs of the national historic landmark are up the hill.

Bear Lake State Park is 45 miles northeast of Logan on UT89 and is nestled high in the Rocky Mountains near Garden City. The lake's color, an intense turquoise-blue, is created by limestone deposits suspended in the water and has prompted its nickname "Caribbean of the Rockies."

Logan Canyon Scenic Byway travels through an area rich in beauty and natural resources that have attracted people for hundreds of years.

Bear Lake has a rich history. Nomadic Indians were hunting and gathering around Bear Lake when trappers first arrived. The Indians told the newcomers stories about a serpentine monster patrolling the lakeshore. The Oregon Trail marker north of Bear Lake Marina shows where immigrant wagons once traversed. The Old Mormon Trail Marker, 10 miles from the Wyoming border, also points out a route used by Sioux, Cheyenne, and Crow raiding parties on their way to Ute and Shoshone encampments.

Between 1825 and 1840, Bear Lake was a site where mountain men and Indians traded goods and stories at annual rendezvous. The locals still gather some Septembers at Rendezvous Beach on the south end of the lake for a rendezvous re-creation.

Bear Lake is Utah's second largest freshwater lake, and its white sandy beaches provide a wealth of opportunities to enjoy water sports such as swimming, fishing, jet skiing, and boating. During the winter, snowmobiling and skiing are popular in the surrounding area.

SOUTH OF LOGAN

The **American West Heritage Center** is 6 miles south of Logan just off UT89/91. This 160-acre living-history center is dedicated to the diverse cultures that made their homes there from 1820 to 1920. At the Native American Encampment, you can learn more about the indigenous Northwestern Band of the Shoshone. Other exhibits include a pioneer settlement with displays of a wagon encampment and homesteader's cabin, a historical farm with equipment from the early twentieth century and farm animals, and a mountain man camp.

If you have the time, reserve a spot for the Tipi Overnight Experience, which includes an overnight stay in a tipi equipped with the trappings of a typical Shoshone home, along with a Native American interpreter to educate you about how the items were used in daily life. Each tipi sleeps eight to ten people, and you will need to bring or rent a sleeping bag.

The center also sponsors Festivals of the American West, which are events held throughout the year that focus on related themes.

At **Crystal Hot Springs** you can partake of the Ute Indian custom of soaking in pools of healing mineral water. This particular hot springs is one of only two places in the world that have both a hot and cold spring near each other. Utes used it as a favorite winter campsite, with the Wasatch Mountain Range providing a natural windbreak and the hot springs providing heat. Travelers can now swim in the crystal-clear waters and camp for the night.

OGDEN
Map #2

Around Town: D.U.P. Museum and Relic Hall, Fort Buenaventura, Natural History Museum, Museum of Natural Science, Ogden Nature Center, Ogden Canyon
Nearby: Antelope Island State Park, Bear Lake State Park, Bear River Battle Monument, Bear River Migratory Bird Refuge, Golden Spike National Historic Site, Heritage Museum

The confluence of the Weber and Ogden rivers was a popular place for nomadic Shoshone, Ute, and prehistoric Indians to fish and hunt. Remains of some of their camps have been found nearby. At one time, American trappers and their Indian wives and children shared the spot, making it a major rendezvous site in the mid-1820s. Around 1845,

Miles Goodyear built a cabin of cottonwood logs near the Weber River. In 1846, he built a traveler's way station and trading post and called it Fort Buenaventura. The Mormons arrived in 1847, and Goodyear, feeling the pinch of overcrowding, sold them his settlement and moved to California. The Mormons renamed it first Brownsville, and then Ogden.

On the eighty-eight acres of **Fort Buenaventura** is an accurate reconstruction of Miles Goodyear's first permanent European settlement in the Great Basin. You can tour the stockade and cabins, and at several times throughout the spring and summer watch the reenactment of various mountain men's activities. The *visitor center* displays Ancestral Puebloan artifacts, and the park has a picnic area, a pond with canoe rentals, and camping sites. To reach the peaceful setting of the fort, from downtown take 24th Street west across the railroad yard and the river, turn left on A Avenue, and follow the signs.

You can visit Miles Goodyear's cabin (probably the oldest non-native structure in Utah) and view pioneer furnishing, clothes, crafts, and photos at the **Daughters of Utah Pioneers Museum** in Tabernacle Square. The cabin, moved from its original site to behind the museum, can be seen even when the museum is closed.

Southeast of downtown is Weber State University. On the northeast corner of the campus, on the main floor of Lind Lecture Hall, is the university's **Museum of Natural Science**. In addition to displays on geology, dinosaurs, and other natural history topics, the museum displays petroglyphs, Basketmaker artifacts, katsinas, and Edward S. Curtis photographs.

Ogden Canyon is an international attraction for professional and amateur geologists. The trail high on the south wall was once the only route through this narrow, pink quartzite gorge. Indian Trail can still be hiked for 4.3 miles from the trailhead in the canyon to 22nd Street. To reach the canyon, take 12th Street east, which becomes UT39—a nationally designated scenic byway. For more information, contact the U.S. Forest Service Intermountain Regional Office.

To better understand the natural environment of the area, hike the trails at **Ogden Nature Center**, a 152-acre wildlife sanctuary that preserves the woods, wetlands, and open fields where indigenous people once roamed freely. Indoor and outdoor exhibits help to interpret what you see, and the visitor center offers workshops and activities year-round. Take I-15 to the 12th Street exit, and travel east 1.5 miles.

Bear River Migratory Bird Refuge provides a sanctuary for migrating birds.

Golden Spike National Historic Site keeps alive the historic moment when the Central Pacific and the Union Pacific railroads joined the American West to the East.

The *Ogden-Weber Convention and Visitor Bureau* is located in the historic Union Station Museum Complex at 25th and Wall Avenue. In the same office is the *Forest Service Information Center* for the Wasatch Range forest. The huge Union Station Building was built in 1924 and now houses four museums (car, railroad, firearms, and natural history) and an art gallery. The **Ogden Natural History Museum** displays Indian artifacts and crafts along with its primary displays of gems, minerals, and fossils. Ask at the visitor bureau for a brochure about historic 25th Street, a wide boulevard that leads east from the station and is now a pleasant and convenient place for strolling, shopping, and eating.

NORTH OF OGDEN

The Shoshone once claimed the land west of Bear River, but through a combination of force and trickery, they lost it for a few "beeves" (cattle) and several hundred pounds of flour. It has long been a favorite of migrating birds such as duck, black ibis, trumpeter swans, snowy egret, and terns.

Bear River Migratory Bird Refuge is on the northern tip of the Great Salt Lake, 15 miles west of Brigham City on Forest Street. It consists of thousands of acres of marsh, open water, and mud flats. This impressive refuge offers exceptional bird viewing of shorebirds and waterfowl, especially in spring and early summer. You can take the 12-mile-long loop road by auto, bicycle, or hiking, year-round from sunrise to sunset. Be advised to call ahead in the spring and winter to check if the road is accessible. Restrooms, a fishing pier, and an interpretive site are near the beginning of the route. The Wildlife Education Center, west of I-15, exit 363, has interactive exhibits and a trail.

Golden Spike National Historic Site is where Central Pacific's Jupiter and Union Pacific's #119 steam engines officially met on Promontory Summit on May 10, 1869, thus connecting the east and west coasts of the United States.

As the transcontinental railroad wedged through the West, it ultimately doomed the existence of the frontier and forever changed the Indians who lived there. What was once a six-month journey now took less than a week. Machinery, livestock, and manufactured goods from the East were soon streaming into the area, along with miners, workers, settlers, and entrepreneurs. As the voices for national unity strengthened throughout the country, native peoples were increasingly seen as a hindrance to progress.

Today, replicas of the original locomotives steam along a short section of track every day from May through Labor Day. Each Saturday during that same time, the Golden Spike ceremony is reenacted, complete with local volunteers in period costumes. For a more in-depth experience, follow a self-guided auto tour along the old railroad bed, or listen to one of the ranger-led lectures in the summer. The main building has displays, films for viewing, a gift shop, and vending machines.

Golden Spike is located northwest of Brigham City. From I-15 take Brigham City exit 368, turn west (right) onto UT13 and UT83, and follow the signs for 29 miles.

SOUTH OF OGDEN

The Great Salt Lake has eight islands in it, some of which have Fremont rock art on them. **Antelope Island State Park**, the largest of the islands, is connected to the mainland via a 7-mile paved causeway, although in times past, water fluctuations have flooded the land as far as the nearby freeway. The island is now 15 miles by 5 miles of rocky slopes, grasses, marshes, and dunes, with Frary Peak rising 6,596 feet in the center. Prehistoric archaeological sites are on the island, as well as elk, pronghorn antelope, bighorn sheep, and around five hundred free-roaming bison. The yearly bison roundup in late October keeps the herd to a manageable size. You can enjoy the island's beaches, visitor center, bird watching, historic ranch house, marina, hiking trails, and camping. To reach the park, take I-15, use exit 335, and drive 9 miles to the causeway and park entrance. For more information on the Great Salt Lake, see "Around Town" under Salt Lake City below.

Heritage Museum covers the local historical and cultural development. Its small Native American collection includes arrowheads, grinding stones, beadwork, Hopi katsinas, and a few Navajo items. The museum is located in the town of Layton, west of the high school and south of city hall.

PRICE
Map #3

Around Town: College of Eastern Utah Prehistoric Museum
Nearby: Emery County Museum of the San Rafael

Price, the seat of Carbon County, is surrounded by dozens of coal mines and oil and natural gas fields within 30 miles of town.

The **College of Eastern Utah Prehistoric Museum** is best known for its paleontology and archaeology exhibits, which include two floors of artifacts from early hunting, gathering, and agricultural societies. Displayed are unfired clay Pilling figurines at least eight hundred years old, painted buffalo robes from five hundred years ago, a replica of a Fremont village, a full-sized tipi, a reproduction of the Barrier Canyon mural, and casts of petroglyphs from Nine Mile Canyon. The museum also sponsors guided tours and special events focusing on the local rock art. To reach the museum, take exit 240 onto 100 North and travel east to the Utahraptor statue on the right.

For brochures, maps, information, and a self-guided tour of Nine Mile Canyon (see South of Vernal for more information) and other nearby rock art, stop at the *Castle Country Regional Information Center* in the lobby of the museum.

SOUTH OF PRICE

Emery County Museum of the San Rafael, south on UT10 in the town of Castle Dale, features life-size dinosaur skeletons, award-winning displays of plants and animals found in and around San Rafael, Indian artifacts from some of the unique archaeological finds in Emery County, and native folk art. Also at the small museum are Fremont and Ancestral Puebloan pottery, tools, jewelry, baskets, split-twig figurines, and a tool-making kit called the Sitterud Bundle.

SOUTHEAST OF PRICE

The remote **Range Creek Wildlife Management Area** protects significant well-preserved Fremont rock art and ruins. Public access is limited and permits are required.

PROVO
Map #4

Around Town: Museum of People and Cultures
Nearby: Goshute Reservation, Fairview, Lehi (John Hutchings Museum of Natural History, Pony Express Trail), Stagecoach Inn State Park

Provo, the third largest city in Utah, sits in the center of a lush green valley. The Timpanogos Utes living here in 1776 were friendly to friars Dominguez and Escalante when they passed this way. Later relations between the Indians and Europeans were not always so cordial, and skirmishes prevented Mormon settlement until Fort Utah was built in 1849.

Today, Brigham Young University, operated by the Church of Jesus Christ of Latter-day Saints, is an active presence in the community. The public is welcome at any of the university's four museums—Monte L. Bean Life Science Museum, Museum of Art, Earth Science Museum, and Museum of People and Cultures. The **Museum of People and Cultures**, on the six-hundred-acre campus in Allen Hall, has archaeology and ethnography collections from around the world, including modern and ancient cultures of the Great Basin and the Southwest. BYU students produce all of the exhibits and change them periodically. Topics have included Hopi katsinas, the notable Casas Grandes culture, the use of rituals and ceremonies in seeking the divine, and the life and art of the Western Anasazi.

NORTH OF PROVO

At least nine thousand years ago, people camped near what is now the quaint town of **Lehi** (17 miles northwest of Provo on I-15). Later, Ancestral Puebloans and Fremonts moved here, followed by the Shoshone and Bannock as they roamed north of the Point of the Mountain. You can still see *petroglyphs* downtown on the north side of the wash. The *chamber of commerce* has a booklet detailing the site of a Fremont camp near the Jordan River, as well as other places of interest. It is housed in the historic train station.

In town, the *John Hutchings Museum of Natural History* houses a diverse collection covering the history and natural history of Utah. Visit the Native American room to view various artifacts that include Fremont pitch-sealed water baskets, arrowheads, Clovis points and clay pots, prehistoric flaking tools, hide scrapers, and bead drills. You can also see examples of the ceremonial dress and shelter of the Ute, Paiute, Goshute, and Shoshone cultures. The gift shop sells native crafts and provides guided tours for groups.

West of town is the old *Pony Express Trail*, which carried mail through Wyoming, Utah, and Nevada between stage stops and hot springs. Marked with wayside exhibits and interpretive signs, this is the most completely preserved section of the trail in Utah. You can follow it on a day-long, 133-mile, remote, backcountry drive. Begin at Camp Floyd State Park near Fairfield and end at Canyon Station near the small town of Ibapah. Other wayside exhibits are at Faust Junction, Boyd Station, and Simpson Springs, a reliable source of water used by the Indians long before it became a Pony Express and Overland stage station. Water is still available here March through October. For road information and an interpretive brochure, contact the BLM Salt Lake District.

Camp Floyd/Stagecoach Inn State Park marks the spot where nearly one-third of the entire U.S. Army was stationed in the mid-1850s to suppress a rumored rebellion in Utah. Only the fort cemetery and one commissary building remain of the original four hundred buildings. Also in the park is the historic *Stagecoach Inn*, once an overnight stop on the Overland stage and Pony Express route. The adobe hotel, built in 1855, has since been restored with original period furnishings. The state park is 21 miles southwest of Lehi on UT73.

SOUTH OF PROVO

In 1859, Mormon settlers founded the town of **Fairview** (south of Provo on US89). In the mid-1860s during the Black Hawk Indian War, a thick, ten-foot-high rock wall was constructed around town center for protection. You can learn more about the town's history at the unique *Fairview Museum of History and Art*, with displays that often exhibit a sense of humor as well as culture. Included are oral and family history collections and a full-size replica of a Columbian mammoth found on the Wasatch Plateau.

WEST OF PROVO

The **Confederated Tribes of the Goshute Reservation**, established in 1914, lies isolated in the heart of the Great Basin and spans the border with Nevada about 70 miles south of the town of Wendover. The Goshutes are considered to be one of the seven distinct, but related, Shoshone groups that lived in the Great Basin and Snake River areas in 1840. Their name is either derived from that of a leader named Goship or from the word *Gutsipupiutsi*, which is Shoshone for "Desert People."

In 1940, the Goshute people incorporated as the Confederated Tribes of the Goshute Reservation. Tribal enrollment today is around 425, which includes 125 people who belong to the Skull Valley band (see below). Headquarters for the Goshute Reservation are in the village of Ibapah (*EYE-buh-paw*), from Ai-bim-pa, meaning "White Clay Water." It was founded in 1859 by Mormons who came to teach agriculture to the Indians. Groceries and gas are available at *Ibapah Trading Post*.

The reservation is in White Pine County, Nevada, and Juab and Tooele counties in Utah. To reach Ibapah, take Alternate US93 south of Wendover to Ibapah Road and turn left. The road to the reservation is unimproved, and once there, you will need permission to enter. You can ask for it at tribal headquarters. For backcountry travel, write the tribal council well in advance (they meet infrequently) and explain the purpose and dates of your travel. Wilderness experience and topographical maps are required.

SALT LAKE CITY
Map #5

Around Town: Chase Home Museum of Utah Folk Art, Fort Douglas Museum, Pioneer Memorial Museum, State Capitol Building, This Is the Place Heritage Park and Old Deseret Village, Utah Museum of Fine Arts, Utah Museum of Natural History, Utah State Historical Society Museum

Nearby: Skull Valley Reservation, Utah Cultural Celebration Center

In the Pleistocene era, much of western Utah and small portions of eastern Nevada and southern Idaho were covered by the twenty thousand square miles of Lake Bonneville. Over thousands of years, this massive lake either drained out over Red Rock Pass or evaporated. By the time the Goshutes entered the Lake Bonneville Basin, the expanse of water had shrunk to a fraction of its original size, leaving behind the Great Salt Lake and the Great Salt Lake Desert, which contains Bonneville Salt Flats.

The Great Salt Lake is still enormous, 48 miles wide and 98 miles long, but the depth is only about 35 feet. It is a terminal lake, meaning no rivers flow out of it; any water lost is through evaporation. Because of this, the level of the lake can fluctuate dramatically, rising during times of heavy mountain snow runoff and falling after summer heat has increased the rate of evaporation. Historically, the salinity of the water has ranged from an amount just above seawater (a little less than 5 percent) to a level beyond which water cannot hold more salt (almost 27 percent). Goshutes called the lake *Titsa-pa*, meaning "Bad Water," and avoided it.

When the first members of the Church of Jesus Christ of Latter-day Saints (L.D.S.) entered Salt Lake Valley, one of them described it as a paradise for lizards, crickets, and rattlesnakes. Despite this, leader Brigham Young called it the Promised Land, and the people set about the hard work of turning it into his vision. What emerged was a lovely city laid out on a grid, with blocks that are ten acres large and tree-lined streets that are 132 feet wide.

Temple Square, with the famous Mormon Temple and Tabernacle, is at the center of the grid. Visitor centers here have exhibits and provide daily tours to sites important to the LDS Church. Three blocks north is Utah's **State Capitol**, where you can view the historical displays and enjoy expansive views of the city, valley, and Wasatch Mountains. Free guided tours are available in summer.

On the west side of the capitol grounds is **Pioneer Memorial Museum**, which displays the Daughters of the Utah Pioneers' huge collection of photographs, furniture, textiles, toys, dolls, and other memorabilia dating from the time of the first settlers to the joining of the railroads at Promontory Point. Scattered among the eclectic displays are a few Native American items.

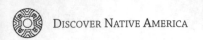
SALT LAKE CITY

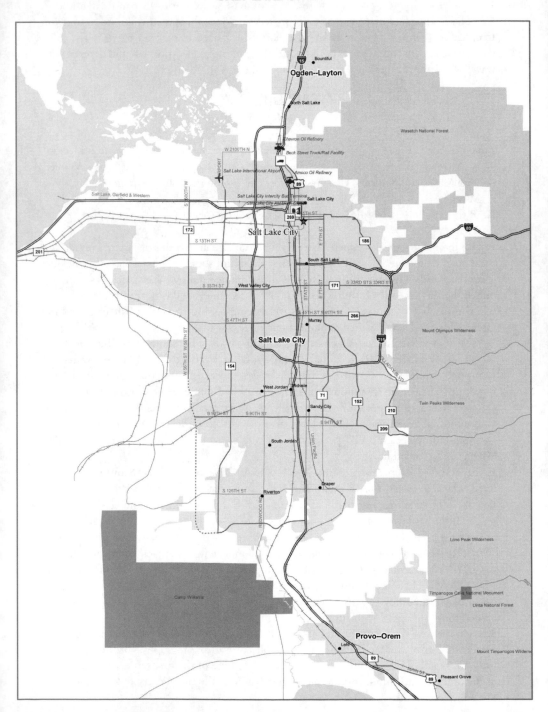

South of the capitol is Council Hall, the original meeting place of the territorial legislature. The *Utah Office of Tourism* now has its offices in the building. Stop here for information about sites and activities throughout the state. You can also obtain tourist information and a combined site pass at one of the *Salt Lake City Convention and Visitors Bureau* in the Salt Palace Convention Center or the airport.

In the mid-1800s, Isaac Chase and Brigham Young built a flour mill and two-story adobe home in the middle of a 110-acre farm. The land became Liberty Park and the home is now the **Chase Home Museum of Utah Folk Art**. Although some of the pieces in the museum follow a historical style, all have been fashioned by contemporary Utah folk artists. Native artists are represented with Navajo baskets, Ute, and Shoshone beadwork, and other items in the Native Gallery. The museum also sponsors music and dance performances from Utah's various cultures. Liberty Park is 1.5 miles from downtown. Enter the park on 600 East at either 1300 South or 900 South.

The University of Utah, established in 1850, is on a terrace east of town. On the west edge of the campus is the **Utah Museum of Natural History,** which owns an archaeology collection of items excavated from around 3,800 Native American sites in Glen Canyon, Dead Man's Cave, Cowboy Cave, and other places in the region. Cultures include the Archaic, Fremont, Ancestral Pueblo, Paiute, Hopi, Pueblo, Shoshone, Navajo, and Ute. The Range Creek canyon exhibit interprets the extensive remains left by the Fremont people who lived there from A.D. 500 to 1350. An additional one thousand traditional pieces from the Great Basin, Southwest, Pacific Northwest, Northwest Woodland, and Great Plains cultures constitute the well-documented Anthony Taylor Collection. Temporary exhibits also often have a Native American focus. The museum sponsors field trips, special events, and lectures, and the gift shop sells Indian-crafted items.

To reach the museum from I-80, go north on 1300 East to 200 South. Turn right (east) for one block to University Street, then right onto University Street, and then left into President's Circle to the south corner.

In 1862, Colonel Patrick Connor and his California-Nevada volunteers built Camp Douglas to defend the mail route, control the local Indians, and keep an eye on the Mormons. **Fort Douglas Military Museum** preserves the history of the fort with indoor and outdoor exhibits. In the historic Quartermaster's Victoria Infantry Barracks are artifacts and photos of military life at the fort, as well as information about other Utah forts. You can take a self-guided tour of the museum campus or peruse the volumes on military history in the large library. The museum is located within the grounds of the University of Utah, east on Wasatch Drive. Look for the large flagpole on the south side of the parade grounds.

Also on the university's campus is the **Utah Museum of Fine Arts,** which displays a rotating series of objects from its collection of over seventeen thousand items. Included are representations of art styles from Old and New World cultures, ranging from Egyptian antiquities to twentieth-century lithographs. Native American items such as Navajo weavings, Mimbres pottery, pottery by famous Pueblo potter Maria Martinez, and artwork from northwest coast indigenous cultures are sometimes displayed. The museum also hosts traveling exhibits in its 74,000-square-foot Art and Architecture Center south of the library.

This Is the Place Heritage Park and Old Deseret Village is a living-history museum near the mouth of Emigration Canyon that marks the place where Mormon pioneers first

THE DEER

Deer range widely across the plateaus and mountains of the Southwest, and for centuries they provided not only food but many other necessities to the people who lived near them. Tanned deerskin was made into dresses, shirts, leggings, and moccasins. Scrapers fashioned from deer jawbones were used to remove corn from the cob, and antlers and bones became awls, spearpoints, needles, and decoration. Hooves became rattles, and long hollow leg bones made musical instruments to accompany ceremonial and social dancing.

entered Salt Lake Valley. In addition to immersing yourself in a re-creation of frontier life between 1847 and 1869, you can view "This Is the Place" National Historic Landmark, which commemorates the various people who have lived in and traveled through the valley, including Indians such as Washakie, leader of the Eastern Shoshones.

SOUTH OF SALT LAKE CITY

The **Utah Cultural Celebration Center** at the Riverfront in West Valley City highlights the music, dance, performance, and visual arts of various cultures of the Wasatch Front, including its Native Americans. The sixty-acre center sponsors exhibitions and public events designed to preserve and perpetuate cultural traditions and promote cultural exchange. The center displays an Olmec stone head sent to them from Veracruz, Mexico, their sister city. Their two-story Spirit of Diversity mural aptly portrays the mission of the center.

WEST OF SALT LAKE CITY

Skull Valley, about 35 miles south of the Great Salt Lake in a remote part of Tooele County, is home to the Skull Valley band of the Goshute Indians. (See above for the Confederated Tribes of the Goshute Reservation.) The **Skull Valley Reservation** (18,560 acres) was established in 1917 and 1918 and is governed by a traditional council. Today only about 30 of the 124 enrolled tribal members live on the reservation, the rest having moved to other places in search of better opportunities.

The reservation is surrounded by a variety of environmental threats, including Dugway Proving Grounds (where the U.S. government tested chemical and biological weapons), the world's largest nerve gas incinerator in the world, a Magnesium Corporation plant, and radioactive waste disposal sites. Recently, after consideration of the possibility of other economic ventures, the group itself has offered to lease land to a private utility company for storage of spent nuclear fuel. Controversial lawsuits have ensued, and the plan has been blocked for now.

VERNAL
Map #6

Around Town: Utah Field House of Natural History and Dinosaur Gardens, Western Heritage Museum
Nearby: Dinosaur National Monument, Dry Fork Canyon petroglyphs, Flaming Gorge National Recreation Area, Nine Mile Canyon, Uintah-Ouray Ute Reservation

Vernal is one of the largest towns in northeastern Utah and a good base camp for exploring the unique geology, paleontology, and archaeology of the region. The *Visitors Center* on Main Street has information, self-guided tour brochures, and a short video of area highlights.

It is in the **Utah Field House of Natural History State Park and Dinosaur Gardens**, a state-of-the-art museum with an assortment of displays in anthropology, geology, paleontology, and natural history that highlight the area's ecological diversity. Many of the exhibits are hands-on. Archaeology exhibits in the Amerindian Hall range from Fremont artifacts to Ute ceremonial attire. In the Dinosaur Gardens, you and the children can wander among the life-size sculptures of Mesozoic dinosaurs.

The small **Western Heritage Museum** houses the Thorne Collection of prehistoric and historic Indian artifacts. Included are Fremont petroglyphs and artifacts, Ute baskets, beadwork, musical instruments, arrowheads, and Ancestral Puebloan sandals. Historical photographs taken by Leo C. Thorne between the late 1800s and early 1900s are an added bonus. The museum also has other historical displays ranging from a country store to a one-room schoolhouse. The gift shop sells katsinas, pottery, and other crafts. The museum is at the Western Park complex.

NORTH OF VERNAL

Flaming Gorge National Recreation Area spans northeastern Utah and southern Wyoming. It includes over 200,000 acres of rugged mountains, expansive deserts, and a ninety-one-mile-long reservoir formed by Flaming Gorge Dam on the Green River. In this isolated place, moose, Rocky Mountain elk, pronghorn antelope, and bighorn sheep still roam, much as they did in the past, when Fremont, Comanche, Shoshone, and Ute hunters stalked big game here.

John Wesley Powell named many local landmarks, including the gorge itself, in the 1800s. Today, several scenic drives provide splendid vistas, roadside exhibits, and nature trails that highlight the abundant wildlife, native plants, and spectacular geology of the region.

Red Canyon Visitor Center perches at the edge of flaming red cliffs and affords an impressive view of the Flaming Gorge. A nature trail around the center has information about the local flora and fauna. The archaeological and historical exhibits in the center include artifacts from the Fremont and Ute people.

Flaming Gorge Dam Visitor Center, on US191 on the east side of the recreation area, features displays on regional geology, history, and natural history. A tour of the dam is also available.

Flaming Gorge National Recreation Area also provides abundant opportunities for outdoor recreation, including hiking, biking, backcountry travel, and water sports such as rafting, boating, and fishing. In winter, cross-country skiing, ice fishing, snowshoeing, and snowmobiling are popular along the many miles of trails. Facilities include marinas, lodges, campsites, picnic areas, and river guides. The main facilities are in the southeastern section, accessed by taking US191 north about 42 miles from Vernal or US191 south from I-80 in Wyoming. The towns of Manila and Dutch John offer lodging, restaurants, and other travel services.

SOUTH OF VERNAL

Dry Fork Canyon boasts petroglyphs etched by the Fremont Indians between A.D. 1 and 1200, famous for their quality and accessibility. The large panels cover two hundred square feet of the sandstone canyon walls, and some of the figures are up to nine feet tall. The rock art is on private land owned by the McConkie Ranch but remains accessible to the public as long as the signs are obeyed and the sites not damaged.

From the center of town, take Maeser Hwy (UT121) west to 3500 West Street. Turn north (right) and continue about 10 miles to a major fork in the road and the sign reading "Red Cloud Loop." Turn right, cross the bridge, and continue for 2 miles to the trees, canyon walls, and Dry Fork Creek. Trails take you to the petroglyphs. A self-guided brochure is available from the visitor center in Vernal.

If you are interested in prehistoric rock art, don't miss **Nine Mile Canyon,** the longest corridor of Fremont rock art ever found. As early as A.D. 300, Fremont Indians made their home in the canyon, hunting, farming, and storing their corn, beans, and squash in granaries built high in the cliffs. The ruins of the granaries, subterranean pithouses with rock and adobe-lined walls, and other Fremont dwellings can still be seen, both beside the road and in the distance with binoculars. When they abandoned the canyon, the Fremont also left behind some of their best and most numerous examples of pictographs and petroglyphs, including animals, hunting scenes, and stylized humanlike figures.

Among the thousands of rock art images is the famous Hunter Panel, which depicts a hunting scene with almost three dozen mountain sheep, six hunters, and over forty other figures. The panel is in Cottonwood Canyon, accessed from the Nine Mile Canyon Road.

The main route to Nine Mile Canyon is from Price. From town, travel 8 miles east on Hwy6/191 to Soldier Creek Road (2200 East, at Walkers Chevron gas station). Turn north (left) and stop at the Back Country Byway sign and kiosk on the corner for information on the canyon. Alternately, you can take US40 west from Myton for 1.6 miles and exit onto the first paved road to your left. A Back Country Byway sign and information kiosk are one-third mile down the road.

The all-weather dirt and gravel road through Nine Mile Canyon also passes ghost towns and other historic sites as it follows the old wagon route between the towns of Wellington and Myton, which was once an Indian trading post. Despite its name, Nine Mile Canyon is over 40 miles long, and the road between Wellington and Myton is 78 miles. For information, contact the BLM Vernal Field Office. Be advised that travel here can take most of the day; the area is primitive, so come prepared.

EAST OF VERNAL

At least 9,500 years ago, Paleo-Indians hunted the remnants of the Pleistocene game herds in what is now **Dinosaur National Monument**. Around 6000 B.C., Desert Archaic people built pithouses in the lower valleys for protection from the bitter winter winds and dug sego lily bulbs and bitterroot to eat in the springtime.

Fremont Indians, here from about A.D. 100 to 1250, gathered fruits, nuts, berries, and roots, hunted small game, practiced horticulture, and carved petroglyphs throughout the area. Later, Utes and Shoshones camped here in their conical-shaped brush wickiup shelters.

The majority of the monument is still rugged wilderness. The *Quarry Visitor Center,* 7 miles north of Jensen on UT149, was built over a working quarry for dinosaur bones. Once the most popular parts of the park, it has been closed indefinitely because of safety issues. You can take a virtual tour of the dinosaur quarry at the monument's Web site. A *temporary visitor center* has been erected just down the hill from the original. This is a good place for information on the petroglyphs and other Indian sites in the monument, as well as directions to more remote places.

A 12-mile *auto tour* that leads past rock art and other cultural sites begins from here. The park offers guides for the tour for a nominal fee. The Fossil Discovery Trail also begins at the center and shows dinosaur bones still encased in the earth.

Petroglyphs were left at Cub Creek at Dinosaur National Monument.

Diamond Mountain Road, north of the visitor center, will take you to *Jones Hole National Fish Hatchery* 48 miles away. A 4-mile (one-way) hiking trail here leads past rock art and Deluge Shelter, where Fremont and Desert Archaic cultural remains have been found. The site is about 1.5 miles from the trailhead. Ask at the visitor center for directions.

McKee Spring, which is near Island Park, has some of the finest examples of rock art in the monument, including geometric designs and large, humanlike figures. To reach this site, take UT149 south of the entrance near Dinosaur Quarry to Brush Creek Road (the first road south of Brush Creek). Turn right and go 4.1 miles to Island Park Road. Turn right and travel 12 miles to McKee Springs. This dirt road is often impassable after a heavy rain, so ask at the visitor center before embarking.

The *river corridor* also has petroglyphs and sites such as Mantle Cave, which is an alcove once used for storing grain and where a headdress of flicker feathers and ermine over 1,200 years old was found. Access to the Green and Yampa rivers is by permit or by guided float trips. A list of concessionaires is available at the visitor center, as are backcountry permits for camping and wilderness hiking to petroglyphs and archaeological sites.

The temporary visitor center is 30 minutes from the town of Vernal. Take Main Street (US40) east of town about 20 miles to UT149 and follow the signs to the monument. The center is about 7 miles from the turn.

Another small visitor center with exhibits and slide show, as well as much of the backcountry section of the monument, are located in Colorado (see Chapter 13, Northwest Colorado, page 215, for information).

WEST OF VERNAL

The 4.5 million acres of the **Uintah and Ouray Ute Reservation** lie in the mountains between Vernal and Provo. The northern Ute bands that live here are the Uintah, whose traditional home was Utah, and the Whiteriver and Uncompahgre, who moved here from Colorado. Tribal enrollment is 3,154 people, who are governed by a council consisting of two elected members from each band. Community enterprises include farming, forestry, and development of mineral resources, while many individuals work as farmers and stockmen.

Much of the reservation is now in a patchwork pattern and it comprises a small fraction of the Ute's original homelands. Fishing, hunting, and camping at backcountry lakes are the major tourist activities. Roiling rivers, deep canyons pecked with petroglyphs, and alpine trails provide a lovely natural setting for visitors to enjoy a taste of wilderness.

The group is currently working to develop other facilities for visitors, including more recreation facilities at *Bottle Hollow Reservoir,* so named because soldiers once hid their whiskey bottles here. The reservoir, about 1 mile west of Fort Duchesne, is an off-stream lake. It is now a place you can fish for channel catfish, bass, and trout.

Permits are available for boating, camping, hunting, fishing, and sightseeing from Utah Outfitting and Guide Services through the Fish and Wildlife office 1.5 miles south of US40, as well as at sporting goods stores in Vernal, Price, Salt Lake City, and other towns. Permits can also be purchased online at the tribal Web site.

Fort Duchesne (doo-SHAYN), east of Roosevelt and on the northern end of the reservation near the confluence of the Uintah and Whiterocks rivers, is headquarters for the reservation. In 1886, Major Benteen established a fort here with infantry troops that included two companies of buffalo soldiers. Logs were hauled from nearby canyons to build a commissary, storehouse, hospital, and living quarters. The fort was abandoned in 1912, but some of the nineteenth-century buildings are still being used today. The historical marker at 7600 E 800 South has information about the fort.

Ute Bulletin is a biweekly newspaper that reports on items of interest to tribal members. *Ute Lanes* provides bowlers with a chance to hone their skills.

Traditional dances include the Sun Dance, an important religious and social ceremony held in summer, the Turkey Dance, performed on various social occasions, and the Bear Dance in the spring.

The *Duchesne County Chamber of Commerce*, in the nearby town of Roosevelt, has information on places to eat and stay. When visiting the reservation, be advised that tourists should keep to the main roads.

EVENTS

APRIL/MAY *Native American Awareness Week:* Sponsored by several colleges and universities in Utah to promote cultural exchange and awareness of the various native groups in the state. Events can include lectures by nationally known speakers, powwows, arts and crafts vendors, film series, and the crowning of Miss Indian University of Utah. Call the various university multicultural centers for more information.

MAY *Bear Dance:* This ceremony traditionally celebrated the emergence of the bear from hibernation in the spring and includes traditional dancing and a feast. Held on Memorial Day weekend at Ft. Duchesne. Call 435-722-5141 for information; www.utetribe.com.

Living Traditions: A Celebration of Salt Lake's Folk & Ethnic Arts: Celebrates the arts and crafts of Salt Lake's various cultures. Held at Brigham Young University for three days on the weekend before Memorial Day. Washington Square, Salt Lake City. Call 801-596-5000 or visit http://arts.utah.gov/folk_arts_program.

Old Ephraim's Mountain Man Rendezvous: One of the largest mountain man rendezvous still around. Held in Blacksmith Fork Canyon on Memorial Day weekend. Call 435-245-3778 for information.

Utah Prehistory Week: Lectures, hands-on activities such as spear and atl-atl throwing, demonstrations on flint-knapping and creating rock art, lectures, and tours of prehistoric sites are held statewide and provide insight into the lives of those who lived in Utah thousands of years ago. Sponsored by the Utah Division of State History. Contact the Utah History Research Center, 801-533-3500, 300 South Rio Grande Street, SLC, UT 84101.

JUNE *Goshute Annual Powwow:* Powwow held in early June. Call Goshute tribal headquarters for information.

Heber Valley Powwow: Dancing, storytelling, food, arts and crafts. At Soldier Hollow, 435-654-2002, www.soldierhollow.com/pow-wow.php.

JULY *Black Hawk Mt. Man Rendezvous:* Recreation of a traditional rendezvous. Held in Mt. Pleasant. Call 435-462-0152 or 801-785-6639.

Native American Celebration in the Park: Includes an intertribal powwow, cultural displays, fireworks, live music, entertainment, and vendors. Liberty Park in Salt Lake City in late July. Call Chase Home Museum of Folk Art or go to www.nativeamericancelebration.com.

Northern Ute Indian Powwow and Rodeo: Indians come from all over the West to Fort Duchesne on July 4th weekend to participate in the dancing, all-Indian rodeo, Indian Market Days, and hand-game tournament. Call 435-722-5141 for information.

Sun Dance: A spiritual renewal ceremony taught to the Ute by the Shoshone. Held for several days in mid-summer at Sun Dance Grounds 10 miles north of Ft. Duchesne. No photography or recording is permitted at this religious ceremony. Call the Uintah-Ouray Ute Reservation for information.

AUGUST *Railroaders Festival:* Includes activities such as handcar races and rides, contests, Old Time Fiddlers' Concert, and buffalo-chip-throwing contest. On second Saturday in August. Contact Golden Spike National Historic Site for information.

SEPTEMBER *Bear Lake Mountain Man Rendezvous:* During the summers of 1827 and 1828, fur trappers and local Indians held large rendezvous at Bear Lake with over one thousand people attending. A Mountain Man Rendezvous recreates the experience each year in mid-September at Rendezvous Beach.

NOVEMBER *Indigenous Day:* Dinner and awards ceremony held to honor native peoples who live in Utah. Sponsored by Utah Division of Indian Affairs, held in Salt Lake City.

Ute Thanksgiving Powwow: Large powwow in late November at Fort Duchesne. Call Uintah-Ouray Ute Reservation for information, 435-722-8541.

Utah Valley State College Contest Powwow: Powwow on the campus of Utah Valley State College in Orem. Call 801-863-7276 for information.

CONTACT INFORMATION

American West Heritage Center
4025 South Hwy. 89/91, Wellsville, UT 84339
800-225-3378 *or* 435-245-6050
www.americanwestcenter.org
Tues-Sat 10am-4pm, and during festivals, Memorial Day-Labor Day; Mon-Fri 10am-4pm, Labor Day-Memorial Day; living-history site closed in winter; fee

Antelope Island State Park
4528 West 1700 South, Syracuse, UT 84075
801-652-2043; fee area
camping reservations: 800-322-3770
http://stateparks.utah.gov

Bear Lake Convention & Visitors Bureau
PO Box 26, Fish Haven, ID 83287
800-448-2327 *or* 208-945-3333
www.bearlake.org

Bear Lake State Park
1030 N Bear Lake, Garden City, UT 84028
435-946-3343
camping reservations: 800-322-3770
http://stateparks.utah.gov/parks/bear-lake/

Bear River Migratory Bird Refuge
2155 West Forest Street, Brigham City, UT 84302
Office: 435-723-5887
Visitor information: 435-734-6425
http://bearriver.fws.gov
Refuge: open sunrise to sunset daily
Visitor Center: Mon-Fri 8am-5pm; Sat 10am-4pm

Bridgerland Travel Center
160 North Main Street, Logan, UT 84321-4541
801-752-2161 *or* 800-882-4433.
www.utahtravelcenter.com/travelregions/bridgerland.htm

Bureau of Land Management
www.blm.gov/ut/st/en.html
Information on Utah's prehistoric rock art sites
www.ut.blm.gov/antiquitiescentennial/places.htm
Price Field Office
125 South 600 West, Price, UT 84501
435-636-3600
Salt Lake Field Office
2370 South 2300 West, Salt Lake City, UT 84119
801-977-4300
Vernal Field Office
170 South 500 East, Vernal, UT 84078
435-781-4400
For GPS guide to Nine Mile Canyon:
http://climb-utah.com/Misc/ninemile.htm

Cache County DUP Museum
160 North Main Street, Logan UT 84321
435-752-5139 *or* 435-753-1635
Tues-Fri 10am-4pm, June-Labor Day, or by appt

Cache Valley Tourist Information Center
199 North Main Street, Logan, UT 84321
800-882-4433 *or* 435-775-1890
www.tourcachevalley.com

Camp Floyd/Stagecoach Inn State Park and Museum
18035 West 1540 North, Fairfield, UT 84013
Mailing address: PO Box 446, Riverton, UT 84065-0446
801-768-8932
http://stateparks.utah.gov/parks/camp-floyd
Visitor Center: hours vary, daily Apr-mid Oct & Mon-Sat mid Oct-Mar; fee

Castle Country Regional Information Center
155 E. Main Street, Price, UT 84501
(at College of Eastern Utah Prehistoric Museum)
800-842-0789 *or* 435-637-5060
www.castlecountry.com

Chase Home Museum of Folk Art
900 South 700 East, (at Liberty Park), Salt
Lake City, UT 84105
801-533-5760
http://arts.utah.gov/experience_arts/galleries/
chase_home_museum/index.html
Mon-Thurs 12 noon-5pm & Fri-Sun 2pm-
7pm, summer; weekends, 12 noon-5pm,
spring and fall; no fee

College of Eastern Utah Prehistoric Museum
155 East Main Street, Price, UT 84501
Mailing address: 451 East 400 North, Price,
UT 84501
800-817-9949 *or* 435-613-5060
http://museum.ceu.edu
Daily 9am-6pm, Memorial Day-Labor Day;
Mon-Sat 9am-5pm, rest of year; donation

Confederated Tribes of the Goshute Reservation
Box 6104, 195 Tribal Center Road, Ibapah,
UT 84034
801-234-1138 *or* 435-234-1138
www.goshutetribe.com
　Ibapah Trading Post
　Ibapah, UT 84034
　435-234-1166

Council Hall
300 N. State Street, SLC, UT 84111
801-538-1900

Crystal Hot Springs
Rt. 1, Honeyville, UT 84314
801-279-8104 • www.crystalhotsprings.net
Call for hours; fee

**Daughters of Utah Pioneers Museum/Miles
Goodyear Cabin**
2148 Grant Avenue, Ogden, UT 84401
801-393-4460
Mon-Sat 10am-5pm, mid May-mid Sept; no fee

Dinosaur National Monument
www.nps.gov/dino
　Canyon Area Visitor Center
　4545 E. Highway 40, PO Box 210,
　Dinosaur, CO 81610
　970-374-3000
　Daily 8:30am-4:30pm, Memorial Day-
　Labor Day; Wed-Sun 8:30am-4:30pm,
　spring and fall; closed winter; no fee
　Temporary Visitor Center
　11625 E 1500 S, Jensen, UT
　435-781-7700
　Daily 8:30am-5:30pm, Memorial Day-
　Labor Day; daily 8:30am-4:30pm, rest
　of year; fee

Dinosaurland Travel Board
55 E. Main Street, Vernal, UT 84078
800-477-5558 *or* 435-789-6932
www.dinoland.com

Dry Fork Canyon petroglyphs
10 miles north of Vernal, McConkie Ranch;
donation
435-789-6932

Duchesne County Chamber of Commerce
50 E. 200 South, Roosevelt, UT 84066
435-722-4598 • www.duchesne.net

Emery County Museum of the San Rafael
64 North 100 East, Castle Dale, UT 84513
435-381-5252
http://castlecountry.com/what_to_do/
san_rafael_museum.html
Mon-Fri 10am-4pm; Sat 12 noon-4pm; fee

Fairview Museum of History and Art
85 N. 100 East, Fairview, UT 84629
435-427-9216
Mon-Sat 10am-6pm & Sun 1-6pm, mid May-
mid Oct; no fee

Flaming Gorge National Recreation Area
Jointly administered by the Ashley National
Forest District, USDA Forest Service and
the US Bureau of Reclamation
www.fs.fed.us/r4/ashley/recreation/
flaming_gorge/index.shtml
　Ashley National Forest District Ranger
　PO Box 279, Manila, UT 84046
　435-784-3445 • www.fs.fed.us/r4/ashley
　Bureau of Reclamation
　Flaming Gorge Field Division
　Box 278, Dutch John, UT 84023
　435-784-3445
　Camping reservations
　www.recreation.gov
　Flaming Gorge Dam Visitor Center
　435-885-3135
　Daily 8am-6pm, summer; Sat-Sun 10am-
　4pm, winter; recreation area use fee
　Red Canyon Visitor Center
　435-889-3713
　Daily 8am-6pm, summer; closed in winter;
　recreation area use fee

Fort Buenaventura
2450 A Avenue, Ogden, UT 84401-2203
801-399-8099
www1.co.weber.ut.us/parks/fortb
Daily, hours vary, Apr-Nov; fee

Fort Douglas Military Museum
32 Potter Street, Salt Lake City, UT 84113
801-581-1251 • www.fortdouglas.org
Museum: Tues-Fri 12 noon-5pm & Sat 12
noon-4pm; no fee; Grounds: 24 hours

Golden Spike National Historic Site
PO Box 897, Brigham City, UT 84302-0897
435-471-2209 • www.nps.gov/gosp
Visitor Center, daily 9am-5pm; fee

Heritage Museum of Layton
403 North Wasatch Drive, Layton, UT 84041
801-336-3930
www.laytoncity.org/public/museum
Tues-Fri 11am-6pm & Sat 1pm-5pm; no fee

John Hutchings Museum of Natural History
55 N. Center Street, Lehi, UT 84043
801-768-7180 • www.hutchingsmuseum.org
Tues-Sat 11am-5pm & first Mon of month
6pm-8pm; fee

Lehi Chamber of Commerce
235 East State Road, Lehi, UT 84043
801-766-9657 • www.lehiareachamber.org

Logan (*See* Bridgerland Travel Center)

Miles Goodyear Cabin (*See* Daughters of Utah
Pioneer Museum)

Museum of Anthropology at Utah State University
Room 252, Second Floor, Old Main, Utah
State University, Logan, UT 84322
435-797-7545
www.hass.usu.edu/~anthromuseum
Mon-Fri 8am-5pm, or by appt; no fee

Museum of People and Cultures
700 N 100 E, Allen Bldg., Provo, UT 84602
Mailing address: 105 Allen, BYU, Provo, UT
84602
801-422-0020 • http://mpc.byu.edu
Mon-Fri 9am-5pm; no fee

Museum of the San Rafael (*See* Emery County
Museum of the San Rafael)

Nine Mile Canyon (*See* BLM at Vernal)
www.blm.gov/utah/price/9mile.htm

Nora Eccles Harrison Museum of Art
Utah State University, 650 N 1100 East,
Logan, UT 84322
435-797-0163 • www.hass.usu.edu/~museum
Tues, Thurs, Fri 10am-4:30pm & Wed
10:30am-7pm & Sat 12 noon-4pm; closed
during exhibition installations; no fee

Northwestern Band of the Shoshone
Brigham Tribal Office
707 N. Main Street, Brigham City, UT
84302
800-310-8241 *or* 435-734-2286
Pocatello Tribal Office
427 N. Main Street, Ste. 101, Pocatello, ID
83204
888-716-5712 *or* 208-478-5712

Ogden (**town**)
www.utah.com/culture/ogden

Ogden Natural History Museum
Union Station, 25th & Wall Avenue, Ogden, UT
801-393-9884
www.theunionstation.org/museums

Ogden Nature Center
966 W. 12th Street, Ogden, UT 84404
801-621-7595 • www.ogdennaturecenter.org
Mon-Fri 9am-5pm & Sat 10am-4pm; fee

Ogden-Weber Convention and Visitor Bureau
2501 Wall Avenue, Suite 201, Ogden, UT
84401
866-867-8824 *or* 801-778-6250
www.ogdencvb.org
Mon-Sat 8am-8pm & Sun 10am-7pm, Memorial Day-Labor Day; Mon-Fri 8am-5pm,
rest of year

Pioneer Memorial Museum
300 N Main, Salt Lake City, UT 84103
801-532-6479 • www.dupinternational.org
Mon-Sat 9am-5pm & Sun 1pm-5pm, June-Aug;
Mon-Sat 9am-5pm, Sept-May; donation

Price
City Hall, 185 E Main Street, Price, UT 84501
http://city1.price.lib.ut.us

Provo (**town**)
www.utah.com/provo
Utah County Travel Council
51 S. University Ave., Suite 111, PO Box
912, Provo, UT 84601
800-222-8824 *or* 801-370-8393
www.utahvalley.org

Range Creek Wildlife Management Area
Utah Division of Wildlife Resources
435-613-3700
www.wildlife.utah.gov/range_creek

Salt Lake City (**town**)
www.visitsaltlake.com

Salt Lake City Convention and Visitors Bureau
90 S West Temple, SLC, UT 84101
800-541-4955 *or* 801-534-4902
Airport: Terminals 1 and 2
801-575-2800 • www.saltlake.org

San Rafael Swell (*See* BLM Price Field Office)
www.ut.blm.gov/sanrafaelohv

Skull Valley Band of Goshute Indians
PO Box 150, Grantsville, UT 84029
435-831-6163 • www.skullvalleygoshutes.org

Temple Square
Main and N, S, and W Temple streets, Salt
Lake City, UT 84101
800-537-9703 *or* 801-240-1245
Daily 9am-9pm; half-hour to one-hour tours
every ten minutes; no fee

**This Is the Place Heritage Park and Old
Deseret Pioneer Village**
2601 E. Sunnyside Avenue, Salt Lake City, UT
84108
801-582-1847 • www.thisistheplace.org
Old Deseret Village
Mon-Sat 10am-6pm with Mon & Fri hours
extended until 9pm; Living History
Season, Memorial Day weekend
through Labor Day; fee
Monument and Grounds
Daily dawn to dusk; no fee
Visitor Center
Mon-Sat 9am-5pm, summer; no fee

Uintah and Ouray Ute Indian Reservation
PO Box 190, 910 South 7500 East, Ft.
Duchesne, UT 84026
435-722-5141 • www.utetribe.com
Fish and Wildlife Department
901 South 6500 East, PO Box 190, Ft.
Duchesne, UT 84026
435-722-5511
Northern Ute Indian Powwow
435-722-5141
Ute Bulletin (annual subscriptions $25)
6700 E Highway 40, PO Box 100, Ft.
Duchesne Utah 84026
435-722-8541
www.utetribe.com
Ute Lanes
435-722-2341
Ute Tribe Outfitting and Guide Services
PO Box 807, Ft. Duchesne, UT 84026
435-722-5511

United States National Forest Service
Intermountain Regional Office
324 25th Street, Ogden, UT 84401
801-625-5306 • www.fs.fed.us/r4
Ashley National Forest
355 N. Vernal Avenue, Vernal, UT 84078
435-789-1181
Duchesne Ranger District
PO Box 981, Duchesne, UT 84021
435-738-2482
Flaming Gorge Ranger District
PO Box 279, Manila, UT 84046
435-789-3445
**Vernal Ranger District, District
Headquarters**
355 North Vernal Avenue, Vernal, UT 84078
435-789-3445
Uinta National Forest Supervisor
88 West 100 North, Provo, UT 84601
801-377-5780

Utah County Visitors Center
51 S. University Avenue, Provo, UT 84601
800-222-8824 *or* 801-370-8394
www.utahvalley.org/cvb

Utah Cultural Celebration Center
1355 West 3100 South, West Valley City, UT 84119
801-965-5100
www.wvc-ut.gov/CulturalCenter
Mon-Thurs 9am-7pm, Fri-Sun times vary depending on events

**Utah Field House of Natural History and
Dinosaur Gardens**
496 E. Main Street, Vernal, UT 84078
435-789-3799
http://stateparks.utah.gov/parks/field-house
Daily 8am-7pm, summer; daily 9am-5pm, rest
of year; fee

Utah Museum of Fine Arts
410 Campus Center Drive, Salt Lake City, UT
84112-0350
801-581-7332 • www.umfa.utah.edu
Tues-Fri 10am-5pm & Wed 10am-8pm & Sat-
Sun 11am-5pm; fee

Utah Museum of Natural History
1390 East President's Circle, University of
Utah, SLC, UT 84112
801-581-4303 (info line) *or* 801-581-6927
www.umnh.utah.edu
Mon-Sat 9:30am-5:30pm & Sun 12 noon-
5pm & first Mon of month 9:30am-8pm;
call for holiday hours; fee (first Mon of
month free)

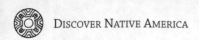

Utah Office of Tourism
Council Hall, 300 N State Street, SLC, UT 84114
800-200-1160 *or* 801-538-1030
www.utah.travel
Mon-Fri 8am-5pm & Sat 10am-5pm

Utah State Capitol
350 N. Main Street, Salt Lake City, UT 84101
800-200-1160 *or* 801-538-1563
tours: 801-538-1800
www.utahstatecapitol.utah.gov
Mon-Fri 8am-8pm; Sat-Sun 8am-5pm; no fee

Utah State Parks and Recreation
1594 W. North Temple, PO Box 146001,
    SLC, UT 84116
801-538-7220 • http://stateparks.utah.gov

Vernal Area Chamber of Commerce
134 West Main, Vernal, UT 84078
435-789-1352 • www.vernalchamber.com

Vernal Convention and Visitors Bureau
147 East Main Street, Vernal, UT 84078
435-789-6730 • www.utahconventions.org

**Weber State University Museum of Natural
    Science**
Lind Lecture Hall, 3705 Harrison Blvd,
    Ogden, UT 84408
801-626-6653
http://community.weber.edu/museum
Mon-Fri 8am-5pm; no fee

Western Heritage Museum
328 E. 200 South, Vernal, UT 84078
435-789-7399
www.co.uintah.ut.us/museum/whMuseum.php
Mon-Fri 9am-6pm & Sat 10am-4pm, Memo-
    rial Day-Labor Day; Mon-Fri 9am-5pm &
    Sat 10am-2pm, Labor Day-Memorial Day;
    donation

CENTRAL UTAH

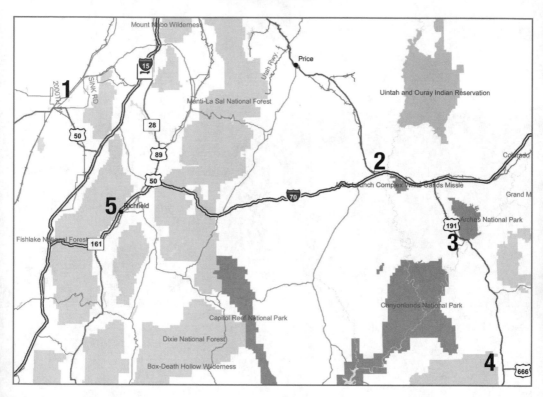

1. Delta
2. Green River
3. Moab
4. Monticello
5. Richfield

CHAPTER 22

CENTRAL UTAH

CENTRAL UTAH IS A SCENIC SPECTACLE of deserts, national forests, and the grand geological wonders of Canyonlands and the San Rafael Swell and Reef, which were carved out of the rocky land by rivers rather than rain. The environment here is hot and arid, and to survive, plants and animals have been forced to adapt. Many of the plants did so by shrinking their leaves and overall size to minimize water loss through evaporation. Others evolved a period of dormancy to survive the driest times of the year. Most animals avoid the worst of the relentless heat by hiding out during the day and becoming active only after the blazing sun has set.

One good way to explore remote areas in central Utah is with a guide. Guides can lead you to ancient ruins, rock art, and other Native American sites that might otherwise be inaccessible to you. *Utah Guides and Outfitters* is an association of outdoor outfitters in Utah, all of whom offer low-impact adventures. Visit their Web site for information on individual companies.

DELTA
Map #1

Around Town: Great Basin Historical Society Museum
Nearby: Fort Deseret State Monument, Great Stone Face

People inhabited the land around Delta as early as twelve thousand years ago, when they lived on the shores of an inland sea that has long since dried up. By the time Spanish explorers Dominguez and Escalante came through in 1776, Utes were living there.

The **Great Basin Historical Society Museum** displays rocks, arrowheads, desert fossils, photographs, and historical and cultural artifacts of the area, along with a video about Topaz, the nearby World War II Japanese internment camp.

SOUTH OF DELTA
Mormon settlers built Fort Deseret in 1865 during the Black Hawk War, a Ute uprising. The mud and straw adobe walls were erected in only eighteen days for protection

against possible attack, but the fort was never used. Instead, when Black Hawk and his followers came through, he and the settlers successfully negotiated a peace. Today, the fort walls have been partially restored at **Fort Deseret State Monument**, south of town near Mile Post 65 on UT257.

About 3 miles past Fort Deseret on UT257 is a turnoff leading to a large black lava rock called **Great Stone Face**. Many believe the rock's profile resembles the face of Mormon prophet Joseph Smith. Petroglyphs you pass on the way to the rock may relate to ancient hunting and water rights along the Sevier River.

GREEN RIVER
Map #2

Around Town: John Wesley Powell River History Museum
Nearby: Goblin Valley State Park, San Rafael Swell and Reef (Buckhorn Wash, Rochester Creek Panel), Sego Canyon Rock Art

Green River was founded in 1878 where the Old Spanish Trail, once the main trade route between New Mexico and California, crossed the Green River. Today, the town is a popular departure point for expeditions down the Green, Colorado, and San Juan rivers. It is also a good place to begin your exploration of the surrounding wilderness and its wealth of prehistoric and historic sites.

John Wesley Powell River History Museum commemorates the courage of the river runners who explored Utah's rivers. Creative exhibits range from the prehistory of the rivers and the round-hulled boats used by the Indians to the intrepid explorers who risked their lives before the advent of rubber rafts. You can also watch a multimedia presentation and buy maps and river charts in the gift shop. For a first-hand experience of river running, book a raft trip here from one of the numerous outfitters. An added bonus of these trips is a chance to see the rock art, prehistoric dwellings, and rock shelters hidden deep within the nearby canyons. The museum is on the east side of town just across the river bridge.

The *Green River Visitor Center* on east Main Street and the *Emery County Travel Bureau* on Farrer Street have visitor information.

WEST OF GREEN RIVER
San Rafael Swell and Reef is nine hundred square miles of amazing wilderness reminiscent of a miniature Colorado Plateau. This rugged and remote area is a geological maze of desert, red-rock canyons, hogback ridges, and intriguing rock formations. Dozens of outlaws, including Butch Cassidy and his gang, have found refuge in its isolation and intricacy. The Indians called it *Sau-auger-towip*, or "Stone House Lands." If you use your imagination, you can still see the same temples, buildings, and ruined cities that prompted early tourists in Green River to call it the "silent city."

Today, I-70 enters San Rafael Reef, the region's eastern boundary, 17 miles west of Green River and then continues west to bisect the swell. Although a few roads into this wilderness are passable by automobile, much of it is only accessible by dirt roads and trails suitable for mountain bikes, ATVs, 4x4s, horses, and hikers. Raft trips down the San Rafael River during seasons of high water are another access option.

No matter how you travel into San Rafael Swell, be sure to take your camera for some unforgettable photographs. Hidden in the magnificent scenery is a treasure trove of pre-history and history, as well as prolific dinosaur quarries.

Numerous pictographs and petroglyphs, the oldest dating back well over two thou-sand years (some say closer to 8,000 years), give silent witness to the people who once lived here, including Basketmakers, Fremonts, and Utes. Some of the examples still visible today are at Rochester Creek, Temple Mountain, Box Canyon Devil near Swayze's Cabin (south of I-70), Head of Sinbad at Locomotive Point (30 miles south of San Rafael Campground), Three Fingers Canyon, Moore Cutoff Road, and Buckhorn Wash.

Cottonwood Wash Road, which becomes Buckhorn Wash Road after crossing the San Rafael River, provides well-maintained access to the center of San Rafael Swell. South of the river is Cottonwood Wash Road, which travels through rolling hills of high desert. North of the river is Buckhorn Wash Road, where the scenery turns to towering canyon walls, rock art, and dinosaur tracks.

Buckhorn Wash has a mysterious Barrier Canyon–style pictograph panel created by an archaic culture two thousand or more years ago. Fremont Indians later added their own messages on the rock in the form of petroglyphs, and today you can see ancient images sprawling across two hundred feet of the canyon wall.

The Barrier Canyon culture was a hunter-gatherer society of people who made their homes in caves or brush shelters and used the atl-atl (a spear-throwing stick) as their main weapon. The original red figures they painted on the sandstone at Buckhorn Wash were created with powdered hematite that may have been mixed with animal fat or eggs. After decades of abuse by modern-day vandals, this panel has recently been restored to its orig-inal glory.

The site is about 22 miles north of I-70, near the San Rafael campground, the only official campground in the swell, which has ten dusty sites but no water. Buckhorn Wash can also be accessed from the town of Castle Dale.

Rochester Creek Panel has a variety of unique rock art on it. Archaeologists still disagree over who created these bizarre images–the Barrier Canyon culture or the Fremont culture. The site can be reached from either Moore Cutoff Road or UT10. A gravel road then trav-els 5.5 miles to a trailhead that marks the start of a half-mile hike to the panel.

The BLM is working on the San Rafael designation route to connect these and other cultural sites in the swell. If you plan to explore, a good map is vital (the BLM office in Price and the Castle Country Regional Information Center in Castle Dale have them), along with other wilderness necessities—water, food, spare tire, and a full gas tank. No services are available, and cell phone coverage is spotty. Also, be aware that this is flash flood coun-try. Do not camp or park in dry washes—they can become raging torrents after a sudden cloudburst.

SOUTH OF GREEN RIVER

Goblin Valley State Park is a good base for campers who want to explore the adjacent San Rafael Swell. The park itself looks like a landscape from another planet, with weirdly shaped rocks called "hoodoos" littering the valley floor. While here, you can follow a hik-

Strange shapes in Goblin Valley State Park evoke visions of aliens.

ing trail through the intricately eroded rock formations or enjoy a picnic amidst the bizarre scenery. The state park is off UT24, between Hanksville and Green River.

EAST OF GREEN RIVER

North of the town of Thompson Springs in **Sego Canyon** are some of the best panels of easily accessed rock art in Utah. The images, left from three different periods of settlements, are clustered on three adjacent panels on your left, plus two additional panels about 100 yards farther up the canyon and on your right. Vandals have taken their toll on the site, but restoration efforts on the main Barrier Canyon–style panel have brought back much of its original quality. Fremont and historic Ute images are also visible on the panels.

From I-70, take exit 185 to the small town of Thompson Springs, where you will cross the railroad tracks and follow the signs north about 3 miles to the junction of Sego Canyon and Thompson Canyon. When the road curves, stay to the right on the dirt road. Contact the Moab BLM offices for more information.

MOAB
Map #3

Around Town: Museum of Moab (formerly the Dan O'Laurie Museum)
Nearby: Arches National Park, Canyonlands National Park (Island in the Sky, the Maze, the
    Needles), Dead Horse Point State Park, Rock Art Auto Tour, Sevenmile Canyon

Moab is a convenient place to stay while touring the nearby canyon country. It is also a mecca for outdoor enthusiasts. With Canyonlands and Arches national parks, as well as miles of national forest and BLM land easily accessible from town, Moab has become a bustling hub for hikers, mountain bikers, four-wheelers, campers, and river rafters.

The **Museum of Moab** (formerly the Dan O'Laurie Museum) displays regional items dating from the time of the dinosaurs to early ancient inhabitants to the twentieth-century mining era. Native American artifacts include a model of a pithouse, a large burden basket,

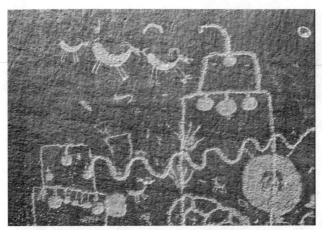

A large concentration of petroglyphs near Moab can be viewed from Potash Road.

tools, jewelry, and pottery. The gift shop sells books on the Four Corners states, and the museum publishes the *Canyon Legacy*, which includes articles of archaeological interest.

One of the easiest ways to explore the wilderness that surrounds Moab is via the river. The *visitor center* downtown on the corner of Main and Center streets has a brochure listing float trips that lead past numerous prehistoric sites. This multi-agency facility also provides information on the nearby national parks, national forest, and BLM lands. Interpretive displays include Ancestral Pueblo and Ute baskets, prehistoric points, pottery, and other artifacts found near Moab. A multimedia production about the Colorado Plateau includes Ancestral Pueblo and Navajo stories and is shown daily during the summer. The gift shop sells maps and books.

The **Rock Art Auto Tour** brochure, also available at the visitor center, provides a description and directions to several easily accessible rock art sites outside of town, including Potash Road, Golf Course Rock Art, Kane Creek, Courthouse Wash, and Wolfe Ranch in Arches National Park.

Canyonlands Field Institute is an organization dedicated to promoting stewardship of the land through direct experience. With that in mind, they lead hiking, camping, and river-running trips for all ages to study local natural and cultural history. Tours to the Navajo, Hopi, and Ute reservations are also offered.

NEAR MOAB

Canyonlands National Park is 527 square miles of colorful sandstone carved by the Colorado River and its tributaries into a labyrinth of winding canyons, spires, deep gorges, and precipitous bluffs. Most of Canyonlands is wilderness inaccessible by car, so hiking, mountain biking, and four-wheeling are some of the best ways to explore its interior. Another good way to the heartland is via the Colorado and Green rivers.

Paleo-Indians hunted in these canyons ten thousand years ago, and Archaic hunter-gatherers wandered through, leaving their marks on the rocks darkened with desert varnish. Ancestral Puebloans, living in small family groups, cultivated maize, beans, and squash here until A.D. 1200. Their neighbors were Fremonts, who left behind simpler dwellings. A wealth of rock art panels, stone tools, pottery sherds, and abandoned settlements provide a glimpse into the lives of these people, who lived here in ages past. Although less

*An ancestral Pueblo granary
lies hidden in an alcove in
Canyonlands National Park*

than 3 percent of the park has been surveyed for prehistoric sites, at least 1,380 prehistoric sites have been identified.

Canyonlands is divided into three districts, delineated by the Y confluence of the Green and Colorado rivers: *Island in the Sky* just north of Moab, the *Maze* to the west, and the *Needles* between the towns of Moab and Monticello. Even though the districts are geographical neighbors, they are not linked directly by roads, so traveling from one to the other will take from 2 to 6 hours by car. A fee is charged for all backpacking and four-wheel-drive trips into Canyonlands. Permits are available at visitor centers, ranger stations, and park headquarters.

NORTH OF MOAB

Some of the most breathtaking views of Canyonlands can be seen at Island in the Sky and Dead Horse Point State Park. To reach them, take US191 north of Moab for 10 miles to UT313. The first part of UT313 travels through **Sevenmile Canyon**, a gorge filled with giant cottonwoods and unusual rock configurations. For the first few miles, you can see petroglyphs on the right-hand side of the road. At about 18 miles, the road forks, with the right branch leading to Island in the Sky and the left continuing 5 more miles to Dead Horse Point.

Dead Horse Point is an isolated mesa six thousand feet above sea level on the rim of the Orange Cliffs escarpment. The view from this promontory is magnificent, stretching over countless square miles of vivid colors, towering spires, and buttes in southeast Utah's canyon country.

Stop at the *Dead Horse Point State Park Visitor Center* and interpretive museum to see the geological displays and obtain information about ranger-led activities, canyon rim hikes, and backcountry maps and permits. The twenty-one-unit campground has electrical hookups and sewage dump stations for recreation vehicles, but water for them is limited. Near the end of the point is a picnic site, a large shade pavilion providing a welcome respite from the summer sun, and walkways to the cliff rim, where two thousand feet below you can see a loop of the Colorado River eating its way through layers of sandstone, mudstone, conglomerate, and 300-million-year-old limestone.

Delicate arch graces a sandstone ledge in Arches National Park.

Island in the Sky, the northern border of Canyonlands, is an elevated plateau between the Green and Colorado rivers. From this island of rock, the land plummets to the river gorges over a thousand feet below in a series of terraces resembling huge stair steps. Overlooks provide vast, superlative views of an amazing landscape.

Be sure to bring your own water when visiting, as only bottled water is available in the park. Stop at the visitor center for exhibits, maps, publications, and information on the various trails and four-wheel-drive roads that lead into the park. Ranger-led walks and talks are held April through October. The twelve sites at Willow Flat Campground are available on a first-come, first-served basis.

Closer to Moab, but also accessed from US191, is **Arches National Park.** The landscape in Arches was sculpted by wind and rain, rather than rivers, into a spectacular architecture of windows, arches, pinnacles, and balanced rocks. The *visitor center* has archaeological displays and a short self-guided nature trail that highlights native plants. Interpretive programs are offered daily, March through October.

An 18-mile scenic drive from the visitor center travels past unusual rock formations, viewpoints, and short hikes to the base of many of the arches. In addition to providing fantastic scenery to contemporary travelers, Arches was once visited by prehistoric Indians. Ancestral Puebloans and Fremont Indians quarried the chert and jasper rocks for spear points and arrowheads. They left behind their unique rock art on the walls of *Courthouse Wash*.

Utes, who camped here in the 1830s and 1840s, also left their markings on the soft sandstones. Near *Wolfe Ranch*, homesteaded in 1888, you can see a hunting scene panel attributed to the Ute. To reach it, follow the signs to Delicate Arch and Wolfe Ranch, then hike the trail from the parking lot about 600 feet past the cabin and across the wash to a branch of the main trail.

SOUTH OF MOAB

The wild western district of Canyonlands is the **Maze**, a complicated labyrinth of gorges sliced into the layered sandstone below the Orange Cliffs. For the serious hiker or four-wheeler, this is an unparalleled opportunity to be immersed in wilderness. Because of its remoteness, visiting the Maze requires planning and time. Expect to spend at least three days, or more, when you travel here.

Primary access to the Maze is via a dirt road passable to regular vehicles except during stormy periods of weather. To reach it, take UT24 south from I-70 for 24 miles, and turn left just past the turnoff to Goblin Valley State Park. The dirt road travels 46 miles southeast to *Hans Flat Ranger Station*, where you can obtain backcountry and natural history information, topographical maps, and emergency aid. From the ranger station, you will need another 3 to 6 hours to reach the canyons of the Maze via a high-clearance, four-wheel-drive road. Be aware there is no food, gas, or potable water.

One of the star attractions in the Maze is *Horseshoe Canyon* (a.k.a. Barrier Canyon), which has some of the most significant and intriguing examples of rock art in the Southwest. The somber, life-sized beings on the *Great Gallery*, the most famous panel here, were created either by the Fremont or a culture that predated them. Horseshoe Canyon can be accessed from the ranger station via a four-wheel-drive road, but most people use the two-wheel-drive graded dirt road that travels 32 miles from UT24 to the west rim of the canyon, or they follow the dirt road from Green River for 47 miles. Please note that a storm can render any of these roads impassable.

Camping is permitted at the canyon's west rim trailhead but not in the canyon itself. From here a hiking trail (6.5 miles round-trip with a 750-foot descent) leads to the 280-foot panel of the Great Gallery, where dozens of anthropomorphic figures, lined up below a large, ominous image nicknamed the "Holy Ghost," stare out from the rock. Many consider these pictographs to be the oldest rock art in the Southwest, and it is the defining example of the Barrier Canyon style. No signs direct the way here, so be sure of your destination before you begin, and check with the ranger station for regulations about hiking the canyon.

The Great Gallery panel in the Maze is famous for its haunting petroglyphs.

Another four-wheel-drive road leads to the Maze Overlook, and an awe-inspiring view of a labyrinth of canyons made of red and white sandstone. From here a trail leads deep into the canyon complex to another famous rock art site, the secluded *Harvest Scene pictographs*.

MONTICELLO
Map #4

Around Town: Frontier Museum
Nearby: Beef Basin Towers, Needles District of Canyonlands, Newspaper Rock State Historical
  Monument, Ruin Park, Shay Canyon Petroglpyhs

The small town of Monticello, about 55 miles south of Moab on US191, has several lodging and dining options. The **Frontier Museum** on Main Street has historical exhibits featuring local cultures.

Four Corners School of Outdoor Education offers education programs on archaeology, outdoor skills, natural sciences, and the cultural heritage of the Colorado Plateau and Four Corners regions. Programs are offered from February to November and last from three to six days.

For maps and information, visit the *San Juan County Regional Travel Center* for Canyon Country on south Main Street.

NORTH OF MONTICELLO
The southeastern district of Canyonlands, to the east and south of the river confluence, is called the **Needles**. This is a complex jumble of unusual canyons, *grabens* (flat-bottomed valleys), and spectacular arches and is named for its hundreds of colorful rock spires made of Cedar Mesa Sandstone. An extensive trail system makes this the most popular backpacking destination in the park.

Much of the Needles is composed of the *Salt Creek Archaeological District*, which has the highest density of prehistoric sites on the Colorado Plateau, estimated to be almost sixty sites per square mile.

Chesler Park is a popular destination for an all-day hike in the Needles portion of Canyonlands National Park.

The only paved road to the Needles is UT211, which turns off US191 about 14 miles north of Monticello. The road descends through Indian Creek Canyon and past **Newspaper Rock State Historical Monument**. On this smooth, protected panel that the Navajo call *Tse Hane*, "The Rock That Tells a Story," over 350 distinct petroglyphs and pictographs were chipped and painted by Ancestral Puebloans, Utes, Navajos, and Europeans. A quarter-mile interpretive trail explains the natural areas on both sides of the road, and a primitive campground has a pit toilet, grills, and picnic tables, but no water.

Also nearby are the **Shay Canyon Petroglyphs**, which include a wide variety of styles and motifs. Featured are several Kokopelli figures, an animal fertility scene, and a large figure similar to a mastodon. The turnoff to the short trail is about 12 miles west of US191 on UT211.

Another prehistoric site is **Beef Basin Towers**, which has numerous square and circular stone towers constructed in the thirteenth century. Primitive trails lead to the towers, most of which are at the edge of an open area called *Ruin Park*. The park also contains *Farm House Ruin*, the site of a small village located at the west end of Canyonlands. Summer and fall access is over gravel roads 35 miles southwest of UT211 at Dugout Ranch. Contact the Bureau of Land Management Monticello Field Office for information on both Shay Canyon and Beef Basin.

The Needles District is 35 miles west from US191 on UT211. At the edge of the national park is a graveled road to *Canyonlands Needles Outpost*, which has a snack bar, general store with camping equipment and maps, gasoline, and a private campground with showers.

A short distance inside the park on the main road is the *visitor center*. Stop here to see the exhibits, to ask about the rock art and ancient ruins, and to purchase maps and backcountry permits.

One mile west of the visitor center on the paved road is an easy quarter-mile nature trail to *Roadside Ruin*, a well-preserved prehistoric granary built about seven hundred years ago. A brochure available at the trailhead points out many of the indigenous plants and their Indian usage.

In the park, the *Squaw Flat Campground* offers interpretive programs March through October. The campground has water, bathrooms, and twenty-six sites available on a first-come, first-served basis. Be advised that it usually fills from late March through June and again from September through mid-October.

RICHFIELD
Map #5

Nearby: Cove Fort, Fillmore, Fremont Indian State Park, Kanosh

Richfield Park was the site of a five-room house built centuries before Mormons settled in the area. Modern archaeologists found agricultural implements and earthen pots left by these earlier inhabitants, as well as four skeletons. Numerous other artifacts have been discovered in town, and a display in the foyer of the Sevier Valley Applied Technology School includes some of them.

Ten Mormon men settled the town in 1864 and called it Big Springs, only to abandon the site during the Black Hawk War of 1867. The town was resettled in 1870. At the Sevier Stake Mormon Tabernacle is a plaque marking the site of the 1865 Fort Omni, built by residents who feared the local Utes.

Today Richfield is a convenient place to stay along I-70 when visiting south-central Utah.

NORTHWEST OF RICHFIELD

As early as A.D. 1380, the Western Utes lived around the town of **Fillmore**, inhabiting this and other valleys on the eastern margin of the Great Basin. The Western Utes called themselves *Timpanogos,* meaning "Fish Eaters." Dominguez and Escalante, passing through in 1776, commented on them and their encampments near the shores of Utah Lake. In early pioneer days, one of their greatest leaders, Walkara, became known as the "Hawk of the Mountains."

In the park outside the *Territorial Statehouse State Park Museum* are descriptive panels detailing the Walkara (a.k.a. Walker) War of 1854, and the burial ground that contains his grave and those of twenty others killed in the conflict. The museum itself is housed in a red sandstone building that once served as the territorial capitol before Utah became a state. Its small display of Indian artifacts includes pottery, arrowheads, a baby basket, and a bow of Paiute leader Kanosh, for whom a nearby town was named.

SOUTHWEST OF RICHFIELD

When the Utah Highway Department built I-70 through Clear Creek Canyon, they uncovered an archaeological treasure trove. On a knoll called Five Finger Ridge, over one hundred Fremont structures were discovered, making it the largest Fremont site known in Utah. The structures date from A.D. 500 to 1300, and at peak occupation, the settlement was home to around 150 people.

Clear Creek Canyon was probably also used by Hopis, Paiutes, Utes, Goshutes, and Shoshones. Even today, Paiutes return to a sacred site in the canyon where a font collects rainwater.

At **Fremont Indian State Park,** you can see some of the seven tons of artifacts excavated from the site, as well as one of the most extensive collections of pictographs and petroglyphs in existence today. The visitor center has engaging displays, including a detailed replica of a Fremont dwelling, Pilling figurines, Fremont moccasins, and a bighorn sheep horn that has been heated, flattened, and then used as a scythe. The oldest item in the museum is a ten-thousand-year-old Folsom point. Also look for the life-size mannequin. A technique called cranial overlay was used to model the facial features of the mannequin according to the structure of an actual skeleton of a Fremont woman found near Salina, Utah.

An auto tour and interpretive trails will take you past prehistoric structures and numerous and unusual examples of rock art, including some that may have been used in coming-of-age ceremonies. With advance notice, you can make arrangements for a guided walk.

Outside the visitor center is a replica of a pithouse made of mud and poles. Unlike the ones the Fremont built with entrances through holes in their roofs, this pithouse has a doorway.

A primitive campground is situated at a pleasant, shady spot along the creek and is not usually crowded. The Paiute ATV Trail, a 200-mile loop through central Utah, also has an access point at the park.

Fremont Indian State Park is on I-70, about 24 miles southwest of Richfield.

Several miles past Fremont Indian State Park is **Cove Fort**, built in 1867 primarily as a rest stop for travelers along the "Mormon Corridor" between Salt Lake City and St. George. Relations between the settlers and the local Paiutes remained largely peaceful. In fact, Paiute leader Kanosh and about seventy of his followers eventually converted to Mormonism. At least one Indian girl worked at the fort, and others erected tipis in the sunflower fields and harvested the seeds.

The fort is constructed from volcanic rock and limestone. The Mormon Church has restored it with period furnishings, and costumed guides now explain its history to visitors. One of the rooms displays blankets and other items typically used for trade between Mormons and Indians.

Cove Fort is 2 miles south of exit 135 off I-15 and 1 mile north of exit 1 off I-70.

WEST OF RICHFIELD

The village of **Kanosh** was named for a Pahvant Ute leader who often acted as an intercessor between the Indians and white settlers and was a representative at the signing of the treaty to end the Walker War. He is now buried in the town cemetery.

North of town between Kanosh and Meadow is the home of one of the five bands of Paiutes administered from Cedar City. They own *Paiute Fabric Products*, where many Paiutes are employed sewing items for the U.S. Coast Guard, among other clients. Public tours of the small factory can be arranged by calling 435-759-2434.

To reach the town, take I-70 south of Richfield to I-15. Turn north on I-15 to exit 146, and follow UT133 to town.

EVENTS

MAY *Utah Prehistory Week:* Sponsored by the Utah Division of State History. Lectures, hands-on activities such as spear and atl-atl throwing, demonstrations on flint-knapping and creating rock art, lectures, and tours of prehistoric sites are held statewide and provide insight into the lives of the people who lived in Utah thousands of years ago. Contact the Utah History Research Center, 801-533-3500, 300 South Rio Grande Street, SLC, UT 84101.

Blue Mountain Festival of the Old West: Mountain man events, Native American dances, and food. In Dodge Canyon near Monticello. Call for information, 435-587-2332, www.bullhollow.com/blue.mountain.festival.html.

CONTACT INFORMATION

Arches National Park
PO Box 907, Moab, UT 84532-0907
Visitor information: 435-719-2299
Headquarters: 435-719-2100
www.nps.gov/arch
Visitor center: daily 8am-4:30pm, with
extended hours spring-fall
Park: daily, 24-hours; fee

Bureau of Land Management
www.blm.gov/ut/st/en.html
Information on Utah's prehistoric rock art sites
www.ut.blm.gov/antiquitiescentennial/
places.htm
Fillmore Field Office
35 East 500 North, Fillmore, UT 84631
435-742-3100
Moab Field Office
82 East Dogwood, Moab, UT 84532
435-259-2100
Monticello Field Office
435 North Main, PO Box 7, Monticello,
UT 84535
435-587-1500
Price Field Office
125 South 600 West, Price, UT 84501
435-636-3600
Richfield Field Office
150 East 900 North, Richfield, UT 84701
435-896-1500

Canyonlands National Park
www.nps.gov/cany
Main Office
2282 SW Resource Blvd, Moab, UT 84532
Visitor information: 435-719-2313
Backcountry information: 435-259-4351
Island in the Sky District
435-259-6577
Visitor Center: daily 9am-4:30pm, with
extended hours spring-fall
Park: open during daylight hours
Maze District
Hans Flat Ranger Station
435-259-2652
Daily 8am-4:30pm
Needles District
Ranger Station
435-259-6568
Daily 9am-4:30pm, with extended hours
Mar-Oct

Canyonlands Field Institute
PO Box 68, 1320 S. Hwy 191, Moab, UT
84532
800-860-5262 *or* 435-259-7750
www.canyonlandsfieldinst.org

Canyonlands Needles Outpost
PO Box 1107, Monticello, UT 84535
435-979-4007
www.canyonlandsneedlesoutpost.com

Cove Fort
HC74 Box #6500, Cove Fort, UT 84713
435-438-5547 • www.covefort.com
Daily except in inclement weather; 8am-1 hour
before sunset, Apr-September; daily 9am-1
hour before sunset, Oct-Mar; no fee

Dead Horse Point State Park
PO Box 609, Moab 84532-0609
435-259-2614; Visitor Center: 435-259-6511
www.stateparks.utah.gov
Visitor Center: daily 9am-5pm, winter; daily
8am-6pm summer
Park: daily 6am-10pm; fee

Delta (town)
76 North 200 West, Delta, UT 84624
435-864-2759 • www.deltautah.com

Emery County Travel Bureau
48 Farrer Street, Green River, UT 84525
888-564-3600 *or* 435-564-3600
www.sanrafaelcastlecountry.com

Fort Deseret State Monument
Contact: Millard County Tourism
PO Box 854, Delta, UT 84624
888-463-8627 *or* 435-864-1400
www.millardcountytravel.com/placestosee/
oldfortdeseret.htm

Four Corners School of Outdoor Education
Dept UT, East Route, Monticello, UT 84535
800-525-4456 *or* 435-587-2859
www.fourcornersschool.org

Fremont Indian State Park
3820 West Clear Creek Canyon Road, Sevier,
UT 84766
800-322-3770 *or* 435-527-4631
http://stateparks.utah.gov/parks/fremont
Daily 9am-6pm, Memorial Day-Labor Day;
daily 9am-5pm, winter; fee

Frontier Museum
233 S Main, Monticello, UT 84535
435-587-3401

Goblin Valley State Park
PO Box 637, Green River, UT 84525-0637
Park: 435-564-3633
Reservations: 800-322-3770
http://stateparks.utah.gov/parks/goblin-valley

Great Basin Historical Society Museum
PO Box 550, 328 W. 100 North, Delta, UT 84624
435-864-5013
www.greatbasinheritage.org/gbmuseum
Mon-Fri 10am-4pm & Sat 1pm-4pm, summer;
   winter hours may vary; no fee

Green River Visitor Information Center
885 E. Main, Green River, UT 84525
435-564-3427 • www.greenriverutah.com

John Wesley Powell River History Museum
1765 East Main Street, Green River, UT 84525
435-564-3427 • www.jwprhm.com
Daily 8am-8pm, summer; daily 8am-5pm,
   winter; fee

Moab Visitor Center
PO Box 550, 125 E. Center Street, UT 84532
800-635-6622 *or* 435-259-8825
www.discovermoab.com
Map and auto tour of rock art:
www.discovermoab.com/rockart.htm

Monticello (town)
PO Box 457, 17 North 100 East, Monticello,
   UT 84535
435-587-2271 • www.monticelloutah.org

Museum of Moab
118 East Center, Moab, UT 84532
435-259-7985
www.moab-utah.com/danolaurie/museum.html
Mon-Fri 10am-6pm & Sat-Sun noon-6pm,
   summer; Mon-Fri 10am-3pm & Sat-Sun
   noon-5pm, winter; no fee

Richfield (town)
75 E Center Street, PO Box 250, Richfield,
   UT 84701
435-896-6439 • www.richfieldcity.com

San Juan County Regional Travel Office
117 South Main Street, PO Box 490, Monticello, UT 84535
800-574-4386 or 435-587-3235
www.utah.com/visitor/travel_offices

Territorial Statehouse State Park Museum
50 W. Capitol Street, Fillmore, UT 84631
435-743-5316
http://stateparks.utah.gov/park/
   territorial-statehouse
Daily 9am-6pm

Utah Guides and Outfitters
www.utah-adventures.com

Utah State Parks
1594 West North Temple, Salt Lake City, UT
   84116
877-887-2757 *or* 801-538-7220
http://stateparks.utah.gov

SOUTHERN UTAH

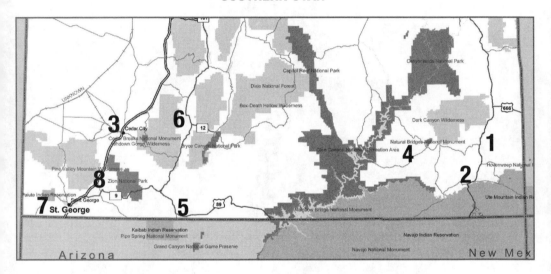

1. Blanding
2. Bluff
3. Cedar City
4. Glen Canyon National
   Recreation Area

5. Kanab
6. Panguitch
7. St. George
8. Zion National Park

CHAPTER 23

SOUTHERN UTAH

MOTHER EARTH IS FRACTURED in southern Utah, with mesas and spires, pinnacles and needles, and natural bridges and arches all shuffled into an astonishing rocky jumble. Words to describe the scenery range into the superlative: unbelievable, spectacular, awesome, gorgeous. Climate varies with the altitude, which swings from 2,350 feet at Beaver Dam Wash to 12,721 feet in the La Sal Mountains, but in general, it is hot in summer and cold in winter.

Southwestern Utah, also called Utah's "Dixie," has the mildest temperatures in the state. Here you will find ranching, retirement communities, forests, lakes, red rocks, and national parks of exceptional beauty. By contrast, much of the southeastern portion of the state is a wilderness of deserts, mountains, and portions of the rugged Colorado Plateau, where remnants of ancient cultures still infuse the land with an otherworldly mystery and where a portion of the Navajo Reservation provides an opportunity for visitors to learn more about contemporary Native Americans.

A good way to explore remote areas in southern Utah is with a guide who can lead you to ancient ruins, rock art, and other Native American sites that might otherwise be inaccessible to you. *Utah Guides and Outfitters* is an association of outdoor outfitters in Utah, all of whom offer low-impact adventures. Visit their Web site for more information on individual companies.

BLANDING
Map #1

Around Town: Blue Mountain RV Park and Trading Post, Cedar Mesa Pottery, Edge of the Cedars Sate Park, Huck's Museum and Trading Post, Nations of the Four Corners Cultural Center, White Mesa Institute for Cultural Studies
Nearby: Butler Wash, Grand Gulch Primitive Area, Mule Canyon Ruins, Natural Bridges National Monument, Trail of the Ancients, Westwater Ruin, White Mesa Ute Indian Reservation

Blanding, in the southeastern corner of Utah, is a mix of Wild West cowboys, prehistoric sites, and modern-day Native American cultures. With around 3,500 people, it is the largest town in San Juan County and a good place to stay and eat.

On the northwest edge of Blanding is the **Edge of the Cedars State Historical Park**, which preserves the ruins of an Ancestral Puebloan village built on a slight rise with an unobstructed view. The pueblo, inhabited between about A.D. 700 and 1220, had ten kivas and seventy-five surface rooms. A short, self-guided trail now leads through a stabilized ruin and includes a climb into a kiva.

The *visitor center* has a museum that is the repository for Ancestral Puebloan artifacts recovered in the southeastern part of the state, and its exhibits are some of the finest around. The history of people in the Four Corners area from prehistoric times to the historic Ute and Navajo is covered. Exhibits include the largest collection of prehistoric Puebloan pottery on display in the Four Corners region, a seven-hundred-year-old Bullet Canyon loom of the type still used by Pueblo weavers, an eight-hundred-year-old macaw feather sash, baskets, stone knives, and wooden plates.

You can also view living-history films, Indian crafts demonstrations, and gardens of native plants at the park. Special programs, exhibits, and workshops, such as Ute flute making and Navajo astronomy, are offered throughout the year. Park staff has information about other activities in the Four Corners connected to native peoples and where to find rock art.

Edge of the Cedars is also a departure point for the **Trail of the Ancients**, a 180-mile scenic loop past prehistoric ruins, the site of the last armed encounter between Indians and whites on the frontier (1923), national monuments relating to the Native American experience, and many other attractions. The route passes some of the best Ancestral Pueblo sites open to the public (including some of those we have listed separately), as well as sites of natural wonders and those on the Navajo Reservation. A map is available at Edge of the Cedars State Park, as well as at the multi-agency visitor center in the nearby town of Monticello.

The corn ground by prehistoric Indians with manos and metates was smaller than modern varieties.

Nations of the Four Corners Cultural Center is dedicated to the cultures that have inhabited San Juan County. You can tour replicas of traditional Navajo, Ute, Anasazi, Mexican, and Anglo dwellings while hearing about the heritage of the diverse cultures. Following the tour, you can enjoy an ethnic dinner and performance of traditional music and dance. The center is located 1 mile west of Blanding Cultural Center on the rim of Westwater Canyon.

Cedar Mesa Pottery employs Navajos and Utes for production and hand-painting of their ceramics. Many of the designs used are original creations of the employees. On a tour of the pottery factory (available on weekdays), you can watch the pottery being produced and painted. The enterprise also sells rugs, jewelry, sand paintings, and other crafts.

You can also shop for pieces made by native artisans from nearby reservations at several other places in town. Unique items for sale at **Blue Mountain RV Park and Trading Post** include award-winning Tohono O'odham baskets with exterior beading by Navajo artists. In addition to items for sale, **Huck's Museum and Trading Post** has an extensive private collection of Indian artifacts from the past thousand years, including arrowheads, beads, pendants, and Anasazi pottery.

The **White Mesa Institute for Cultural Studies** offers educational programs on the native cultures and natural history of the Southwest. The institute is sponsored by the College of Eastern Utah.

SOUTH OF BLANDING

Just south of town is **Westwater Ruin**, a cliff dwelling with storage structures, work areas, five kivas, and dwelling rooms. Take US191 south from the stoplight for 1.7 miles to the paved road leading west. Two miles down this road is the viewpoint to the ruin.

About 12 miles south of Blanding on US191 is **White Mesa Ute Indian Reservation**, part of the larger Ute Mountain Ute tribe with headquarters 100 miles east in Towaoc, Colorado. About 380 people live here in the village of White Mesa at an elevation of 6,200 feet.

Indian Canyon on the reservation has been set aside as a refuge for sacred ceremonies and prayerful retreats. Sweat lodge frames, dancing and arbor grounds, and fire circles are used by tribal members and others for vision quests, sweat lodges, coming-of-age rituals, and other important ceremonies. Plans are to build a Village House to extend the use of the site.

Also south of Blanding on US191 is the intersection with UT95. Turn west onto UT95 and travel about 11 miles to **Butler Wash**, with twenty-three Ancestral Pueblo cliff dwellings and storage structures that date to the mid-thirteenth century. Three of the kivas at Butler Wash are of the round, common Mesa Verde type, but the fourth is square, which indicates influence by the Kayenta culture found in Arizona. A 1-mile loop trail leads to an overview of the ruins; an interpretive brochure is available at the trailhead or from the BLM San Juan Resource Area in Monticello.

Mule Canyon Ruin, off UT95 about 26 miles southwest of Blanding and 10 miles west of Butler Wash, has several Ancestral Pueblo surface dwellings, a reconstructed kiva, and a tower. There are also an interpretive sign explaining the site, restrooms, and disabled accessibility.

A few miles farther west on UT95 is the intersection with UT261. Turn south here to **Grand Gulch Primitive Area**, an excellent place for the serious backpacker or horse-back rider to find Anasazi ruins. The 50-mile long canyon has several hundred cliff dwellings, kivas, and an uncounted number of impressive petroglyphs and pictographs. Access to the box canyon is via a 5-hour round-trip hike. Permits are required to enter this natural/archaeological preserve. The Kane Gulch Ranger Station, beside UT261, 4 miles south of UT95, provides permits on a limited basis, plus a self-guiding booklet. To purchase a permit in advance, contact the BLM office in Monticello.

UT95 continues a short distance to UT275 and the entrance to **Natural Bridges National Monument**. The bridges here were carved by streams, not wind and rain, and once decorated the backyard of prehistoric cultures. Between A.D. 100 and 1300, Ancestral Puebloans grew corn on the nearby mesa tops and eventually built small pueblos here. Cass Hite was the first recorded Anglo to see the sandstone bridges. A Paiute guide who called the bridges *ma-vah-talk-tump,* meaning "under the horse's belly," led him here in 1883.

Stop at the *visitor center* for exhibits, a slide show, and information about Native American sites in nearby Allen Canyon, White Canyon, and Grand Gulch Primitive Area. For scenic overlooks and hiking trails to the bridges, prehistoric rock art, cliff dwellings, and hunting camps, follow the 9-mile loop road.

The grandest of the bridges is *Sipapu.* The dome of the U.S. Capitol building would almost fit underneath it. *Kachina Bridge* stands over two hundred feet high and continues to grow as the river underneath it carves deeper into the earth. It is decorated with more prehistoric artwork than any other bridge in the monument. Cliff dwellings are scattered two hundred yards to the left of the bridge. Under the pale pink *Owachomo Bridge* is a pothole known as Zeke's Bathtub, named for the first curator of the monument, and once a source of drinking water for prehistoric residents.

A major attraction at the monument is *Horsecollar Ruin,* a well-preserved Ancestral Puebloan site abandoned over seven hundred years ago. The ruin is named for two structures with perfectly round doorways that resemble a horsecollar. The usage of the unusual structures remains a mystery. Much of the site is the same as it has been for hundreds of years, such as the original roof and interior of the kiva.

If possible, plan to stay until after sunset for an extraordinary view of the Milky Way rising over Owachomo Bridge. In 2007, Natural Bridges became the first international Dark Sky Park, which means it has one of the darkest, starriest skies you can find in any park. Join one of the summer astronomy ranger programs to learn more about the thousands of stars and planets visible here at night.

The thirteen-site primitive campground, comfortably situated in the juniper forest, is available on a first-come basis. No backcountry camping is allowed in the monument.

You can download a map and visitor guide at the monument's Web site.

BLUFF
Map #2

Nearby: Fourteen Window Ruin, Sand Island Petroglyphs, St. Christopher's Episcopal Mission, Three Kiva Ruins

Bluff is an isolated town of about three hundred people, founded in 1880 by Mormon pioneers who named it for the red sandstone hills edging the town. The first prehistoric Clovis hunting site found on the Colorado Plateau is nearby, along with abandoned Ancestral Puebloan dwellings built in cliff alcoves along Comb Ridge. Historical native groups in the area have included the Navajo and the Paiute. Today, the Navajo Reservation borders the town. Galleries and trading posts in town feature the arts and crafts of regional native artists, and local Navajos occasionally sponsor public dance performances, rodeos, and other get-togethers.

Recapture Lodge, in addition to being a good place to stay, sponsors naturalist tours and features a nightly slide show of the region. The lodge is run by longtime outfitters who are well-versed in the local backcountry Indian ruins and stunning scenery.

EAST OF BLUFF

St. Christopher's Episcopal Mission, 2 miles east of town on UT163, was established for the Navajo in 1943, and the architecture of the sandstone building reflects native influence. A statue of the Navajo Madonna and Child stands on the site of the original church. Tours of the grounds are available.

One mile past the mission on UT163, just after mile marker 4 on the right, is a parking area and cable-supported footbridge that spans the San Juan River. The swaying San Juan footbridge was once the only way to get from the Navajo Reservation to Bluff. Today, it will lead you to the trail to **Fourteen Window Ruin**, an Anasazi cliff dwelling. After crossing the bridge, follow dirt roads past Navajo farmlands for a half mile to a road at the bottom of the cliffs. Turn right (west) for a half mile; the ruins are in an alcove on your left. The trail is an easy walk of about 2 miles round-trip from the parking lot.

Three Kiva Ruins, a side trip on the Trail of the Ancients Scenic Byway, is a fine example of an Ancestral Puebloan dwelling. It includes a kiva with a restored roof that you can enter the traditional way, via a ladder through the roof. Occupied between A.D. 1000 and 1300, the main Three Kiva Pueblo once had fourteen rooms, a ramada work area, three kivas, a trash mound, and what is thought to have been a turkey run. The ruin is in an isolated place in Montezuma Creek Canyon. Take US163 east of Bluff to Montezuma Creek Road and the junction with UT262. Turn left (north) onto UT262 and follow the road to SJC Road 414. Turn right (east) onto SJC Road 414 and follow it to SJC Road 446. Turn left (north) onto SJC road 446 and follow it to boundary of the Navajo Nation, where the road becomes SJC Road 146. Follow SJC Road 146 to the pueblo.

UT262 south and east of Blanding leads to Hatch Trading Post (see Chapter 7, The Navajo, page 102, for more on trading posts) and Hovenweep National Monument (see Chapter 15, Southwest Colorado, page 270).

WEST OF BLUFF

Sand Island Campground on the banks of the San Juan River is 3 miles west of Bluff on US163. The boat launch here is a principal departure point for San Juan River trips. Several tour guides offer popular float trips past geological and archaeological sites along the river, including River House, the largest cliff dwelling on the river.

The dirt road to the right of the campground leads to the **Sand Island Petroglyphs**, a fifty-yard-long panel of rock art etched by people from the San Juan and Basketmaker cultures. Five of the figures are depictions of Kokopelli, a hump-backed flute player sometimes called the Anasazi Casanova because of his role in assuring the fertility of the women of the villages. Kokopelli is also said to have traveled across the Southwest giving kernels of life-giving corn to the people. Legend claims he came from the Yucatan.

US163 continues southwest of Bluff toward the small town of Mexican Hat. If you feel adventurous, turn at milepost 29 (about 15 miles southwest of Bluff) onto a fair-weather dirt road that winds for 17 miles through the spectacular scenery of Valley of the Gods, which is a small-scale version of Monument Valley on the Navajo Reservation. Plan 1 to 1.5 hours for the drive.

Further west off US163 is Goosenecks State Park, with primitive camping and an amazing view of the tight curves of the San Juan River a thousand feet below. Turn onto UT261 for 1 mile, and then left onto UT361 for 3 miles.

A short drive from the state park is Muley Point Overlook, with a wonderful panorama of Monument Valley that makes for one of the best views in the Southwest. Take UT261 northwest from the Goosenecks turnoff for 9 miles. This is a dry-weather gravel road with sharp curves and steep grades.

US163 continues to the Navajo Nation Indian Reservation. Sites in Utah that are on the reservation include Monument Valley and Goulding Trading Post (although the visitor center is in Arizona), Oljato Trading Post, Poncho House, Hatch Trading Post, Four Corners National Monument and Navajo Tribal Park, and Rainbow Bridge National Monument (see Chapter 6, The Hopi, and Chapter 7, The Navajo, for more information).

CEDAR CITY
Map #3

Around Town: Iron Mission State Park and Museum, Paiute Indian Tribe of Utah
Nearby: Cedar Breaks National Monument, Parowan, Parowan Gap Petroglyphs

The land around Cedar City has been home to Paiutes for hundreds of years. In the 1800s, the five Paiute bands were closely associated with the Shoshone. In 1954, official United States government recognition and services were withdrawn from the Paiute, with disastrous results. In addition to losing fifteen thousand acres of land, they experienced a mortality rate of close to 50 percent due to lack of income and health services. After many years of lobbying the federal government, the tribe was finally re-recognized in 1980, and a constitution was approved in 1981. Today the **Paiute Indian Tribe of Utah** has a village in northeastern Cedar City, and the five bands are administered from the offices there. The annual Paiute Restoration Gathering is held here in mid-June to commemorate federal recognition of the tribe.

When Mormon pioneers settled Cedar Fort, it was as a base for iron mining and manufacturing. Today, the town of Cedar City makes a good base for touring Zion, Bryce Canyon, Cedar Breaks, and other sites. The *chamber of commerce*, located in the park downtown, publishes a brochure of sights to see, as well as cultural and sporting events in town. Ask here for information on lodging and places to eat in town.

If you are interested in backcountry travel to find prehistoric sites, visit the *BLM Escalante Resource Area* office on the west side of town for maps and information.

Iron Mission State Park and Museum tells the story of development in Iron County that began with Mormon missionaries in the 1850s. Among the displays of pioneer arti-facts, horse-drawn vehicles, farm equipment, and historic buildings are a few Indian games collected by William R. Palmer and a small collection of Indian hunting tools, weapons, and clothing.

NORTH OF CEDAR CITY

The small town of **Parowan**, north of Cedar City off I-15, is the seat of Iron County and the oldest community in southern Utah. For information on places to stay and eat in town, stop at the town's *visitor center* on Main Street.

To view Fremont rock art, travel north on Main Street to 400 North (the last street) and turn west (left) to **Parowan Gap Petroglyphs**, about 10 miles northwest of town. When Fremont Indians passed through this deep gorge in the Red Hills, they pecked into the rock, leaving behind images of snakes, lizards, mountain sheep, geometric designs, and human figures resembling spacemen. Between A.D. 750 and 1250, other groups also tra-versed Parowan Gap and left the remnants of their passing in the form of pithouses, tools, pottery, and rock art. A map and interpretive brochure of the site are available at the BLM office in Cedar City.

EAST OF CEDAR CITY

Cedar Breaks National Monument is a three-mile-wide amphitheater of eye-piercing white and orange cliffs. Fremont Indians once gathered fruit here during the summer. His-torical Indians visited, too, and called the place "Circle of Painted Cliffs."

The *visitor center* has information on the geology, wildlife, and wildflowers in the park. The 5-mile *Rim Drive* provides four breathtaking views of the canyon, and one of the two hiking trails passes bristlecone pine trees over one thousand years old. Although the road and visitor center are closed by snow from mid-October to late-May, you can still enjoy the park during that time on cross-country skis and snowmobiles.

GLEN CANYON NATIONAL RECREATION AREA (LAKE POWELL)
Map #4

Around Lake Powell: Defiance House, Glen Canyon Dam, marinas, Rainbow Bridge National Monument

Glen Canyon Nation Recreation Area encompasses 1.25 million acres of canyons, buttes, deserts, and lakes in Arizona and Utah. The heart of the recreation area is Lake Powell, which holds 27 million acre-feet of water and is 186 miles long at capacity. Back-ing up behind Glen Canyon Dam into a maze of sandstone gorges, the lake creates a swatch of vivid blue surrounded by desert red. It is an anomaly in a place that gets fewer than eight inches of precipitation a year, and while environmentalists and local Native Ameri-cans have mourned the loss of the beautiful Glen Canyon (which now lies under the lake), many others have enthusiastically embraced the new opportunities for outdoor recreation.

Some of the first evidence of people living here was left by hunters and gatherers of the Desert Archaic culture. Then, around two thousand years ago, Basketmakers moved into the area and farmed along the Colorado River. Eventually, the area inhabitants began to build cliff dwellings and irrigation systems and learned to craft pottery. Around 1250 A.D. they abandoned Glen Canyon, and soon after, Utes, Navajos, and Paiutes moved in.

Today Lake Powell provides an abundance of water sports, as well as excellent backcountry hiking and mountain biking. Four of the marinas—*Wahweap*, the largest and 6 miles from Page on the south shore, *Hite* in the north, *Bullfrog* near mid-lake, and *Hall's Crossing*, across the lake from Bullfrog—offer numerous facilities for visitors, including motor- and houseboat rentals, lodging, gas, camping and trailer sites, boat tours and trips, a picnic area, supplies, guided tours, and food. Ranger offices at each marina have current information on backcountry roads, camping, and sites. In addition, gift shops sell Navajo, Hopi, and Zuni handcrafts. *Antelope Point*, the newest marina, has boating facilities and a restaurant. *Dangling Rope*, accessible only by boat, is a floating marina 42 miles from the dam. See Chapter 7, The Navajo, page 104, for more on Antelope Marina.

A *ferry* transports cars and passengers the approximately 3 miles between Bullfrog and Hall's Crossing, thus saving visitors a 130-mile drive.

Carl Hayden Visitor Center, 2 miles north of Page and in Arizona, sits on the western end of the lake at **Glen Canyon Dam**. Here, a detailed relief map of the Colorado Plateau region will help orient you to the area. You can also view exhibits illustrating the history of the construction project and take a free guided tour of the massive dam, which was made with 5 million cubic feet of concrete and now rises 710 feet above the Colorado River. This is a good place to ask for information on the Indian dwelling, storage, and ceremonial structures and petroglyphs easily visible in the lake canyons and surrounding backcountry.

Two miles from the Carl Hayden Visitor Center, on a mesa overlooking the lake, is the town of Page, Arizona. It is the largest community in far northern Arizona and a good place to spend the night. Just remember that Arizona does not observe daylight savings. Fifteen miles downriver from the dam is Lees Ferry (see Chapter 5, Grand Canyon Country, for more information on Page and Lees Ferry).

The other visitor center at Lake Powell is the *Bullfrog Visitor Center*. It is located along UT276 near the eastern end of the lake and features natural and cultural exhibits.

Indian ruins and petroglyphs are around the lake, including **Defiance House**, which is 15 miles northeast of Bullfrog Marina in Forgotten Canyon. The site has Indian ceremonial, storage, and dwelling structures, which have been stabilized and can be explored. It was occupied around A.D. 1050 to 1250 and was home to approximately twenty individuals. The rock art panels here originally included figures of animals, a flute player, and anthropomorphs, which blend animal and human characteristics. Note that Defiance House and Three Roof Ruin are no longer accessible by water.

The most popular destination at Lake Powell is **Rainbow Bridge National Monument**, which soars 290 feet high and spans a width of 275 feet. It is the largest natural stone arch in the world and is considered sacred by the Navajo. One of their legends claims that *Nonnezoshi,* meaning "Rainbow Turned to Stone," was created by a spirit who, upon hearing the prayer of another supernatural being who was trapped in the canyon by a flash flood, threw down a rainbow for him to tread to safety. Beneath the spirit's feet, the rainbow turned to stone.

Rainbow Bridge is 50 miles upstream from Wahweap marina and is part of the Navajo Reservation (which includes 134 miles of Lake Powell's southern shoreline). The easiest way

Nonnezoshi, "Rainbow Turned to Stone," is the Navajo name for Rainbow Bridge.

to get to the monument is by boat, either your own or on a tour boat leaving from Wahweap, Hall's Crossing, or Bullfrog. Depending on the lake's water level, tours may involve a hike.

Overland access is more challenging. Rugged trails through the Navajo Nation leave from Navajo Mountain Trading Post (14-mile foot and horse trail) or the abandoned Rainbow Lodge (13-mile foot trail). If you hike either trail, you can plan an easier trip by hiking to the bridge and hiring a boat for your return. The trail from Navajo Mountain Trading Post follows a route used for centuries, first by Anasazi and later by Navajos. In 1909, John Wetherill, the first white man to see Rainbow Bridge, was guided along this same route by a Paiute named Nashja-begay.

Permits for the trails can be purchased from the Navajo Nation. Write early for the permit, take along a good map, and ask the park ranger about trail conditions and if trading posts are open along the way. "Hiking to Rainbow Bridge" trail notes are available from Glen Canyon National Recreation Area.

A good time to view Rainbow Bridge is in the late afternoon, when the sun highlights the natural pink hue of the rock. The best times to follow the trails are April to early June and September through October.

For rentals and reservations at Lake Powell, contact *Lake Powell Resorts and Marinas*, administered by ARA Leisure Services. This concessionaire also has publications and videos about the recreation area. Be sure to make reservations well in advance, especially for houseboats; they are often booked a year ahead.

KANAB
Map #5

Around Town: Frontier Movie Town
Nearby: Coral Pink Sand Dunes State Park, Hell Dive Canyon Pictographs, Moqui Cave, Paria
Canyon-Vermilion Cliffs Wilderness, South Fork Indian Canyon pictograph site

Kanab is a Paiute word meaning "Place of the Willows," and you can still see them growing along Kanab Creek. The town began in 1864 as Ft. Kanab, which was intended as an outpost for explorers and to provide protection for settlers. Hostilities from local Indians, though, forced the army to abandon the fort. Mormon missionaries eventually moved here and founded the town.

Today Kanab sits at the base of the Vermilion Cliffs near the southern border of Utah on US89. It is a crossroads for major driving routes to the national parks, monuments, and other sites in the area. A variety of accommodations and inexpensive places to eat make this small town a convenient place to stay while touring southwestern Utah and northwestern Arizona.

In the twentieth century, the area became a popular setting for filmmakers, and the town earned the nickname "Little Hollywood." Many movies and television series projecting the stereotypical image of Indians and life in the American West were filmed near here. In town, **Frontier Movie Town** is a replica of a typical movie set, complete with exhibits of memorabilia, entertainment, and gift shops that sell Indian arts and jewelry. To walk through an actual 1930s movie set, take the Paria Valley Road (off US89 at milepost 31) to the abandoned buildings. The original set was destroyed by fire in 2006. Plans are to rebuild it with replicas.

For more information on the Kanab area, contact the *Kane County Office of Tourism* on US89. For information on prehistoric sites and backcountry exploration, visit the *BLM Kanab Field Office*.

NORTH OF KANAB

The privately owned **Moqui Cave** is 5.5 miles north of town on US89. This natural cave features exhibits of Indian artifacts, many of them found locally, and a replica of an Anasazi ruin found in nearby Cottonwood Wash. Dinosaur tracks, an extensive black-light mineral display, and a gift shop selling Indian crafts are also on-site.

EAST OF KANAB

From town, scenic US89 travels east along the southern edge of Grand Staircase–Escalante National Monument between the town of Kanab and Lake Powell.

Some of the sites between Kanab and Page, Arizona, include Johnson Canyon Road, the Old Pahreah and Paria movie set, Paria Canyon and Vermilion Cliffs National Monument, Cottonwood Canyon Road, and Big Water.

Paria Canyon–Vermilion Cliffs Wilderness comprises over 112,000 acres in Utah and Arizona. The Paria (Paiute for "Muddy Water") River is the only major tributary of the Colorado River between Lake Powell and the Grand Canyon. As it flows through this rocky desert landscape, in some places the river runs wide and shallow, with a ribbon of greenery edging its banks. In other places, where the water is confined by cliffs up to two thousand feet high, it rushes through twisting, rugged slot canyons.

Over seven hundred years ago, Ancestral Puebloans hunted bighorn sheep and mule deer along the Paria and its tributaries, and they cultivated corn, squash, and beans in the broad, lower end of the main canyon. You can still see some of the petroglyphs and campsites they left behind.

Hiking the canyons of the Paria River and its tributaries, whether on a day-hike or an extended backpacking trip, is a memorable experience. For those with backcountry experience, a hike through the stunning main canyon begins at the Paria Canyon Information Station on US89 (43 miles east of Kanab near milepost 21) and travels downstream for 37 miles to Lonely Dell Ranch at Lees Ferry in Arizona, where the Paria and Colorado rivers unite.

This rigorous hike takes 4–6 days and includes about three hundred river crossings and long stretches of walking in the river. Like all overnight hikes in this wilderness area, it requires a BLM permit, which can be purchased up to four months in advance. Be advised that the number of available permits is extremely limited, so make your request early to the BLM or the Arizona Strip Interpretive Association. On occasion, permits may be available that day from the Paria Information Station (March 15 to November 15) or the BLM Kanab Field Office (November 16 through March 14). Both the information station and the Kanab office post weather forecasts (important in an area prone to flash floods, especially from July through September) and provide maps and information.

WEST OF KANAB

Coral Pink Sand Dunes State Park is 6 square miles of colorful sand dunes where you can hike, picnic, drive off-road vehicles through the soft dunes, and camp. To reach the state park, take US89 about 8 miles northwest of Kanab to the paved Hancock Road and turn left. Follow Hancock Road for 9.3 miles and turn south (left) onto a paved road that leads in 3 miles to the ranger station.

In the Moquith Mountain Wilderness Study Area near the state park are two pictograph sites you can visit with a four-wheel-drive vehicle—South Fork Indian Canyon and Hell Dive Canyon. The **South Fork Indian Canyon pictograph site** has outstanding examples of pictographs dating to A.D. 1200. To reach them, take Hancock Road 3.3 miles from the Coral Pink Sand Dunes Visitor Center and Campground to Hancock Road. Turn right onto Hancock Road and travel about 3.5 miles to Sand Spring Road, a four-wheel-drive road that will take you within a half mile of the site. Turn right onto Sand Spring Road and travel about 1 mile to Sand Spring. Continue for another 1.5 miles and look for the winding, narrow road on your left that leads 1.75 miles to a parking lot. From there, walk northeast to find a path through the sand. This leads to the easy trail, which travels a half mile to the canyon, where the pictographs were painted at the back of a large alcove. Since a fence prevents you from approaching closer than 30 feet, be sure to bring zoom and wide-angle lenses if you plan to take photographs. The visitor center has an area map.

Hell Dive Canyon rock art includes a unique pictograph of a baby's foot, as well as depictions of a family set in a massive alcove. To reach the site, continue on Sand Spring Road past the turnoff to South Fork Indian Canyon. Travel three-fourths of a mile to the

Y intersection and take the left fork of the road. Follow it for about three-fourths of a mile until driving becomes too difficult. Hike the remainder of the way to the bottom of Water Canyon, up the ridge, and then to another intersection. Turn left at the intersection and follow the path south (stay on the main path avoiding any turn-offs) to the footpath descending into Hell Dive Canyon Alcove. The hike is about 6.6 miles round-trip.

LAKE POWELL. See **GLEN CANYON NATIONAL RECREATION AREA.**

PANGUITCH
Map #6

Nearby: Grand Staircase–Escalante National Monument, Scenic Highway 12 (Anasazi State Park, Bryce Canyon National Park, Calf Creek Recreation Area, Capitol Reef National Park, Escalante archaeological sites, Escalante Petrified Forest State Park, Paunsagaunt Western Wildlife Museum)

Panguitch means "big fish" in the Paiute language. With numerous inexpensive choices for accommodations and dining, this pleasant town on US89 is a popular place for tourists who are visiting Bryce Canyon National Park and Cedar Breaks National Monument.

SOUTHEAST OF PANGUITCH

Grand Staircase–Escalante National Monument, Utah's newest national monument, contains about 1.9 million acres, which makes it the largest national monument in the lower forty-eight states. Situated between Glen Canyon National Recreation Area, Bryce Canyon National Park, and Vermilion Cliffs National Monument, it is a pristine wilderness with plenty of eye-popping scenery and prehistoric sites.

In the 1870s, this rugged, remote region became the last place to be mapped in the continental United States. In general, it consists of three separate districts. In the west are sparsely treed uplands lying on the edge of the Grand Staircase cliffs. In the center is the wilderness of the Kaiparowits Plateau, with its arid canyons and rangeland.

The eastern district, which is what most people come to the monument to see, includes the winding slickrock canyons of the Escalante River and its tributaries. Ancestral Puebloans and Fremont Indians lived here from A.D. 1050 to 1200, and they left behind rich reminders of their habitation. Hikers often stumble across abandoned villages, rock art, small stone granaries in canyon alcoves, and artifacts such as mats, sandals, corncobs, arrowheads, and pottery pieces on the floors of sandstone caves. By contrast, the Southern Paiute, who arrived in the area in the 1500s and stayed until being displaced by white settlers, left behind little evidence of their time here.

Catstair Canyon, near Paria Contact Station, has a 1-mile round-trip hike to a prehistoric rock-art panel. The trail leaves from the road that turns south off US89 near milepost 24.

The national monument has six visitor center/ranger stations where you can obtain backcountry permits, books, maps, and information about current conditions in the monument. Headquarters is in Kanab, with regional centers in Escalante, Cannonville, Boulder, Big Water, and Paria Canyon. Camping is available at the three developed campgrounds. In general, no services or water are available in the monument.

There are two main roads that pass through the monument—UT12 and US89. High-clearance vehicles are recommended for some of the dirt roads.

SCENIC HIGHWAY 12 FROM PANGUITCH

Scenic Highway 12 runs 124 miles from Torrey to Red Canyon, linking Bryce Canyon and Capitol Reef National Parks, and also providing access to the Escalante canyons. As scenic drives go, this one is not to be missed. It has been rated one of the ten most scenic drives in the entire United States.

Beginning in the east at Capitol Reef National Park, some of the sights you pass are Anasazi State Park, Calf Creek Recreation Area and Falls, Escalante Petrified Forest State Park, Grosvenor Arch, Kodachrome Basin State Park, Cottonwood Canyon Road, Bryce National Park, and Red Canyon. Pick up a brochure at an area visitor center.

The Navajo called **Capitol Reef National Park** the "Land of the Sleeping Rainbow," and when you see its rainbow of colors ranging from vivid blues and greens to purples and orchids, you may agree. Fremont Indians once used the river here to irrigate fields of corn, beans, and squash, and then they stored the surplus in sheltered bins called *moki* huts. Years later, Utes and Southern Paiutes passed through on hunting expeditions. They were followed by Mormon pioneers, who homesteaded in the area and eventually planted orchards and settled the town of Fruita.

Capitol Reef, a hundred-mile section of the Waterpocket Fold, ranges in elevation from 3,900 to 8,800 feet. The land itself is arches, spires, and red sandstone cliffs topped with white sandstone domes. The park is divided into north, south, and central districts. The central district contains its most renowned canyons, its only paved road (UT24), and the *visitor center*. Dirt roads provide access to the other two sections.

Fremont Indians carved unusual human figures on the rocks.

In the central district, Fremont Indians grew corn along the Fremont River between A.D. 700 and 1350. Scenic UT24 now travels through *Fremont River Canyon.* A wayside exhibit a half mile east of the visitor center highlights their petroglyphs, and the self-guided, 1-mile hike to Hickman Natural Bridge leads past one of their granaries.

The *visitor center,* also on UT24, features an orientation slide program, a three-dimensional relief map, replicas of Fremont petroglyphs, and prehistoric objects found in rock shelters in the park. Included are eight-hundred-year old corn and squash, a cedar bark rope, mountain sheep-hide moccasins, and gray undecorated pottery. The center also provides interpretive programs, information on where to find the rock art and prehistoric structures in the park, and backcountry permits. *Ripple Rock Nature Center,* .75 miles from the visitor center, has interactive exhibits.

Scenic Drive travels south from the visitor center for a 25-mile round-trip to Capitol Gorge, where a 1-mile hike leads past Basketmaker petroglyphs and to the Tanks, natural basins that collect water. Unfortunately, the petroglyphs here have been badly defaced. Allow a minimum of 1.5 hours for the Scenic Drive. A self-guiding brochure is available at the visitor center; a less elaborate one is available at the first stop on the drive.

At the historic town of *Fruita,* you can pick several types of fruit in season and will often see deer and other wildlife. The developed Fruita campground is on a first-come, first-served basis.

Ask the park rangers about hikes and road conditions for the north and south districts. Although Capitol Reef is open all year, trails and unpaved side roads may be closed during rains or in midwinter.

Outside of the park, UT24 connects with Scenic Highway 12. Turn onto Scenic Highway 12 and follow it to the town of Boulder.

The tiny town of Boulder is so isolated that it received its mail by mule until the 1940s. The *visitor information booth* in the center of town is open May-October.

Anasazi State Park, in town, preserves the remains of a village occupied between A.D. 1160 and 1235 that was one of the largest Ancestral Puebloan settlements west of the Colorado River. Historical and cultural displays in the *visitor center* include a diorama of the original village, a storage granary, replicas of rock art, and a sampling of the thousands of artifacts found at the site. Outside is the Coombs site, a partially excavated village that once contained eleven pithouses and sixty-seven surface rooms that provided homes for around two hundred people. You can still see remnants of grinding and mealing bins against the outside wall and explore a life-size, six-room replica of a dwelling. Signs explain how archaeologists predicted where to find the ruin.

Advance arrangements can be made for atl-atl throwing and flint-knapping demonstrations. Packages of Anasazi beans and blue popcorn are sold in the visitor center. You can also obtain information on the Grand Staircase–Escalante National Monument.

From Boulder, continue on Scenic Highway 12 to the beautiful **Calf Creek Recreation Area,** used extensively by both Fremont and Ancestral Pueblo Indians. The 5.5-mile round-trip hike to Lower Calf Creek Falls is along a self-guided nature trail that leads past small Indian ruins and a rock art panel. Be sure to wear appropriate footgear. The trail leads through the shallow Escalante River several times, as well as through sand. A trail guide is available at the trailhead. The BLM campground has thirteen lovely campsites beside the river, and the shallow water makes this a popular spot for tubing and wading.

About 15 miles farther west on Scenic Highway 12 is the small town of **Escalante.** Dixie National Forest, which surrounds the town, has archaeological sites where you can see pictographs, petroglyphs, and cave dwellings. Contact the Escalante Forest Service office for information.

Escalante Petrified Forest State Park has an abundance of petrified wood, as well as the remains of a Fremont village and petroglyphs estimated to be nearly a thousand years old, although no developed trail leads to them. The *visitor center* displays a few Fremont artifacts.

Continue on Scenic Highway 12 to the turnoff to **Bryce Canyon National Park** at UT63. Bryce Canyon is a dramatic place of intensely colored pink pinnacles that stand in a canyon washed out of the side of a plateau by thousands of rain-filled cascades. The Paiute called the gorge *Unka-timpe-wa-wince-pack-ich*, which means "Red Rocks Standing like Men in a Bowl-Shaped Canyon." According to their legends, the beings that lived in this fairyland long ago were birds, animals, lizards, and those who looked like humans. Coyote was their leader, and he had built this place for his followers. Never satisfied, the residents kept beautifying their homes until Coyote, angry at how ungrateful they were for his initial efforts, knocked over their paints and turned everything to stone.

The *visitor center* is at the entrance to the park. It has exhibits, maps, an orientation film, a schedule of the numerous ranger-led programs and hikes, and information on the two park campgrounds. A shuttle bus service runs throughout the park from May through September.

Rim Road, possibly the most colorful 18 miles of geology in the world, leads past stunning lookout points. Hiking trails also provide access to scenic overviews and into the canyon, and an easy 1-mile loop trail leads past 1,700-year-old bristlecone pines.

Lodging in the park is available at *Bryce Canyon Lodge*, open from April 1 to November 1. The lodge operates a gift shop and dining room. Arrangements can be made here for horseback rides and van tours. These are often filled, so make your reservations early. North Campground is open year-round. Sunset Campground is open late spring to early fall. Look for more information in the park newspaper, *The Hoodoo*.

Calf Creek Falls is a popular hiking destination from Scenic Highway 12.

Hikers in Bryce Canyon National Park get a closer view of its dramatic spires.

The closest lodging outside of the park is the Best Western *Ruby's Inn*, which is 1.5 miles north of the park. In addition to motel rooms, Ruby's Inn also operates a campground, RV park, restaurants, and other tourist services. It also conducts horseback rides, scenic flights, and a guided ATV tour to the rim of Bryce. The park shuttle stops in front of the inn.

Bryce Canyon is open year-round, but the road south of Inspiration Point is usually closed by snow November through April. During that time, the rest of the park is accessible on snowshoes, available at the visitor center.

A few miles west of the turnoff to Bryce Canyon on Scenic Highway 12 is **Paunsaugunt Western Wildlife Museum**, where you can see taxidermy animals native to the Southwest in dioramas that depict their natural habitats and tour an elk preserve. The museum also has a good collection of Indian pottery, weapons, tools, and other artifacts.

ST. GEORGE
Map #7

Nearby: Amasazi Trail, Jacob Hamblin Home, Little Black Mountain Petroglyph Site, Old Fort Pearce, Red Cliffs Recreation Area, Shivwits Paiute Reservation, Snow Canyon State Park

St. George is in the heart of Utah's "Dixie." Once home to Paiutes, it is now a retirement mecca with dozens of golf courses and spas. As the largest town in southern Utah, it makes a good place to stay while visiting Zion and other nearby natural wonders.

St. George was settled in the 1860s by members of the "Cotton Mission," a group of faithful Mormons sent from Salt Lake City to find a hot, dry climate to grow cotton. In the center of town they built a temple in 1877, making it now the oldest active Mormon temple in the world. The town was also important as the winter home of Brigham Young, who was drawn here by the mild climate. Today, pioneer artifacts are on display here and at the Daughters of Utah Pioneers Museum.

The museum is next to the Pioneer Courthouse and the *chamber of commerce*, which has brochures, maps, information on other city attractions, and a walking tour of the city covering local history. The chamber also provides information on tours and scenic flights over nearby national parks and Lake Powell.

NORTH OF ST. GEORGE

North of St. George is **Red Cliffs Recreation Area**, which has enjoyable hiking trails, camping, and picnicking. *Red Cliffs Trail* leads to a small Anasazi ruin with an interpretive sign to explain the site. From northbound I-15 take Leeds exit 22 and follow the frontage road 3 miles south of Leeds. Turn west onto a paved road that travels 1.7 miles through a narrow underpass to the BLM recreation area. From southbound I-15, take exit 23.

Zion National Park is north of St. George on Highway 9 (see page 444 for more information).

SOUTH OF ST. GEORGE

You can see outstanding examples of rock art at the **Little Black Mountain Petroglyph Site**, where people from various cultures, including the Great Basin, Western Ancestral Puebloan, and lower Colorado River, left over five hundred individual designs on the cliffs and boulders as they traveled through the natural corridor here. Turtles, bear paws, and lizards are some of the representations. Access to the site is via dirt road. From St. George, take River Road 5 miles out of town to the Arizona state line. Travel a third of a mile beyond the state line and turn left (east). The road leads 4.5 miles to the site. Contact the BLM office near the I-15 exit on Riverside Drive in St. George for more information.

Old Fort Pearce, named for the leader of Mormon troops in the 1865–68 Black Hawk War against the Utes, was built at a spring long used by Indians as the only reliable water source for miles. A large portion of the eight-foot walls and corral still remain. Just south of the fort (about 20 feet down the slope) is a small group of petroglyphs. The fort is 10 miles southeast of St. George in Warner Valley. The BLM office in St. George has directions to the fort and to nearby rock art sites.

WEST OF ST. GEORGE

Five miles west of St. George off I-15 is the town of Santa Clara and the **Jacob Hamblin Home & Museum.** Hamblin was a nineteenth-century Mormon missionary who knew the Paiute and Ute languages and was known as a peacekeeper with the Indians. The sandstone house he built here in 1862 had a bedroom for each of his two wives, one of whom was Paiute. The house has been nicely restored with many of the original furnishings.

Continuing north on UT8 from Santa Clara, you will come to the town of Ivins. Turn right here to stay on UT8 to **Snow Canyon State Park**, a 3-mile long trough of cliffs intricately sculptured from Navajo sandstone and splashed with desert varnish. Cradled between the cliffs that rise between 50 and 750 feet are soft dunes of silky sand, Indian pictographs and pottery sherds, and a valley floor blobbed with lava. Hiking, picnicking, biking, and camping are popular here. The campground has trailer hookups, water, electricity, and showers; the picnic area has interpretive displays.

The left fork of the road from Ivins travels a short distance to the **Shivwits Paiute Indian Reservation**. The Shivwits band of Paiutes probably came to southern Utah around A.D. 1100. They lived in small bands of families that foraged for wild seeds, roots, nuts, and berries and hunted rabbits, deer, and mountain sheep. The people also cultivated corn, squash, melons, gourds, and sunflowers in irrigated fields along the banks of the Virgin, Muddy, and Santa Clara rivers. Fall was the time for large celebrations, dancing, and marriages. Winter was filled with stories of the supernatural world and spirit animals.

The traditional Paiute lifestyle was unable to withstand the arrival of the Mormons and other settlers in the 1850s. In 1891, the first Paiute reservation was established here at Shivwits on one hundred acres of land. Today the Shivwits band has 279 people. Although most of the early homes have been replaced with newer ones, the cemetery remains.

Also off old US91 west of Ivins is the *Anasazi Trail*, which passes Native American rock carvings. Look for the Anasazi trailhead sign and turn left onto a dirt road and go .4 miles. A relatively easy 1-mile walk leads from the parking area to the site.

ZION NATIONAL PARK
Map #8

Around Zion National Park: Kolob Canyons Road, Kolob Terrace Road, Southgate Petroglyphs, Zion Canyon Field School, Zion Canyon Scenic Drive, Zion Human History Museum, Zion-Mount Carmel Highway, Zion Nature Center
Nearby: Springdale, Village of Many Nations

Zion, which means "place of refuge or sanctuary," is a fitting name for this timeless and stunning place of rich natural and cultural resources. The Colorado Plateau, Great Basin, and Mojave Desert provinces all meet here to create a unique geography and various life zones that support a diversity of plant and animal life. In the 229-square-mile park is a magnificent collection of enormous rock monoliths, delicate arches, forested plateaus, colorful mesas, and mazes of spectacular canyons with cascading waterfalls. Large sections of the park are wilderness, but three paved roads and several hiking trails provide access for the average visitor to enjoy the dramatic scenery.

Evidence of human occupation in the park includes four major cultural periods. With less than 15 percent of the park surveyed, over 430 archaeological sites have been found.

People from the Archaic culture lived here and across the entire western Colorado Plateau and Great Basin from around 6000 B.C. to A.D. 500. They lived in small groups, hunted game animals, and foraged for wild plants, but they left few traces of having been here. Most of their cultural remnants have been found in dry caves and burials that include yucca-fiber sandals, baskets, nets, stone tools, and atl-atls.

Around 300 B.C., members of the Basketmaker culture called the eastern section of the park home. They planted corn and squash along the rivers, crafted coiled baskets, and lived in pithouses.

From A.D. 500 to 1300, members of both the Virgin Anasazi and Parowan Fremont cultures lived in Zion. They established permanent pueblos, crafted ceramic vessels, de-

Many rock formations are on a massive scale at Zion National Park.

veloped the use of the bow and arrow, and relied heavily on cultivated foods. These two groups disappeared from southwestern Utah about A.D. 1300. Either the alternating extended droughts and floods in the eleventh and twelfth centuries or competition from the Southern Paiute and Ute may have driven them away. These newcomers were nomadic hunters and gatherers, just as the Archaic people were, although the Southern Paiute also cultivated corn, squash, and sunflowers to supplement their diets.

In the 1860s, Mormon pioneers settled along the upper Virgin River and near Oak Creek, although flooding and poor soil created unfavorable conditions.

Zion Canyon Visitor Center, at the south entrance of the park, features a topographical map and relief model of the park; an informative film about Zion; excellent exhibits on the park's early Indian cultures, geology, and wildlife; an extensive bookstore, with trail guides and maps; and booklets for the self-guiding trails in the park. Rangers are on duty to answer questions, sell backcountry permits, and provide information about naturalist-led hikes and evening talks available from late March through early November. Ask here for directions to the few accessible prehistoric sites in the park, including Southgate Petroglyphs across the road from Watchman Campground.

Zion Canyon Scenic Drive winds for 7.5 miles from the visitor center through the chasm of Zion Canyon. For most visitors, this drive is the highlight of their trip here. Carved out by the North Fork of the Virgin River, the canyon's massive walls, which are multicolored in shades of red, blue, yellow, and white, rise over 2,400 feet from the canyon floor.

The **Zion Human History Museum** is a half mile north of the park entrance on the scenic drive. Permanent exhibits here showcase the human history of the park, from the prehistoric Indians through the pioneers and to the growth of Zion as a national park. The dynamic effect of water at Zion is also highlighted. A short video provides an overview of the park, rangers are available to answer questions, and the bookstore sells a variety of books and maps.

The road continues to Canyon Junction, where it divides into Zion Canyon Scenic Drive to the left and UT9 to the right. From April through October, Zion Canyon Scenic Drive is closed to all vehicles except park shuttle buses. The shuttle departs every ten minutes or so during busy times, and it makes eight stops in the park. Total trip time is 90 minutes. Eliminate the parking hassle (visitor center lots fill early in the day) by boarding the shuttle at one of its six stops in Springdale. Alternately, you can walk the short distance from Springdale to the visitor center and board a shuttle there. Enter the park at the Zion Canyon Giant Screen Theater.

From Canyon Junction, the scenic drive leads to Zion Lodge, the Grotto, Weeping Rock, and the Temple of Sinawava. The right branch becomes the **Zion-Mount Carmel Highway**, which travels 10 miles to the east entrance of the park. This road is steep and passes through a narrow mile-long tunnel that requires large vehicles to have an escort. You can make arrangements for this at a park entrance.

Kolob Canyons is the northwestern section of the park. *Kolob Canyons Visitor Center* is 17 miles south of Cedar City off I-15 at exit 40. The small center has geological exhibits and rangers on-site to answer questions. Also available are books, maps, and backcountry permits. **Kolob Canyons Road** travels 5 miles from here to Kolob Canyons Viewpoint and a picnic area. Several hiking trails lead from this paved road deeper into the canyons.

Kolob Terrace Road is accessed from the town of Virgin, on UT9 between La Verkin and Springdale. This steep, winding road leads past Lava Point (dramatic, panoramic view of Cedar Breaks, Zion Canyon, Mount Trumbull, and other geological wonders) and continues to Kolob Reservoir, a good place to fish for trout. The narrow road is not advisable for trailers, and the upper portion of it is not plowed in winter.

Zion Lodge, operated by Xanterra Parks and Resorts, provides lodging, dining, a gift shop, and guided tours of the park. It is located on Zion Canyon Scenic Drive. Campgrounds in the park include *Watchman Campground*, open year-round with reservations six months ahead, and *South Campground*, open mid-March through October, available on a first-come basis. Other lodging options, campgrounds, and restaurants are outside of the park near the east entrance and in the towns of Cedar City, Kanab, Mt. Carmel Junction, Springdale, and Rockville.

If you have children with you, check out the Junior Ranger Program at **Zion Nature Center**. If you are interested in more in-depth exploration of Zion, contact the **Zion Canyon Field Institute**, which offers educational programs combining classroom time and outdoor field trips to explore the park's archaeology, geology, and ecosystem.

For a map and extensive online guide, visit the park's Web site.

SOUTH OF ZION

Springdale, just outside the south entrance of Zion, is a small village of about 500 people that is geared to serving tourists. Numerous motels, B&Bs, and restaurants, plus a frequent shuttle bus service to Zion, create a convenient base for those touring the national park. Other amenities in town include tour companies, bicycle rentals, a dog boarding facility, and a medical clinic. If you enjoy shopping, the local art galleries, rock shops, and gift shops are added attractions.

Zion Canyon Giant Screen Theatre by the south entrance to the park shows the

IMAX movie *Zion Canyon: Treasure of the Gods* on a daily basis. The **O.C. Tanner Amphitheater** presents multimedia productions and a performing art series.

EAST OF ZION

Village of Many Nations is on UT9 near the east entrance to Zion. Visitors here can participate in Native American cultural activities, spend the night in a tipi, and enjoy the summer nightly entertainment by members of area tribes.

EVENTS

Edge of the Cedars Museum: Near Blanding, the museum sponsors a variety of educational programs throughout the year. Contact the museum for a schedule.

MAY *Amazing Earthfest:* Scientific and cultural events and hikes. Kane County. Call 800-733-5263, www.amazingearthfest.com.

Utah Prehistory Week: Sponsored by the Utah Division of State History. Lectures, hands-on activities such as spear and atl-atl throwing, demonstrations on flint-knapping and creating rock art, lectures, and tours of prehistoric sites are held statewide to provide insight into the lives of those who lived in Utah thousands of years ago. Contact the Utah History Research Center, 801-533-3500, 300 South Rio Grande Street, SLC, UT 84101.

JUNE *Paiute Restoration Gathering and Powwow:* Held in mid-June to commemorate the 1980 federal re-recognition of the Utah Paiute. Powwow, arts and crafts, princess pageant, parade, softball tournament, and cultural activities. Contact Paiute Cultural Center in Cedar City.

Parowan Gap Summer Solstice Celebration: Lectures and barbecue at Parowan Gap prehistoric site. Sponsored by town of Parowan.

JULY *Boulder Heritage Festival:* Celebrates the diversity of cultures that have lived in the area with arts, crafts, music, and history. Held mid-July at Anasazi State Museum and Park in Boulder. Call 435-335-7422 or email Boulderheritagefestival@yahoo.com.

Ute Stampede: PRCE Rodeo and Western celebration, family activities. At San Juan County Fairgrounds in Nephi, 435-623-1735.

AUGUST *Jedediah Smith High Mountain Rendezvous:* Rendezvous with mountain men and Indians. Black-powder shoots, games, and other activities. In the mountains above Cedar City.

Western Legends Round-up and Western Festival: Celebration of Western culture with cowboy poetry, Navajo weavers, mountain man camps, Western film festival, movie set tours, and more. In Kanab at the end of August; www.westernlegendsroundup.com.

SEPTEMBER *Utah Navajo Fair and Rodeo:* Traditional song and dance, rodeo, food, and arts and crafts. Held in Bluff at the end of September.

White Mesa Ute Council Bear Dance: Traditional Bear Dance and celebration. Hand games, Powwow, softball tournament, Country & Western dancing and bands. White Mesa Ute Reservation, Labor Day weekend. Call 435-678-3397.

OCTOBER *Zion Canyon Art and Flute Festival:* Flute enthusiasts can enjoy three days of art and Native American and world flute workshops, concerts, and vendors. Held in Springdale. For information, call 480-984-5820 or visit www.zioncanyonartandflutefestival.com.

CONTACT INFORMATION

Anasazi State Park
PO Box 1429, 460 North Hwy 12, Boulder,
UT 84716
435-335-7308
http://stateparks.utah.gov/parks/anasazi
Daily, 8am-6pm, summer; daily 9am-5pm,
winter; fee

Archaeology Plus
BLM parking lot at 345 E. Riverside Drive, St.
George, UT
435-688-7325
Guided hikes 8am-noon, 4th Sat of month,
Sept-May; fee

Arizona Strip Interpretive Association
www.blm.gov/az/asfo/asia.htm
Visitor Information Center
345 East Riverside Drive, St. George, UT 84770
435-688-3246
Mon-Fri 7:45am-5pm & 10am-3pm Sat

Blanding Chamber of Commerce
50 W 100 S, Box 792, Blanding, UT 84511
435-678-3662 • www.blandingutah.org

Blue Mountain RV Park and Trading Post
1930 S. Main, Blanding, UT 84511
435-678-7840 *or* 435-678-2570

Bluff (town)
www.bluffutah.org

Brigham Young Winter Home
67 W 200 North, St George, UT 84770
435-673-2517 • www.lds.org/placestovisit
St. George Temple Visitor Center: 435-673-5181
Daily 9am-6pm, summer (extends to 7pm as weather improves); daily 9am-5pm, winter; no fee

Bryce Canyon National Park
Superintendent, PO Box 640201, Bryce Canyon,
UT 84764
435-834-5322 • www.nps.gov/brca
Bryce Canyon Lodge
www.brycecanyonlodge.com
Open April-October
Dinner reservations
435-834-5361
Lodging reservations
Xanterra Parks and Resorts
Central Reservations
6312 S. Fiddler Green Circle, Suite 600N,
Greenwood Village, CO 80111
888-297-2757

Seasonal
PO Box 640079, Bryce Canyon
National Park, UT 84764
435-834-5361
Year-round
Regional General Manager, c/o Zion
Lodge, Zion National Park, PO
Box 925, Springdale, Utah 84764
435-772-7700
Campgrounds
North
877-444-6777 • www.recreation.gov
Open year-round; reservations only
mid May-Sept 30, can be made up
to 240 days ahead
Sunset
Closed in winter; no reservations accepted
Visitor Center
435-834-5322
Daily 8am-8pm, May-Sept 30; daily 8am-
6pm, Apr & Oct; daily 8am-4:30pm,
Nov-Mar; fee

Bureau of Land Management
www.blm.gov/ut/st/en.html
Information on Utah's prehistoric rock art sites:
www.ut.blm.gov/antiquitiescentennial/
places.htm
Arizona Strip Field Office
345 East Riverside Drive, St. George, UT
84790
435-688-3230
Cedar City District Office
176 East D.L. Sargent Drive, Cedar City,
UT 84720
435-586-2401
Kanab Field Office
318 North 100 East, Kanab, UT 84741
435-644-4600
Escalante Interagency Office
PO Box 225, Escalante, UT 84726
435-826-4291
**Grand Staircase-Escalante National
Monument**
190 E. Center Street, Kanab, UT 84741
435-644-4300
Henry Mountain Field Station
PO Box 99, Hanksville, UT 84734
435-542-3461
Paria Information Station
Near milepost 21 on US89, 43 miles east of
Kanab
Daily 8:30am-4:15pm, mid March-mid
Nov; closed mid Nov-mid March

Permits for hiking Paria Canyon
Arizona Strip Interpretive Association
435-688-3246
www.blm.gov/az/paria/checklist.cfm
San Juan Resource Area (Monticello Field Office)
435 North Main, PO Box 7, Monticello, UT 84535
435-587-1532
St. George Interagency Office
345 East Riverside Drive, St. George, UT 84790
435-688-3200

Capitol Reef National Park
HC70, Box 15, Torrey, UT 84775
435-425-3791 • www.nps.gov/care
Ripple Rock Nature Center: Tues-Sat 10am-3pm, Mem. Day-Labor Day
Visitor Center: daily 8am-7pm, June-Sept; daily 8am-4:30pm Oct-May; fee for Scenic Drive

Cedar Breaks National Monument
2390 W Hwy 56, Suite 11, Cedar City, UT 84720
Visitor Center: daily 8am-6pm, June-mid Oct (depending on snow); fee
435-586-9451 • www.nps.gov/cebr

Cedar City Chamber of Commerce
581 N. Main Street, Cedar City, UT 84720
435-586-4484 • www.cedarcity.org

Cedar Mesa Pottery
333 S. Main Street, Blanding, UT 84511
800-235-7687 or 435-678-2241
www.cmpottery.com

Coral Pink Sand Dunes State Park
PO Box 95, Kanab, UT 84741
435-648-2800
Camping reservations: 800-322-3770
www.utah.com/stateparks/coral_pink.htm
Camping and Day-Use fee

Daughters of the Utah Pioneers Museum
145 N 100 East, St George, UT 84770
435-628-7274

Edge of the Cedars State Historical Park
PO Box 788, 660 West 400 North, Blanding, UT 84511
435-678-2238
http://stateparks.utah.gov/parks/edge-of-the-cedars
Daily 9am-6pm, mid May-mid Sept; daily 9am-5pm, mid Sept-mid May; fee

Escalante Petrified Forest State Park
PO Box 350, 710 N. Reservoir Road, Escalante, UT 84726
435-826-4466
Campground reservations: 800-322-3770 or 801-322-3770
http://stateparks.utah.gov/park/escalante
Park: Daily 7am-10pm, summer; daily 8am-10am, winter; fee
Visitor Center: Daily 8am-5pm, summer

Frontier Movie Town
297 W. Center, Kanab, UT 84741
800-551-1714 or 435-644-5337
www.onlinepages.net/frontier_movie_town
www.frontiermovietown.com
Daily 9am-11pm; no fee

Glen Canyon National Recreation Area (Lake Powell)
Superintendent, PO Box 1507, Page, AZ 86040
928-608-6200 • www.nps.gov/glca
Bullfrog Resort and Marina
PO Box 4055, Hwy 276, Lake Powell, UT 84533
800-528-6154 or 435-684-3000
Boat tours (including Rainbow Bridge)
Lake Powell Resorts & Marinas; PO Box 56909, Phoenix, AZ 85079
800-528-6154 • www.lakepowell.com
Charles Hall Ferry Hours vary
Clinic 435-684-2288 • Daily mid May-Sept
Defiance House Lodge (includes Anasazi Restaurant & RV park)
800-528-6154 or 435-684-3000
Visitor Center
Open intermittently beginning in May
435-684-7420
Carl Hayden Visitor Center
928-608-6072
Daily 8am-6pm, Memorial Day-Labor Day; daily 8am-5pm, rest of year
One-hour guided dam tour (leaves every half hour); 8:30am-3:30pm, May-Oct
Dangling Rope
928-645-2969
Hall's Crossing Marina
Highway 276, Lake Powell, UT 84533
435-684-7400 or 435-684-7460 (boater contact info)
Hite Marina
PO Box 501, Lake Powell, UT 84533
435-684-2278
Lake Powell Ferry
Bullfrog Marina on Hwy 276, Lake Powell, UT 85431
435-538-1030

Glen Canyon National Recreation Area (*continued*)
Lake Powell Motel
Contact Lake Powell Resorts
Lake Powell Resorts and Marinas/ARA Leisure Services
PO Box 56909, Phoenix, AZ 85079
800-528-6154 *or* 602-278-8888
www.lakepowell.com
Navajo Bridge Interpretive Center
www.nps.gov/glca/historyculture/navajo bridge.htm
Daily 9am-5pm, mid Apr-oct; weekends only 10am-4pm, early Apr & Nov
Navajo Nation Recreational Resources Department
Box 308, Window Rock, AZ 86515
602-871-6647
Stateline 928-645-1111
Wahweap Lodge and Marina
PO Box 1597, Page, AZ 86040
800-528-6154 *or* 928-645-2433
Boat tours (including Rainbow Bridge)
928-645-1070 • www.lakepowell.com

Grand Staircase-Escalante National Monument
www.ut.blm.gov/monument
Anasazi State Park Visitor Center
60 N. Hwy 12, Boulder, UT 84716
435-335-7382
Daily 9am-5pm, mid March-mid Nov; closed mid Nov-mid March
Big Water Visitor Center
100 Upper Revolution Way, Big Water, UT 84741
435-675-3200
Daily 8am-5pm, mid March-mid Nov; closed mid Nov-mid March
Cannonville Visitor Center
10 Center Street, Cannonville, UT 84718
435-826-5640
Daily 8am-4:30pm, mid March-mid Nov; closed mid Nov-mid March
Escalante Interagency Visitor Center
755 W. Main, Escalante, UT 84726
435-826-5499
Daily 7:30am-5:30pm, mid March-mid Nov; Mon-Fri 8am-4:30pm, mid Nov-mid March
Kanab Visitor Center
745 E. Hwy 89, Kanab, UT 84741
435-644-4680
Daily 8am-5pm, mid March-mid Nov; Mon-Fri 8am-4:30pm, mid Nov-mid March
Paria Contact Station
Hwy 89 (44 miles east of Kanab)
Daily 8:30am-4:15pm, mid March-mid Nov

Hovenweep National Monument
McElmo Rt., Cortez, CO 81321
970-562-4282 • www.nps.gov/hove
Park: daily year-round; fee
Visitor Center: daily 8am-5am; extended summer hours

Huck's Museum and Trading Post
1387 South Hwy 191, Blanding, UT 84511
435-678-2329
Museum: daily 8am-5pm; fee

Iron Mission State Park and Museum
585 North Main Street, Cedar City, UT 84720
801-586-9290
stateparks.utah.gov/parks/iron-mission
Museum: daily 9am-6pm, summer; Mon-Sat 9am-5pm, winter; fee

Jacob Hamblin Home & Museum
Santa Clara Boulevard & Hamblin Drive, Santa Clara, UT 84765
435-673-5181 (St. George Visitor Center)
www.utah.com/mormon/hamblin_home.htm
Daily 9am-7pm, spring; daily 9am-8pm, summer; daily 9am-5pm, winter; No fee

Kanab (town)
76 N Main Street, Kanab, UT 84741
435-644-2534 • http://kanab.utah.gov
Mon-Fri 9am-5pm

Kane County Office of Tourism
78 South 100 East (Hwy 89), Kanab, UT 84741
800-733-5263 *or* 435-644-5033
www.kaneutah.com

Lake Powell (*see* **Glen Canyon National Recreation Area**)

Moqui Cave
Hwy 89 North, Kanab, UT 84741
435-644-8525 • www.moquicave.com
Mon-Sat 9am-7pm, season; Mon-Sat 10am-4pm, off-season; fee

Nations of the Four Corners Cultural Center
707 West 500 South, Blanding, UT 84511
435-678-2027

Natural Bridges National Monument
HC-60, Box 1, Lake Powell, UT 84533
435-692-1234 • www.nps.gov/nabr
Visitor Center: daily 8am-5pm; fee

Navajo Nation Parks and Recreation Department
PO Box 2520, Bldg 36A, E. Hwy 264 at Rt. 12, Window Rock, AZ 86515
928-871-6647 • www.navajonationparks.org

O. C. Tanner Amphitheater
Dixie State Collelge, Springdale, UT 84767
435-652-7994 • www.dixie.edu/tanner

Paiute Indian Tribe of Utah
440 N. Paiute Drive, Cedar City, UT 84720
435-586-1112
www.indian.utah.gov/utah_tribes_today/
    paiute.html

Paunsaugunt Western Wildlife Museum
PO Box 640009, 1945 W. Scenic Highway 12,
    Bryce, UT 84764
435-834-5555 Apr-Oct; 702-877-2664 Nov-Mar
www.brycecanyonwildlifemuseum.com
Daily 9am-10pm, Apr-mid Nov; fee

Panguitch Chamber of Commerce
PO Box 400, 200 East 25 South, Panguitch,
    UT 84759
433-676-8585 • www.panguitch.org

Rainbow Bridge National Monument
PO Box 1507, Page, AZ 86040
928-608-6200 • www.nps.gov/rabr

Recapture Lodge
PO Box 309, Bluff, UT 84512
435-672-2281 • www.bluffutah.org/recapturelodge

Ruby's Inn
1000 South Hwy 63, Bryce, UT 84764
800-468-8660 (toll-free reservations) *or*
    435-834-5341 • www.rubysinn.com

San Juan County Visitor Center
117 S Main Street, Box 490, Monticello, UT
    84535
800-574-4386 *or* 435-587-3235
www.southeastutah.com

Shivwits Paiute Indian Reservation
PO Box 2656, Tuba City, AZ 86045
928-283-4587
http://indian.utah.gov/utah_tribes_today

Snow Canyon State Park
PO Box 140, Santa Clara, UT 84765
800-322-3770 (reservations) *or* 435-628-2255
www.utah.com/stateparks/snow_canyon.htm
Daily, year-round; camping and day-use fee

St. Christopher's Episcopal Mission
PO Box 40, Bluff, UT 84512
435-672-2296

St. George Chamber of Commerce
97 E. St. George Boulevard, St. George, UT 84770
435-628-1658 • www.stgeorgechamber.com

St. George Temple Visitor Center
490 South 300 East, St George, UT 84770
435-673-5181

Three Kiva Ruins
www.byways.org/browse/byways/61345/
    overview.html

United States Forest Service
    Dixie National Forest
    345 E. Riverside Drive, St. George, UT
        84790
    435-688-3246
    Cedar City Ranger District
    1789 Wedgewood Lane, Cedar City, UT
        84720
    435-865-3200
    Escalante Ranger District
    PO Box 246, 755 W. Main Street,
        Escalante, UT 84726
    435-826-5400

Utah Guides and Outfitters
www.utah-adventures.com

Utah State Parks
1594 West North Temple, Salt Lake City, UT
    84116
877-887-2757 or 801-538-7220
http://stateparks.utah.gov

Village of Many Nations
800-871-6811 or 435-648-3227
www.utahtrailsresort.com

Washington County Tourist and Visitor Center
97 East St. George Boulevard, St. George, UT
    84770
801-628-0505

White Mesa Institute for Cultural Studies
639 West 100 South, Blanding, UT 84511
435-678-2200

White Mesa Ute Reservation
PO Box 7096, Blanding, UT 84511
435-678-3735
http://indian.utah.gov/utah_tribes_today/
    whitemesa.html

Zion Canyon Theatre
145 Zion Park Blvd., Springdale, UT 84767
888-256-3456 *or* 435-772-2400

Zion National Park
Superintendent, Springdale, Utah 84767
Park Headquarters: 435-772-3256
www.nps.gov/zion
(continued)

Zion National Park (*continued*)
Zion Canyon is open year-round; Kolob
  Canyon is closed by snow in winter; fee
  Backcountry information
  435-772-0170
  Campground reservations (Watchman)
  800-365-2267 *or* 877-444-6777
  www.recreation.gov
  Horseback riding
  435-679-8665
  Kolob Canyon Visitor Center
  435-772-3256
  Daily 8am-4:30pm, with extended spring
      & summer hours
  Zion Canyon Field Institute
  800-635-3959 *or* 435-772-3264
  www.zionpark.org
  Zion Canyon Visitor Center
  Daily 8am-5pm, with extended spring and
      summer; call for winter hours
  Zion Human History Museum
  Daily 10am-5pm, with extended spring,
      summer, & fall hours
  Zion National Park Lodge
  888-297-2757 or 435-772-7700
  Dining reservations (recommended spring-
      fall): 435-772-3213
  www.zionlodge.com
  Zion Natural History Association
  Zion National Park, Springdale, UT 84767
  800-635-3959
  Zion Nature Center
  Mon-Fri, Memorial Day-Labor Day

A SWIRL OF COLOR AT A NATIVE
AMERICAN POWPOW

NAVAJO GIRL

(TOP, LEFT) ARIZONA DESERT SUNSET OVER RED ROCKS

(BOTTOM, LEFT) COLORADO RIVER IN GRAND CANYON

(TOP, RIGHT) POOL AT STEELE INDIAN SCHOOL

(BOTTOM, RIGHT) COLORADO RIVER IN HAVASU-TOPOCK
   NATIONAL WILDLIFE REFUGE

ARIZONA SUNSETS

GRAN QUIVERA NATIONAL MONUMENT, ARIZONA

WRINKLED LAND OF
THE COLORADO
PLATEAU, ARIZONA

NAVAJO CODE TALKERS AT THE 2005 SANTA FE INDIAN MARKET
Seated: Samuel Tsosie Sr., Merril Sandoval, Peter MacDonald Sr., Frank
Thompson, Samuel Tso, and George Willie
Standing: Bill Toledo, Arthur Hubbard Sr., Chester Nez, Samuel Smith, Jack
Jones, and Alfred Peaches

DISPLAY AT GILA RIVER INDIAN CENTER/MUSEUM, ARIZONA

GALLUP CEREMONIAL, NEW MEXICO

Above: SPRAGUE LAKE, ROCKY MOUNTAIN NATIONAL PARK, COLORADO
Below: CLIFFS NEAR KREMLING, COLORADO

Quiet lakes and pine forests nestle near Grand Lake, Colorado

SAN ILDEFONSO DRUMMERS, NEW MEXICO

ZUNI MAIDENS, NEW MEXICO

NATIVE AMERICAN CEREMONY IN NEW MEXICO

Top: **VALLEY OF THE GODS NEAR BLUFF, UTAH**

Bottom, left: **POTHOLE HOLE, CANYON-LANDS NATIONAL PARK, UTAH**

Bottom, right: **GREEN RIVER OVERLOOK, CANYONLANDS NATIONAL PARK, UTAH**

RED CANYON ARCH

BOY AND GIRL IN
NATIVE DRESS

GLOSSARY

NATIVE AMERICAN LANGUAGES ARE RICH, DIVERSE, AND NUMEROUS. Unfortunately, many that were actively used before the first European contact are no longer spoken. Since these languages were traditionally oral, it was often Europeans who first wrote them down, using their own Eurocentric understanding of how to spell and pronounce the words. Today, reviving the use of their traditional language is an important component of contemporary Indians' reclaiming their heritage, and this often includes standardizing a written form of it. Because in many cases this is a recent venture, you will still find a diversity of spellings and translations for words in the various languages. Below are some words and phrases in several native languages, along with the common way they are written.

ENGLISH	NAVAJO	JICARILLA APACHE	UTE	TEWA	O'ODHAM
One	Láá'íí	Dalaa	Suu	Wî'	Hema
Two	Naaki	Naakii	Waini	Wíyeh	Gohk
Three	Táá'	Kai' ii	Peini	Poeyeh	Waik
Four	Dii"	Dii' ii	Wacuwini	Yôenu	Gi'ik
Five	Ashdla'	Ashdle'	Manigini	P'áanú	Hetasp

HELLO

Apache (Jicarilla)	Dad'atay
Apache (White Mountain)	Dago Te
Hopi	Um waynuma?
Hopi *(answer)*	Owí, nu' waynuma
Hopi	Um pitu?
Hopi *(answer)*	Owí
Hualapai *(How are you?)*	Gumu
Navajo	Yá'át'ééh
O'odham	Shap ai masma
(How have you been?)	
Ute	Mique wush tagooven
Zuni	Kesh'shi

GOODBYE

Apache	Ka dish day
Apache *(Farewell)*	Yadalanh
Apache *(See you later)*	Ánágodziih doleel
Apache *(Until we meet again)*	Egogahan
Hopi	
(to person leaving)	Um ason piw a'ni
(by person going)	Nu' tus payni
(response)	Ta'á, um ason piw a'ni
Hualapai *(See you later)*	Met nyi u ya
Navajo	Hágoónee'
Navajo *(response)*	Lá'aa, hágoónee'
O'odham *(I'll see you again)*	Tom ñei
Ute *(See you later)*	Pooneekay vatsoom ahdtuih

WELCOME

Apache *(Come in)*	Ha'ándáh
Hopi	Keuwawata
Hualapai	Goan u
Navajo *(Come in, to one)*	Yah aninááh
Navajo *(Come in, to two)*	Yah ooh'aash
Navajo *(Come in, to three +)*	Yah oohkááh
Yavapai	Gum yuu j'eh

WHAT IS YOUR NAME?

Apache	Hant'é gonlzéé?
Hopi	Um hin maatsiwa?
Navajo	Haash yinílyé?
O'odham	Shap chegig?
Ute	Ani ümüí nia?

MY NAME IS ...

Apache	... gonszee
Hopi	Nu'... yan maatsiwa
Navajo	... yinishyé
O'odham	... bun chegig
Ute	Nünai nia ...

THANK YOU

Hualapai *(It is good)*	hangu
Hopi *(said by men)*	Kwakwhá
... very much	Is kwakwhá
Hopi *(said by women)*	Askwali
... very much	Is askwali
Jicarilla Apache	Ihe edn
Navajo	Ahé hee'
Tewa	Kuunda
Ute	Towyak, Tog'oyak, Tokhoyak

YES

Apache	Ha'oh
Apache	Ha'ah
Hopi	Owí
Navajo	Aou'
Navajo	Aoo'
Navajo	Ooa
Ute	Üü
Zuñi	Haugh

NO

Apache	Dah
Hopi	Qa'é
Hopi	Gae'
Hopi	K'ae'
Navajo	Dooda
Navajo	Ndaga'
Ute	Kach
Ute	Ka-
Zuñi	'Ella

I DON'T UNDERSTAND

Apache	Doo nidists'ad da
Ute	Kanükaiwa

A FEW MODERN ADDITIONS IN NAVAJO

Cell Phone **Bi níjoobaím**, which literally means "one spins around with this," possibly referring to the way teens often turn in circles while talking on a cell phone. Slang term.

Computer **Béésh ntsikeesí**, which literally means "the metal that thinks." Slang term.

Microwave **Bee na'niildóhó**, which literally means "what you warm things up with." Slang term.

Telephone **Béésh bee hane'é**, which literally means "the metal you use to talk with."

INDIAN CODE TALKERS

Because American Indian languages are so unique, they have been used to carry codes in war times. In World War I Comanche recruits devised a code based on their language that was used to aid the U.S. war effort.

During World War II in the spring of 1942, twenty-nine Navajo servicemen were recruited by the United States Marine Corp and trained in special signal work. More Navajo recruits were added, until around four hundred were trained. The platoon adapted the Navajo language to encode military commands in the Pacific Theater of Operations, and it became a vital part of the Allied victory there. The code was finally revealed in 1969 at a Marine reunion, where it was shown that the code included not only words from the Navajo language, but also a code within a code that assigned Navajo words to English letters. Eventually, the twenty-nine code originators received the Congressional Gold Medal of Honor, and the rest of the code talkers received the Congressional Silver Medal of Honor. Below are a few of the words that were used.

English	Navajo	Literal Translation
Alaska	Beh-Hga	With winter
America	Ne-He-Mah	Our mother
India	Ah-Le-Gai	White clothes
Britain	Toh-Ta	Between waters
Spain	Deba-De-Nih	Sheep pain (Sheep was *S*)
Mine sweeper	Cha	Beaver
Battleship	Lo-Tso	Whale

English	Navajo	Literal Translation
Bulldozer	Dola-Alth-Whosh	Bull sleep (bull dozer)
Cemetery	Jish-Cha	Among devils
Creek	Toh-Nil-Tsanh	Very little water
Not	Ni-Dah-Than-Zie	No turkey (Turkey was *T*)
Notice	Ne-Da-Tazi-Thin	No turkey ice
Tank	Chay-Da-Gahi	Tortoise
Village	Chah-Ho-Oh-Lhan-Ih	Many shelter
Will	Gloe-Ih-Dot-Sahi	Sick weasel (Weasel was *W*)

PHOTO, MAP, AND ILLUSTRATION SOURCES

Denver Metro Convention and Visitors Bureau: page 242

Denver Public Library Western History Collection: pages 14, 17, 24, 27 (Walker Art Studio), 33, 40 (John K. Hillers), 54, 55 (Jesse L. Nusbaum), 86, 88 (H. S. Poley), 152 (A. Frank Randall)

EPCVB (Estes Park Convention and Visitors Bureau): pages 218, 225; photo insert, page 10 (top)

Experience Colorado Springs at Pikes Peak: page 237

Limon, Janet: pages 30, 46, 71, 75, 102, 107, 154, 161, 170, 180, 214, 217, 234, 249, 252, 276, 317, 326, 330, 332, 334, 339, 369, 414; photo insert, page 6 (bottom), 8 (top), 11

McCall, Jim: page 150

Minear, Tish: pages 6, 9, 42, 47, 52, 57, 84, 120, 140, 158, 172, 175, 178, 179, 181, 193, 197, 199, 221, 286; photo insert, pages 1 (top), 2 (bottom), 3, 4, 6 (top)

Mohave Museum of History and Arts: pages 18, 20, 74, 122

National Park Service: pages 32, 50, 66, 68, 97, 98, 132, 135, 137, 143, 190, 191, 204, 222, 262, 267, 319, 329, 391, 398, 416, 418, 419, 428, 435, 442, 445; photo insert, pages 14 (bottom), 15 (bottom)

National Scenic Byways (www.byways.org): pages 38 (Greg Gnesios), 246, 268 (Dennis Adams), 274 (Dennis Adams), 352 (Carla Ward), 388 (A. E. Crane), 415 (Greg Gnesios), 441 (A. E. Crane); photo insert, pages 10 (bottom/Jean Landess), 14 (top/Utah Canyon Country Visitor Services), 16 (top/W. Dyde)

New Mexico Tourism Department: pages 36, 287, 289, 291, 293, 301, 303, 321, 336, 337, 351, 355, 360, 372, 375, 379, 380; photo insert, pages 1 (bottom), 8 (bottom), 12, 16 (bottom)

Perkins, M. Diane: pages 26, 34, 156, 200, 270, 361

Phoenix Visitors Bureau: photo insert, pages 2 (top), 5, 9

Sandoval, Jeannie: pages 95, 100, 106; photo insert, page 7 (bottom)

Sante Fe Convention and Visitors Bureau: pages 35, 296; photo insert, page 13

U.S. Fish and Wildlife Service: page 390

USGS: pages 401, 417, 439

White, Sara: pages 4, 12, 247, 318, 368

Maps are courtesy of the Federal Highway Administration except where noted.

LIST OF MAPS

INDEX

References in bold refer to text graphics.

Index

Index

Other Titles of Interest from Hippocrene Books

TRAVEL

Navajo Nation: A Visitor's Guide
Patrick and Joan Lavin

The Navajo are the largest Native American tribe in the United States. Numbering a quarter million, the Navajo Nation spans 25,000 square miles in northeastern Arizona, northwestern New Mexico, and southern Utah. Navajo country (known as *Diné' bikéyah)*, extends well beyond these boundaries. The area, which draws thousands of visitors each year, boasts some of the most awe-inspiring scenery in the world. In every direction there are spectacular views of distant mesas, expansive plateaus, and towering mountains, specifically the Painted Desert, Monument Valley, and Canyon de Chelly.

This unique guidebook opens with a section on the history of the Navajo from pre-colonial times to the present, with a special focus on the development of their culture and religion. The next section is a comprehensive visitor's guide to the region, covering sites of historical interest and natural beauty and including driving directions, accommodations, and other helpful information. Finally, a section on the Navajo language gives readers a flavor for speaking Navajo and includes useful words and phrases.

- Covers attractions, routes, dining, and accommodations
- Suggested itineraries for 3-day to 10-day trips
- Includes special details for RVs, camping, and hiking
- 16 pages of color photos bring Navajo country to life

283 pages • 5½ x 8½ • 978-0-7818-1180-4 • $21.95pb

HISTORY

Arizona: An Illustrated History
Patrick Lavin

From prehistory through the Spanish conquest and the "wild west," here is the complete illustrated history of Arizona, the Grand Canyon State. Patrick Lavin explores the "land of contrasts," whose history is as varied and fascinating as its landscapes. No other North American region offers such environmental diversity, including the native plants, animals, and people that inhabit it. Complemented by over 60 photographs and maps, this concise history recounts the story of the state from the prehistoric days of the Paleo-Indians to the twenty-first century.

225 pages • 5 x 7 • 0-7818-0852-9 • $14.95pb

New Mexico: An Illustrated History
Patrick Lavin

Known as the "Land of Enchantment," New Mexico is living witness to the coexistence of Native American, Spanish, and Anglo civilizations. In *New Mexico: An Illustrated History,* Patrick Lavin takes an all-inclusive approach to New Mexico's past by vividly reconstructing the state's key historical events in a concise and accessible format.

Citing fascinating material from newspapers, journals, and personal accounts of pioneers and explorers, this compelling volume relates the arrival of the Paleo-Indians, Spanish exploration and colonization, the Mexican-American War and subsequent territorial period, as well as New Mexico's early statehood and the post-World War II era. Today, New Mexico continues to inspire visitors and artists who come to pay tribute to the state's magnificent natural beauty and cultural heritage.

With more than 50 illustrations, photographs, and maps, *New Mexico: An Illustrated History* provides a thorough and lively historical overview that reveals the heart and soul of this fascinating southwestern state.

253 pages • 5½ x 8½ • 0-7818-1053-1 • $14.95pb

DICTIONARIES & LANGUAGE GUIDES

Navajo-English Dictionary
Leon Wall & William Morgan

The dictionary is designed to aid Navajos learning English as well as English speakers interested in acquiring knowledge of Navajo.
- Over 9,000 entries
- A detailed section on Navajo pronunciation
- A comprehensive, modern vocabulary
- Useful, everyday expressions

164 pages • 5½ x 8½ • 0-7818-0247-4 • $11.95pb

Colloquial Navajo: A Dictionary
Robert W. Young and William Morgan

The dictionary addresses the inadequacy of literal translation when working with idioms by offering interpretations based on the general meaning of a phrase rather than the individual words that comprise the expressions. This volume is ideal for Navajos interested in learning English, as well as English-speakers interested in studying the Navajo languages.

461 pages • 5½ x 8½ • 0-7818-0278-4 • $16.95pb

Yoeme-English/English-Yoeme Standard Dictionary
Felipe S. Molina, Herminia Valenzuela, David Shaul

Yoeme is an expressive language traditionally spoken by the Yaqui tribe in northern Mexico and the American Southwest region. This is the first Yoeme dictionary ever published. It includes over 8,000 entries, a comprehensive grammar of the Yoeme language, and informative facts about the Yaqui culture.

351 pages • 8,000 entries • 6 x 9 • 0-7818-0633-X • $16.95pb

Instant Spanish Vocabulary Builder with CD
Tom Means

Many words in Spanish are nearly the same as their English counter-parts, except for the word ending. This unique book identifies the 24 most common word-ending patterns between these languages and provides over 4,000 words that follow them. Perfect as a classroom supplement or for self-study, it is appropriate for all ages and levels of experience. The enclosed CD allows the reader to master pronunciation of the most common words and phrases from each chapter by repeating them after a native speaker.

209 pages • 6 x 9 • 0-7818-0981-9 • $14.95pb

Spanish-English / English-Spanish Compact Dictionary (Latin American)

• Concise and portable
• Side-by-side pronunciation
• 3,700 total dictionary entries
• Brief guide to Spanish grammar and pronunciation
• Ideal for travelers, students, and businesspeople
170 pages • 3 x 4½ • 0-7818-1041-8 • $8.95pb

Spanish-English / English-Spanish (Latin American) Concise Dictionary
Ila Warner

• Over 8,000 word-to-word entries
• Phonetic pronunciation in both languages
• An informative guide to Spanish pronunciation
• A concise, easy-to-use format
• Completely modern and up-to-date entries
• A list of culinary terms from Spanish-speaking countries

310 pages • 4 x 6 • 0-7818-0261-X • $12.95pb

COOKBOOKS

Aprovecho: A Mexican-American Border Cookbook
Teresa Cordero-Cordell and Robert Cordell

Aprovecho, which means "I make best use of," is a celebration of the food and culture found along the U.S.-Mexico border. This comprehensive book contains more than 250 recipes, including such traditional fare as enchiladas, quesadillas, and margaritas, along with more exotic delights, such as Cactus Salad, Lobster and Tequila, and Watermelon Sorbet. In addition to appetizing recipes, this entertaining cookbook contains special sections that relate popular legends, explain how tequila is made, and provide instructions for making your own festive piñatas. Also included are a glossary of chiles and cooking terms as well as a Mexican pantry list so you'll always be prepared for a fiesta!

PB: 377 pages • 6 x 9 • $16.95 • 978-0-7818-1206-1
HC: 377 pages • 6 x 9 • $24.95 • 978-0-7818-1026-4

Mexican Culinary Treasures: Recipes from Maria Elena's Kitchen
Maria Elena Cuervo-Lorens

This cookbook provides insight into modern Mexican cooking and the history behind it. The recipes range from very traditional dishes like tacos to the modern cuisine of Mexico City such as chicken in prune and red wine sauce. Maria Elena Cuervo-Loren's extensive knowledge of the nation's culinary traditions combined with an enthusiasm for sharing the vibrant flavors of her native Mexico make this book a fascinating journey through Mexico's culinary treasures.

266 pages • 6 x 9 • 0-7818-1061-2 • $24.95hc

Prices subject to change without prior notice. **To purchase Hippocrene Books** contact your local bookstore, visit www.hippocrenebooks.com, or call (718) 454-2366.